A GLIMPSE OF HELL

A GLIMPSE OF HELL

☆

THE EXPLOSION ON THE USS *IOWA* AND ITS COVER-UP

☆

CHARLES C. THOMPSON II

W. W. NORTON & COMPANY
NEW YORK · LONDON

The text of this book is composed in Electra
with the display set in Latin Condensed
Desktop composition by Gina Webster
Manufacturing by Quebecor Printing, Fairfield, Inc.
Book design by JAM Design

Library of Congress Cataloging-in-Publication Data

Thompson, Charles C.
A glimpse of hell : the explosion on the USS Iowa and its cover-up /
Charles C. Thompson.
p. cm.
Includes bibliographical references and index.
ISBN 0-393-04714-8
1. Iowa (Ship) 2. Marine accidents—Investigation—United States.
3. United States. Navy. I. Title.
VA65.I59T46 1999
363.12'3'0973—dc21 98-42061
CIP

W. W. Norton & Company, Inc., 500 Fifth Avenue, New York, N.Y. 10110
http://www.wwnorton.com

W. W. Norton & Company Ltd., 10 Coptic Street, London WC1A 1PU

2 3 4 5 6 7 8 9 0

Contents

Illustrations

Preface

SOME STORIES, ESPECIALLY those involving cover-ups, are like will-o'-the wisps. The harder you chase, the more elusive the truth seems. This was such a story. In 1989, during a routine training exercise in the Caribbean, the center gun in Turret Two of the forty-six-year-old recommissioned battleship USS *Iowa* blew up. The fireball that surged through the seven-story structure released clouds of poisonous gases and ignited bags of powder, setting off further explosions. A botched investigation began mere hours after the explosion that killed forty-seven men. Evidence was literally tossed overboard. Material as big as two 2,700-pound projectiles simply vanished. Testimony was doctored. Test results were fabricated or misinterpreted. Supposedly reputable institutions turned out suspect autopsy reports and issued conclusions that were scorned by independent medical examiners. Pop psychology supplanted reality.

Less than a week after the disaster, I received a call from an *Iowa* gunner's mate from Turret One, which was located forward of Turret Two. He had helped fight the fires in the stricken turret and had participated in the grisly chore of identifying and removing badly mangled bodies. He told me that the investigation had been dishonest from the beginning. I began pursuing the story at that time and never stopped. Often, as I interviewed high-ranking naval officers, I felt as if I were in a house of mirrors with distortions everywhere. But like water dripping, slowly wearing away stone, stubbornness and the passage of time paid off. Officers and crewmen from the USS *Iowa* and other commands left the service and were able to tell their stories without fear of retribution. A number of admirals did the same thing. Fellow journalists, friends on Capitol Hill, and the families of the men who died in Turret Two provided a wealth of details, including the final letters from their loved ones. I filed a Freedom of Information Act lawsuit against the Navy and won a stack of documents. Historians in the United States and in Great Britain furnished me with priceless background information.

I FIRST became seriously enamored of battleships and their mammoth guns during the summer of 1966, when I was a student at the Naval Amphibious Warfare School at Little Creek, Virginia. I was part of a class of about twenty young officers who were preparing to return to Vietnam for a second tour as naval gunfire spotters, artillery observers, and forward air controllers. Our manuals dated back to World War II, and we had to memorize such things as how many direct hits by sixteen-inch high-explosive shells could demolish a bunker reinforced with sandbags and palm logs. This seemed absurd to us, because at the time the Navy had no battleships armed with sixteen-inch guns on active duty. The largest guns were eight-inchers and six-inchers mounted on aging cruisers; most of our shore-fire bombardment had to be accomplished with five-inch guns mounted on destroyers. We compared these relatively puny weapons with the main armament of a battleship and prayed that the Navy would recommission at least one of these great ships then in mothballs in the Philadelphia and Bremerton, Washington, Naval Shipyards.

In Vietnam, I was part of the First Air Naval Gunfire Liason Company (ANGLICO), a hundred-man outfit that provided the U.S. Army and other allied forces the same gunfire and naval air support that U.S. Marines received. When a ship first arrived on the "gun line," several of us would fly out by helicopter, talk to the captain and navigator and the gunnery and fire-control officers, examine her records and equipment, and see if she were qualified to fire in close support of troops. All the ships I worked with did well, except one, which regularly overshot her targets by two miles.

About two months before my tour ended, the Navy announced that it was going to overhaul the battleship USS *New Jersey* and send her to Vietnam. I seriously contemplated extending my time on active duty to serve aboard her. If I had, I would have met Captain Ed Snyder years before I did.

Snyder was a tinkerer who bought scrap cars when he was in his early teens, transforming them into racers. He was a nuclear weapons designer and a veteran sea captain. That made him the ideal choice to transform the *New Jersey* into a fighting ship after ten years in mothballs. A self-confessed "gadget nut," Snyder outfitted the ship with navigational equipment and computers, and brought along a remotely controlled helicopter on an accompanying destroyer, which was equipped with a television camera and transmitter for spotting gunfire. He also spent a great deal of time personally ensuring that the gunpowder was stable and devising ways to reduce barrel erosion.

The battleship received rave reviews from the "grunts on the ground" in Vietnam. Marine Staff Sergeant Robert Gauthier told the *New Jersey* sailors that he had gone back into an area that had been blasted by her sixteen-inch guns. "There was nothing, just nothing. It was like someone had come along with a big eraser and wiped everything clean. And these were big, heavily fortified bunkers, targets our own artillery couldn't touch."

WHEN THE *Iowa* explosion occurred, Snyder, by then a retired rear admiral, was the Navy's foremost expert on battleships and sixteen-inch guns. He volunteered to help with the investigation, but the Navy rejected his offer. I asked him to help me, and he stayed at my side every step of the way. This book is dedicated to Admiral Snyder and to my wife, Betty Cole Thompson. I couldn't have written it without both of them. They gave me the nerve to go back to the Navy over and over, seeking answers. They examined the documents, helped me decipher them, and made insightful suggestions on the manuscript.

I'd like to thank Mike Wallace for his support. As a former naval officer, he was just as reluctant as I to believe the Navy's bogus account about how the *Iowa* explosion was initiated. He gave me a wide mandate to research the story and called upon some of his own sources to substantiate details. He was never buffaloed by the admirals. He encouraged me to produce two *Iowa* segments on *60 Minutes*, which resulted in an apology from the Navy to the family of Gunner's Mate Second Class Clayton Hartwig, the sailor the Navy falsely accused of triggering the fatal blast in Turret Two. Mike also spurred me to write this book.

I'd also like to express my appreciation to Donald S. Lamm, my editor at W. W. Norton, who shaped and gently improved the manuscript; Mary Cunnane, my former editor at Norton, who moved to Australia; Charlotte Sheedy, my agent; Ari Allan, Ann Volkes, Paul Hoven, Howard Rosenberg, and Gail Eisen, my former colleagues at *60 Minutes*; John C. Reilly Jr. of the Naval Historical Center; Paul Stillwell, director of the history division of the U.S. Naval Institute; Benis M. Frank and Richard A. Long of the U.S. Marine Corps History and Museums Division; retired Chief Robert Sumrall, curator of ship models at the U.S. Naval Academy; author Joseph Goulden; attorneys Robert Seldon and Sarah Levitt of the Project on Liberty and the Workplace and Joanne Royce, Jeff Ruch, and Don Aplin of the Government Accountability Project (GAP) for litigating my Freedom of Information Act lawsuit against the Navy; Louis Clark and Tom Devine of GAP and Conrad Martin, executive director, and the board of the Fund for Constitutional Government, for financial and technical assistance in obtaining documents; Rear Admiral Dennis Brooks (USN-Ret.); Captain Larry Seaquist (USN-Ret.); Captain Stan Sirmans (USN-Ret.); Captain Jay Coupe (USN-Ret.); Commander John Alexander (USN-Ret.); Commander Kevin Mukri (USN-Ret.); Colonel Don Price (USMC-Ret.); Lieutenant Colonel Roger Charles (USMC-Ret.); Doris Lama, the Navy's Privacy Act coordinator; and to the courageous families of the forty-seven men who died in Turret Two aboard the *Iowa*.

A GLIMPSE OF HELL

PROLOGUE

"Sir, What Happens If That Damned Tomahawk Hits Us?"

THE FORTY-SIX-year-old battleship USS *Iowa* was steaming leisurely through the Caribbean 260 miles northeast of Puerto Rico at fifteen knots on Wednesday morning, April 19, 1989. The frigates USS *Ainsworth* and USS *Aylwin* formed a ragtag column about five thousand yards behind the battleship's foamy, creamy wake, with the *Ainsworth* in the lead. Tropical winds gusted from the southeast at thirty miles per hour, churning up the waves. Each succeeding swell and trough pitched and rolled the two frigates, which were a twelfth the *Iowa*'s size, making life decidedly unpleasant for their crewmen. The 1,600 officers and enlisted men on the 59,000-ton battleship, on the other hand, enjoyed a much smoother ride. The choppy seas didn't trouble the *Iowa* in the slightest. She had been designed back in 1938 to navigate her way through a monsoon or ride out a typhoon and suffer no appreciable damage. Her proud, jutting, clipper-style bow neatly furrowed the waves, flecking a light spray back over her forecastle, slightly wetting down Turret One, the forwardmost sixteen-inch gun mount. At sunup, the sea was a bright royal blue; the skies were clear, the horizon seemed to stretch forever.

The *Iowa* was near the center of a task force composed of some thirty U.S. Navy vessels, including the aircraft carrier USS *Coral Sea*, seven cruisers, three guided-missile destroyers, two conventional destroyers, seven frigates, three amphibious assault craft, a communications ship, two oilers, a minesweeper, two ammunition ships, plus three South American frigates—two from Venezuela and one from Brazil. Strung out over hundreds of miles of ocean, this unwieldy task force had been cobbled together to participate in war games known as "FLEETEX 3-89." Vice Admiral Jerome Johnson, the trim, dapper commander of the U.S. Second Fleet, was in charge. The *Iowa* was now his flagship.

FLEETEX had gotten off to a desultory start. For the previous two days, the weather had stubbornly refused to cooperate with the fleet's operational schedule. A low-pressure front hovered off the Puerto Rican coast, periodically drenching the ships with rain showers and obscuring some of the target areas with patches of dense fog. The weather had twice postponed a secret missile experiment involving the *Iowa*. This morning's clear skies put the experiment back on the schedule. However, the *Iowa*'s staff meteorologist said that this window of opportunity was limited, predicting that there probably would be intermittent rains, patchy cloud cover, squalls, and rougher seas in late morning or early afternoon.

A sizable number of the battleship's sailors hoped that the missile experiment would be scrubbed again. Most of the enlisted men didn't possess the proper security clearances and weren't supposed to know anything about the experiment. However, nearly every one of the ship's gunner's mates was well aware of the details of the experiment and thought it sheer lunacy. Some sailors were so disturbed that they drew up new wills. Talk about the experiment continued to dominate conversation this morning as the men clutched their compartmentalized aluminum trays and filed through the breakfast lines in the crew's mess in the after portion of the ship.

ONE OF those who knew about the missile experiment was Dale Eugene Mortensen. A petty officer first class, he was known simply as "Mort" by his shipmates and drinking buddies. A well-built thirteen-year Navy veteran, Mortensen, thirty-two, had dark brown hair and a mustache to match. He stood five feet eight inches tall, with a faded tattoo of an eagle and an anchor on his right forearm. Sometimes sullen, the first class gunner's mate was tightly wound and fast with his fists. He had enlisted in the Navy before his twentieth birthday, after frittering away two years in Detroit in a dead-end job as a shoe salesclerk. He first arrived on the *Iowa* on a crisp autumn day in 1983 at the Ingalls Shipyard in Pascagoula, Mississippi, where the *Iowa* was being overhauled for recommissioning after having spent twenty-six years in mothballs following the Korean War.

Mortensen had volunteered for the *Iowa* because Master Chief W.O. Tisdale, in charge of assigning gunner's mates to ships for the Navy Department, convinced him that a tour on a battleship would be good for his career. Mortensen stressed that his volunteering was contingent on a promise that he would never be assigned to one of the ship's three gargantuan sixteen-inch gun turrets. He was a five-inch gunner, and he intended to remain a five-inch gunner, convincing himself that he didn't have "the stuff it took" to master one of the ship's three gargantuan sixteen-inch gun turrets. The chief smoothly reassured Mortensen that he foresaw "no problem whatsoever accommodating your request." The recommissioned *Iowa* retained twelve of her original five-inch, .38-caliber guns. Tisdale didn't inform Mortensen that the Navy had mandated that any experienced gunner's mate coming to the *Iowa* would automatically be assigned to the sixteen-inch guns. The ease with which the chief agreed to Mortensen's request, without ever consulting anyone higher up in the Navy chain of command, should have alerted the normally wary Mortensen that something was not right. But he accepted the chief's word and did not demand anything in writing.

Suspicion of authority figures came naturally to Mortensen. He carried a semipermanent chip on his shoulder after a traumatic experience aboard the destroyer USS *Newman K. Perry*. While Mortensen was on a lengthy cruise in the Mediterranean, his wife learned that she was dying of leukemia. The Red Cross sent numerous messages to the *Perry*, requesting that Mortensen be granted immediate emergency home leave. But his department head was an officer who had counted on Mortensen's expertise to help the ship pass an upcoming fleet gunnery inspection. The officer pocketed the messages and never informed his subordinate that his wife was dying. A full eight weeks after the messages began arriving, a yeoman in the ship's communications department became outraged by the gunnery officer's action and informed Mortensen of his wife's illness.

Mortensen went berserk. Having access to the ship's armory, he took out a .45-caliber, semiautomatic pistol and several magazines of ammunition. He shoved his way into the lieutenant's stateroom, jacked a round into the chamber, and stuck the cocked pistol under the chin of the terrified officer, who muttered, "You weren't issued a wife with your seabag." That crass remark almost cost the officer his life. He was rescued when the yeoman, along with several of Mortensen's fellow gunner's mates, rushed into the lieutenant's stateroom. They pleaded with Mortensen not to shoot the officer, arguing that he would be executed, leaving his two small daughters without either a mother or a father. Mortensen released the lieutenant, uncocked the pistol, and surrendered the weapon to his shipmates. The destroyer's commanding officer declined to press charges against him for assaulting the officer and sent him on emergency leave. His wife died in his arms shortly after Mortensen arrived home.

From then on, although outwardly respectful of authority, Mortensen inwardly seethed over the Navy's rigid caste system, which caused so many officers to treat enlisted men like scum. He was still proud to be a part of the U.S. Navy, but he expected little or nothing in return. He summed up his ambivalent feelings this way: "The Navy's like a fan. You stand behind it, it sucks you. You stand in front of it, it blows you. You stand beside it, it doesn't do a damned thing for you."

THE NAVY "fan" was in good working order the day Mortensen reported onboard the *Iowa*. Shortly after he bounded up the aft gangway and handed his orders to the junior officer of the watch, he was greeted by George Steffan, a civilian technician hired by Sea Systems Command, the Navy outfit supervising the overhaul of the *Iowa*. Steffan, a retired chief petty officer who was in charge of training the *Iowa*'s sixteen-inch gunners, was hardly an inspiring sight. Leathery, grizzled, and badly stooped, he had been in charge of a turret on a battleship during World War II. Strapped to his side was a colostomy bag, evidence of a bout with cancer. Steffan had received a call from Chief Tisdale that Mortensen would make an ideal candidate to become a sixteen-inch gun-turret captain.

Grabbing Mortensen's arm, Steffan instructed the young first class petty officer to follow him to a sixteen-inch turret. "Why are we going to a sixteen-inch turret? Chief Tisdale promised me I could stay in five-inch guns," Mortensen insisted. Steffan asked him if he had anything in writing, and Mortensen shook his head. "Well, then you're mine," the retired chief said, leading Mortensen up through the tail hatch of a gun turret. He had selected Turret Three, which was on the after portion of the ship behind the superstructure. Like its two sister turrets, it was a heavily fortified, rotating citadel. Each had three sixty-eight-foot-long guns that could accurately lob a shell more than twenty miles.

Steffan demonstrated the turret officer's control booth to Mortensen, explaining the function of the two periscopes, the bank of switches to train the guns, and the large cylindrical range finder, transversing the rear of the compartment. He had Mortensen scrunch past a hollow brass column—the opening of the shell hoist into the narrow, two-deck-high center gun room. Steffan unlatched the gun's one-ton breechblock and invited Mortensen to poke his head into the gun barrel, but Mortensen declined.

Steffan expanded the cradle, an aluminum, spark-free trough used to slide the shell and powder bags into the breech. He pointed out the chain-linked rammer. "Ramming is the most dangerous part of loading a gun," he said. "A high-speed overram can ruin your whole day." The two men meandered through the other two gun rooms and then crawled down a narrow, steep ladder to the mechanical decks below. From there they descended farther to the two projectile decks, where 370 shells would stand in six-foot-high ranks on well-greased rotating brass turntables. More shells would be secured to the bulkheads (walls) by heavy-link chains. The brass turntable rotated to bring a shell toward the hoist. A line was passed around the shell's base and looped three times around a power-driven capstan to move the shell into place for the hoist.

Steffan said, "We use real big fellows down here," adding that a high-capacity shell, used for shore bombardment, weighed 1,900 pounds, while an armor-piercing projectile, used for fighting other ships, weighed 2,700 pounds. The two men scrambled down the ladder into the bottom of the six-story turret. They were well below the waterline in the powder flats. Steffan demonstrated the operation of the other hoists, used to haul smokeless powder up to the gun rooms. He unfastened six latches—or "dogs"—on a watertight, blastproof door and pushed it open. He signaled for Mortensen to follow him out of the circular, revolving portion of the turret and into the surrounding magazines, where powder bags, each weighing 110 pounds, would be stored in galvanized steel cans.

"We put our new men, our donkeys, our bad boys down here in the magazines. It's hard, dirty work," Steffan said. Gunner's mates had to open the powder cans and manhandle the cylindrical nitrocellulose, smokeless powder bags into scuttles (hatches with movable lids). From the powder-handling rooms, these bags were put on hoists and hauled up to the gun rooms.

The tour of the turret overwhelmed Mortensen. Steffan could see it in the younger man's eyes. He had taken other gunner's mates on tours and had witnessed the same reaction in their faces. Mortensen thought there was too much to learn, too much that could go wrong. Steffan assured him that within a matter of months, he would master the turret and its oversize guns.

And the old man's prediction proved correct. Almost six years later, when the *Iowa* sailed to the Caribbean for FLEETEX, Mortensen was serving as turret captain for Turret One. He had earned a reputation as the ship's most knowledgeable sixteen-inch gunner. Known as "Mr. Fixit," he knew how to cope with broken powder bags, shorted firing switches, and malfunctioning rammers. On more than one occasion, he had risked his life by wetting down a smoking powder bag with a bucket of water, hauling it from the turret, and heaving it over the side. He had served as the top enlisted man in all three turrets, and whichever one he served in became the ship's top performer. He had no hesitation about decking a misbehaving sailor, no qualms about allowing disputing sailors to settle their differences in the turret with boxing gloves.

Mortensen had taken over that turret almost two years earlier, after five gunner's mates had been arrested on drug charges and thrown out of the Navy and the chief petty officer had been fired. "Mortensen banged heads, busted knuckles, and within twelve months succeeded in ousting his former turrets, Two and Three, from their positions as *Iowa*'s gunnery leaders," according to Ensign Dan Meyer, the officer in charge of Turret One. Solemn and bookish, Meyer had graduated from Cornell University, where his father, a U.S. Naval Academy graduate and highly respected submarine captain, had commanded the Naval Reserve Officer Training Corps (NROTC) detachment.

Ensign Meyer had joined the *Iowa* in the summer of 1987. After a five-week break-in period in Turret Three, Meyer was sent to the Surface Warfare School in Newport, Rhode Island. When he returned to the ship three months later, the weapons officer, Commander Gene Kocmich, told Meyer that he was sending him to Turret One to work with Dale Mortensen. Kocmich advised Meyer to follow Mortensen's lead.

"After about six months, I was no longer Dale's appendage," Meyer said. "I was making independent decisions, but there was no question in my mind that if I had a disagreement with him, it would be decided in his favor. Any well-trained monkey can do the turret officer's job," Meyer said. "It's not a very demanding job. Your main function is to be there for misfires. Mortensen's job required him to coordinate the actions of all the men throughout the turret and to actually give the loading orders." Even though their relationship involved mutual respect, Mortensen never let down his guard or dreamed of calling the ensign anything but "Mr. Meyer."

Meyer and Mortensen became good friends, but Mortensen resisted the ensign's efforts to promote him to chief petty officer, claiming that if he became a chief he could no longer associate with his men in the same manner. The chiefs had their own mess and berthing quarters well away from the lower-ranking crewmen. Mortensen claimed that the chiefs "belonged to a goat locker." He wanted no part of them, staging his reenlistment ceremony six levels down in the turret's powder flats, because he knew the majority of the chiefs on the ship were so fat they couldn't climb down the ladders to attend the ceremony.

TWO DAYS before the *Iowa* departed from her Norfolk, Virginia, homeport for FLEETEX, the crew of the *Iowa* got its first clue that something unusual was going to take place in the Caribbean. A dockside crane pulled alongside the battleship and deposited a mysterious, white-painted, reinforced-steel van, about the size of a tractor-trailer, on the battleship's fantail, the aftermost section of the main deck. "That white van was so big that it was impossible to ignore," Meyer said. "The men were frantic to find out what was inside it and learn what it was doing on the *Iowa*."

Four or five civilian technicians—whom the sailors termed "spooky types"—arrived shortly after the van was secured on the fantail. Tight-lipped, these men were clearly nerds, geeks with plastic pocket protectors, polyester pants, and suede Hush Puppies shoes. When asked where they were assigned, they would only say, "Range Target Support Section . . . Range Directorate . . . Naval Air Test Center . . . Patuxent River, Maryland." They spent most of their time in private staterooms and obviously weren't saltwater sailors.

The first night the *Iowa* was at sea, Dale Mortensen broke into the white van, which was unguarded. Inside, he found documents detailing the battleship's role in a cat-and-mouse game to be played out with an incoming Tomahawk cruise missile. Mortensen sought out several fellow first class petty officers, electronic technicians who had security clearances and could tell him more about the experiment. The next morning, Mortensen assembled the fifty or so men assigned to Turret One and told them everything he had learned. The men were petrified by what they heard. "Everybody was very distressed. Nobody, not one person wanted to be on the ship that day," said David Smith, a stocky, twenty-year-old sailor, who'd been on the *Iowa* for about three weeks. Smith had never witnessed the big guns fire and was already jittery about being in a turret during a live-fire mission.

Mortensen learned that during the experiment the guided-missile cruiser USS *San Jacinto*, positioned over the horizon some 150 miles from the *Iowa*, would aim and fire a Tomahawk cruise missile at the battleship. He had not been able to determine whether the twenty-foot-long Tomahawk would be carrying a live warhead, containing 1,000 pounds of explosives, or would have a dummy warhead. The missile would be heading at the *Iowa*, skimming above the waves at about the speed of sound. When it neared the battleship, the Tomahawk would pop up, gain altitude, and home in for the kill.

Once a Tomahawk struck its target, its solid-fuel boosters would behave like blowtorches, boring fiery holes through the target's hull and igniting secondary explosions in the powder magazines and fuel tanks. "The same thing could happen to us that happened to the *Stark*!" screamed Scott Ragan, a second class gunner's mate.

Ragan was referring to a 1987 attack on the guided-missile frigate USS *Stark*. The *Stark* had been on patrol in the Persian Gulf when she was struck by two French-made Exocet missiles fired by an Iraqi F-1 Mirage jet fighter. The *Stark* nearly sank. Thirty-seven of her crewmen were killed, and twenty-one others were wounded. Most of the damage and casualties resulted not from the missiles' explosive warheads but rather from fires started by the fuel carried aboard the two Exocets.

Mortensen reminded Ragan that unlike the *Iowa*, the *Stark* was a thinly armored, aluminum-hulled ship. The missiles' propellant had superheated the aluminum, causing it to burn. Still, Ragan and the other sailors were not persuaded by Mortensen's assurances that they would be safe if the Tomahawk struck the *Iowa*.

What was the point of this dangerous exercise? the men demanded. It was supposed to test electronic equipment located in the white trailer on the fantail, Mortensen said. Just as soon as the *San Jacinto* launched the Tomahawk and the missile began zeroing in on the *Iowa*, the technicians in the trailer would activate a special piece of electronic equipment designed to mimic the output of a Soviet ECM jammer. The trailer was crammed with electronic countermeasures (ECM) emitters, radar antennas, transceivers, transmitters, transponders, simulators, and banks of computers. During most of the time the trailer had been on the ship, the technicians had been huddled inside it—playing with electronic gadgets, peering at pale green scopes, and hacking away on their computer keyboards.

"I was to supply a third-rate simulation of a frequency," Toby Larkin, a civilian technician stationed in the white trailer during FLEETEX, later testified. Larkin said he planned to actuate the frequency for fourteen minutes after launch of the Tomahawk. Fourteen minutes was the time it took the missile to fly from the *San Jacinto* and arrive at the *Iowa*. In theory, Larkin's jamming equipment would obscure the *Iowa* in an electronic fog and make her "invisible."

Rendering the *Iowa* electronically "invisible" would be no mean feat, especially since there was so much of the battleship to hide. She was long, almost comparable to three football fields placed end-to-end. And 108 feet wide—so wide that she squeezed through the locks of the Panama Canal with only two feet to spare. She was so tall that she had had to fold her radio and radar masts in order to slip under the stately old Brooklyn Bridge when she emerged from the shipyard in 1943.

TURRET ONE'S sailors were so upset after Mortensen's briefing that the turret captain decided to talk with Ensign Meyer, who had said he had overheard a great deal of talk about it from the ship's senior officers while he was standing watch on the bridge. Meyer was able to learn that if the jamming were successful, and the Tomahawk did indeed veer away from the *Iowa*, it was preprogrammed to climb to a higher altitude and go after another target, a World War II Liberty ship positioned about one hundred miles away from the battleship. And if the Tomahawk failed to sink the Liberty ship, then A-6 Intruder jets from the carrier *Coral Sea* would bomb it. And if this bombing failed to sink the Liberty ship, then the *Iowa* would be allowed to close in on the target and finish it off with shells. "I was told that sinking the hulk was our payback for coming down here," Meyer said. "We would get the chance to compare our sixteen-inch guns to other naval strike weapons."

Ensign Meyer, anxious to find out if the Tomahawk would be carrying a live warhead, sought out someone he believed would know, Master Chief Stephen Skelley, a diminutive fire-control expert. Skelley, who enjoyed a close working relationship with the mysterious civilian technicians aboard the *Iowa*, told Meyer that according to his sources, the Liberty ship had been altered to make her harder to sink. Bulkheads had been reinforced and hatches welded shut. "The Tomahawk would almost certainly have to carry a live warhead, or there would be no way it could sink the old Liberty ship," Skelley said.

Meyer asked Mortensen to reassemble the men on the main deck behind Turret One. He told the gathered sailors that the ship's four Phalanx Gatling-type guns would be manned during the experiment. These guns could each pump out 3,000 rounds of 20-mm depleted-uranium ammunition per minute. Their effective range was only 1,625 yards, not a safe margin with a missile packed with high explosives closing in at more than six hundred miles per hour. Besides, the Phalanx system had a well-known history of jamming and developing other technical problems when it was most needed.

In addition to the Gatling guns, Meyer said an A-6 chase plane would be pursuing the Tomahawk. The chase plane would be equipped with a remote-controlled steering device; theoretically, it could blow up the Tomahawk if it got too close to the *Iowa*. Meyer's information failed to alleviate anyone's fears. They had seen Tomahawk missiles in operation on the *Iowa*, and they were not impressed.

The sailors who had been on the battleship the longest informed the others that the *Iowa* had herself been involved in a Tomahawk mishap on August 2, 1986, under the previous skipper, Captain Larry Seaquist. The day before it happened, the *Iowa* had launched her very first Tomahawk since her recommissioning. Nothing out of the ordinary happened then. But the next day's launch was an entirely different story. The missile ran amok and attacked the state of Alabama. The Tomahawk was programmed to fly box squares around the missile range at Eglin Air Force Base in the Florida Panhandle. After completing a predetermined number of ninety-degree turns, the missile was supposed to shut down its engine, deploy its parachutes, and plummet harmlessly back to earth, where it would be retrieved by chase helicopters. But its preset terrain guidance system malfunctioned, and the missile continued across the Florida border, finally plowing into an Alabama hilltop far from the government reservation.

Several months after the screwup, Captain Seaquist was in Washington, where he attempted to explain what had gone wrong to the head of the surface Navy, Vice Admiral Joseph Metcalf. Admiral Metcalf told him to relax and not worry about it. Seaquist learned that the hilltop where the Tomahawk crashed had been occupied by some "good ol' boys" harvesting marijuana. Nobody was killed, or even seriously injured, but the sight of the incoming missile, trailed by helicopters filled with heavily armed security agents, convinced the dope growers to throw their hands into the air and surrender. The Navy didn't want any publicity about the fiasco, because at the time the Pentagon was solemnly swearing to Congress that a Tomahawk was so accurate and reliable that you could fire it, forget it, and fully expect it to streak through an enemy's bedroom window some fifteen hundred miles away.

And there was another problem. This was the first time since the Civil War ended in 1865 that a federal warship had launched an unprovoked attack on Alabama. So if any reporters asked questions about the debacle, the Navy's public relations specialists were prepared to tell them that the unguided missile was actually on a reconnaissance mission, part of a well-planned, well-orchestrated, federal law-enforcement and military crackdown on illicit marijuana growing in Alabama. "It would be the world's first cruise-missile drug bust," one admiral told Seaquist. But the Navy lucked out, and there were no stories about what had actually happened in Alabama.

After Ensign Meyer's briefing, most of the crewmen remained doubtful that a Tomahawk was actually capable of going where it was programmed to go. Some cried out, "Sir, what happens if that damned Tomahawk hits us?" Meyer was unable to come up with a satisfactory answer. The briefing broke up on that dismal note.

Details about the Tomahawk experiment didn't remain long within Turret One. Rumors about it spread like wildfire to the men in the other two sixteen-inch turrets and to the gunners crewing the five-inch batteries.

Clayton Hartwig, an experienced gun captain assigned to Turret Two, wrote a letter to his girlfriend in his hometown of Cleveland, Ohio, describing the experiment and telling her that the men feared "that the missile could hit us instead."

The twenty-four-year-old Hartwig had been in the Navy for six years and planned to make the service his career. Discussing the Tomahawk experiment, Hartwig told a sailor from Turret One, "I'm with you. I don't like to have people shooting at me." One of the other men joined in to say that he intended to have his will made out as soon as possible. Hartwig laughed at the sailor and said that a sixteen-inch turret was "the safest place on the ship." "You've got seventeen and a half inches of armor around you. And if something hits you, so what," he said. "There would be so little damage that it would only require a slight repainting of the side of the turret."

Very few of the other gunner's mates were as optimistic as Hartwig about a Tomahawk not being able to seriously damage the *Iowa*. Their fears were further stoked by a lack of confidence in their senior officers, most notably the *Iowa*'s skipper, Captain Fred Moosally. Under Moosally's command, the *Iowa* had in one day nearly rammed four other Navy ships. In late August 1988, she had become mired in Chesapeake Bay mud and had nearly beached herself. A month after that, she had dumped 20,000 gallons of fuel oil in Norfolk Harbor while taking on ammunition. The captain failed to report the harbor pollution to higher authorities, even though Navy regulations required such notification. And if that were not enough, the ship had come within a hairbreadth of shooting off her own bow during a gunnery exercise in January 1989. Training and maintenance were a joke, especially in the weapons department. By the time of FLEETEX, there was abundant evidence that the *Iowa* was a 59,000-ton accident looking for a place to happen.

1

"Mr. Secretary, That Ship Is Unsafe!"

THE *IOWA* HAD been anything *but* an accident waiting to happen when Captain Larry Seaquist had been her skipper. Things started to change the day Seaquist left the ship. That day, Seaquist had stood on the forecastle on the teak-covered main deck of the *Iowa*, facing the muzzles of Turret One's three guns, and felt a wave of melancholy wash over him. The *Iowa* was moored bow-first at the main pier at the Norfolk naval base. In his two years as the *Iowa*'s commanding officer, the fifty-one-year-old Seaquist had transformed the battleship into a well-honed fighting machine.

In his twenty-six years in the Navy, Seaquist, who had commanded three other warships—a gunboat, a frigate, and a destroyer—had earned a service-wide reputation as a natural and gifted ship handler. "The sea is always in session," he said. "You point your ship in the wrong direction, and you kill somebody. A warship at sea is extremely powerful and can do a lot of damage. You have an absolute responsibility to ensure that damage is not inflicted upon your own crew."

At work on the bridge, Seaquist resembled a maestro frenetically directing a symphony orchestra. He barked out multiple orders and had the ability to solve simultaneously up to fifteen tactical solutions in his head without breaking into a sweat. He enjoyed steering his colossal craft, which had two rudders and four propellers, in and out of packed formations at twenty-five knots. The *Iowa* could generate 212,000 horsepower, giving her a top cruising speed of thirty-three knots (or about forty miles per hour). This made her as fast or faster than a modern guided-missile cruiser or aircraft carrier, but not so fast that it overly strained her engines.

Seaquist's penchant for fast steaming, coupled with his daredevil ship-handling habits, earned him the nickname "25-Knot Larry." Even though the *Iowa* could turn on a dime in deep water, she was sluggish and tricky to handle in shallow water. Almost every other battleship skipper employed tugs when docking his ship or getting her underway in port. Not Seaquist. He usually docked his ship without assistance and left the harbor the same way. But the *Iowa* had some serious problems that Seaquist had inherited when he took over command of the battleship.

SECRETARY OF the Navy John Lehman had shaved nearly a year off the time the *Iowa* was supposed to spend in the Ingalls Shipyard being refitted before she was to be returned to active duty. This accelerated overhaul had two consequences: (1) The $450 million price tag went up an additional $50 million, due to excessive overtime; (2) many badly needed repairs, especially to the engineering plant and the guns, were never made, because there was no time. To meet Secretary Lehman's schedule, the ship's commanding officer, Captain G.E. Gneckow, simply skipped the final contractor's trials. These trials, required by law, are administered by the Naval Board of Inspection and Survey (InSurv). Since 1964, the board had been headed by Rear Admiral John D. Bulkeley. A Congressional Medal of Honor winner, Bulkeley had been the captain of the PT-boat that had ferried General Douglas MacArthur in March 1942 from the doomed fortress of Corregidor more than five hundred miles through a Japanese air/sea blockade to the Philippine island of Mindanao. The seventy-five-year-old Bulkeley, known as "the Sea Wolf," was rough as a cob. His inspections had ruined many promising naval careers, and any officer who deliberately avoided his team of InSurv inspectors did so at his own peril.

It was nearly two years after the ship had been recommissioned that Admiral Bulkeley and his staff arrived on the *Iowa* for an inspection. Despite Navy regulations requiring the commanding officer to document in detail any of his ship's deficiencies on cards, Captain Gneckow had very few cards to give Bulkeley's InSurv team, which met the ship in Port Everglades, Florida, on March 17, 1986. The lack of documentation was enough to flunk the InSurv.

The *Iowa*'s guns were hemorrhaging hydraulic fluid (averaging about fifty-five gallons per turret per week). All the Cosmoline (an anticorrosion lubricant smeared on metal) had not been removed from the guns. Clots of Cosmoline sometimes caused the sixteen-inch barrels to oscillate uncontrollably. Turret Three leaked oil, hydraulic fluid, and water so badly that it was known as "the rain forest." All three five-inch gun mounts on the port side were frozen and could not be fired. Down below the waterline in the engineering spaces, the bilge piping had deteriorated; the electrical system regularly shorted out; pumps failed; the engineers worried that a boiler might explode and scald the sailors tending it; soft patches went unrepaired on high-pressure lines; and some valves to the ship's firefighting system remained frozen shut.

Bulkeley "was really pissed," witnesses say. He told Gneckow to take the battleship—which had just returned from a goodwill tour of Central America—out of the harbor, past the hundred-fathom (600-foot) mark, and then attempt a full-power run. The jittery captain jumped the gun and began increasing the power to the engines before he reached deep water. About the time the ship sped up to twenty-five knots, a huge rooster tail (much like the wake of a fast-moving ski boat) reared up behind the fantail, soaking the after portion of the ship. Bulkeley instructed Gneckow to slow down and not to speed up again until he reached deep water. When his fathometer indicated that he was in sufficiently deep water, the captain told the engineers to throttle up to maximum speed. But the power plant failed to respond. The engineering plant was in such disrepair that it was incapable of generating thirty-three knots.

Bulkeley and his staff wrote page after page of notes concerning the *Iowa*'s failures. Not only did the admiral flunk the ship, he also wrote up the captain and many of his officers for dereliction of duty. When he arrived back in Washington, Bulkeley plopped a copy of his report on the desk of the Chief of Naval Operations. Then, the cantankerous InSurv chief marched down the hall to the Navy Secretary's "E-Ring" office on the fourth floor of the Pentagon, where he told John Lehman, "Mr. Secretary, that ship is unsafe! I demand that you take her out of service!" Lehman refused to take such a drastic step, but he did tell the top admirals of the Atlantic Fleet to ensure that the *Iowa*'s problems were remedied.

By this point, Gneckow, who had already been selected to be a rear admiral, knew he was in trouble. Then things got even worse. In addition to dodging Admiral Bulkeley's InSurv for almost two years, Gneckow had also neglected to have his ship undergo another mandatory test, known as the Operation Propulsion Program Evaluation (OPPE). Within the Navy, the OPPE was called "the world series of exams." The *Iowa*'s OPPE took place in Norfolk about a month after the ship had failed the InSurv. The test went on for three punishing days, and the ship again performed miserably.

Larry Seaquist had already been designated to take over the *Iowa* when he was summoned to a meeting with Vice Admiral William F. McCauley, commander of Surface Forces Atlantic. "I don't know what's going to happen, whether I leave Gneckow onboard until he can fix the mess or send you onboard to clean it up," McCauley said. The admiral said he wanted to see the *Iowa* shoot a lot more when Seaquist took over, informing the prospective captain that he would not be held to a strict ammunition training allowance. "You do the shooting, and I'll do the counting," McCauley added.

The *Iowa* was given a second OPPE and just managed to pass it. But even with the OPPE out of the way, the *Iowa* was still not out of the woods. She was also long overdue for a requalification on the Navy's gunnery range at Vieques, Puerto Rico. Seaquist took a helicopter out to the ship, which was sailing off the Virginia Capes, and rode her down to the Caribbean.

The ship shot miserably during her first day at Vieques, and if she couldn't improve her score on the second day, then Seaquist would be unable to relieve Gneckow. It was touch and go, but she finally managed to hit a target.

The change-of-command ceremony took place on April 25, 1986, an hour before sunset. The formalities were conducted on top of Turret Three. One gun in Turret Three was fully loaded and primed to fire when the ceremony began. The weapons officer told the turret captain to swivel his weapons to the centerline and lock them in place. Turret Three's loaded center gun was now aimed directly at the crewmen standing in a packed formation on the fantail for the change of command. If the gun had discharged, the concussion would have blown Captains Gneckow and Seaquist, three admirals, the Undersecretary of the Navy, and the U.S. Marines detachment off the turret and probably into the Caribbean, and it would have inflicted horrendous casualties on the crew.

AFTER ASSUMING command, Seaquist spent countless hours roaming through the ship looking for things that didn't work. It didn't take him long to realize that he was doomed to failure unless he was able to obtain some topflight help. He desperately needed a dependable weapons officer (preferably somebody who had extensive mechanical training). And he also required the services of an experienced chief engineer, a magician who could patch up the ship's rotting power plant. He didn't know it at that time, but a weapons officer with the credentials and temperament he desired was already on his way to the *Iowa*.

The new weapons officer assigned to the *Iowa* was Gene Kocmich, who had served as damage-control assistant, main propulsion assistant, weapons officer, and chief engineer on various ships. He also had been Admiral Bulkeley's aide for two and a half years and knew how to fix things. Kocmich arrived a week after Larry Seaquist took command. Seaquist told his new weapons officer, "If anything is on my ship, it will work or be jettisoned!"

As Gene Kocmich made his way through the turrets, magazines, and fire-control spaces with Master Chief Chuck Hill, the ship's gunner, he began to realize the seriousness of the situation he had inherited. But he felt lucky that he had the services of a tough chief petty officer like Chuck Hill, who was no stranger to adversity. The fifty-three-year-old Hill had participated in shore-fire bombardment in the waters off Korea while aboard the heavy cruiser USS *St. Paul*. Turret One of that ship blew up on April 21, 1952, while she was shelling enemy installations. Thirty men died from suffocation and burns. The accident was traced to the left gun, which was loaded but had the breech open. The gun captain thought the weapon had fired and told the rammerman to shove another projectile into the gun. The gun blew up, setting off the other two powder bags that were in the hoist. Chuck Hill, then a deckhand, had gone to boot camp with fifteen of the dead men. He helped sew up the canvas shrouds in which they were buried at sea.

HILL INFORMED Kocmich that when the Navy recommissioned the *Iowa*, overage sailors who had battleship experience dating back to World War II, Korea, and Vietnam were allowed to return to active duty. Kocmich had very little use for over-the-hill gunner's mates of this sort: "They were all a lick and a promise. They could talk the talk, but they couldn't walk the walk. They were good storytellers, but they didn't have the physical stamina to keep up with the young sailors." The weapons officer quickly figured out that each turret had its own unique way of loading and firing. There was little or no continuity. And when he questioned somebody about why something was done in a particular way, he always got the same answer: "That's the way we've always done it." The men were accustomed to shooting their projectiles into the sea rather than at fixed targets. This was meaningless.

Kocmich began relighting and rewiring the turrets. He also established a way to filter impurities from the hydraulic fluid to keep the equipment from freezing up. Then he replaced the piping. Priorities were set, and by the time Larry Seaquist's time as skipper was up, the work in the forward two turrets had been completed. Turret Three still was a wreck. Since it was the rearmost turret, hidden behind the superstructure, it was fired much less often than the other two. "Out of sight, out of mind" was the outlook adopted by the officers and chiefs who served back there. Turret Three sailors still used twenty-five-watt light bulbs, because seventy-five-watt bulbs would blow fuses. If a hatch cover fell off its hinges, it was seldom reattached. The gunner's mates in Turret Three employed bent and shaved-down coat hangers to jury-rig their receiver regulators (devices used to accept train and elevation orders to the guns from the fire-control computers).

In addition to the wiring, the leaks, and inadequate training, another concern in the weapons department begged for a solution. When the ship had been overhauled between 1982 and 1984, she had been equipped with state-of-the-art electronic devices, which could either be shattered or knocked out of registration whenever the ship fired a broadside. The weapons officers solved this problem. Every time a turret fired a three-gun salvo, the shots from the left and center guns were staggered ten milliseconds, and the right gun eighty milliseconds, thereby lowering the shock waves that reverberated off the superstructure.

SHORTLY AFTER his arrival aboard the *Iowa*, Gene Kocmich was introduced to the most controversial character in the ship's company, Master Chief Fire Controlman Stephen Skelley. A physically fit, small, wiry-haired, self-educated "battleship nut" from Decatur, Illinois, the forty-year-old Skelley had joined the *Iowa* in the fall of 1983, during her recommissioning in Mississippi. He had devoted almost his entire life to studying the minutiae of battleships and their armament.

When discussing battleships, Skelley's eyes became pinwheels. His dialogue harked back to the glory days of the 1930s, when the "gun club" ran the U.S. Navy. This was a clique of admirals opposed to naval aviation except to provide long-range aerial spotting for naval gunfire and scouting for the surface fleet. Skelley had enlisted in the Navy in 1965. He went to the aircraft carrier USS *Ranger* as a fire controlman. Three years of that was enough for Skelley, and he quit the Navy and returned to civilian life. For the next fifteen years, his only steady employment was a job selling pots and pans door to door. He conceded that he wasn't very successful peddling kitchenware, because he devoted almost every waking hour to researching little-known facts about battleship gunnery. While he was a civilian, Skelley had remained in the reserves and took numerous correspondence courses. Even though he had very little experience at sea, he was promoted to master chief (the highest rank a Navy enlisted person can hold), returning to active duty at that level.

Unlike most of the *Iowa*'s other chief petty officers, Skelley had no home other than the ship. He'd also never learned how to operate a car, never held a driver's license, and hardly ever bothered to cash his paychecks. He just stuffed the checks in his locker inside a battleship publication. He didn't know how to type, so he hand-printed his reports in block letters. "He was a total squirrel, who should have been locked up in a cage and only let out when he was needed," said Chuck Hill. "He was like a hand grenade with the pin pulled. He could go off in your face at any time."

Hill made the turrets and magazines strictly off limits to Skelley and refused Skelley's requests to fire certain powder lots or to conduct experiments. "Skelley wanted to go to my turrets to tell my guys what to do—what to fire. I said, 'Skelley, you stay the fuck out of my magazines and stay out of my turrets. If you want to find out something you ask me. If you go in them again, I'll break your fucking neck!' " Skelley contended that he had a right to visit the turrets, arguing, "I'm the master fire-control chief; I've got to know what's going on."

Shortly after becoming commanding officer, Larry Seaquist heard Chief Hill's grievances against Skelley. Seaquist watched Skelley closely for several months, and then said, "I decided that Skelley was brilliant, but was also a very weird little fellow who required a very tight leash. . . . He could be dangerous if left to his own devices, because he was totally fixated with getting more accuracy and range out of the guns, even if that entailed cutting corners and compromising safety." Gene Kocmich respected Skelley's impressive knowledge: "Skelley opened a window and let fresh air blow in. He would give you a different way of looking at things. If you asked him a question, he could always come up with an answer. But you absolutely couldn't let him supervise anybody, because he couldn't communicate with sailors."

IN ADDITION to fixing the guns and repairing the engineering plant, Seaquist was given another priority assignment, this one by the Secretary of the Navy. John Lehman was committed to having remotely piloted vehicles (RPVs) operate off a battleship. An RPV is an overgrown model airplane controlled by an electronic linkup. It carries a television camera and infrared sensors and can transmit images of the target back to ship. The Pentagon had spent ten years and $2.8 billion attempting to develop its own RPV, the "Aquilla." When that system proved a bust, Lehman contracted to buy the Israeli-made "Pioneer." Lehman also personally selected the officer to make this brand of RPV work on the *Iowa*. He was Lieutenant Commander Dana Griffin, a dark-haired naval flight officer.

Griffin had flown Army helicopters and then switched over to the Navy flight program in 1973. He reported to the *Iowa* in the fall of 1986. The RPVs proved troublesome at first. Griffin launched four of the drones, and three promptly crashed. After recovering the wrecked RPVs, Griffin and his men dissected them and discovered that they had all experienced vapor locks in their carburetors. The Israelis had designed the drones for a type of fuel not used by the U.S. Navy. Tinkering with the engines and employing low-lead, 100-octane aviation fuel, Griffin's men managed to get optimum performance from their RPVs.

EVEN AFTER a year on the *Iowa*, Larry Seaquist hadn't been able to make the same progress on upgrading the ship's power plant as he had with the sixteen-inch turrets. He needed a new chief engineer, and the man sent to do that job was Commander Jerry Ware, a short, sincere North Carolinian and an experienced engineer. Before his assignment to the *Iowa*, Ware was called to the office of Admiral McCauley. Ware was kept standing at attention before the admiral's desk for a considerable period of time. Finally, McCauley looked Ware squarely in the eye and said, "The *Iowa*'s engineering plant is fucked up. I want you to unfuck it. If you don't unfuck it, I'm going to fuck you!" End of interview.

Ware's first inspection tour of the *Iowa*'s engineering spaces confirmed his worst forebodings. "It was obvious that there was very little training. Records were almost nonexistent. I couldn't see how the plant had ever passed the 1987 OPPE." Terming the plant "a chamber of horrors," he said the chiefs and junior officers informed him that they were "petrified because they were working on a system which would not be legal in engineering school." Flammable liquid flowed everywhere, especially from boiler number three.

Insulation was missing from much of the piping, which had been repaired at some time or other with temporary soft patches. The metal was in an advanced stage of deterioration, and a number of eight-inch valves had been frozen open since the early 1940s. Ware feared that the engineering plant might blow up. He went to Seaquist and informed him that the engine rooms were "ticking time bombs." The chief engineer requested permission to take the whole system down and begin emergency maintenance on it. Seaquist said that was impossible, as they were facing an upcoming foreign deployment. Seaquist did consent to taking individual portions of the plant off-line to begin repairs, even if that caused a drop in the ship's speed.

Seaquist unlocked his safe and handed Ware a copy of Admiral Bulkeley's 1986 InSurv report. Ware read the report and said, "Admiral Bulkeley is right. This ship is unsafe to steam." Seaquist also showed Ware a thick sheaf of letters from three- and four-star admirals referring to the Bulkeley report. "If Congress ever got their hands on this file, it would be extremely incriminating. We put this ship back in commission, and it is a floating disaster. It's very clear a lot of high-ranking officers are trying to cover this up," Ware said. The chief engineer and his men didn't waste any time beginning the repairs. They began removing large portions of corroded pipe and replacing them. They made other at-sea quick fixes, but Ware had serious doubts that this was any way to "unfuck this mess" as Admiral McCauley had ordered.

LARRY SEAQUIST ousted his original executive officer and named Gene Kocmich his acting second-in-command. The captain admired Kocmich's laidback way of getting things done and attempted to make the job permanent. But after four months, the Norfolk group commander, Rear Admiral Jeremy "Mike" Boorda, told him that was impossible. Boorda, a rising star in the Navy, told Seaquist that Commander Mike Fahey was on his way to the *Iowa* to become executive officer. Boorda told Seaquist he had no say in the matter, emphasizing the fact that Fahey "was politically well connected in the Navy." "You have to swallow Fahey," he said. Kocmich reverted to his original job as weapons officer.

Fahey was lean and rugged, standing six feet two inches tall. Shortly after he came to the ship, relations between Seaquist and his executive officer ruptured and never mended. A Chicago native, Fahey was a practicing believer in the bare-knuckles school of leadership. He manhandled at least three officers during his time on the *Iowa.* As he jogged his daily ten miles in circuits around the *Iowa,* Fahey carried a hand squeezer to strengthen his grip. When he was irate, he rapidly squeezed the device.

He was proud of his nickname, "Iron Mike," and soon Jerry Ware became one of "Iron Mike's" favorite scapegoats. Fahey had never served on a ship with a power plant as old as the *Iowa*'s. According to Gene Kocmich and Larry Seaquist, Fahey had no comprehension about how the engines worked and was disinclined to make any allowances for the difficulties Ware was experiencing in his attempts to make major repairs at sea. While the *Iowa* was on a six-month deployment in the Eastern Mediterranean, the two men clashed openly. Not far from the Suez Canal, waves buffeted the ship and salt water cascaded over the bow, seeping into some of the electrical equipment. The seepage shorted out a major electrical switchboard. All the electrical power to the ship was knocked off-line.

The executive officer dashed from the bridge to the main engineering control room, brandishing a flashlight like a club in one hand and his grip squeezer in his other. "We're dead in the water! We're dead in the water!" he howled. "You're going to get us all killed! We're in a war zone!"

Ware scornfully aimed the beam of his own flashlight at the engine revolution indicator and calmly replied, "I've got four engines doing 120 revolutions per minute. The engines are still functioning. We're still moving through the water. We're doing sixteen knots. This is a battleship, not an aircraft carrier. She's built to take hits. Just because you lose electrical power doesn't mean you lose propulsion on a battleship." Just then, the electrical generators kicked in and the lights went back on. Fahey stormed off in a funk.

Another time, when Larry Seaquist was off the ship during the Mediterranean cruise, Ware and Fahey exchanged insults, and Fahey informed Ware that he was fired for insubordination. When Seaquist returned, Fahey told the captain that he had dismissed the chief engineer for cause. Seaquist shouted, "Don't compromise my engineer anymore!" Fahey rushed off the bridge, tracked down Ware, and told him that Seaquist had saved his job. The executive officer then shook a balled fist in Ware's face and said Seaquist wouldn't be there forever, and he would get even.

From then on, Fahey openly exhibited his intense hatred of Seaquist. On Christmas Eve, Seaquist was again off the ship, attending a Bob Hope show with Rear Admiral Dennis M. Brooks, commander of the Joint Task Force Middle East, on the nearby carrier USS *Midway*. After the show ended and Seaquist and the admiral were headed back to the battleship, their forty-foot utility boat developed engine troubles. The coxswain radioed the *Iowa* for help. The officer of the deck (OOD) asked Fahey what to do. "Train a sixteen-inch battery out and blow the mother fuckers out of the water. I hope Seaquist drowns," Fahey snapped. Everyone on the bridge—the three junior officers on watch, the navigator, the helmsman, the boatswain's mate of the watch—overheard this and was shocked. The OOD had a rescue boat dispatched to pick up Seaquist and Brooks. Seaquist heard about what had happened and wanted Fahey off his ship. The captain also didn't appreciate Fahey's open declaration about the sixteen-inch guns: "If those fuckers never fire again, it will be too soon for me!" But Seaquist knew that he would never get away with sacking somebody so wired to some of the Navy's top officers.

MOST BATTLESHIP captains were promoted to rear admiral after successfully completing their tours. When he relinquished command of the USS *Bradley* in 1970, Joseph Metcalf, who became a vice admiral, quoted from Joseph Conrad's essay *The Captain*: "In each ship there is one man who in the hour of emergency or peril at sea, can turn to no other man. There is one who alone is ultimately responsible for the safe navigation, engineering performance, accurate gunfiring and the morale of his ship. He is the commanding officer. He is the ship." When asked why his protégé, Larry Seaquist, wasn't selected to become a rear admiral, Admiral Metcalf sighed and called Seaquist an "iconoclast." "The admirals didn't quite understand Larry. He never paid attention to the flag officers' [admirals'] community. Not many flag officers went aboard his ship. It takes politics to become an admiral in the United States Navy. That's a sad commentary, but true, and Larry wasn't a very good politician."

2

☆

"The Moose"

CAPTAIN FRED MOOSALLY, the man who would take Larry Seaquist's place as commanding officer of the *Iowa*, was a consummate politician. Most changes of command aboard U.S. naval warships were ostentatious affairs, but Larry Seaquist, who had started life as an Idaho farm boy, had great disdain for pomp and ceremony. As the outgoing commanding officer of the *Iowa*, he had the final say on the format and content of his change of command. He determined that the officers' uniform of the day would be dress whites with medals, but he had banned the wearing of swords, saying they were too pretentious, too much like the Royal Navy. That didn't sit well with the man standing next to Seaquist on the forecastle, the man who was scheduled to relieve Seaquist as commanding officer, Captain Fred Moosally. There probably never were two naval officers more dissimilar. For one thing, Moosally was a darling of the Chief of Naval Operations, and he was also closely allied with some very important congressmen. The burly, forty-four-year-old officer designated to command the *Iowa* had paved the way to be selected as a rear admiral on the completion of his two-year tour on this ship.

Nearly as bald on top as a billiard ball, Moosally had long sideburns bracketing his ears. He was proud of his nickname, "the Moose," which he'd acquired on the gridiron, playing defensive tackle at the U.S. Naval Academy in two championship football seasons during the mid-1960s. His college yearbook, *The Lucky Bag*, referred to him as "a big aggressive athlete" who "lost no time distinguishing himself on the Navy football fields." He still considered himself a jock, and he was quick to point out, to almost anyone with whom he talked, these three accomplishments: (1) He had played on the Navy's 1963 Cotton Bowl team, led by future Dallas Cowboys quarterback Roger Staubach; (2) he had been a member of the 1965 Blue-Gray All Star Team; (3) he'd won the Annapolis Touchdown Club's Silver Helmet trophy in 1965 as the Navy's most valuable player.

FRED MOOSALLY was born and grew up in Youngstown, Ohio, the heartland of America's Rust Belt. Bisected by the Mahoning River, Youngstown was a blue-collar, steel-producing town with a reputation for tolerating municipal corruption, gambling, prostitution, dope, shakedowns, and other organized-crime schemes. Although many of his school friends thought he was Italian, Moosally actually was of Lebanese descent. He still had relatives living in Lebanon. The Moosally family was prominent in the old country, including physicians, the director general of the Ministry of Trade, a diplomat, and powerful businessmen. Fred and his family were Maronites, a Christian sect taking its name from a priest and hermit who roamed through the Middle East in the fourth century AD. There were 1,500 Maronites in Youngstown. Most attended services at St. Maron's Church, where Fred and his family were communicants. Fred's father was an insurance salesman; his mother was a member of a prominent Youngstown Maronite family, the Saadys. There were six children in the Moosally family, three boys and three girls.

Fred graduated from Ursuline High School in 1962. He was an outstanding tackle on the high-school football squad and was selected to be a second-string member of the All-City squad. He also lifted weights, ran track, and played summer baseball. A neighbor, Loretta Latronico, whose children grew up with the Moosally children, said Fred "was a terrific kid" and "was wonderful to his parents." His Ursuline coach, Tom Carey, said, "I remember Fred as a leader, as a student outstanding academically, and as an athlete. He was an easy-going individual to work with." Moosally was courted by the football coaches of Pennsylvania State University and the University of Pittsburgh. But he made up his mind to attend Annapolis after talking with the Naval Academy's football coach, Bill Elias.

Moosally apparently wasn't much of a scholar at the academy; he graduated near the bottom of his class in 1966, ranking 812 out of 868. But he was a typical Annapolis "ring knocker," meaning that he conspicuously displayed his USNA class ring to Navy ROTC and OCS graduates to impress upon them that he had a much better chance of becoming an admiral than they did.

After his commissioning, Moosally spent six months at the Naval Academy doing odd jobs before reporting to the guided-missile destroyer USS *K.D. Bailey*. He served a tour off the coast of Vietnam, attended destroyer department head school in Newport, Rhode Island, and then went to another guided-missile destroyer, the USS *Lynde McCormick*. Returning to Annapolis in 1971, he worked in the recruitment and candidate guidance office. He also worked with the varsity football team. As a thirty-year-old lieutenant, he was assigned to the frigate USS *Bronstein* as executive officer. Her skipper was Lieutenant Commander William J. "Bud" Flanagan, a close friend of Moosally's, who also belonged to the Navy's elite group of youthful, politically well-connected movers and shakers.

Flanagan, a graduate of Massachusetts Maritime Academy in nautical science, would, like Moosally, spend time on Capitol Hill as a Navy lobbyist. A wheeler-dealer, Flanagan ultimately became a four-star admiral in charge of the entire Atlantic Fleet.

After the *Bronstein*, Moosally went to Washington to the Bureau of Naval Personnel, where he worked for Vice Admiral Joseph Metcalf. He then served another tour as an executive officer, this time on the guided-missile destroyer USS *Mahan*. After that, he was promoted to commander and went to work for the Chief of Naval Operations (CNO) as a surface-warfare program coordinator. Two years later, he became administrative assistant and aide to the Chief of Naval Operations, Admiral Thomas Hayward.

Moosally was in a very high-visibility job, entitling him to wear on his left shoulder four gold aiguillettes (ornamental braids signifying that he worked for a four-star admiral). Seagoing officers scornfully refer to aiguillettes as "loafer's loops." Moosally's time in this rarefied atmosphere turned him into a "water walker" (Navy jargon for someone akin to Jesus Christ) when he was only thirty-seven years old. He got this job not because he had demonstrated that he was a particularly good ship handler, or a brilliant tactician or a strategic thinker. Rather, those in the Navy who really knew Moosally rated him a first-rate politician. His Naval Academy classmates, in awe of his political acumen, said he was "way ahead of the power curve."

As one of the CNO's "junior gatekeepers," Moosally was astute at advising the executive assistant (a senior captain who actually ran the day-to-day affairs of the office) whom to admit and whom to decline politely. He was the type of aide who never acted as if he were "trying on his admiral's stars for size." He unruffled feathers, heaped flattery on fleet commanders, and accumulated an impressive stack of IOUs from flag officers—ever mindful that some of these same officers would sit on the selection board that would decide his fitness to wear the gold shoulder boards and silver star of a rear admiral (lower half).

FRED MOOSALLY had one potential career-killer. He didn't have one single day of sea-command time on his record. If Moosally were really serious about making admiral, he had to remedy this situation, and fast. He had many patrons high up in the Navy, among them Vice Admiral Joseph Metcalf—the same Joseph Metcalf who had picked Larry Seaquist to command the *Iowa*. "I thought a great deal of Fred," Metcalf said. "He was excellent in carrying out things I wanted done. He was personable. He never behaved like the typical executive assistant in the greaseball sense." The admiral cautioned Moosally: "You're turning into a professional executive officer. Get you a command at sea or forget about your future in the Navy."

Moosally applied for command and was made skipper of the guided-missile destroyer USS *Kidd*. Homeported in Norfolk, she carried a crew of 341. The man Moosally relieved as captain of the *Kidd* was his old buddy and former commanding officer on the *Bronstein*, "Bud" Flanagan. Flanagan had very nearly been cashiered for the opulent manner in which he had decorated the captain's quarters on the *Kidd*. He had painted his cabin black and hung lots of mirrors on the bulkheads, but the real kicker was the couch. It cost $6,000. The press reported on Flanagan's extravagance, which made Navy Secretary John Lehman livid. Lehman wanted to throw Flanagan out of the Navy, but he was dissuaded from doing so by the Democratic Speaker of the House Thomas "Tip" O'Neill, the red-faced, white-maned Boston politician. Flanagan had gone to college in O'Neill's district, and he asked the speaker to convince Navy Secretary John Lehman to lay off. O'Neill went to bat for him, and Flanagan survived the mini-scandal, ending his career as a four-star admiral.

Admiral Metcalf thought that Moosally did "a terrific job" as skipper of the *Kidd*. Following this command, "the Moose" returned to Washington to work for the Navy's Office of Legislative Affairs (OLA) as a liaison officer on Capitol Hill for the House of Representatives. His OLA boss was an Annapolis football teammate, Rear Admiral Thomas Lynch.

Dedicated saltwater officers, who sought desperately to avoid Washington duty, were openly scornful of OLA, referring to it as "the office of pimps, liars, con men, thieves and charlatans." Retired Captain Stan Sirmans, who had served a tour in OLA, compared those who worked for the Navy on Capitol Hill to the principal character in Arthur Miller's *Death of a Salesman*, saying, "They're Willy Loman types, all salesmen, with a handshake, a shoeshine and a smile." However, OLA was highly valued by the brass hats who ran the Navy and counted on the largesse of Congress to fund the Navy's ships, planes, fuel, and sailors.

Fred Moosally fit in just fine at OLA. Well liked and affable, he exuded locker-room bonhomie. He was a master at spinning "sea stories." His appearance was always flawless. Most of the time he wore civilian suits and ties. But on those days when he wore his blue uniform, he looked like a recruiting poster of a naval warrior, with four rows of multicolored ribbons and a gold Surface Warfare badge pinned above his left breast. His white cap with its black bill encrusted with "scrambled eggs" was tucked under his arm as he made his rounds of congressional offices.

He was good with names, and he cultivated staffers with the same intensity that he devoted to their bosses. "I never saw the guy flustered. I never saw him in any way but grace under pressure," Jim Hickey, a congressional aide, told the *Daily Press* newspaper in Hampton, Virginia. "He's intelligent, politically savvy and well respected not only by the people in the liaison office but by the Navy folks as well." When he was lobbying Congress,

Moosally often worked out of the office of Representative Ike Skelton, who provided him with a desk and a phone.

A Missouri Democrat, Skelton was a military groupie. He had attended high school at the Wentworth Military Academy but never spent a day in the armed services. A former prosecutor and state attorney general, he was a heavy hitter on the House Armed Services Committee, serving on the Procurement, Military Nuclear Systems Subcommittee and as chairman of the Military Personnel Subcommittee. Skelton was strongly in favor of the Navy's reactivation of the four *Iowa*-class battleships. "When there was bad news, Fred made sure that it was palatable, that it was sweetened," said Russ Orban, a former Skelton aide.

When Skelton and other members of the House Armed Services Committee wanted to visit the USS *Stark*, which had been badly shot up by an Iraqi jet fighter in 1987, Moosally made all the arrangements for the trip to Bahrain, where the frigate was undergoing repairs. OLA seemed to have an unlimited pocketbook when it came to financing congressional junkets of this sort. Its budget was tightly held. Moosally regularly squired the lawmakers and staffers on field trips to aircraft carriers and submarine forces and always made sure that they were introduced to key flag officers. "Whenever the Navy got in trouble," said a source in the Navy Secretary's office, "OLA would have a party on the Hill for members and staffers with all the shrimp you could eat and all the whiskey you could drink."

According to a number of congressional staffers, Moosally spent a great deal of time on Capitol Hill campaigning to get command of a battleship, which would almost certainly guarantee that he would one day become an admiral. His friend "Bud" Flanagan, who was commanding a destroyer squadron and had been selected as a rear admiral, helped his old shipmate. Moosally was also assisted by Rear Admiral Richard Milligan, the Navy battle group commander in Charleston, South Carolina. Another one of his biggest promoters was the Norfolk group commander, Rear Admiral Mike Boorda, a man whose own star was rising. Boorda had been selected to head the Bureau of Naval Personnel, and as such would become a three-star admiral. This support was helpful, but what tipped the balance was the decisive role Moosally played in winning a battle to get Congress to approve the construction of two new aircraft carriers at Virginia's Newport News Shipbuilding Company. Admiral Carl Trost, Chief of Naval Operations, appreciated Moosally's efforts. Trost was also aware that Moosally had persuaded his pals in Congress to tuck the funding for a couple of extra frigates and a nuclear-powered cruiser into the Defense Department's annual appropriations bill.

IN LATE 1987, Moosally visited his former boss, Vice Admiral Joe Metcalf, and told him how much he wanted to command a battleship. "I had confidence that he could do the job," the admiral later said, dividing those Navy officers who obtain a command at sea into three categories. He put about 20 percent in his first grouping: "They do it because it's a way to get their ticket punched. They're not very happy. Some of them would be very happy to go through their entire Navy career without ever going to sea." Fifty percent went into Metcalf's second grouping: "They'll go to sea and do the job. But the characteristic that distinguishes these people is that they don't have any imagination. I wouldn't want to go to war with them." Finally, there was the remaining 30 percent: "They are the Nelsons [British Admiral Horatio Nelson, who won the Battle of Trafalgar in 1805] and the Moorers [Admiral Thomas H. Moorer, chairman of the Joint Chiefs of Staff during the Vietnam War]. They have the imagination. They don't go by the book, because warfare doesn't go by the book. It takes boldness to beat the enemy. You've got to show that son-of-a-bitch that you're better than he is, show him that you can't screw around with the United States Navy." Metcalf added, "You have to go on gut instincts in picking men for command, and sometimes your gut is just plain wrong."

With endorsements in hand from Admiral Metcalf and the CNO, Moosally sought to obtain command of the battleship USS *Missouri*. His name was penciled in for that ship, but he ultimately lost out to Captain John J. Chernesky, who had been executive officer of the *Iowa* during most of the time that G.E. Gneckow was her skipper. When Chernesky won the *Missouri*, Moosally went after the *Iowa* and got her.

LARRY SEAQUIST was well aware of Fred Moosally's reputation as a politician and the fact that he had only commanded one other vessel. Still, he did not want to do anything to undercut Moosally's authority with the crew. That was bad business. In the Navy, the captain of a ship is often referred to by his crew as the "Old Man"—signifying, regardless of his chronological age, that he is a father figure. Every Old Man inspired a certain measure of awe and fear in his men. On the bridge it was said, "On a ship there's god. And when you can't find god, you can always find the captain. The captain always outranks god."

Seaquist strove to make the transition as painless as possible for his successor. He had invited Moosally to join the ship in New York and sail her back to Norfolk. "This would allow him to get a feel for her. The change of command was going to be on a Friday, and then the ship was going into the yard the following Monday for a three-month overhaul. If he didn't ride her from New York down, he wouldn't be able to do it for quite some time," Seaquist said. But Moosally turned him down without offering any explanation.

On the day of the change-of command, both Seaquist and Gene Kocmich warned Moosally to watch out for "Iron Mike" Fahey, the executive officer, hinting that Fahey "could be a bit rough on the wardroom." (The wardroom, where the officers ate their meals, came to be used as a synonym for the officers themselves.) Seaquist and Kocmich understated the problem, as was demonstrated just before the ceremonies began, when Fahey waylaid Dan Meyer and Terry McGinn, telling them, "You cocksuckers are dog meat just as soon as Seaquist leaves this ship!" McGinn had spilled coffee on his dress-white blouse and wondered if his messy uniform might have sparked that outburst. Earlier that same morning, Fahey informed Jerry Ware that he "had planted a poison pill" with the new captain and that Ware's "ass was grass." Even before the day was over, Fahey would start making good on his threats to Meyer, McGinn, and Ware.

SEAQUIST AND Moosally did tussle over one issue that would generate great animosity in the chiefs' quarters. Almost all of the 110 chiefs on the *Iowa* had more than twenty years of experience in the Navy, and a large number of them were pushing or exceeding thirty years. They wore the same khaki work uniforms as the officers and had their own mess and berthing spaces. They were tough, proud men who jealously guarded their status and prerogatives. There was an old saying in the Navy: "The officers merely rent the sailors. The chiefs own them." These senior ranking enlisted men had tremendous influence over the low-ranking sailors—managing their work, their behavior, their likelihood for promotion, and deciding whether or not they could leave the ship on liberty. They were also the technical experts. And when an officer was unsure how to do something or was stumped by a convoluted technical manual, it was common for him to call out, "Where's the chief?"

During their many years in the Navy, the chief petty officers had seen many captains come and go; some were splendid ship handlers and tacticians, others were fools and poseurs. A wise captain would cultivate the chiefs and seek their advice and counsel. He wouldn't go out of his way to alienate them or treat them with contempt. And he most certainly wouldn't make war on them. But that's exactly what Fred Moosally did, beginning his war with the *Iowa*'s chiefs even before he was officially in charge of the ship.

The top enlisted man on the *Iowa*—and probably the most popular person aboard her—was Command Master Chief Bobby L. Scott. On his left sleeve, he wore a gold chevron and a silver eagle topped by two gold stars, as well as nine gold hash marks, signifying that he had completed thirty-six years of honorable service. Born in a small town in western Tennessee, he had enlisted in the Navy on August 2, 1952, one month after his graduation from high school. A personable boatswain's mate with a ruddy complexion and a bulbous nose, he served as the captain's problem-solver and goodwill ambassador to the crew. During his Navy career, he had been assigned to five separate ships. He served a tour as an enlisted instructor at the U.S. Naval Academy and had been the last enlisted man to teach seamanship at Annapolis. He had also served in Vietnam with the riverine forces and had been decorated with a Bronze Star with "V" for valor.

Bobby Scott presided over the chiefs' mess, setting the agenda on how the other senior enlisted men interacted with the officers above them and the sailors below them. He could be tough and unbending, and he refused to let the chiefs show "skin flicks" on the ship. Scott loved the young sailors and treated them like his sons. He lined them up before they went on liberty, saw to it that their uniforms were immaculate, and counseled them, "Make sure you boys have fun on the beach, but be real sure you uphold the *Iowa*'s good name and honor while you're there." On his desk, he kept a big jar full of peppermint patties and hard candy for his visitors. "Bobby's attitude was infectious with the other chiefs. They vied with one another to be just like Scott," Larry Seaquist said. "He was the best sailor on the ship," added Chuck Hill.

About a month before Fred Moosally was scheduled to take over the *Iowa*, Moosally informed Seaquist that he planned to replace Scott when he became skipper. Seaquist wrote Moosally that he was making a serious mistake that could dramatically lower morale. Unpersuaded, Moosally claimed that Bobby Scott was totally lacking in leadership qualities. Moosally's plan to relieve Scott leaked all over the ship, causing an uproar.

Shortly before the change of command, Larry Seaquist received a call from Rear Admiral Boorda, the group commander: "I've got Fred Moosally here, and 'the Moose' has got a burr up his ass about this command master chief business. I've told him that you two guys could work it out. We're on our way up there now to settle things." Seaquist walked down the gangway and met the admiral and Moosally on the pier. Boorda said, "I just brought Fred here. I'm heading back to my headquarters. You two guys square this away." Seaquist nodded. The admiral drove off in his black limousine. Moosally told Seaquist that his mind was made up. He was going to replace Bobby Scott with Master Chief T.C. Waters.

Seaquist argued that Scott was the type of leader that "troops would walk over coals to please." He attempted to convince Moosally to let some time pass before he named a replacement. The ship was going into the yards, he said, and the new skipper would need help from people like Scott. Their discussion became heated, and crew members watched goggle-eyed from the main deck as the two captains verbally sparred with each other on the pier.

Finally, Moosally promised that he would retain Scott for a time. But several days later, he sent a message saying he was definitely getting rid of Scott and announcing that Waters would take Scott's place. Chuck Hill was so furious about what Moosally had done to his shipmate that he put in his retirement papers a month early. He didn't want to be on the ship when the new captain took over.

Hill's early departure created some major problems in the weapons department. And things worsened further for Fred Moosally when Gene Kocmich transferred to the staff of the Atlantic Fleet commander. But at the time, Moosally didn't seem to be overly concerned with the guns. The captain's enthusiasm was reserved for the missiles, according to Chief Bob Sumrall. "With the new people [in the Navy] their careers revolved around missiles. Being assigned to a sixteen-inch gun was a real career stopper," Sumrall said. "They were all oriented toward sophisticated, high-tech weapons. The only ones who cared about the guns were the old-timers," he added, dismissing missilemen as "winged weenies."

THE CHANGE of command took place on Friday, May 23, 1988, while the ship was tied to the main pier at the Norfolk naval base. It was a splendid, slightly overcast spring day. All the ammunition had been unloaded in preparation for the ship's being towed to the shipyard the following Monday for its three-month overhaul. Without the weight of the ammunition and a full load of fuel, the ship rode somewhat high in the water.

A tent had been set up amidships for refreshments after the ceremony. The teakwood on the main deck had been scrubbed until it was almost white. The ship's brightwork and brass gleamed. Seaquist frequently said, "A battleship is not a pretty face, it's a working warship." But on this day, the *Iowa* displayed a comely face to visitors and dignitaries who attended the ceremony.

The principal speaker was Rear Admiral Mike Boorda. Born in South Bend, Indiana, Boorda had been an enlisted man for six years. He attended Officers' Candidate School (OCS) and was commissioned in 1962, but he didn't obtain his college degree from the University of Rhode Island until 1971. He aspired to become Chief of Naval Operations. That was quite a goal, since aviators and nuclear submariners dominated the upper ranks of the Navy and had a lock on the top job. After his speech, Boorda pinned the Legion of Merit on the left side of Larry Seaquist's white blouse.

Seaquist quoted Joseph Conrad's work *The Captain*, just as his "sea daddy (patron)," Vice Admiral Joseph Metcalf, had done eighteen years earlier at his change of command aboard the USS *Bradley*. Seaquist praised the crew effusively for their hard work and for the support they'd given him. He attempted to convey just how much he hated to leave this ship. Tears welled in his eyes, and his voice broke. Then he read these lines from poet Emily Dickinson:

Exultation is the going
Of an inland soul to sea,
Past the houses—past the headlands—
Into deep Eternity—

Bred as we, among the mountains,
Can the sailor understand
The divine intoxication
Of the first league out from land?

Fred Moosally read his orders giving him command of the ship. Lacking Larry Seaquist's eloquence, "the Moose's" maiden speech was more like a locker-room exhortation. Command Master Chief Bobby Scott presented Seaquist with the tapering red, white, and blue pennant with seven stars, which had flown day and night on the main truck (tallest mast) of the ship. The reception was a spartan affair, consisting of lemon pound cake, chocolate chip cookies, and sugary red punch, unspiked. (U.S. Navy warships became dry after President Woodrow Wilson appointed Josephus Daniels, a Southern newspaper editor and passionate prohibitionist, to be Secretary of the Navy in 1913.)

LARRY SEAQUIST and his wife, Carla, hadn't reached the end of the pier before Fred Moosally began putting his imprint on the *Iowa*. The Seaquists heard the boatswain's pipe shrill over the 1MC (the main public-address system), followed by the announcement, "All officers report to the wardroom." Responding to the order, the officers filed into the wardroom wearing a mixed bag of uniforms. Some still had on their dress whites, while others had dropped by their staterooms and changed into wash khakis. The executive officer was one of the first to arrive. The officers segregated themselves by rank—lieutenant commanders and above sitting up front and lieutenants and below positioning themselves in the rear of the shabby, white-painted compartment. The new captain, lugging a thick stack of memos under his arm, was one of the very last to arrive. He seated himself at a table covered with garish blue Naugahyde next to his second-in-command and had an officer pass out memos to the others.

Almost everyone present thought that Fred Moosally was largely uninformed about the *Iowa* and her officers. He'd never conducted any kind of inspection of the ship. The only other time he'd even been aboard was about a week earlier, when he had spent about twenty-five minutes on the ship before departing in the red Datsun convertible in which he had driven down from Washington. But it soon became apparent that Moosally had absorbed a lot about the ship and her officers from a well-placed source on the ship.

"Iron Mike" Fahey had carried out the threat he had made earlier to Jerry Ware. The executive officer had indeed sought out the new captain and planted a poison pill against Ware and many other officers.

"Iron Mike" opened the meeting. Standing up and pounding the table, he roared, "These fuckers don't have any idea about how to do anything!" He referred to the officers as "cocksuckers," "assholes," and "dumb motherfuckers." Anyone who disagreed with him or the new captain, he pledged, would be summarily fired and drummed out of the Navy in disgrace.

Moosally followed the executive officer and offered no conciliatory words to the assembled officers. He said he'd heard that the ship, contrary to its sterling reputation on the waterfront, was a pigsty, a real rat's nest.

The engineering department, Moosally said, was a dank, foul, fetid cesspool. It would receive priority treatment during the upcoming shipyard overhaul. If the mess were not cleaned up soon, heads would roll. "I demand fierce loyalty, and anybody who doesn't give it can kiss their asses and their careers good-bye!" he shouted. He then called Larry Seaquist's seamanship and tactics "overrated." He said the junior officers had been pampered by Seaquist and the chiefs were loafers and over-the-hill time-servers. His harsh words intimidated as well as offended many of the solemn-faced officers. Typical was the reaction of Lieutenant Commander Dana Griffin, commander of the remotely piloted vehicle (RPV) detachment. "Up to that point, we'd thought of ourselves as super-stars, and then in waltzes this dumb, crude ex-jock, acting like we'd lost a football game for him. It was an obscene and degrading way to meet a man who had such power over your life."

Moosally was far from through. Not one to shy away from the liberal use of clichés, he invoked the role and verbiage he knew best—straight from the gridiron. "I'm the coach, and you're the team. You can forget everything you learned under Larry Seaquist. I'm calling the plays now. If you guys are out to screw me, you can forget about it!"

The officers were stunned. "It was obvious that self-preservation and survival had set in that wardroom. Everybody was just trying to preserve some kind of professional decorum, but sedition of a sort was rampant," said Jerry Ware. Ensign Jeff Turner, a deck officer who had recently been assigned to the Tomahawk and Harpoon missiles, correctly guessed that Moosally was going to engage a game known as "Devour your young," practiced by some of the Navy's predatory commanding officers.

As the degrading session ended, the officers began to read the twelve-page memo that Moosally referred to as "my manifesto." It was a loyalty oath, larded with boilerplate prose about leadership and tactics.

WORD SPREAD quickly from the wardroom to the chiefs about Moosally's contemptuous comments, setting off a near-mutiny in their quarters. These chiefs were especially infuriated about the new captain describing them as "that damned labor union—the AFL-CIO." Chief Bob Sumrall called Moosally nothing more than "an admiral striker." *Striker* is a Navy term for an apprentice or learner, and Sumrall didn't intend this epithet to be a compliment.

If Moosally intended to mistreat some of the senior officers and all of the chiefs and junior officers, he had mapped out an entirely different type of strategy for dealing with the lower-ranking enlisted men, becoming their benevolent, paternalistic best friend. "Moosally and Fahey launched a khaki attack [officers and chiefs], but they treated the blue jackets [sailors] like gods," Jerry Ware said.

Moosally started making frequent tours around the *Iowa*, exuding geniality to the sailors he encountered along the way. He winked at the crewmen and acted like he was one of the boys. He slapped backs, patted fannies, and told the sailors that if they had any trouble whatsoever with their chiefs and officers, they should not hesitate to come in and see "the Moose."

ALTHOUGH LITTLE had been said about gunnery during the captain's wardroom session, it was evident, given Iron Mike's apparent closeness to the captain and his avowed disdain for the sixteen-inch guns, that gunnery would be deemphasized. This suspicion was confirmed about a week later, soon after the *Iowa* had been towed to the Newport News Shipyard for her scheduled overhaul. Larry Seaquist, Gene Kocmich, and Master Chief Chuck Hill had compiled a detailed $1 million gunnery-repair package. It was supposed to repair most of the lighting and electrical, powder hoist, and hydraulic discrepancies that had not been fixed in the three turrets.

Moosally and Fahey canceled everything in the gunnery-repair package and transferred these funds to the engineering department to overhaul the power plant. This was folly, because the "ready safe switches," which prevent the guns from discharging after they were loaded and primed, were inoperable on most of the nine sixteen-inch guns. Some seventy-five deficiencies were documented in the magazines alone.

To keep their turret operational, Dan Meyer and Dale Mortensen had employed a time-honored (if unofficial) Navy custom known as "cumshaw" to procure spare parts. According to the *Naval Terms Dictionary*, "a 'cumshaw artist' is adept at getting cumshaw work done, usually by liberal handouts of food and coffee to shipyard workers." The word was picked up in China, where the United States had formerly maintained a fleet of river gunboats to protect American interests. Sailors heard Chinese beggars say *kam sia*, meaning, "thank you very much." The beggars' word was bastardized to fit the American tongue.

Mortensen and Meyer were able to mend their "ready safe switches," but they couldn't do a thing about repairing the turret officers' panel. This board of colored lights indicated when the guns were loaded and primed to fire. The panel had an important safety function, giving the turret officer the ability to prevent the guns from firing in an emergency. Turret One's panel was patched with duct tape and could short out the turret's entire electrical system. This situation had existed for more than four years.

And they faced yet another hazard. When a gun is fired, compressed air is forced down the barrel. The air, which must have a pressure of 175 pounds per square inch, purges cinders, gas, and burning debris from the barrel. Known as gas ejection air, it is essential to the safety of the gunners and to the ship as a whole. If the compressed air does not function properly, an accident could occur in this manner: A shell is fired; new powder bags are inserted; the breechblock is not yet closed; residue and gases ignite the bags of propellant; and a firestorm ensues. Turret One's compressed-air reservoir was out of commission, and the turret was forced to secure its air from main engineering. However, the gunner's mates could never count on obtaining a uniform flow of air, and sometimes they couldn't get any air at all.

Turret One also had a large crack in the water main used for firefighting. In some slick "cumshaw" dealings with the yard workers, Meyer and Mortensen arranged to have the fire main welded. But other welding projects needed to be done, and with the shells and powder off the ship, this was an ideal time to do them. Even Meyer and Mortensen, however, weren't able to persuade the "yard birds" (shipyard workers) to undertake any other projects. And since the *Iowa*'s own engineering force was being overworked by the executive officer in overhauling the power plant, the engineers were in no position to help the turrets.

Mike Fahey for the most part avoided the weapons department during the ship's time in the yard, but he constantly prowled the engineering spaces, tossing insults in his wake. One day, Fahey became infuriated at something Jerry Ware was doing and lunged at Ware, grabbing the chief engineer by his collars. "You're not a fucking commander!" Fahey roared. "You're a fucking wimp!"

EVEN THOUGH they had no money, almost no assistance from the shipyard, and no backup from their own engineers, Meyer and Mortensen vowed that they would do whatever it took to repair their turret. During the summer months when the ship was in the yard, they mustered their men before first light and kept them working until long after dark.

Meanwhile, the repair of broken equipment in the other two sixteen-inch turrets was languishing, bogged down by a lack of motivation. The hydraulic leaks had gotten so out of control in Turret Two that one newly arrived petty officer wrote his mother that people in the turret were forced to "stumble over the piles of sand" spread on the decks to absorb the oil.

The dominant personality in Turret Two was thirty-nine-year-old Senior Chief Reginald Ziegler, a nineteen-year Navy veteran. Ziegler was a big man, standing over six feet tall and weighing 230 pounds. He had a mustache, wore thick black-rimmed glasses, and still retained most of his dark brown hair. Calm and ponderous, he was immensely popular with his fellow chiefs. Ziegler was one of the very few chiefs who got along with Master Chief Skelley.

Reggie Ziegler had met his wife, Sharon, in a youth group connected to the Methodist Church in central New York when they were both seventeen years old. After his draft number came up, he enlisted in the Navy. Sharon learned to condition herself to the frequent geographic moves and Reggie's long absences at sea, but she longed to start a family. However, before that could happen, tragedy struck. Sharon was diagnosed with Hodgkin's disease when she was twenty-six. Over the years, her cancer had worsened, requiring her to use a wheelchair, and she had to reconcile herself to the fact that she was never going to have children.

Reggie volunteered and was accepted for duty on the *Iowa* in August 1987. He did it largely because he wanted to see what a battleship was like before he retired from the Navy (scheduled to occur in January 1990). Ziegler had a lot on his mind during the time the ship was in the yard. Foremost was reaching his retirement date alive, so that Sharon would not be deprived of his full pension. Second, he was not a sixteen-inch-gun expert. He was considered to be a genius with five-inch guns, but he was a rookie when it came to operating and repairing the sixteen-inch monsters. He had relied on Master Chief Chuck Hill to get him through, but Hill had retired, and his replacement proved to be a disappointment.

Ziegler did have an outstanding leading petty officer, Ernest E. Hanyecz. A good-natured, competent first class gunner's mate, Hanyecz was twenty-six years old and had been in the Navy almost ten years. After completing basic training at Great Lakes, Illinois, Hanyecz returned home and married his high-school sweetheart. He then volunteered for duty on the battleship USS *New Jersey* and accompanied the vessel to Lebanon. He next completed a tour of shore duty and then asked for more battleship duty. He was assigned to the *Iowa* in 1986.

Ernie Hanyecz and Dale Mortensen became best buddies, making Chief Ziegler feel more comfortable asking Mortensen for assistance repairing equipment or for advice on how to train green replacements. Ziegler, who had served two combat tours in Vietnam, also developed a good rapport with Ensign Dan Meyer. Most Friday evenings that the ship was in port, when the majority of the other chiefs were off the ship spending time with their families, Ziegler and Meyer ate steaks together in the chiefs' mess. Sharon Ziegler's illness made it impossible for her to move from their home in upstate New York to Norfolk, where the *Iowa* was based.

REGGIE ZIEGLER was constantly at odds with the officer assigned to his turret, Lieutenant (junior grade) Philip Buch. An immature, emotionally fragile young officer, Buch regularly broke the Navy's taboo about fraternizing with enlisted men. He alienated Ziegler by routinely crossing that forbidden line and getting drunk with his sailors. Buch arrived on the *Iowa* in June 1986 and was assigned to the operations department. He didn't perform well there, so when the ship departed for the Middle East in 1987, Larry Seaquist left Buch and another officer behind, claiming that he did it to make room for the battle group commander's staff. Seaquist later said he actually did it to give the two officers some remedial education, believing that both young men were not "natural sailors." They were assigned to take some technical courses in Norfolk and in Newport, Rhode Island.

When Buch got back to the ship, Seaquist assigned him to Turret Two. It had formerly been commanded by Lieutenant (junior grade) Ed Dooling, probably one of the best junior officers aboard the *Iowa*. Seaquist's thinking in assigning Buch to Turret Two was "that Dooling left it in such good shape that nobody could screw it up."

Nevertheless, Buch managed to make a mess out of the turret. The twenty-three-year-old officer, who had graduated from Purdue, told other gunnery officers that if there were no funds for the yard workers to fix his turret, he had no intention of doing anything. Among other things, Turret Two's sprinklers, especially the ones in its powder magazines, were not functioning. That meant that the turret had no way to put out a propellant fire. Buch didn't bother to keep an accurate duty roster. He said he wasn't good at keeping records. Dan Meyer and Terry McGinn—who, like the other young officers on the *Iowa*, were fond of Buch—nagged him about his failure to keep accurate records, but Buch merely shrugged and said, "I don't give a shit about paperwork, because if this turret blows up, I'll be dead, and who'll give a rat's ass about paper work!"

THERE WERE no full-time senior officers assigned to the weapons department during most of the yard time. Gene Kocmich left the ship two weeks after Larry Seaquist's departure, and he was not replaced during the entire period. The *Iowa* also had no permanent gunnery officer for two months of the overhaul. Lieutenant Commander Mark Ruprecht, a missiles officer, filled Kocmich's job on a temporary basis. Ruprecht stood six feet four inches tall in his stocking feet, had a head like a block of hardwood, powerful biceps, and the swagger of a nineteenth-century Prussian officer. Junior officers knew it could be hazardous to their physical well-being to try to snow Ruprecht. Any time somebody attempted it, Ruprecht would yell, "That's the goddamnedest line of shit I've ever been handed!" Retaliation would be swift and sure.

One morning during the yard period, Phil Buch tumbled down a ladder, picked himself up, and then went reeling down a passageway. Smelling like a distillery, Buch staggered into the acting weapons officer's office and crumpled at Ruprecht's feet. "You dumb motherfucker, you're drunk!" Ruprecht shouted. He ordered the splayed-out Buch to pick himself up and put himself in "hack" (a punishment meted out to officers, involving restriction to quarters). Hack apparently had little effect on Buch. When he was freed, he continued to let things go steadily downhill in his turret and continued to booze it up on the beach with the sailors who worked for him.

3

"Terror on the Bridge!"

IF THINGS WERE in atrocious shape in Turret Two, they were even more harrowing back in Turret Three. Fred Moosally needed a take-charge, kick-ass ship's gunner to take Chuck Hill's place and deal with the problems in Turrets Two and Three. But instead of doing that, the captain made an unfortunate choice by selecting Master Chief James Hickman. A barrel-chested, twenty-six-year Navy veteran, Hickman only stood five feet nine inches tall, but he was built like a battering ram. He was so blocky that he couldn't squeeze through turret hatches. Hickman had spent four years as a gunner's mate on the heavy cruiser USS *Canberra* and had also served a combat tour in Vietnam on small boats. Despite his experience, he had developed a spotty reputation in the *Iowa*'s weapons department for skirting responsibility, dodging work, and adroitly covering his tracks.

Hickman mostly kept his own counsel, and only spoke when spoken to. Before his retirement, Chuck Hill had alerted Hickman that it was absolutely imperative for him to keep accurate PQS (personnel qualification standard) training records. Knowing that Hickman was a lousy recordkeeper, Hill emphasized that training was critical, and PQS was the best gauge of its being done systematically. Hill told Hickman he had to stay current on PQS, because untrained troops could cause accidents. Droves of men in the turrets were scheduled to rotate off the ship in the fall of 1988, perhaps as many as 40 percent, Hill said, and the apprentice replacements would be in need of intensive indoctrination. A sixteen-inch turret should not be manned by ignorant, untrained amateurs. For one thing, the guns weren't all that easy to operate. The crews had to be physically strong and agile, and mentally alert.

A coal miner or even a steelworker on an open-hearth blast furnace probably enjoyed better working conditions than a turret crew. The environment was one notch above hell. It was hot, grimy, nasty, hazardous, and cramped. The *Iowa* turret decks, coated with hydraulic fluid and oil, were slippery. A tumbling shell could pulverize a man. One misstep in the gun house and a sailor could plunge into the pit, where he might be crushed to death by moving machinery or by an elevating or traversing weapon. Friction and static electricity were constant sources of anxiety. A spark could trigger an explosion. Some men couldn't handle life in the turrets. They were prostrate with fear every time the guns were discharged.

The guns were dinosaurs, throwbacks to naval warfare as it had existed at the turn of the twentieth century. To call the *Iowa*'s sixteen-inchers "big" was to grossly understate their dimensions. There was nothing any bigger anywhere else in the world. (The "sixteen-inch" designation represented the diameter of the gun bore.) Their closest competitors were circus cannons, which shot clowns out of their barrels. The next biggest guns in the U.S. Navy's arsenal were eight-inchers, which fired a relatively puny 200-pound shell. By contrast, the *Iowa*'s shells were brutes, weighing 1,900 and 2,700 pounds. According to the Navy, each one of these gargantuan shells "weighed as much as a Volkswagen Beetle." When they exited the sixty-eight-foot-long barrels, the shells traveled at twice the speed of sound at ranges up to twenty-five miles. A Navy press release extolled the fact that each one of these shells could blast its way through "thirty feet of reinforced concrete," and if fired "into a tangled jungle, it would create a hole fifty feet across and twenty feet deep."

They were breechloaders, meaning they were loaded on the opposite end from the muzzle. A projectile and six cylindrical bags of smokeless powder were rammed into the breech; a mushroom-shaped breechblock was slammed shut; a primer shell was inserted; an electrical firing circuit was closed; and the gun went "Bang!" Well, not exactly. The six bags, which weighed about 600 pounds, didn't explode. Rather, they burned very, very rapidly and created a gas buildup, which squeezed and thrust the projectile from the muzzle at high velocity.

HICKMAN HAD been warned by Hill that when the *Iowa* left the shipyard, under no circumstances should he agree to take back onboard the gunpowder for the sixteen-inchers that had been stored on barges by the Navy. "They'll fuck with that shit, and it won't be worth a damn!" Hill said. The powder was antiquated. The Navy hadn't manufactured any of it since 1952, and some of the *Iowa*'s propellant dated back to the 1930s. The battleship's powder had been reblended in huge vats, but, as was revealed later, a large percentage of it had been faultily rebagged and was potentially lethal.

The Navy failed to monitor the temperatures or humidity on the barges where the *Iowa*'s powder had been stored for five months, from April to August 1988. Nitrated cotton was the primary ingredient of the propellant,

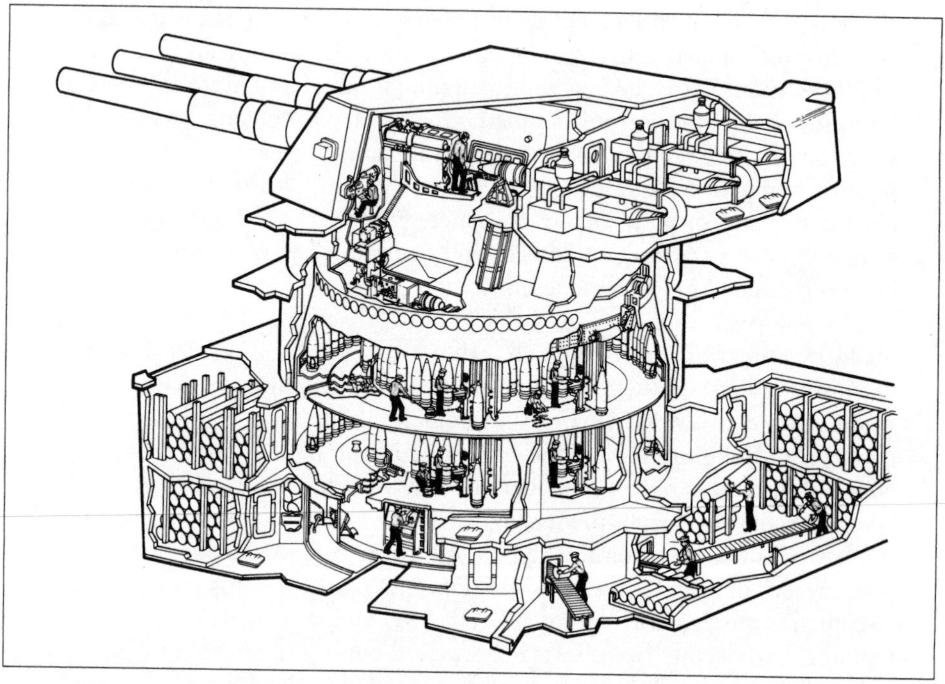

This schematic of one of the USS *Iowa*'s three sixteen-inch turrets shows bags of propellant being removed from the magazines, thrust through scuttles into the annular space, and then muscled into the powder flats at the base of the turret, where they were hoisted up to the gun rooms on a dumbwaiter-type device. The cutaway also shows massive shells, standing about six feet tall and weighing as much as 2,700 pounds, being sent up to be rammed into the breeches of the guns. The thickly armored turret was supposed to be able to withstand a catastrophe in one gun room without the other two being affected, but that didn't happen on April 19, 1989. (U.S. Navy)

which consists of two-inch-long, pencil-like strands. It was mixed with ether and alcohol and combined with one part nitric acid and three parts sulfuric acid. Components of the powder could become unstable if stored under hot and humid conditions. To reduce the likelihood of combustion when the powder is aboard a ship, the bags are stored in water-chilled magazines whose temperatures are monitored constantly.

According to *Navy Manual OP5*, the official guide to storage of munitions, when powder is improperly stored, decomposition begins at temperatures above 70°F. At 100°F, the decomposition is relatively high, and at 110°F, it is dangerous. The *Iowa*'s powder was subjected to temperatures of up to 125°F on the unventilated, aluminum-covered barges on the York River.

Hickman disregarded Hill's admonition about accepting the stored powder at the end of the yard overhaul. Much of this "smokeless" powder arrived back on the ship coated with mold. Some 2,100 bags were in wretched shape and smelled strongly of ether. The Navy doesn't like to intermix powder lots, because the lots burn at different rates, causing the initial velocity of the shell to vary radically and making accurate fire control virtually impossible. Despite this well-stated, service-wide policy, Hickman allowed powder lots to be intermingled when he had them struck down below to the individual magazines associated with the three turrets.

Senior Chief Reggie Ziegler took violent exception to what Hickman was doing. "This is garbage! It's no good! I don't want it!" Ziegler ranted. Stomping around the main deck, Ziegler pointed out that the majority of the metal canisters, each holding three bagged charges, were banged up, some having their airtight seals broken. Ziegler assigned a party of boatswain's mates and gunner's mates to mark the worst-looking canisters with chalk before they were lowered below. He wanted to make sure these were never fired and were easy to identify. Also enraged by Hickman's lack of safety consciousness, Dale Mortensen began throwing over the side any powder bags he considered dangerous.

After Hickman allowed the contaminated powder back onboard, there were frequent instances of bags arriving in the gun rooms and spilling out nitrocellulose pellets on the deck. These broken bags were supposed to be immersed in a water tank and later heaved over the side. But that hardly ever happened. Reggie Ziegler explained what was going on to Emmett C. Dunn Jr., a Navy civilian technician who came aboard the *Iowa* for an inspection. "Senior Chief [Ziegler] told me that on more than one occasion powder bags came up the hoist ripped, torn or damaged in some manner. Instead of stopping the process, returning the damaged bags and cleaning up the loose grains, he said he used the torn powder bags and merely scooped up the loose grains and threw them into the guns behind the bags, then closed the breech and fired," Dunn said.

TURRET THREE'S condition continued to go downhill during the *Iowa*'s stay in the yard. The biggest problem was its inept management team. Chief J.C. Miller became turret captain when the ship entered the yard. Miller was a twelve-year Navy veteran who announced to anybody who would listen to him, "I'm not an expert on sixteen-inch guns." He was an expert, he claimed, on much smaller three-inch and five-inch guns. "Miller was loud, very loud, and he talked, talked, talked about things he knew absolutely nothing about. When he got caught, he would screw his men," Dan Meyer said.

Miller's turret officer was Ensign Kevin Hunt, a Navy ROTC graduate from Virginia Tech. When Hunt arrived on the ship in June 1987, he was assigned for six months to Turret One, where he and Dale Mortensen fought constantly. Mortensen thought Hunt didn't know what he was doing, even though the ensign pretended that he did. Hunt left the ship for six months to attend surface warfare and engineering schools. When he came back, he was assigned to Turret Three. He and Dan Meyer were roommates, but they didn't get along, largely because Meyer criticized the pathetic shape of Hunt's turret and his arbitrary treatment of his sailors.

Hunt adopted Phil Buch's laissez-faire manner of doing business in the yard, except that his training records were in even worse shape than Buch's. "They really looked like somebody wiped their butt with them," Meyer said. Hunt and his men frequently called it a day at 1:30 P.M. when the ship was in the yard. "At times Kevin would get wistful about his problems in Turret Three," Meyer added. "There was no way out. He couldn't solve the problems. There never was a team in Turret Three."

IN MID-July 1988, Captain Fred Moosally discovered for himself what a horror show Turret Three had become. The captain crawled down a trunk to reach an engineering pump room adjacent to Turret Three's base. He grabbed a hatch by a handle and the hatch fell to the deck. It hadn't been attached to anything; its hinges were broken. He asked a young sailor, who worked for the engineering department, who was responsible for maintaining the hatch. The sailor, who had been on the ship eighteen months, told the captain that it belonged to Turret Three and said it had been inoperable ever since he'd been aboard. "A lot of Turret Three's hatch covers are like that," the sailor volunteered.

Moosally sought out Kevin Hunt and demanded to see the "Yoke and Zebra" documentation—for damage-control conditions. Each day, the chief responsible for a particular compartment must certify that the hatches there are capable of being secured. This is critical in time of war or in case of a fire or some other kind of emergency. The secured hatches and doors are designed to keep any flooding or fire from spreading. Moosally became furious when he determined that the broken hatch had been signed off as meeting "Yoke and Zebra" damage-control standards during the entire eighteen months that the engineer told him it had been broken. Clearly, somebody had "gun-decked" (falsified) the records.

"The Moose" sent for Mike Fahey. They inspected Turret Three and found a profusion of soft patches, hydraulic leaks, poorly grounded wiring, low-wattage light bulbs, sound-powered phones that were inoperable, and watertight fittings that leaked. And then they heard the kicker. Turret Three was incapable of rotating. Moosally could see his career going to pieces. He needed some expert help, so he told Fahey to call retired Master Chief Chuck Hill and see if Hill would return to the ship to talk with him.

Fahey did as he was told. He informed Hill, "We have some really big problems in the weapons department, especially in Turret Three." That came as no real surprise to Hill, who agreed to see Moosally the next day. When Hill arrived, he was promptly ushered into the captain's in-port cabin. Moosally had a tape recorder on his desk and a Marine sentry at his side. "Turn off that damned tape recorder!" Hill demanded, also telling the captain to dismiss the guard. Moosally complied and then rattled off an unbelievable list of inoperable equipment in Turret Three. Moosally asked Hill how to make the paralyzed turret rotate. Hill said that it was probably as simple as rewiring a circuit board.

Hill told the captain that the equipment troubles were related to several lazy master chiefs in the weapons department. "They never leave their offices and see what's going on. You've got to get them off their fat asses!" Moosally begged Hill to return to active duty and assume his old job. "I can't do that, Captain," Hill said, preparing to leave. He had only come to this meeting out of curiosity and was still seething over the churlish way Moosally had treated his best friend, Command Master Chief Bobby Scott.

Fred Moosally decided that if he couldn't get Chuck Hill, the next best thing was to put Senior Chief Reggie Ziegler in charge of Turrets Two and Three. When Ziegler heard about Moosally's plan, he panicked and told Dale Mortensen that he couldn't handle it. He was practically drowning in Turret Two. Ziegler told the captain that he desperately needed more time to make corrections in Turret Two, and Moosally let the chief off the hook.

Moosally then threatened Ensign Kevin Hunt with the end of his naval career unless he got his turret fixed so it rotated and repaired the hatch covers. Turret Three's gunner's mates began welding hatches, installing new lighting, and rewiring the gunnery phone circuits. Moosally, temporarily appeased, was blissfully ignorant about what had just been papered over. Some of the supervisors showed some enterprise for a time but then reverted to their old ways.

JUST BEFORE the *Iowa* left the shipyard, Fred Moosally acted as cheerleader at a ceremony for the assembled crew on the fantail of the ship for his favorite officer, Mike Fahey. The executive officer was being "frocked"—that is, given the insignia of the higher rank to which he had been newly selected. He had been promoted to captain, allowing him to wear four gold stripes on each sleeve of his dress-blue uniform. A USS *Iowa* baseball cap jammed on his head, Fred Moosally held up the two silver eagles that Fahey was now entitled to wear on his shirt collars to denote his new rank. Moosally chanted, "Do you know what these are made of? I'll tell ya. They're made of iron, because Mike Fahey is made of iron!" A demonstration of this sort was astonishing, because the vast majority of naval captains absolutely refuse to have any other officer on their ships wear comparable rank, even if that officer has already been selected by a promotion board and his upgrade has been officially announced. These officers feel that there should be only one captain on a ship at a time.

The yard period for the *Iowa* came to an end the third week of August. By canceling the overhaul on all the guns, Fred Moosally got his ship out of the yard a week early. The gunpowder that had become contaminated during the time it was stored on river barges came back aboard—with only Reggie Ziegler, Dan Meyer, and Dale Mortensen offering any real resistance. "The

Moose" was anxious to see how the *Iowa* handled in deep water. Still wary of the ability of junior officers to conn (control the movements of a ship—the officer in control has the conn) his ship, he decided that there needed to be some "adult" supervision of the junior officers standing bridge watch.

The captain designated Commander Bob Finney, the tall, thin operations officer, to control everything on the bridge. It was a very bad choice, because Finney had a vicious temper and was not a particularly good seaman, having once run a minesweeper aground in the Chesapeake Bay. In his post, Finney became a divisive influence on the bridge, a place that by its very nature required calmness and coolness.

Simply put, the bridge is the ship's brain and central nervous system, the chief command-and-control point. It's the place where the ship is steered and navigated; where orders are issued; where tactics are formulated and communications are evaluated. From the bridge, information is passed along to the crew via the main announcing system. The name *bridge* dates back to the days when the Navy shifted from sail to steam. Sailing ships had been steered since time immemorial from the main deck behind the aftermost mast. The early steamers came equipped with oversize paddlewheel boxes, which blocked the watch-stander's field of vision, so, to gain a better vantage point, the officers shifted their operations up to the "cross-over bridge" connecting the paddle boxes. At that point, *bridge* became part of the official lexicon. Even after the evolution from wooden- to metal-hulled ships, and a corresponding relocation of the steering functions forward to the structure above the main deck, a naval vessel's principal command-and-control station continued to be known as the "bridge."

The bridge is a serious work environment, a place where protocol is inflexible and discipline is rigidly enforced. The officer of the deck (OOD) heads up the bridge watch team, acting as the captain's surrogate, and as such speaks with the captain's full power and authority. Next to the captain and the executive officer, the OOD has more responsibility than any other officer on the ship, even though he's normally very junior in rank and length of service. With the exception of the Coast Guard, none of the other services has seen fit to entrust a junior officer with such unfettered power and awesome responsibility. The OOD is assisted by the junior officer of the deck (JOOD) and the junior officer of the watch (JOOW), who are in effect apprentice OODs.

A miscalculation or an error in judgment by either the OOD or his two assistants can easily lead to a collision at sea, a grounding, or some other disaster. And should that happen, the captain becomes personally accountable. That doctrine tends to make most naval captains choosy about those they deem qualified to stand watch on the bridge. The captain can assume the conn anytime he's on the bridge. But, as Vice Admiral Joe Metcalf said, there is no requirement that the captain of a major combatant be a great ship handler, although it is greatly appreciated by the crew if he happens to be one. Most of the watch-standers on the bridge were accustomed to the way Larry Seaquist handled a ship. He was a virtuoso performer. They had never seen Fred Moosally in action on the bridge, and nobody knew anything about his abilities as a seaman, but they hoped for the best. However, they were in for a rude shock.

THE *IOWA* headed out the Norfolk channel early on the morning of August 24, 1988, without incident. In addition to an untried captain on the bridge, there was a grass-green navigator plotting her course: Lieutenant Commander Joe Jones. As the ship made her way out the dredged channel, Jones quickly demonstrated that he was in over his head. He was filling some pretty large shoes. The man he replaced, Lieutenant Commander Gary Scott, an exceptional navigator, had once piloted the *Iowa*'s course from Europe to Norfolk without relying on the Navy's modern satellite tracking system.

The *Iowa* easily threaded her way through the mile-wide expanse between Fort Wool, a kidney-shaped island in the center of the Chesapeake Bay, and Old Point Comfort. She steered on past the fifty-five-foot-tall red brick Thimble Shoals Lighthouse and exited the channel. She went out about sixty miles, loitering off the Virginia Capes for some twenty hours, running routine exercises. Then came a string of potentially hazardous incidents: An electrical short repeatedly caused the loss of steering control to the bridge; a minor fire broke out in the engineering spaces; and one of the eight boilers flamed out. But even with these minor nuisances, Fred Moosally was still relishing how well his new command handled in deep water.

THE *IOWA*'S deft maneuvering capability vanished in shallow water, where she assumed the handling characteristics of a soggy log. She was flat-bottomed and slab-sided (meaning that her sides dropped steeply downward, rather than sloping inward to form a sharp "V" at her keel). Viewed from below the waterline, with the exception of her rakish clipper bow, she looked like a floating box. The boxy hull design accounted for her great stability in rough seas, but that advantage became a liability in shallow water. She was a "bottom sucker." Her prodigious size and weight made her displace an enormous amount of water from under her hull. She was so weighty that she literally squeezed out the water and suctioned the bottom dregs upward.

The only other ship Fred Moosally had commanded was a destroyer, which was one-seventh the size of the *Iowa* and had nowhere near her draft (the depth measured vertically from the waterline to the keel). It required at least forty feet of water to keep the *Iowa* afloat when she was fully loaded with men, fuel, ammunition, and supplies. The *Iowa* had another disturbing handling characteristic: Once battleships of the *Iowa* class gained momentum, it was virtually impossible to stop them, making it easy for them to turn a pier into matchsticks if a skipper didn't know what he was doing and didn't use a tug. In restricted waters, rudder and engine orders—which worked well in deep water—either had no effect or had just the opposite effect of what was intended. Every experienced battleship captain worth his salt knew this and avoided shoal water like the plague. These were the very waters where Fred Moosally would soon take the *Iowa,* and they had spoiled more than one promising naval career—as the commanding officer of the battleship USS *Missouri* had discovered on January 17, 1950, when he grounded his vessel while transiting these same waters.

THE *IOWA* experienced serious difficulties when she reentered the channel on the morning of August 25, 1988, and crossed over the Chesapeake Bay Tunnel. At 6:44 A.M., she crossed the boundary that required her to abide by inland rules of navigation. She was creeping along at a bare steerageway of five knots. The visibility was wretched. A thick fog enveloped the ship, greatly inhibiting the lookouts' ability to sound the alarm if any other vessel got too close. The bridge ordered that a prolonged blast be sounded on the foghorn every two minutes. Due to the fog, the running lights also were on. At that point, the *Iowa*'s surface search radar ceased to function and the combat information center (CIC) went on the blink. The CIC electronically tracks everything around the ship on the surface of the water or in the air. It makes recommendations to the bridge on courses to steer and speeds to take to avoid collisions at sea, and it alerts the bridge whenever it detects that there is a danger of running aground.

Poor visibility, no surface radar available, the combat information center down, an unproven captain on the bridge, an unskilled navigator plotting the course, an unpredictable senior watch officer overseeing the bridge watch—all the variables were in place for a catastrophe. And it almost happened between 7:22 and 7:34 A.M. The *Iowa* nearly collided with three other naval vessels—the frigate *Moinster,* the destroyer *Farragut,* and the nuclear-powered cruiser *South Carolina.* In each instance, the deck log records that the *Iowa* "rendered honors" to each ship, but witnesses say that the *Iowa* almost rammed the other vessels. ("Rendering honors" means attention was sounded on the IMC and the hand salute was rendered by everyone on the main deck.) To say the least, the Navy frowns on near collisions, and captains who engage in them can expect, at the least, to have a letter of censure inserted into their permanent personnel folders. But that didn't happen to Fred Moosally.

Following those close encounters, the *Iowa* continued a westerly course in the channel, finally winding up in shoal water, where she very nearly beached herself. According to her deck log, at 7:37 A.M., she struck a red buoy, marking the safe water channel, on her port side. The captain took the conn. "That wasn't a buoy. We didn't hit a buoy," Moosally insisted. Nobody disputed him. Hitting the buoy should have alerted the captain to the fact that he was outside the safety of the dredged channel and in treacherous water.

For the next thirteen minutes, "the Moose" issued a disjointed stream of thirty wildly inconsistent and often contradictory rudder orders, course adjustments, and speed changes. The three young watch officers, oversize binoculars slung around their necks, warily danced around the burly captain like a trio of chipmunks dodging a grizzly with a splinter in its paw. One of those watch-standers later termed what went on around him "a bitter comedy." Lieutenant Commander Jones was totally flustered. He had lost his navigation track in the fog. Commander Finney was trying to stay out of the captain's line of fire and not having much success.

Moosally clung to the conn. He was on the northern lip of the channel. Following the captain's orders, the helmsman zigged and zagged in the channel and then collided with a second buoy, the "red #18 buoy on the port side." Calamity was at hand. Just a few more yards and another *Iowa*-class battleship would be embedded in the mud. The OOD noted the impending disaster in the official deck log: "*Iowa* is in danger of running aground at Thimble Shoals." She was close to the spot where the *Missouri* had grounded herself in 1950. The "red #18's" anchor chain scraped along the hull, clanging as it neared the propellers. If the chain wrapped itself around the four revolving propellers, the ship would be crippled.

In the bowels of the ship, in main engineering control, Jerry Ware heard the racket of the chain on the hull and became alarmed. He had listened to the captain's torrent of orders on the intercom and thought an emergency of some sort must be occurring. Ware called the bridge on his "bitch box" (intercom). "Hey, did we hit something?" he asked. The bridge was in pandemonium. Finney, standing directly behind the captain, was being verbally flayed by "the Moose." Finney, who had been conning the *Iowa* when she hit the first buoy, walked over to his own "squawk box" and angrily toggled the key to speak. "Shut the fuck up!" he screamed at Ware. "We almost hit a goddamned nuclear submarine! There's terror on the bridge! The captain has gone bonkers!"

That was enough to scare Ware. But there was more to come. The captain ordered the anchor dropped at 7:51 A.M. A minute later, he changed his mind and had the anchor hauled back up. The OOD recorded it this way: "Emergency bring up the anchor." And another minute after that, Moosally directed Ware: "Stop all engines." Ware, baffled, called the bridge once more to see if he could find out if there were some method to this madness. All Finney would say was, "The captain is taking some time to calm himself down."

The *Iowa* remained stuck in soft mud for more than an hour. During that time, Ware ordered his engineers to spin the propellers at a relatively high speed to prevent the mud and bottom sludge from clogging the cooling-water intakes. If Ware had not taken this initiative, the engines could have been ruined, turning the battleship into a huge scrap heap. After weighing anchor from waters off Thimble Shoals, the *Iowa* finally managed to get back in the channel.

Fred Moosally took the precaution of picking up a civilian pilot and getting a tug so that she could travel to "Whiskey Anchorage" in the outer harbor, where she was supposed to pick up some ammunition. She remained at Whiskey Anchorage for seven hours and then made her way back up the channel to deep water. The next day, she ran some routine tests along the Virginia coast. On the way back to the *Iowa*'s regular pier, Moosally again obtained a pilot and two tugs . She tied up at 1 P.M. on August 26 without further incident. It had been quite a baptism of fire for the new captain.

During the hour when the *Iowa* was stuck in the mud off Thimble Shoals, a number of other Navy vessels sailed by, noting her predicament. Normally, the *Iowa*'s performance would have resulted in disciplinary proceedings against the commanding officer, but Fred Moosally escaped this fate. This proved to a number of officers on the ship that "the Moose" was "Teflon-coated." It was widely speculated on the ship that Vice Admiral Boorda, Chief of Naval Personnel, had played some kind of role in protecting Moosally's career following the Thimble Shoals incident.

Moosally's amateur seamanship caused an uproar in the wardroom. One of the officers most distressed about it was Lieutenant Commander Dennis "Strike" Flynn, who was in charge of determining tactics and strategy for the ship. He worked for Commander Finney, the operations officer, and was either Finney's "godsend or nemesis," depending on the mercurial operations officer's mood swings. Many of the young officers who stood bridge watch were in awe of Flynn's expertise in formulating complex maneuvers for the ship. Speaking scornfully of Moosally's inability to conn a ship, Flynn informed a group of young officers: "We've gone from being a superstar ship to a goddamned buoy bender all in the course of four months."

"Iron Mike" Fahey cautioned the officers that they were never to tell anybody (including their Navy superiors) about what had happened at Thimble Shoals, nor were they ever to use the word *aground* in connection with the incident, even though that word was plainly recorded in the *Iowa*'s official deck log.

THE VERY day that the *Iowa* departed for her three-day expedition and near-grounding, a new weapons department head, Commander Robert John Kissinger, reported aboard. A compact jogger, Kissinger had dark hair, beginning to gray at the temples. The new weapons officer had what can best be described as "a reptilian mouth." According to Dan Meyer, Kissinger "flicked his tongue incessantly when he was nervous." Kissinger had served as gunnery officer on the destroyer USS *Perry*, completed a tour in Vietnam on fast attack boats in the Mekong Delta, had been a weapons officer on a frigate, and then became executive officer of the destroyer USS *Hayler*.

Known within the Navy as a missile man, Kissinger had spent three years developing the Tomahawk and had served another tour as a missile specialist working for the three-star admiral who commanded the Atlantic Fleet's surface forces. Fred Moosally said Kissinger was considered to be "the number one commander" on the Surface Forces Atlantic staff.

Soon after Kissinger arrived, he summoned the three sixteen-inch turret officers and the five-inch battery officer to a meeting and announced that he was a missile man and intended to remain a missile man. From his years on destroyers, he said, he "thoroughly" understood the five-inch guns, but sixteen-inch guns were beyond his comprehension. Just as soon as a full-time gunnery officer reported aboard, Kissinger said, he was planning to cede all responsibility for the big guns to that officer. In the meantime, he would rely on the junior officers and chiefs to keep things on a steady course.

A MONTH after Bob Kissinger arrived to head the weapons department, a new gunnery officer came aboard. He was Lieutenant Commander Kenneth Michael Costigan, a 1972 U.S. Naval Academy graduate who been twice passed over for promotion to commander and spurned as a department head. Costigan's Naval Academy class yearbook had this to say about him: "Known for his ever present smile and his quick wit, he was always one to brighten up a room. An athlete of distinction, and a lover of renown, many a study hour was spent rehashing his exploits in both fields." If those words were true in 1972, something drastic had happened to change him in the intervening sixteen years. There was an air of desperation about him. His naval career wasn't going anyplace, and he knew it.

His movements were halting and unsure, but his uniform was always impeccable, as one would expect from an Annapolis graduate. His shrill voice did not inspire confidence in those he addressed. He was a battleship devotee who (just like Master Chief Steve Skelley) could rattle off obscure battleship trivia. Costigan's father had served on the battleship USS *Nevada*, which had been heavily damaged by Japanese aircraft attacking Pearl Harbor in 1941 and then salvaged to fight the remaining war in the Pacific. This was not Costigan's first battleship tour; he had been gunnery officer on the *New Jersey* from 1984 to 1986. He arrived on that ship as she was completing bombardment duties off Lebanon. His commanding officers on the *New Jersey* had been Captain Richard Milligan and then Captain Lewis Glenn. Costigan owed his present job to Glenn, who had since been promoted to rear admiral. Glenn wrote Fred Moosally and asked him to take on Costigan as gunnery officer. At the time, Costigan was occupying a dead-end shore billet at the Fleet Combat Training Center at Dam Neck, Virginia. Moosally reluctantly agreed to accept Costigan.

Once aboard the *Iowa*, the new gunnery officer failed to make a good first impression on the captain. Moosally told other officers that Costigan was "weird." As a nondrinker, Costigan had nothing in common with Mike Fahey or with any of the other party animals in the wardroom. He hardly ever frequented an officers' club when the ship was in port. His habit of standing on a wing of the bridge when he was not on watch and "zoning out" (staring into space, trancelike, for up to four hours at a time) caused a number of officers to question his stability. "He didn't seem to be playing with all the cards in his deck," said Terry McGinn.

Costigan did something else that his fellow officers thought was bizarre. He arranged to have the use of two staterooms. In addition to his regular space, he coaxed a steward into giving him the key to another cabin, which was assigned to Fred Moosally and located high up in the superstructure. Moosally never used this space, so Costigan made it his hideaway, often vanishing there for long periods of time, occasionally from 9 A.M. until sunset, without telling anybody where he was. He dressed eccentrically when he went on the beach on liberty, frequently wearing a threadbare Mickey Mouse shirt, baggy Bermuda shorts, and sandals.

Costigan's odd behavior spooked the gunner's mates and fire controlmen who worked for him. And they became even more skittish about the lieutenant commander when a rumor circulated on the mess decks and in the berthing spaces that Costigan had been responsible for the death of a gunner's mate aboard the *New Jersey*. Although false, the rumor was still widely accepted by the enlisted men in the weapons department. Costigan made matters even worse by initiating what he termed "*New Jersey*-style" modifications in the way the *Iowa*'s guns were controlled. The crew of the *Iowa*, for some reason, considered the *New Jersey* unlucky. Among other changes, Costigan made alterations to the sound-powered phone system. Standard gunnery procedure makes the main battery plotting-room officer, who is located in one of the most heavily armored portions of the ship, responsible for deciding when to fire the sixteen-inch turrets. Costigan's phone changes allowed the bridge and the captain to talk directly to the turrets rather than going through the plotting-room officer. It also allowed Costigan, whose battle station was in an exposed area one level above the bridge, to control the guns. He wore a headset attached to a fifty-foot extension cord, permitting him to roam around and still be able to give the order to fire.

Dan Meyer asked Costigan whose orders he was to follow when his turret was firing. Costigan said there were a number of options, depending on what the captain was doing. The net result of the change was to leave both the turret crews and the fire-control supervisors hopelessly confused about who would actually be in charge during a live-fire exercise.

Costigan hadn't been on the ship long when he became bosom buddies with Master Chief Skelley, "the pots and pans man." Both were battleship junkies, two kindred spirits. Costigan referred to Skelley as "a scientist," even though the chief only had a high-school diploma. Although Costigan was aware that Skelley was not trained to operate the guns, that didn't matter to him.

In some ways, Fred Moosally concurred with Costigan's assessment of

Skelley. The captain said he believed that the chief was "a very intelligent guy," but added, "I think he belongs in a laboratory somewhere." Moosally correctly decided that Skelley "could be a loose cannon." "Master Chief Skelley drives me nuts. I can only stand to spend about five minutes with him." The captain did his best to ignore Skelley and the gunnery experiment he proposed.

Moosally also did his best to ignore Costigan. During World War II, the *Iowa* had carried a crew of 3,000 men (about twice the number of officers and men she had aboard in 1988). Costigan repeatedly badgered Moosally to ask the Navy for the same number of men in the turrets as had been there in 1943. "The Moose" thought Costigan's idea was absurd and told the gunnery officer so. From then on, Moosally stayed away from the guns and allowed Costigan and Skelley to operate the sixteen-inch turrets pretty much as they saw fit.

The pair set about turning the *Iowa* into a "research-and-development platform," where they performed "kitchen-sink" experiments not sanctioned by the Navy. In addition to Moosally, nobody else in authority seemed to care what they did. Whenever Moosally was asked about the chronic lack of training in the turrets, according to Dan Meyer, the captain responded that it would be addressed when the ship deployed to Europe in June 1989. The executive officer, who hated the guns, was no help either. And the weapons officer remained absorbed in the missiles, to the exclusion of the guns. Master Chief Hickman, the ship's gunner, allowed Skelley access to the turrets and let him give instructions to the gunner's mates. Hickman also authorized Skelley to select which powder lots to fire. Skelley went from being almost a hermit with nobody to supervise to the premier member of the weapons department.

LIEUTENANT LEO Walsh, the fire-control officer, was in an ideal position to be the voice of reason and restraint. But Walsh, known to the turret officers as the "Cheshire Cat," didn't like to make waves. A former enlisted man who had completed twenty years of active service, he had been a senior chief fire controlman before receiving his commission in 1983. He was an LDO (limited duty officer), meaning that he was restricted to his fire-control specialty and did not stand bridge watches.

Candidly admitting that he wasn't very knowledgeable about sixteen-inch gunnery when he first came aboard the ship, Walsh proved to be a quick study. When the *Iowa* was firing, Walsh was in forward main plot, where he oversaw the operation of the oversize Mark 8 range keeper, an analog computer that solved aiming problems and transmitted those solutions to the turrets. By today's standards, the Mark 8, with its whirring and clicking noises as its gears and disks meshed, would be considered obsolete and sluggish, but it was very reliable and accurate.

There were two plotting rooms on the *Iowa*, one forward and one aft. Each plotting room was equipped with three electrical firing keys capable of discharging nine guns at a time.

Leo Walsh exhibited a wry sense of humor when he was around other junior officers, but he became very inhibited around superior officers—even to the point of being careful about the inflections of his words. He wasn't exactly a go-along-to-get-along type of guy, but he was no rebel, either. As an LDO, he sensed that he did not fully belong in the wardroom or back in the chiefs' mess. He felt that he was in a never-never land, not completely accepted by either the officers or the chiefs. So he hunkered down and tried to keep a very low profile.

On one occasion, Leo Walsh did get into a disagreement. He told Ken Costigan that his rewiring of the gunfire communications system was unsafe, but his views were disregarded. A fire controlman who worked for Walsh, Master Chief Dale Miller, also attempted to derail some of Costigan's and Skelley's hair-raising ideas, with no success. Miller, who was senior in date of rank to Skelley, had the mustache, build, and temperament of a walrus. He met several times with Reggie Ziegler, Dale Mortensen, and Dan Meyer to form an underground opposition to Costigan and Skelley.

In the weeks after the fiasco at Thimble Shoals, the executive officer continued his campaign to get Jerry Ware discharged as chief engineer. One day, as the ship was taking on ammunition at Whiskey Anchorage—about ten miles away from the piers but still within Norfolk Harbor—20,000 gallons of fuel oil spilled. Although Ware was not at fault, Fahey blamed him anyway. A fuel spill in harbor waters was a very serious matter. Fred Moosally was required to report the spill and could have been held personally financially liable for the damages. According to a number of officers, this spill was grossly underreported to the Navy. Zeroes mysteriously disappeared, and the 20,000 gallons became a mere two hundred gallons. This was such a small amount of spillage that the captain was assessed nothing. Once the ship returned to the pier, Fahey summoned Ware and Lieutenant Commander Dan Kimberlain, Ware's deputy, to his stateroom for a raw hiding. Fahey was toying with his ever-present hand squeezer as the two engineers entered his stateroom.

Fahey accused Ware of being incompetent, pointing to the fuel spill. He said Ware was incapable of leading anyone and had endangered the lives of the crew and crippled the ship at sea while she was in the Middle East. The executive officer liberally laced his accusations with profanity and expletives. Finally, Ware had had enough. "I'm tired of your bullshit!" he shot back. Fahey sprang from his seat and snatched the much smaller chief engineer by the collars of his shirt. Fahey shook Ware like a rag doll and smacked him several times. Kimberlain stood by and did nothing.

The executive officer finally tired of cuffing Ware and dismissed him, but Fahey ordered the chief engineer to return to his stateroom the next morning. Even though he was apprehensive, Ware did as he was told. Another round of verbal abuse resulted, but no more fisticuffs. Fahey told Ware that he was fired and taunted him, saying that Larry Seaquist was no longer around to save his job. Fahey and Ware adjourned to what they thought was an empty wardroom and continued screaming at each other. But there was a witness. Dan Meyer, who had entered the dining area earlier to get a cookie, heard the altercation and hid behind a milk machine. The young officer was shocked to learn that Ware, whom he considered to be the very best department head on the ship, had been fired.

After Fahey left the wardroom, Meyer revealed his presence to Ware, whose hands were shaking uncontrollably. "Are you all right, Commander?" Meyer asked. "Have you been here the whole time?" Ware inquired. Meyer nodded, and Ware said he needed some time to steady his nerves. They drank glasses of milk, and Meyer expressed sorrow about what had happened. Ware quickly regained his composure, because he had little time to spare. Fahey had told him to get off the ship immediately. He rushed from the wardroom to pack his bags and catch a utility boat back to the Norfolk piers.

A month after Jerry Ware was booted off the *Iowa*, the ship sailed to Guantanamo Bay, Cuba, to undergo the Operation Propulsion Program Evaluation tests again. She passed, and there is almost no chance that would have occurred without the remedial work on the engines that Jerry Ware had initiated during his tenure as chief engineer.

MIKE FAHEY next attacked Lieutenant Gary Avery, the *Iowa*'s senior officer of the deck. A soft-spoken Southerner with straight dark hair, he was unflappable under pressure and was regarded by everyone who stood watch with him as a soothing influence in a normally frenzied environment. Avery was routinely called upon to handle complicated at-sea maneuvers, such as underway replenishments, refuelings, tight-formation steaming, and sailing in and out of port. He was good at coaching prospective OODs, impressing on the junior officers he trained the gravity of having the lives of 1,500 men in their hands when standing watch on the bridge.

There is a contemporaneous written account of the executive officer's September 27, 1988, assault on Gary Avery. Lieutenant Terry McGinn kept a personal log of the events on the *Iowa*. McGinn recorded that at 10:03 A.M. that day: "I just came off the bridge from a hectic GQ (General Quarters) where the XO physically pushed Lieutenant Avery. It was chaotic up there." The *Iowa* was firing her sixteen-inch guns that day for the first time since Fred Moosally had become commanding officer. McGinn said Fahey "grabbed and threw" Avery against a bulkhead and told the lieutenant he "wanted to fire him."

4

"These Dumb Bastards Are Gonna Kill Us!"

THE *IOWA* SCARCELY ever shot her sixteen-inch guns during the fall of 1988. She went out of the Chesapeake Bay on September 27-28 and fired about fifty rounds off the Virginia Capes. All three turrets participated. There were no targets, just water splashes, which were measured on radar in a feeble attempt to determine how close the shells actually came to where they were supposed to land. During this short voyage, Chief Skelley conducted an experiment employing some unique shells that he had personally designed.

Skelley had prevailed on the Navy's ordnance facility in Louisville, Kentucky, to shave 25 percent off the walls and hollow out the cores of some sixteen-inch-high explosive shells, repacking them with 424 antipersonnel bomblets and resealing and refusing them. Skelley referred to this tailored ordnance as "my baby killers."

Safety studies done by Louisville and also by the Naval Surface Warfare Center at Dahlgren, Virginia, were less than thorough. There were no metallurgical estimates on how well the thinned-out walls of the shells would hold up as they spun out of the rifled barrels at 4,000 revolutions per minute. Dan Meyer, whose turret had been designated a "test platform" in August by Commander Kissinger, Lieutenant Commander Costigan, and Master Chief Skelley, termed Skelley's experiment "very, very scary."

Skelley and Costigan prevailed upon Meyer and Mortensen to fire ten of the EX-136 cluster-bomb shells from Turret One's left gun. Fortunately, there were no incidents. Each EX-136 made a splash 600 yards in diameter and threw up a circular wall of water thirty feet in the air. Meyer said it was "a spectacular sight."

For the next two months, Fred Moosally would schedule gun shoots and then cancel them. It takes a lot of dry-run practice and live-firing exercises to keep the gun crews proficient. Not firing the weapons on a regular basis was a bad idea. "Those guys need that training," Chief Bob Sumrall said. But Chief Hickman had turned the training program into a farce. He wasn't even making a pretense of having the PQS (personnel qualification standard) forms filled out, much less making sure that the training was actually being performed. With the guns silent, Lieutenant Commander Dana Griffin's remotely piloted vehicles were grounded. "Moosally did not want the RPVs to fly," Griffin said. "He had other things to do. It was not in his plan. He was not shooting the guns. The weapons department and the aviation department were out of favor."

Master Chief Skelley was hyper. "He was kinda like a terrier dog scratching at the door to take a pee. He wanted to shoot. He wanted to experiment," Meyer said. In addition to the experimental EX-136 shells, Skelley had designed an "urgent attack" antisubmarine shell, which had an electronic timed fuse and could explode hundreds of feet below the surface. He wanted to test it, as well as another long-range projectile-and-powder combination that he was sure could break long-distance records established by Army coastal artillery batteries using sixteen-inch guns in Hawaii and Panama during the 1930s. Skelley begged Meyer to intercede with the weapons officer, and maybe even the executive officer, to have the ship shoot her guns more regularly. Not anxious to have his head bitten off by "Iron Mike," Meyer told Skelley to do it himself.

The ship went to Guantanamo Bay for her mandatory Operation Propulsion Program Evaluation in mid-October 1988. Dan Meyer and the other two sixteen-inch turret officers, Phil Buch and Kevin Hunt, knew the turrets fell far below minimum standards and expected the OPPE team to detect the deficiencies and "to ream our butts." But that didn't happen. The *Iowa*'s officers were supposed to demonstrate to the satisfaction of the inspectors that their men were fully capable of fighting a full-blown turret fire. That requirement was waived. According to Meyer, "The inspectors said, 'You're the *Iowa*. You know more than we do. Just take us on a tour of your turrets, and let's call it a day.' "

While in Guantanamo, Meyer shared breakfast in the officers' club one morning with two officers he greatly respected, Lieutenant Gary Avery and Lieutenant Commander Dennis Flynn. Avery said that ship handling had taken a nosedive ever since Moosally had begun having lieutenant commanders and commanders—who hadn't driven a ship in years—stand bridge watches rather than the qualified junior officers who normally handled this duty. The battleship was frequently being waved off by the supply ships and forced to make multiple attempts before attaining a linkup. This degradation in seamanship was scandalous.

Flynn, who directed the ship's strike warfare center, said he doubted that the *Iowa* could now survive war games with NATO's standing naval forces based in the Caribbean. "This ship has never been 'sunk' in a fleet exercise,"

Flynn said. But he predicted that she would be "sunk" (electronically destroyed by simulated gunfire, missiles, or torpedoes) the next time she took part in a fleet or NATO tactical exercise. Flynn was correct. Later that fall, the *Iowa* engaged NATO forces and was "sunk" by a Dutch frigate lurking behind a civilian oil tanker.

THERE WAS plenty of recreational time in Guantanamo Bay, and consequently lots of heavy drinking and partying by the ship's company. Much of the fun-and-games was organized by Mike Fahey. "He would stir us up and have a big party," said Ensign Jeff Turner. The majority of the junior officers followed the executive officer's lead and partied with him.

One young officer who chose to avoid Fahey's parties in Cuba was Phil Buch. The twenty-three-year-old officer had already aroused Senior Chief Reggie Ziegler's displeasure by his regular fraternizing on liberty with the gunner's mates assigned to Turret Two. Buch had hoarded a bottle of Wild Turkey whiskey, which he told Terry McGinn he intended to drink from noon to midnight with some of his sailors while at the Guantanamo Enlisted Men's Club.

A brawl broke out at the club on October 21 while Buch was there. He entered the fray, swapping punches just like one of the guys. Many of the brawlers, aware that Buch was a commissioned officer, were mystified by his conduct. That same night, on the way back to the *Iowa*, Buch, who had many cigarette burns all over his arms, got into an altercation with an enlisted man in the utility boat. When Chief Ziegler, who had been on shore patrol, heard about Buch's misconduct, he wrote off the junior officer as an overgrown juvenile delinquent. From then on, Ziegler had as little as possible contact with Buch. The chief had no respect for the lieutenant and never again trusted his judgment.

During the time in Guantanamo, Dan Meyer received the unsettling news from Dale Mortensen that three men who filled critical gunnery slots in Turret One had openly discussed suicide. The young sailors had been under tremendous pressure and just couldn't handle it, according to Mortensen. Meyer visited Chaplain Fred Thompson and asked what he should do. Thompson advised Meyer to talk to the men and not make a formal issue out of it, or the men would most likely be sent to a psychiatric hospital. Meyer talked to the men confidentially and reduced their workload for several weeks. He informed the weapons officer about what he had done, and Bob Kissinger offered no objections. The men seemed to get better.

The gun captains who talked about suicide; the forlorn state of affairs on the bridge; the ship's greatly diminished tactical capabilities; the steadily worsening materiel condition of the turrets; the lack of training of the gunner's mates—all combined to depress Meyer's spirits. So when the ship returned to Norfolk, he headed home to discuss these problems with his father. A 1954 Naval Academy graduate and former submarine skipper, retired Captain

Donald Meyer was astonished by his son's account. The senior Meyer told his son to create a paper trail and document the serious irregularities in the *Iowa*'s gunnery department. "Cover your ass, son," he warned.

MEYER TOOK his father's advice and drafted a memo for Commander Bob Kissinger on October 23, 1988. The memo pointed out that a scarcity of shooting practice had led to "a deterioration in the quality of our main battery [three sixteen-inch turrets]." Meyer said that "the chaotic performance of Turret Three over the last six months" showed that the gunners there "are not capable of safe, efficient gunnery." The men in Turrets One and Two believed the captain's bad opinion of Turret Three might account for his reluctance to shoot all of the sixteen-inch guns. Bob Kissinger glanced briefly at Meyer's memo before handing it to Ken Costigan, telling him "to take whatever action you deem fit." Costigan did not respond to the memo. The ship didn't shoot again for another month. And morale worsened.

THE NEXT time the *Iowa* fired her guns, the ship was back in the Caribbean at Vieques during late November and early December of 1988. She was undergoing naval gunfire support qualifications when she was called upon to put on a "smoke-and-fire show" for a high-powered Washington delegation consisting of Secretary of the Navy William L. Ball III and three congressmen—Ike Skelton (D—Missouri), Owen Pickett (D—Virginia), and Bob McEwen (R—Ohio). The visiting dignitaries were squired by Moosally's old Annapolis football teammate, Rear Admiral Tom Lynch, chief of the Office of Legislative Affairs (OLA).

The Navy Secretary and the congressmen proved to be easy to impress. The ship didn't hit anything with her sixteen-inch guns during a gunnery exercise Fred Moosally staged for the Washington luminaries. She simply lobbed shells into the Caribbean. But the visitors were awed just the same. In his after-action report, Moosally reported, "SECNAV [Secretary of the Navy] appeared impressed and commented several times on appearance and readiness of ship and crew. . . . visit considered a total success." Tom Lynch was even more fulsome. "The *Iowa* shone from stem to stern and topmast to the bilges. The *Iowa* crew represented the best and brightest in the surface force. The *Iowa* said a lot about what is right with today's Navy."

The day after Lynch and the VIPs flew off the *Iowa* in a helicopter, the battleship reverted to her customary slovenly ways. Turret Two was supposed to shoot first but was unable to carry out its mission. The turret was disabled by electrical problems, traceable to the duct tape on the turret officer's panel. Forward main plot shifted the fire mission to Turret Three, but it failed a pre-fire safety check and was out of action. Turret One was not scheduled to fire anything that day. The whole mission was a bust.

THE *IOWA* spent the next two months in Norfolk moored to a pier. When she returned to Vieques in late January, it would be to conduct a long-range gunnery firing. Chief Skelley and Lieutenant Commander Costigan had persevered in their efforts to persuade Fred Moosally to allow them to conduct some gunnery experiments aboard the *Iowa*. They had the support of some technicians working for Sea Systems Command, which was in charge of the Navy's weapons. Skelley and Costigan wanted the *Iowa* to be able to shoot farther and more accurately than any battleship had during World War II. Captain Moosally, under the false impression that the experiments had been approved by the top management of Sea Systems Command rather than by some midlevel bureaucrats, agreed to conduct the experiments.

WHEN THE *Iowa* arrived in the Caribbean, "Iron Mike" Fahey wasn't aboard. He had completed his tour as executive officer earlier in the month and had joined the surface warfare section in the Pentagon. There were mixed feelings aboard the *Iowa* when Fahey left. On the one hand, he was a despot, but on the other, he was the one who had actually run the ship, not Moosally. The younger officers and the chiefs were worried that Moosally wasn't capable of handling a ship as large and as complex as the *Iowa*. If Fahey's replacement turned out to be a paper shuffler instead of a kick-ass "ship driver," the *Iowa* might be in for an even worse time than she had experienced under Fahey.

THE NIGHT before Fahey's final departure, the *Iowa*'s wardroom staged a farewell party for him at the officers' club at the Norfolk Naval Air Station. Dan Meyer arrived very late. When he did, he was sweaty, bedraggled, and in a foul mood. Meyer had been left onboard to receive and store below some specially designed shells and baglets of powder that the ship would use in Chief Skelley's upcoming long-range experimental gun shoot. The ordnance was shipped from the Yorktown, Virginia, Naval Weapons Station and did not arrive until nightfall. It was highly irregular to take on propellant and shells at night. Meyer and Senior Chief Reggie Ziegler only had a reduced complement of sailors to stow the ammunition. There was no time or sufficient lighting to conduct more than a superficial inspection of the experimental ordnance. Meyer had very little faith in the 2,240-pound shells, which had been used on pre–World War II vintage battleships. Skelley called these reworked shells DX-149s.

In addition to using six bags of D-846 propellant for each of the six test shells Skelley planned to fire, he also intended to add a fifty-pound baglet of D-834 "supercharge" powder. A copy of a five-page hand-lettered memo showed that Skelley estimated the reconfigured shells boosted by the baglets would extend the gun range by as much as ten miles. But what would this do to the *Iowa*'s aged gun barrels? Would the baglets increase the pressure to such an extent that the barrels would rupture?

Once the DX-149 shells and baglets had been stowed onboard, Meyer checked with some naval ordnance officers and found out that technicians at the Naval Surface Warfare Center at Dahlgren, Virginia, had only test-fired six of the projectiles and baglets in a shore-based gun before deciding that it was safe for the *Iowa* to proceed with the long-range experiment. John McEachren, a civilian assigned to Sea Systems Command, authorized the test. McEachren later told the Navy's Inspector General, Rear Admiral Ming Chang, that he "hid" the *Iowa* gunnery experiments and their costs from his superiors, because "they would stop the project."

MEYER HAD a vested interest in determining whether Skelley's experiment was safe. His turret was supposed to fire the shells. He sought out every source he could think of, including discussing the experiment and the erosion of his gun barrels with some of his former fraternity brothers at Cornell University who had majored in engineering. Meyer was also worried about whether the breech plugs would blow out due to the increased pressure generated by the baglets. His former fraternity brothers told Meyer that there was no way they could provide him with solid data without making a personal inspection of the gun barrels. But they gave him a crash course on tensile strength, told him how to look for evidence of brittleness, and asked whether the metal had significantly eroded over the years. Meyer told them that the barrels had worn down about 20 percent, but that was "only a guesstimation." They told him to search for hairline cracks, which would mean that the guns couldn't handle the stress generated by a more powerful powder charge.

And that's what he did. He realized that his inspection would be limited to the eight feet inside the barrel where the powder was seated, because he had no means of reaching the sixty or so other feet of circular rifled steel inside each barrel. Meyer asked Dale Mortensen to help. They recruited two petty officers in their turret, Shane Cline and Mark Harden. The four men used masking tape to label anything that looked out of the ordinary. They found one burr in the left gun barrel, but on closer inspection, they agreed that it was just an inconsequential flaw.

Cline and Harden pleaded with Meyer to try to get the tests canceled, or at least to get them transferred to another turret. Both men had been jittery when they fired Skelley's "baby-killer" shells, worrying that the shell would burst before it exited the muzzle. They reminded Meyer that he had often told them that their turret "ran on oil, electricity, and blood," and that "blood [manpower] was the most important commodity." They were not willing to spill their blood being Skelley's guinea pigs. The Navy wasn't supposed to operate that way.

The more Meyer reflected over what Cline and Harden said, the more convinced he became that there was solid Navy precedent outlawing the testing of experimental ordnance on a working man-of-war. Meyer, who had soaked up nautical lore from his father, dug deep into the recesses of his memory. And there it was, the "Peacemaker." He headed to his stateroom and retrieved a well-thumbed, blue-bound copy of *The United States Navy:*

200 *Years*, by Captain Edward L. Beach, USN (Retired). He flipped to the index, located the pages referring to the "Peacemaker," and turned to them to refresh his memory.

THE "PEACEMAKER" was a wrought-iron gun conceived in 1843 by Captain Robert F. Stockton, a wealthy officer whose grandfather had signed the Declaration of Independence and whose father had served in the U.S. Senate. Stockton was offered the post of Secretary of the Navy by President John Tyler, but he declined, instead requesting authority to design a new ship that would incorporate some advanced fire-control and propulsion features. Her guns would be the largest and most powerful ever made at that time—twelve inches in diameter and capable of firing a 225-pound solid shot about five miles, using a fifty-pound charge of black powder. The guns would be mounted on swivels, one on the forecastle and one near the stern.

Stockton had his wrought-iron gun made by a New York firm, then bypassed standard ordnance testing procedures. He towed the gun to sea aboard a barge, fired five shots with gradually increased powder charges, and pronounced his "Peacemaker" fully tested. Nobody in the Navy dared contradict him. He docked the *Princeton* at the Washington Navy Yard and regularly took celebrities on excursions down the Potomac River. These junkets sometimes included gun-firing exercises near Mount Vernon. About 1 P.M. on February 28, 1844, a blustery, clear day, the *Princeton* got underway for an outing. In addition to the ship's company, there were 150 female and 200 male guests onboard. Among them were President Tyler and his fiancee, Julia Gardiner, the Secretary of State, and the Secretary of the Navy. Meyer held his breath as he read what Captain Beach wrote next.

> Four hours later, her bell tolling, the *Princeton* crept upstream and anchored off Alexandria. A big section of her starboard bow bulwark was missing, her bowsprit was damaged, black soot covered her once immaculate forecastle. In the center of the desolation, still on its rotatable carriage, stood the Peacemaker, but with a horrible difference. All of its breech was gone, as was part of the barrel forward of it, up to the trunnions. The heavy iron gun carriage with [Swedish designer John] Ericsson's patented recoil mechanism was bent and covered with soot, but it still supported what remained of the huge gun, now a ridiculous tube of heavy iron open from one end to the other. Its muzzle sagged almost to the forecastle deck in the destroyed gun carriage, looking as though it were aimed to shoot a hole right through the deck and out the side of the ship. But half of the Peacemaker was gone, the jagged broken end where the breech had been was raised into devastating view. One could see through the heavy iron tube from end to end.

There were eight bodies near the *Princeton*'s gangway, unceremoniously wrapped in canvas hammocks. They were Secretary of State Abel Upshur; Navy Secretary Thomas W. Gilmer; Colonel David Gardiner, the father of President Tyler's fiancée; Virgil Maxcy, U.S. chargé d'affaires at The Hague; Commodore Beverly Kennon, chief of the Navy's Bureau of Construction, Equipment and Repair; two members of the gun crew; and President Tyler's personal servant. Stockton did a masterful job of dodging the blame and was exonerated of any guilt by both Navy and congressional investigations. However, the House Naval Affairs Committee found that the flawed weapon had been procured in a nonregulation manner and declared that in the future, full approval of the Naval Bureau of Ordnance and Hydrography was required before any experimental weapons could be installed on a warship. Rigorous standards had to be met. And for years, there was a policy that no guns were to be fired with more than half of the powder charges the guns were designed to handle.

MESMERIZED BY Captain Beach's account of the "Peacemaker" catastrophe, Meyer was struck by the similarities of the 145-year-old accident to what he felt was about to happen on the *Iowa*. Captain Robert Stockton had fired too much powder in a weapon that was not adequately tested. Skelley and Costigan were planning to have more powder rammed into the guns than they had been designed to handle.

Meyer stewed over this information for a day and then unburdened himself to Commander Kissinger. As the ensign patiently explained the planned *Iowa* experiment in relation to the "Peacemaker" explosion, the weapons officer's tongue began flicking in and out of his mouth. He said, "What do you think, Dan? If you're not convinced the guns will take the pressure . . . that it's unsafe . . . we won't do it." Meyer replied, "We're up to the maximum limits that the guns are supposed to take. If in the past forty or so years, the guns have had too much wear and tear and are brittle, they could blow back in the crew's face." Meyer bore down on Kissinger. Did he plan to have any further discussions with the captain about the safety of the experiment? Kissinger hemmed and hawed. He said he preferred to deal with situations such as this within his own department. He said he wasn't personally qualified to make the decision to cancel it and told Meyer that it would have to be his call. "Jesus Christ!" Meyer thought as he headed back to Turret One. "Kissinger's going to leave the decision up to a lowly fucking ensign, a first class petty officer, and two third class petty officers!" Meyer told Mortensen that Kissinger wasn't going to do anything. "Fucking spineless wimp!" Mortensen exploded.

Several days later, Meyer was drinking coffee after lunch in the wardroom with Lieutenant Commander Kimberlain. The lanky assistant engineering officer queried Meyer about the experiment. Meyer described the nonregulation shells and powder. "God! That sounds dangerous to me! We would never do something like that in engineering," Kimberlain exclaimed. For example, he said, before an engineer would put more than the rated pressure on a boiler, he would demand a mountain of paperwork certifying that extensive shore-based tests had been performed and that the chance of a catastrophic failure was nonexistent.

COMMANDER JOHN Morse, Mike Fahey's replacement as executive officer, was the antithesis of the man he relieved. A 1970 ROTC graduate of Dartmouth College, Morse was a talker, not a brawler. The new executive officer wasn't on the ship long before a consensus developed in the wardroom that he couldn't take over the ship in an emergency, despite the fact that Morse had been the executive officer of the patrol gunboat USS *Canon*, which had been ambushed and nearly sunk in Vietnam. He was awarded the Bronze Star with "V" for heroism and the Navy Commendation Medal. He had also served on a heavy cruiser and two destroyers, as well as commanding the destroyer USS *Nicholson*.

Morse toured the turrets, as he did every other space in the ship, soon after he came aboard. He was dismayed at some of the things he observed in the gun rooms. But he didn't do anything about them, and it soon became painfully clear that he wasn't going to say or do anything that might offend the captain. The conditions in the turrets continued to go downhill. PQS training remained a nonpriority item. Some 350 men, who handled ordnance but were not gunner's mates, received no formal safety training.

ON JANUARY 20, 1989, on the way down to Vieques for the long-range shoot, the *Iowa* participated in war games with the standing NATO forces in the Caribbean. She was trounced by the British, Canadian, and West German forces. Then the *Iowa* took a two-day excursion to St. Martin, a tiny island in the West Indies. During this port call, Phil Buch, the Turret Two officer, disgraced himself once again. Buch joined Dan Meyer and Terry McGinn for several hours at a thatch-roofed beach bar, where they tossed down shots of 151-proof rum. Meyer and McGinn said they had exceeded their limit and were going to get some food. Buch declined to join them, saying he was going to meet some sailors from his turret at another bar to continue to raise hell. Eventually, Buch passed out on the beach, awaking the following morning to discover that he had been rolled, his wallet with his ID card, checkbook, and credit cards stolen. His two enlisted companions, neither of whom was robbed, were both ex-jailbirds. One was John Michael Mullahy Jr., a tall, fast-talking, Boston Irishman. The thirty-four-year-old Mullahy, who joined the Navy in 1971, had spent five months in the Philadelphia Naval Brig before coming to the *Iowa* in December 1988. He had pleaded guilty to misuse of about $4,000 in housing-allowance money, although he contended at his court-martial that he did nothing wrong.

Primarily because of his criminal record, Mullahy, who had previously served on a half-dozen other ships before coming to the *Iowa*, was treated as an outcast, a virtual untouchable, on the battleship. He was banished to the bowels of Turret Two, some sixty feet below the main deck, to labor in the magazines toting 110-pound powder bags. It was a humiliating experience for a man who had earned the right to wear the three red V-shaped chevrons of a first class gunner's mate when he was only twenty-one years old. To make matters worse, his boss in the magazines, Kendall Truitt, fourteen years his junior, was a self-confessed car thief and loan shark.

Truitt, a rail-thin third class gunner's mate, was Lieutenant Buch's other companion on the beach. Truitt, unlike Buch and Mullahy, hardly drank at all. He had been in the Navy three years and on the *Iowa* two years. He had flunked out of an electronics program at the Great Lakes Naval Training Center in Illinois and was sent to the *Iowa* to become an apprentice gunner's mate. But before leaving the training center, Truitt stole a Camaro automobile and drove it to his hometown to see his girlfriend.

Not satisfied with the first car, Truitt dumped it and stole a replacement, a 1986 Cutlass Supreme. He drove that car to Tampa, Florida, to see his mother, then back to Illinois, and finally to Norfolk to join the *Iowa*. The hot car was parked where the *Iowa* was normally berthed at the Norfolk base for several months before security checked its registration and requested the Naval Investigative Service to arrest Truitt. He confessed, spent fourteen days in jail in Virginia, and was shipped back to Illinois for another night behind bars. His father, Walter Truitt, bailed him out and provided him with an attorney. He was allowed to plead guilty to a misdemeanor, paid $4,000 in restitution, and was released without having to serve any prison time. The Navy took no additional punitive action against him.

Truitt was Turret Two's resident loan shark. He advanced money to his turret mates at usurious rates. Senior Chief Reggie Ziegler assigned Truitt—who was probably the smartest sailor in Turret Two—down in the magazines, hoping it would deter his unsavory financial practices. The assignment had no effect. Truitt made more money than ever before. He was open about what he did, saying, "I did loan money from time to time. I was one of the preferred people, because I had better rates than a lot of people. For me, if I loaned you $10, you could pay $15. A lot of other guys charged $10 for $20." Those were weekly interest rates. So many men in Turret One had been in hock to Truitt that Dale Mortensen took action. Mortensen wrote out a check, squaring his men's debts with Truitt, and then warned the third class gunner's mate never to come into Turret One again, "or I'll kick your ass."

TRUITT'S AUTO-theft conviction and his loan-sharking were not the only reasons for his controversial shipboard reputation. In early 1987, when Larry Seaquist was captain, Truitt and a second class gunner's mate, Clayton Hartwig, were written up for "dereliction of duty." Reticent and pliant, Hartwig made up his mind when he was in grammar school that he would follow his father's footsteps and become a gunner's mate in the Navy. He was devoted to his job and was considered one of the best sixteen-inch gun captains on the ship. He was also mechanically clumsy, to the point of being unable to install a radio in his car. Hartwig, a Seventh-Day Adventist, also a light drinker, became best friends with Truitt. The pair were inseparable during their free time off the battleship, frequently renting motel rooms together and hanging out in malls ogling girls. They shared an interest in cars, music, and guns.

Despite the fact that both Truitt and Hartwig engaged in heterosexual relations and both adamantly denied they were homosexuals, rumors slowly spread around the ship's berthing compartments that they were "fairies and faggots" and that they enjoyed a "special relationship." Those rumors blossomed when two sailors spotted the pair wrestling on the port side of the main deck during their midnight-to-4-A.M. watch. "The next day I find myself being questioned for an indecent act with another. I was outraged," Truitt said. Larry Seaquist assigned Master Chief Chuck Hill to investigate what had happened. "If they're homosexuals, I want them out of the Navy. That's the law," Seaquist said.

After his investigation was completed, Hill told Seaquist, "Those boys are not queers, Captain. They were goofing off while on watch and should be punished for it, but they're not faggots. Hartwig was the senior man and should receive more punishment." Seaquist took away one of Hartwig's stripes, but told him he could win it back in short order if he behaved himself. Truitt was fined and given additional duty.

Chuck Hill's verdict about Hartwig and Truitt didn't stop the rumormongering. From time to time, graffiti scrawled in the crew's heads (bathrooms) suggested that Hartwig and Truitt were gay lovers. The relationship between the pair cooled considerably after December 1988, when Truitt married Carole Smith, the twenty-year-old daughter of a former Detroit policeman.

AT ABOUT 5:30 P.M. on January 26, 1989, the *Iowa* was steaming off the island of Vieques, preparing to fire six of Master Chief Skelley's DX-149 experimental shells. Skelley positioned himself in "Spot 1," 116 feet above the main deck. He intended to use a twenty-six-foot stereoscopic range finder to adjust optically the fall of shot on the target. He would not employ radar, nor would he rely on an aircraft spotter for adjustments in range and deflection. His target was an abandoned school bus on Vieques, located 23.4 nautical miles away from the *Iowa*. Due to curvature and rotation of the earth, the Mark 38 range finder Skelley was using could measure distances no farther than fifteen nautical miles from the ship on a clear day. And it wasn't a clear day. It was steamy and misty, with a badly blurred horizon. The fact that Skelley would be firing blind didn't deter him. J. Harold Jones, a Navy civilian ordnance expert, stood near the chief to observe the experiment.

Shane Cline was in charge of Turret One's left gun, which would fire three shells, each one packed with more than two hundred pounds of high explosives. Turret One's right gun would fire the other three shells. Using the gunfire net, Skelley instructed Cline and Ron Griffith, the right gun captain, to ram their shells, followed by six bags of propellant per gun. Cline and Griffith were also told to insert fifty-pound "supercharge" baglets.

Dan Meyer and Dale Mortensen were still debating whether to obey an order to fire their guns. "Are we doing the right thing?" Mortensen mused. "If we're not, and something goes wrong, we're going to blow up a turret and kill a hell of a lot of people," Meyer responded.

Word about Meyer's safety concerns regarding the experiment had circulated throughout the wardroom. Before the shooting began, the new executive officer urged Fred Moosally and other senior officers to get into the "citadel," a reinforced steel booth designed to protect the helmsman if the bridge is hit by enemy fire. According to Terry McGinn, John Morse shouted, "Get everybody in here in case the guns blow up!" There's not a whole lot of room in the "citadel," and the helmsman was hard pressed to keep the ship on course as the department heads hustled into the armored cubicle.

TURRET ONE fired six rounds—nothing out of the ordinary occurred. The first shell from Shane Cline's left gun climbed to an altitude of 20,000 feet before impacting seventy-five yards away from the yellow bus, making it a "direct hit," according to Skelley. The next two rounds dropped about fifty yards from the target, and the final three rounds pulled to the right and plopped down sixty to seventy yards from the bus. Skelley claimed that the *Iowa*'s guns had hit a target 48,000 yards away, or 6,000 yards farther than had ever been achieved by any battleship. He also insisted that he had broken the Army's 1935 record by 7,000 yards. The *Iowa* had broken the world's record for seaborne naval gunnery, but Skelley made it sound like he had beaten every existing distance record for sixteen-inch gunnery. But what he conveniently failed to mention was that in the early 1950s, the U.S. military had fired a sixteen-inch projectile that could carry a nuclear warhead thirty-six nautical miles, or approximately thirteen nautical miles farther than Skelley's much-ballyhooed Vieques experiment.

Declaring the experiment "really kind of incredible" in the ship's newspaper, *The Iowan*, Skelley boasted that he had seen a target 49,000 yards away, a physical impossibility. "We could have hit the target at that range," he asserted. "Over the past five years we've done a lot of experimenting and we hope to do more in the future."

Fred Moosally emerged from the armored "citadel" strutting like a peacock. He had glowing press releases transmitted to the Chief of Naval Information in Washington for wide dissemination to the news media. And then he updated his resume to take credit for the *Iowa*'s long-range gunnery exploits.

JUST A week after the long-range shoot, the *Iowa* engaged in another unsafe experiment. This one was conceived by the executive officer,

Commander Morse. Morse had seen a picture somewhere of a battleship simultaneously shooting all six guns in her forward two turrets just off the bow. This is possible, because Turret Two is one full deck higher than Turret One, but it is risky. Although there are safety cutouts built into the fire-control system to prevent the loaded guns in both turrets from slewing around and shooting off the bow, these cutouts are not fail-safe. The executive officer called this macho exercise the "John Wayne Shoot."

When Dan Meyer and Dale Mortensen heard what Morse wanted to do, they were apoplectic. Meyer told the weapons officer that Commander Morse was courting disaster. Kissinger assured Meyer that the executive officer, who had no previous experience with large-caliber guns, knew what he was doing. Kissinger said he was not about to question the judgment of an officer who was senior to him. Ken Costigan, who was present in the weapons office when Meyer and Kissinger discussed the impending shoot, said he had conducted a similar exercise when he had been gunnery officer aboard the *New Jersey*. Nothing had gone wrong then.

The "John Wayne Shoot" took place on a hazy, humid day, midway up the east coast of Florida. The ship was plodding along at about eight knots. There was a slight chop. Turrets One and Two were pointed out on the starboard beam about fifteen degrees off the bow. Turret One was encountering difficulties with broken powder bags. There was a lengthy delay, but all three guns finally fired. The left and right guns were reloaded and both misfired. The center gun got off another round. And then all hell broke loose. Turret Two let go with a three-gun salvo over the top of Turret One. The right gun in Turret Two was pointed directly over the left gun in Turret One, which meant that Turret Two was shooting diagonally across the port bow. "We lined up incorrectly. We endangered those guys' lives," said John Mullahy, who was in Turret Two that day.

"Being inside Turret One was the most frightening experience I have ever had in my life," Dan Meyer said. "Things were flying everywhere and dropping from the overhead. Wires were blown. Welding tacks popped out. The shock wave blew out the turret officer's switchboard and the leads. We had no power, no lights for a time. Men were screaming. There was a panic."

The concussion shredded the bucklers around all three of Turret One's guns. Bucklers (also known as bloomers) are flexible rubberized canvas covers attached externally to a turret so that guns are free to move about, but water is kept out. The bucklers for each turret cost $90,000 and are virtually impossible to replace. Matt Price, who was the right gun captain in Turret Two, wrote his parents that when his weapon fired over Turret One, "It ripped that black bag at the base of the barrel. It tore it completely off and ripped the other two. So now Turret One has no bloomers. All the bloomers are shot." With the bucklers in rags, three fireballs arced into Turret One, followed by a thick pall of acrid yellow smoke. The fireballs vaporized the water that had accumulated in the bloomers, turning it into steam. This steam, combined with the smoke generated by the gunpowder, made it appear for five minutes or so that Turret One was ablaze. "There is a problem in Turret One!" Master Chief James Hickman yelled into the gunfire net. As the turret slowly rotated to port, Fred Moosally became increasingly agitated over Turret One's failure to unload her guns.

It was then that Chief Mark Cable, who was standing on the bridge near Chief Hickman, stepped forward with a suggestion that the captain eagerly embraced. A thin, red-headed gunner's mate who was assigned to the five-inch guns, Cable said, "Captain, they can attach lanyards and fire by percussion." Moosally turned to Chief Hickman and ordered, "Have Turret One attach lanyards and fire by percussion." Hickman merely shrugged his shoulders and passed the captain's order along to Meyer and Mortensen. Ken Costigan also came up on the net, echoing the order.

A lanyard is a short orange-nylon rope with a wooden handle fastened to one end. It looks rather like the cord used to start a lawn mower. Attached to the other end of the lanyard is a hook (similar to one found on a dog leash). A gunner's mate connects this hook to a clip found near the center of the breechblock and then yanks back on it. This activates a small, spring-loaded hammer inside the breechblock. After the lanyard is hauled back a certain distance, the hammer is released and strikes the primer cartridge, causing the powder in the gun to ignite. It's a last-ditch method of firing, and it's dangerous. A gunner's mate yanking on the lanyard can easily be crushed by the recoiling gun. Shooting by percussion overrides the ship's redundant fire-control safety features. If the guns are pointed at the bow, the odds are excellent that the bow will be blown off when the weapons discharge.

Shane Cline, Turret One's left gun captain, rebelled when he heard the order from the bridge. Cline hurled his orange lanyard into the gun pit. "Fuck you!" he shouted at nobody in particular. Ron Griffith, whose left gun was loaded, held onto his lanyard and refused to carry out the order. Mark Harden's center gun was empty. Meyer and Mortensen knew they had the makings of a mutiny on their hands.

"Fire those fucking guns!" Costigan screamed on the gunfire net. "Check fire! Check fire!" Mortensen yelled back. This is an emergency order given whenever there is imminent danger from the guns to the crew, the ship, or anything around the ship. "What the fuck is going on?" Costigan whined. "Commander, look at where my guns are pointed," Mortensen replied. Meyer was then engaged in a heated dialogue with the bridge. Chief Hickman told the turret officer that the captain was "really pissed" that Meyer wasn't firing his guns. "Master Chief, look at where my turret is pointing. I'll shoot the bow off," Meyer said. There was a short pause on the circuit, and then Meyer heard Hickman gasp, "Oh, shit!" Meyer then heard a chorus of "Oh, shits!" coming from Captain Moosally and Commanders Morse, Kissinger, and Finney.

AFTER ALLOWING the guns to cool off and then having the crews unload them, Meyer hurried to the weapons-department office, where he assailed Commander Kissinger. "Come look at my turret! My bucklers are in shreds! I've got rags around my guns! I damned near blew the front of the ship off! We've got to debrief this, Commander, so all the men in the weapons department can hear what happened," Meyer raged. Kissinger shook his head: "There's no need to have a debriefing."

MEYER WAS too disturbed to let matters drop there. He followed Ken Costigan from the weapons office to his stateroom. Meyer said that he adopted "my best drill sergeant voice" when he bearded the pale gunnery officer. Costigan quickly tired of being railed at by a subordinate, and he warned, "Remember who you're talking with, Ensign." "I know who I'm talking to, you're the commander who almost blew off the front of the ship!" Meyer countered. "Get the fuck out of here!" Costigan barked. As Meyer left, he punched a wall locker decorated with a picture of the battleship on which Costigan's father had served during World War II.

Still determined to have a debriefing, Meyer asked for help from Dale Mortensen, Senior Chief Reggie Ziegler, and Master Chief Dale Miller. Even Master Chief Hickman was willing to be of assistance. The event was held on the main deck behind Turret One. Meyer's men were there, as were the vast majority of the men assigned to Turret Two. "These dumb bastards are gonna kill us!" Reggie Ziegler predicted. Describing the "John Wayne Shoot," Chief Hickman said, "That was the most fucked-up shoot we ever had!" Chief Miller stated that if the senior officers continued to dodge responsibility, the chiefs, leading petty officers, and junior officers had to find ways to avoid "another fuck-up like today."

MEYER AND Mortensen decided that they would never again subject their men to any more of Skelley's experiments or to harebrained exercises dreamed up by senior officers who knew nothing about sixteen-inch gunnery. Skelley's experiments were like playing Russian roulette with a six-shot revolver with six bullets in the cylinder. Meyer and Mortensen called on Skelley in his tiny, cluttered office and told him that they were no longer going to participate in his experiments. Skelley's mouth puckered. His dark eyes took on a soulful quality as he fought back tears. He tried to argue, but he'd become tongue-tied. "I'm sorry, Master Chief, but my men are in revolt," Meyer said.

SO SKELLEY needed another turret to conduct his experiments. Turret Three was out of the question. First of all, in Skelley's words, there was "all the cluttered shit back there." That was his way of saying that the ship's boats were stacked around Turret Three and interfered with the turret's ability to rotate and fire. Second, Turret Three hadn't properly maintained the hydraulic system on the powder-car hoist to the left gun. Recently, a loaded powder car had tumbled six decks below and shattered the 2.5-inch-thick brass base of the car. It was out of operation, perhaps forever, and this effectively reduced the turret by one gun. Finally, Turret Three was a cesspool, literally and figuratively.

That left Turret Two. Skelley knew that Senior Chief Reggie Ziegler hated his experiments. Even though Ziegler was Skelley's closest friend in the chiefs' quarters on the ship, he regularly took Skelley to task about breaking, or at the very least skirting, safety regulations with his "kitchen-sink" experiments. Ziegler was a "short-timer," having only seven months left before he retired in August from the Navy after twenty years of service. The strapping senior chief believed that he had reached the outer limits of his competency with the sixteen-inch guns. In his opinion, he wasn't qualified to supervise Skelley's projects. Moreover, Turret Two was low on manpower, and a number of the sailors assigned to the turret were completely untrained. And finally, Ziegler had no confidence that his division officer, Lieutenant Phil Buch, could handle an emergency if it developed while the turret was shooting.

So when Skelley asked Ziegler to turn Turret Two into an "experimental platform," Ziegler yelled, "No! And hell no!" Skelley then took his case to Lieutenant Phil Buch. He found Buch in his cubbyhole office, which had once been a 40-mm antiaircraft gun magazine. Skelley immediately asked to use Turret Two as his "research platform," and he was dumbfounded when Buch agreed. Skelley didn't tell Buch that Reggie Ziegler had already turned him down.

THE *IOWA* pulled into New Orleans on February 5, 1989, for a four-day Mardi Gras bacchanalia. Drunkenness by the officers and sailors reached an all-time high. Dan Meyer and some of the junior officers favored a hole-in-the-wall bar that served a potent dark-green witches' brew in hurricane glasses. It tasted like antifreeze and made your teeth ache when you swilled it down. Early one morning, after a particularly bad night, Meyer barely managed to make officers' call. Badly hungover, he was unshaven and dressed in a filthy, rumpled, sweat-stained, wash-khaki uniform with a fore-and-aft cap (commonly referred to as a "piss cutter") jammed down his head, almost covering his bloodshot eyes. Ken Costigan reprimanded him for his disreputable appearance. As Meyer shambled off, he bumped into one of the men in his division. "Mr. Meyer, do you think the officers are drinking more in the past six months than they did before?" Meyer was embarrassed.

He went below to his stateroom to shower, shave, and change into a fresh uniform. While he was scraping the stubble off his face, the question posed by the sailor made him think. "Things were so grotesque that they had not seemed so strange when they were happening," he reflected. "Fahey's beating people up. Officers getting rolled on the beach. It was dysfunctional conduct. Mardi

Gras was awful. The whole wardroom was hungover. It wasn't the troops. It was the officers. The 'John Wayne Shoot' was insanity. Safety had gone out the window. We didn't have any right doing these gunnery experiments."

WHEN SHE left New Orleans, the *Iowa* steamed to Port Everglades, Florida. Along the way, she did some routine shooting. Turret Two was out of action, due to a major electrical breakdown. The ship also carried out an exercise designed to simulate mine warfare. A large charge was detonated near the ship to see how well she could withstand the pressure. Four fuel lines were severed in the process. Commander Edwin Jankura, who had replaced Jerry Ware as chief engineer, informed the captain that damage was so extensive that the Port Everglades visit had to be canceled so the ship could return to Norfolk for repairs. Even with the shattered fuel lines, the ship managed to fire twenty-two rounds of conventional ammunition off the Virginia Capes before entering the Chesapeake Bay. Turrets One and Three each shot eleven times. Turret Two was still out of commission.

CHIEF REGGIE Ziegler called his wife, Sharon, soon after the *Iowa* was moored to the pier in Norfolk. He didn't want to worry her, but at the same time he had to talk to somebody about the dread that seemed to permeate the *Iowa*. "Reggie told me how unsafe and how old that gunpowder was," Sharon said. He told her that he had to mill parts in the ship's machine shop to keep the guns operating. He gave her a detailed description of the "John Wayne Shoot," revealed that Steve Skelley was a menace, and said that Lieutenant Buch had lost the respect of the sailors in Turret Two.

Sharon had been physically unable to tour the *Iowa*, so Reggie had shot an elaborate video of the vessel and sent it to her to give her some notion about the ship's size and complexity. Reggie told Sharon that some of the apprentice gunner's mates the Navy had recently been sending to the *Iowa* were so lacking in mechanical skills that they didn't even know how to tighten or loosen a bolt. "I tell them, 'righty tighty, lefty loosey.' " An intensely proud, meticulous man, Ziegler said, "Some of the chiefs just sit in the lounge on their butts drinking coffee and won't work with the kids. I can't do that. I have to set an example for these boys."

"We're losing guys left and right," he told his wife. "We're shorthanded. Chiefs with seventeen years of service are quitting. I've got to teach these kids to push the right button, or they'll blow us to kingdom come! My butt is on the line!" he added. The decorated Vietnam veteran reminded Sharon, as he had in the past, that if he died at sea, he wanted to be buried at sea. "No, you'll be buried next to me!" she cried.

After they hung up, Sharon was agitated. Reggie had always been her pillar of strength. He had always been so stoic about whatever happened to him in the Navy. He was the type who sat back, said nothing, and sized up another person or situation. If he were so willing to emerge from his shell and talk to her as candidly as he had, then conditions on the *Iowa* must really be terrifying.

REGGIE ZIEGLER wasn't the only husband in Turret Two to call his spouse from Norfolk and report that things were ghastly. Jack E. Thompson Jr., a third class gunner's mate from eastern Tennessee, telephoned his wife, Leasa, and complained about the lack of training and the poor condition of the gunpowder. There was more. Something dreadful had happened to Jack's gun during a recent gun shoot, but the twenty-two-year-old, who was Turret Two's left gun captain, would wait until he was home on Easter leave to talk about that.

Leasa had visited Jack on the ship in Norfolk the previous Christmas. She didn't think he had been his normal optimistic self back then. He took her on a tour of the ship with his best friend and turret mate, Errick Lawrence. Lawrence, twenty-nine, was seven years older than Jack, but he always respectfully deferred to the younger man, acting as if Jack hung the moon. Jack was the real article, a full-fledged gun captain, and Errick was only a wannabe. Even though Errick had completed three years of college, he was judged to be "clumsy" by the gunner's mates assigned to Turrets One and Two. Errick was continually "under instruction," but so far he had failed to qualify as a gun captain. That was unfortunate, considering that he was a second class petty officer with seven years of service.

During her Christmas visit, Leasa climbed up through the tail hatch with Jack and Errick into Turret Two. They checked out the turret officer's booth and entered the left gun room, where Jack was assigned. He explained the layout and then almost casually said, "If anything ever happens in here, we'll all be killed." An outdoors man, Jack said that he felt cooped up in the gun room, comparing himself to a caged animal. When he told Leasa how old the powder was, she gasped, "My god! That powder is fifty years old! . . . You've got to be crazy to work here. Jack, this looks dangerous." "It's dangerous, if you don't know what you're doing," Jack said. "If anything did happen, you wouldn't have time to pray."

Several months after Leasa Thompson toured the *Iowa*, Jack sent her a letter saying that a "dangerous" gun shoot was in the works. "But [they're] always scary, because I'm getting too short for this shit!" he wrote. Then, he dropped this tantalizing non sequitur: "Oh, Errick seen the ghost today." It seemed that the *Iowa* was haunted by a ghost of a dead seaman who reportedly had made periodic appearances on the ship since World War II. Sometimes, the battleship's sailors swore, he materialized in his dress-blue uniform, walking arm-in-arm with a beautiful woman wearing a long taffeta gown and straw bonnet. The supernatural pair had been observed in the past just before something really awful occurred.

5

"Mort! . . . Mort! . . . Mort! . . ."

ON MARCH 29, 1989, some six weeks after the "John Wayne Shoot" threw the *Iowa* into turmoil, Naval Sea Systems Command held a sixteen-inch-gunnery improvement seminar in a hotel near Washington's National Airport. About two hundred battleship officers, chiefs, and petty officers attended, as well as civilian technicians and officers from ordnance facilities around the country. Master Chief Steve Skelley, Lieutenant Commander Kenneth Costigan, the *Iowa*'s gunnery officer, and Ensign Dan Meyer attended.

Rear Admiral Robert T. Reimann, Sea Systems Command's deputy commander, a veteran destroyer and cruiser skipper, was the keynote speaker. The blunt-spoken Reimann said he wasn't there to warn everyone that trouble was on the horizon. "The handwriting is on the walls," he said. "The budget cutters are looking for reasons to kill the battleship program. You all know battleships are manpower-intensive and expensive to operate. Guys, lie low and don't do anything stupid for God's sake! Don't give the fiscal snipers anything to cut your system. Avoid accidents at all costs! Avoid negative publicity!"

Up until this point, Dan Meyer had been under the impression that the experiments had all been formulated by Sea Systems Command and that Skelley had merely implemented them. "I was amazed to find out that all of the ideas originated with Skelley. He was the dog who wagged Sea Systems's tail," Meyer said.

Dan Meyer was not the only person to become upset by Skelley's experiments. In the three weeks following the battleship conference, and before the ship's departure to the Caribbean for FLEETEX, relatives of a number of the *Iowa*'s sailors learned firsthand just how perilous the ship had become for their sons, husbands, fathers, and brothers.

During this period, twenty-nine-year-old Gunner's Mate Third Class Robert W. Backherms called his wife, Susan, in Ravenna, Ohio, and told her that no substantive gunnery training had taken place on the *Iowa* since he reported aboard in January 1989. Tall and gangly, with graying hair, Backherms was assigned to Turret Two. On one occasion, after being told to wax the deck of a compartment, he accidentally locked himself in the cubicle and spent the night on the deck curled up in a corner. When he was set free the next morning, he couldn't coherently explain to the chief why he had failed to use the phone in the compartment to summon help.

On another occasion, he was told by the chief early one morning to polish a brass shell case. When the chief returned late that evening, he found Backherms still buffing the gleaming case, even though it was obvious that he had completed the task many hours earlier. Backherms had not paused for lunch, or even taken time to go to the bathroom. He told the thoroughly perplexed chief that he thought he had to keep shining until he received a direct order to stop.

GUNNER'S MATE Backherms was assigned a job considered to be one of the most dangerous on the *Iowa*. He was the center gun's rammerman. He had never operated the rammer during a gun shoot. Each sixteen-inch gun had a five-man crew consisting of: (1) The powder-car operator, who controlled a small elevator that hauled the propellant up to the gun room from the magazines; (2) the cradle operator, who made sure that a large, aluminum tray was properly aligned so that the powder and the projectile could be loaded into the gun; (3) the gun captain, who directed the activities of the other four crewmen and synchronized the loading and firing cycles; (4) the rammerman, who used a variable-speed device to shove the powder bags and shell into the breech; (5) the primerman, who stood on a platform below the gun and inserted a .30-caliber rifle cartridge into the open breechblock to trigger the detonation.

The rammer operator sat on a bicycle-style seat and used a chain-driven mechanism that thrust the shell into the breech at a maximum speed of fourteen feet per second. Next, he used the same rammer to nudge the six pelletized powder bags into the breech behind the projectile at no more than 1.7 feet per second. There was no safety feature to prevent the operator from confusing the fast projectile-ramming speed with the much slower powder-ramming speed. The farther a rammerman pressed down on the control lever, the faster the rammer would go into the breech. Many sailors were able to qualify at every other position in the gun room but could not overcome their fear of ramming powder. A veteran sixteen-inch gunner put it this way: "If you fuck up and ram the powder as fast as you ram the shell, kiss your ass good-bye! Your parts are going into a body bag, that's if we can find them!"

After Backherms told his wife that he was going to be shoving explosive

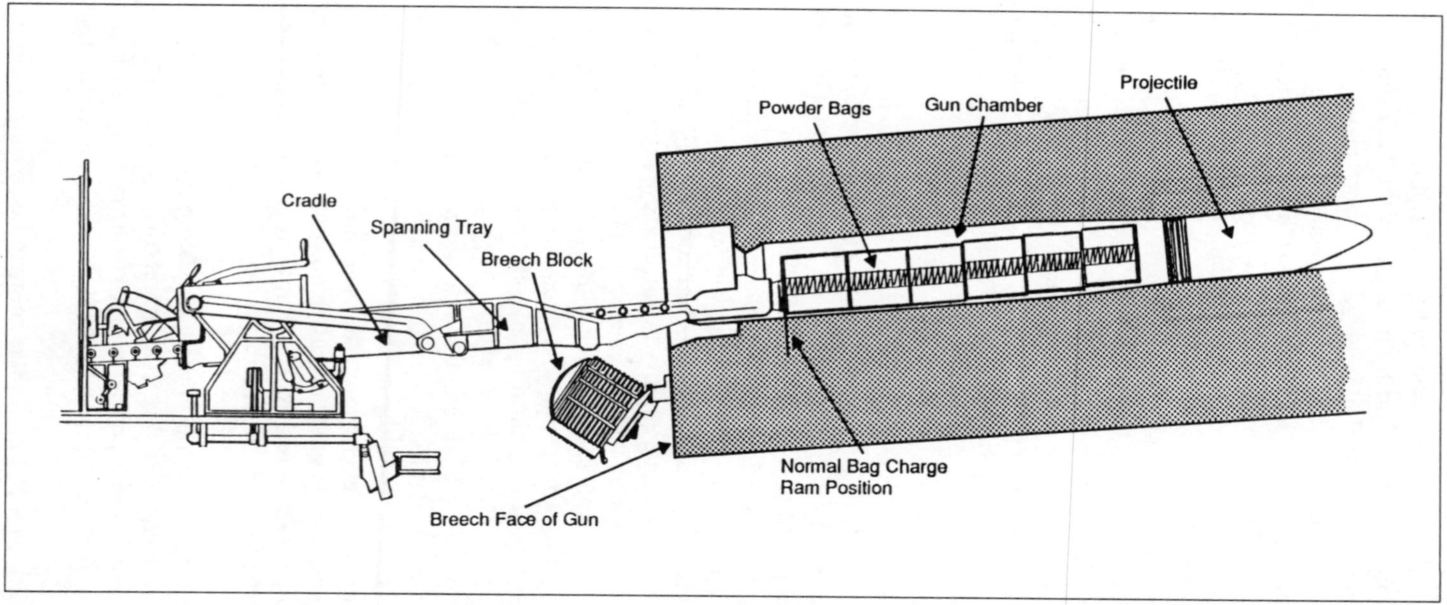

A loaded sixteen-inch gun. It has six powder bags seated behind the projectile, rather than the five that were in Turret Two's center gun when it exploded. The breech is open and the chain link rammer is still extended into the rear of the barrel, as they were on the day of the accident. The spanner tray, used to support the shell and powder bags before ramming, is still extended. The rammerman's position can be seen behind and to the side of the cradle. It is almost directly in line with the blast. (U.S. Navy)

shells and powder into a gun barrel with a chain rammer, she said, "I don't like what you're telling me, Robert. You get too lax and things happen. You're working with dangerous materials, and you need all the training you can get." Susan Backherms later described her husband as "a good man, a fine sailor, but a klutz, completely uncoordinated." Robert Backherms would receive no more training before he attempted to ram live ordnance in Turret Two's center gun.

In early April, Scot Blakey, a third class gunner's mate assigned to Turret Two, traveled home on leave to Eaton Rapids, Michigan, a small town near the state capital. One night, as his mother, Mary Lou Blakey, was preparing dinner in the kitchen, she overheard twenty-year-old Scot talking to his eighteen-year-old sister, Julie. "I'm not thrilled with some of the things we're doing on the *Iowa*," he said. "We shouldn't be doing them. Something could go wrong." "Why are you doing them?" Julie inquired. "We don't have a choice," Scot replied.

TWENTY-YEAR-old Matt Price, Turret Two's right gun captain, arranged to get home on leave to Burnside, Pennsylvania, a hamlet located on the west branch of the Susquehanna River in bituminous coal mining and timbering country. During Matt's brief visit, his seventeen-year-old sister, Didi, noticed that her brother wasn't his customary high-spirited self.

Didi asked her older brother to give her a ride into town to do some shopping, hoping that she could find out what was bugging him. As they drove down a twisting, two-lane country road, they had the radio on, listening to the plaintive Madonna melody, "Like a Prayer." "I don't like that song," Matt remarked. "It reminds me of death." "Are you afraid of dying, Matt?" Didi probed. "I'm not afraid of dying, but I just don't want to. I'm ready, but I have a lot of things I want to do," he said. Then, he told her about everything that had gone wrong on the *Iowa*, especially in his turret. "That turret just shakes, and it's scary. I'm frightened," he said.

JACK THOMPSON, Turret Two's left gun captain, went home on leave to Greeneville, Tennessee. Jack nosed his red 1984 Mazda into the drive of his parents' red brick rambler on March 26, 1989. The rugged, blond third class petty officer was eager to see his wife, Leasa, and his parents, Jack Sr. and Mildred. But he was hesitant about telling his parents too much about the problems on the *Iowa*.

Early one morning, as Jack was working in the carport changing the oil in Leasa's red Volkswagen, his mother, a nurse, came out of the kitchen and sat in a swing near him. "Good morning, Jack, get your head out of the motor or you're liable to get blown up," Mildred said, teasing her son. But her words had just the opposite effect. Jack blurted out, "Momma, I'm afraid my whole ship is going to blow up!" Tears were streaming down his face. His anguished mother inquired, "If it's that dangerous, son, why don't you report it?" "We did report it, and they don't believe us," Jack replied. "Jack, I wish you could get out of this Navy," Mildred said. Jack's face turned chalk white and his hands shook.

That same day, Jack drove out into the countryside to get an expert opinion from his uncle Rubel. A prickly, tight-lipped, hickory-hard mountaineer, Rubel had served in the field artillery and was well acquainted with bag propellant and big guns. Jack explained the "John Wayne Shoot" to his uncle. He said that the projectile and powder had been rammed home in his gun, the breechblock was ajar, and the powder began to smolder. He was just able to latch the breechblock when the sixteen-inch gun "went off by itself." No primer had been inserted. Jack said there were "a bunch of goof-offs" in his turret, and he called it "a death trap." He was certain the powder was "bad."

THE *IOWA* sailed from Norfolk on Thursday, April 13, heading toward the Caribbean at a respectable rate of twenty knots. While Dale Mortensen and Dan Meyer were occupied investigating the details of the Tomahawk missile experiment, Turret Two's leadership was frantically trying to keep its turret from falling apart. Lieutenant Philip Buch had agreed to carry out Chief Skelley's experiments in Turret Two, but his senior turret chief, Reggie Ziegler, had so few trained gunner's mates that he seriously doubted he could carry out an elementary fire mission, much less participate in one of Skelley's elaborate exercises.

On Sunday, April 16, Ziegler and Buch walked into the ship's technical supply office and asked two petty officers working there, Donald Schultz and Robert Enochs, if they could use their microfiche machine. The chief and the lieutenant scrolled through the microfiche for fifteen minutes, asked the petty officers some questions, and then filled out a handful of requisition forms. As they were getting ready to depart, Ziegler told Buch, "Something just don't feel right, but we can't pinpoint the problem. I can't put my finger on it." Buch replied, "I just hope we can get it fixed or figured out before someone gets hurt."

ALL OF Turret Two's personnel were pressed into service doing major overhaul during the entire night of April 18-19. The center gun was in the worst shape. The "firing lock," the mechanism in the breech containing the firing pin, had to be disassembled and cleaned. The compressed-air system, which cleansed the bore of sparks and debris each time a shell was fired, wasn't operating properly. This gas ejection air system was turned on and off with a valve located in a pit about twenty feet directly below the gun room. Dale Mortensen later inspected the center gun and said that he was certain that after the repairs had been completed, the gas ejection air valve was left in the closed position.

The door of the center gun's powder hoist was jury-rigged with a part from a flattened Pepsi can, but even with this stopgap repair, the hoist still didn't work properly. It no longer stopped automatically.

On Wednesday morning, April 19, with the launching of a Tomahawk missile from the cruiser USS *San Jacinto* toward the *Iowa* still a distinct possibility, the battleship also made plans to fire her sixteen-inch guns. The day before the gun shoot, Lieutenant Walsh, the fire-control officer, along with Chiefs Skelley and Hickman, held a pre-fire briefing at 10 A.M. on the port side of Turret Three for about forty officers, chiefs, and petty officers from the weapons department.

Far from being an amorphous bull session, a pre-fire briefing has to rehearse realistically the actual event. Everyone involved needs to know precisely what and where the targets are, which guns will shoot, the order in which they will fire, what kind of powder and projectiles will be used, and how to communicate with one another. Walsh's meeting, which he strangely referred to as a "pre-pre-fire briefing," was notable for who was not there. Absent were Captain Fred Moosally; Commander Morse, the executive officer; Commander Kissinger, the weapons officer; and Lieutenant Commander Costigan, the gunnery officer.

Walsh often deferred to Skelley during the briefing. Skelley planned to complete an unauthorized gunnery experiment that he had first begun in November 1987 and that Commander Gene Kocmich had expressly forbidden him ever to undertake again. He was going to use D-846 powder charges to propel 2,700-pound projectiles. He intended to do this despite a prominent notice stenciled on every D-846 canister, saying, WARNING: Do Not Use with 2,700 lb. Projectile. D-846 powder was old. It had been used on battleships several generations older than the *Iowa*. It came in bags that weighed ninety-four pounds, sixteen pounds lighter than normal propellant, but it burned faster. D-846 was considered fine when shooting 1,900-pound shells, but the Navy feared that this powder could build up too much pressure behind 2,700-pound shells and cause the barrel to burst. And if the warnings on the canisters were not enough to deter Skelley from this experiment, he should have remembered Admiral Reimann's admonition at the recent battleship gunnery conference to "lie low and don't do anything stupid." Skelley was thumbing his nose at authority. Neither Lieutenant Leo Walsh nor Master Chief James Hickman did anything to halt Skelley, who rationalized the experiment by saying that he was just trying to squeeze some more accuracy from the guns.

The briefing was like attending the Mad Hatter's tea party. Everything was up in the air. It was unclear whether the turrets would fire on the port or the starboard side. That was important to Turret Three, which had the captain's gig and the ship's utility boats stacked on the starboard side near the turret and thus couldn't fire to starboard. However, if the shooting was to occur on the port side, Turret Three was told to fire all three of its guns. That wasn't possible, because Turret Three's left gun was inoperable. The hoist had not been repaired since the powder car tumbled six decks below, shattering itself, several months earlier. Neither Walsh nor Skelley seemed to be aware of this problem, and Turret Three's division officer, Ensign Kevin Hunt, didn't speak up and clarify the situation.

Each of Turret Three's guns was to be loaded with four bags of D-846 powder and one 2,700-pound projectile. Properly seating four bags rather than a regulation six-bag load is an awesome task for a rammerman. A quilted red silk patch on the tail end of the last powder bag must be positioned very near the breech plug. This plug, which bulges inwardly like a toadstool, is called "the mushroom." The quilted patch, known as a "red end," contains the same kind of black powder used in antique muzzle-loading rifles. If the rammerman does a proper job of lining up the bags, it is said that "the red end is kissing the mushroom." The .30-caliber primer cartridge is fired through an aperture in the "mushroom" into the "red end," prompting a chain reaction. If the bags are shoved too far into the powder chamber, the gun will misfire. None of the *Iowa*'s gunner's mates had any training on how to ram nonstandard loads of four or five bags.

Reggie Ziegler and Phil Buch were told that Turret Two would fire ten projectiles—two rounds in the left gun and four rounds in both the center and the right guns. No targets would be involved. Turret Two would be firing 2,700-pound practice shells (containing no explosives) more than 10,000 feet in the air and have them splash into the ocean seventeen miles away. The turret was to use a five-bag load of D-846 propellant for every projectile it fired. Ziegler didn't like anything about this gun shoot, but he didn't say that to Walsh and Skelley. Instead, he waited until after the briefing ended and arranged a meeting with Master Chief Hickman.

When they met that evening, Ziegler told Hickman that he only had the trained manpower to fire two guns at a time. He didn't have enough gunner's mates in the magazines, powder-handling room, and projectile decks to handle three guns. "I told Reggie that if he only had the trained men to fire two guns not to attempt to fire three," Hickman said.

Skelley ran into an immutable object when he attempted to involve Dale Mortensen in his forbidden experiments. "Mortensen doesn't like the idea of a five-bag shoot. I'll have a hard time selling it to him," Skelley had earlier told Dan Meyer. "You're not going to sell him anything, because he knows that's illegal. He's not going to risk the lives of his men for one of your experiments," Meyer responded. Skelley informed Mortensen at the pre-fire briefing that since he objected to firing four or five bags of D-846 in combination with 2,700-pound projectiles, he could fire whatever he pleased. Mortensen said that Turret One would fire six "reduced charges" of D-845 powder (which weighed about sixty pounds) with each 1,900-pound high-explosive projectile. The powder-and-projectile combination that Mortensen selected was in full compliance with all of the Navy's ordnance manuals for sixteen-inch guns. His would be the ship's only legally operated turret on April 19.

Walsh and Skelley sowed more confusion at their briefing by raising other complicating possibilities. The *Ainsworth* and the *Aylwin*, the two frigates trailing the *Iowa,* might take part in the gun shoot. The *Ainsworth* would remain four miles behind the *Iowa* and fire her five-inch guns to starboard, and the *Aylwin* would trail a mile behind her sistership and fire her five-inch guns in the same direction. The *Iowa* might fire her sixteen-inch guns to port, rather than starboard, and could also fire three five-inch turrets to port. None of this was engraved in stone. Contrary to standard practice, no misfire procedures or safety precautions were reviewed at the pre-fire meeting. "After the briefing, a lot of stuff was very flexible," Walsh said.

AFTER TALKING with Chief Hickman about his manpower shortages and seeing to it that his men were still engaged in making repairs to the turret, Reggie Ziegler sat down in the main battery office over coffee with Ernie Hanyecz, his leading petty officer, and Dale Mortensen to figure out what they could do to make the gun shoot go smoothly the next day. Dan Meyer arrived later and offered several suggestions. Mortensen was miffed over "how easily Phil Buch had gone along with Skelley about shooting five bags of D-846 powder." Ziegler said the center gun, where every single crew member was either untrained or a partially trained beginner, was where he expected the most trouble.

Ernie Hanyecz thought that the inexperienced center gun rammerman, Robert Backherms, should be removed from that position. The primerman, Seaman Recruit Reginald L. Johnson Jr. of Warrensville Heights, Ohio, a Cleveland suburb, had been on the *Iowa* less than two months and had never been involved in a live shoot. The bright twenty-year-old sailor, who hoped to make a career in electronics, had already told his father, Reginald L. Johnson Sr., that the *Iowa* was a "dangerous ship."

The powder-car operator, Gary Fisk, a twenty-three-year-old second class boatswain's mate from Oneida, New York, had been assigned to the battleship a mere three weeks. Fisk had enlisted in the Navy in 1985 after spending his first six months out of high school stapling coffin liners for a casket company. He had served four years on the USS *Canopus*, a submarine tender that almost never went to sea, and had become a specialist in operating the tender's giant cranes. The stubby, barrel-chested boatswain's mate hadn't even completed the sixteen-inch indoctrination course and had never operated a powder hoist during a gun shoot. The center gun's hoist, a dumbwaiter that hauled the powder bags seven decks up from the ammunition-handling rooms below, was not working properly and could be a headache even for an experienced seaman.

But the biggest potential problem, according to Reggie Ziegler and Ernie Hanyecz, was Errick Lawrence, who was "under instruction" to become the center gun captain. This would be Lawrence's first time filling that position without an experienced gun captain looking over his shoulder. According to Dale Mortensen, "Reggie said, 'If I have any trouble whatsoever, it will be that gun. It's because Lawrence is the gun captain.' " Dan Meyer said that

Ziegler had decided that Lawrence was "slow as far as intelligence, one of those guys you had to repeat orders to three or four times." Actually, Lawrence was book-smart but was not mechanically inclined. Hanyecz considered Lawrence to be "excitable, a real screamer who might go to pieces in an emergency."

Ziegler and Hanyecz decided that they had to dragoon somebody not on the duty roster to be present in the center gun room to keep a close eye on Lawrence and handle any emergencies that arose. For that job they picked Clayton Hartwig, a second class gunner's mate from Cleveland. Hartwig was the normal center gun captain, but he had been excused from duty after he had been notified in March that he had been nominated for a Navy physical security assignment in London. Since the hour was late, Ziegler decided not to inform Hartwig what he would be doing during the gun shoot until the next morning. Lawrence worked on the center gun that night and signed the pre-fire paperwork the next morning as gun captain.

Chief Ziegler had some misgivings about the third class gunner's mate assigned to the left gun. He was twenty-two-year-old James D. "Jay" White of Norwalk, California. A scruffy, corpulent sailor, White was the cradle operator. Several men in Turret Two, including Errick Lawrence, had complained to Ziegler that White was a safety hazard and was a "burned-out druggie." White told many other sailors in his division that he had once deliberately ridden his motorcycle at high speed into a concrete abutment under an interstate-highway overpass. "Jay didn't have a real good childhood, but he never tried to kill himself," said his wife, Shelly.

In a turret full of young men where the majority were country-music fans, White was a devotee of heavy-metal music. Not only did he play it loudly on a tape recorder in Turret Two's berthing space, he also sang the lyrics and sometimes tacked stanzas of it on the bulletin board in the berthing compartment. White had recently posted a song entitled "Disposable Heroes," his rewrite of lyrics taken from an album called *Master of Puppets*, by the heavy-metal group Metallica. White's version ended with the line, "Left to die alone in a sixteen-inch gun," and was illustrated with dripping blood and a skull. Everyone who shared the berthing compartment was well aware that this was White's handiwork.

JOHN MULLAHY, the third class gunner's mate who came to the *Iowa* in December 1988 after spending five months in the Philadelphia brig, ran into Clayton Hartwig in Turret Two's berthing compartment at 9 P.M. on April 18. Mullahy talked to Hartwig for almost an hour about what Hartwig ought to take with him when he went to his new assignment in London. Mullahy had been in the Navy for eighteen years; had served in Spain, Vietnam, Lebanon, and the Philippines; and had visited London a number of times. "Clay was in a jovial mood and was excited and looking forward to the physical security posting," Mullahy said. As the more experienced sailor talked,

Hartwig jotted down a list of items, such as transformers and electrical adaptor plugs, that he might need overseas.

The tall, slender Hartwig had borrowed Navy Exchange catalogues from several of the other men on the ship to see what things were available in London and what he should buy in the United States before going abroad. Hartwig told Mullahy that he was corresponding with a girl who lived in Portsmouth, England, to obtain additional information. Chief Hickman, the ship's gunner, also had an extended discussion with Hartwig and gave the second class gunner's mate some tips about what kind of civilian clothing he might require on a security detail. Hickman thought Hartwig "was steady, a good sailor, if not brilliant."

WHEN DAN Meyer stopped by the main battery office at 6:30 A.M. on Wednesday, April 19, on his way to the bridge to stand a five-hour watch, several gunner's mates were hanging around the office bitching about the Tomahawk experiment. Meyer told them that although the missile launch had not been permanently canceled, the weather was unlikely to remain favorable long enough for such a complicated operation to proceed. However, since Lieutenant Walsh and Chief Skelley were only talking about firing twenty-five sixteen-inch shells, the gun shoot probably would occur on schedule.

Meyer rummaged through the main battery office looking for a copy of the firing plan, but he was unable to locate one. A firing plan is not an optional document. In peacetime, a skipper cannot shoot his guns or launch his missiles without one. He is not supposed to deviate from the written plan without a very good excuse. The plan is not supposed to contain the large numbers of contingencies, hedges, and what-ifs that Walsh and Skelley had piled on at their pre-fire briefing. Meyer had seen a partially completed (but unsigned) firing plan the previous evening; it had listed him as being inside Turret One during the gun shoot, when in reality he was assigned to the bridge standing watch. The officer who would be in Turret One was Ensign Ephraim Spencer Garrett IV. An easygoing Naval Academy graduate, Garrett had received no training on the sixteen-inch guns during his paltry sixteen days aboard the *Iowa*. Meyer took into consideration Garrett's lack of experience and designated Dale Mortensen as turret officer during his absence. Garrett didn't have a problem with that, but Meyer wanted to make sure that it was duly noted in the firing plan in case there were any questions about it later. He asked Yeoman Third Class Vergil Marshall, the administrative assistant to the weapons department, to correct the firing plan on his word processor.

While Meyer was tearing apart the main battery office in his search for a firing plan, Clayton Hartwig was eating breakfast on the mess deck with David Smith. Smith was nervous about the upcoming gun shoot. The twenty-year-old from Rockville, Maryland, had been in the Navy less than two years and on the battleship only nineteen days. He had been assigned to Turret One's magazines and asked Hartwig how the guns worked, what could go wrong, and how he could protect himself in case something did occur. Smith said he was petrified of handling powder: "I was working handling the powder. They said the powder was, you know, the other gunner's mates said it was very unstable, easy to set off. Some of the guys said, you know, you could drop one, and it could go off. You know, you had to be real careful." Hartwig told Smith to calm down, just listen to his petty officers, and everything would be fine. "I was very nervous. I was very, you know, jittery. I mean it was just a big day for me, you know," Smith said.

DAN MEYER climbed five decks from the main battery office to the bridge at 6:40 A.M. and began poring over the deck log, familiarizing himself with what had gone on during the previous watch, as well as determining where the other ships were located in relationship to the *Iowa*. The battleship, headed due south at fifteen knots, was scheduled to remain on this course for several more hours, although she would increase her speed to twenty knots at 8:14 A.M. The watch team cracked open the bridge windows, removed their blue baseball caps, and allowed the mild subtropical wind to stream through their hair. "It was a marvelous day. It was the kind of day which made you grateful just to be alive," Meyer said. He saluted the officer he was relieving, assumed the duties of junior officer of the watch, and took the conn, retaining it nearly the whole time he remained on the bridge.

The officer of the deck was the ship's electrical officer, Lieutenant Kenneth MacArthur, a jug-eared Californian in his late twenties. He had been in the Navy four years and on the *Iowa* six months, coming to her from an amphibious craft. He had qualified as OOD in January.

The junior officer of the deck was Lieutenant Carl Cusaac, a tall, slender Citadel graduate in his early twenties. Cusaac spoke in a soft Southern drawl. He had been in the Navy two years, almost all of that time on the *Iowa*, and he was assigned to the engineering department as assistant boilers officer. This was the first time he had been back on watch since Captain Larry Seaquist, unimpressed by Cusaac's abilities as a "ship handler," had banished him from the bridge.

Shortly after Meyer arrived on the bridge, he began poking around looking for a firing plan. Ken MacArthur also searched for the elusive document. The boatswain's mate of the watch, who supervised all the enlisted men on duty on the bridge, informed MacArthur and Meyer that no firing plan had been delivered by the weapons department. At 7:30 A.M., the OOD called the weapons-department office and told Yeoman Marshall, "The bridge needs a firing plan. Mr. Meyer's on the bridge and is concerned that there is no firing plan."

"Sir, there's several versions of the firing plan floating around," Marshall responded. The OOD insisted that the bridge needed an accurate firing plan as soon as possible. For the next two and a half hours, the bridge watch team made periodic calls to the weapons department office demanding the document, but it never materialized.

At 8 A.M., just before the turret crews were sent to their gunnery stations, Commander Bob Kissinger held an abbreviated briefing behind Turret Two. The weapons officer told the gunner's mates and fire controlmen that the ship would fire on the port side, when the opposite was true. He had no idea whether or not Turret Three was going to shoot, and he also stated that the frigates *Aylwin* and *Ainsworth* would participate in the exercise, which was wrong. Kissinger specifically mentioned Skelley's nonregulation powder experiments, thus endorsing them. He would later claim that he told Captain Moosally about the experiments before the shooting started. Kissinger advised the gun crews to tuck their pant legs into their socks, button their shirt collars, and roll down their sleeves as a safety precaution. He told them not to take "spark-producing items," such as cigarette lighters, dog tags, knives, tape players, radios, watches, rings, and keys, into the turrets. As events would later reveal, his advice mostly went unheeded.

AT 8:17 A.M., Dan Meyer directed the lee helmsman (the assistant steersman) to signal twenty-two knots to the engine room via the annunciator, a device that transmits orders through a series of bells. The engineers increased the revolutions of the propellers. At that point, Captain Moosally appeared on the bridge. The three officers and the enlisted men on watch visibly tensed with "the Moose's" arrival. With the captain tensely pacing around the bridge, nobody wanted to make any mistakes. Several minutes after the captain's appearance, Meyer told the lee helmsman, "All ahead full." "Aye, aye, Sir," answered the sailor, tugging down on the annunciator's handle.

IN LESS than a minute, the *Iowa* was doing twenty-five knots, deliberately outrunning her two escorts. The frigates were only capable of making twenty-seven knots, but considering the choppy seas and the fact that the relative winds were gusting off the port bow at thirty-five knots, the frigates would have taken a pounding if they had unwisely attempted to keep pace with the battleship. The *Ainsworth* lost power to both her generators at 8:09 A.M. and remained dead in the water for thirty-three minutes. She remained well behind the *Iowa* for most of the morning. The *Aylwin* dawdled along at seven knots and didn't increase her speed to twenty-seven knots until 10:42 A.M., when she finally tried to catch up with the battleship. "Captain Moosally put as much space between ourselves and the frigates as possible. He was afraid of hitting one of the escorts [with sixteen-inch shells]," Dan Meyer said.

At 8:31 A.M., Meyer, who was standing at the center of the bridge behind a pelorus, a gyrocompass, turned to the captain and asked, "Request permission to pass the word to man up gun stations." Rather than using the formal command "Very well," Moosally simply told Meyer, "Do it." Meyer told the boatswain's mate of the watch, "Man up all five-inch mounts, secondary plot, Turrets One, Two, and Three, main plot, Sky One, the combat information center, and the Marine detachment's spotters." The boatswain's mate headed to the port side of the bridge and flipped a switch activating the ship's public-address system, the 1MC. He put to his lips a curved silver whistle (called a "boatswain's pipe"), blew a series of shrill notes into the 1MC, and then loudly repeated the instructions Meyer had given him. Hundreds of sailors began scurrying along the ship's teak-covered main deck and down a spacious interior passageway, known as "Broadway," connecting Turrets Two and Three. Seaman Patrick Shedd, the twenty-year-old helmsman, was relieved of his duties on the bridge so that he could go to his assigned gunnery duty station in the base of Turret Two, where he was a powder handler.

IT TOOK almost thirty minutes for the gunnery and fire-control personnel to reach their assigned duty stations and report that they were ready to fire the guns. "Zebra," the strictest damage-control condition, had also been set, meaning that all watertight and blastproof doors and hatches had been sealed and "dogged." These hatches were not supposed to be opened as long as the ship was involved in the gun shoot. But Commander Kissinger, after realizing he still didn't have a firing plan, violated that rule and summoned Yeoman Marshall at 9:45 A.M from Turret Two's powder-handling spaces to type one. Shortly after Marshall departed, a mess cook, Seaman Nathaniel Clifford Jones, arrived in Turret Two. "Zebra" was again "broken," so that Jones could reach his assigned duty station on the projectile decks.

After the order was passed sending the crewmen to their gunnery stations, Senior Chief Robert Porter, the master-at-arms, the ship's top cop, began prowling the ship searching for idlers and malingerers to send to the sixteen-inch turrets. Porter, who looked and acted like a small-town sheriff, was instructed by Commander Kissinger to escort Legalmen First Class Robert Kenneth Morrison and Michael William Helton to Turret Two. Kissinger claimed that the two paralegals "were goofing off," drinking coffee in their broom-closet office. Despite the fact that neither Morrison nor Helton had any training on the sixteen-inch guns, they were delivered to the right gun room of Turret Two, where they took up valuable space and had no duties to perform. Morrison came from a Navy family. He had been born in the Portsmouth, Virginia, Naval Hospital; his father, Robert Morrison, was a retired chief boatswain's mate who had served in the Navy for a quarter of a century. A television reporter later asked the retired chief boatswain's mate, "Why would a legalman be assigned to a gun turret?" "I don't have any answer for that," Chief Morrison replied.

Ken Truitt arrived late for his job as petty officer in charge of Turret Two's magazine. Chief Ziegler fumed over Truitt's tardiness and told John Mullahy over the sound-powered phones to have Truitt report to Ziegler following the gun shoot. Truitt sauntered in just before the turret was sealed. He claimed he was late because he had to go to the head. Everybody giggled.

Mullahy and Truitt and seven other sailors toiled in magazine A-515-M, a ten-by-fifteen-foot compartment crammed from deck to ceiling with high explosives. They sweated prodigiously in the heat. They rolled forty-two bags of powder across the rough, steel-plated deck from the magazine before lifting the bags and pushing them up through a "scuttle," a quick-closing slot, into a powder flat, an ammunition-handling space within the armored rotating portion of the turret. One of Truitt's men, Seaman Recruit Carlos Bernard Washington of Shreveport, Louisiana, had only been in the Navy six months and on the *Iowa* two months. This was his first gun shoot. As he pried the lids off the powder tanks, Washington was startled when he read the inventory cards inside the cans. "Almost all the powder dated back to 1945. Some of it dated back to 1943," he said. He thought this powder was much too old to shoot. The other men working alongside him agreed.

First Lieutenant John Brush and his Marine Corps spotter team, consisting of one sergeant and three corporals, arrived on the starboard bridge wing to adjust the *Iowa*'s fall of shot. That wouldn't be easy, considering the fact that the ship would be flinging shells into an empty ocean with no targets to hit. Moreover, the twenty-six-year-old Brush and his shore-fire bombardment team would be using optical equipment with a maximum effective range of only eight nautical miles on the bridge, and the *Iowa* would be firing at a minimum range of seventeen miles.

The short, gung-ho Marine lieutenant checked in with forward main battery plot and talked with Lieutenant Walsh. Despite the fact that Walsh still didn't have a written firing plan, the fire-control officer said the ship would be firing twenty-three rounds. Turret One would fire two rounds from each gun; Turret Two would fire three rounds from the left gun and four rounds from the center and right guns; and Turret Three would fire three rounds each from the center and right guns. The shells would be fired separately. There would be no multiple-gun salvos. Despite what Walsh told the Marine spotter, Commander Kissinger later testified that Captain Moosally had other plans in mind. The captain wanted to fire at least one three-gun salvo from a turret to put on a show for Vice Admiral Jerome Johnson, commander of the Second Fleet, who was on the bridge to observe the gunnery exercise.

GUNNER'S MATE Third Class Cletus Guffin was slated to be the first sixteen-inch gun captain on the *Iowa* to fire his weapon. A Sioux from South Dakota, Guffin had been in the Navy three years and was making his debut as Turret One's left gun captain. He had mastered every other position in the turret—magazines, projectile decks, gun layer station, rammerman, cradle operator, powder-hoist operator, and primerman.

Turret One's center gun captain was Gunner's Mate Third Class Mark Harden, who had occupied that slot for a year. The right gun captain was Gunner's Mate Third Class Murray Cunningham, a bodybuilder with immense hands. Gunner's Mate Third Class Shane Cline was substituting for Dale Mortensen as turret captain. Mortensen, in turn, was filling in for Dan Meyer as turret officer.

Ensign Ephraim Garrett was present in the turret officer's booth, but since he was "under instruction," he gave no orders to Mortensen and Cline and deferred to their opinions. Chief Gunner's Mate Benjamin Droweinga was also in the turret officer's booth. As a newcomer on the ship, he was also content to let Dale Mortensen and his petty officers run the turret.

At 9:33 A.M., forward main battery plot told Turret One's left, center, and right guns to load. Guffin's left gun was to fire first. Vice Admiral Johnson was sitting in Captain Moosally's raised swivel chair on the starboard side of the bridge, chatting with the captain. Guffin's crew sent up a 1,900-pound projectile and six "reduced charges" of D-845 powder. This was rammed sequentially into the barrel, and the breechblock was secured with a primer in place. Gears meshed, and the back portion of the gun was lowered into the pit, the muzzle rising to the firing position. Guffin informed Mortensen on the sound-powered phones that he was prepared to shoot. Ready-fire lights simultaneously blinked on in the turret officer's booth and in main battery plot. Mortensen relayed what Guffin told him over the sound-powered phones to the plotting room. The salvo alarm was sounded; a brass trigger was squeezed in the plotting room; and a 25-volt charge was transmitted to the primer in Guffin's gun. There was a slight popping noise in the gun room. The gun had misfired.

Guffin had a potential "hang fire," a precarious situation. The black powder in the "red end" patch on the last bag in the chamber might be smoldering, and if so, it could "cook off" at any moment. If Guffin unlatched the breechblock to see what was wrong, the powder could ignite and blow back, destroying the gun room and perhaps the entire turret. Mortensen told Guffin to "super-elevate" his gun (raise the barrel to its highest angle) and see if the last powder bag would slide down against the primer in the mushroom (the bulging portion of the breechblock). After super-elevating, Guffin was to check and see if the primer had actually ignited. Guffin raised the barrel and then brought the breech back to the load position.

Gunner's Mate Second Class John Keerl, who was in charge of repairs in Turret One, entered Guffin's gun room to assist him. The gaunt second class petty officer carried "a repriming tool," a sawed-off broomstick with oversize tweezers attached to one end. Guffin and Keerl prudently remained behind a painted line that designated how far back the gun recoiled when it fired.

"We were worried that the gun might go off and impale us," Guffin said. Keerl poked his handmade tool into the firing lock and extracted a spent primer cartridge. The primer had evidently fired. He inserted another primer into the closed breechblock. Mortensen advised forward main battery plot and the bridge that they had reprimed and were prepared to fire again. The salvo alarm sounded; the firing circuit was closed; and another jolt of electricity was transmitted to the left gun. "I heard a click and then nothing. The gun had misfired again," Guffin said.

Mortensen told Mark Harden to fire his center gun. It went off without any difficulty. Murray Cunningham was told to fire his right gun. He encountered no difficulties. In the meantime, Guffin and Keerl had inserted another cartridge. They went through the entire firing drill and for the third time got another infuriating click. Harden and Cunningham each successfully fired a second round. Before the day was over, Guffin would superelevate and reprime his gun eight times, but he was never able to get it to discharge. "This is my first day as a full-fledged gun captain, and this can't be happening to me," he thought.

While Guffin and Keerl were striving to clear the left gun, Captain Moosally was in a dither on the bridge. It had taken a full five minutes from the time his order to fire had first been passed to Turret One until the first shell emerged from the center gun. This was a lackluster show for Admiral Johnson, so Moosally decided to ignore established gunnery procedures and have Turret Two start firing, even though he was well aware that Cletus Guffin still had a loaded gun. The captain turned to Commander Kissinger on the bridge and instructed him to fire a three-gun salvo from Turret Two. Kissinger did as he was told. The executive officer, Commander Morse, later said that he thought Captain Moosally was very interested in showing Admiral Johnson what a three-gun salvo looked like.

Kissinger told Marine Lieutenant Brush, the spotter, that Moosally wanted a three-gun salvo from Turret Two for Admiral Johnson. The weapons officer relayed this information to Chief Hickman, who was on the bridge to coordinate the exercise with Lieutenant Walsh in main battery plot and with Chief Skelley, who was four levels above the bridge operating the optical range finder. Chief Hickman had anticipated that Turret Two would fire only one gun at a time, so he did not inform Moosally or Kissinger that Chief Ziegler had told him the night before that Turret Two didn't have the trained manpower to fire a three-gun broadside.

Hickman pressed the button on his sound-powered phone and said, "Turret Two, left, center, and right guns, one round, load." He also told Lieutenant Phil Buch that his turret would be firing a three-gun salvo. In main battery plot, Lieutenant Walsh was alarmed when he heard Hickman relay the captain's orders to Turret Two. Ripping off his headset and hurling it to the deck, he screamed, "Who's in charge here? I've totally lost control!" According to the gunnery manual, Walsh was the only individual who was authorized to order any of the turrets to load and fire. Chief Skelley was also disturbed by the turn of events. "This was not the first time we found out the bridge had loaded the guns without telling us," said Skelley. He would later insist the gun shoot had degenerated into "a worthless smoke-and-fire show" staged solely to impress a visiting brass hat.

Dale Mortensen, outraged that the bridge was disregarding the rules, registered his protest with Lieutenant Walsh. "Forward main plot, don't forget that I'm sitting here with a misfire. My left gun is reprimed," Mortensen said. Walsh told him that there was nothing he could do. Ensign Garrett remembered that the basic weapons training he had received at Annapolis had taught him enough to know that the captain's order was wrong. "If you have a misfire in one turret, it just struck me as surprising that you wouldn't clear a gun before you started loading other guns."

On the bridge, Fred Moosally was telling Vice Admiral Johnson that his weapons department was normally very sharp. Pointing to Turret Two, he said, "This is my best turret. Watch those guys shoot." In the hour before Turret Two was given the order to load its guns, Chief Ziegler had been under such pressure to find trained or at least partially trained crewmen to operate the turret that he had reassigned eight men to different duty stations. Consequently, there was no roster detailing the position of each of the fifty-nine men in the turret. The Navy would later state that only thirteen men were qualified for the positions they were filling.

And other major problems existed. There weren't enough emergency-escape breathing devices to go around. A sprinkler system that was supposed to be remotely activated from Turret One had been broken for months. An external water line from the ship's main damage-control system, known as a "jumper hose," was not connected, so the turret's fire hoses and sprinklers were useless when they were desperately needed.

Forty-four seconds after Phil Buch received the order to load his three guns, he reported that the right gun was ready to fire. Seventeen seconds later, he gave the same report for the left gun. High above the bridge, three officers attached to the Second Fleet staff had their personal cameras trained on Turret Two. One of them, Commander Thomas J. Kilcline Jr., a fighter pilot who was Admiral Johnson's operations officer, had toured the turret the day before and had been invited to observe the gun shoot from inside the turret. Kilcline, a Naval Academy graduate and the son of a retired vice admiral, declined the invitation, saying he'd take a rain check. He began snapping 35-mm still pictures as the guns were loaded. Standing next to him were Lieutenant Commanders Elton Kelly and Warren Krull. Kelly was operating a Japanese-made camcorder and Krull had a still camera.

Monitoring Turret Two's phone circuit, Dale Mortensen heard Jack Thompson and Matt Price report that the gas ejection air in the left and right guns worked properly. But nobody said that about the center gun. Down below in Turret Two's magazine, John Mullahy heard someone say that the center gun's gas ejection air did not function. Mortensen and Mullahy independently decided that something was amiss with the center gun. Mullahy continued to monitor the XJ circuit, listening to the cross talk between the gun captains and Chief Ziegler in the turret officer's booth. Mullahy heard Errick Lawrence in the center gun room tell Ziegler, "We have a problem here. We are not ready yet. We have a problem here." "Ziggie was yelling over to Mr. Buch to tell him to tell plot there is a problem in the center gun and they are not ready yet," Mullahy said. Seaman Carlos Washington, who worked on Mullahy's magazine team, said Mullahy talked of hearing something like "friction . . . friction" on the phones, then something about "static," and finally Chief Ziegler screaming, "Oh, my God!"

Boatswain's Mate Second Class Robert Burch, Seaman Recruit Cecil Croft, and Seaman Patrick L. Shedd had been taking the powder bags that Truitt's and Mullahy's sailors passed through the scuttles from the magazines and transferring them through a thick armored partition into another compartment containing the powder hoists. Burch heard Chief Ziegler say on the sound-powered phones, "Left gun loaded, good job. Center gun is having a little trouble. We'll straighten that out."

On his phones, Mortensen overheard Lieutenant Buch in Turret Two say, "Left and right guns are loaded." Then, Ernie Hanyecz, Turret Two's leading petty officer, cried, "Mort! . . . Mort! . . . Mort! . . ." Gunner's Mate Third Class Michael Estes, who was in charge of Turret One's powder flats, said he heard Chief Ziegler on a sound-powered circuit cry, "Oh, my God! The powder is smoldering!" Estes believed that Ziegler opened the door to the center gun room and shouted at the crew to ram the powder home and close the breech. He then heard Ernie Hanyecz holler into the sound-powered phones, "Oh, my God! There's a flash!"

AT 9:53 A.M. on April 19, the center gun in Turret Two blew up. The fireball that surged from the open breech was between 2,500° and 3,000°F, traveling at a velocity of 2,000 feet per second and at a pressure of 4,000 pounds per square inch. The rammer chain flew backward from the breech, the links parting and whirling around the compartment like shrapnel. The explosive force caved in the door between the center gun room and the turret officer's booth and simultaneously buckled the reinforced-steel bulkheads segregating the left and right gun rooms. Fire and clouds of deadly gases, including cyanide produced by burning polyurethane foam surrounding the powder bags, billowed downward into the lower levels of the turret through the powder-hoist shafts and ventilation ducts. When the fire reached the powder-handling area servicing the turret, it ignited twenty-one bags stacked there. Nearly a minute after the first explosion, another detonation occurred when sparks landed on some loose powder bags in the turret. Nine minutes later, another blast, probably caused by a buildup of carbon monoxide gas, rocked the turret.

Down below, Seaman Apprentice Ricky Frambo was passing a powder bag through a scuttle when the first explosion rocked the turret. "Hey, that didn't sound right!" Frambo yelled. John Mullahy screamed, "We just lost all communications!" None of the twenty men normally connected to the phone circuit answered Mullahy's calls. The lights flickered and then went off. The big Irishman used a monkey wrench to pound open the armored hatch into the space where Boatswain's Mate Second Class Robert Burch and two other sailors worked. Burch and Seaman Recruit Cecil Croft snatched up all the powder bags that had accumulated in their space, dumping them into water tanks. Mullahy opened the hatch to the powder flats. He saw several powder bags on fire, observed a number of bodies, and repeatedly called the name of Gunner's Mate Second Class Stephen Welden, the petty officer in charge of the flats. Welden didn't answer. He was dead, as were the ten men who worked for him. Burch, Croft, and Seaman Patrick Shedd darted from their work space, yelling, "Fire! Explosion! Everybody get the fuck out of here!" Mullahy, who had inhaled too much smoke, staggered after them. He knew that they had to abandon this area before the 2,500 pounds of high explosives on the red-hot deck of the flats exploded.

Truitt had his men replace a number of powder bags in the canisters and put them back in the magazines before evacuating the area. The magazine area was rapidly filling up with acrid yellow smoke and gas. Mullahy told everyone to get an OBA (gas mask) and slip it on before trying to climb the steep ladder that would take them to safety on the third deck. But there were not enough OBAs to go around. Ricky Frambo was first to start up the rungs, followed by Seaman Recruit Carlos Washington.

The last man up was Seaman Michael Drowns. Mullahy wouldn't have made it without Drowns's help. He was hacking up black substance and blood. "He [Drowns] is about two inches taller and about forty pounds heavier than me. He literally picked me up and threw me up the ladder," said Mullahy, who is hefty himself. Many of these survivors would voluntarily return to the turret numerous times to fight fires and retrieve the bodies of their dead shipmates. Mullahy and Burch would be decorated for heroism for their actions on this day.

6

☆

"Turret Two Just Blew Up!"

Several seconds after Dale Mortensen heard Ernie Hanyecz's cry, "Mort! . . . Mort! . . . Mort! . . ," Turret One filled with white smoke. The first thing that crossed Mortensen's mind was that his turret was on fire and that Cletus Guffin's left gun with the stubborn "hang fire" had finally exploded. "I had no idea. I just couldn't figure out what happened, and then I heard another explosion," Mortensen said. He disconnected the electrical firing circuit to Guffin's loaded gun, so that no one on the bridge or in main plot could accidentally discharge it. Then he sent Gunner's Mate Second Class John Keerl down to the electrical decks to see if it were ablaze. "There was no sign of a fire anywhere. The phone rang on the electrical decks and in the booth, I picked it up, and it was Mr. Meyer on the bridge saying that Turret Two had just had a detonation," Keerl said. Keerl tried to activate Turret Two's sprinkler system by vigorously turning a crank at the base of Turret One. The system failed to operate.

Mortensen and Keerl decided to leave their turret and join the firefighting efforts at the base of Turret Two, leaving Gunner's Mate Third Class Cline in charge. When Ensign Garrett, who was only in the turret as an observer, was instructed by main battery plot to evacuate everyone from the turret, Cline said, "Don't do it, Sir." The spunky petty officer then called the bridge to protest and was advised that the captain wanted all "nonessential personnel" out of Turret One immediately. Cline, Garrett, and fifteen men opted to stay behind, including Cletus Guffin's jinxed left-gun crew. They remained at their stations until nightfall.

When Turret Two's center gun blew up, Chief Skelley was scanning the horizon with the large optical range finder. Skelley thought the "booming and whooshing" noises below him sounded a lot like a jet-assisted takeoff

(JATO) bottle used to help launch the ship's remotely piloted vehicles (RPVs). "What in the fuck are they doing with the RPV, and did one of the JATO mags [magazines] go?" Skelley asked a nearby sailor. But before he received an answer, he heard Chief Hickman shout on the sound-powered phones, "Turret Two just blew up!" "I heard several secondary bangs going off and then saw ocher brown and gray smoke coming up," Skelley said.

BUTTONED UP in Turret Three behind the superstructure and some 400 feet from the inferno raging in Turret Two, Chief J.C. Miller and Ensign Kevin Hunt detected the distinctive odor of burning powder and thought their own turret had caught fire. Gunner's Mate First Class Verlin Allen, the turret's leading petty officer, began getting ready for the worst. "We smelled the smoke and we didn't know where it was at so, for safety, we went ahead and had our powder struck back into the magazines, shut down all of our electrical equipment," Allen said. He buckled on a gas mask and left Turret Three, becoming one of the first experienced petty officers to venture inside Turret Two.

On the bridge, Dan Meyer was staring fixedly at Turret Two when he heard a deep rumbling sound and saw the guns' bloomers shred. Then he saw "orange-tinted" smoke gush out of the turret's vents and thought that perhaps as many as two gun rooms and the turret officer's booth had been wiped out, probably killing fifteen men. He had been taught that an *Iowa*-class sixteen-inch turret could contain a catastrophic event, such as a shell hit or a powder explosion in one gun room, without the remainder of the turret's being appreciably damaged. When the second explosion occurred, Meyer was sure that Lieutenant Phil Buch had not survived. "Phil, damn it. Phil, damn it. What did you do?" Meyer exclaimed.

Commander Bob Kissinger was on the right bridge wing when he heard the first throaty boom. "I thought the gun went off, and I was about to tell Master Chief Hickman, 'What the hell are those guys doing down there? They're not supposed to be firing!' and as soon as I turned and looked and I saw smoke coming out, then I realized it was something different," Kissinger said. Also on the bridge, Lieutenant Commander Costigan, the gunnery officer, told Dan Meyer that there were no reliable schematics of the turret's interior on the ship. Costigan had ordered the schematics more than a year earlier, but he had never received them.

Captain Moosally wasn't exactly tranquil. Dan Meyer recalled that "the Moose" had the thousand-yard stare of a death-row inmate who had recently learned that his last appeal had been rejected by the Supreme Court. Moosally ordered Meyer to send the ship to General Quarters (GQ). A boatswain's mate rushed to the main public-address system (1MC) and bellowed, "General Quarters! General Quarters! All hands man your battle stations!" At the same time, a quartermaster turned on a clanging alarm. Men darted through the ship, slamming hatches shut and dogging them down.

The dogged hatches would subsequently impede the firefighters' efforts to shift critically needed equipment from the rear of the ship forward to Turret Two.

Following the sounding of General Quarters, the executive officer, Commander John Morse, notified the crew on the 1MC that there had been an "unknown detonation in Turret Two."

On hearing the GQ call, the chief engineer ordered the number-one circuit board shut down, cutting off electrical power to the forward portion of the ship. Lieutenant Commander Dan Kimberlain wasted no time taking over and informing the electricians to disregard the chief engineer's instructions. Kimberlain announced over the main engineering communications circuit, "This is Lieutenant Commander Kimberlain, the main propulsion assistant. I have relieved the chief engineer." If Kimberlain hadn't restored the power when he did, there would have been no water pressure in the firefighters' hoses. And the magazines might have exploded, ripping the ship apart.

After GQ was sounded, Vice Admiral Johnson rose from the captain's swivel chair and went one deck below to flag plot to transmit messages to the Atlantic Fleet commander in Norfolk and the Chief of Naval Operations in Washington, alerting them to the disaster and saying that no efforts would be spared to save the *Iowa*. Admiral Johnson's first "flash" message said in part: "Detonation in Turret Two during open ocean NGFS [naval gunfire support]. Extent of casualties unknown. Currently closing [heading to] *Coral Sea* [aircraft carrier] for additional medical assistance." Many of Admiral Johnson's staffers dashed off the bridge to their staterooms in order to change into cotton wash-khaki uniforms. Unlike the ship's officers, they had been wearing form-fitting, tailor-made, polyester khaki uniforms with rows of brightly colored ribbons and shiny, plastic-coated black shoes. They realized that if the flames in Turret Two spread throughout the ship, their synthetic outfits could melt to their skins.

As the sailors rushed to their GQ stations, Chief Hickman walked over to the port wing of the bridge and then climbed a ladder up one level to get a better vantage point of Turret Two. He noticed a group of men from one of the starboard five-inch mounts spraying water on the immense steel box with a fire hose. He then listened as telephone talkers in forward main plot and the combat information center (CIC) reported that their areas were filling with smoke. He climbed back down to the bridge and asked the captain for permission to evacuate both areas. Moosally agreed.

According to the deck log, Dan Meyer steered the ship sixty degrees to starboard, hoping that the wind would help put out the fire in the turret. He also slowed the vessel from twenty-five to five knots. His efforts were not successful. OOD Kenneth MacArthur assumed the conn and had no better luck, so the captain took over. Moosally told the helmsman, "Left full rudder, come to course two-five-five." The captain asked the gunnery officer for the blueprints of Turret Two. When informed that none existed, he became choleric, saying, "How the hell do I know where the fire is going to spread, if I don't have any schematics?" Fearing that the captain's temper was about to erupt, Meyer asked permission to go below and survey the damage. Moosally agreed.

LIEUTENANT OLIVER Demery was directing the firefighters encircling Turret Two. The powerfully built gunnery officer was in charge of the ship's six five-inch mounts. He had his men spraying water over the entire surface of the turret. Chief Hickman shouted from the bridge, "Lieutenant Demery, we still have guns loaded, we have the left and the right barrels loaded, keep the water cooling the barrels down." Demery had his hosemen redirect their streams of water onto the two outboard barrels. He was joined by three Marines—two officers and a first sergeant.

Marine Captain Jeffrey W. Bolander and First Sergeant Bruce W. Richardson attempted to open the turret's escape hatch with their bare hands, but they had no success because it was rusted shut. Richardson, a tough, twenty-two-year Marine veteran, had been in the chiefs' mess enjoying a cup of coffee when he'd heard GQ on the 1MC, and then the announcement about the explosion. He had double-timed forward to help. He sent one of his Marines to the forecastle to ask Chief Warrant Officer Wilfred Patnaude, the ship's boatswain, for sledgehammers and a steel crowbar to crack open the escape hatch. About half of the men in the burning turret worked for Patnaude, and he promptly rounded up these tools.

When Meyer reached Turret Two, Captain Bolander and Sergeant Richardson were standing directly under the escape hatch, banging away with sledgehammers. Meyer told them to stand to the side of the hatch when they swung, in case it fell and crushed them. He also recommended to Lieutenant Demery that his men spray the turret vents in order to get as much water as possible down inside the turret. "I told Oliver that there had to be loose powder in the handling rooms, and if it ignited, we could be blown out of the water," Meyer said. He made his way back up on the bridge to ask the captain for permission to descend to the base of Turret Two.

The captain kept the conn and was maneuvering the ship when Meyer interrupted him, saying, "Request permission, Captain, to lay below to fight fires and assess the damage." Moosally gave his permission, and Commander Kissinger asked if he could accompany Meyer. Moosally told the weapons officer to go ahead. Neither man took time to obtain a gas mask (OBA) before scaling down to the base of Turret One and then inching their way to Turret Two through a narrow space partially filled with electrical cables. They were engulfed in dense smoke and squirmed back through the crawl space, knowing they had to find a better way to reach the base of the damaged turret. They were also convinced that before trying again, they needed to don OBAs.

Back up on the main deck, Kissinger obtained two OBAs. He and Meyer were joined by Gunner's Mate Third Class Noah Melendez, who removed the expired canister in Meyer's OBA and inserted a new one so that Meyer had a steady airflow. This time, they went down the same ladder that John Mullahy and the other Turret Two survivors had used to escape.

At the bottom of the turret, the first thing they noted was that the magazines had not been flooded. They undogged the armored double doors to the annular space (the area where the powder bags were passed before being relayed into the flats). Some of the water that Lieutenant Demery's firemen had directed into the vents had made its way down, and about eighteen inches of it had accumulated inside the annular space. Kissinger circled to the left around the rotating portion of the turret, and Meyer proceeded to the right. Both men were able to open watertight doors on each side of the powder flats, even though the metal handles were hot and they weren't wearing gloves.

When the doors swung open, they had a glimpse of hell. The water inside the flats was at knee level. A body tumbled out the door that Kissinger opened. He struggled with the corpse for more than a minute before shoving it back into the flats. Meyer saw a "tangle" of three or four bodies entwined with two inoperable fire hoses. Meyer also saw "a pile of four or five" other men who lacked oxygen masks and had tried to use "chemical/biological filters" as substitutes. The filters hadn't protected the men from poisonous gases. "It was obvious that they knew what was coming, and they were scared out of their minds. It was slow and excruciating, and they had to wonder why none of their equipment worked," Meyer said.

Something else inside the flats grabbed Meyer's and Kissinger's attention. Nearly a ton and a half of powder, not in canisters, lay in the flats. "Twenty-five to thirty bags were glowing a bright cherry red. It looked like charcoal briquettes at a Sunday afternoon barbecue," Meyer said. Neither he nor Kissinger was aware that the burning powder bags were producing poisonous cyanide gas. They resealed the flats and the annular space, and as they were preparing to leave, they heard a thunderous clap above them. Improperly stowed flammable lubricants and several hundred gallons of antifreeze in the center gun room had blown up.

Meyer, Kissinger, and Petty Officer Melendez scrambled up the ladder to the third deck. "What do we do with the sprinklers, Dan?" Kissinger inquired. Meyer said that Captain Moosally needed to flood Turret One's magazines in order to protect the turret. Kissinger agreed and hustled off to tell the captain to flood the magazines, annular spaces, and powder flats. Meyer went to the weapons-department office to get the captain a small schematic of the turret from a training manual. When Commander Kissinger told the captain about what he, Meyer, and Melendez had seen below, Moosally agreed to flood the magazines.

LIEUTENANT TIMOTHY P. Blackie, the *Iowa*'s damage-control assistant, was sitting in a dental chair having a tooth extracted when GQ sounded. He had held this job on the *Iowa* for just twenty-four days. "I grabbed a wad of cotton from the dentist, stuffed it in my mouth, and proceeded to DC [damage control] central," Blackie said. But before he got there, he encountered thick smoke, so he backtracked and got an OBA. There was no way he could personally handle all of the phone circuits, control panels, knobs, levers, cranks, handles, and squawk boxes in DC central. But fortunately, John Mullahy and Dale Mortensen showed up when he did to lend a hand. Blackie had Mullahy and Mortensen twirl cranks like those on an old Model-T Ford, opening valves in Turret Two's eleven magazines, allowing 16,000 tons of seawater to flow in and drench the powder canisters. The additional weight of the water made the ship ride "bow down."

Despite the fact that he was wearing an OBA, Blackie was overcome by smoke and fell to the deck. At first, Mullahy and Mortensen thought the short, forty-year-old damage-control assistant had suffered a heart attack. Mullahy scooped up the lieutenant and carried him to the wardroom, which was serving as an emergency medical clearing station. The doctors treated Mullahy for smoke inhalation. He was released after forty-five minutes, but Blackie had to stay in sick bay for six hours.

Lieutenant Commander William Barbra hastened to DC central to take over for Lieutenant Blackie. Barbra was alarmed because the *Iowa* was listing noticeably to starboard due to the amount of water that had been poured into her magazines. Nine magazines and adjacent compartments were inundated, some containing up to ten feet of water. This was in addition to at least twenty feet of water in Turret Two's powder flats. Using submersible pumps, Barbra's damage controlmen siphoned off the water, then routed it up two decks and dumped it over the side. It was a slow, touch-and-go procedure, because some of the pumps malfunctioned, and body parts from the demolished turret clogged the flexible piping.

Lieutenant George Anderson, considered to be one of the very best engineers aboard the *Iowa*, said, "No other class of ship in the Navy could have taken that kind of punishment without sinking. The water pressure would have buckled any other class of ship's bulkheads and collapsed her sides."

George Anderson's men, normally assigned to fight fires in the engineering spaces, were the first sailors who actually got inside Turret Two. They received this assignment by default, since they were the only sailors on the ship wearing one-piece, heat-resistant "proximity" suits, oxygen masks, fire boots, and Kevlar helmets. This gear had only been provided to them the day before they sailed on this cruise, and they had not had an adequate opportunity to check it out.

On the main deck, Marine Captain Bolander had finally succeeded in bashing in and popping open Turret Two's escape hatch. The larger tail hatch was gone, blown off when the center gun exploded. The 250-pound tail hatch had ricocheted off the teak deck, caroming over the side. Twenty-year-old Fireman Brian R. Scanio was the first firefighter to arrive at the turret equipped with an OBA and wearing a proximity suit. Hull Technician First Class Thomas Smith showed up ten seconds later and asked, "Who's ready to go? Whose OBA is already lit off and is getting good oxygen?" Scanio raised his gloved right hand and began scaling the fire-blistered ladder up through the escape hatch into the blazing turret.

Scanio hadn't gotten very far before he was blocked by a steel grate. He wrestled with it for five minutes and then backed down. The three Marines ascended and used a long crowbar to shift the obstacle out of the way. Once they did that, Ernie Hanyecz's torso, which had rested on the inch-thick grate, dropped to the deck. One of his severed hands was later found fused to a latch. There was no doubt in Scanio's mind that Hanyecz had seen something in the turret that scared him and led to his attempt to flee through the escape hatch.

Scanio was helped back up the escape hatch with fire hoses wetting down his backside. "I kept hearing this rumbling. The smoke was so intense. I just saw small glows and—it's just the noise, it was so intense, and the heat, you could feel it searing," he said. There was no light except for the flames. It was like falling into Dante's *Inferno*.

Shortly after Scanio climbed into the turret, a secondary explosion hurled him fifteen feet against a bulkhead near the range finder in the turret officer's booth. Two minutes later, a smaller explosion that had a "sucking sound" buckled his knees and rattled his teeth. The center and right gun rooms continued to burn out of control. The door to the turret officer's booth had been blown away. The first body he stumbled over belonged to Chief Ziegler. The chief's anchors, denoting Ziegler's rank, were still affixed to the collars of his khaki shirt. The body was headless. That was enough to make Scanio think seriously about abandoning this charnel house. "I was terrified when I was in there because for one, I was alone. Another thing. I didn't know a whole lot about the turrets. How much powder would be in the space, you know, I wasn't sure what I should do first," he said. He then stumbled over the corpse of someone else he knew, Boatswain's Mate Second Class Michael Williams. He recognized Williams by the distinctive tattoos on his arm.

Ten minutes after Scanio entered the turret, he was joined by four of his colleagues. The engineers were able to drag in three hoses with two-and-a-half-inch nozzles. They also hauled in foam applicators and battle lanterns, as well as "red devil blowers" to suck the smoke out of the turret through flexible, accordion-style, wide-diameter tubing. All of the bodies they saw in the upper portion of the turret were badly mangled. "The first body that I saw didn't have a head," said Repairman Third Class Thad Harms. "And the second one I couldn't see the top half of him, so I don't know if it was there or not. And then the third one, I just noticed a person in front of me. I didn't know how much of him was left."

Over the next several hours, Scanio had to leave the turret three times, because the forty-five-minute chemical supply in his OBA was nearly exhausted. On one of his trips back into the turret, his OBA mask melted to his face. When the fire was finally extinguished in the center gun room, by a combination of water and foam, Scanio cautiously entered it. He was able to identify the body of Gary Fisk, the center-gun powder-hoist operator. It appeared that Fisk had been attempting to escape when he was cut down by the blast.

Straddling a catwalk in the center gun room, Scanio peered through the gaps where the deck plates had been. He saw two bodies below him. The first was located about six feet down, on a platform where the primerman stood to insert a cartridge into the breechblock. The other was at the bottom of the deep pit, where the gas ejection air for the gun was turned off and on. Scanio removed the clear plastic face plate of his breathing apparatus for a brief period in order to get a better view. He was the first to admit that he was no expert on a sixteen-inch turret, but he had gone through an indoctrination in one of the turrets when he first came to the *Iowa*. That, and what he'd learned from some of his friends who were gunner's mates, was enough to make him realize that nobody was supposed to be in the bottom of the pit just before the guns were fired. Had that fellow down there been doing some last-minute repairs when he was cut down by the explosion? He wouldn't forget this body in the pit.

Photographs were critical, since Chief Ziegler had made so many last-minute assignment changes that there was no accurate duty roster. "They didn't bring the naval photographers in to take the pictures before they moved the bodies," said Scanio. He had been a volunteer fireman before joining the Navy and was familiar with the care taken by civilian police and fire departments to preserve and document accident and crime scenes. He said sailors started "haphazardly moving" the bodies in Turret Two, trying to identify them. "Bodies were just moved, and then after the fact, everybody said, 'Well, I think that's where we found him. I don't remember, but I think that's where we found him.' Nobody was preserving the evidence."

After two nerve-racking hours inside the turret, the temperature inside Scanio's proximity suit was 140°F. He slowly descended through the escape hatch and sprawled on the wooden deck. "I was exhausted, basically. And the corpsmen were taking off, you know, my suit and everything and they were cooling me down with water and giving me something to drink, you know, so I really was out of it at that time," he said. Scanio would later return to the turret to haul out bodies and then go back once again to remove wrecked equipment.

WHILE MOST of the 1,550 surviving members of the *Iowa*'s crew were fighting fires, recovering the bodies, or just trying to keep the ship afloat, a small band of thieves broke into the lockers and looted the possessions of

Captain Larry Seaquist (in dress whites) greets President and Mrs. Ronald Reagan and navy Secretary John Lehman (on Mrs. Reagan's right) aboard the *Iowa* in New York Harbor on July 4, 1986, to commemorate the 100th birthday of the Statue of Liberty. (U.S. Navy)

Captain Larry Seaquist presents the Navy Achievement Medal to Gunner's Mate First Class Dale Mortensen.

Admiral "Bud" Edney, the Vice Chief of Naval Operations, micro-managed the Navy's flawed investigation of Clayton Hartwig. (U.S. Navy)

Dan Meyer's father, Donald, a retired Navy captain, and mother, Mary, attach his shoulder boards following his commissioning as an ensign.

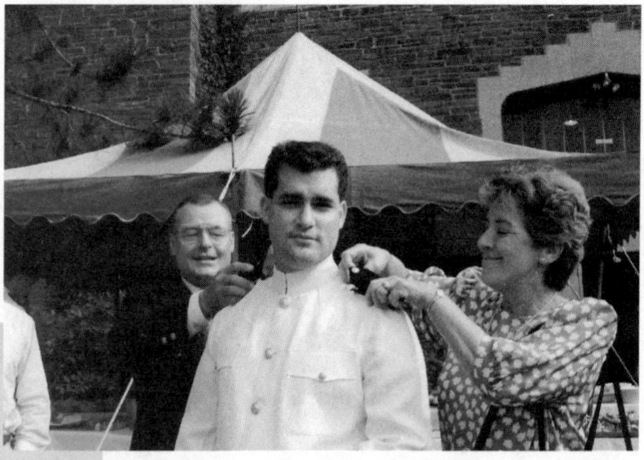

Captain Larry Seaquist departed the *Iowa* as Skipper ten months before the disaster. (1987 *Iowa* Cruisebook)

Master Chief Gunner's Mate Chuck Hill put in his retirement papers when he heard Fred Moosally was coming to the *Iowa*. (1987 *Iowa* Cruisebook)

Commander Michael "Iron Mike" Fahey (in khaki uniform) was Second-In-Command of the *Iowa* and a proponent of the "bare knuckles" school of leadership.

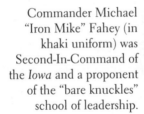

Captain Fred Moosally shakes hands with Gunner's Mate Second Class Clayton Hartwig while the *Iowa* is in the shipyard during the summer of 1988.

Aerial view of the USS *Iowa* firing a nine-gun broadside to starboard. (U.S. Navy)

Turret Two trained to port.
(U.S. Navy)

Senior Chief Reggie Ziegler standing in front of Turret Two.

Fire Control Master Chief Stephen Skelley was known as the "pots and pans man" by the other *Iowa* chiefs, because selling kitchen wares door-to-door was the only other job he ever held.

Lieutenant Phil Buch (seen as an ensign) did not put a high premium on training or maintenance in Turret Two.

Clayton Hartwig as a third class gunner's mate on Turret Two's Projectile Deck in 1987.

Earl Hartwig, father of Clayton Hartwig, as an eighteen-year-old gunner's mate in 1945 on the USS *Adams*, a destroyer/mine layer.

Gunner's Mate Third Class Jack Thompson told his family a month before his death that Turret Two was a "deathtrap."

Master Chief Gunner's Mate James Hickman (standing to the right of Commander Kissinger, who is wearing sunglasses). (1989 *Iowa* Cruisebook)

Commander John Morse, Executive Officer when the explosion occurred. (1989 *Iowa* Cruisebook)

Fire Control Master Chief Dale Miller. (1989 *Iowa* Cruisebook)

Commander Robert Kissinger, Weapons Officer at the time of the explosion.
(1989 *Iowa* Cruisebook)

Lieutenant Leo Walsh, Fire Control Officer at the time of the explosion.
(1989 *Iowa* Cruisebook)

Captain Fred Moosally shakes hands with Gunner's Mate Third Class Matt Price. Price was the Right Gun Captain in Turret Two when the explosion occurred.

Gunner's Mate Second Class Errick Lawrence, following a playful shaving cream fight in Turret Two, was listed as Gun Captain on the day of the explosion.

Captain Ed Snyder and Commander James Elfelt (to Snyder's left) observe a replenishment of the USS *New Jersey* off the coast of Vietnam. Elfelt was the vessel's Executive Officer.

This photograph taken by a second fleet officer shows the billowing smoke following the explosion and black pieces of the "Bloomer," the rubberized fabric gasket surrounding the center gun shred and blasted into the sea. (U.S. Navy)

Firefighters attempt to extinguish the flames inside Turret Two. (AP/Wide World Photos)

Admiral Jerome Johnson was on the *Iowa*'s bridge at the time of the explosion. Later, as Vice Chief of Naval Operations, he supported an apology to the Hartwig family. (U.S. Navy)

(1)

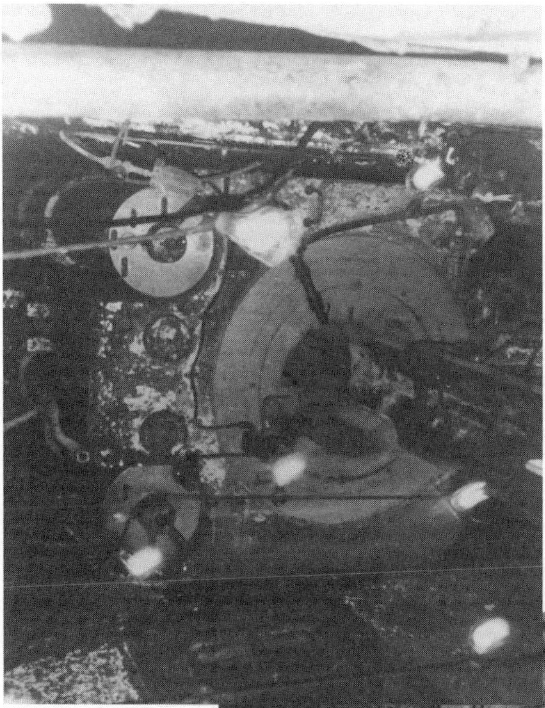

These bootleg pictures of Turret Two were taken by an *Iowa* gunner's mate after the bodies were removed, but before the cleanup effort began. The center gun's (1) massive breech block has been blown away. The wiring (2) at the rear of the Turret Officer's booth is charred. The center gun's "cradle" (3), which holds the powder bags and shell before they are rammed, is crushed.

(2)

(3)

(1)

A Navy photography team entered Turret Two about two weeks after the explosion and discovered that even after an intensive effort had been made to clean it up, the space was still in shambles. The Turret Officer's booth (1) had been burnt to a crisp. The chain housing (2) for the center gun's rammer was demolished, and the rammer control mechanism (3) was totaled. (U.S. Navy)

(2)

(3)

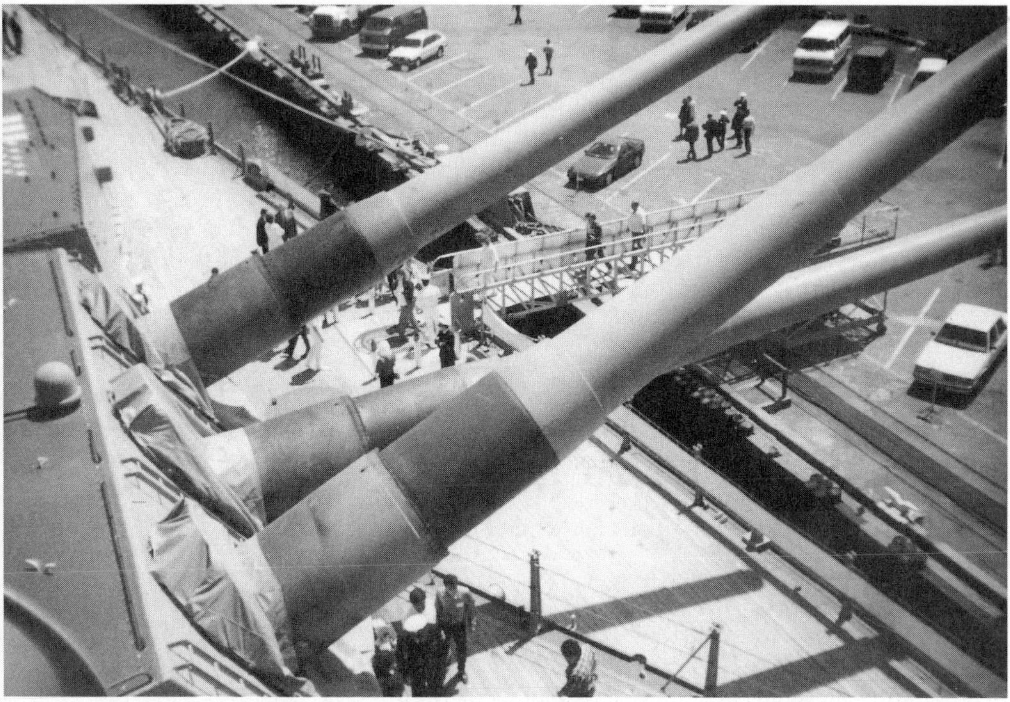

Five days after the explosion, as relatives come aboard the *Iowa* in Norfolk, Turret Two remains trained to starboard, with the center gun canted downward. (Mary Welden)

Military pallbearers carry one of the 47 bodies flown into Dover Air Force Base from the USS *Iowa*. (AP/Wide World Photos)

Turret Two's casualties, as well as the lockers of some of the live crewmen who were occupied with damage-control efforts. Money, checks, insurance policies, jewelry, and other personal possessions were filched. Navy public-relations officers in Washington would at first deny that there had been any looting. Later they admitted that burglary had taken place, but that it had not been widespread.

Dan Meyer had seen "three or four lockers" in Turret Two's berthing compartment "popped open" during one of his many trips to the base of the turret. He reported the looting to the boatswain's mate of the watch, who called the master-at-arms. Meyer said, "That turret was burning and those people were in the process of dying and somebody was looting their possessions." Brian Scanio, whose locker was looted, said, "I was ready to lynch those bastards. They broke into my locker while I was fighting fires to save lives."

SHORTLY AFTER the explosion, the *Iowa*'s bridge team radioed the two frigates trailing the battleship. At 10:36 A.M., forty-one minutes after the first explosion, the *Aylwin* deployed a helicopter to aid the *Iowa*. The *Ainsworth* darted alongside the starboard quarter of the *Iowa* at 10:48 A.M. She was waved away and told to drop back and reapproach on the port side in order to avoid the *Iowa*'s three loaded guns. The *Aylwin* joined the *Ainsworth* off the battleship's port quarter just three minutes later. She had a motor whaleboat ready to go and had rigged a high line in case the *Iowa* wanted to transfer any of her casualties. Three choppers containing a medical team and an explosive ordnance disposal unit from the carrier *Coral Sea* landed on the *Iowa*'s flight deck between 11:45 A.M. and noon.

The battleship's executive officer, Commander Morse, concerned about the three loaded guns on the *Iowa*'s starboard side, radioed other helicopters and ships to give her a wide berth. A team of Naval Investigative Service accident specialists was aboard the *Coral Sea*, but they were told they were not needed aboard the *Iowa*. Not utilizing the services of professional investigators while the accident scene was still fresh would come back to haunt the Navy.

At noon, Admiral Johnson cabled the Atlantic Fleet commander in Norfolk, saying, "*Iowa* under full power, fires under control, initial casualty report 15 dead. Appropriate actions taken, will inform of *Iowa* approach to R.R. [Roosevelt Roads, Puerto Rico]. Maneuvering to keep smoke out of other compartments; NBC News already broke story. Request our position not be given to keep sightseers away. Assure you things are in good order. Ship responded in timely manner."

Admiral Johnson knew of the early NBC broadcast because he had brought a state-of-the-art satellite transmitter/receiver aboard the *Iowa*. Twenty-six minutes after that message was sent, the Second Fleet commander advised Norfolk that the *Iowa* had just been buzzed by an aircraft chartered by CBS News. Most of the other ships under Admiral Johnson's control continued to conduct FLEETEX war games while the *Iowa* burned and fought for her life. The modern nuclear cruiser USS *Mississippi*, which was not far away from the *Iowa*, launched a Tomahawk cruise missile at 2:40 P.M. One of the *Iowa*'s two escorts, the *Aylwin*, no longer shadowing the battleship, was accompanying the *Mississippi*.

Fred Moosally also dispatched a stream of messages to higher headquarters, including one to Admiral Powell Carter, the Atlantic Fleet commander. All of the captain's messages attempted to put the best light on the situation. Some of them contained glaring errors. For example, Moosally stated that the explosion "took place in loading tray of center gun Turret Two, which was in process of being loaded with six powder bags." In another message, the captain asserted, "Right and left gun Turret One still loaded with high-cap and powder." Hours after the explosion, Moosally apparently was still unaware that Turret Two was loading five bags in each gun when the accident happened, or that Turret One only had a "hang fire" in one gun.

During much of the afternoon and into the evening, gloomy roll calls were periodically sounded on the public-address system. Since there was no accurate roster of who had been in Turret Two, best-guess estimates were assembled by Master Chiefs Hickman and Skelley, Commander Kissinger, and Lieutenant Commander Costigan. Then the boatswain's mate of the watch would read dolorous lists of about fifty-five names: "Gunner's Mate Third Class Matthew Price, report to the mess deck. . . . Gunner's Mate Third Class Milton DeVaul, report to the mess deck. . . . Seaman Apprentice Leslie Everhart, report to the mess deck. . . ." "Calling those names was like scraping a knife on a raw wound. The seamen reacted as if they had been slapped in the face every time a new name was read," Dan Meyer said. If a sailor whose name had been called appeared on the quarterdeck, his name was deleted and replaced by another likely candidate.

Brian Scanio was still recuperating from heat exhaustion on the deck near Turret Two when one of those roll calls of the dead began. It was interrupted by an announcement: "Commander Second Fleet [Vice Admiral Johnson] departing." "Jesus Christ! The cowardly motherfucker is deserting us!" Scanio screamed. Dan Meyer and Dale Mortensen heard the same announcement. Mortensen, who wasn't enraptured by flag officers, grumbled, "What do you expect from a fucking airdale [aviator]." Admiral Johnson later said that he had most probably been leaving the battleship to fly over to the *Coral Sea* for a briefing. He did return to the *Iowa* later in the afternoon and remained aboard her until the next morning, when he flew off for good to Roosevelt Roads, Puerto Rico. Before his departure, Johnson went inside Turret Two. An experienced fighter/bomber pilot, the fleet commander had often served as an aviation accident investigator. "I saw this mass destruction in the turret, and I knew we'd never find out the cause of this. I've seen my share of catastrophic explosions in aviation accidents. It's been my experience that sometimes you can't reconstruct the cause," he said.

7

"It Was Just Hell, Pure Hell!"

AFTER DAN MEYER obtained a schematic of the turret from a training manual, he returned to the bridge and presented it to the captain. Moosally asked Meyer, whose mouth was scorched and who was hacking up phlegm, what he had seen in the powder flats. Someone gave Meyer a glass of water. He gulped the water and then told the captain that there were at least ten dead men inside the flats. The captain told Meyer to try to go below one more time and bring back more information. Meyer saluted and walked off the port side of the bridge, encountering Chief Skelley. The stubby chief slapped the ensign on the back and told him that the ship's senior officers thought he was doing such a terrific job that he should get a medal. Glancing at the smoking turret, Meyer said, "Screw the medal, Master Chief, I think we'll all be lucky to get out of here alive!"

Meyer took the same route to the base of the turret as he had used with Commander Kissinger and Petty Officer Melendez. When he reached the magazines, it was quickly apparent to him that too much water had been pumped into the ship. The water pressure had crushed a number of sturdy powder canisters in the magazines. Meyer talked to the engineers, who told him that they were routing water up to the third deck and over the side. There was nothing that could be done about the flats, which would remain submerged for some time. Removal of the water and the bodies in the flats would have to be accomplished by climbing down from the gun rooms and then through the mechanical, electrical, and projectile decks.

Meyer returned to the bridge and told the captain that there were tens of thousands of gallons of seawater washing around in the magazines and in Turret Two's powder flats. Without giving Meyer a chance to recuperate, the executive officer told him to report to Turret Two and assist with the identification of bodies.

WHEN DALE Mortensen reached Turret Two, the flames had abated and the smoke was not so bad. Mortensen combed through the rubble to see if he could determine what had happened. He examined the powder hoist. The door was closed and dogged, but the car was still up. It should have descended to the flats. Something was definitely wrong here. Either the hoist had malfunctioned, as it was prone to do, or the operator had screwed up. He examined what was left of the rammer. The links littered the rear of the gun house. He decided that the rammer had still been inside the breech when the detonation occurred, indicating that it had been rammed too far, most likely at a speed that was too high. He made note of the fact that the door connecting the center gun room to the turret officer's booth had been blown off its hinges. That could mean that somebody was trying to leave the center gun room, or more likely, Chief Ziegler had observed something terribly wrong and was entering the gun room to take care of it. Mortensen peered into the breech and saw that the projectile had been driven into the rifling. That meant that immense force had been applied to the base of the shell. He checked to see if a primer had been inserted into the open breechblock. It had, but he could not tell if it had been fired until he had a tool to extract it.

Then he stared into the same pit that Brian Scanio had and observed one body on the primerman's platform and another body at the base of the pit. Mortensen scrambled down the badly warped ladder to the base of the pit. The first thing he checked out was the gas ejection air valve to determine if it were on. He recalled hearing on his sound-powered phones that the gun did not have compressed air on when the breechblock was opened. But it was on now, meaning that Chief Ziegler had sent somebody into the pit to turn it on. Mortensen was able to determine who that somebody was without much difficulty. The forearms of the body near the air valve had been severed near the elbows, both legs had been blown off below the knees, and much of the face was missing. In addition, the cadaver was partially charred, coated with soot, and "stippled" (peppered) with gun powder. But there was a distinctive sailing ship with the words "USS *Iowa*" tattooed on the upper left arm. The only man on the ship who had a tattoo like that was Clayton Hartwig. Mortensen checked the body on the platform and was fairly sure that it was the primerman, Reginald Johnson, a twenty-year-old seaman recruit who had only been in the Navy six months.

Dan Meyer entered the center gun room as Dale Mortensen emerged from the pit. Mortensen told Meyer about locating Hartwig's body in the pit. He said that in his opinion Hartwig had been sent down there by Chief Ziegler to turn on the gas ejection air after the trainee gun captain, Errick Lawrence, had forgotten to turn it on. "Dale and I theorized that Lawrence had gone ahead and loaded the gun while Hartwig was down in the pit. The rammerman, Backherms, didn't know what he was doing and had shoved the powder in way too far and way too fast and blew everything up," Meyer said. Proceeding farther into the center gun room, cautiously avoiding the gaps in the deck plating, Meyer stared into the pit and recognized the body that Mortensen had described in graphic detail.

As Meyer began the grisly chore of attempting to identify bodies, Mortensen and a group of damage controlmen began shoring up the three guns, so the weapons wouldn't "fall out of battery" and crush the sailors who entered the turret once the fires had been extinguished. "Identifying those bodies was virtually impossible. Those guys didn't mark their clothes with their names like they should. They weren't allowed to wear dog tags in the turret, and most of them didn't have wallets on them," Meyer said. He located Lieutenant Phil Buch's body—headless and in three parts—in the rear of the turret officer's booth near the fire-control computer. Meyer recognized Buch from the khaki uniform he was wearing and the single silver bar affixed to each of his collars. Meyer was then directed to what some of the men were calling the body of rammerman Robert Backherms. Both arms and one leg were gone, and the trunk was carbonized. "It looked like a smoking pile of ashes. It didn't look human to me," Meyer said.

In the rear of the right gun room, he stumbled across what was left of the two legalmen, Robert K. Morrison and Michael W. Helton, who had been sent to the turret for punishment. There was a torso and "a pile of body parts" in the center gun room that Meyer thought belonged to Errick Lawrence, the trainee gun captain. The body of Matt Price, the right gun captain, was in the turret officer's booth just behind the center gun. Sound-powered phones were burned into Price's head. Gunner's Mate Third Class Peter E. Bopp was "blown out aft" into the turret officer's booth. Navy investigators would later insist that Bopp had been working below on the electrical deck when he died. They would also confuse Bopp's body with Clayton Hartwig's, although Hartwig was more than fifty pounds heavier and at least seven inches taller than Bopp. Jack Thompson, the left gun captain, and Jay White, the left cradleman, had been hurled from their gun room. Two fire controlmen, Tung Thanh Adams and Richard Lewis, apparently were trying to escape when they were caught by the blast. Adams was stretched out next to where the tail hatch had been, and Lewis was lying adjacent to the escape hatch.

Meyer made a rudimentary sketch showing where bodies or parts of bodies were found. It was the only sketch ever made by anybody who actually visited the turret, and it contradicted some key points the Navy would later assert to be absolutely true. The corpses were placed in zippered plastic bags. One of these black bags had masking tape on which was written, "unknown human remains." Meyer was physically and spiritually numbed by the time he completed this stomach-wrenching assignment, but there was much worse to come.

DALE MORTENSEN worked with Operations Specialist First Class James Bennett Drake, an explosive ordnance disposal expert, who arrived from the *Coral Sea* about 3 P.M. to unload the powder in Turret Two's left and right guns. Drake toured the bombed-out turret, asked a number of perceptive questions, and then said, "It's my opinion that the explosion started in the center gun room caused by compressing the powder bags against the sixteen-inch shell too far and too fast with the rammer arm." Using a chain hoist, Mortensen and Drake unfastened the breech plugs of the left and right guns. When the breeches were open, buckets of water were tossed into the powder chambers. The bags were then cautiously removed. None of them showed any damage. They were passed by hand out of the turret and then heaved over the side.

Once this harrowing chore was completed at 5:22 P.M., Mortensen conferred with Dan Meyer about getting the captain's permission to clear the fouled bore in Turret One. Meyer went up to the bridge and received permission to attempt again to fire Cletus Guffin's gun. By then, Guffin and his crew had been at their stations for nearly ten hours. They weren't allowed to leave the turret, even to go to the head; they had to use a bucket in the gun room. Galley stewards had brought them box lunches.

All the sailors assigned to Turret One were notified on the 1MC to return to their battle stations, and everyone else was warned to stay clear of the forecastle. "We'll try to shoot the left gun to clear the muzzle," the captain stated. Guffin reprimed. The salvo alarm blared. Then came a click. Guffin tweezed the primer out with a sawed-off broom-handle contrivance, inserted a new cartridge, super-elevated, and tried once more. Click. He repeated the cycle. Another click. While Guffin sweated, the range was frequently obstructed by two aircraft chartered by television networks. The ship was forced to alter her course several times to obtain a clear range.

After five clicks and no discharges from the .30-caliber primers, Mortensen was positive that Guffin's gun couldn't be cleared in the normal manner, so he decided to let it cool off a bit before undoing the breech and jerking out the powder. Jim Drake, the explosive ordnance disposal man from the *Coral Sea*, was with Meyer and Mortensen in Turret One, but he let Mortensen do most of the work. Mortensen had Shane Cline, the acting turret captain, get a bucket of water and perch atop the gun barrel. Drake had a fire hose. When Guffin opened the breechblock, Cline threw the water from his bucket into the powder chamber, and Drake aimed a steady stream on the bags. Mortensen pulled on the bag nearest the breech. It was "cocked" (turned sideways) and had a two-inch hole burned into its side. A number of the powder granules were singed. "It looked like mice had been nibbling on it," Meyer said. "I mean it was scary. It was a goddamned scary thing," Mortensen said. All six bags were removed, "had the shit soaked out of them" in immersion tanks, and were taken to the main deck, where they were tossed into the Caribbean. It was 6 P.M. The turret was swiveled around and pointed at the bow. Turret Two remained trained on the starboard beam, with 2,700-pound projectiles trapped in all three barrels.

As soon as Cletus Guffin's gun was cleared, Meyer went to the wardroom to get some dinner. He was disheveled, wearing undersized, short-sleeved blue coveralls soiled with oil, hydraulic fluid, and blood. He smelled strongly of smoke and worse. His hair was standing up in greasy spikes. His face and hands were permeated with soot. He walked over to Commander Morse, immaculate in his starched khakis, and asked, "Sir, request permission to join the mess." The executive officer granted permission. Meyer seated himself next to Ensign Raymond Gorski, a thickset deck officer from western Pennsylvania. The boatswain's mates who had died in Turret Two had belonged to Gorski's division. The mess steward brought Meyer a limp salad and a plate of overcooked green beans and potatoes and some unrecognizable meat floating in grayish gravy. He gagged, his stomach roiling. The steward took Meyer's untouched plate away and brought him an extra-large salad and a fistful of "battleship" cookies, which he ate."

After finishing his meal, Meyer visited the executive officer in his stateroom. Commander Morse walked over to talk to him. The executive officer told Meyer that he was setting up a panel composed of *Iowa* officers and chief petty officers to investigate the explosion. He wanted Meyer to suggest an unbiased officer and a chief from the weapons department to serve in this group. Meyer recommended Lieutenant Commander Mark Ruprecht, the missiles officer, and Senior Chief Fire Controlman Donald Larrick, who worked for Ruprecht. Larrick was vetoed because he was too fat and wouldn't look good appearing as an *Iowa* spokesman on network television.

It was dark on the main deck when Meyer emerged from the wardroom, but there was a full moon in the sky. The ship's running lights were on, and the vessel was poking along at eleven knots in a southwesterly direction. Meyer sought out Dale Mortensen and told him about their latest disgusting assignment. Mortensen recoiled. He felt that he had already done his fair share, but he ultimately agreed to go along. He snared Shane Cline, Cletus Guffin, Mark Harden, Michael Estes, and Murray Cunningham. The seven men obtained battle lanterns and made their way down a ladder in the center gun room to the electrical deck, where they discovered the body of Gunner's Mate Third Class Heath Stillwagon, seated in a chair with his hands folded, as if he were in church. "This man realized that he was so far down in the turret that he wasn't getting out. He had time to think about it and to pray," Meyer said. He also found the body of his regular tennis partner, Gunner's Mate Third Class Scot Blakey, off the electrical deck in the train operator's position. The tall, athletic Blakey had been scheduled to rotate out of the turret. Meyer was convinced that both Stillwagon and Blakey would have survived if they had been provided with OBAs.

Meyer's men despised their assignment. "It was dark. There was no light.

It was just hell, pure hell," Cletus Guffin said. The bodies they located with their battle lanterns were mostly bloated and blackened by the fireball that had raged through the rotating decks below the gun house. They next found Seaman Apprentice Leslie Allen Everhart Jr. curled up in a fetal position behind four projectiles, with sound-powered phones clamped to his ears. He had apparently suffocated. His hair, eyebrows, and skin were scorched, but his eyes were "crystal clear." A former theatrical set designer and lighting specialist, Everhart had toured England with a dramatic company before enlisting in the Navy eight months earlier. He had hoped to gain admission to a technical school that offered training in illustrating and drafting.

The men tiptoed around the body of Seaman Recruit John Goins, lying flat on his back on the upper projectile deck. He seemed to have suffocated. Another man was seated on the deck with a charred book clutched in his blistered hands. Meyer desperately searched for the body of Gunner's Mate Third Class Geoffrey Schelin, another frequent tennis partner. He finally spotted Schelin's corpse off the electrical deck in the right gun layer's position. Schelin had been in charge of elevating and depressing the barrels and evidently had strangled on the cord of his sound-powered phones. The top of his skull had also been bashed in from being hurled into the steel overhead (ceiling). Close to tears, Meyer was examining his deceased friend when a stream of graymatter and cranial fluid from Schelin's corpse dripped from the overhead, splattering a clipboard he was holding. "Jesus Christ, Geoff. No, no, not this way," he wailed, nearly vomiting. The Navy would later erroneously inform Schelin's parents that his body had been found in the right gun room, where he had been the rammerman.

Mortensen located another dead sailor he couldn't identify. The body was wearing a headset, only it wasn't a sound-powered phone headset. It was a Sony Walkman. He popped it open and saw that a cassette inside still was revolving. Slipping on the earphones, he heard rock star David Lee Roth. Walkmen were strictly forbidden in the turret, because they could generate sparks and distract a man when he was involved in hazardous work. A charred Sony Sports Walkman, with earphones, two cassette tapes, and a pair of sunglasses, had also been located near the remains of Robert Backherms, the center gun's rammerman. Mortensen wanted to submit a written report listing the Walkmen and other contraband items, but he was ordered by the executive officer to forget about it.

When the team from Turret One reached a thick hatchway leading from the lower projectile deck to the powder flats, they were confronted by an even more gruesome spectacle. They saw a heap of six or seven sailors who had died while attempting to flee. Meyer called the macabre scene "straight carnage." The seaman at the bottom of the mound had been crushed, battered, and scratched by his frenzied comrades, all of whom had either suffocated or been poisoned by the gas that permeated the turret. Rigor mortis had begun to set in, and there was no way for Meyer's men to untangle the bodies and reach the flooded powder flats below them, so they headed back up to the gun house and then out on the main deck. The foul taste of burnt plastic remained in their mouths, and their nostrils were inflamed by what they had been forced to smell.

Gratefully sucking in lungfuls of fresh air, Meyer crumpled on the teak planking and quickly fell into a fitful slumber. His fatigued men retired to their berthing compartment. About 1:30 A.M., Meyer felt someone kicking his high-top Navy-issue "boondocker" work shoes. It was Ken Costigan, the gunnery officer, who told Meyer to take a shower, go to his stateroom, and get into his bunk. Meyer did as he was told, but he spent the remainder of the night tossing and turning, tormented by the sights, sounds, and smells he had endured in that ghastly turret.

While Meyer slept, Lieutenant Commander Bob Holman, who was in charge of the deck divisions, sent teams of boatswain's mates squirming through a maze of compartments in Turret Two to retrieve the corpses that Meyer and his men had tried to identify. Sometimes the sailors had to rig blocks and tackles to extract the bodies. In other cases, they broke the stiffened limbs of the dead men so they would fit through narrow hatchways. They had a shipfitter standing by with an acetylene torch in case a hatch had to be enlarged. As many as twenty bodies, immersed in twenty feet of water, had to be extricated from the powder flats. This meant carrying centrifugal pumps and hoses and diving into water fouled with charred gunpowder, cyanide, sulfur, distillate fuel oil, hydraulic fluid, and firefighting foam. As the pumps slowly lowered the water level, corpses bobbed to the surface, petrifying the swimmers.

The search in the foul witches' brew sent some of the sailors over the edge. The day after the explosion, the Navy dispatched psychiatrists, psychologists, and chaplains—all members of the Special Psychiatric Rapid Intervention Team—to the *Iowa*, but the counseling and/or treatment they carried out was superficial at best. One day later, a psychiatrist sent a message to the psychiatry department of the Portsmouth, Virginia, Naval Hospital, saying, "Assessment complete, intervention underway. Officers and crew doing well."

AS THE bodies were transferred to the main deck, the exact numbers of the casualties and where they were discovered became increasingly speculative. According to Lieutenant Eugene F. Smallwood Jr., a medical service corps officer from the *Coral Sea*, the extraction of bodies from the powder flats was not completed until 4:30 A.M. Smallwood said a total of fifty-one bags had been filled with corpses or body parts. Twenty-nine were "Presumptive/tentatives," meaning the face had been identified by two crewmen who knew the person or had been identified by stencil markings on their clothing. Nine were "guesstimates," meaning that there were partial stencils on their clothing or somebody said they "thought it was Smith, Jones, Thomas."

Nine were "unidentifiables." And four bags "contained partial, unidentifiable remains which could not be associated with any specific corpse."

At 2:58 A.M., the OOD recorded in the ship's official log: "Removed from Turret 2 final body count 44." By 7:38 A.M., he listed the names of forty-seven men who might have been in Turret Two at the time of the explosion and had failed to appear at any of the numerous sight musters held on the forecastle since the explosion. However, it would take the FBI's disaster squad considerably longer to positively identify the dead men. By April 22, FBI technicians could say with certainty that they had identified thirty-two individuals by fingerprints. Four more were identified by fingerprints three days later. Forty-seven *Iowa* men were identified by a combination of fingerprinting, dental X-rays, and blood and bone marrow typing by May 16, nearly a month after the explosion. But by that time, the funerals of all forty-seven had been conducted, and the Navy had aggressively discouraged the relatives from opening the coffins to determine if they were burying the right body.

WHEN DAN Meyer woke up on April 20 and walked out on the main deck, he noticed that the ship was creeping through the water at three knots, heading in an easterly direction. A little before 9 A.M., the fifty-one body bags were removed from "reefers" (large refrigerators), where they had been stored, and carted back to the ship's flight deck behind Turret Three. Helicopters began landing to transport the bags to the naval base at Roosevelt Roads, Puerto Rico.

Meyer was startled by all the activity going on around Turret Two. A boatswain's mate told him that the executive officer had ordered that the turret be sanitized before the ship got back to Norfolk. Lieutenant Commander Holman had inspected the turret after the bodies were removed. Sickened by the stench and evidence of the slaughter, Holman told the executive officer that they should thoroughly scour the turret before the *Iowa* returned to Norfolk and the relatives of the dead men saw it. Commander Morse agreed with Holman and gave him permission to paint over whatever he thought necessary.

One of the men who volunteered for Holman's cleanup detail was Gunner's Mate Third Class David Jones, who had spent the night hauling bodies out of the projectile decks and the powder flats. Medical personnel from the *Coral Sea* had run out of body bags, so Jones and the other men in the flats were issued black garbage bags. Jones was forced to put a human leg in one of these bags. "I had a hard time dealing with that," he said.

The 250 or so sailors assigned to Holman were instructed "to make the turret look as normal as possible." They swept, sponged down machinery, and painted accordingly. Some of the seamen pocketed souvenirs. One man stole the brass trigger from the turret officer's booth. Another pilfered a knob. Others carried items out and simply pitched them overboard. One boatswain's mate tossed a human foot into the ocean. Cletus Guffin disdainfully watched what was unfolding and told Meyer, "Here we're supposed to be having a big investigation, and they're throwing stuff over the side." And not only small items were being stripped from the turret. Meyer watched in disbelief as groups of sailors dragged huge steel plates and pieces of equipment back to the fantail, where it was all shoved or heaved overboard. Dale Mortensen said, "I was close to screaming my head off on the main deck about what they were doing."

One of the most meaningful pieces of evidence to vanish was the center gun's primer. Gunner's Mate Second Class John Keerl, Turret One's leading petty officer, used a screwdriver to disassemble the firing lock. He tapped out the cartridge. Inspecting it, he determined that it did not fire. He passed it to a gunner's mate standing behind him. Dale Mortensen, who was also present, said the primer accidentally dropped into a bilge (a repository for waste water, etc.). "There was a mess down there and nobody wanted to stick his hand in it," Mortensen said. When this particular bilge was pumped out later in the shipyard, a human hand was found blocking a drain, but there was no primer.

The executive officer wanted to train Turret Two back on the centerline of the *Iowa*, so the vessel would look "normal" when she steamed into Norfolk. He told Meyer and Mortensen to take care of this, and also to elevate the skewed center gun so that it matched the left and right guns. They balked, explaining that if they released the brakes and rotated the turret, they might crush some men.

THE MORNING after the accident, Captain Moosally and his senior officers correctly discerned that the Navy had no intention of permitting them to investigate the disaster themselves. Fred Moosally had his legal officer, Lieutenant Commander Richard Bagley, convene meetings with the officers in the wardroom and the enlisted supervisors in the first class petty officers' mess. Although Bagley would later claim that these assemblies concerned how to handle "the press when the ship got back to Norfolk," Terry McGinn and others who attended the meetings said the officers were told how to limit their testimony in the forthcoming investigation. McGinn said Bagley made no attempt at being subtle: "He told everybody what to say. It was a party line pure and simple."

Lieutenant Leo Walsh told Dan Meyer and Terry McGinn that if the Navy called him as a witness, he intended to keep his testimony to an absolute minimum: "These motherfuckers on the other side of the table [the investigators] have axes to grind, and they're after you."

Dan Meyer and Dale Mortensen were working in their turret and didn't attend Lieutenant Commander Bagley's sessions, so they were unaware that when their testimony was taken, they weren't supposed to let it all hang out.

Several hours after the explosion, the Chief of Naval Operations (CNO), Admiral Carl Trost, placed a moratorium on the firing of all sixteen-inch guns "until the investigation into the accident aboard USS *Iowa* is completed." Trost said he was taking this action to "preclude any possibility of a similar occurrence on the other [three] battleships." Rear Admiral Richard Milligan, a one-star group commander stationed in Charleston, South Carolina, was appointed by Vice Admiral Joseph S. Donnell, commander of Surface Forces Atlantic, to conduct "an informal one-officer" investigation of the *Iowa* disaster.

Admiral Milligan's investigation would be closely scrutinized and at times micromanaged from the Pentagon by an aggressive four-star admiral. The military calls this kind of interference with an official investigation "command influence," which is expressly forbidden by the Uniform Code of Military Justice and also by Navy Regulations. The man who had more influence on how the *Iowa* investigation was conducted than Admiral Milligan or anyone else in the Navy was Admiral Leon "Bud" Edney, Vice Chief of Naval Operations, the service's second highest ranking officer. The fifty-four-year-old Edney was a 1957 Annapolis graduate and highly decorated jet pilot who had flown numerous bombing missions over North Vietnam. He had also commanded the aircraft carrier USS *Constellation.*

Admiral Edney had served six tours in Washington, one of them as Chief of Naval Personnel, and had been a White House Fellow and commandant of midshipmen at Annapolis. He had a well-deserved reputation for being a ruthless political infighter. Admiral Trost, considered to be an ineffective administrator by many of the other four-star admirals, had ceded the day-to-day running of the Navy to Edney, who didn't wear his stars lightly or silently suffer fools.

Two admirals who worked for Edney said that as an aviator, the admiral really had no interest in what happened to the battleships in the aftermath of the *Iowa* explosion. He thought they were fossils. His attitude was—what do you expect when you play with fifty-year-old relics? But there was a hitch. Each of the battleships led a battle group commanded by a rear admiral. Scrap the four battleships (*Iowa*, *New Jersey*, *Missouri*, and *Wisconsin*), and you forfeited four flag officers and god knows how many cruisers, destroyers, frigates, oilers, and ammunition and supply ships that supported them.

It would be beneficial, then, if Admiral Milligan concluded that the battleships and their ammunition were safe. But, most important, this verdict would protect the reputation of the Navy. It would be a political and public-relations nightmare for the Navy if Milligan found that the Navy had knowingly allowed an unsafe ship to operate, permitted its sailors to fire hazardous guns and propellant, and subjected these same crewmen to unauthorized and risky experiments.

Admiral Edney would admit to making frequent phone calls to Vice Admiral Donnell, who had appointed Milligan to head the *Iowa* investigation. Donnell had the power to approve or disapprove of Milligan's findings. The surface forces commander willingly accepted Edney's suggestions about how to conduct the investigation and passed them on to "Rich" Milligan, according to Rear Admiral John E. "Ted" Gordon, the Navy's Deputy Judge Advocate General.

"I like Bud Edney, and I warned him about the dangers of 'command influence,' but he wouldn't listen. He constantly got Joe Donnell on the horn and told him exactly what to do," Gordon said. "He thought that there was no use in having rank, in being an admiral, if you couldn't tell your subordinates what to do. This totally undercut any kind of an independent inquiry. Milligan was nothing more than Edney's clone. Nobody who knows Rich thinks he has any independence or is in any way a technical expert on anything, especially gunnery."

8

☆

"Dropping the Bomb"

REAR ADMIRAL RICHARD Milligan took a helicopter out to the *Iowa* at 11 A.M. on April 20 while she was anchored fifteen miles off Roosevelt Roads, Puerto Rico. From the air, the seventeen-inch-thick steel turret appeared trained to starboard with its center gun canted downward like a broken toy. Milligan could see dungaree-clad sailors thronging around the turret, slapping haze-gray paint over burn marks.

Shortly after embarking from the helicopter, the admiral toured Turret Two to see for himself the destruction to the three gun rooms, the turret officer's booth, the electrical and mechanical decks, and the two projectile decks. He couldn't get into the powder flats, because that space was still partially flooded. He made no effort to halt the cleanup.

THE FIFTY-two-year-old Milligan had graduated from Annapolis in 1959. Stocky and bespectacled, with thinning sandy hair, he looked more like a finicky schoolmaster than a battle group commander. Although he had commanded five vessels, a small electronics craft, two destroyer escorts, a cruiser, and the battleship *New Jersey*, and was considered by his former boss, Vice Admiral Joseph Metcalf, to be "a first class ship handler," seamanship wasn't his primary interest. He took pride in being a "bean counter," and he had served six tours as a budget analyst or a comptroller.

He hoped to become the Navy's comptroller general, a three-star job, and officers who served with him say that he was always trimming his sails rather than saying something that might offend someone senior to him. Milligan once stumbled so badly that he nearly ruined his chances of attaining his goal. It happened off the coast of Lebanon in 1983-84, when he commanded the battleship *New Jersey*. She had been the first ship of her kind to emerge from mothballs and be recommissioned in late 1982 as part of Navy Secretary John Lehman's ambitious plan to increase the Navy's size and striking power. The overhauled *New Jersey*—the only battleship to fire her guns during the Vietnam War—ran into serious problems soon after she left the shipyard. Captain Bill Fogarty, the commanding officer, was on the bridge as the *New Jersey* inched southward down the California coastline to fire her guns for the first time. "The guns boomed, and all this shit, all of this electronics, tumbled to the deck from the bulkheads all over the place," Fogarty said. "Nothing had been hardened to withstand the concussion from the guns. We had this fancy phone system. And the first time we fired, we couldn't talk to anybody. We had fancy paneling, chandeliers. We fired, and they're gone. Fancy, sexy command-and-control gear. Boom! It blew apart!"

That was bad, but there was worse to come. Fred Ralston, a fire controlman assigned to forward main plot, noticed that while the ship was firing on the San Clemente, California, gunnery range, the velocity of the projectiles exiting the barrels was wildly erratic. Some projectiles left the muzzles traveling 120 feet per second faster and some 120 feet per second slower than the 1,725-feet per second norm for a 2,700-pound armor-piercing shell. Gunnery experts say that a deviation of only two or three feet per second is cause for alarm. The excessive deviation made it almost impossible for the *New Jersey* to aim her guns accurately. It also indicated that the powder could be unstable.

The *New Jersey*'s fire-control officer, Lieutenant Ken Conklin, determined that the accuracy of the guns degenerated even more when the ship shot at targets farther than 8,000 yards. Captain Fogarty informed Sea Systems Command about the defective powder, saying that the initial velocity (exit speed from the muzzle) sometimes varied by a whopping 300 feet per second. "I told them what was going on with the guns. They said they would work on it, but it didn't seem to be a big deal to them. I guess they expected the guns to work, because they had always worked."

The powder problems were not corrected in 1983. When the ship was in the Philippines and fired her sixteen-inch guns on the Tabones mountain range, Fred Ralston said she was beset by repeated misfires. "A lot of things were just not making sense. It was very surprising that we didn't have a serious accident on the *New Jersey*. We were lucky, very lucky."

In the fall of 1983, the *New Jersey* was ordered to transit the Panama Canal and head to Lebanon. Fogarty, who had been selected to become a rear admiral, sought to remain in command, but he was told to turn the ship over to Captain Richard Milligan once she reached the Caribbean. Fogarty said that before a hasty change-of-command ceremony on the forecastle, he informed Milligan about the unstable powder. It took twelve days, steaming at twenty-five knots, for the *New Jersey* to reach her destination. For the next two and a half months, the battleship ran tightly constricted rectangular patterns off Lebanon and Israel. Not once during this period, or even on her way to the Middle East, did she test-fire her guns.

A COUNTRY no larger than Connecticut, Lebanon had three million people and seventeen officially recognized religious sects. The United States had injected itself in 1982 into a civil war among Maronite Christians; the Druze, a sect that dominated a large section of Lebanon's central mountains; Sunni Muslims, mostly businessmen and wealthy families; and Shiite Muslims, the poor, many of whom were radical fundamentalists, making up about half of Lebanon's population. Syria, Iran, the Palestine Liberation Organization, and Israel were also involved, each backing one or more of the factions. The Reagan administration sent 1,200 Marines to Lebanon as part of a multinational peacekeeping force. The Marines were bivouacked on a flat coastal plain behind a thinly guarded perimeter near the Beirut airport, where Druze gunners in the Shouf Mountains overlooking the airport could easily rain down artillery shells on them.

Responding to calls for help from the Christian-dominated Lebanese Army, the Pentagon, in the early fall of 1983, ordered Navy destroyers and cruisers to fire their five-inch guns at Syrian-backed Druze militiamen. Following this bombardment, some of the Muslims decided to retaliate. At 6:22 A.M. on Sunday, October 23, 1983, a smiling, bearded Muslim driving a nineteen-ton yellow Mercedes-Benz truck sped through a barbed-wire obstacle at the U.S. Marines compound. The truck sped on, crashing into the central lobby of the four-story headquarters building, where the driver detonated a huge bomb. The explosion killed 241 Marines, wounding more than 100 others.

Navy Secretary John Lehman advocated using the *New Jersey*'s sixteen-inch guns to avenge the Marines' deaths. The Joint Chiefs of Staff agreed to let the battleship fire on December 14, 1983. Eleven 1,900-pound high-explosive shells were lobbed into the Shouf Mountains. There were no spotters in the air or on the ground to adjust where the shells fell. The results were pitiful. Tim McNulty, a *Chicago Tribune* correspondent based in Lebanon, said, "Everybody loved the *New Jersey* until she fired her guns. Once she fired, it was obvious that she couldn't hit anything."

Even after this failure, Milligan did nothing to get better powder so that the *New Jersey* could hit her targets the next time she was called upon to fire. She was cleared for another fire mission the afternoon of February 8, 1984. The targets—all located by satellite—were Druze and Syrian gun positions near a mountain village about fifteen miles east of Beirut. Again, no spotters were present. For eight hours, the *New Jersey* hurled nearly 300 sixteen-inch shells. She fired another thirteen shells on February 26 before heading back to her homeport in Long Beach, California. The results of these two missions were even worse than in December.

Marine Colonel Don Price, who had served in combat in Vietnam and was familiar with naval shore-fire bombardment practices, investigated the *New Jersey*'s gunnery in Lebanon and concluded that she missed her targets by as much as 10,000 yards (about six miles). Price was convinced that some of the *New Jersey*'s errant shells killed civilians living in the Shouf Mountains, although the Navy denied this. "You have a multimillion-dollar weapons system, and nobody knows how to put the rounds anywhere near the target," Price said.

ALTHOUGH THE Navy publicly claimed that the *New Jersey* hit her targets, the Chief of Naval Operations, Admiral James Watkins, thought otherwise. Watkins met with Rear Admiral Bill Fogarty and asked him if there had been a powder problem when he commanded the *New Jersey*. Fogarty said the initial velocity of the shells was often unpredictable. Watkins had a pained expression on his face.

The Vice Chief of Naval Operations requested retired Rear Admiral Ed Snyder, who had commanded the *New Jersey* in Vietnam, to look into what went wrong in Lebanon. Snyder discovered that the propellant had been rebagged after being blended in 500,000-pound vats. Before this occurred, powder "lots" (propellant that had been manufactured at the same time and place) had been strictly segregated. "It was my experience that all powder bags in the same lot burned at the same rate. As long as you fired from the same lot, you wouldn't experience any nasty surprises like erratic initial velocity," Snyder said. He rebuked some of the officers and civilian technicians at Sea Systems Command who were responsible for intermixing the powder, saying, "That's the dumbest thing I ever heard of. Do you have any idea of the damage you people have done? It's going to be virtually impossible ever to get those guns to shoot accurately again."

THE PERSON who was probably the most embarrassed by the *New Jersey*'s poor gunnery was Navy Secretary John Lehman. He had laid his professional reputation on the line in 1981 by assuring the Senate that he could reactivate the four *Iowa*-class battleships without any great inconvenience. It had not been easy for the Navy Secretary to sell the lawmakers on bringing back the timeworn vessels. The late Barry Goldwater, a Republican senator from Arizona, hooted, "Reviving old battleships is like trying to revitalize the Army by digging up old General Custer." The safety of the powder and shells was a major concern to the senators. However, after Lehman guaranteed that everything—ships, guns, missiles—would work as they should, the appropriations bill had passed by a vote of fifty-one to twenty-nine.

When news of the *New Jersey*'s wretched marksmanship leaked out, there was talk on Capitol Hill about killing the whole battleship program. Lehman begged for and received time to correct the powder problems. Once that was done, he said, the Navy would stage a gunnery demonstration in Vieques to prove that sixteen-inch guns were capable of hitting their targets. This would take place after the *Iowa* completed her overhaul in the shipyard in Pascagoula, Mississippi, and had a short shakedown cruise.

Although Lehman was galled by the *New Jersey*'s sorry show, according to one of his aides, he took no disciplinary action against Richard Milligan, because it would only make the Navy look worse. Milligan remained aboard the *New Jersey* as commanding officer for another year, at which point he was promoted to rear admiral. He became a battle group commander in 1987 and occasionally used the *Iowa* as his flagship.

To help him investigate the fatal explosion aboard the *Iowa*, Rear Admiral Richard Milligan brought three officers who had served under him on the *New Jersey* in Lebanon. The admiral's chief of staff was Captain Edward Messina, who had been the *New Jersey*'s weapons officer. Another *New Jersey* veteran was Lieutenant Benjamin Roper, who had been in charge of Turret One on that ship. Roper was proud of the fact that he had fired forty-eight rounds in Lebanon, and, shortly after arriving aboard the *Iowa*, he made sure that Dan Meyer knew that he had been hardened in combat. Meyer, who had just been promoted to lieutenant (junior grade), wasn't impressed and told Roper that the forty-eight rounds he had shot aboard the *New Jersey* was pitiful compared to Meyer's 320 aboard the *Iowa*. The third old hand from the *New Jersey* was Lieutenant Commander Timothy Quinn. Unlike Captain Messina and Lieutenant Roper, Quinn was a much calmer individual who treated the *Iowa*'s officers with respect.

Milligan's legal counsel, Commander Ronald Swanson, was already on the *Iowa* when the admiral arrived. Swanson, who had participated in the Navy's shallow investigation of the USS *Vincennes*'s 1988 shoot-down of an Iranian airliner, was aboard the *Iowa*, serving on Vice Admiral Johnson's staff, when Turret Two blew up. He was assigned to the Milligan investigation by the Atlantic Fleet's legal officer, Captain Ed Ellis. Two Navy lawyers, junior to Swanson, were also appointed.

During the twenty-three hours from the explosion until Admiral Milligan and the other team members arrived on the *Iowa*, Swanson, by his own admission, was aware that "potential evidence" from Turret Two was being pitched over the side. Although he had an advanced degree in criminal justice and had been a prosecutor for years, he did nothing to stop what was going on.

Given the number of *Iowa* crewmen who had been killed in the blast, and the damage inflicted upon the *Iowa*, many active-duty and retired flag officers believed that a panel of three to five admirals would have been more appropriate than Milligan's "informal one-officer" investigation. In fact, the Navy's JAG (Judge Advocate General) manual encouraged a formal panel of this sort any time a large loss of life was involved. Warren Nelson, longtime staff director of the House Armed Services Committee's Investigations

Subcommittee, was adamantly opposed to an "informal" format. "The only thing for which I would use a one-officer investigation would be to find a lost mop on a ship," Nelson said. "Informal" meant that testimony was not necessarily taken under oath; witnesses weren't advised of their rights; defense attorneys weren't present; and no one could be charged with a crime no matter what the evidence revealed.

In addition, Admiral Milligan's appointment order, signed by Vice Admiral Donnell, enjoined him from pursuing one line of inquiry, stating, "No opinion may be expressed concerning the line of duty and misconduct status of deceased members." In other words, Milligan was forbidden to accuse anyone who died in Turret Two of causing the accident. According to Commander Swanson, that April 27, 1989, order was never modified.

Admiral Milligan hadn't been aboard the *Iowa* long when he heard that Master Chief Skelley had been conducting powder experiments in Turret Two when the explosion occurred. The admiral had authorized similar experiments when he had been on the ship in November 1987 during a European deployment. Skelley had approached Commander Gene Kocmich, the weapons officer back then, and requested permission to fire five bags of D-846 powder with each 2,700-pound shell. Kocmich had told Skelley this combination was illegal and denied his request in no uncertain terms.

Shortly after that, Kocmich flew back to the United States on a two-week leave. Skelley then went to Captain Larry Seaquist with the same request. Seaquist, unaware that his weapons officer had previously refused permission, told Skelley that he would approve the experiment only if Admiral Milligan, the battle group commander, concurred. Milligan agreed to the experiments, and they went forward without a hitch. When Kocmich returned and learned what Skelley had done, he was ready to skin the chief alive. He emphatically forbade Skelley never again to conduct any unlawful experiments; as long as Kocmich was weapons officer, Skelley obeyed the rules.

A number of military-law experts say that once Admiral Milligan became aware of the powder experiments on April 19, he should have informed his superiors that he had previously been involved in analogous experiments on the *Iowa*. And either he should have recused himself from the investigation or Admiral Donnell should have dismissed him. Milligan never told Admiral Edney of this potential conflict of interest.

WHILE ADMIRAL Milligan was examining Turret Two, the bodies of the dead *Iowa* crewmen were being loaded on a mammoth Air Force C-5A Galaxy cargo plane squatting on the runway at Roosevelt Roads. Eight honor guardsmen shifted the metal coffins from dark blue Chevrolet vans to the plane's cargo bay. A color guard, consisting of two sailors in dress whites and three Marines in dress blues, stood rigidly near the ramp of the aircraft, carrying the Navy, Marine Corps, and United States flags, which fluttered in the balmy Caribbean winds. When the last casket was positioned and secured for the journey, the doors were shut and the plane turned on its engines, taxied, and lifted off for a four-hour flight to the military mortuary in Dover, Delaware.

Six-man teams of sailors and 500 onlookers were on hand when the plane landed in Dover. As the teams of pallbearers respectfully bore the flag-draped caskets to an open hangar, a military band played the Navy hymn. Navy Secretary Will Ball, who had visited the *Iowa* off the Vieques gunnery range the previous fall and inspected Turret Two, had traveled to Dover to pay tribute to the men who had died. "I had sailed with them and had crawled around their turret, shaken their greasy hands, felt the strong, sure grip that only a gunner's mate can give, seen the ready grins on their faces, and watched the steady rough way they went about their work," Ball said. "They were good sailors. Their deaths were a jolting reminder of the dangers faced by those who freely make that choice and serve at sea." He walked to the front of the coffins, knelt on the rough concrete floor, and bowed his head in silent prayer.

The Dover facility was the largest military mortuary on the East Coast, handling twenty to thirty bodies per week. Sixty-two military pathologists and FBI technicians began their grim work as soon as the services concluded and the dignitaries departed. In a third of the cases, they had to match body parts with torsos. Fifty-one body bags had been flown off the *Iowa*, yet Navy public-relations officers were claiming that they were "almost positive" that there had been forty-seven victims. The FBI did not want to release any of the bodies for burial until all of them had been positively identified, but the Navy insisted on releasing the remains, even though the identities of some of them had not been established by DNA testing before they were interred.

MANY HOURS before the bodies of the dead *Iowa* sailors were loaded on the jumbo transport for the trip to Dover, bleak-faced Navy teams fanned out across the country to notify parents, spouses, children, and siblings that they had most likely lost their loved ones in Turret Two. Their messages were often deliberately ambiguous, because there was as yet no substantive proof of who had been killed in the blast. The Navy was speculating.

At 4:45 A.M. Pacific time on the day following the explosion, four somber junior officers drove up to Dale and Darleen Schelin's home in Coast Mesa, California, forty miles southeast of Los Angeles, in a white official Navy vehicle. The Schelins had been up until 2 A.M. watching television and praying that their twenty-year-old son Geoff had not been one of those killed on the battleship. When the officers knocked on their front door, Darleen looked out her bedroom window and saw the uniformed group fidgeting on the doorstep. "My heart sank. I knew what they were going to tell me. I screamed and fell down on the floor," she said. One of the officers read from the prepared statement, which said, "We regret to inform you that your son, Gunner's Mate Third Class Geoffrey S. Schelin, is missing and presumed dead." They said they couldn't answer any questions and departed, promising to return when they had more information.

At the time this heart-wrenching tableau was taking place, no positive identification had been made of Geoff's body. The Schelins, a tight-knit Mormon family, had been happy when their son signed up for a four-year hitch in the Navy in 1987. "He was good looking and could charm the bark off the trees," his father said, "but he was also the most difficult of the nine children we had to raise. We went head-to-head several times, and he almost didn't graduate from high school, even though he was very smart."

Geoff told his mother that he had enlisted "to get some discipline in my life." He had first been assigned to the aircraft carrier *Coral Sea* and then arranged a transfer to the *Iowa* because he wanted "to shoot those guns" and believed the carrier was "a rust bucket."

After the *Iowa* returned from the exercises in the Caribbean, Geoff had been planning to drive his Honda cross-country for two weeks of leave with his parents, brothers and sisters, and many friends and former schoolmates. He had matured in the Navy and had recently informed his father that after his enlistment was up, he wanted to work in the family business of rehabilitating and reselling foreclosed property. He also wanted to go to college.

Four Navy officers returned at 10 A.M. that same day and said that Geoff's death "has been confirmed." He had been identified by the stenciling on his uniform and his military ID card. In addition, several of his shipmates recognized his body.

AT 7 A.M. central time, a Navy chaplain and another officer appeared at the door of the two-story bungalow belonging to Mrs. Dorothy Williams and her daughter, Linda Williams, in Elgin, Illinois, a Chicago suburb. Dorothy was the grandmother and Linda the aunt of Boatswain's Mate Second Class Michael Williams. They had helped raise Michael, and both regarded him as a son. The two women had spent a sleepless night—reclining on couches, catching snippets of television news about the explosion, and being worried sick about Michael. As the two officers climbed the twelve steps leading to the front door, Linda screamed, "They're here! They're here!" "Who's here?" her mother asked. "It's just like in the movies," Linda said, "the men in white hats are here."

Linda unlocked the front door, regarded the two officers in white hats with trepidation, and said, "I don't even want to let you in here." "You have to let us in," the chaplain said. "Please let us in." After a lengthy pause, the officer accompanying the chaplain announced, "We regret to inform you that Boatswain's Mate Second Class Michael Robert Williams was killed in Turret Two on the battleship USS *Iowa*." The officers said Michael had been identified by the tattoos of girls on his body. They had precious little else to say, except that they were sorry about what had happened to Michael and would be back in touch about funeral arrangements.

After the Navy men left, the two women discussed their tall, twenty-one-year-old grandson and nephew. They remembered his thick, wavy, often tousled auburn hair, and the fact that he never wanted to hurt anyone's feelings. His tattoos had once been topless, but he had had tops added so they wouldn't offend anyone, especially his grandmother and aunt. He'd loved to tinker with cars and drag-race his souped-up 1967 Chevelle.

AT 7 A.M. eastern time, another white Navy van entered the driveway of Mrs. Lucille Young in Rock Hill, South Carolina. Mrs. Young was the mother of Seaman John Rodney Young. She turned off the television, glanced out the window, and saw two officers get out of the van and begin trudging toward her home. "I didn't want to open the screen door," she said. "I thought if I could keep them out, then it wouldn't be so." But she couldn't keep them at bay, and after some hemming and hawing, they informed her that her twenty-one-year-old son had "presumably died" in Turret Two.

Less than an hour after they left, Red Cross workers in Columbia, South Carolina, told Rodney Young's stepmother, Mrs. Mary Coleman Chambers, that he was dead. "I went into denial, I didn't believe it," Mrs. Chambers said. Rodney had been a timid thirteen-year-old when his father, John Willie Chambers, brought him to Columbia to live with his new wife, Mary. Rodney had joined the Navy when he was eighteen, planning to make it a career and hoping to become a Navy commando, a SEAL. He had informed his family that all was not right in Turret Two, but he had offered no details. He'd been home a month before the explosion and told his family, "If anything happens to me, I don't want anybody to wear black. Wear white. I don't want anybody to mourn over me."

AT 6 A.M. eastern time, yet another of the Navy's white vans rolled into the driveway of Alvin and Mai-Anh Adams's home in Alexandria, Virginia, outside Washington. A Navy chaplain and a warrant officer gently tapped on the Adamses' front door. They were admitted and told the stunned couple that their twenty-five-year-old Vietnamese-born adopted son, Fire Controlman Third Class Tung Thanh Adams, had died in the turret explosion. Although he was practically felled by sorrow, Al Adams was a career State Department officer, and he could empathize with these two uniformed emissaries. There had been times when duty had required him to be in the same position. Since he was an attorney, it was in character for Adams to ask the officers a stream of questions, which they politely deflected.

Tung Adams had astonished his parents in late 1986 when he told them he was going to enlist in the Navy. He said he wanted to see the world, learn more about electronics, and serve his adoptive country. He was often seasick, but he stuck it out and became a capable fire controlman. "I think he realized the risks of working with those big guns. He was a gentle boy in a rough business," his father said.

SOME OF the *Iowa* families received their grim news in a packed gymnasium located on the Norfolk, Virginia, Naval Base. More than 300 people milled around the gym all through the night following the disaster. Rear Admiral Jimmy Pappas, the base commander, had to locate about ten families in the anxious crowd and tell them that there was almost no hope that their relatives had survived. "How do you find the needles in the haystack? Emotions ran high," Pappas said.

Reluctantly, he decided to have the names of the families he was seeking announced over the public-address system. Chaplains then led those who answered the pages into private rooms in the rear of the gym and broke their hearts. This process was called "dropping the bomb."

A chaplain "dropped the bomb" on Mary Ogden at 1:30 A.M. He walked over to the twenty-six-year-old wife of Gunner's Mate Third Class Darin Ogden and said that he needed to have a talk with her. She followed him to one of the rooms in the rear, where he told her her husband was "presumed dead."

Ogden, twenty-four, had worked in the powder flats, and at the time the chaplain spoke with Mary, the flats were still flooded, so the bodies had not been removed, much less identified. Mary and Darin had been high-school sweethearts in Shelbyville, Indiana. She couldn't believe he was dead. He had taken her on several tours of the ship. "It seemed so safe," she said.

9

☆

"Your Best Witnesses Are All Dead."

THE NAVY'S FORMIDABLE public-relations apparatus revved up the day after the explosion. Two "flacks" from Washington, Captain Paul Hanley and Lieutenant Commander Steve Burnett, flew to Roosevelt Roads to assist Vice Admiral Jerome Johnson at a press conference. While Hanley prepared Admiral Johnson, Burnett supervised the dubbing of four one-minute copies of the amateur videotape shot by Lieutenant Commander Elton Kelly, a Second Fleet staff officer, as the blast ripped apart the inside of Turret Two. Burnett was going to give them to CNN and the three other major television networks, but first he had to edit them. For instance, when the turret exploded, Kelly had yelled, "Holy shit!" That expletive was deleted.

About a hundred reporters swarmed over the Roosevelt Roads naval base, begging to get on the *Iowa*. Captain Hanley turned them down, claiming that the crewmen were not emotionally ready yet to deal with newsmen. He offered Admiral Johnson as a substitute. While Johnson made it clear that he was not an expert on battleships, he downplayed the danger the fires and the flooding of the turret and magazines had posed to the *Iowa*. Insisting that "there was no confusion at all," he then added, "The team was qualified that was operating the guns. They had undergone a rigorous training program and recently had undergone inspection." He dismissed out of hand a suggestion that the advanced age of the battleship and the gunpowder could have had anything to do with the explosion. According to Johnson, the Navy had "no firm idea" of what had caused the blast.

Another press conference took place in the Pentagon at about the same time. Captain Larry Seaquist, who had left as commanding officer of the *Iowa* almost a year earlier, faced print and broadcast reporters gathered in the Secretary of Defense's briefing room and conducted a tutorial on how to load and fire sixteen-inch guns. Seaquist compared the turret to a seven-story building that weighed about the same as a World War II destroyer. When asked how the explosion could have happened, Seaquist replied, "We simply don't know." Why had there been so many deaths? He had no explanation. "There has never been an *Iowa*-class battleship accident. We've never had this happen."

ABOUT THE same time that Larry Seaquist was holding his press conference, retired Rear Admiral Ed Snyder drove to the Pentagon in his white diesel-powered Volkswagen Jetta sedan, heading south along the George Washington Memorial Parkway. The former commanding officer of the battleship *New Jersey* was engrossed in what he'd seen on television and read in the newspaper about the turret explosion on the *Iowa*. Considered by many to be the foremost authority on sixteen-inch gunnery in or outside the Navy, Snyder believed that he could help whoever was investigating the *Iowa* explosion, perhaps even head up the inquiry himself. He was certainly qualified, and he expected that his opinions would be accorded the weight they deserved by the officers in the Navy's surface warfare section, which he was planning to visit that day. After all, he had been instrumental in a successful campaign to persuade Congress to reactivate the battleships in 1981 and had been asked by the Navy to look into the *New Jersey*'s poor gunnery in Lebanon.

Snyder had been a member of the board that selected Carl Trost to become an admiral. Trost, the current CNO, was a nuclear submariner, and Snyder was an esteemed nuclear weapons designer. The CNO and Snyder were friends who respected each other's intellectual achievements. A courtly, slender man who hated hats and invariably had a lock of dark hair cascading over his forehead, Snyder was a legend among surface sailors. The 5,866 sixteen-inch rounds fired by the *New Jersey* in Vietnam meant that he had directed more shelling in combat than any other living battleship captain. By contrast, the *New Jersey* shot one-tenth of that during World War II. The son of a Methodist minister, Snyder entered Annapolis when he was sixteen and graduated in 1944 when he was nineteen. After he was commissioned, he was assigned to the twenty-nine-year-old battleship USS *Pennsylvania*, which had been badly damaged during the Japanese attack on Pearl Harbor. Snyder was on the bridge the night of October 24-25, 1944, serving as tactical watch officer, when the *Pennsylvania* and five other elderly battleships sank two Japanese battleships steaming down the Surigao Strait in the Philippines. It was the last engagement between opposing battleships.

After the war, Snyder served back-to-back tours in the gunnery departments of the heavy cruisers *Toledo* and *Macon*. He then designed and assembled atomic warheads, depth charges, and artillery and naval shells at the Los Alamos National Laboratory in New Mexico. He was gunnery officer of the destroyer USS *Holder* and earned a master's degree in nuclear physics from the Massachusetts Institute of Technology. His first command was a destroyer escort, a radar picket ship, which sat in the turbulent waters of the North Atlantic for a month at a time, scanning the horizon for possible incoming Russian bombers. The weather was so rough that Snyder was forced to strap on a canvas harness before he got in his bunk to keep from being flung to the deck during the night.

After that, Snyder helped design the nuclear warhead that went on the submarine-launched Polaris fleet ballistic missile. He then commanded a destroyer, USS *Brownson*, during the Cuban missile crisis. When his command of the *Brownson* was over, Snyder didn't get to go back to sea for five years. He spent that time in the Pentagon as a deputy to the Assistant Secretary of the Navy for Research and Development and became a recognized authority on oceanography and underwater engineering.

WHEN SNYDER first came aboard the *New Jersey* in drydock in the Philadelphia Naval Shipyard on January 12, 1968, he was startled by what a mess she was. Her hull had already been sandblasted and painted; her propellers had been replaced; and her eight boilers had been fired and tested. Some work had been done. However, he thought that he and his crew were going to have to work around the clock to get her out of the yard for engineering sea trials, which were scheduled in less than three months. He looked on her as the biggest challenge of his career.

He was surprised that the guns and shells were in such good shape, but the powder was another matter. Visiting ammunition storage facilities around the country, he often gagged when powder canisters were opened and the unmistakable aroma of ether wafted out, indicating that the powder had chemically deteriorated. When some of the powder bags were pulled from the canisters, the silk covering crumbled from rot.

He requisitioned powder lots that seemed to be in the best shape, and he had acquired a huge supply of brass needles and bolts of virgin raw silk, so that the sailors could sew up split bags. He purchased a portable "oven" to burn powder granules to check their stability. And he had a Doppler radar installed to measure the velocity of the projectiles as they exited the barrels.

He knew that barrel erosion was going to be a big headache. The Navy found out during World War II and the Korean War that the rifling in the sixteen-inch barrels wore out after firing just 290 armor-piercing shells. Changing a barrel at sea was impossible; even in a shipyard, it was a daunting task. Snyder heard about some newly developed titanium dioxide wrappers that could be tied around the powder bags and virtually eliminate barrel erosion. So he got his hands on several bales of them. The waxlike substance in the wrappers melted as the powder burned, forming a protective coating that allowed the projectiles to practically slide out of the barrels without impairing the rifling.

Forced to resort to "hook and crook" to obtain spare parts, Snyder nevertheless got the *New Jersey* out of the yard on schedule and began steaming to Vietnam, arriving in the South China Sea in late 1968.

Once in the Tonkin Gulf near the nineteenth parallel, the battleship blasted away with her sixteen-inch guns at coastal artillery batteries located in caves on Hon Matt Island, near the port city of Vinh. As her shells impacted on the island, a Navy airborne spotter radioed, "You've blown away a large slice of the island, it's down in the ocean!" Stories about the "island sinking" received wide play around the world.

The *New Jersey* was popular with "grunts" (Marine and Army infantrymen) and saved a forty-two-man Marine outpost, located just a thousand yards south of the DMZ, from annihilation by 130 North Vietnamese troops on February 23, 1969. At 1:06 A.M., the ship received a cry for help. She responded with two five-inch mounts, then with four, and finally five. Snyder shifted the ship's position during the night to rotate the firing between the port and starboard five-inch batteries. A ring of steel steadily dropped around the outpost for five and a half hours. Some 1,710 shells were expended. There was never time to cool off the guns, which had long strips of gray paint peeling off their barrels the next morning.

In the early morning hours of April 1, 1969, the *New Jersey* completed her time on the "gun line." Despite the fact that the Navy had promised to deploy Snyder and the *New Jersey* back to Vietnam for another tour, on the rainy afternoon of December 17, 1969, at the Bremerton, Washington, Naval Shipyard, the *New Jersey* left active service for the third time in twenty-six years. Undersecretary of the Navy John Warner had planned to attend the decommissioning ceremony, but he had been discouraged from doing so by the Navy's public-relations people, who said the service wanted the *New Jersey* to "go quietly and attract as little attention as possible." Twelve years later, Warner, by then a Republican senator from Virginia, advocated recommissioning the *New Jersey* and the other three *Iowa*-class ships. He startled his colleagues by disclosing that he had been personally ordered by the Nixon White House to get rid of the *New Jersey* in 1969 "because she was impeding the peace negotiations" with North Vietnam.

After Snyder left the *New Jersey*, he became chief of staff of the Atlantic Fleet's Cruiser/Destroyer Force, based in Newport, Rhode Island. He was then promoted to rear admiral and served as the Navy's oceanographer for six years. Retiring from the Navy in 1979, Snyder undertook projects for the National Academy of Sciences and worked for George Washington University.

When Snyder reached OP 03, on the fourth deck of the Pentagon, the Navy's surface warfare section, he was told that Vice Admiral John Nyquist, the chief of surface warfare, would be away all morning. The admiral's aide said that the Navy had already selected Admiral Richard Milligan to direct the *Iowa* investigation and offered to take Snyder up one deck to be briefed by the *Iowa*'s former executive officer, Captain Mike Fahey, and to review some of the recent messages from the *Iowa*.

Studying the messages, Snyder learned that the center gun in Turret Two had not been fired before the explosion. That meant it was a "cold gun," thus eliminating smoldering debris as the culprit. He also discovered that the four-inch-thick steel tail hatch had been blown off and bounced overboard. That startled him. It was hard to comprehend the pressure it must have taken to snap steel bolts three quarters of an inch thick.

The number of casualties also astounded him. Snyder had been trained to believe that a blast on an *Iowa*-class vessel would be contained within an individual gun room. It amazed him that the fireball and concussion had ripped through the other two gun rooms, then into the turret officer's booth and down the trunk to the powder flats. According to messages from the ship, the three gun rooms had "totally disintegrated." Snyder noted that the left gun in Turret One had experienced eight misfires and that the ship's captain had attempted to load and fire three guns in Turret Two while he still had a fouled bore in Turret One. Unbelievable! Fahey asked Snyder what caused the explosion. "You're in a never-never land now. Your best witnesses are all dead," the retired admiral said.

Fahey gave Snyder a card and a telephone number to call if he had any additional questions or thoughts. As he left the Pentagon, Snyder was aware that he had received a polite brush-off. He didn't know why that had happened. He was disappointed and thought about calling Admiral Trost, the CNO, but he didn't. However, this was not to be Admiral Snyder's last involvement with the *Iowa* case.

SOON AFTER Admiral Richard Milligan arrived on the *Iowa*, word was passed on the 1MC public-address system that anyone who had information about the explosion should muster in the passageway outside the legal office. A queue of more than one hundred officers and men soon formed. That was more people than Lieutenant Commander Richard Bagley, the legal officer, could handle. His work space was only slightly larger than a broom closet, and his two assistants, Legalmen First Class Robert Kenneth Morrison and Michael Helton, had been killed in Turret Two.

Captain Ed Messina, Milligan's chief of staff, wandered up the passageway outside Bagley's office, eyed the snaking line of potential witnesses with displeasure, and told Bagley to pick out twenty or thirty and get rid of the rest. Some of the men were turned away outright. Others were dismissed after writing out unsworn statements. Of the men who were rejected, most were never interviewed.

The admiral and his staff met in Captain Fred Moosally's sea cabin below the bridge and took testimony from fourteen witnesses on April 20. They heard from the men who had escaped from Turret Two's magazines and annular space. Kendall Truitt was one of the first witnesses called. The twenty-one-year-old third class gunner's mate described Master Chief Skelley's experiment, which was being attempted when the center gun exploded. "Master Chief Skelley likes experimenting a lot. He coordinates a lot of the gun shoots," Truitt said. He explained that this was not the first time Skelley had been involved in such an experiment on the *Iowa*. The admiral asked who had authorized the experiment. Truitt wasn't sure where Skelley obtained his authority.

Truitt testified that the entire center gun crew was inexperienced, especially the gun captain, Errick Lawrence, and the rammerman, Robert Backherms. Calling Backherms "kind of a weird guy," he added, "He [Backherms] had a problem looking you in the eye when you talked to him and it kind of made you wonder. He wasn't really a competent person and Lawrence intimidated him a lot, anyway. Lawrence was a type of guy that was very nervous and, when he was nervous, he'd yell a little." The officers were impressed with Truitt's intelligence, his facility with words, and his clean-cut appearance.

JOHN MULLAHY, the third class gunner's mate from Boston who helped eleven colleagues to safety from the bottom of the burning turret, told the panel of hearing Errick Lawrence screaming over the sound-powered phones about having a problem. "Lawrence was a very excitable person," Mullahy testified. The eighteen-year veteran told about helping the damage-control assistant, Lieutenant Blackie, flood the magazines. Mullahy explained that he had picked up Blackie after he had collapsed from smoke inhalation and carried him to safety. Mullahy also disclosed that Turret Two's sprinkler system "was trashed" and had been that way for a number of months.

Boatswain's Mate Second Class Robert Burch, who had been in charge of the annular space, testified that he heard Senior Chief Reggie Ziegler remark on the sound-powered phones, "Left gun is loaded. Good job. Center gun has some trouble." There was a lag of approximately five minutes, and then the explosion jolted the turret. Burch pressed the button on his phones and yelled, "Explosion in the powder flats!" He received no response from anyone. Seaman Recruit Cecil Croft, who worked for Burch, said that prior to the explosion, he had not been taught to handle ammunition. Seaman Patrick Shedd, who had nearly died in the annular space with Croft and Burch, said the center powder hoist had been broken since 1987. Chief Ziegler was aware of the problem but had not repaired it. According to Shedd, the center hoist operator on April 19, Boatswain's Mate Second Class Gary Fisk, was "new on board" and didn't know how to control the hoist, which malfunctioned on a fairly regular basis.

Seaman Recruit Donovan Housley, who had been on the *Iowa* four months and was assigned to the magazines April 19, told Admiral Milligan and his staff how panicked he had been when "the big explosion" boomed above him. "Truitt started yelling, saying, 'Get the powder bags back in the canisters!' That's when I was kind of scared. I never heard Truitt yell before, so we started putting the powder bags back in the canisters, and Petty Officer Mullahy went to investigate and to see what was going on. When he came back he told us to get out of there as quick as we could." Housley also stated that he'd never received any formal training.

Seaman Apprentice Harry Freeman was assigned to the magazines with Housley. Freeman was upset because some members of the *Iowa*'s crew were saying that the accident had occurred because the men in Turret Two "were playing grab-ass and not paying attention to what they were doing." Absolutely untrue, he said. "There is never any level of complacency in the turrets, because everybody is very, very aware of the potential for death and destruction that the weapons have."

Seaman Recruit Carlos Washington said that he was working in the magazines for the first time during an actual gun shoot. At the conclusion of Washington's brief testimony, Commander Swanson, Admiral Milligan's legal officer, asked the sailor if he had any questions. "How old should the gunpowder be before they get rid of it?" Washington inquired. "We are going to try to develop all the information. Okay?" Swanson replied.

Commander Swanson asked Seaman Apprentice Frank Gerstenslager, another one of the twelve men who had escaped from the base of the turret, if there was anything he wanted to say. "The only thing I know is that I lost all my friends and nobody knows why," the sailor replied. Milligan called the accident "very unfortunate" and said he could sympathize with him. Gerstenslager looked intently at the admiral and said, "I would like to talk to you about the *Iowa* and the sheet that was just printed. I don't think that it was accurate." "What are you talking about?" Swanson asked. Gerstenslager excused himself and walked out into the passageway to obtain an April 20 Associated Press story. When he returned, Swanson wanted to know what was wrong with the story. "I feel like this accident was not mishandling of ammunition, because our turret was so careful about ammunition handling," Gerstenslager said. "We took it easy with bags. We were extremely careful. I feel that is wrong and they shouldn't print it." "That is the purpose of this investigation," the admiral replied. "It's really to put on record what we really believe is the cause of the accident. The press will undoubtedly speculate. We will try to set that straight in time."

Chief J.C. Miller of Turret Three said his center and right guns were prepared to fire four-bag powder loads. The powder hoist on his left gun was smashed, putting the gun out of action. Admiral Milligan asked Miller whether, if he were disturbed about the lack of training of the gun crews, he would raise the issue at a pre-fire briefing with the gunnery and weapons officers. Miller, who wasn't even properly trained himself, said that he would raise the issue. "If you go through the records, we get a lot of [technical] school flunkies," Miller said, adding that there was considerable concern "that the sixteen-inch gun system was a dumping ground for unqualified gunner's mates."

DAN MEYER and Dale Mortensen testified on April 21. Neither man had attended the preparatory sessions conducted by the ship's legal officer, Lieutenant Commander Richard Bagley, so they didn't know that they were supposed to limit what they said. Meyer had been performing maintenance in the bottom of his turret and showed up for his testimony inappropriately attired in blue coveralls smeared with hydraulic fluid and oil. The verbal fisticuffs began to fly when Meyer conceded that he had had an officer (Ensign Garrett) in his turret taking orders from a first class petty officer (Dale Mortensen). Such arrangements were discouraged in the United States Navy.

Meyer testified that when he attended the battleship conference in Washington three weeks before the explosion, he had been stunned to learn that the Navy was unaware that the *Iowa* was "running a real research and development program." Admiral Milligan inquired if the research program was "a Master Chief Skelley program." It was strictly Skelley's operation, Meyer said. He gave Milligan a summary of Skelley's long-range gunnery experiment at Vieques the previous January. "Excuse my French, but, as turret officer, I was scared shitless to do that DX-149 (long-range) shoot. The guns had never been fired at such a level of over-pressure." Meyer called Skelley's experiments "kitchen-sink research and development," a term coined by Senior Chief Ziegler.

He said that Captain Fred Moosally and the weapons officer, Commander Kissinger, allowed Skelley to "do his thing" without interference or supervision. Captain Messina instructed the stenographer to stop typing and took Meyer out into the passageway. "You little shit, you can't say that!" Messina, a short, white-haired man, roared. "The admiral doesn't want to hear another word about experiments!"

At this point, Meyer knew that he had stepped into a hornet's nest and thought that he might end up becoming one of Admiral Milligan's targets. He was very glad that he had written the weapons officers a memo more than six months earlier, detailing the problems with the sixteen-inch guns. That memo might be the only thing standing between him and a court-martial.

When a chastened Meyer reappeared in the inquiry room, Admiral Milligan asked him why he had been on the bridge and not in his turret when the explosion occurred. Meyer said he was on the duty roster and had a number of petty officers fully qualified to fill in as turret captain. Mortensen had served as turret captain many times before.

He said that none of the *Iowa*'s three sixteen-inch turrets routinely connected their fire hoses to the "jumper hose" before a gunshot. The Navy's gunnery manual requires that the connection be made and the lines pressurized before the turrets could fire, but for some unknown reason, the *Iowa* didn't follow the rules. He was asked about where the various men were supposed to be assigned in Turret Two the day of the explosion. He said that Jack Thompson had been the left gun captain. "I know that [Errick] Lawrence was debuting that day as gun captain, center gun, and I believe that [Matt] Price was right gun captain."

He said he also informed Admiral Milligan where Clayton Hartwig's body had been discovered in the gun pit after the blast, but when he later obtained a copy of his testimony, he discovered that some of what he had said had either been expunged or never been transcribed, including what he had said about the location of Hartwig's body.

Meyer told Milligan that when he, Dale Mortensen, and the Turret One gun captains reached Turret Two's projectile decks almost twelve hours after the explosion, they confronted some ghastly sights. He described his two nerve-racking trips to the base of Turret Two and told the admiral about the bags that were on fire in the powder flats and the horror he experienced when he saw the sailors' bodies entangled in fire hoses in the flats. On the projectile decks, he said, "There were life preservers, looked like they had been used as pillows, and there was a Walkman, looked like somebody had kicked back to listen to the Walkman, and some sunglasses and some books," he said. The dead men there had loaded the projectiles and they had stretched out, expecting to spend the next two hours of the shoot doing as little as possible.

Meyer had handed over Turret Two's training records to Admiral Milligan's aide, Lieutenant Chip Buckley, that morning, but he inspected them first. The documents revealed: "They [Senior Chief Reggie Ziegler and Lieutenant Phil Buch] were miserable recordkeepers. They had training files of people who had left five years ago."

After completing his testimony, Meyer sought out Dale Mortensen and told him to be careful about what he said, because Milligan and his officers had a hidden agenda. Mortensen informed Admiral Milligan of the eight misfires that Cletus Guffin had experienced in his left gun in Turret One. He said that he was notifying forward main battery plot that he still had a fouled bore when he heard Chief Hickman tell Turret Two to load all three guns and simultaneously fire them. After recounting how his friend Ernie Hanyecz had called his name three times just seconds before the explosion, he slumped back into his chair and rubbed his eyes. Commander Swanson called a brief recess. When Mortensen recovered his composure, he speculated that the explosion might have been caused by ramming the powder into the chamber too far and too fast.

The thirteen-year Navy veteran said, "Something, I think, distracted that rammer operator. I really do." He indicated that friction or static electricity also could have caused the blast. The polyurethane foam wrappers surrounding the powder bags "were as rough as sandpaper" and could easily generate sparks. And there was another possibility. Maybe Errick Lawrence didn't have the gas ejection air on? The admiral didn't debate that point with Mortensen. In fact, Milligan said another witness had corroborated the fact that the gas ejection air had not been on when Lawrence opened the breech. If that were so, Mortensen said, Reggie Ziegler would have had to send someone down into the gun pit to twist open the air valve. "What's to say while he was down there turning the valve on, what's to say that somebody else didn't step on the platform, spin the cradle, and ram the projectile and go into the sequence of a loading." This was the scenario that Mortensen had described to Dan Meyer on the day of the explosion, except that he didn't tell Admiral Milligan that Clayton Hartwig was the person Chief Ziegler had sent down into the pit.

The panel didn't finish with Mortensen until 10:16 P.M., and by the time he was through, he was convinced that Meyer had been correct about these officers having an agenda. They certainly weren't interested in hearing anything that suggested the equipment or the propellant might have been at fault. He noticed that during his testimony, the stenographer's tape frequently was turned off, and when he received a copy of his transcript, he discovered, like Meyer, that much of what he had said had either been edited out or gone unrecorded.

For some reason, Admiral Milligan's panel initially had decided not to talk to Brian Scanio or the other firemen who had been the first sailors to enter the burning turret. These men then bitterly complained to their division officer, Lieutenant George Anderson. Concerned about these men—some of whom were experiencing terrible nightmares and displaying symptoms of post-traumatic stress syndrome—Anderson escorted the firemen down to the *Iowa*'s legal officer, Lieutenant Commander Richard Bagley. "These are the guys who know exactly where the bodies were found," Anderson informed Bagley. "They ought to be allowed to testify." The legal officer didn't want to do anything that might upset Fred Moosally, but Bagley didn't think that having the firefighters testify would affect the captain one way or the other, so he told Lieutenant Anderson that he would see to it that the sailors were added to Admiral Milligan's witness list. Scanio was called to testify on April 22, and the others were fitted in soon after that.

Before Scanio testified, Dan Meyer and Dale Mortensen and six petty officers from Turret One held a meeting. Mortensen asked Meyer if he had informed Admiral Milligan about seeing the two bodies in the gun pit. Meyer said he had, unaware that his testimony had not been recorded. "This kid Scanio is going to come in and commit hara-kiri by saying that he saw Clayton Hartwig's body at the bottom of the pit. It's essential that he has an officer to back him up," Mortensen said. "He's shaky and needs all the support he can get."

Brian Scanio's testimony came three days after the turret explosion. "I told them everything that exactly happened. I told them about the secondary explosion," he said, "and it seemed that when I said certain things, they just stopped the recorder. There was a recorder sitting behind the staff on a table. They'd stop the recorder, and there'd be inaudible phrases between the admiral and his captains, and then they'd go on and ask a different question, and they wouldn't finish the question that they were on." The burly fireman was asked about the location of the bodies he found in the turret. Scanio tried to give answers, but he was constantly interrupted. "They wouldn't let me elaborate on what I saw or what I felt happened. They didn't want any opinions or what I thought happened," he said.

Scanio thought Admiral Milligan was intentionally discourteous. He told the admiral that he had observed a body at the bottom of the gun pit, but he wasn't allowed to say who he thought it was. The admiral softened his demeanor near the end of Scanio's testimony, asking, "Knowing what you know now, would you go back in like you did on the 19th of April?" Without pausing, Scanio said he'd do it again. "If I wouldn't have put out that fire a lot worse could have happened. I was thinking that there could be an explosion," he said. Had the fires reached the powder magazines, he said, the ship could have been blown apart. Scanio wanted to ask Milligan why he had allowed so much evidence from Turret Two to be thrown over the side. But he thought better of it.

Yeoman Third Class Vergil Marshall was the last man to get out of Turret Two before the blast snuffed out the lives of forty-seven of his colleagues. Marshall testified that he had been called out of the powder flats minutes before the accident by the weapons officer and ordered to type up a firing plan. Admiral Milligan had been provided a copy of that plan. It had been time-stamped April 18, 1989, and had been signed by Captain Fred Moosally. If Marshall didn't even begin typing the document until after the explosion on April 19, then it would be logical to assume that it had been backdated. The document Marshall had typed shielded the captain, allowing him to claim that he was unaware of Chief Skelley's experiments, because they were not listed on the firing plan he had signed.

The day after Brian Scanio testified, three of his colleagues who helped extinguish the fires in the upper part of the turret told their stories. Fireman Recruit Ronald Robb was asked by Commander Swanson if he ever thought about refusing to enter the blazing turret. "No," he replied. Was there any hysteria among the firefighters? Or was a disciplined approach to fighting the fire maintained inside the turret? "Yes, it was." Did his teammates perform their tasks in a heroic manner? "Yes, they did." Machinery Repairman Third Class Thad Harms, who had been a member of the *Iowa*'s crew two and a half years, was asked by Commander Swanson, "Were you scared?" "Yes, Sir," Harms replied. Were the casualties Harms viewed in the turret mutilated? "All of the ones that I saw there." Engineman Robert Shepherd had been the second fireman to enter the turret and the first one to drag in a hose. He confirmed Scanio's account about seeing a body in the pit. He had crawled down below and had a look at it, but he didn't have enough time to identify it properly because he was running out of oxygen and a fire was blazing in the pit.

The fire-control officer, Lieutenant Leo Walsh, testified the same day as Robb, Harms, and Shepherd. And as Walsh had confided to some of his fellow officers, he did not volunteer any information that was not asked, including the fact that Turret Two was scheduled to fire an unauthorized five-bag load and that Turret Three was planning to fire a four-bag load. Asked his opinion of what might have happened in Turret Two, Walsh said the question could be better answered by Chief Skelley.

Skelley was called next. Almost every time Admiral Milligan or his staffers asked a question, Skelley rambled far afield. "Only respond to our questions. All right?" Commander Swanson warned Skelley. Following one incomprehensible monologue, Swanson admonished Skelley: "But in terms of being responsive to the questions. Let's try 'yes', 'no', or 'don't know.' Okay?" When he was asked what caused the explosion, Skelley said the red silk patch filled with black powder sewn on the end of the propellant bag was probably culpable.

Skelley said that one of the first bags rammed into the chamber might have spilled black. The remaining bags then could have scraped over the loose grains, generating a spark. He said he knew of three or four occasions "of where a smoldering pad had been viewed in a gun." "On what ship?" the admiral asked. "On this ship here," Skelley replied. Admiral Milligan said that he and Captain Messina had fired a thousand sixteen-inch rounds on the *New Jersey* and had never encountered anything remotely similar to what Skelley had described. Skelley couldn't resist taking a poke at the admiral. "Well, Sir, I've been tracking the rounds, and right now *Iowa* has fired twice as much ammunition as all of her sisters combined," he gloated. "I'm not making a comparison, Master Chief, on who fired the most rounds," Milligan snapped.

Skelley was questioned about his powder experiments. He admitted that he was aware that it was illegal for him to use six bags of quick-burning D-846 propellant with a 2,700-pound projectile. Did anyone in the Navy authorize him to fire five-bag loads of D-846 powder with a 2,700-pound projectile? Skelley said he didn't have any paperwork from anybody in Sea Systems Command giving him permission to conduct his experiments. Then he claimed that gunnery officers in the 1930s and 1940s had used their own "prerogative" to shoot any combination of powder and shells they pleased.

He was quickly reminded that this was not the 1930s or 1940s. He then freely admitted that the four- and five-bag D-846 experiments were his own idea. But that didn't end his lecturing about the glory days of battleship gunnery back in the 1930s. Reading from notes, he said, "This is: *West Virginia*, long range battle practice, shoots 80 rounds, nine minutes 42 seconds, 31,003 yards, she's got 6.4 percent hits on a battle target; *Tennessee*, long range battle practice, 115 rounds, seven minutes 41 seconds, 26,530 yards, shoots seven percent which is good hitting percentage for that many rounds on a battle practice target. *California*, 103 rounds, nine minutes 46 seconds, 26,571 yards, you got 9.7 percent hits."

He droned on through 1937. The investigative officers bit their lips and cracked their knuckles. As Skelley began 1938, animosity displaced boredom. Was this guy for real? Forty-seven sailors were dead, the *Iowa* was in shambles, and this weird little fellow was jabbering interminably about the halcyon days of battleship gunnery before Pearl Harbor. The panel had more questions for Skelley, but the officers couldn't take any more of him. They abruptly dismissed him, informing him that they would call him back when and if they needed him.

DAN MEYER gave Lieutenant Buckley, Admiral Milligan's aide, a copy of the October 23, 1988, memo his father had urged him to write concerning the gunnery problems on the *Iowa*. The memo acquainted Buckley with Turret Three's "chaotic performance," Fred Moosally's "gun shyness," Phil Buch's carousing and brawling with his enlisted men, as well as defects with the guns' hydraulics and turret sprinkler systems. Buckley was elated, because Meyer's memo proved that a number of significant problems had existed for a long time and had not been addressed by the gunnery officer, the weapons officer, the executive officer, or the commanding officer. Buckley confided to Meyer that Admiral Milligan was already planning to "administratively hang" the *Iowa* for failing to maintain proper training records and for not sticking to the personnel qualification standard (PQS) guidelines.

Back at the Pentagon, Rear Admiral Brent Baker, the Deputy Chief of Naval Information, said it was apparent from a stream of messages emanating from Captain Fred Moosally that the *Iowa* skipper was becoming increasingly perturbed by the questions asked by Admiral Milligan and by what he considered to be a spate of disparaging stories written about his ship after the explosion. With the vessel drawing ever nearer to Norfolk, Rear Admiral Jimmy Finkelstein, who was scheduled to retire in several months as the Navy's Chief of Naval Information, transmitted a four-page, saccharine-coated telegram to Moosally.

Finkelstein, a short, frog-voiced Mississippian, reminded the *Iowa* captain that Vice Admiral Johnson, Captain Seaquist, and Navy Secretary Ball had all lauded the crew's heroic efforts to save the ship and extolled the sixteen-inch gun system. Finkelstein said that Captain Paul Hanley, a shrewd public-affairs operative, had already arranged for Moosally and some of his crew members to talk with the national press when the ship reached port. Finkelstein estimated that the news coverage would "peak" on Monday, April 24, when President George Bush arrived for the memorial service. "Seize the moment to praise your crew, and it will get national coverage," Finkelstein recommended.

Captain Moosally and his public-affairs officer, Lieutenant Commander Brad Goforth, met to choose three suitable candidates to appear with Moosally at a "press conference for heroes" in Norfolk. The chunky, balding Goforth thought that John Mullahy would be an ideal choice. He would subsequently be replaced by Kendall Truitt, which would turn out to be a public-relations headache. Goforth's and Moosally's other two candidates were Commander Kissinger, the weapons officer, and Captain Jeffrey Bolander, the Marine detachment commander, who had hammered and pried off the escape hatch, making it possible for Brian Scanio and the other firemen to enter the turret and put out the fires. Word about who had been designated a "hero," and the impending press conference, rapidly made the rounds of the mess deck and berthing compartments.

Dale Mortensen was only briefly considered to be a "hero" by Goforth and Moosally. There was no one else on the *Iowa* better qualified to receive a medal. He had stopped Turret One from participating in Skelley's illegal experiment. He had battled fires in Turret Two, helped flood the magazines, shored up the guns in Turret Two, identified bodies, and unloaded guns. But he had also struck Fred Moosally and Admiral Milligan as an outspoken individualist who had the gall to order around a rookie ensign.

Dan Meyer was another "hero" candidate, having made several trips to the bottom of the burning turret, obtaining a schematic of the turret for the captain, and recovering bodies. But he had also shot off his mouth to Admiral Milligan, telling the admiral more than he wanted to hear. Meyer had also appeared for his cross-examination attired in dirty work clothes. They never would have medals pinned on their chests.

10

"Miceli Confuses Motion with Progress."

AT 1:39 P.M. on Sunday, April 23, as the *Iowa* neared the channel into Norfolk, Navy jets flew low over the ship, executing the poignant "missing man formation." An hour later, as the ship continued northwest at fifteen knots, Admiral Powell Carter Jr., the Atlantic Fleet commander, arrived by helicopter on the battleship's flight deck behind Turret Three. Carter was an uncommon individual. A 1955 Annapolis graduate and nuclear submariner, he had been openly opposed for his current job by some of his fellow admirals who did not believe he had spent enough time at sea to be able to oversee the hundreds of ships in his command. He liked to don threadbare clothing and a ratty wool watch cap, pedal his bicycle around the waterfront where the ships of the Atlantic Fleet were moored, and ask ordinary seamen for their opinions. He didn't think the enlisted men would tell him the truth if they knew he was a four-star fleet commander. Most of the sailors recognized the admiral and told him "sea stories"—harmless fables guaranteed not to get their ships or their skippers in any trouble. Admiral Carter remained on the *Iowa* for about thirty minutes, talking to Admiral Milligan and Captain Moosally and taking a cursory look at the exterior of Turret Two, which by then was covered with a freshly applied coat of haze-gray paint. The fleet commander then flew back to Norfolk. He would visit the ship when she docked.

The *Iowa* took a pilot onboard at 4 P.M. to guide the ship into port and began sounding prolonged blasts on her whistle. Deckhands doubled up her mooring lines at the Norfolk Naval Base's Pier 5 at 5:41 P.M. and put her forward and aft brows in place. Three Marines in dress blues trooped smartly to the stern of the ship, ran the national ensign up the flagstaff, and then dipped it to half-mast as a sign of mourning. There was a nippy breeze, but the entire crew was dressed in summer whites with black armbands. Three thousand relatives and friends of the crewmen clogged the pier. Family members, worried sick ever since they heard about the explosion, were allowed up the gangplanks thirty minutes after the battleship had been tied to the pier. Hordes of reporters were kept at bay outside a chain-link fence some three hundred yards from the *Iowa*'s bow. It had only been ten days since the ship had departed Norfolk.

IN THE hubbub of relatives and friends of crewmen streaming aboard the battleship, the arrival of Captain Joseph Dominick Miceli on the *Iowa* went virtually unnoticed. Miceli, who worked for Sea Systems Command, had been assigned as Admiral Milligan's technical investigator. He would direct the scientific testing to establish, among other things, the stability of the powder and the operability of the rammer and ammunition hoist, and he would investigate whether radio or radar signals had anything to do with initiating the blast.

Bald, with a prominent, fleshy nose, pursed mouth, eyes shielded behind tinted lenses, and great protruding ears, Miceli came from a hardworking coal-mining family in Wilkes-Barre, Pennsylvania. Considered one of the most controversial officers on active duty, he had a bigger potential conflict of interest involving the *Iowa* investigation than Admiral Milligan did. Miceli was not a graduate engineer, but he had served for three decades as an ordnance specialist, which was an engineering billet.

Chuck Bernard, director of land warfare for the Pentagon, and Tony Battista, an influential House Armed Services Committee staffer, both worked with Miceli at the Naval Surface Warfare Center at Dahlgren, Virginia. "Joe Miceli comes to a conclusion first and then proves it," Bernard said. "Miceli confuses motion with progress. He's kind of a legend inside the Navy. He's an asshole," Battista said.

Both Bernard and Battista sneered at Miceli's attempts to make the 76-mm, rapid-fire, Italian-designed OTO Melara cannon work. No matter how many changes were made, the OTO Melara, which was designed to be used on frigates, routinely jammed and was incapable of accurate fire. Miceli decided that if the gun had a more substantial platform, it wouldn't recoil so badly and might perform better. So he had a humongous concrete slab poured, which scornfully became known as "Miceli's folly." Miceli had the gun bolted to the slab. "It became a big joke. We said, 'Hey, Joe, even if that big slab of concrete works, if you put it on a ship you're going to sink it," Chuck Bernard said.

Miceli, who hadn't been assigned to sea duty since 1967, had a history of offending skippers when he was onboard their vessels as a passenger. Once, while aboard a destroyer from Key West, Florida, to Norfolk, he got into a heated argument with the ship's commanding officer, who became so incensed that he made an unscheduled stop in Mayport, Florida, in order to throw Miceli off his ship. The captain swore that if Miceli ever set foot on his ship again, he would have him "keelhauled."

Miceli's biggest troubles began when he was commanding officer of the Naval Weapons Support Center in Crane, Indiana, from 1982 to 1985, and ineptly handled the powder for the four *Iowa*-class battleships. The Crane facility was responsible for the indiscriminate mixing of powder lots in 500,000-pound vats. That goof, according to Admiral Ed Snyder, was primarily responsible for the *New Jersey*'s deplorable shooting in Lebanon. Miceli almost had his career ruined then. However, he partially redeemed himself by discovering a large cache of unblended powder, much of it nearly sixty years old, in an upstate New York ammunition-storage facility. It was remarkably well preserved and stable. Miceli had it rebagged and this time was fastidious about maintaining the integrity of each lot. Even so, during the rebagging process, a potentially lethal flaw was introduced into a large number of these bags, some of which were eventually shipped to the *Iowa*.

THE *IOWA* used some of this unblended powder during a June 1984 firepower demonstration at the Vieques gunnery range to show Congress that battleships were capable of hitting their targets. The *Iowa* fired twenty-five projectiles at ranges between thirteen and eighteen miles. Marine Colonel Don Price was aboard the battleship, serving as Navy Secretary John Lehman's liaison. Price thought the gun shoot bore no real resemblance to what he had experienced in combat in Vietnam. The ship was anchored; her position was firmly established by radar and transponders (electronic beacons) on the beach; the targets were located by powerful optics or radar or both; and one of the foremost Marine Corps spotters was aloft in an A-6E Intruder to walk the shells onto the targets. "It was like shooting fish in a barrel. They couldn't miss," Price said.

Colonel Price noticed that there weren't enough trained gunner's mates on the *Iowa* to operate more than one turret at a time. After Turret One shot, its tail hatch dropped open and about fifty men scooted to Turret Two. After Turret Two fired, the same gaggle of sailors sprinted aft to Turret Three to repeat the process. "It was like watching a car full of clowns at a circus. It was funny. Some of those clowns were really, really old. They looked like they had fought in the Spanish-American War," Price said. Even so, the *Iowa* didn't experience the erratic initial velocity problems that the *New Jersey* had. Most of the *Iowa*'s projectiles landed on or near the targets.

Price went back to Washington after the gun shoot. Arriving at the Pentagon, he headed directly to John Lehman's office and told him what had happened. "If she had been a Marine on the rifle range, she would have shot high expert. I wouldn't want to be on the beach with her shooting at me," Price said. Lehman was ecstatic and had Price prepare a chart of Washington with an overlay showing where the *Iowa*'s shells would have landed had she been blasting away at the capital. Lehman sent the chart and overlay to Congress with the following notes: "What it indicated is that the battleship could have dropped eight sixteen-inch shells directly on the Capitol and five on the Rayburn House Office Building to the south, with a half-dozen near misses, and only a couple of stray shells out on Independence Avenue." That was enough to save the battleship program.

SOME SENIOR Navy and Marine Corps officers who knew Captain Joseph Miceli became alarmed when they heard that he had been appointed to head the technical side of the *Iowa* investigation. Rear Admiral Ming Chang, the Navy's Inspector General, first met Miceli when they were both gunnery officers aboard rival destroyers in the Pacific, nearly three decades earlier. Chang had been Miceli's superior at Sea Systems Command and had a very low opinion of Miceli's technical abilities and integrity.

Rear Admiral Ted Gordon commanded the Naval Investigative Service during the preliminary stages of the *Iowa* probe and then became the Navy's Deputy Judge Advocate General. Gordon and Miceli were from the same hometown and had served together on the destroyer leader USS *Josephus Daniels* in the mid-1960s. "Joe Miceli had his own turf to protect," Gordon said. "The guns, the shells, the powder were all his responsibility. He had a vested interest in seeing that they were not at fault in the *Iowa* accident." As the *Iowa* inquiry progressed, the fifty-five-year-old Miceli confided to Gordon that his high-visibility assignment with Admiral Milligan was going to guarantee that he became a rear admiral. Gordon was doubtful. "I have the inside track. I have been promised the job," Miceli insisted.

Boarding the *Iowa* shortly after the ship was moored on April 23, Miceli loitered around the exterior of Turret Two for about thirty minutes before asking the *Iowa*'s in-port officer of the deck to unlock the turret's escape hatch. Miceli climbed up the ladder into the turret, followed by an entourage consisting of a lieutenant commander, a chief gunner's mate, and two civilian ordnance specialists. They spent several hours inspecting the damage that day and devoted most of the following day to that task. At the end of April 24, Miceli's first full day aboard the *Iowa*, Dan Meyer and a number of gunner's mates from Turret One heard Miceli say, "I know there is nothing wrong with the powder or the guns; it must have been sabotage."

THE NAVY flew 370 family members of the dead sailors from all over the country to Norfolk to attend a memorial service at 9 A.M. on Monday, April 24. The keynote speaker would be President George Bush. Expecting an overflow crowd, Rear Admiral Jimmy Pappas, commander of the Norfolk Naval Base, had his sailors set up 4,000 folding chairs in a vast hangar and wired loudspeakers outside.

Crisply uniformed sailors from the *Iowa* began arriving in the hangar two hours before the memorial service was scheduled to begin. John Mullahy was one of those who headed to the hangar early. He was being driven from the ship in a staff car by Lieutenant Commander Deborah Burnette. She and her co-worker, Lieutenant Commander Steve Burnett, were public-affairs officers assigned to work for Admiral Powell Carter as well as for Admiral Frank Kelso, who commanded all U.S. forces in the Atlantic. Lieutenant Commander Goforth, the *Iowa*'s public-affairs officer, rode in the car with Mullahy and Deborah Burnette. When they neared the hangar, Goforth informed Mullahy that he wouldn't be part of the post-service press conference with Captain Moosally. "Why not?" Deborah Burnette demanded. "Because he's been court-martialed and spent time in the brig," Goforth replied. He said that Mullahy was being replaced at the press conference by Kendall Truitt. Mullahy was crushed.

President and Mrs. Bush sat in the first row of the family section—between the widows of twenty-one-year-old Seaman Apprentice Jose Luis Martinez, who had died in the powder flats, and thirty-one-year-old Seaman Apprentice Leslie Allen Everhart Jr., who had died on a projectile deck. It was standing-room-only in the hangar, and another 3,000 people stood outside in the chilly morning air, listening to the ceremony on loudspeakers. President Bush, a former naval aviator who was shot down in World War II, said, "Let me say to the *Iowa* crew, I understand your grief. I, too, have stared at the empty bunks of lost shipmates, and asked, 'Why?' I promise you today, we will find out 'why,' the circumstances of the tragedy. But, in a larger sense, there will never be answers to the questions that haunt us. We will not, we cannot, as long as we live, know why God has called them home."

As he neared the end of his remarks, Bush was overcome by grief. His voice caught when he told the audience, "Your men are under a different command now, one that knows no rank, only love; knows no danger, only peace." Then, removing his glasses, his eyes brimmed with tears. He and Mrs. Bush moved slowly up and down the rows of relatives for twenty minutes, shaking hands and offering words of condolence and an occasional embrace. Later, on Air Force One en route to Chicago, the president told reporters that some of the families had asked him to "please help us find out what happened." He said he was determined to keep the four battleships on active duty despite what had happened to the *Iowa*. "They're a useful platform for our missiles. There's a hell of a lot of firepower there. I don't think the guns are obsolete. The firepower is enormous, the accuracy is supposed to be pretty good."

AFTER THE president departed, Fred Moosally, Kendall Truitt, Robert Kissinger, and Jeffrey Bolander held their press conference. Moosally claimed that the ship "had finished firing Turret One" before he gave the order to switch to Turret Two. He failed to say that Turret One's left gun had a fouled bore. That omission would come back to haunt Moosally a week later when reporters for the *Virginian-Pilot* and *Ledger-Star* newspapers in Norfolk uncovered the truth and printed it. The captain was asked if he'd talked with Admiral Milligan's investigators. He refused to say, but, in fact, he hadn't been called as a witness yet. What were his theories about the cause of the explosion? "There's a lot of theories," he said. "We're just going to have to look at every aspect, all the experts, all the arson experts, fire experts, the weapons experts."

Had he seen any hint of a problem before the accident? No, he'd had congressmen, the Secretary of the Navy, senators, and reporters all aboard his ship, and everything had always seemed to work fine. Why was the turret still trained to starboard? "It's not moved by choice," he hedged. He said that "two observers" had been killed in Turret Two, but he failed to explain that Legalmen First Class Michael Helton and Robert Morrison had been escorted to the right gun room by the ship's master-at-arms as a punishment. "They were just looking, observing," he lied.

Had anyone drowned when he gave orders to flood the magazines? No, but he wouldn't have hesitated to drown somebody if that's what it took to save the ship. Was anybody in the turret unqualified? His nose should have sprouted when he said, "Nobody in there—that turret—did anything unless they had the qualifications to do it." He claimed that all of the secondary explosions had ceased before he ordered any firefighters into the turret—disregarding the fact that Brian Scanio had been flattened by a secondary explosion soon after he had entered the turret. Had anybody brought "spark-producing items," such as cigarette lighters, tape recorders, knives, watches, rings, or dog tags, into the turret? He seriously doubted that had happened, because Chief Reggie Ziegler was the best noncommissioned officer on the ship.

Kendall Truitt spoke next, calling the explosion a "freak accident." The third class petty officer seemed clean-cut and as wholesome as apple pie in his dress blues with a single row of campaign ribbons and a gleaming silver Surface Warfare badge pinned on the left breast of his jumper. He spoke in perfect sound bites. Truitt's death-defying escape tale was so riveting that it was prominently featured on all the television networks.

Commander Kissinger, the weapons officer, claimed that an exhaustive inspection had been conducted on all nine sixteen-inch guns before the explosion, and that nothing out of the ordinary had been detected. This was curious, because Turret Three only had two guns that worked. Marine Captain Jeffrey Bolander said that at first he didn't think the accident was as serious as it turned out to be. Bolander, who banged and pried open the escape hatch with a sledgehammer and a crowbar, said, "When I saw the first casualties, I knew."

Lieutenant Commander Steve Burnett arrived back at the fleet public-affairs office satisfied that the day had gone beautifully. The president's speech had been well received by the audience and the media. The *Iowa*'s skipper, Fred Moosally, was right out of central casting, another Horatio Hornblower, and that lanky, fresh-faced sailor, Kendall Truitt, was a Norman

Rockwell original. It had all been a brilliant public-relations triumph. And then his telephone rang. "Hey, Steve, I got another strange one for you," said a naval officer Burnett knew well. "That guy Truitt you used as a spokesman at the press conference this morning. Well, he's a car thief, does loan-sharking on the ship, and probably is a faggot to boot. You've stepped in shit, old buddy." Burnett hung up with a sinking feeling. Maybe the press wouldn't hear about Truitt's shady background? Fat chance, he thought.

FOLLOWING THE memorial service, the Navy allowed the families of the deceased sailors to go aboard the *Iowa*. The family of Gunner's Mate Third Class Geoffrey Schelin walked up the forward gangplank and asked the officer of the deck if he could locate Lieutenant Dan Meyer for them. Dale and Darleen Schelin and their surviving four sons and four daughters knew that Meyer regularly played tennis with Geoff, and was his friend. Perhaps the lieutenant could shed some light on the events of April 19? Meyer approached the family with some anxiety. "They all looked like Geoff, boys and girls alike. They were all tall, good-looking, athletic, dark-haired, and had those penetrating blue eyes. It was like looking at ghosts," Meyer said. He told the Schelins that while he was not allowed to take them inside Turret Two, he could show them his turret. It was essentially the same as the one in which Geoff had died. Meyer left Darleen Schelin and Geoff's siblings in the turret officer's booth and took Dale Schelin down to the right gun layer's position off the electrical deck. "I found Geoff right here, the very same spot in Turret Two," Meyer said. The Navy had informed the family that Geoff had died in the right gun room, and that he had been the rammerman. "That's not true. Here's where he died," Meyer said.

Meyer was uneasy about revealing the circumstances of Geoff's death, but Dale Schelin pressed him. So Meyer told him that Geoff had strangled on the cord of his sound-powered phones, and he had been flung into the steel overhead, where the top of his skull had been split. Dale asked Meyer if there was anything else he could tell him. There was, but Meyer said he didn't want to talk about it. Dale implored Meyer not to hold back, to be completely forthcoming about Geoff's death. Meyer told how, as he was standing near where Geoff had died, some of Geoff's brain matter had dripped from the overhead onto his clipboard. He had experienced an emotional catharsis when that had occurred, and he experienced another one as he talked to Geoff's father. The senior Schelin thanked Meyer, hugged him, and they both wept over Geoff.

CLAYTON HARTWIG'S family also sought out Dan Meyer after the memorial service. They found him at a brunch held at the base's enlisted men's mess hall for the *Iowa* families and members of the ship's crew. Meyer walked up with Dale Mortensen. "It looked like Hiroshima did after the atom bomb had been dropped. All you could see in the gun rooms were outlines of bodies," Meyer told Hartwig's father and mother, Earl and Evelyn. He didn't inform the family that their twenty-four-year-old son's body had been located in the pit below the center gun. Mortensen stood by, shuffling his feet, saying nothing. But Gunner's Mate First Class Verlin Allen, who was adjacent to Mortensen, interjected himself into the conversation, telling the Hartwigs that their son's name had not even appeared on the duty roster the morning of the gun shoot. "He wasn't even supposed to be in that turret," Allen declared.

Kathy Kubicina, Clayton Hartwig's sister, tried to wheedle more specifics from Meyer. She asked him if he were aware of rumors that a homosexual liaison had existed between her brother and Kendall Truitt. Meyer said that such rumors were widespread. He didn't say whether he believed them or not.

LATER, EVELYN Hartwig asked the lieutenant who was assigned to be their escort if he would locate Kendall Truitt. Truitt arrived several minutes later, grasped Evelyn in a bear hug, and kissed her. He had visited the Hartwigs' home in Cleveland a number of times and was well liked by all the family members, including Kathy and her husband, Frank Kubicina. Truitt introduced his twenty-year-old wife of four months, Carole, to the Hartwigs. He said he would help them locate Clayton's black 1977 Chevrolet Monte Carlo and reclaim his personal effects. The Hartwig family and the Truitts found the dented, rust-pitted automobile in a parking lot near the pier where the *Iowa* was moored.

The car's rubberized gaskets around the windows were so decomposed that Kathy was able to slip her fingers inside the window on the passenger side and shove the glass down, allowing her to unlock the vehicle. Rumpled uniforms and dirty civilian clothing were piled high on the back seat. Military publications, paperback novels, a Vivitar 35-mm camera, road atlases, a sack of cassette tapes, a Seiko calculator, a FM transceiver, several cheap watches, an owner's manual, fuses for the car, D-cell flashlight batteries, a Radio Shack antenna, a set of handcuffs, and a miniature flashlight were strewn throughout the car. An unloaded 9-mm, semiautomatic Beretta pistol was stashed under the driver's seat. There were several Navy-issue duffel bags in the trunk, so the family pitched in and stuffed the motley contents inside the bags for the flight home to Cleveland. They planned to have the car driven home at a later date or sold for scrap.

Once the duffel bags were filled, Truitt shocked the Hartwigs with an announcement. He said that the year before, Clayton had taken out a $50,000 double-indemnity life-insurance policy. "I doubt that it's still in effect, but if it is, I'm the sole beneficiary. I don't want the money. Anything that comes from it you can have," he said. He proposed that they drive to the Atlantic Fleet Federal Credit Union on the naval base and check the status of the policy. Truitt and sixty-two-year-old Earl Hartwig, a retired railway worker who had served as a gunner's mate on the USS *Adams*, a destroyer, in the Pacific during World War II, went inside the credit union, remaining there for nearly an hour. When they emerged, Earl's face and ears were flushed, and he was staggering. "Ken's rich," Earl croaked. "His name's still on the policy." "Well, Ken, he must have liked you a whole lot," Carole Truitt said. "Mr. and Mrs. Hartwig, I don't want anything out of this. The money's yours. I'm giving it to you," Ken vowed.

Soon after leaving the credit union, the Hartwig family drove to the Norfolk airport and prepared for the flight back to Cleveland. Once they were airborne, Frank Kubicina turned to his wife and said, "I don't trust Truitt. I don't think he's going to give your parents any money, and I don't think that's right. Somebody should write the Navy and get them to do right by your parents." For a week, Kathy fretted over what Frank said. Then she drafted and mailed letters concerning the insurance policy to Captain Moosally; Commander Morse, the executive officer; Lieutenant Commander Costigan, the gunnery officer; Lieutenant Commander James Danner, the ship's Catholic chaplain; and to Ohio Senators Howard Metzenbaum and John Glenn. These letters would boomerang on her. Her parents would receive no more than $2,500 of the insurance money. And the act of seeking the money would turn the family's lives inside out.

THE DAY after the service in Norfolk, Mary Welden arrived back home in Oklahoma City. Five hours after her return, she received a telephone call informing her that the body of her twenty-four-year-old son, Gunner's Mate Second Class Stephen J. Welden, would be arriving at the airport on a commercial flight from Philadelphia. She was also informed that Steve's body would be escorted by a sailor who was well acquainted with her son. "The escort was a nice kid, but he had no idea who Steve was. He was just a sailor stationed in Philadelphia that the Navy told to accompany Steve's body to Oklahoma. After the coffin came off the plane, we never saw this sailor again," Mrs. Welden said. Lieutenant Commander Terry Sanner, the casualty assistance officer, advised her that Steve's remains were "unviewable."

That didn't sit well with Mary Welden, forty-six, a registered nurse, who remembered how in the mid-1980s the military had hoodwinked Kathryn Fanning, the wife of an Air Force officer missing in action in Vietnam. Mrs. Fanning, an Oklahoma City native, buried what she thought were the remains of her husband, Major Hugh Fanning, in 1984. The military also informed Mrs. Fanning that the body of her husband, who had been missing in action for seventeen years, was "unviewable," but that a positive identification had been made by matching the major's teeth with his dental records. A year after the interment, Mrs. Fanning had second thoughts and had the body exhumed. She hired two board-certified anthropologists to examine the contents of the coffin. The scientists told her that there was no skull present, nor were there any teeth that could have been compared with dental records. "These remains could not be identified as Major Hugh Fanning or any other particular individual," the anthropologists concluded.

"I didn't trust the Navy. For all I knew, they could have put rocks in Steve's coffin or just parts of his body," Mrs. Welden said. She and Steve's brothers—Mike, twenty-three, and Bill, twenty-two—visited the funeral home that was in charge of the arrangements and obtained the undertaker's permission to open Steve's casket. Steve's face was covered with a sheet, which they folded back. There was a dress-blue uniform jumper lying atop his chest. After thoroughly checking the body, there was no doubt in any of the three Weldens' minds that this indeed was Steve. Even so, Mrs. Welden began battling the Navy and the Armed Forces Institute of Pathology, which had conducted autopsies on the *Iowa* sailors, to obtain Steve's postmortem records and photographs. When she finally secured them, she asked several physicians at Oklahoma City's Baptist Medical Center, where she was employed, to determine what had killed her son. "The doctors told me it was a toss-up between the head and the chest wounds he received," she said. Steve was buried with full military honors in Resurrection Cemetery, following a requiem mass.

THE BODY of Gunner's Mate Third Class Jack Thompson Jr. arrived in Greeneville, Tennessee, the same evening that his mother and father, Mildred and Jack Thompson Sr., and his wife, Leasa, returned from the memorial service in Norfolk. Like Mary Welden, Mildred Thompson, who was also a nurse intended to inspect the body of her son before burying him. Mrs. Thompson, too, had been warned by the Navy that her twenty-two-year-old son's corpse was "unviewable." She liked and respected the family's casualty assistance officer, who had pleaded with her not to open Jack's coffin, but she also recalled the blood-curdling conversation that she had had with Jack during his last visit home less than a month before he died. She had nightmares about what he'd told her, how untrusting he'd been about the officers who ran his ship and how he'd called his turret "a death trap."

The casualty assistance officer, Lieutenant Tim Kindred, a naval reservist from Kingsport, Tennessee, told Mildred Thompson that if she did open the coffin, she had to have a physician, an attorney, and a minister present. She said that funeral-home director Robert Jeffers would be plenty of company for her. When she refused to back down, she was allowed to inspect the badly burned body. She recognized a distinctive chipped tooth her son had had since he was a small child. That convinced her this was really Jack, even though his body was coated with gunpowder. She asked Lieutenant Kindred for an explanation and never received an answer.

Several hundred mourners, many of them members of Jack's extended family, squeezed into the rural Cedar Grove United Methodist Church for his funeral. He was buried on a windswept hill dotted with maple trees, overlooking the red brick church and meandering, pristine Horse Creek. Seven white-clad sailors from the Naval Air Station in Atlanta, Georgia, bearing M-14 rifles, fired three loud volleys into the air. Several hundred yards away from the flag-draped coffin, a solitary sailor placed a bugle to his lips and blew Taps.

Mildred Thompson, who had lost a leg to diabetes, hobbled off the hill on her artificial leg, still seething over an encounter she'd had with Fred Moosally earlier in the week in Norfolk. "Mrs. Thompson, it was just an act of God," Moosally said. "I believe in God, but you can't blame him for this," she hissed. She considered the balding captain to be "a lying son-of-a-gun." There was just something about Moosally that wasn't right, she had told her husband. Jack Thompson Sr. had agreed, calling the *Iowa* skipper "a phony bastard" to his face.

A COFFIN containing Clayton Hartwig's remains arrived at the Cleveland airport on Wednesday evening, April 26, seven days after the explosion. By that date, the FBI's disaster squad had only been able to identify positively the "bodies and/or parts of 36 individuals." The FBI forensic technicians would not be able to identify the additional eleven bodies until May 16, some three weeks after they had been interred. After the Navy announced it was releasing all the bodies for burial before the identifications had been completed, FBI technicians severed the fingers from the corpses to obtain prints. Body parts that had not been matched to torsos by April 25 would be discarded. The Navy would later insist that all of the identifications had been completed by April 24. FBI records refute that assertion.

A list compiled by Ensign Kevin Hunt on the *Iowa* during the first twenty-four hours after the bodies were removed from the turret proved to be so inaccurate that it was little help during the identification process. According to Hunt's records, Clayton Hartwig died on the projectile decks. A second *Iowa* inventory was also filled with errors, stating that as many as forty-nine sailors (rather than forty-seven) died in the turret, including thirteen "unknowns" and six "questionables." Clayton Hartwig's name didn't appear in that inventory. A third tally didn't show Hartwig as working in the center gun room at all. It claimed that he had perished due to "blast" wounds, but there was no indication of where he had died. The inventory and sketch, which Dan Meyer had drawn inside the turret before the bodies were removed, was the most accurate, but it was still incomplete. Hartwig's corpse was the very last one to be identified by the FBI, even though the distinctive clipper-ship tattoo with the name "USS *Iowa*" could be distinguished easily on his upper left arm.

Hartwig's sister, Kathy Kubicina, wanted to open the casket the Navy shipped to Cleveland to make sure that her brother's corpse was in it. Lieutenant Renee Lewis, the casualty assistance officer assigned to the Hartwig family, sought to dissuade her, saying that if she did look inside, she had to have a Navy representative present, plus a minister, a representative from the funeral home, an attorney, and a physician. Like many of the other relatives of the sailors killed in Turret Two, Kubicina had formed a bond with her casualty assistance officer, but she had also become suspicious of many things the Navy told her, so she planned to ignore Lieutenant Lewis's advice and look in the casket.

Earl Hartwig planned to do the same thing, but the funeral-home director promised that he would personally inspect the corpse and tell Earl and Kathy what he found. The mortician went back to an embalming room and reappeared an hour or so later, saying that the coffin contained a human torso inside a gray flannel bag labeled UNITED STATES NAVY in large block letters. He pleaded with Earl and Kathy not to look themselves, and they reluctantly agreed.

Rebecca Shaw, a reporter for the local ABC television affiliate, visited the two-story Hartwig home, in a blue-collar neighborhood that had fallen on hard times. For the evening newscast, Shaw taped an emotional piece centered on Clayton's bedroom. Located in a partially finished attic adjacent to ceiling-to-floor metal shelving jammed with Evelyn Hartwig's canning Clayton's room had a wall poster of the *Iowa* and two Aegis cruisers steaming past the Statue of Liberty into New York Harbor. The walls were also adorned with certificates proving that Clayton had crossed the equator and entered the Arctic Circle, a photograph of his boot-camp company, another of his gunnery-school classmates, and an antique cavalry saber. There was a large collection of grinning "Garfield" cat dolls, another of gray plastic World War II battleship and destroyer models, two 20-mm polished-brass shell casings, and bookshelves brimming with military histories, Bible stories, nature books, and the children's classic *Little House on the Prairie*. The room had a twin bed covered with a blue-and-white afghan. A black footlocker was positioned at the foot of the bed. The clock had been stopped at the hour and minute when Clayton had last left this room to return to the *Iowa*. Stopping the clock was a tradition that Evelyn had unfailingly observed each time her son left home for any long trip. She always restarted and reset the clock when he returned. The television reporter told the Hartwigs that the room's martial decor clearly demonstrated Clayton's patriotism and his pride in the Navy. Shaw recorded her on-camera close, saying, "How tragic it is that Mrs. Hartwig will never be able to start this clock again."

Two days after Clayton Hartwig's body arrived in Cleveland, his funeral was held at the Lakewood Seventh-Day Adventist Church, where he and his parents had regularly attended services since his birth. The Reverend Tim Bailey, pastor of the Seventh-Day Adventist Church in Wheeling, West Virginia, officiated. Hartwig and Bailey attended church-sponsored preschool together and later went together to Mount Vernon Academy, another Seventh-Day Adventist institution in Ohio. Bailey said that as long as he had known Clayton, his friend had made it abundantly clear that he intended to follow in his father's footsteps and become a gunner's mate in the United States Navy. "Ironically, it's against our religion and belief to carry any kind of gun, and it's the biggest gun in the world that killed Clayton," Bailey said, losing his composure and sobbing. The youthful minister apologized for falling apart, but many of the more than two hundred people attending the service weren't listening. They were too busy weeping themselves.

After the funeral service, a caravan of more than a hundred automobiles moved out on Route 83 and then hastened down Interstate-90 North for fifteen miles to Avon, Ohio, and a military cemetery. The sky was leaden and the morning crisp as seven naval reservists inserted magazines into their M-16 rifles and fired three volleys of .223-caliber blanks into the air. After Taps was sounded, six other reservists, serving as pallbearers, lowered the casket into the grave. Then they painstakingly folded the American flag that had been draped over Clayton's coffin into a tight triangle and handed it to the commander of the reserve unit, who in turn tendered it to a tearful Evelyn Hartwig, saying, "I present this flag to you on behalf of a grateful nation." After her son's funeral, Evelyn put the folded flag on top of Clayton's afghan.

MATT PRICE'S family in Burnside, Pennsylvania, had opted not to attend the memorial service in Norfolk after the Navy balked at reimbursing them for the airfare for Matt's brother and three sisters. His father, Arthur R. "Butch" Price, told his wife, Peggy, "We're private people. I want to be by myself. I want my grief to myself. I don't want to share it with a lot of other people, or have a lot of reporters poking microphones in our faces and asking us how we feel." The Navy said that it would fly Matt's body to Pittsburgh, about 120 miles north of Burnside, and would have it at the Pittsburgh airport by 5 P.M. on Monday, April 24. The government had agreed to pay the Prices and the other forty-six *Iowa* families up to $2,100 to bury their kin. At 5:30 p.m. on Monday, a casualty assistance officer assigned to the Price family called Matt's twenty-three-year-old sister, Karen Fetterman, and asked her if she knew where Matt's body was. Karen was bewildered. She didn't know anything more than what the Navy had already told her. The officer said he would check with the Bureau of Naval Personnel in Washington and call her back.

He telephoned thirty minutes later, informing Karen that there had been "a huge screwup." Matt's and Ernie Hanyecz's bodies had been switched. Matt's body had been driven by hearse to Ernie's hometown in Bordentown, New Jersey, and Ernie's body had been airfreighted to Pittsburgh. The Navy was in the process of "unscrewing this mess," and Matt's body would arrive in Burnside by hearse in a matter of hours. The officer asked Karen not to tell her parents about the mix-up, saying that he didn't want to "unduly trouble them." A hearse containing Matt's body did arrive in Burnside five hours after the initial panicky call to Karen.

Matt's funeral was held three days later at the 121-year-old, white clapboard Christian and Missionary Alliance Church, situated forty yards from the Price homestead. Two hundred of the town's 1,200 residents filled the church, and many more stood outside the whitewashed structure. Cletus Guffin, Matt's good friend from Turret One, attended the funeral. Burial was in a graveyard on a gently sloping hill four hundred yards from the church. The Odd Fellows Cemetery, nearly as old as the church, is surrounded with mature pines and cedars. The day was unseasonably hot, with temperatures approaching 100°F. A seven-man squad of naval reservists fired volleys and sounded Taps, and then the Prices' friends, neighbors, and relatives trekked back to their tree-shaded front lawn for buckwheat cakes, sausage, and coffee served off trestle tables.

Several weeks after her brother's funeral, Karen would tell her parents how the Navy had mixed up Matt's and Ernie Hanyecz's bodies. That did it for Peggy Price, who had come to doubt anything the Navy said about the *Iowa*. "For all I know, I might have Ernie Hanyecz's body buried up on that hill," she said.

To make matters worse, Ila Lane of Manheim, Pennsylvania, mother of Boatswain's Mate Third Class Todd McMullen, insisted that Matt's and Todd's bodies had been exchanged. So, despite her husband's objections, Peggy Price asked the Armed Forces Institute of Pathology in Bethesda, Maryland, for Matt's autopsy records and photographs. It would take her more than a year to obtain them, but when she did, she had more questions. Matt had a mermaid tattooed on his upper left arm, but there was no mention of it in his autopsy report. When she asked the pathologists at Bethesda about this inconsistency, they had nothing to say. The autopsy photograph revealed that the body's fingertips had been sliced off. When she asked about it, she was informed that it was a "customary practice" in disaster situations. She demanded the return of her son's fingertips and was informed they had been thrown away. Officials at the Armed Forces Institute of Pathology asked her to return the autopsy records and photographs and stop asking questions, but she refused. "I could take anything if they would have just told me the truth. But they either told outright lies or failed to tell me and the other *Iowa* families what they had done," she said.

SUSAN BACKHERMS of Ravenna, Ohio, wife of Gunner's Mate Robert Backherms, the center gun rammerman, also rejected the Navy's advice not to look inside her husband's sealed casket. Mrs. Backherms said her husband's remains were wrapped in "a cheap gray flannel bag." She had Robert interred in historic Arlington National Cemetery, across the Potomac River from Washington, because he had once seen a movie, *Gardens of Stone*, containing scenes shot there, and told Susan that if he ever died on active duty, he wanted to be buried there. After she buried her husband, Susan Backherms launched a media campaign to hold Captain Moosally and senior officers of the *Iowa* accountable for operating a chaotic, unsafe vessel.

She told the *Navy News*, a weekly newspaper published in Hampton Roads, Virginia, that the "kicked back" attitude her husband had experienced on the battleship must have been a contributing factor to the explosion. She also asked why the gun shoot had not been halted on April 19 after Turret One experienced multiple misfires. "Why didn't they just shut down training? It wasn't imperative that training go on. There is no reason for people to die like that in peacetime." Rear Admiral Gneckow, who had commanded the *Iowa* when the ship had been reactivated in 1984, wrote the *Navy News*, attacking Backherms. "[She] knows zippo about the Navy. That's why we hired Captain Moosally, and not a seaman's wife!" Gneckow wrote. "I got terribly mad," Susan Backherms said. "They took the position that I was a housewife and I should know my place."

11

☆

"Master Chief Skelley Drives Me Nuts!"

SOMEHOW CAPTAIN FRED Moosally received daily summaries and sometimes transcripts of the testimony by the *Iowa*'s officers and enlisted men before Admiral Milligan's panel. Moosally was displeased when he learned that Dan Meyer had testified about Chief Skelley's "kitchen-sink" experiments, the chaos that existed in Turret Three, and the absence of training in the weapons department. Meyer was summoned to Moosally's stateroom and chewed out. Moosally called Meyer "disloyal." The captain sat glowering behind his desk while Meyer stood at attention. Moosally said he couldn't understand why Meyer had divulged so many of the ship's secrets, especially after attending the briefings conducted by Lieutenant Commander Bagley, the ship's legal officer. "I wasn't at the briefings, Captain. I didn't know anything about them. I was working in my turret," Meyer said, backing out of the captain's stateroom. Moosally dismissed him after warning him to be more circumspect in the future. "Aye, aye, Sir," Meyer said. Meyer's friend, Terry McGinn, said, "Dan was pretty stung at being accused of being disloyal for just telling the truth."

CAPTAIN JOSEPH Miceli faced a major problem as he started his technical investigation. He had to find some way to extract the three projectiles from Turret Two's gun barrels. The center gun would be the most trouble, since the explosion had driven the 2,700-pound projectile forty-four inches into the barrel. Miceli borrowed a 750-pound "swinging hammer" from the U.S. Army to knock out the three shells. The noisy contraption crashed away incessantly for a week before the left and right shells popped out. However, the hammer didn't budge the center projectile. The shell's rotating band was a major impediment. The rotating band—a strip of malleable copper alloy located at the rear of the shell—formed a gas-tight seal once the shell was fired, engaging the rifling and imparting a ballistic spin.

The explosion had fused the center shell's rotating band to the rifling, and Miceli figured that a tremendous amount of force would be required to free the projectile. To ease the task somewhat, hundreds of gallons of PD-680 (a lubricating solution) and Break-Free (a chemical compound used to cleanse powder residue from the bore) were poured down the muzzle. Sailors also used steel-wool swabs attached to wooden poles to channel the PD-680 and Break-Free around the rotating band.

An oversize drilling rig was crammed into the narrow center gun room, and another week was consumed boring a succession of holes five inches in diameter and a foot deep into the base of the projectile. The base was literally bored out, alleviating the pressure on the rotating band. The hammer was then able to pound the projectile from the barrel. This laborious exercise was not completed until May 24, almost five weeks after the explosion. When the center gun shell finally emerged from the barrel, it was in wretched shape—bobtailed, abraded, and gouged. Nevertheless, Miceli would later testify that chemical evidence of sabotage had been discovered under the rotating band. This despite the fact that thousands of gallons of water, firefighting foam, PD-680, and Break-Free had coursed down the barrel, and that metal fragments from the drilling and hammering and steel-wool fibers coated the shell.

After the three projectiles had been removed from the turret, the center gun shell was trucked away for tests. The left and right projectiles would "disappear" for eighteen months. Miceli had made no effort to remove the 1,900-pound projectile stuck in Turret One's left gun. It would remain in the barrel for four more months and then be fired in the Mediterranean the next time the *Iowa* was permitted to shoot her guns.

CAPTAIN MICELI had three hundred bags of the D-846 powder lot involved in the explosion shipped for analysis to naval ammunition facilities at Crane, Indiana; Dahlgren, Virginia; Indian Head, Maryland; Yorktown, Virginia; and Seal Beach, California. Miceli also sent the parts of the center gun's hydraulic rammer that hadn't been tossed overboard to the Naval Ordnance Station in Louisville, Kentucky. Most of his testing was conducted at the Naval Surface Warfare Center at Dahlgren.

Since the height of the Vietnam War, when more than 250 military and civilian specialists had worked on a full-time basis on ordnance and ballistics, there were no more than fifteen technicians left at Dahlgren when the *Iowa* tests were conducted. Its facilities were not in the best shape. The sixteen-inch gun barrel primarily used at Dahlgren to test-fire projectiles was little more than a rusty elongated sewer pipe that was 93 percent eroded. By contrast, Turret Two's center gun had only been 20 percent eroded at the time of the explosion.

Miceli would later brag that 20,000 tests had been conducted to establish a cause of the *Iowa* explosion. That sounded like a lot, but photographs and documents reveal that a large percentage were no more than replications performed under lax scientific standards. One Dahlgren veteran, who had served as a turret chief on the battleship *Pennsylvania* and worked at the ordnance facility for thirty-eight years, said, "Where did Joe Miceli come up with the figure of 20,000 tests? I'll tell you. He pulled it out of his ass." Another gunnery specialist with thirty-four years of service said, "Based on my experience at Dahlgren and on shipboard, the whole damned *Iowa* investigation looked like a sham."

One test involved holding the flame of a Zippo lighter under the quilted igniter pad of the propellant bag to see what would happen. Another involved tossing a lighted cigarette on a pile of loose black powder. Other tests consisted of dropping propellant bags from a hundred-foot tower onto a steel plate affixed to a concrete block. The technicians also sliced powder grains at different angles, counting each cut as a separate test.

WHILE MICELI was toiling to remove the three projectiles from the barrels, Admiral Milligan took testimony from the *Iowa*'s most senior officers. Commander Robert Kissinger, the weapons officer, was called to testify on four separate occasions. He wasn't quite sure which turrets had been supposed to be firing what kind of ammunition on April 19, or why. He confirmed that the ship had been conducting experiments for some time, but he was unable to cite anyone in the Navy's chain of command who had given him permission to violate the regulations.

Often rattled, Kissinger was unable to answer almost any of Milligan's technical questions, and had to keep reminding the admiral, "I'm not a sixteen-incher." Captain Ed Messina reeled off a laundry list of Kissinger's shortcomings: "Your turret officers are very junior, your Turret Three chief is not qualified, and you have a first class [petty officer] apparently running the show in Turret One." Was a lack of trained personnel in Turret Two "the proximate cause of the accident"? "I don't believe so," Kissinger answered, but he didn't sound sure.

On May 10, during Kissinger's second-to-last appearance before the panel, Admiral Milligan stated that he was "relatively convinced" that Clayton Hartwig had been the Turret Two's center gun captain on April 19. The admiral provided no explanation for that statement. Instead, he said witnesses had testified that during muster the morning of the explosion, Lieutenant Buch, Chief Ziegler, and Petty Officer Hanyecz had all stated that Errick Lawrence would be the center gun captain. Lawrence had also signed the pre-fire checks as gun captain. "Do you know any history, any background whatsoever, that resulted in that switch [from Lawrence to Hartwig as gun captain]?" the admiral asked. "No, Sir, I don't," Kissinger said. Why had as many as eight or nine personnel changes been made in

Turret Two in the last minutes before the explosion? Kissinger didn't have a clue.

What steps had Kissinger personally taken to notify the sailors in Turrets Two and Three that they would be firing fewer than the standard load of six powder bags in their guns? The weapons officer said he had done nothing. Hoping to salvage his reputation and nineteen-year naval career, Kissinger added, "Sixteen-inch [gunnery] was completely new to me when I arrived onboard the ship and I've spent the last eight months trying to learn a lot of the information." Admiral Milligan and his staff, unimpressed, recommended that disciplinary action be taken against Kissinger for dereliction of duty.

LIEUTENANT COMMANDER Kenneth Costigan's testimony and his dejected demeanor were an ordeal for Admiral Milligan and three other investigative officers who had served with Costigan when he had been gunnery officer on the *New Jersey*. Now the gunnery officer of the *Iowa*, Costigan was properly deferential, and his answers were generally lucid, but it was obvious to his former shipmates that his spirit had suffered a serious blow on April 19. Following the explosion, some of the junior officers aboard the *Iowa* feared that Costigan might try to kill himself. They confiscated his pistol and established a "suicide watch" on him. They had stewards bring all his meals to his stateroom, and they tried unsuccessfully to get him to talk.

Admiral Milligan asked Costigan if he were aware that D-846 powder could not be used with a 2,700-pound projectile. Costigan told his former commanding officer that he was well aware of this restriction. Did he have a document from anybody from Sea Systems Command or Surface Forces Atlantic allowing him to bypass regulations and conduct the experiments? "I cannot recall a specific document relating to that, no, Sir," Costigan replied. He told the incredulous officers that he did not believe the multiple misfires experienced by Turret One's left gun on April 19 constituted an "unusual or an unsafe condition." Captain Messina emphatically disagreed, saying that he could not comprehend why Costigan had not communicated with Turret One during the entire time that Cletus Guffin was attempting to clear his weapon. Costigan said there was no reason to talk to Guffin or anybody else in the turret, since they were complying with established procedures.

Costigan had no idea about which men had been assigned to Turret Two's center gun room on the day of the explosion, or whether any of those men had been qualified to fill their jobs. He confirmed that Chief Skelley had planned to fire four bags of powder with each 2,700-pound projectile in Turret Three. He said he could not "specifically" remember briefing Captain Fred Moosally about the powder experiments. He had been aware for months that Turret Two's sprinkler system had been broken, but he had done nothing to see that it was fixed.

Shortly after this dismal performance, Costigan was fired by Fred

Moosally. He became an outcast in a shabby cinderblock building along the waterfront less than half a mile from where the *Iowa* was berthed. His job was keeping track of obscure technical publications. For all practical purposes, his career was over.

AT 1:22 P.M. on Monday, May 1, twelve days after the explosion, Captain Fred Moosally testified for the first of two times. Commander Swanson read the *Iowa*'s commanding officer his rights, informing him that he was suspected of dereliction of duty and warning him that anything he said could be used against him at a court-martial. The captain was bracketed by two Navy attorneys, a lieutenant and a commander, who had been designated to defend him. He waived his rights and agreed to answer the questions put to him by Admiral Milligan and his officers. His language was simple and direct.

According to Moosally, gunnery training under his predecessor, Captain Larry Seaquist, "was in pretty poor shape." Moosally also disparaged the engineering department he had inherited from Seaquist. He said that he had not wanted to accept Lieutenant Commander Costigan as his gunnery officer, because he "didn't want a wardroom full of passed-over guys who are not going to go anywhere." He accepted Costigan only as a favor to Rear Admiral Lewis W. Glenn Jr., a former commanding officer of the *New Jersey*. In his opinion, Turret Three had been "a mess" when he became commanding officer.

Moosally said he had sacked officers without having anyone to replace them. "I knew that the officer wardroom had been mismanaged on that ship for two years," Moosally added, taking another swipe at Seaquist. The skipper was subjected to a withering barrage of questions from Admiral Milligan, Captain Messina, and Commander Swanson. A jumbled set of answers by Moosally indicated that he had no idea about who was qualified to operate the equipment in the turrets. The admiral and his officers were startled by Moosally's declaration that he had been kept in the dark about the illegal powder experiments on April 19.

"Would it surprise you to learn that they intended to fire Turret Three with four bags of powder?" Admiral Milligan asked. "Very surprising, very alarming," Moosally replied. The admiral said he was incensed that the *Iowa* had been used as "a research and development platform," not bothering to mention that he had personally given Master Chief Skelley permission to conduct an illegal experiment on the *Iowa* in November 1987.

Damning his weapons officer with faint praise, Moosally said, "I still think Bob Kissinger's a well-meaning, intelligent guy." He again savaged Kenneth Costigan, his gunnery officer: "I don't know what Ken Costigan has told you, but Ken Costigan is a basket case, right now. He completely collapsed on me during this whole thing. He had to see a psychiatrist. On the way back, he was totally useless." Moosally said that he had never been pleased with the quality of his officers, claiming that he had raised the issue in a letter to Vice Admiral Mike Boorda, Chief of Naval Personnel.

The captain was far from finished shredding the reputations of his officers and some of his chiefs. His operations officer, Commander Finney, would never be deemed fit for command, because he "ran a minesweeper aground back when he was a lieutenant commander." His assistant operations officer had been evaluated as not "worth a damn" on his previous ship. Admiral Milligan interrupted Moosally's diatribe to inquire about Master Chief Skelley. Moosally exclaimed, "Master Chief Skelley drives me nuts! I can only stand to spend about five minutes with him!"

When Moosally returned nine days later to complete his testimony, he accused the Navy of losing interest in the battleships. He cited as his evidence the inferior quality of enlisted men who had been assigned to his ship by the Bureau of Naval Personnel. He was thirty-seventh on the bureau's priority list to obtain replacement gunner's mates. He asked for 130 gunner's mates and received eighty-eight. "If I was to disqualify all the guys I've got on the *Iowa* that have problems, I'd be in a hurt locker. I mean, I've got guys that were kicked out of submarines, kicked out of being SPs [shore patrol]—that I've got as gunner's mates. That's what the Navy sends me."

He claimed that there were many sailors serving on the *Iowa* who were "dopers, marginal performers, constant UAs [unauthorized absences]." He said he'd been advised by the Navy's brass to "straighten these guys out." He stated that he had booted out "hundreds" of sailors since becoming commanding officer.

Moosally said he received several messages from the Atlantic Fleet commander, Admiral Powell Carter, complaining, "We're losing too many guys. You better keep some of these jerks around, because you can straighten them out if you're a good leader." Moosally claimed that if he had kicked out every sailor who was a troublemaker, had legal difficulties, or was incapable of doing his job, "I don't think I'd have many guys left." The *Iowa* had experienced a 48 percent turnover of personnel since January 1989. "I don't know how you run a ship effectively with that large of a turnover."

Moosally's slashing, self-serving testimony about his crew would remain under wraps for nearly five months. When it first surfaced in the independent weekly newspaper *Navy Times*, it would cause a major morale problem aboard the *Iowa*. His remarks about "dopers, marginal performers, and constant UAs" were especially resented by sailors and the families of the forty-seven men who had died on April 19. Many of the officers and chiefs had become inured to Moosally's ad hominem attacks, beginning with the wardroom meeting the day he assumed command of the ship. But his remarks were considered to be a stab in the back by those sailors who were accustomed to seeing him strutting through their work spaces, slapping them on the back and regaling them with sports stories. He had been their buddy. How could he heap this load of shit on their heads? He had double-crossed them. When Moosally's testimony became public, the Navy wasted no time distancing itself from his slurs, insisting that the *Iowa* had always received "high quality sailors."

THE SHIP'S executive officer, Commander John Morse, testified that he was aware that Turret Two would be firing five bags of powder on April 19, but he did not know how many bags Turret Three would shoot. He said he was unaware that firing a 2,700-pound projectile with D-846 powder was prohibited. Despite having arrived on the *Iowa* four months before the explosion, Morse said he knew next to nothing about basic sixteen-inch gunnery procedures. He had no technical training in the subject, hardly ever attended pre-fire briefings, and had no idea what to do if a gun misfired. By his own admission, he was "not exceptionally technical." As with Admiral Milligan, his primary field of expertise was financial management.

Morse said he heard Chief Skelley referred to "as a civilian in uniform" and knew that Skelley was doing some strange things with gunpowder and shells. Even so, Morse hesitated: "I was convinced that there was nothing that was going on [aboard] the *Iowa* that wasn't proposed or approved by the proper level of authority. And that's not Master Chief Skelley." What was his opinion of Skelley? "He's not the type of chief petty officer who I would like to have running a division. If you ask him a fairly simple question, you'll probably get more information than you need."

THE SHIP'S operations officer, Commander Bob Finney, also testified that he was not conversant with sixteen-inch gunnery procedures. One of Finney's duties was ensuring that the ship's training was accomplished in a timely and orderly fashion. Commander Swanson advised Finney that his training program was an embarrassment. The legal officer pointed to Turret Three's J.C. Miller as a prime example. Chief Miller had been on the ship for six months and had not completed a single training requirement. Swanson said a review of the three sixteen-inch turrets revealed that "damn near half of the people assigned to watch stations weren't qualified for those stations, and the CO [commanding officer], apparently, did not know it." Unlike the captain and the weapons officer, the gangly operations officer did not try to defend his actions.

COMMANDER GENE Kocmich, who had served as the *Iowa*'s weapons officer and executive officer under Captain Seaquist, appeared before the investigative panel on April 29. Captain Messina asked Kocmich about Chief Skelley's powder experiments on the *Iowa* in 1987. Kocmich said he had been on leave when they took place. "I didn't think there was anything to be gained from it [the experiments]," he said, reminding Admiral Milligan that the experiments had occurred when the admiral was aboard the *Iowa* as battle group commander.

Commander Swanson asked Kocmich where would have been the best place to conduct Skelley's experiments. The former weapons officer said the Naval Surface Warfare Center at Dahlgren was ideal. What about Master Chief Skelley's leadership and technical qualifications? "He's not a leader, he's not the leading petty officer of his division. I understand that before my time, they tried it and it didn't work," Kocmich said. "Skelley would piss me off, and I would throw him out of the office. He would do things that would drive me up the wall. At the same time I would listen to him in the areas I thought he was the expert."

CHIEF J.C. Miller was re-called for additional testimony. Miller said he was positive the center gun's gas ejection air valve wasn't functioning in Turret Two on April 19. Had Chief Ziegler informed Miller about any manning problems in the turret? "Senior Chief Ziegler was leery of [Gunner's Mate Second Class] Errick Lawrence's overall capabilities to a certain extent," Miller said. "He [Ziegler] had made comments to me, not on that morning [of the explosion], but earlier, such as 'Lawrence had been on the turret for two years and still was kind of absent minded or lost.'" Had Senior Chief Ziegler said anything to Miller the morning of the explosion that he was replacing Errick Lawrence as center gun captain with Clayton Hartwig? "No, not at all," Miller said.

Gunner's Mate Second Class John R. Keerl of Turret One testified that he had spoken with Errick Lawrence immediately after the pre-fire briefing the morning of April 19, and Lawrence still believed he was assigned to be the center gun captain in Turret Two. Admiral Milligan told Keerl that it was his "belief" that Clayton Hartwig was center gun captain, even though Hartwig's name did not appear on the watch bill (duty roster). "I recall Petty Officer Lawrence being excited about getting to finally be a gun captain and being able to shoot. I was talking to him the night before and he was pretty excited about it," Keerl said, obviously unimpressed by the admiral's "belief."

MASTER CHIEF James Hickman, the ship's gunner, was called to testify and would later claim that he was treated with such disrespect by Admiral Milligan and his staff that, "I got so mad I got tears in my eyes." Hickman was asked why "Zebra" [the watertight and blastproof hatch fastenings] on Turret Two had been "broken" just before the guns were scheduled to fire. He replied that Commander Kissinger, the weapons officer, wanted Yeoman Marshall "to go down to the office and finish" typing documents, such as the firing plan, which should have been completed before the gunnery exercise began. After Hickman communicated Kissinger's instructions to Lieutenant Buch to detach the yeoman the lieutenant refused to comply. An argument ensued, and ultimately Yeoman Third Class Vergil Marshall left the powder flats minutes before the turret blew up.

Captain Messina asked Hickman about Clayton Hartwig. Hickman said he believed that Chief Ziegler might have substituted Hartwig for Errick Lawrence as the center gun captain in Turret Two in the last minutes before the hatches were sealed, because Lawrence "was a little shaky." The morning of the explosion, Hickman had talked with Hartwig about the sailor's upcoming assignment to a security post in London. Hickman told Hartwig it would be pleasant duty, that he would wear civilian clothes and carry a pistol. While he was in Turret Two gabbing with Hartwig, Hickman noticed that the door to the center gun's powder hoist was still inoperable. Chief Ziegler had attempted to mend it with a shim cut from a flattened Pepsi can. Hickman examined a piece of malfunctioning electrical equipment located near the powder hoist door. It had been known to shower sparks in the past. Although it was a safety hazard, Hickman said there was no time to do anything about it before the gun shoot.

GUNNER'S MATE Second Class Michael Carr of Turret Three testified that he was a friend of Errick Lawrence and Clayton Hartwig. Captain Messina asked Carr his opinion of Hartwig. "He was a very quiet individual. He was very dedicated to the Navy, from what I knew of him," Carr said. "It seemed his whole life revolved around it. I worked for him once before. It was during the time of an ammunition load-out. He was very professional about the whole thing." Just before the men manned up the sixteen-inch turrets on April 19, Carr said he and Lawrence were "just joking around," and Lawrence told him that he was slated to be center gun captain in Turret Two. Admiral Milligan wanted to know if Carr was positive about Lawrence being gun captain. "That's what I was led to believe," Carr replied.

WITH GREAT qualms, Admiral Milligan re-called Chief Skelley. His answers continued to be so confusing that Commander Swanson passed him a piece of blank paper and told him to write down Admiral Milligan's questions before he attempted to answer them. The plan failed, because Skelley regularly interrupted Milligan. Asked when the *Iowa* had first used fewer than six bags in an experiment, Skelley said that happened in 1987. When he was asked who had authorized this on the day of the explosion, Skelley ignored the question and digressed at length about "pounds per square inch" and "initial velocities." He declared that he had already given the panel the answers and materials they sought. In that case, Milligan said, Skelley had no authority to conduct experiments aboard the *Iowa*.

Not so, Skelley replied; he had history on his side. He referred to Rear Admiral Willis Lee's gunnery work during World War II, but he was unable to provide any specific dates or ship names to prove that Admiral Lee's experiments were in any way analogous to what he was doing aboard the *Iowa*. Skelley jabbered on and on about dispersion (spread of shells when they impact) and about velocity rates of battleship projectiles in 1927 and 1937. He said the Navy's fourteen-inch gun "was ridiculous in the 20s and 30s for dispersion." "Master Chief, we're looking at sixteen-inch guns and an explosion that took place in 1989, okay?" Captain Messina said dourly. "Yes, Sir, but they're all tied together," Skelley said. "They're all related in design. That's it. They're all tied very, very closely together because they carried over everything they learned, and, of course, we've forgotten a lot of what they learned, that's just it." Everyone in the cabin, with the exception of Skelley, was numb. Skelley was dismissed. There was obviously nothing more to be gained from him.

DURING THE two weeks following Clayton Hartwig's fiery death on the *Iowa*, thirty-six-year-old Kathy Kubicina existed largely on Pepsi, More cigarettes, and adrenaline. She hardly slept or ate. Over the couch in the living room, she had hung a collage of photographs of her brother. And every afternoon at the same time, her mother and father, Evelyn and Earl Hartwig, drove to her unassuming home and sat under the pictures of their deceased son, saying nothing for hours on end. As the days dragged on, Kathy became angrier and angrier about Clayton's insurance-policy money going to Kendall Truitt instead of to her grieving parents. Truitt had promised to give her parents the proceeds from the policy, but he had not kept his word.

She contemplated the advice her husband, Frank, had given her to write somebody in the Navy and ask for help with the policy. Her parents had "lived near the poverty line their entire lives," and this cash would allow them "to get a little house somewhere" and flee their neighborhood, which had become a mecca for drug dealers and drive-by shooters. The corpse of a young female murder victim had recently been discovered alongside some garbage cans in the alley behind their home.

KATHY WAS trying to decide whom to write and how to phrase her letter when she received a call from her congresswoman, Mary Rose Oakar. Oakar, forty-nine, had previously interceded with Secretary of Defense Richard Cheney, who persuaded the Navy to pay Kathy and Frank Kubicina's airfare from Cleveland to Norfolk to attend the *Iowa* memorial service. The congresswoman also had one of her staffers attend Clayton's funeral to see if there were anything she could do for the Hartwigs. A former Ohio Bell telephone operator and a schoolteacher, the seven-term representative referred to the voters in her twentieth congressional district as "my people." Oakar listened to Kathy's doleful tale about her brother's insurance policy and then said, "I want you to write to every senior officer on that ship who might have known your brother and see if they can do anything to straighten this mess out." Kathy agreed to write the letters and telephone Oakar as soon as the Navy responded.

She located Clayton's electric typewriter and set it up on a large, rectangular Formica table in the kitchen of the home where she had lived her whole married life. She did her writing at night, while Frank was at work as an electrician for the Ford Motor Company and her three children were sleeping. Sitting at the kitchen table, barefoot, dressed in baggy shorts and a T-shirt, Kathy pecked out six letters—the first one to Captain Fred Moosally, three more to other officers on the ship, and one to each of Ohio's two senators.

In the course of her lifetime, she had worked in a bakery, been a waitress in a fast-food restaurant, been a bank teller, sold souvenirs and programs in a football stadium, been a bartender and a bouncer in a lounge, and managed a video store. But this was the most daunting task she had ever undertaken. She was telling the United States Navy that something was wrong and ought to be fixed. That was pretty heavy for a housewife. In fact, it was even heavier than she ever imagined when she rolled the first piece of paper into the typewriter. The Navy didn't take kindly to unsolicited advice.

After completing a paragraph of a letter, Kathy raked her hand through her short-cropped brown hair, then took a swig of Pepsi and a drag on a cigarette fished from an overflowing ashtray. Her greenish-brown eyes were fogged with fatigue. She hit the carriage return and the space bar, touched the tab key with her left little finger, and continued to type. The letters told how her brother had decided to make Kendall Truitt the beneficiary of his life-insurance policy. She said the friendship between her brother and Truitt had dissolved after Kendall reneged on a promise to have Clayton as the best man in his December 1988 wedding. Truitt didn't deserve the insurance money, she claimed, because he had not even bothered to attend Clayton's funeral. Nor had he sent condolences or flowers to her parents. She asked the *Iowa* officers to talk to Truitt and persuade him to abandon his claim on the money.

It took Kathy six days to compose the letters, which she mailed on Thursday, May 4. Four days later, on Monday, May 8, the executive officer, Commander Morse, called her at 10 A.M. to say that he and Captain Moosally had received the letters and would have someone look into the matter. Morse told her, "This was just your way of handling your grief. I know exactly how you feel."

MANY FBI agents, other federal investigative agents, criminal defense lawyers, and U.S. attorneys considered the Naval Investigative Service to be the bottom of the barrel, an agency that had more than its share of rank amateurs and ham-handed scoundrels. Within the Navy, the reputation of NIS was even worse. "The Naval Investigative Service is the Gestapo for the admirals," said former Secretary of the Navy John Lehman. "The admirals frequently employed NIS to cover up their mistakes." Rear Admiral Ted Gordon, who commanded NIS for two years before becoming the Navy's Deputy Judge Advocate General and then Judge Advocate General, said NIS wasn't an investigative agency in the "truest sense. . . . They were incapable of solving a crime on their own. They more or less would decide on a culprit and then go out and prove he did it."

While he was in charge of NIS, Gordon said, agents were not authorized to open criminal investigations on naval personnel "solely because they were homosexuals. . . . This, of course, went contrary to the thinking of a lot of the individual NIS agents who had a thing about gay bashing," Gordon said.

Gay bashing is exactly what attorney Charles Macloskie of Beaufort, South Carolina, encountered in 1988 when he defended a young female Navy petty officer assigned to a Marine Corps boot camp who had been brought up on charges by NIS, because she was allegedly a member of a lesbian ring. Macloskie, a former Marine officer, termed the Parris Island, South Carolina, handling of his client and several female Marines "the NIS lesbian witch hunt." "They [NIS] are very, very even handed with everyone. They treat everyone nastily. They have a few good agents, but the vast majority of their agents don't give a rip about human decency," he said.

Macloskie subpoenaed the agency's interrogation manual and showed that it advocated deception when interrogating witnesses or suspects. The NIS manual contained statements such as: "Interrogate the weakest [easiest appearing] suspects first. . . . Pen and paper should be out of sight as much as possible during the early stages of interrogation and minimally present thereafter, because notes are a grim reminder of the seriousness of the situation and emphasize the legal significance of an incriminating remark. . . . Avoid terminology such as 'murder,' 'steal,' 'rape,' 'confess,' as it is more desirable from a psychological standpoint to employ milder terminology—'shoot,' 'take,' 'intercourse,' 'tell the truth.'. . . Tell the suspect, 'You better tell your side of the story before you're left holding the bag. You know the others are going to exaggerate your guilt to make themselves look better. Besides, if you are the last to talk, no one is going to believe your story even when you decide to be truthful.' "

Gay bashing and deception weren't the only thing wrong with the way NIS conducted investigations. The agency had been embarrassed in 1987 following an espionage investigation known as "Moscow Station." Members of the Marine security-guard force at the U.S. Embassy in Moscow were accused of trading classified documents and admission to the embassy's most secure spaces to Soviet spies in return for sexual favors and money from women controlled by the KGB. NIS hurried a hundred agents to Russia; interviewed 487 Marines and 1,285 other people; opened criminal files on 136 Marines; and conducted 260 polygraph exams. This extraordinary expenditure of manpower and resources resulted in the arrest of just four Marines.

And even then, the charges against these men began to crumble after defense attorneys proved that NIS agents had browbeaten their clients into signing bogus statements. Due to the misconduct of the NIS agents, the charges were thrown out against every Marine except Sergeant Clayton J. Lonetree, twenty-five, who had voluntarily approached a CIA agent and told him of his contact with a Soviet intelligence operative. Lonetree received a twenty-five-year sentence. Former *Washington Post* investigative reporter Ronald Kessler, author of the book *Moscow Station*, said the Bill of Rights is rarely respected by many NIS agents. "There is a Gestapo tendency, definitely," Kessler said. "They seem to think that since they are part of the Navy, they can do with Navy people whatever they want. They think it's like boot camp. And that is not the way to run an investigation, and it also tramples on people's rights."

12

☆

"We Are the FBI of the Navy."

LESS THAN AN hour after the *Iowa*'s executive officer turned Kathy Kubicina's letters over to Admiral Milligan, the admiral picked up the phone and called Claude Rollins, the NIS regional director in Norfolk. Milligan informed Rollins about Kathy's letters and requested the agency's assistance in the *Iowa* investigation. The two men arranged for representatives of their various staffs to meet the next morning. Admiral Milligan had exceeded his authority by going directly to Rollins. NIS guidelines required that a request come from the "convening authority," which was Vice Admiral Donnell, the Surfaces Forces Atlantic commander. But since Rollins and his superior, Brian McKee, had been angling to get NIS involved in the investigation ever since the explosion, they were not very conscientious about making sure that all the legal niceties were observed.

Rollins called NIS headquarters, located in the two-century-old Washington Navy Yard on the banks of the Anacostia River, to inform Brian McKee that Admiral Milligan wanted the agency's assistance in the *Iowa* investigation. Following his conversation with Rollins, McKee walked into the office of Rear Admiral Ted Gordon to inform the NIS commanding officer that the agency was now cooperating with Milligan.

Gordon was only the second Navy admiral to command NIS. The Navy's top brass had never been comfortable with how NIS operated, so the service began assigning a one-star admiral to command the organization and tighten up discipline. The agents reacted badly to this. They were career civil servants, and if they didn't like the admiral's methods, they dragged their feet, knowing he'd be gone once his two-year tour ended. Ted Gordon was in command of NIS, but Brian McKee, the civilian director, had more influence over the agents. Gordon liked McKee and respected him even when they had disagreements over policy issues.

Gordon told McKee that he had serious misgivings about the legality of having NIS involved in Milligan's administrative inquiry. Milligan had only been authorized to conduct an "informal investigation." The *Manual for Court Martials* did not allow Milligan to bring criminal charges against anyone. Gordon thought that the *Iowa* disaster should be addressed by a "formal" inquiry, in which all the testimony would be taken under oath, with accurate transcripts maintained and constitutional safeguards observed. "I fought to keep our investigation separate from Milligan's," Gordon later said. "NIS should have done an investigation only to show who might be criminally responsible and how they did it. It was a mistake to intermix the two [informal and criminal]. It just polluted the process." Gordon said he also related these thoughts to Admiral Bud Edney, the Vice Chief of Naval Operations. Edney said that having Milligan supervise the NIS investigation did not bother him in the slightest. Edney later confirmed that he had this conversation with Gordon.

THE NIS and Admiral Milligan's staffers met for the first time on the morning of May 9 at the investigative agency's regional headquarters in Building 1AAA at the Norfolk Naval Air Station, in what had formerly been a bowling alley and a movie theater. Admiral Milligan brought three of his subordinates—Captain Ed Messina, Commander Ron Swanson, and Lieutenant Commander Timothy Quinn. NIS had six agents, led by Robert Nigro, a fifteen-year veteran who was the number-two man in the regional office. A short, husky man in his late thirties, Nigro would soon have 150 agents assigned to the *Iowa* case. Admiral Milligan only remained in the briefing room a short time. Captain Messina, Milligan's number-two man, dominated the meeting once his boss departed. NIS agent Mike Dorsey kept detailed notes.

Messina flatly stated that Clayton Hartwig had been the center gun captain in Turret Two when the explosion occurred, even though Errick Lawrence had been assigned to that position and had signed the pre-fire checklist as gun captain shortly before the explosion. Furthermore, Messina said, Hartwig was staring into the breech when the fireball erupted from the barrel. Hartwig's position had been determined by the nature of his wounds, the captain claimed. This was absurd, given the fact that the FBI's disaster squad still hadn't been able positively to identify Hartwig's body. Mike Dorsey wrote: "Possible suicide by Hartwig, because he can control everything. Truitt had little control [of triggering the explosion], because he was not in the gun house."

Messina explained that Hartwig had made Truitt the beneficiary of his life-insurance policy and depicted Hartwig as "a quiet loner type." He asserted that the explosion had not been an accident. Dorsey underlined that statement six times. At the time, Captain Joseph Miceli's technical team was still fifteen days away from freeing the 2,700-pound shell from the center gun. If there were any evidence of sabotage—especially evidence indicating that a detonating device had been utilized—it would most likely be located under the shell's copper rotating band.

Mike Dorsey sketched a powder chamber containing five powder bags, calling a black swatch located between the first two cylinders a "lead bag." When a sixteen-inch weapon is loaded, the gun captain inserts a four-by-four-inch piece of lead foil, stitched into a rough silk pouch, between two bags of propellant. When the lead burns, it cleanses the barrel of impurities, such as the copper residue from the rotating band. Messina told the NIS agents that a "possible ignition device was inserted in the lead bag" and then put between the first two powder bags by the gun captain, whom he contended was Clayton Hartwig. He had no scientific proof to support his thesis. Even though he seemed to be confident of this, he offered an alternative hypothesis. If Hartwig wasn't guilty, then the crime had most likely been perpetrated by Hartwig's "aggrieved lover [Kendall Truitt]."

Agent Dorsey drew up a list he called "Knowns of *Iowa* Investigation," including such items as: (1) Truitt's previous car-theft charges; (2) "Possible '8G' [homosexual] relationship between Truitt and Hartwig"; (3) Truitt's gain of $100,000 from Hartwig's insurance policy; (4) "No mechanical/accidental explanation for explosion."

WHEN THE meeting ended, Agent Tom Goodman called Kathy Kubicina to see if he and his partner, Ed Goodwin, could meet with her and her parents in Cleveland the next afternoon. Kubicina told Goodman she would make sure that the whole family was available. Goodman claimed he only wanted to help her untangle her brother's insurance policy. Subsequently, both Commander Ron Swanson and Admiral Gordon said Goodman had been obligated to advise Kubicina that he was conducting a murder investigation in which her brother was the prime suspect. Goodman should have sought a warrant from a U.S. District Court in order to search the Hartwigs' home. If the agent didn't get a warrant, he had to obtain the family's permission to search the residence after candidly informing them that he was looking for evidence of a crime. Goodman never did any of this.

A former Norfolk Police Department detective, Goodman had been with NIS for seven years, and in that time he had conducted more than twenty homosexual investigations, some of which resulted in convictions. He was familiar with the *Iowa*, having flown aboard her in 1987 to investigate the destruction of some hydraulic lines in a sixteen-inch gun turret. He had failed to come up with any suspects during the three days he spent on the vessel during that investigation.

Like Tom Goodman, Ed Goodwin had spent much of his career tracking down and jailing homosexuals. Early on Thursday morning, May 11, the two

NIS agents took a commercial airline flight to Cleveland. They were met at Hopkins Airport by an agent from the NIS Cleveland office and lent a car. Neither man had ever been in Cleveland before, so they obtained maps and directions to Kathy Kubicina's house from the resident agent.

When Kathy answered the knock on her front door to admit them, Goodman flashed his gold agent's shield and gave her a business card. "We are the FBI of the Navy," he said. Goodman settled into the most comfortable chair in the room, a recliner. He unbuttoned his suitcoat and crossed his right ankle over his left, exposing the revolver holstered just above his sock. Kathy, who was perched on the sofa near Ed Goodwin, gaped as the Velcro fasteners strained around Goodman's calf. Frank Kubicina tensely paced from the living room to the dining room and back. He barely opened his mouth during the agents' stay, but he became increasingly agitated over their questions and statements. "I didn't like them one damned bit. I didn't like their looks. They gave me the creeps. They were sneaky," Frank said later. Evelyn Hartwig propped herself against the door frame to the dining room, looking much like she had been mugged. Earl Hartwig rested uneasily on a love seat, a dejected expression on his face.

Evelyn said that Clayton, her youngest child, didn't have many playmates due to the schedule dictated by his religion. Unlike his two sisters, Clayton had been raised in the Seventh-Day Adventist Church. On Saturdays, when other children were romping around the neighborhood, he was attending services. Sabbaths began for him at sundown Friday and lasted through sundown Saturday. When he was free to play on Sunday, the other children were in church with their families.

Clayton had wanted to join the Navy ever since he was a toddler, Earl said. Once when Clayton was less than ten years old, he appeared in the dining room, where his whole family was waiting for dinner, wearing Earl's World War II dress blues. The jumper swallowed him, and the bell bottoms dragged on the floor, but he had made a statement. His father told him, "When you do enter the Navy, pick good friends, do your best, and your officers will stand behind you."

CHARLENE METER, the Kubicinas' nineteen-year-old adopted daughter, was also present for the meeting with the two agents, as were the three Kubicina children—Jami, thirteen; Katie, five; and Mark, four. Preschoolers Katie and Mark whooped and hollered, played tag, and continually begged for snacks and sodas and asked to be taken to the bathroom. Their eleven-year-old cockapoo, Buster, added to the confusion, barking and romping round and round the crowded living room. "It was chaos, absolute chaos," Kathy said. The two NIS agents gamely tried to ignore the madhouse environment, pressing on with their questions. Neither agent took notes, nor did they tape-record the conversation.

"Are you a liberal person?" Goodman asked Kathy. She was baffled by the question and didn't answer it. Goodman continued: "What if I told you the evidence shows that your brother was a homosexual?" She said she didn't believe he was telling the truth. He claimed that pictures had been found on the *Iowa* showing Clayton engaging in sex with another sailor. Kathy challenged him to produce the photographs. Since he had no such pictures, he refused. Although he did not include it in his official interview report, Goodman later claimed that Kathy referred to her brother as a "faggot" a number of times. "I don't recall how many times, but a number of times she referred to him as a faggot, sometimes with adjectives," he said. "I don't recall the adjectives. Sometimes with 'little faggot,' sometimes with 'that faggot,' those kinds of terms." Kathy and Frank Kubicina, Earl and Evelyn Hartwig, and Charlene Meter all insist that Goodman was "lying."

Goodman asked Kathy if she believed that her brother had committed suicide. "How do I even know that my brother is dead?" she retorted. "I saw the autopsy photos," Goodman contended. "I dare you to produce them," Kathy shouted. He said he wasn't authorized to show them to family members, because the graphic photos might upset the family. As of that date, the FBI still had not identified Clayton's body.

Due to the disturbance created by the two younger Kubicina children and Buster, Tom Goodman was having a difficult time concentrating. He attempted to talk to Charlene Meter but was able to hear hardly anything she said. She had lived with the Kubicinas five years and had dated Clayton, exchanging romantic letters with him while he was on the *Iowa*. Goodman did learn that Charlene had nine letters from Clayton, the latest dated April 16, 1989. Goodman proposed that he and his partner leave the Kubicina home, check into their hotel, and interview Kathy and Charlene Meter there.

Despite Goodman's offensive allegations about her brother's sexual orientation, Kathy still hoped that the two NIS agents were going to help her family straighten out Clayton's insurance policy. Frank Kubicina was suspicious, saying, "I don't see why you guys can't interview Kathy and Charlene here. Something's not right. You're out to pull a fast one."

"We can't hear a thing in this house. We need some privacy, Mr. Kubicina," Goodman said. Kathy shushed her husband and told Goodman that she would go to their hotel room and would permit Charlene to go there, too. The two agents drove to the Residence Inn, located between the Kubicina home and the airport.

Goodman phoned Kathy and asked her to come over first. Her interview took place in a downstairs living-room area of the two-story suite. The agents sporadically jotted notes on stenographic pads, but they made no real attempt to keep an accurate record of what was said. Kathy believed that her remarks were being secretly tape-recorded, but the agents later swore they never taped anything. The men kicked off their shoes, removed their coats, and loosened their ties. Both agents had 9-mm pistols holstered on their belts. Often while one man questioned Kathy, the other tiptoed to a bedroom loft and spoke softly into a telephone. Kathy characterized the agents' attitude as being "extremely homophobic."

Goodman later claimed that Kathy said some "unsettling things" about her brother. "She told me that her brother was a recluse, that she hadn't seen him in years. She told me that he was a homosexual. She told me things that caused little flags to go up as an investigator," he said. Kathy told him that her brother didn't have a temper, and she never recalled seeing him angry. Goodman told her again that he was interested in seeing that her parents obtained Clayton's insurance money. That mollified her somewhat, and she left the Residence Inn thinking that it might still be all right for the agents to talk with Charlene.

Charlene, or Char as she preferred to be called, arrived fifteen minutes after Kathy left. She told Goodman and Goodwin that Clayton always wore his uniform when they went out on dates because he was proud of it. She had a hard time getting him to talk about anything but the Navy. "Whenever a stranger walked up and inquired about the Navy, Clayton would become a totally different person and really open up and start talking with that person," she said. Char, who was completing her freshman year in college, described Clayton as being a good-looking, unassertive young man who enjoyed watching police and war movies. She had dated him off and on for eighteen months and was able to provide the agents with incidental information, such as the fact that Clayton thought it was ridiculous to purchase a newer car to replace his clunker, because he would soon be assigned to London on security duty.

But these incidental details about Clayton Hartwig were not the reason the agents had invited Char to their suite. Cutting to the chase, they asked the young woman about Clayton's relationship with Kendall Truitt. "Did Clay and Ken have something going?" Goodman inquired. "No way. I can't believe you brought me to this hotel room to ask me such an outrageous question. Why dance around the question? Just say, 'Is Clayton a homosexual?' The answer is no. No, he was not," she said with some irritation. They restated variations of that question over and over during the next two hours. And each time they did, Char angrily shook her blonde ringlets, denouncing them as "rumormongers."

In their report, the NIS agents wrote that Char informed them she had never been sexually intimate with Clayton, but that she had been "coming on rather strong" through her letters. They pleaded with her to turn over the letters she had received from Clayton. She said she would give them copies but not the originals. "We need the originals for handwriting analysis," Goodman said. What did handwriting analysis have to do with straightening out Clayton's insurance policy? Goodman did not answer her question. Instead, he said they would check with her in the morning to see if she were willing to part with the original letters. "You can try, but I don't think I'm going to give you anything," she said as she left their suite. Her cheeks were still flushed when she returned to the Kubicina home. "What happened?" Frank asked. "It was awful, just awful," Char said. "I don't want to talk about it, ever!"

About the same time that Char returned home, Earl phoned Kathy and told his daughter that he had discovered a copy of Clayton's will neatly folded inside a Bible in his footlocker. Kathy said she would call Goodman and Goodwin at the Residence Inn and then guide them to her parents' home. The agents' line was busy, so she drove to their hotel and told them about the will. It was 11 P.M., yet they were still anxious to see the document. But first Goodman asked Kathy what kind of neighborhood her parents lived in. "It's kind of rough, to tell you the truth," she responded. "Well, I guess I better take me some more bullets," he said. He unlocked his briefcase and fished out two boxes of ammunition, one of 9-mm and the other of .38-caliber. He stuffed handfuls of the two types of bullets in separate pockets of his suitcoat. "You never can be too careful," he said with an abashed look on his face. Kathy left her car at the hotel and rode with the two agents in their gray Chrysler. They had to drive through a seedy strip of adult bookstores, bars, and burned-out structures on the city's decaying West Side in order to reach the Hartwig residence.

Once Kathy and the two agents entered her parents' home, Earl handed Tom Goodman the typed will. The four-page document was dated February 15, 1988, and had been drawn up by Lieutenant Commander Stephen Stallings, then the *Iowa*'s legal officer, while the ship was patrolling the Strait of Hormuz. The document stipulated that all of Clayton's personal possessions were to go in equal shares to Bryan Hoover, a high-school friend, and Kendall Truitt. Earl Hartwig was listed as executor, and it was witnessed by Legalmen First Class Robert Morrison and Michael Helton, who died in the explosion with Clayton. The document also signified Clayton's desire to be buried in Arlington National Cemetery if he died on active duty. Goodman asked Earl if he and Ed Goodwin could "look around" Clayton's room. Earl consented, but Evelyn warned the Navy agents "not to mess anything up." "I want this room to remain exactly the way Clay left it," she said. The Hartwigs and Kathy escorted the agents up to the attic. Earl showed them the 9-mm Smith & Wesson pistol he had found under the front seat of Clayton's car after the memorial service in Norfolk. The agents recorded its serial number. Goodman located a year-old muster of gunner's mates assigned to Turret Two lying on a manual typewriter. Clayton had brought the list home during the summer of 1988, along with a "cruise book" (much like a high-school yearbook) to show his parents what his shipmates looked like.

Clayton had seven Bibles, and Goodman wanted to search them all to see if there were any more wills or documents. Vigorously shaking one of the Bibles, he dislodged a hand-printed nine-line note. Dated January 23, 1984, when Clayton was nineteen years old, it was addressed to his mother and said, "I know this isn't a legal document or anything, but it will have to do till a real one can be made. If anything should happen to me while I'm gone, all of my possessions are to go to Bryan [Hoover]. This includes my radios, T.V., books, guns, everything. I'm changing my life insurance policy so that Bryan will be the beneficiary. All of the money I have in the bank is to go to Gordon Hackler [another former Mount Vernon student]. I hope you can understand why I'm doing this. They mean more to me than anyone else. Love, your son, Clay."

The agents examined Clayton's "Rambo-style" survival or hunting knives, his muzzle-loading musket, a BB pistol, a toy M-16 rifle, Earl's Japanese bolt-action rifle that he had brought home from World War II as a souvenir, an empty 105-mm brass shell casing. They also rummaged through Clayton's alphabetized military-book collection, consisting of more than 250 volumes, and leafed through his scrapbook of commercial vessels that had sunk, caught fire, or collided in the Great Lakes. They were rough when they handled these keepsakes, and that greatly upset Evelyn. They told her they'd do better, but they didn't, and Evelyn rebuked them. When Goodman had had enough of her, he said, "Mr. Hartwig, would you please take your wife downstairs and stay with her?" As her parents descended the stairwell, Goodman told Kathy, "You're lucky this is not a criminal investigation or we would go through this room with a fine-tooth comb."

The two agents located a picture of Clayton when he was sixteen years old, wearing the shoulder boards of a Navy commander. He also had on four rows of ribbons, a blue baseball cap with the gold "scrambled eggs" of a senior officer encrusted on the bill, and his father's captured Japanese saber belted on his left side. He had embellished the khaki uniform of the Pathfinders, the Seventh-Day Adventist Church's equivalent of the Boy Scouts, and was on his way to a costume party pretending to be the captain of the popular television series *The Love Boat*. The picture had been snapped with a Polaroid camera by Evelyn Hartwig, who dated the back of it "12/30/80." The agents never asked Kathy Kubicina or Evelyn Hartwig for an explanation of the photograph. But the agents would later claim that it proved that Clayton "had delusions of grandeur" and had violated the Uniform Code of Military Justice by "impersonating an officer."

While the agents were examining some of Clayton's personal correspondence, they came across letters from a young English woman, Sandie Denford, with whom he had been communicating in anticipation of being stationed in Great Britain. He had met her when the *Iowa* visited Portsmouth, England, in October 1986. They also made a perfunctory inspection of stacks of audiotapes of naval battle sounds recorded during World War II and looked at the labels of his extensive collection of movies about that war, a number of them starring John Wayne. They found another videotape of a very different sort. Entitled *Faces of Death*, it was a gruesome collection of people getting killed in different ways. One man steps out of a car and attempts to film a grizzly bear and is ripped to pieces; another person commits suicide on camera. The agents did not attempt to seize anything as evidence. After spending several hours in the bedroom, they told Kathy they wanted to go downstairs and talk with her parents some more.

Sixty-year-old Evelyn Hartwig was seated in a chair at the kitchen table. When Goodman and Goodwin walked into the room, her face had a tortured expression. She was distressed about the two wills her son had left. "She used profanity against her son," Goodwin said. The agent claimed that he ordered her to stop cursing her son. "He's dead, let's respect the dead and, Mrs. Hartwig, you are a religious woman. Stick to those beliefs through these hard times and please do not do that." Tom Goodman claimed that it was Kathy Kubicina, not her mother, who cursed Clayton. "She [Kathy] began berating her brother," Goodman said. Both agents were liars, Kathy later said. "My mother never, ever uses profanity, and I certainly never called my dead brother those terrible names. I loved him," Kathy said. Earl Hartwig corroborated his daughter's account.

Evelyn Hartwig let the agents read a letter dated December 26, 1988, of which she was especially proud, terming it the "sweetest letter Clay had ever written." Clayton thanked his parents in the letter for making his ten-day Christmas leave so extraordinary. It was the first Christmas leave he'd been able to arrange since he had joined the Navy in 1983, shortly after graduating from high school. "I know I very rarely say it, but I love you both very much," he wrote. "I wish I didn't have to say good-bye so often, but that's the life of a sailor I guess, and that's the life I've chosen. All I can do is make you proud of me." The agents asked if they could copy the letter. They promised to return the original on their way to the airport the next morning. The Hartwigs agreed to that.

Earl was asked why his son would make another sailor the beneficiary of his life-insurance policy. He said that during Clayton's boyhood he had often discussed his own experiences aboard the destroyer/minesweeper *Adams*. The senior Hartwig told his son that it had been a common practice during World War II for single sailors to name shipmates as their beneficiaries.

IT WAS 2:10 A.M. when Kathy Kubicina and agents Goodman and Goodwin left her parents' home. She hardly uttered a word during the ten-minute drive back to the Residence Inn to pick up her car. When they arrived at the hotel, Goodman said that he and his partner would drop by her home about 10 A.M. to try to persuade Char to relinquish her letters from Clayton. Kathy tossed and turned the rest of the night and consequently was groggy when the agents appeared on her doorstep in the morning.

Char, still feeling "violated" by her encounter with the two agents the night before, didn't want to go to the front door or have any more to do with them. When she finally emerged, Tom Goodman, a heavyset man with slick black hair, began his pitch. Char cut him off: "I don't want you to take these letters. You don't know what they mean to me." She finally relented, but only after Goodman promised to make copies and promptly return the originals. He failed to keep his word, and it took nearly three years and a legal battle before they were returned.

CLAYTON'S LETTERS to Char described life aboard the *Iowa*. Some of them were filled with his fantasies about the glamorous life he hoped awaited him as a naval security agent based in Europe. "Did you tell your friends I'm going over to London to be the next James Bond?" he wrote. Occasionally, he referred to Char as his "little sister" and himself as her "big brother," but the letters made it very clear that he had more on his mind than a purely platonic relationship with her. He mailed her $80 so she could have a special picture taken of herself, which he planned to show off to his shipmates. His last letter, dated April 16, 1989, three days before he was killed in Turret Two, described the Tomahawk experiment in some detail. He said some of the gunner's mates were scared that the cruiser *San Jacinto* might accidentally hit the *Iowa* with a missile. He eloquently described the "bright, royal blue" Caribbean washing against the battleship's hull, whales swimming alongside her, and the "crystal clear" horizon.

Once Tom Goodman had obtained Clayton's letters to Char, he was impatient to return to Norfolk. He told Kathy that he would remain in close touch with her and that he should be back in Cleveland in a week or so. On their way to the airport, the agents stopped at the Hartwigs' home and returned Clayton's post-Christmas letter.

13

☆

"I Just Can't Visualize Clay Killing Himself."

WHILE NIS AGENTS Tom Goodman and Ed Goodwin were in Cleveland interviewing the Hartwigs and rummaging through their dead son's room, Admiral Milligan's men, led by Captain Ed Messina, continued to question several *Iowa* gunner's mates, hoping to bolster the theory that a detonator had been secreted in a lead-foil packet and inserted between the first two powder bags.

For the theory to work, it was absolutely essential to show that the *Iowa*'s gun captains customarily inserted a lead-foil packet between these bags every time they fired their weapons. Shane Cline, a gun captain assigned to Turret One, was asked about his experience. Cline said he had fired more than two hundred projectiles in the previous year. Did he insert a lead foil every time he fired his weapon? Commander Swanson inquired. "No, normally it's one for every two rounds," Cline replied. He had been inside Turret Two on several occasions, observing his colleagues fire their guns. Was Turret Two's practice concerning the lead foil the same as Turret One's? Yes, the Turret Two gun captains put the foil flush against the projectile, not between two powder bags, he said.

Michael Mielens, a gun captain from Turret Three, was asked where he put the lead-foil packet. "I usually put it between [powder bags] three and four," Mielens said. Did he insert one every time he fired his gun? "No, Sir," he said. Verlin Allen, a first class gunner's mate assigned to Turret Three, was recalled for the third time. Allen had also served as a gun captain on the battleship *Missouri* and had formerly been the leading petty officer in Turret Two. He had played a vital role in saving the *Iowa* on April 19. He stated that apprentice gun captains on the *Iowa* were instructed to place the lead foil either up against the base of the projectile or behind the first three bags, "depending on which one, at the time, is easier for the gun captain." Cline, Mielens, and Allen totally undermined the thesis by revealing that there was no set placement for the lead-foil packets in the *Iowa*'s guns. Despite their testimony, Captain Messina and Admiral Milligan refused to abandon their theory.

BY MID-May, Captain Joseph Miceli was still two weeks away from extracting the 2,700-pound projectile from Turret Two's center gun. The task was consuming an exorbitant amount of time and manpower, and Miceli had developed the habit of roaming around the battleship to let off steam. During one of his forays, accompanied by a lieutenant commander from Sea Systems Command, Miceli asked Commander Kissinger, the ship's weapons officer, to loan him Dan Meyer and one of Meyer's petty officers to check out Turret One's magazines. Meyer asked the two investigating officers if the technical tests at Dahlgren had been able to replicate what had happened in Turret Two on April 19. The lieutenant commander began answering in the affirmative when Miceli interrupted him, insisting that no such thing had happened. Miceli wheeled and whacked the lieutenant commander in the stomach with the back of his hand, ordering him to keep his mouth shut.

ABOUT THE same time that Miceli silenced his subordinate, he and Captain Ed Messina became involved in forensic pathology, a field in which neither had been trained. Their aim was to show that Clayton Hartwig had been in the center gun room and in a perfect position to sabotage the weapon. Yet none of the firefighters, who were the first sailors inside the turret after the explosion, placed Hartwig's body in the center gun room.

The investigators needed a credible witness to place Clayton Hartwig's body behind the open breech, so Captain Messina took Master Chief James Hickman, the ship's gunner, into Turret Two's center gun room and told him that the experts from the Armed Forces Institute of Pathology knew exactly where every crewman in the room was at the time of his death. Messina claimed that Hartwig was in the gun captain's position, standing on a slightly raised platform, and that he had been peering into the breech. "That proves that Hartwig did it. He blew up the gun," Messina declared.

Hickman had been on the bridge when the explosion occurred and had not ventured into the turret until several hours after the fires were out and many of the bodies had been removed. Still, he saw his share of gore and severed limbs. "I'd seen the slaughter first hand, and there was no way a shore-based doctor could come up with that kind of conclusion," Hickman later said. But in the spring of 1989, Hickman said he was intimidated by Messina and agreed to go along with his story.

Messina then went to Miceli, who had been designated by Admiral Milligan as the liaison officer with the Armed Forces Institute of Pathology.

Messina explained that Chief Hickman had agreed to say that Hartwig had been leaning over, looking into the breech when the blast felled him. Miceli then called Dr. Richard Froede, the Armed Forces Medical Examiner, and, according to Dr. Froede's secretary, supplied the medical examiner with the locations of all the bodies Miceli claimed were found in the center gun room. Froede took Miceli's word at face value and wrote on Hartwig's autopsy report that his injuries were consistent "with those of an individual standing on the gun captain's platform, bending over and looking into the open breech of the gun at the time of the explosion."

ADMIRAL BUD Edney, the Vice Chief of Naval Operations, was not pleased with the speed or the focus of the NIS investigation. Brian McKee said that Edney pressured him to make a murder case against Kendall Truitt. Edney later also acknowledged this. Rear Admiral Ted Gordon, then the Navy's Deputy Judge Advocate General, said, "Admiral Edney always had a thing about Truitt, even after everyone else was saying that Hartwig did it. He was convinced that Truitt was down in the magazine and found a way to send up an exploding device. He kept telling everybody again and again to go back out there and prove Truitt did it." Edney later said, "Anybody who knows me, knows I get pretty steamed up about some things. I remember telling them [NIS] to get busy on that matter [Truitt]."

On May 16, the morning after Kendall Truitt's transfer off the *Iowa* had been approved, NIS agents Goodman and Goodwin took Truitt to their headquarters at the Norfolk Naval Air Station for questioning. They didn't inform him that he had been targeted by Admiral Edney as a murder suspect, nor did they read him his rights or inform him that he was entitled to an attorney. They took him into a back room, four feet wide by six feet deep, that had barely enough space for one chair for the suspect in the center and chairs on either side for the interrogators. The interview lasted three hours, but Truitt said there was no more than forty-five minutes' worth of substantive questions. "They were repetitive. They'd ask the same question four or five times, and put words in your mouth," he said. " 'So, Mr. Truitt, don't you think Clay was gay, huh?' And then about, you know shortly later, they'd say, 'So you were telling us that Mr. Hartwig was gay. Can you go a little further on that?' "

The twenty-one-year-old third class gunner's mate said he had become friends with Hartwig when he was assigned to the *Iowa* in 1986. "Hartwig was a good guy. He didn't drink. I mean, we would go out and maybe have a daiquiri every once in a while, but I mean, we wouldn't come back trashed like everybody else," Truitt said. "You know, he was honest. He did his job well. He was a professional. He was going to either stay in the Navy and retire, or he was looking into law enforcement. He was a good guy." The agents asked Truitt if he had ever had a homosexual affair with Clayton Hartwig or with anyone else. He emphatically denied their allegations.

Truitt later claimed the agents played "good cop" and "bad cop." Goodman was the "bad cop," the one who threatened, insinuated that he knew more than he did, and asked all the questions about homosexual behavior. Goodwin was the "good cop," the one who didn't speak much, but who would say from time to time, "We're sorry to have to ask you these questions. We're only doing our job, you know."

Truitt said that Hartwig wasn't a homosexual, because he had sex with numerous women, including several prostitutes. One of his girlfriends was an attractive blonde go-go dancer who worked in a Norfolk nightclub known as The Body Shop. Truitt also said that Hartwig was a "mechanical klutz" who could never have constructed a workable detonator. "I had to put in his car radio, because with instructions, he could still not install it," Truitt said. He described Hartwig as being serious about his job as a gun captain and a hard worker.

Goodman asked Truitt why he and Hartwig had been punished in 1987 after they had been caught scuffling on the battleship's main deck while they were supposed to be on watch. Truitt said they were engaging in "horseplay," and that Captain Larry Seaquist and Master Chief Chuck Hill had thoroughly investigated the incident and concluded that no homosexual conduct was involved. Goodman asked the sailor for permission to search his locker aboard the ship. "I had nothing to hide, so I agreed," Truitt said.

The agents, accompanied by the *Iowa*'s legal officer, Lieutenant Commander Bagley, went through Truitt's locker and found a 200-gram lead foil. They also discovered a green notebook containing the names of *Iowa* sailors and corresponding dollar amounts these men owed Truitt. It was evidence of Truitt's loan-sharking activities, but the agents barely mentioned the notebook in their official report, because they only seemed interested in evidence concerning homosexuality and murder.

Once they finished with the locker, the agents asked Truitt if he would let them search his apartment. Once again, he consented. They drove him to his two-bedroom apartment, located along a bustling Norfolk boulevard and sparsely furnished with a dining-room table, four chairs, a waterbed, and a chest of drawers. The Truitts had lived in the ground-floor apartment less than a month. Goodwin later testified that after spending most of a day with Truitt, he had developed a strong antipathy toward the sailor. The agents considered Truitt to be "a con man, a manipulator, somebody you couldn't trust."

Goodwin also claimed that when he and his partner entered the apartment, Carole Truitt "was cleaning house and she was naked." Truitt yelled that he had some people with him. "So she ran to put her clothes on. She did, and she was fairly scantily clad," Goodwin said. According to both agents, they saw photographs in the master bedroom of a partially clad Truitt, handcuffed and tied to the bed with ropes. Goodwin said he found handcuffs on a kitchen counter, as well as "sexual aids and novelties" in the bedroom, including a red vibrator, lubricating jelly, and "massage oil and cream that generates heat when breathed on."

If the agents were actually conducting a by-the-book investigation of the *Iowa* explosion, why were they so preoccupied with the Truitts' sex life? "Because both of them came in the bedroom with me, and they started picking it [the vibrator] up and showing it to me and laughing and handling it in front of me," Goodwin said.

Carole Truitt denied that she vacuumed her apartment in the buff or that she and her husband had fondled the red vibrator when Goodwin was searching the bedroom. "They [NIS] looked through my underwear, they read my high-school yearbooks, they read letters that I'd written to my husband. They read letters my husband had written to me. All very personal," Carole said. Both agents grilled her about Kendall's alleged homosexual affair with Clayton Hartwig and her sexual relations with her husband. They wanted to know if she had sex with Clayton, or had simultaneously engaged in sex with Clayton and her husband, or had sex with any other *Iowa* officers or enlisted men. "Like these things are actually relevant? These are the kinds of questions that they ask somebody who was completely uninvolved?" she asked.

Goodman and Goodwin had already made up their minds that her husband and Clayton were guilty, Carole said, and when she finally obtained their reports about her, she said that they had distorted her words and, in some instances, fictionalized her answers to support their preconceived notions. "The men are saying, 'We're the best NIS has got.' If that's the best they've got, they're in trouble," she said. "I don't think that Clay was so upset that Ken married me that he ran off and killed himself. I don't think Clay Hartwig was suicidal. I don't believe it. Not for an instant." Kendall didn't believe that Hartwig had been suicidal either, but even if he were suicidal, the agents' allegations of how he took his life were stupid. "If indeed he were suicidal, and he wanted to kill himself and wanted to go out in the big bang that they say he did, he could have gone into the magazines, taken out a bag of powder and a Bic lighter, and stood there until it blew up," Truitt said. "He would not have gotten caught. If he changed his mind, he could have walked away. No one would have known."

The NIS agents discovered a book in Truitt's living-room closet that caused their eyebrows to rise. Entitled *Unconventional Warfare: Devices and Techniques—Incendiaries; TM31 201-1 (U.S. Army 1965)*, it seemed to them to be a textbook on sabotage. When NIS had searched Hartwig's locker on the *Iowa*, they found the mate to Truitt's publication, *Improvised Munitions Handbook; TM31-210 (U.S. Army 1969)*. "We were at a gun show in Norfolk. And we were walking around, looking at some guns, and we walked up on this little book stand," Truitt said. "We saw a couple of old Army field manuals. And we thought this ought to be funny. Let's see what the technology was like back then. And we picked up a couple of books."

The agents didn't buy Truitt's explanation. They thought he was too glib. It was nearly sunset when they left the Truitts' apartment. Carole Truitt watched them drive away and told her husband that she planned to call her father in Tampa and ask him about hiring an experienced criminal defense attorney to protect them from "these vultures."

ON THE same day that NIS agents were rifling through the Truitts' apartment, two other agents, Mike Dorsey and Rob Cully, interviewed John Mullahy. Like Truitt, Mullahy was taken to the agency's regional headquarters and sequestered in a cramped room. Dorsey and Cully never informed Mullahy that he was a murder suspect, or that he was entitled to an attorney, or that he was under no obligation to talk with them. The agents said that as an authority on plastique explosives, he knew more than any other man in the turret about how to blow up the center gun and live through it. They said that as a former "brig rat," he probably harbored a deep and abiding grudge against the Navy.

And then, seemingly out of nowhere, the agents asked the hefty Irishman if he were a homosexual. Mullahy, who was married to a Spanish admiral's daughter, guffawed. "What the hell is so funny?" Dorsey demanded. "Am I a homosexual? I don't fucking think so, at least not in the past thirty-five years that I've been alive. I don't have the strength to fuck guys," Mullahy said, snickering. Dorsey and Cully were not amused.

Didn't Mullahy know for a fact that Hartwig and Truitt were homosexual lovers? He said that he had heard rumors to that effect when he first came aboard the ship, but after being around the two men for a time, he very much doubted that the rumors were true. He said that Hartwig had been involved in a minor traffic accident on March 22, 1989, with his girlfriend. "She's an English major at Old Dominion University, and at nights she is a go-go dancer in one of the bars and Hartwig often shacked up with her."

The agents asked Mullahy about the poem "Disposable Heroes," which had been posted on the bulletin board in Turret Two's berthing spaces prior to the explosion. It was a rewrite of a song by the heavy metal group Metallica, and the NIS men were trying to prove that Hartwig was the author. "Clay wasn't into that kind of music," Mullahy said, adding that it was common knowledge that the poem was the work of Jay White, the despondent third class gunner's mate from Southern California. White was obsessed with music about death, and Mullahy said he had seen multiple scars on White's wrists.

The agents questioned Mullahy about the book, *Getting Even: The Complete Book of Dirty Tricks* by George Hayduke, found in Hartwig's locker. Mullahy dismissed it as a "joke book." Among other things, the book, published in 1980, told how to construct dog-feces or chemical stink bombs, gave advice on using cat urine to kill a rival's grass, and demonstrated how to put Limburger cheese in the muffler or manifold of an adversary's car to create a sickening odor. The book also suggested that an excellent way to fluster a newly married couple would be to send "a woebegone lady with a young child to troop into the reception and confront the groom with the question of his continued child-support payments." Mullahy said the book was infantile and in poor taste but certainly was not a demolition manual.

As they were ending their interview with Mullahy, Dorsey and Cully asked him how he would have blown up Turret Two. He said he would have placed a mechanical or chemically activated device in the magazines, or hidden a detonator in a pump room between two magazines. "My last choice would be throwing a cigarette lighter into the magazine. I would never consider blowing the turret up in the gun house. It's goofy. It's ludicrous. It makes no sense at all," the eighteen-year Navy veteran said. "I just can't visualize Clay killing himself. And not only that, but taking everybody with him. It just doesn't make any sense. You know from the way he talked to me the night before the explosion, he was really happy."

ON MAY 17, almost a month after the explosion, NIS agents Goodman and Goodwin flew back to Ohio to interview Bryan Lee Hoover, Clayton Hartwig's friend from his student days at Mount Vernon Academy. The two agents checked into the Residence Inn in Dayton and were unpacking when Hoover arrived. Ed Goodwin, whom Hoover called "the skinny one," was upstairs in the loft changing into casual clothes, khaki trousers and a plaid shirt. And Tom Goodman, referred to by Hoover as "the fat one," was downstairs talking loudly on the telephone. Goodman motioned to Hoover to be seated on the couch.

When Goodman hung up and was joined by his partner, they began a well-rehearsed routine with Hoover. "They tried to act just like characters out of *Dragnet*, but they weren't any good at it. The 'fat one' took off his shoes and rolled up his sleeves. He looked like a real slob," Hoover said.

Rather than asking Hoover candidly if he and Clayton Hartwig had been involved in a homosexual affair in high school, the agents beat about the bush. Hoover said he knew where they were going, but he had no intention of answering that question until he provided them some background. He met Hartwig in February 1983, when he was a freshman and Clayton was a senior. He and another student, Gordon Hackler, had roomed with Hartwig for a month before Clayton graduated in May 1983. Hartwig paid Hoover's $1,400 tuition during part of his sophomore year from an inheritance he had received from his grandmother. He also sent Hoover $200 each month from his Navy pay for two years. This allowed Bryan to continue attending Mount Vernon after his family had financial difficulties. "Clay and I aren't gay, if that's what you fellows came here to find out," Hoover said. "Our relationship was loving and caring, but did not involve any homosexual activity."

He said that Hartwig had given him a Navy ring after finishing boot camp at Great Lakes, Illinois. "Lovers give lovers rings," Goodman jeered. The agents then falsely informed Hoover that even though they had explored "the homosexual angle" with him, they hadn't discussed it with Hartwig's parents. "We want you to keep this very hush-hush," Goodman said.

Had Hartwig ever attempted suicide while he was a student at Mount Vernon? Hoover said he had once walked into the room they shared and seen Clayton holding a pocket knife. "He was acting weird, so I took the knife from him, but he definitely wasn't trying to kill himself," he said. In their report, the agents wrote that Hoover informed them Hartwig "was contemplating suicide" with a knife. Hoover asked the agents what the investigation was all about. "They told me, 'You'll find out about it in two weeks,'" Hoover said.

As the three-hour interview was concluding, the agents asked Hoover about Michele Lee Poling, another former Mount Vernon student. Bryan had dated her in high school, but they had not kept in close touch since they graduated. The agents planned to see her the next day. When Bryan got back to his apartment, he said he became "almost hysterical" as he replayed the interview with the NIS agents in his head. He called Kathy Kubicina and told her, "They treated me just like a criminal."

Goodman and Goodwin spoke with Michele Poling at her parents' home in Wapakoneta, Ohio. She had very little to tell them. She remembered hearing a "rumor going around Mount Vernon Academy" that Hartwig and Hoover might be homosexuals. She had no evidence that they were. She hadn't seen Clayton in several years, but he did occasionally write her. She had received a letter from him written on April 8, 1989, that she called "harsh and cynical, not happy." The letter rebuked her for writing that he was "hiding in the Navy." "People are always quick to bad-mouth those of us who chose this job," he wrote. "But when something happens, who do they turn to? I don't think the 1,200 men that went down on the USS *Arizona* were hiding, or the 37 sailors that were killed on the USS *Stark* in the Persian Gulf." He said that he could conceivably "become one of those little, white headstones in Arlington National Cemetery," because the *Iowa* sailed "in harm's way every day." Hartwig's words could be interpreted as a patriotic defense of the Navy and its sailors, but the agents did not see it that way. They would use Hartwig's references to "little, white headstones in Arlington National Cemetery," the deaths of the men aboard the *Arizona* on December 7, 1941, at Pearl Harbor, and the *Stark* tragedy as evidence that he was a suicidal mass murderer.

TOM GOODMAN and Ed Goodwin were back on Kathy Kubicina's doorstep on Thursday, May 18, at 3:30 P.M., just as her husband, Frank, was getting home from work. Goodman was wearing a bright pink shirt. He approached Kathy and whispered in her ear that he was an amateur student of psychology and realized that Frank was sore at him for some of the questions he asked during his prior visit. "Pink is a soothing color. I wore this pink shirt to soothe Frank, to calm him down, to make him like me," Goodman said. Kathy rolled her eyes and responded, "I seriously doubt that's going to work, Tom."

Scowling, Frank wasn't placated by Goodman's pink shirt. He refused to shake hands with the agent. Goodman informed Kathy that NIS wanted to return to her parents' home the next day to take still photos and video footage of her brother's room. He again neglected to say that NIS was conducting a murder investigation and that her dead brother was the principal suspect. Instead, he once again lied, telling her that NIS was doing everything in its power to resolve the family's insurance predicament. Kathy called her parents and said she thought it would be okay for the agents to take the pictures.

The next morning, Goodman and Goodwin—accompanied by a Cleveland-based agent lugging 35-mm and video cameras, strobe lights, tripods, meters, and spare lenses—arrived at the Hartwigs' home. Kathy and her parents followed the two agents and the photographer up to Clayton's room. While the photographer was setting up his lights, Kathy and Ed Goodwin chatted outside the room in front of the shelves where Evelyn Hartwig stored canned soyburgers, artificial hot dogs, and other vegetarian food. In addition to being pacifists who abstain from tobacco and alcohol and observe the Sabbath on Saturday, devout Seventh-Day Adventists do not eat meat. Goodwin ridiculed Evelyn's selection of food. When Kathy explained that it was part of her parents' religious beliefs, he was abashed but did not apologize. He quickly changed the subject, telling her that he found Kendall Truitt to be "a cold fish."

Goodwin said he seriously doubted that the Hartwigs would ever hear from Truitt again. He also described Bryan Hoover as "a wimp who giggled a lot." The "wimp" characterization served as an opening for more questions. Did Kathy think Hoover and her brother were gay? No, they were not. What about Clayton and Truitt? She said he had asked various forms of that question over and over. The answer remained the same. No, they were not.

Clayton's room simply wasn't large enough to accommodate Earl and Evelyn, Tom Goodman, and the photographer and all his equipment, so Goodman offered to accompany Evelyn downstairs and chat with her at the dining-room table. Earl briefly lingered outside his son's room and then crept downstairs. He found a place that was inconspicuous, which allowed him to eavesdrop on Evelyn and Goodman's conversation. Evelyn seemed more relaxed than she had during the agent's previous visits.

Goodman later swore that Evelyn asked him, "Mr. Goodman, do you think my son was a homosexual?" He replied, "I don't know, Mrs. Hartwig, what do you think?" He said she answered, "I think he was." Both Evelyn and Earl said that Goodman invented that exchange. "I'm certainly glad that

I snuck down there to listen. That lying so-and-so did just what I thought he would do," Earl said.

The NIS photographer shot film and tape for more than an hour. Kathy, who periodically peeked into the room, couldn't understand the purpose of some of the shots the photographer was taking. After the work was finished, and the agents were departing, Kathy asked Goodman when she'd learn the results of the investigation. "You'll read all about this soon," he said cryptically.

GOODMAN'S PREDICTION proved true. Less than an hour after the agent had made the remark, Jack Dorsey, the military affairs correspondent for the *Virginian-Pilot* and *Ledger-Star* newspapers in Norfolk (and brother of NIS agent Mike Dorsey), called Earl Hartwig, identified himself, and asked for Kathy's telephone number. Earl gave the number to Dorsey without comment. A resourceful, chain-smoking, twenty-five-year print veteran in his late forties, Dorsey had a reputation for fairness and thoroughness with the officers and sailors of the Atlantic Fleet and with Norfolk's vast number of Navy retirees. He also had a good rapport with the top admirals, but since these hidebound senior officers and their press agents rarely provided him with solid leads for stories questioning Navy policies or revealing mistakes, Dorsey believed that the best way to obtain this type of material was by talking with ordinary sailors. As he drove around Norfolk's sprawling naval facilities, he often picked up hitchhiking enlisted men whom he could pump for information about shipboard scandals. Many of these accounts resulted in front-page stories under Dorsey's byline.

Since the explosion, Dorsey had devoted most of his time to the *Iowa* story. After the ship returned to Norfolk, an officer assigned to the *Iowa*'s weapons department called and furnished him with documents detailing training and manpower deficiencies in the three sixteen-inch turrets. Included in the material was the February 27, 1989, "battle bill" compiled by Lieutenant Commander Costigan, the gunnery officer, for Commander Kissinger, the weapons officer, stating that an additional one hundred men were urgently needed in the turrets. Costigan emphasized that many of the sailors in the turrets were completely untrained. Dorsey was teamed on the *Iowa* story with Tony Germanotta, who had been with the two Norfolk newspapers for ten years. Germanotta, a former police reporter from Philadelphia, talked to John Mullahy, who told him about the multiple misfires in Turret One's left gun prior to the explosion in Turret Two's center gun. The reporter also contacted Kendall Truitt, who was on leave at his father's home in Illinois, and Truitt confirmed everything Mullahy had said.

On Sunday, April 30, Germanotta had a page-one story about Turret One's misfires. That caused a major flap, because both Vice Admiral Johnson, the Second Fleet commander, and Captain Moosally had previously been quoted widely as saying that there had been no difficulties with any of the sixteen-inch guns before the explosion. The story also made the Navy look doubly bad, because it revealed for the first time that there had been *twelve*, not *eleven*, survivors in Turret Two. Once the Navy realized that John Mullahy had spent time in the brig, the "flacks" deleted his name from the list of survivors.

The Navy had no comment on Germanotta's story, but the following day he received a call from a person identifying himself only as "Sergeant York." This mysterious source told him about the improper storage of the *Iowa*'s powder on unventilated barges on the York River during the sweltering summer months of 1988. This source, who claimed to work at the Yorktown Naval Weapons Station, said that the temperatures inside the barges were so hot "that they could dangerously accelerate the decomposition of the chemical used to stabilize the powder."

"Sergeant York" told Germanotta, "People are running around trying to cover their ass. They're really worried about this thing." The source said that internal paperwork still existed at Yorktown that could substantiate his account. The reporter considered filing a Freedom of Information Act request for the documents, but he realized that the Navy would stonewall him, and this story was too important to wither on the vine. So he called Captain Al Becker, chief spokesman for Sea Systems Command, and laid out what he had. To Germanotta's surprise, Becker readily admitted that the *Iowa*'s ammunition had been stored improperly. Becker corroborated virtually everything "Sergeant York" had alleged. Becker also disclosed that Captain Joseph Miceli of Admiral Milligan's staff was investigating this matter.

The Navy responded to the article by ordering that 1,800 powder charges be removed from the *Iowa* and replaced with propellant that had been stored in cool underground bunkers in Seal Beach, California. Three Yorktown supervisors were demoted, and the Navy announced that it would no longer store ammunition on unventilated river barges.

While Jack Dorsey was fleshing out his story about training and manpower problems on the *Iowa*, and Tony Germanotta was verifying "Sergeant York's" account, both reporters were being swamped with tips that NIS had begun a murder/suicide investigation connected to the explosion. "It would be unethical for me to obtain any information from my brother [NIS agent Mike Dorsey] about one of his cases or for me to give him information about something that I was working on," Jack Dorsey said. But he and Germanotta learned independently from other sources that a criminal investigation had begun after officers on the battleship received letters from the sister of a dead sailor, complaining that her brother had named another sailor as the beneficiary of a $50,000 double-indemnity life-insurance policy.

The reporters were able to obtain confirmation that Clayton Hartwig of Cleveland had left the money to Kendall Truitt, with whom Germanotta had been speaking concerning other matters. They asked their boss, metropolitan editor David Addis, how they should proceed on such a sensitive story. Germanotta told Addis that he had already checked around with sailors in the fleet and determined that it was not all that unusual for an unmarried seaman to name a buddy as his beneficiary.

The reporters also informed their editor that they had learned that NIS was chasing the "homosexual angle with a vengeance." "It doesn't follow that just because a guy is a homosexual that he'll murder forty-six of his shipmates. I just don't buy it," Germanotta said. "If he wants to kill himself, all he has to do is slip over the side," Dorsey seconded. "Fellows, be careful. I don't want us to unfairly taint the reputation of a man who isn't alive to defend himself," Addis said. He told the reporters to stay in close contact and check back with him on a regular basis. During the week of May 14-19, Jack Dorsey was inundated by calls from Washington reporters who had heard the Hartwig/Truitt rumors leaking from the Navy and were seeking his help.

One of Dorsey's most persistent callers was George Wilson, a longtime Pentagon reporter for the *Washington Post*. Dorsey said that he did everything in his power to warn Wilson "not to get sucked in by the Navy leaks about Hartwig and Truitt." Dorsey told Wilson there were much more substantive stories to write about the *Iowa*—such as manpower shortage in the turrets, contaminated ammunition, and no training—but Wilson said he wasn't interested in anything but Hartwig and Truitt.

When Dorsey finally reached Kathy Kubicina, he told her that NIS was aggressively "floating a murder/suicide theory" in the Norfolk area. She was jarred by that, but she agreed to answer Dorsey's questions, provided that he agree to keep her name and the names of her parents and brother out of his story. He said he would. After hanging up, he quickly batted out a story for the Friday, May 19, afternoon edition. The headline and lead paragraph of the story concerned lack of manpower and training in the turrets. The NIS investigation did not appear until the fourth paragraph, and it was restrained, not mentioning Kathy, Clayton, Earl and Evelyn, or Kendall Truitt by name. Just four paragraphs were devoted to the investigation. It was the fairest, least sensational, and certainly the most humane treatment that Kathy and her family would receive from the news media for some time.

14

☆

"This Insane Bullshit Could Go On for Months!"

WHEN KATHY KUBICINA finished talking to Norfolk reporter Jack Dorsey, she wrote down the time and date and the gist of the conversation in a spiral notebook she kept beside the kitchen telephone. Her husband had called her incredibly gullible for her previous dealings with the NIS agents, and he urged her to document all her future contacts with the law-enforcement agency, the Navy, and the media. "Jeez, Kathy, you got to keep a careful record! This insane bullshit could go on for months!" her husband yelled. Frank was a hard-working man, a devoted husband and father who had really liked her brother, Clayton, but Kathy could tell that this rapidly escalating pressure from NIS, and now the news media, was taking an emotional toll on him and putting a strain on their marriage.

Before Kathy could write down all the details of the Dorsey interview, the phone jangled again. This time it was Robert Kessler, a reporter from *Newsday*, the New York daily newspaper located on Long Island. Kessler claimed that NIS agents had discovered "a crude detonating device" and a book, *How to Get Even Without Going to Jail,* on the back seat of Clayton's car, abandoned in the parking lot of a restaurant on the Norfolk Naval Base. Kessler was referring to another practical-joke book, similar in name and content to the one found in Clayton's locker on the *Iowa*. This was about forty pages long and had been written by a Florida bail bondsman. The most destructive suggestion it contained was to dump syrup in an automobile's gas tank to disable it.

Kessler was far from his field of expertise on this story. His beat was the U.S. District Court in Brooklyn, where he coaxed tips about the mafia from federal law-enforcement agents. One of Kessler's former editors said, "I doubt if Bob even knew where the Pentagon was located. He didn't know a thing about the military." The only reason Kessler would have been involved in this story, the editor said, would be if one of his NIS sources in Brooklyn was assigned to the *Iowa* case.

Kessler told Kathy that his sources "were certain" that the practical-joke book was "a volume detailing methods of constructing booby traps and other deadly devices." It had been a trying day, and Kathy had reached the end of her tolerance for such nonsense. "That's insane!" she wailed. "We checked the car and nothing like that was found!" And she informed Kessler that his sources were dead wrong about where Clayton's car was found. The *Newsday* story, which appeared the next day, didn't mention anything about a detonating device or the joke book. But it did contain Clayton's and Kathy's names and quoted a "U.S. government official" as saying, "Investigators have probed the possibility of murder–suicide, but have reached no conclusion." Kendall Truitt's name did not appear in the article, even though Kessler often mentioned Truitt's name in his interview with Kathy.

KESSLER'S INTERVIEW and his intimations that he was plugged into NIS so rattled Kathy that she called the NIS Norfolk office hoping to find out "if they were the ones who were spreading wild lies and rumors." Tom Goodman was out of the office, so she spoke with Robert Nigro, the agent in charge of the investigation. She told him about Kessler. Nigro chuckled and said, "Don't believe anything these reporters tell you. You are now in the middle of a media feeding frenzy." "How the hell can the media print this crap when Clay's car wasn't even found where they said it was?" Kathy protested. "They can print anything they want. That's what democracy is all about," Nigro said, advising her to take reporters' remarks in the future with a grain of salt.

When she hung up, her phone rang again. It was Representative Mary Rose Oakar, calling from Washington's Dulles International Airport on her way to a fund-raising event. Oakar said that Molly Moore, a reporter for the *Washington Post*, got in touch with her as she was leaving the office. Moore said that a high-ranking source in the Chief of Naval Information's office had given her a copy of Kathy's letter to Captain Fred Moosally about Clayton's insurance policy. The reporter noticed Oakar's name in the letter and asked the congresswoman to use her influence to get Kathy to do an interview. Oakar agreed. "The Navy is saying your brother committed suicide, because he was mad at Truitt, and then turned around and left Truitt all that money," Oakar said. "That makes no goddamned sense to me! Talk to Molly Moore. She says she doesn't believe the story either. Let's nip it in the bud before this gets completely out of hand." Kathy said she would talk with Moore.

Less than a minute later, Moore phoned and claimed that she was "outraged at the suicide story being spread by NIS." Kathy assured her that her brother had nothing to do with killing all those men. Deluded by Moore's declarations of sympathy, Kathy lowered her guard and told Moore about the NIS agents' visits to her parents' home. Moore arranged to meet Kathy in Cleveland the next morning. After hanging up, Moore coauthored a story with George Wilson for Saturday's paper that identified Kathy and Clayton but failed to name Kendall Truitt. The story quoted an anonymous *Iowa* sailor complaining that the murder/suicide theory "must be something the reporters made up." Jack Dorsey was credited with breaking the life-insurance story and for disclosing that there were chronic manpower shortages and a lack of training in all three turrets.

KATHY WAS logging her conversation with Molly Moore in her notebook when another telephone call interrupted her. It was A.J. Plunkett, a just-the-facts-please female reporter for the *Daily Press* and *Times-Herald* newspapers in Newport News and Hampton, Virginia. These scrappy suburban dailies, owned by the *Chicago Tribune*, had a circulation of about 100,000 and tried to compete with the larger, better-established Norfolk newspapers. Plunkett, a Texan in her later twenties, told Kathy that she heard about the investigation from a lieutenant commander in the Norfolk Naval Base's legal office. Unlike many reporters, Plunkett lacked "a gift for gab." She also wasn't well versed in the *Iowa* story, garbling details. This put Kathy off, and she didn't open up to Plunkett as she had with Jack Dorsey and Molly Moore. Kathy did deny that her brother and Kendall Truitt were gay. Disappointed with how little she learned, Plunkett next phoned Evelyn Hartwig, who reacted to the reporter in much the same way as her daughter had.

While Plunkett was getting the runaround, Charlie Bogino, another *Daily Press* and *Times-Herald* reporter, had better success with his sources aboard the *Iowa*. A former Army intelligence officer and Russian-language specialist in his early thirties, Bogino had met John Mullahy several weeks before the explosion and had kept in touch with him since the damaged battleship returned from the Caribbean. Mullahy told Bogino about the misfires in Turret One, the manpower shortages and absence of training in the turrets, and everything he knew about the NIS investigation. Mullahy scoffed at the notion that Truitt could have triggered the explosion to collect the insurance money, because at least fourteen other sailors had handled the powder bags, and Truitt had not touched them.

Mullahy knew for a fact that Truitt hadn't handled any powder bags on April 19. Truitt had been taking it easy that day and had done no work. He also rejected as asinine a report broadcast on a Norfolk television station that a bag of powder was already smoldering before it went up the hoist to the center gun room. "Who the hell is going to be crazy enough to handle a bag of burning powder?" Mullahy exclaimed, adding, "If you don't believe me, go ask Truitt. He lives in an apartment directly across the street from me."

Mullahy gave Truitt's address to Bogino. That bit of information came in very handy later that evening.

Plunkett and Bogino jointly wrote a story that they asked executive editor Jack Davis to read on a computer terminal. Davis detected a flaw. While the reporters named Truitt in their story, neither of them had reached him for comment. Davis said they had to interview Truitt if they wanted to identify him in print. For the next four or five hours, Plunkett and Bogino took turns dialing Truitt's number and having no success. By midnight, as the presses began to roll, they still hadn't reached Truitt. Davis allowed Truitt's name to remain in the story, but he told the two reporters to stake out Truitt's apartment and stay there until they obtained an interview with him.

Bogino rapped on Truitt's front door about 1 A.M. Truitt, who was dressed in a tank top and sweat pants, opened the door and invited the two reporters inside. Truitt's wife, Carole, wearing jeans and a tight-fitting body shirt, asked Plunkett and Bogino to sit down and talk with them. And that's what they did for the next two hours.

Bogino decided to ask his most difficult questions first. "Did you do it? Are you a murderer?" "No," Truitt replied. There was no hostility in his voice. "Are you a faggot?" Bogino spluttered, almost strangling on his last word. Truitt regarded him quizzically for several seconds, then laughed and said, "No. Why is that important?" Bogino was at a loss for words and looked toward Plunkett for help. She was busy scribbling in her notepad and said nothing. There was dead silence for at least ten seconds. Finally, Truitt got up and walked into the kitchen, returning with a certificate from the state of Illinois commending him for his bravery on the day of the explosion. He handed the document to the reporters. "He shouldn't be accused of anything. He's a hero," Carole said.

Truitt said the NIS agents had all sorts of wild theories. He said they asked him if Clayton were suicidal. "There's speculation that's gone so far as to say that I sent up some powder bags with explosives attached," he said. "C'mon, I was in a magazine full of powder. I had eight other guys in there with me. Right now, NIS has got a closed mind. The agents have decided I somehow was the cause of the explosion, which isn't true. Or, two, that Clay committed suicide. And that, too, I can't believe is true." The life-insurance policy "was a bullshit issue. . . . Clay never expected to die, and I was his best friend."

It was after 3 A.M. when Plunkett and Bogino left the Truitts' apartment. Kendall and Carole walked them to their car. Truitt wanted to know if his name would be used in their story. Bogino nodded his head affirmatively, and Carole gasped, "Oh, my God!" Despite the late hour, the reporters woke managing editor Bob Evans and told him about the interview. Even though he was groggy, Evans listened with interest and told them to go home, get some sleep, and return to the office around noon to write a more comprehensive story for Sunday's edition. Their Saturday and Sunday pieces put

Truitt's name in the public eye for the first time. Many news organizations began publishing with impunity ill-sourced or nonsourced allegations about Truitt. There was little worry that a young sailor with limited funds would sue them for libel or invasion of privacy.

MOLLY MOORE arrived at Kathy Kubicina's home on Saturday morning, May 20. While they were together, Moore constantly told Kathy that her information had come from "CHINFO." "What the hell is that?" Kathy inquired. "That's the Chief of Naval Information, the Navy's public-relations office. They put out information," Moore explained. "Good. Give me their phone number. I want to ask them some questions. I didn't know there was such a thing," Kathy said. "You can't call them," Moore said. "They only answer questions or give information to reporters."

Kathy said that her brother had nothing to do with causing the explosion. "My brother is not a crazed mass murderer who would kill forty-six other innocent men." In the early afternoon, she drove Moore to her parents' home so the reporter could look at her brother's room and interview Earl and Evelyn Hartwig. Moore flipped through Clayton's scrapbook and was given copies of his two wills and several of his letters. Kathy had a good feeling about how the day with Moore had gone, but she was sadly disappointed when the reporter's story appeared in the *Washington Post* on May 25.

Moore's lead paragraph set the tone for the article, stating, "A Navy investigation of the sixteen-inch gun turret aboard the battleship USS *Iowa* that killed 47 men in April now is focused on a possible suicide or murder attempt involving two sailors in the turret, rather than an accident related to poor training or faulty equipment, according to sources close to the probe." Kathy, her parents, and Kendall Truitt were all named in Moore's story, but not a single Navy source was identified. The first positive reference to Clayton didn't appear until the thirteenth paragraph.

Moore would later claim that she never believed the NIS account. "The first day I got this tip about a homosexual love affair, I told the national desk that it's so far-fetched I don't believe it," she said. Then why did she cover the story the way she did? "You have to report the fact that NIS is doing an investigation, even if it's a lie, because it's news," she said. She defended her May 25 article, pointing out that it contained criticism of NIS for botching the 1987 "Moscow Station" investigation and also included allegations from civil rights groups that NIS routinely trampled on the constitutional rights of suspected homosexuals.

AS INTEREST in the *Iowa* story grew by geometrical proportions, Rear Admiral Brent Baker, who was scheduled to become Chief of Naval Information in July, found himself increasingly frustrated trying to control the direction of the story. The forty-eight-year-old Baker, who had served as a Navy lobbyist on Capitol Hill, was a proponent of something he called "pro-active public affairs," meaning planting favorable stories, selectively leaking documents and background information, cultivating friendly reporters, discrediting unfavorable stories and "hostile" reporters, and staging dubious "photo opportunities." These tactics had served him well as long as he was dealing with reporters who were assigned to the Pentagon and grateful for any bone Baker tossed their way. But this unruly mob covering the *Iowa*—which included police reporters, legal specialists, science writers, and even gay-rights advocates—was something quite different. An increasing number of senior admirals were perturbed by the "trashy" stories about the *Iowa* and the Navy that were proliferating in print and on the airwaves. Baker feared that the flag officers' indignation might rebound on him.

For all of his outward cockiness, Baker knew that he was lucky to have gotten as high up in the Navy as he had, since he had been involved in some sticky incidents that almost derailed his career. When he was working on Capitol Hill for the Office of Legislative Affairs, Baker designed a computerized system to rate fifty-seven senators and congressmen who were members of the Military Reform Caucus on their voting records on seven pieces of legislation deemed vital to the Navy. This included appropriations for the FA-18 aircraft, money for more nuclear attack and fleet ballistic submarines, and funding for two *Nimitz*-class nuclear-powered aircraft carriers.

Baker intended to use his ratings system to intimidate "enemy" lawmakers into changing their voting habits or face the possibility that naval installations, contracts, personnel, and vessels might be stripped from their districts. Baker was so carried away with his program that he wrote a detailed memorandum about it that was widely circulated throughout the Navy. It was leaked to *Defense Week*, a highly regarded periodical that covered the Pentagon and the defense industry. After the *Defense Week* article appeared, Senator Ted Stevens, a Republican from Alaska who was a member of the Military Reform Caucus, had it inserted in the *Congressional Record*. Representative Jack Brooks, a crusty Texas Democrat who chaired the powerful House Committee on Government Operations, read the *Congressional Record* item and went into orbit. Brooks, who had been an enlisted Marine in heavy combat during World War II, summoned Baker's boss, Rear Admiral Bruce Newell, to his office and shouted, "I want that dirty, rotten son-of-a-bitch [Baker] off Capitol Hill by sundown!"

Brooks and his staff had good reason to believe that Baker's career had been dealt a mortal blow, but such was not the case. Baker was quietly shifted to a Pentagon job. The Navy was impressed by Baker's ratings system, even though it regretted that he had stirred up a hornet's nest by calling undue attention to it. Nevertheless, he was awarded the Legion of Merit, largely for devising the ratings system. The citation accompanying the medal lauded "his keen, perceptive insight into the legislative process, Congressional personalities, and Navy programs and issues."

DURING THE *Iowa* investigation, Baker denied that he or any of his subordinates leaked any derogatory NIS material about Clayton Hartwig. However, his credibility wasn't helped by reporters like Molly Moore, who proclaimed that her confidential information had come from CHINFO. One day, as Baker was strolling through the corridors of the Pentagon, he ran into an acquaintance who worked for Admiral William J. Crowe Jr., Chairman of the Joint Chiefs of Staff. "Hey, Brent, what about all those leaks about the *Iowa*?" asked the officer, a Navy captain. Without slowing his stride, Baker said, "God damn! I wonder who is leaking all of this." He would later claim that he had never been "personally nor morally happy" with the NIS allegations against Hartwig and Truitt. "I never leaked anything, and I was offended that someone's reputation was destroyed by leaks and innuendos."

Admiral Bud Edney wasn't offended by the substance of the leaked allegations about the two *Iowa* sailors. He believed the information was true, but he was fulminating over the leaks. He didn't believe the media had any right to the material until he told them they did. Edney summoned Baker to his office and screamed at the public-relations man, "I abhor leaks!" The vice chief informed Baker that many admirals were irritated by the unauthorized flow of information. He ordered Baker to stop the leaks or face the possibility of being assigned to Antarctica, where he could practice public relations for penguins.

Rear Admiral Ted Gordon, the NIS commander, also questioned Baker about the leaks and was told that Baker's hands were clean. Gordon was skeptical. They had both served on Capitol Hill, and Gordon had seen Baker in operation. Gordon told Baker that potential witnesses were refusing to cooperate with NIS, fearing that anything said in confidence would end up in print or on television.

Gordon took to task Brian McKee, the NIS civilian director, and Robert Powers, the criminal investigations division head, about the leaks. Both men said they "despised leaks to the press and would lock up any agent they caught passing on investigative material." Gordon flew to Norfolk and personally interrogated agent Mike Dorsey. Dorsey was a logical suspect, because his brother, Jack, had been the first reporter to reveal that NIS was pursuing the murder/suicide angle. Mike Dorsey swore that he had revealed nothing to his brother. Gordon told "Bobby" Nigro, who supervised the agents assigned to the *Iowa* investigation, to gather his men. The admiral wanted to talk to them. "I gave them hell. I told the agents, 'These leaks are killing us!'" Gordon said. "And they all swore that they weren't the culprit." But one of them was not playing straight with Gordon. That agent had slipped to a network television producer computerized diskettes containing everything that NIS had gathered.

THE FIRST hint that the entire NIS *Iowa* investigation had been compromised occurred on Tuesday, May 23, when Fred Francis, the NBC News

Pentagon correspondent, called Kathy Kubicina. Francis had come to the network from the CBS affiliate in Miami, where he had made a name for himself covering organized crime and the booming narcotics trade. In his fifteen years at NBC, he had earned a solid reputation covering the world's hot spots, including Iran, Libya, Northern Ireland, and Nicaragua. An aggressive reporter, he was also adept at allaying interview subjects' fears with a mixture of small talk and empathy. He asked Kathy if they could "talk off the record." At this point, she was still unsophisticated in media jargon and didn't understand that if she agreed, then he couldn't use her name or even say that his information "came from a member of the Hartwig family." She told him that was fine with her.

"You need an attorney," Francis said. "I may help you look for one in Virginia. Virginia is where you need to file the lawsuit [to recover the insurance money]. That's where the ship is docked and the credit union is located." He told Kathy not to tell anyone about his offer to find legal help for her. He then shifted the focus of the conversation, stating that NIS had discovered letters in her brother's locker proving that Clayton had been involved in causing the explosion. Following that shocker, he returned to the Hartwig family's desire to recover the money from Clayton's life-insurance policy. He said they had a good chance of winning a lawsuit, and he would help them "undermine his [Truitt's] integrity."

Francis said he had no faith in the Naval Investigative Service. And then he switched topics again, asking, "You do realize that there was a strong possibility that Clayton was a homosexual?" Kathy said she didn't believe that was true, and added, "He's gone. If he was a homosexual, I still love him. He was my brother." Francis told her "not to talk to NIS agents again." He gave her his office number and said he would call her back before he aired another piece about the *Iowa*. The interview disturbed Kathy so much that she wrote four pages about it in her journal.

Fred Francis was being assisted on this story by Len Tepper, a tubby television producer nicknamed "Mad Dog." Bearded and in his early thirties, Tepper began his TV career in the NBC mailroom and had risen up the network ladder by cultivating federal investigators assigned to the U.S. District Court in Brooklyn. One of Tepper's best sources, and a regular drinking buddy, was James Whitener, the former special agent in charge of the NIS Brooklyn office. Whitener had been busted and shipped to Norfolk, where he had offered to computerize the voluminous NIS *Iowa* files. Whitener would later testify, in a civil suit brought by the Hartwig family against the Navy, that he had almost total control of those files. Tepper, who admitted that he was hopeless with computers, said, "I have enough trouble logging on," then added, "Military stuff is not my bailiwick." Despite those two impediments, Tepper was still able to deliver diskettes containing the complete NIS *Iowa* files to Fred Francis at the Pentagon. Was agent James Whitener his source? Some top NIS officials later claimed that he was. But

Tepper refused to say, and Whitener denied he had anything to do with leaking the diskettes.

On Wednesday afternoon, May 24, Francis asked Brent Baker to drop by his tiny office in the Pentagon, located about a hundred yards down the hall from Baker's. Francis's computer was on and he was fiddling with the keyboard when Baker arrived. The correspondent inserted a diskette and entered a password; a file popped up on the screen. Francis scrolled through the text, pausing from time to time to give Baker an opportunity to be able to identify NIS interviews with Kathy Kubicina, Earl and Evelyn Hartwig, Charlene Meter, Kendall and Carole Truitt, John Mullahy, Bryan Hoover, and others. Baker was slack-jawed. He said he thought, "Fred's got the whole damned file!" "Look, Brent, I've got all this stuff. What do I do with it?" Francis asked. Baker's blank stare led Francis to believe that the admiral had thrown in the towel. "He [Baker] was the admiral in charge of the Navy's entire public-relations apparatus, and he had no idea of what to do," Francis later told a forum of journalists and Navy public-relations people at the Naval War College in Newport, Rhode Island.

Baker was down, but not out. He knew he had to do some major damage control, and fast. He didn't want to be blamed for this massive leak of classified material. He could have tried to have Francis arrested for having the diskettes in his possession, but he didn't. That would create more problems. He had to inform Admiral Edney and the Chief of Naval Operations. "My teeth almost fell out in shock at what I saw on the computer screen," he told Edney. He forewarned the CNO's executive assistant, telling him, "We've got a real problem here."

Fred Francis didn't keep his promise to call Kathy Kubicina before broadcasting a story about her brother. She first learned that Francis was planning a piece the day it was to air. She received a call from Mark Brender, an ABC News Pentagon producer and former naval officer who had distinctly different views about the *Iowa* story than Fred Francis. Brender told Kathy that he had no idea what the NBC piece would contain. She was in such a dither about the upcoming Francis story that she called NIS agent Tom Goodman in Norfolk to see what he knew. Goodman proved to be of no help.

At 6:15 P.M. on May 24, just fifteen minutes before the *NBC Nightly News* was scheduled to go on the air, Len Tepper called Kathy and explained that he worked with Fred Francis. He wanted to know where he could find Kendall Truitt. Kathy had no idea. Could Tepper tell her what would be in the Francis piece? Would it be good or bad? "Just watch it," Tepper said, abruptly hanging up.

Francis led the broadcast that night. He announced that five weeks after the *Iowa* explosion, the Navy was unable to find an accidental cause. He identified Clayton Hartwig and Kendall Truitt and showed photographs of both men, alleging that there had been a "special relationship" between them that had soured. These two sailors were now the hub of the investigation. The words *special relationship* were highlighted on the screen. It didn't take a genius to figure out that Francis was labeling the two men homosexuals. The piece endorsed an unproven theory advanced by Captain Ed Messina that "some sort of detonating device" had been inserted between the first two powder bags inside a lead-foil packet. Francis claimed the Hartwig family confirmed to him that Clayton had been "depressed" when the "relationship" with Truitt ended. The correspondent disclosed that Hartwig had made Truitt the beneficiary of his life-insurance policy.

Francis said "some disturbing facts have been uncovered about Truitt." He explained that Truitt had pled guilty to an auto-theft charge and that a search of Truitt's belongings in 1987 turned up some gunpowder and blasting caps. He correctly reported that Truitt had been working in a powder magazine at the bottom of the turret when the explosion occurred, but he erroneously stated that the lead-foil packets were stored there. Francis also erred by claiming that one of these foil packets had been discovered during a search of Truitt's home. The packet had actually been discovered during a search of Truitt's locker on the *Iowa*. Francis's premise seemed to follow these lines: (1) The detonator had been inserted in a lead-foil packet; (2) Truitt had access to these packets; (3) Truitt had somehow managed to route a powder bag containing a detonator up to the center gun room; (4) Truitt's intention had been to murder his former lover, in order to obtain the insurance money.

Francis ran a videotaped clip of Truitt recorded at the Norfolk press conference in April when the lanky gunner's mate had been praised by the Navy as a "hero." The NBC correspondent said Truitt denied killing forty-seven of his shipmates or engaging in a homosexual relationship with Clayton Hartwig. In his final paragraph, Francis somewhat backed away from the conjecture and innuendo that constituted the rest of his report, saying that the Navy might never know if the blast had been caused by a murderer, someone who committed suicide, or was an accident, because much of the evidence had been washed overboard during a hasty cleanup. As soon as the piece concluded, Kathy dialed the number that Francis had given her, hoping to ask him why he hadn't been fair and given her brother's side of the story. She was unable to reach the reporter. She left numerous messages for him, but Francis never called back.

A short time later, an editor for NBC Radio News called Kathy. He identified himself and said, "I'd like to talk about the detonating device and the other things they found. You are the Hartwig boy's sister. Is your brother available for comment?" Kathy screamed, "Have you been living under a rock for the past month? My brother is dead, you fucking idiot!" She slammed down the phone and sobbed. Before the night was over, she fielded 117 calls from newspeople asking for interviews. The next day, she received an additional eighty calls. Her house was under siege, surrounded by television trucks sprouting satellite transceivers and equipped with bright

Lieutenant Commander Richard Bagley, the battleship's Legal Officer. (1989 *Iowa* Cruisebook)

Kathy Kubincina crusaded for ten years to clear her brother's name.

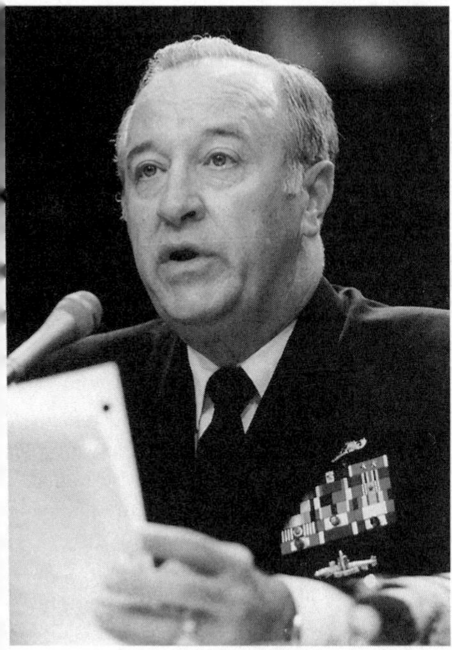

Admiral Carl Trost, the Chief of Naval Operations, defends the Navy's handling of the Iowa investigation to the Senate Armed Services Committee. (AP/Wide World Photos)

Rear Admiral Ted Gordon, the Navy's Judge Advocate General, who assailed Rear Admiral Richard Milligan's investigation of the *Iowa* explosion. (U.S. Navy)

Captain Fred Moosally pins the Navy and Marine Corps Medal, the highest award given for heroism in a noncombat situation, on Gunner's Mate First Class John Mullahy for helping save the *Iowa* after the explosion in Turret Two.

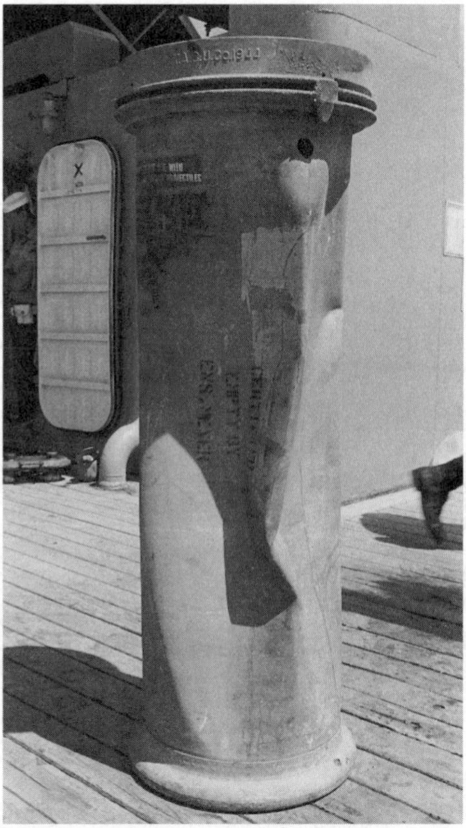

A powder canister crushed by the water that flooded into the magazines following the explosion. Manufactured in 1944, it was certified empty by Dan Meyer.

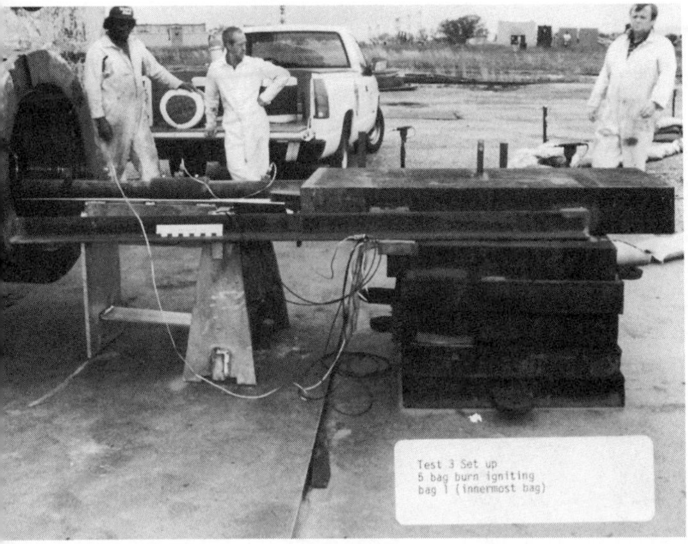

As seen by these Navy photos taken at the Naval Surface Warfare Center at Dahlgren, Virginia, the live fire tests to replicate the explosion aboard the *Iowa* were less than realistic. The ramming apparatus (1) bore no similarity to what was found in the gunroom. The gun barrel (2) was much like an elongated sewer pipe wedged between two concrete and steel partitions. The bore (3) was rusty, badly pitted and almost completely eroded.

)

(2)

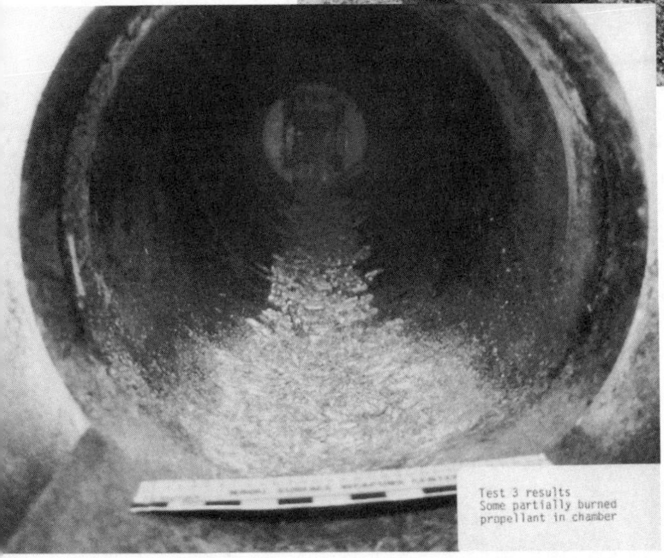

(3)

Turret Two's right projectile shortly after it was dislodged from the barrel. The shell "disappeared" for eighteen months. When it and the left projectile were discovered in a Dahlgren storeroom, they were tested and found to have the same "foreign material" on them as the center projectile, thus discrediting the navy's assertion that a detonator was used to initiate the explosion. (U.S. Navy)

Rear Admiral Brent Baker was Chief of Naval Information and thought the Navy should issue a full, unconditional apology to the Hartwig family. (U.S. Navy)

On August 4, 1989, Turret One fires the first round since the disaster.
(1989 *Iowa* Cruisebook)

Captain Fred Moosally (seated in a chair) beams after the August 4th Gunshoot. Lieutenant Dan Meyer (standing directly behind the captain) doesn't share his exuberance. (1989 *Iowa* Cruisebook)

Douglas Katz (seen as a vice admiral in 1995) came to the Hartwigs' home in 1989 and informed the family that their son caused the *Iowa* explosion. He returned two years later to say that he had given them erroneous information on his previous visit. (U.S. Navy)

Kendall Truitt (center) listens with his wife, Carol, at a Miami press conference while their attorney, Ellis Rubin, attacks the Navy's handling of the *Iowa* investigation. (AP/Wide World Photos)

Captain Joseph Miceli, head of the technical investigation into the *Iowa* explosion, testifies before the Senate Armed Services Committee. (Bob Peterson)

Captain Douglas Katz, accompanied by Commander Sam Falcona, leaves Earl and Evelyn Hartwig's Cleveland home after telling the family that the Navy had concluded that their son intentionally triggered the explosion aboard the USS *Iowa* that killed 47 men. (Photograph by Luci S. Williams. Reprinted with permission from *The Plain Dealer* © 1989. All Rights Reserved.)

Rear Admiral Richard Milligan (right), who was in charge of the *Iowa* investigation, is assisted by his legal counsel, Commander Ron Swanson, as he makes a point before the Senate Armed Services Committee using a diagram of Turret Two. (AP/Wide World Photos)

Captain Joseph Miceli (left to right), Rear Admiral Richard Milligan, and Robert Powers of the Naval Investigative Service testify before the Senate Armed Services Committee about the *Iowa* investigation. (Bob Peterson)

Captain Fred Moosally tells the Senate Armed Services Committee that he doesn't "agree or disagree" with the Navy's findings that Clayton Hartwig sabotaged Turret Two's center gun. (AP/Wide World Photos)

Attorney Kreig Brusnahan (left to right), Evelyn Hartwig, and Kathy Kubicina confront Captain Fred Moosally (back to the camera) following his testimony to the Senate Armed Services Committee. (Bob Peterson)

Gunner's Mate Third Class Kendall Truitt testifies before the House Armed Services Committee. Gunner's Mate First Class John Mullahy can be seen in the background in the space between the two chairs. (AP/Wide World Photos)

FBI Agents Richard Ault (center) and Roy Hazelwood (right) defend their "Equivocal Death Analysis" of Clayton Hartwig at a congressional hearing. (Bob Peterson)

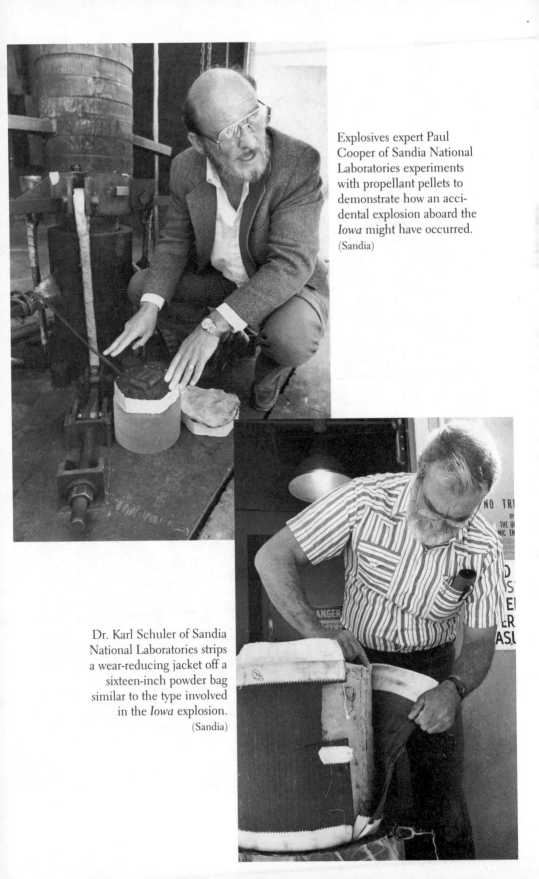

Explosives expert Paul Cooper of Sandia National Laboratories experiments with propellant pellets to demonstrate how an accidental explosion aboard the *Iowa* might have occurred. (Sandia)

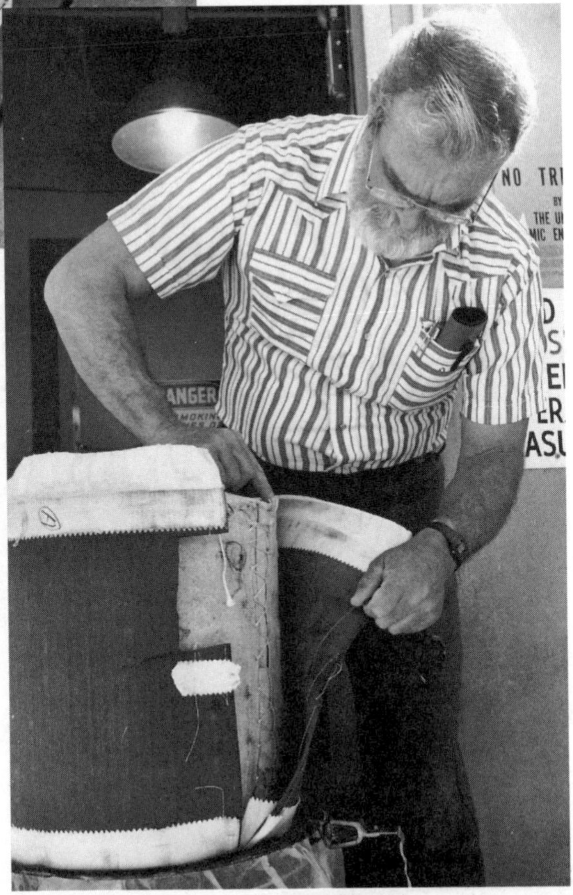

Dr. Karl Schuler of Sandia National Laboratories strips a wear-reducing jacket off a sixteen-inch powder bag similar to the type involved in the *Iowa* explosion. (Sandia)

Rear Admiral Ming Chang, the Navy Inspector General, whose report on the *Iowa* explosion was suppressed by Admiral Bud Edney. (U.S. Navy)

Admiral Mike Boorda attempted to cover up details of the *Iowa* disaster when he was Chief of Naval Personnel. He committed suicide when he was Chief of Naval Operations in 1996. (U.S. Navy)

60 Minutes anchor Mike Wallace interviews Brian Scanio, the first fireman to enter Turret Two following the explosion. (Adriadne Allan)

In 1991, Dan Meyer, by then out of the Navy, appears on *60 Minutes* and says that Clayton Hartwig's body was found in a pit below the gunroom, making it impossible for Hartwig to have triggered the blast. (Bob Peterson)

Mike Wallace questions Admiral Frank Kelso following the Chief of Naval Operations's apology to the Hartwig family. (U.S. Navy)

klieg lights. At one point, she, her three children, and their dog were forced to hide in the basement. She received one death threat, and an anonymous caller told her neighbor across the street to tell "that bitch Kubicina to keep her mouth shut! She's opening a can of worms! Get her ass off TV!"

Earl and Evelyn had been attending a church service when the NBC piece aired. Kathy taped the story for them. When the Hartwigs arrived at Kathy's home, she was standing in the driveway. She told her parents that the story had in effect branded Clayton and Kendall Truitt homosexuals and strongly suggested that one or both had set off the explosion, murdering their friends. Evelyn collapsed, moaning, "Oh, my God! Oh, my God!" Earl, Kathy, and Charlene Meter picked up Evelyn and helped get her inside the house. After she watched the videotape, Evelyn became agitated again, wailing, "This is terrible! This is terrible!"

THE DAY Fred Francis's report aired was the very same day that Captain Joseph Miceli's technical support team finally freed the 2,700-pound projectile that had been stuck in Turret Two's center gun since the explosion. The next day, Miceli released a report rejecting the theory that the explosion had resulted from an intentional act by a crewman. The sabotage theory had dominated NIS efforts since May 9. According to Miceli, friction was the "most likely scenario." Granules of propellant had dribbled out of a bag near the breech; the loose powder was then dragged along the bottom of the chamber by other powder bags; the granules were superheated by friction, producing sparks and igniting the other bags. This was a viable theory, Miceli wrote, because his team had successfully tested it at Dahlgren.

It was a stunner, especially coming from the very same individual who, after his first full day aboard the *Iowa*, had declared that the explosion must have been caused by a person, because there was nothing wrong with the guns or the powder. Miceli's friction report generated shock waves in the Navy, and there was pressure on him to come up with another report that supported the sabotage theory. That happened within three weeks, but in the meantime, NIS went about its business, acting as if the friction report never existed.

DURING THE time that the friction report was agitating some of the Navy's brass, Commander Ron Swanson, Admiral Milligan's chief legal adviser, was in a sweat to complete the *Iowa* report by May 27. This tight deadline had not been mandated by Admiral Milligan, but Swanson was trying to meet it because he had a clerical problem. He didn't know how to operate a word processor. "I didn't even type," he later testified. Swanson had two other attorneys assigned to him, but only one of them, Lieutenant Commander Jeff Styron, a Naval Academy graduate, was computer literate. Styron did the typing while Swanson and the other lawyer, Lieutenant Pat Brogan, took turns dictating.

Styron was leaving the investigation on May 27 to work on a master's degree in environmental law at the College of William and Mary. He finished the first draft of the report before he departed. He later said that when he compared his draft with Admiral Milligan's final version, there were "no significant differences." That's quite a statement, considering the fact that a number of critical scientific tests had not even begun when Styron left.

MOST OF the families of the forty-six other men killed in the *Iowa* explosion rallied around the Hartwigs after the NBC story ran. Bob Gedeon, an eight-year Navy veteran from Cleveland who had served two tours on gunboats in Vietnam's Mekong Delta, called the *Plain Dealer* newspaper and told the editor, "This is nothing but bullshit!" Gedeon's opinion carried some weight, since his son, Seaman Robert J. "Bobby" Gedeon III, had been killed in Turret Two while serving as the primerman of Jack Thompson's left gun. On the morning of his death, Bobby wrote his parents a letter saying he didn't want to go back into the turret, as it was unsafe.

Gedeon was furious about Fred Francis's reporting. The Cleveland NBC affiliate put him on the air, denouncing the leaks and what he considered to be the scapegoating of an innocent sailor. A passionate, articulate man who coached youth-league football, basketball, and baseball teams in his spare time, he began a letter-writing campaign to persuade the Navy to stop chasing shadow conspiracies and return to the serious business of finding out what really happened to Turret Two. He wrote President George Bush, Defense Secretary Richard Cheney, and several members of the House Armed Services Committee. He received form letters from them. And then he did something that proved to be much more productive. He got in touch with a high-ranking Marine Corps officer with whom he had served in Vietnam and asked him to check into Captain Miceli's technical inquiry. The officer poked around and informed Gedeon that the technical side of the investigation was not all it was cracked up to be.

The Marine also supplied Gedeon with a thick stack of photographs that vividly illustrated just how absurd some of Miceli's tests were. Equipment was held together with clamps, masking tape, rubber bands, and glue. Plywood was substituted for steel. The rifling of the sixteen-inch gun barrel used for most of the tests was practically nonexistent. "The photographs bore no semblance to what the Navy claimed in their fancy technical reports. I looked at those photographs, reflected on my son's death, and knew how it felt to be a rape victim," Gedeon said.

In Burnside, Pennsylvania, Butch and Peggy Price, parents of the right gun captain, Matt Price, watched Fred Francis's piece with disgust. They called Earl and Evelyn Hartwig the next day to express their sorrow. "I knew that Clay was Matt's friend, and he wouldn't do something like that to Matt," Peggy said. Evelyn told her how grateful she and Earl were for their support, saying, "When we saw Fred Francis, we thought, 'Oh, my God, are the other families going to think that my son killed them all?' Thank God there's another family out there who believes us!"

After talking with the Hartwigs, Butch and Peggy held a family conference with their other children and their spouses and decided that they needed to take some positive action. The family began making phone calls to senior *Iowa* officers, lobbying members of Pennsylvania's congressional delegation, locating witnesses, and prodding reporters into looking at safety problems that existed on the battleship prior to the explosion. A deeply religious woman, Peggy was willing to employ a poison pen when she thought it was warranted. With a vengeance, she went after Captain Joseph Miceli and Lieutenant Commander Kenneth Costigan, the *Iowa*'s former gunnery officer. And she mailed Captain Fred Moosally a high-school graduation picture of her son, along with his autopsy photo. "This is what I sent you, and this is what you sent me back," she wrote. On another occasion, she wrote Admiral Milligan that he was "Satan" for the treatment "you have inflicted upon the Hartwig family." Moosally and Milligan did not respond.

Another ardent supporter of the Hartwigs was Patsy McMullen, widow of Boatswain's Mate Third Class Todd McMullen. Patsy, who tended bar at the Dockside 21 Restaurant in Port Everglades, Florida, was working behind the bar the day the NBC story ran. The tavern was filled with active-duty sailors and Navy retirees. "The guys heard what that report had to say about Hartwig and Truitt, and they all got pissed off and bent out of shape," Patsy said. Catcalls filled the bar. "Sailors were yelling, 'No way! It's the equipment! The admirals are just using sailors to cover their fat asses! That entire thing about the *Iowa*, that's a bunch of garbage!'" Patsy called Kathy Kubicina the next day and told her about the reaction of the Navy men in the bar to the NBC story.

In Greeneville, Tennessee, the parents of Gunner's Mate Third Class Jack Thompson Jr. came close to throwing a potted plant at their television set while watching Fred Francis's report. They wrote to Earl and Evelyn Hartwig, reassuring them that there were millions of people in America who didn't believe anything that appeared on network television news. "I couldn't take what the Hartwigs took. It would kill me," Jack Sr. said. Mildred Thompson recalled how afraid her son had been about going back in Turret Two. His widow, Leasa, bristled over the NBC story. "It's bullshit! I just don't believe it! . . . The Navy has tried to cover up everything. It's been a bunch of bull from the very first day," she said. "You don't understand how something like this can happen, until it happens to you." Leasa called Kathy and offered her emotional support.

AFTER THE explosion, the Navy went to great lengths to invent the fable that Lieutenant Philip Buch, Turret Two's officer, and Senior Chief Reggie Ziegler, the turret's senior enlisted man, had enjoyed an ideal working relationship. Ziegler's widow, Sharon, knew about the bad blood that had existed between her husband and the callow lieutenant. After watching the NBC piece, Sharon thought, "Oh, boy, the Navy's got them a scapegoat!" She called Kathy Kubicina and told her, "I can't believe that it was murder/suicide. If your brother was nuts and suicidal, then Reggie would have known it."

But Emily Buch-Hague, Lieutenant Buch's mother, reacted differently, telling the *Albuquerque Journal* newspaper, "You can't help but say, 'Why couldn't this man [Clayton Hartwig] have jumped overboard instead of causing the deaths of all these other men who also had things to live for." She and her ex-husband, Joe Buch, became staunch defenders of the Navy's sabotage theory. Joe Buch was confident that his son had been "the victim of a deliberate act." "Well, hell, no one wants to believe their son was killed needlessly, but some maniac did this," he said.

One other *Iowa* family briefly held Clayton Hartwig and Kendall Truitt responsible for the carnage inside Turret Two. Paula Lawrence of Springfield, Ohio, the mother of Errick Lawrence, who died in the center gun room, was shocked by the NBC report. When her husband, Dick, got home from work, she described the television piece. "You mean to tell me that a bunch of queers killed my son over a bunch of junk?" Dick screamed.

The Lawrences turned to their Navy casualty assistance officer, and she told them, "I don't put much stock in the TV report." Both Lawrences then began to question the report. "I did not believe it," Paula said. Her son stood over six feet tall and was strong as an ox. "Errick would have done everything in his power to stop a situation that would have caused the explosion," she said. "If Errick thought it was a life-threatening situation, he would have yelled, 'Get your fannies out of here!' "

15

"We Know That He Did It."

AS THE *IOWA* families reacted to the Fred Francis story, NIS pulled out the stops to locate more potential witnesses. At this point, the agency only seemed to be interested in the sex lives of Kendall Truitt and Clayton Hartwig. Dale Mortensen told agents Tom Goodman and Ed Goodwin that Hartwig was "quiet, stayed to himself, and was a good worker." Mortensen said other crew members had come to him from time to time claiming that Hartwig and Truitt were gay, but he could never prove it.

The morning of the explosion, Mortensen said, Ernie Hanyecz, Turret Two's leading petty officer, informed him that Errick Lawrence, not Clayton Hartwig, was going to be the center gun captain. Mortensen also told the NIS agents that the blastproof steel door was ajar between the turret officer's booth and the center gun room in Turret Two. Someone had to have been entering or leaving the gun room prior to the explosion. This explained why the fireball and shock wave wiped out the turret officer's booth and did catastrophic damage to the right and left gun rooms.

Lieutenant Dan Meyer was very cautious about what he told Goodman and Goodwin. He had seen their confidential reports become front-page news and appear on television before the ink had dried on them. "They sat me down in a chair that had restraining straps for your wrists. It was very intimidating, and I began to wonder when the third degree would commence," Meyer said. He correctly ascertained that the agents were only interested in what he could tell them about Hartwig's and Truitt's alleged homosexual activities. They asked him if Chief Ziegler had once wisecracked that the two sailors were his "faggots." Meyer conceded that was true, but he added that Ziegler had also said that he didn't have a shred of evidence against either man. The NIS agents asked about the 1987 allegations against Hartwig and Truitt. Meyer suggested they talk to Captain Larry Seaquist in the Pentagon or to retired Master Chief Chuck Hill, who was living on a farm outside of Norfolk.

Seaquist was never contacted by NIS, but Hill was visited by an NIS agent who drove out to his farm. The agent had first called the retired master chief gunner's mate and said that he didn't feel like driving "all the way out in the boondocks." "How do I know you're an NIS agent? How do I know whom I'm talking with? If you want to talk with me, you can drive out here," Hill demanded. It was nearing sunset when the agent arrived. The bulky, crew-cut retired chief and the NIS agent spoke in Hill's front yard.

Hill said the agent stammered a lot, had a hard time making eye contact with Hill, and asked questions that didn't make much sense. "What are you really looking for?" the gravel-voiced Hill probed. "Are they [Hartwig and Truitt] queers?" the agent asked in a quavering voice. "Hell, no, but you aren't interested in hearing that they're straight. I'm not answering any more of your goddamned questions!" Hill bellowed. "You've got to, I'm an NIS agent," the investigator said. "And I'm a goddamned bullfrog! You can fuck off! Get the hell off my property! You're probably not even going to write down what I said, because it wasn't what you wanted to hear," Hill shouted. The agent beat a hasty retreat to his car, scattering gravel in all directions as he gunned out of Hill's driveway. Hill was right. The agent didn't write down a thing he said.

The agents put John Mullahy through another interview session. Mullahy, who by then had been eliminated as a murder suspect by NIS, told agents Mike Dorsey and Rob Cully that Truitt had been about twenty-five minutes late arriving in the magazines the morning of April 19. Chief Ziegler had been irritated, but Truitt explained that he had had to go to the head. The agents asked if Truitt had stolen Lieutenant Buch's wallet when Buch and Mullahy passed out on the beach earlier that year. Mullahy said that almost everyone in Turret Two believed that Truitt had taken the wallet, but Truitt denied being a thief and had stalked out of the berthing compartment after his shipmates blamed him.

Dorsey and Goodman dropped by the Mullahys' apartment, across the street from the Truitts, to interview his Spanish-born wife, Geli, who was not completely fluent in English. They asked if Kendall Truitt were bisexual. Geli didn't know, and she said she wouldn't have told them if she did.

Seaman Apprentice Jason Zion, eighteen, told Cully that when he first heard rumors about Hartwig being gay, he confronted Hartwig and told him, "Homos can be homos just as long as they stay away from me." Hartwig denied that he was a homosexual, and Zion said Hartwig had never made any sexual advances toward him, even though they often shared a motel room on weekend leaves. Zion informed agent Cully that Jay White, not Hartwig, had written the poem "Disposable Heroes."

NIS tracked down and interviewed the go-go dancer who dated Hartwig in early 1989. The young woman described Hartwig as "a quiet, self-defeating individual." She said she was astounded when he proposed to her on their second date. They slept in the same bed one night in a motel, but he kept his clothes on and made no attempt to have sex with her. He had written several letters to her, the last one arriving shortly after the explosion and signed, "Love always and forever, Clayton."

On May 25, the same day that Captain Miceli issued his classified report stating that the explosion had most likely been an accident, agents Goodman and Dorsey landed what they thought was their best witness in the case they were constructing against Hartwig. He was Seaman David Smith, who had joined the *Iowa* just nineteen days before the Turret Two explosion. The twenty-year-old sailor had arrived on the battleship after spending a year aboard U.S. warships and commercial tankers in the Persian Gulf. He had been trained by the U.S. Army to operate Stinger shoulder-mounted, antiaircraft missiles and provide the vessels with short-range protection from Iranian aircraft.

Hartwig had befriended Smith several days after the younger man came aboard. "Hartwig was an interesting guy to listen to. He was easy to converse with," Smith said. He later said that he was spooked by the squads of NIS agents roaming around the battleship, searching lockers, and asking questions about Hartwig and Truitt. Truitt made the situation worse by telling Smith that it would just be a matter of time before NIS called him in for questioning.

While it is not clear whether NIS sought out Smith or he sought them out, agents Dorsey and Goodman escorted Smith to their Norfolk headquarters for what would be the first of nine interview sessions with him. The agents parked Smith in one of their sterile white interrogation rooms. "And then they put me in a chair," Smith said. "It's like a big chair with big armrests, you know, and you expect them to like strap you down, and break out the rubber hoses. They have two guys asking you the same question over and over and over."

Smith would remain in the room for seven hours and forty minutes, with only a couple of brief intermissions to go to the bathroom or grab a soda. He was shadowed by an agent whenever he left the room. He was advised of his rights when the interview first began. He waived them and did not ask for an attorney. As the day wore on, agent Ed Goodwin, who did not participate in the interrogation, ordered dinner for everybody from Mama's Pizza. When it arrived, he took a spare pizza and a can of Pepsi to Smith.

Smith was blubbering when Goodwin entered the interrogation room with the food and soda. Goodwin told the distraught sailor that he could eat his dinner in the main room where the agents worked. Smith said he didn't want anything to eat. He wanted to be left alone and went back into the interrogation room while Dorsey and Goodman wolfed down their pizzas.

Smith said the agents wanted him to admit that Hartwig had told him days in advance that he intended to blow up Turret Two. "And when I wouldn't admit this, they told me on several occasions that they could bring me up on forty-seven counts of accessory to murder, perjury, and obstruction of justice," he said. He was scheduled to be discharged from the Navy in six months, and they told him that they could keep him on active duty indefinitely as a material witness. They handed him a document that was a "Testimonial Grant of Immunity," signed by Admiral Milligan. According to the Navy's Deputy Judge Advocate General manual, Admiral Milligan had no legal right to offer immunity. Milligan was only empowered to conduct an administrative inquiry and had no jurisdiction over criminal matters. "They gave me a grant of immunity," Smith said. "They told me point-blank, 'Even if you come out and say you and him [Hartwig] built the bomb and put it in the turret, we can't get you for anything.'" Since he had waived his rights and didn't have an attorney, Smith had no way of knowing that NIS was playing hocus-pocus.

"They said, 'We know that he [Hartwig] did it. We're just trying to find the proof,' " Smith related. The agents didn't audio- or videotape their first session with Smith. According to a typed, three-page statement that Smith signed, he told the agents that he "never really thought Hartwig was gay." Hartwig did talk a lot about girls, and he said that if he died while on active duty, he wanted to be buried in Arlington National Cemetery. But he was looking forward to going to London, where he would be assigned to security duty.

After the explosion, Smith said it crossed his mind that Hartwig had committed suicide, but he hadn't contacted NIS because "I didn't want to see Clay Hartwig labeled by the press as a homicidal maniac who killed forty-seven people." Smith was unable to explain why he felt Hartwig might be suicidal, although he admitted that he, himself, had attempted suicide when he was a child.

Dorsey and Goodman's superiors thought they had made a bad mistake by not taping Smith. His statement could easily be recanted. Smith could claim that NIS had violated his rights and put words in his mouth. If he recanted everything, NIS would be in bad shape, especially if Smith went to the press with his tale about NIS intimidation. Dorsey and Goodman were told to bring Smith back and audiotape him.

Smith had left NIS headquarters at 10 P.M. following his first interview. He reported back to the *Iowa* and was told to stand a nine-hour watch. He had been in his bunk no more than an hour when the NIS agents rousted him and hauled him back to their headquarters to undergo six more hours of interrogation.

Dead on his feet, Smith wept copiously. He also massaged his temples with both hands. The agents asked what was wrong. "I'm tired. I'm tired," he whined. They shrugged and bore down, asking, "Hartwig told you he loved you, didn't he?" They accused Smith of going to motels and sleeping with

Hartwig. "They kept pressing and pressing and pressing, and you know, in my state of mind, I guess I panicked, I don't know. I guess I agreed with them," Smith said. Whenever the agents were unhappy with something he said or the way he said it, Smith claimed they turned off the tape recorders. "So they claimed that they have all the evidence, and it basically comes down to my word against theirs."

During the first four hours of his taped interrogation, Smith repeated what he had already told them the previous day. But finally, he folded, giving them whatever they sought. For two days, he had unwaveringly denied that he had ever seen a timer or an electronic ignition device in Hartwig's possession. But now he said that Hartwig had shown him a timer. What did it look like? It was square, 2.5 by 2.5 inches, about an inch thick, with glowing red numbers from one to ten, and having start, stop, and reset buttons. And where did Hartwig show this timer to him? "Inside his locker, like at the time he was showing me you know his books and stuff and just pulled out a timer."

As the interrogation was drawing to a close, Goodman had Smith renounce his previous statement that he "never really thought Hartwig was gay." Smith claimed that Hartwig told him that when the *Iowa* returned from the Caribbean, he wanted to spend more time with Smith, including sleeping with him in motels. Did Hartwig's sexual propositioning of Smith make him "somewhat frantic"? Smith said it certainly did. When did this occur? Smith was "almost positive" that it took place the night before the explosion. He rejected Hartwig, telling him to "Fuck off!" Even so, he said he ate breakfast with Hartwig the next morning and apologized for cursing him.

Before turning off the tape recorder, Goodman asked Smith if he had been coerced by NIS into providing this information. "No, I had to give it, I've been dragging it around since the 19th [April], and I just had to get rid of it. I just can't carry no more," Smith said. "Have you told us the truth, the whole truth, and nothing but the truth?" Goodman asked. Yes, he had. Well, what about the conflicting statement he had given the day before about Hartwig not being gay? It was truthful, Smith said, but it didn't include everything he knew.

Three days later, Smith was driven back to NIS headquarters to read the transcript of his taped interview. At that time, he recanted all of the meaningful details in the document. NIS scheduled a polygraph examination of him on May 31. Since the taped session, agents had done follow-up interviews with *Iowa* sailors, seeking to corroborate some of Smith's details, and they had come to the conclusion that he was a liar.

BEFORE ADMINISTERING a polygraph to Smith, agent Dave Reppard read the sailor his rights and informed him that he was suspected of the crime of "false swearing." The grant of immunity from Admiral Milligan would not protect Smith from perjury charges. Agent Reppard said that Smith refused to answer any questions once he was hooked up to the polygraph. Reppard turned off the polygraph, and Smith told Reppard that his previous story about Hartwig making gay overtures toward him was a lie. He also told Reppard that Hartwig had never shown him a timer and that the description of the timer he gave to agents Dorsey and Goodman was a total fabrication.

Smith went on to say that Hartwig had never claimed that he could destroy the *Iowa* by planting a detonator in a gun turret. Quite the contrary, Hartwig had assured Smith that the three sixteen-inch turrets could withstand any missile attack. Smith, not Hartwig, was the one who shook in his boots at the thought that an explosion in one turret could start a chain reaction that could sink the *Iowa*. In late July, a polygraph was finally administered, but by that time there was no doubt in anybody's mind—Smith was not credible.

The day after Smith told Agent Reppard that he had lied, he revisited NIS headquarters and formally recanted his negative testimony about Hartwig. He signed a document stipulating that his taped statement to Dorsey and Goodman was not true. He swore that the gay "come-on" incident allegedly involving Hartwig on April 18 took place on the minesweeper USS *Conquest* in the Persian Gulf in 1988, and that the propositioning was done by a communications technician second class.

Despite Smith's record of deception, NIS still called on him in a last-ditch effort to determine who authored "Disposable Heroes." But since Smith had only been on the battleship less than three weeks, and was not assigned to Turret Two, he was no help. So agent Ed Goodwin sent the hand-lettered poem, as well as letters written by Clayton Hartwig to Michele Poling, Charlene Meter, and Kendall Truitt, to the FBI Crime Laboratory in Washington. The lab analyzed the writing samples and was unable to determine who wrote the poem. But that didn't stop NIS and Admiral Milligan's investigative team from claiming that Hartwig was the author.

NIS later brought David Smith to its Norfolk headquarters and scolded him for talking to ABC News producer Mark Brender on the telephone and telling Brender that NIS had browbeaten him into making false statements about Hartwig. Smith's interview with Brender did more damage to the credibility of NIS, but Smith wasn't through avenging himself. In the months to come, he took every possible opportunity to belittle the agency and the Navy. Whenever he was asked by reporters if anyone on the ship really believed that Hartwig caused the explosion, he replied, "No, nobody in the Navy community believes he did it." What did he mean by "Navy community"? "I'm saying the realistic Navy community, not these admirals and all those people." What set the admirals apart from the ordinary sailors, chiefs, and officers below flag rank? "They're politicians. They're not naval officers. You can't make admiral if you're not a politician."

THE NIS agents assigned to the *Iowa* inquiry were sometimes assisted by Lieutenant Commander Thomas Mountz, a clinical psychologist attached to the agency. In his early forties, he had been a naval officer for thirteen years and a psychologist for twenty-one years. Mountz came to NIS after a tour with the SEALS. "Mountz couldn't understand why we refused to let him carry a gun in his boot like he did in the SEALS. I told him that he was a psychologist, a professional staffer, not a gunman," Rear Admiral Gordon remarked.

NIS records show that Mountz provided agent Mike Dorsey the following tips on how to trap John Mullahy: (1) Make him think he's a hero; (2) Ask him if there were any particular times when he felt uncomfortable being around Clayton Hartwig; (3) If Mullahy feels that he is the focus of the NIS investigation, "downplay his involvement"; (4) Explain how Mullahy "is an integral part [of the investigation] and that he can solve this."

Mountz personally interviewed members of the team of psychologists and psychiatrists the Navy sent to the *Iowa* shortly after the explosion to assist the crewmen in dealing with post-traumatic stress disorder. Mountz wanted to know if any of the mental-health professionals had observed anything that might help NIS strengthen the cases it was building against Clayton Hartwig and Kendall Truitt. None of the doctors offered any information.

Mountz met with six representatives of the Armed Forces Institute of Pathology in Bethesda, Maryland, informing them that he was convinced that either Hartwig or Truitt or both had destroyed Turret Two. He learned that Hartwig's toxicological screen for illicit drugs was negative. Navy Captain Robert Karnei, the toxicologist who had performed the screen, told Mountz that Hartwig's corpse had also been tested for the presence of tricyclic medication to determine whether he might have been taking drugs to control depression. That screen was also negative. Hartwig was the only one of the dead *Iowa* sailors whose body was tested for antidepressants. The doctors said they were going to conduct HIV tests, using frozen tissue taken from Hartwig's body, and they planned to run a supplemental toxicological screen to see if an "accelerant" used to start a fire might be present. The results of the HIV and "accelerant" tests also proved to be negative.

MOUNTZ WANTED to compile a "psychological autopsy" of Hartwig, but he didn't think that it would be taken seriously if it came from NIS, so he requested help from other federal investigative agencies with staff psychologists and psychiatrists. A "psychological autopsy" is a reconstruction of a deceased person's character, background, relationships, and habits to understand the individual's way of dealing with life and perhaps to learn how he or she died. The Air Force's Office of Special Investigations (OSI), located at Bolling Air Force Base in Maryland, just off the Beltway, was not receptive to Mountz's proposal that it assemble a "psychological autopsy" on Hartwig. Drs. Neil Hibler and Mark Roman, both Air Force psychologists, spoke with Mountz but tactfully told him to do his own work.

The FBI's Behavioral Science Unit in Quantico, Virginia, was more responsive. Mountz and NIS agents Tom Goodman, Ed Goodwin, and Dawn Teague, a homicide specialist who had received special training in forensics at George Washington University, drove to the FBI Training Academy, on the sprawling Marine Corps base. The NIS group met for several hours with FBI special agents John Douglas, Richard Ault, and Roy Hazelwood, turning over copies of message pads that had passed back and forth between Clayton Hartwig and Kendall Truitt. Mountz did most of the talking, completely ruling out an accidental cause for the April 19 explosion.

At the time of the NIS visit, the Behavioral Science Unit (BSU) was riding a crest of public adulation. The movie *Silence of the Lambs*, about a fictional serial killer, was being filmed. It would be a box-office smash hit and win an Academy Award. The movie's hero, played by actor Scott Glenn, was loosely modeled after John Douglas. Police buffs began ascribing the crime-solving expertise of Sherlock Holmes to the BSU agents. For all the hype, there was no disputing the fact that none of its agents had any experience with a case like the *Iowa*, involving an explosion in a sixteen-inch turret.

Shortly after the four NIS representatives visited Quantico, the FBI notified them that it would accept the *Iowa* case but would adhere to several ground rules. Its agents would not go aboard the battleship or inspect Turret Two. They would not visit any of Captain Miceli's test facilities, nor did they want to be informed about Miceli's test results. They accepted the Navy's word that the explosion had not been an accident. They were not interested in seeing Clayton Hartwig's room or talking with any of his relatives, friends, or shipmates. They would rely solely on NIS's detective work. Even if they suspected that witnesses were lying, they would not ask them to be polygraphed. No one from the Behavioral Science Unit examined Clayton Hartwig's autopsy report or discussed it with the pathologists.

The FBI agents employed a technique they had refined over fourteen years, something curiously called an "equivocal death analysis." Simply put, the agents tried to find everything they could about a dead person and make an educated guess about whether that person died by his own hand, was killed in an accident, or was murdered. They had used the "equivocal death analysis" method in more than fifty cases, but by their own testimony, they obtained "satisfactory results" in only three instances. Since its findings were tentative, the death analysis ordinarily could not be introduced in criminal trials, where it would not meet rigid evidentiary guidelines. "It's not a formal program," agent Ault later testified. "You need a background in looking at crime scenes, analyzing crime scenes; you need a background in the investigative process, in criminal investigations."

JOHN DOUGLAS, the best-known member of the Behavioral Science Unit, did not always see eye to eye with agents Ault and Hazelwood. A tall, urbane man, Douglas had been an FBI agent nineteen years and a member of the Behavioral Science Unit for twelve. He had spent more than a decade interviewing infamous mass murderers and assassins. Among those he visited in prison were Charles Manson; New York serial killer David "Son of Sam" Berkowitz; Sirhan Sirhan, the convicted assassin of Senator Robert F. Kennedy; David Chapman, who was convicted of gunning down singer John Lennon; Richard Speck, the mass murderer of seven nurses in Chicago during the 1960s; and serial killer John Wayne Gacy. Besides being a renowned criminologist, Douglas was also a shrewd bureaucrat who knew a troublesome case when he saw it. The *Iowa* was such a case. Since Ault and Hazelwood were anxious to be involved, Douglas stepped aside. He later told author John Greenya, with whom he worked on a book, that Ault and Hazelwood botched Clayton Hartwig's equivocal death analysis and gave "overblown" testimony about it to Congress. "We never testify to a profile. We use it as an investigative tool, and they [Ault and Hazelwood] used it as tantamount to proof," Douglas said.

Richard Ault became an FBI agent in 1969 and was assigned to Kansas City for a year as a member of the organized-crime squad. He spent five years in Cleveland, handling "extremist matters," which he defined as the White People's Party and the American Nazis. He joined the BSU in 1975, spending most of his time on rape, serial-murder, and spy cases. Sociable and garrulous, he affected a professorial manner. He knew Lieutenant Commander Mountz slightly from another case on which they had collaborated.

Ault's partner, Roy Hazelwood, made no effort to conceal the fact that he was a professional man-hunter. The FBI credited Hazelwood with inventing the equivocal death analysis process. Neither Ault nor Hazelwood claimed to have any expertise with naval vessels. Even though Ault had spent four years in the Marine Corps, Ault said he knew nothing about ships, and he regularly referred to the *Iowa* as "a big boat." Hazelwood had been an Army major assigned to the military police in Vietnam. He seemed grateful that he was not required to crawl through a sixteen-inch turret.

The FBI psychological profilers told NIS that they would begin with Hartwig's and Truitt's notes to each other. In one of these, Hartwig wrote, "When I met Bryan [his high school roommate], he was the best friend I ever had. I love him a lot, and I'm afraid to tell him that, and I know he loves me the same way. With Dan [his roommate at the Guantanamo Bay, Cuba, Naval Base], it's pretty much the same way. With you [Truitt], I'm not sure yet. I'm afraid you might take it the wrong way, and then your and everyone else's outlook towards me would be totally different. Bryan and I were called fags. So were Dan and me. I don't want that to happen here. And believe me, I'm not."

The FBI agents informed Mountz that they needed more material; the Navy psychologist said he would bring them more. About a week later, Mountz, Goodman, Goodwin, and Teague returned to Quantico with the statements of eight people: Kendall and Carole Truitt, Charlene Meter, Evelyn Hartwig, Bryan Hoover, Kathy Kubicina, Daniel McElyea, and John Mullahy.

Dan McElyea had roomed for eighteen months with Hartwig in Guantanamo Bay. He emphasized that Hartwig was never depressed, nor was he suicidal. Hartwig was required to stand watch on the perimeter every four days with a loaded .45-caliber pistol. If Hartwig had wanted to kill himself, McElyea said, he had the ideal opportunity to do so. McElyea said there was no hint of homosexuality on Hartwig's part when he was in Cuba. While he was there, Hartwig had dated a female friend of McElyea's future wife.

The statements of two other witnesses, Angel Baker and Michele Poling, were practically devoid of content. Baker said she threw away her last letter from Hartwig. She couldn't remember the contents but thought he might have been blue. Poling discussed Hartwig's saying he could end up under a white burial marker in Arlington National Cemetery, because the *Iowa* sailed into dangerous waters so often.

The FBI profilers were given photographs of Hartwig's bedroom in Cleveland and a copy of "Disposable Heroes." The NIS agents said they were pursuing a rumor that Hartwig had visited the Naval Historical Center at the Washington Navy Yard and obtained records of the investigations of the two explosions aboard the battleship USS *Mississippi*. The first disaster occurred in 1924 while the *Mississippi* was engaging in fleet exercises near San Pedro, California. Turret Two was loading its three fourteen-inch guns to fire a salvo when flames belched from the breech of the right gun. Forty-eight men died in seconds. The second tragedy happened aboard that same ship in 1943 as she was shelling Makin Atoll in the Gilbert Islands. Turret Two was in the process of reloading its three guns to fire a thirteenth salvo. The left and right gun crews finished their tasks and were prepared to fire, but the crew of the center gun was still not ready. At that point, the turret officer, Lieutenant Richard Leader, activated the sprinkler system and screamed on the sound-powered phones, "Turret Two is on fire!" Those were Leader's last words. He and forty-two other men died. As it later turned out, there was no evidence that Hartwig ever had obtained the two thick courts of inquiry transcripts concerning the *Mississippi* disasters from archivist John C. Reilly Jr.

Tom Goodman said he was returning to Cleveland in the near future to take a closer look at some books and other items in Hartwig's bedroom. Ault and Hazelwood asked him to make a concerted effort to locate anything relating to the two *Mississippi* explosions. Goodman told the FBI agents about David Smith's statements. They asked for transcripts. Goodman promised to drop them off once he returned from Cleveland. He failed to mention that Smith had recanted the incriminating portions.

16

"More Than Just a Friendly Relationship"

WHEN NIS AGENTS Tom Goodman and Ed Goodwin rounded the corner of Kathy Kubicina's street at 2:30 P.M. on June 7, they saw Kathy, her children, and her parents standing in the driveway. The agents got out of their car and said they wanted to search Clayton's room one more time. The Hartwigs were mistrustful, having been burned previously by these same two law-enforcement officers. They asked for time to consult with Cleveland attorney Kreig (pronounced *Craig*) Brusnahan, whom they'd hired to protect their interests. Florid-faced and high-strung, Brusnahan was in his early thirties. He wasn't affiliated with a major law firm and had little experience handling a complicated case such as this, but he was well-meaning and principled. Brusnahan advised the Hartwigs to go along with the search and not force the agents to go to federal court and obtain a search warrant, which could only generate more bad publicity. He would meet them at their home to make sure the agents behaved.

Goodman and Goodwin failed to inform Brusnahan that they were seeking any material the Hartwigs might have squirreled away on the two *Mississippi* explosions for the FBI's psychological profile unit. They also didn't tell the attorney that they wanted to look at Clayton's 9-mm Smith & Wesson pistol again as a favor to a Norfolk-area sheriff's department to see if the gun might have been used in a homicide near the naval-base piers. Brusnahan wasn't informed that the agents also were seeking evidence to solve two explosions that occurred on April 10, 1989, on the Naval Amphibious Base at Little Creek, Virginia. Finally, the Hartwigs' lawyer was not informed that the agents were seeking a timing device similar to the one David Smith had lied about seeing in Clayton's locker.

No *Mississippi* disaster material from the Naval Historical Center was uncovered; Clayton's Model 469 Smith & Wesson had nothing to do with the homicide near the piers; there was nothing to connect Clayton to the Little Creek explosions; and no timer was found. The agents did unearth one innocuous reference to the *Mississippi* on page 35 in the book *The Iowa Class Battleships* by Malcolm Muir. It said, "While bombarding Makin [Island] on 20 November 1943, the old battleship *Mississippi* suffered a blowback in No. 2 turret which burned 42 men to death." Another passing reference to the 1943 disaster was found on page 200 in the book *Battleship at War: The Epic Story of the USS Washington* by Ivan Musicant. The agents didn't seize the books, but they copied down the headlines from ten articles pasted in Clayton's scrapbook. None of these involved the loss of life of anyone in a gunnery mishap. Eight stories concerned civilian or Coast Guard accidents on inland waterways. One newspaper story involved the observance of Pearl Harbor Day in Cleveland in 1980, and the final item concerned the sinking of an unmanned Navy submarine. The agents ended their search at 8:30 P.M., after being in the room ninety minutes. They told Kathy and her parents that the Cleveland end of the investigation was over and they probably would not return.

A WEEK later, Tom Goodman, Ed Goodwin, Dawn Teague, and Tom Mountz again drove south from Washington to Quantico, carrying with them selected portions of David Smith's interviews. They discussed "Disposable Heroes" with FBI agents Ault and Hazelwood but did not tell them that Kendall Truitt, John Mullahy, and Jason Zion all maintained that the poem had actually been written by Jay White. Agent Hazelwood later told Congress, "As to whether or not it [the poem] was written by Hartwig is immaterial; it is quite likely that he saw it."

Agent Ault later testified that if NIS had administered a polygraph to David Smith, it was essential for the FBI to have been told about it before beginning the work on the death analysis. And he said that NIS had not provided him any information about that. Consequently, Ault and Hazelwood relied heavily on Smith's statements in formulating Hartwig's equivocal death analysis.

The day after they received this material, the agents sat down at their computers and wrote Hartwig's equivocal death analysis. The fifteen-page document was completed in a single day. The nucleus of the report, appearing on the first page, stated, "It is the opinion of SSAs [Supervisory Special Agents] Hazelwood and Ault that the victim, Clayton Hartwig, died as a result of his own actions, staging his death in such a fashion that he hoped it would appear to be an accident."

The report was repetitious, with some incidents being cited four and five times to make disparate points. Fourteen pages were devoted to "victimology." Earl Hartwig was described as being "subservient to his wife when in her presence." Neither Ault nor Hazelwood had ever met Earl and Evelyn

Hartwig. No source was given for this statement, and Earl, while solicitous of his wife, had never been shy about expressing his views to NIS agents Goodman and Goodwin, even when Evelyn was present.

Ault and Hazelwood claimed that in high school Bryan Hoover had taken a knife away from Hartwig, "who was making a suicidal gesture with the weapon." Hoover had taken great pains to explain to agents Goodman and Goodwin that Hartwig was not acting suicidal with the knife. The FBI agents declared that the Navy did not believe that Hartwig was "sufficiently aggressive to be a good leader." Again, no source was cited. And if the Navy really rated him thus, why was it processing his papers to be a security agent in London?

Charlene Meter's gibes about the lack of style of Clayton's civilian wardrobe and his indifference to the shape of his car were used to show that Hartwig was a hopeless loser. Ault and Hazelwood rejected the NIS allegations that Hartwig and Truitt were gay. The death analysis said simply, "The evidence to substantiate that is circumstantial." The two agents did find it odd for Hartwig to name Truitt as the beneficiary of his life-insurance policy.

The psychological profilers made much of the picture of Hartwig as a high-school student masquerading as the captain of *The Love Boat*, writing, "He was also known to wear unauthorized insignia on his uniform." Even though they had never been inside Turret Two, the agents described the death scene and speculated that Hartwig "was only slightly out of position [as gun captain] when he died." They realized they were on thin ice, because they added the following disclaimer: "Because the scene was not preserved for a criminal investigation, the writers cannot comment further on the death scene." The agents devoted a full page to debating the pros and cons of whether Kendall Truitt could have blown up the turret, and they decided that although it was possible, it was "the least likely scenario."

In order to bolster their suicide theory, Ault and Hazelwood went to great lengths to show that Hartwig lacked self-esteem. They claimed that it could be "documented" that Hartwig had only three "close" male friends—Bryan Hoover, Daniel McElyea, and Kendall Truitt. He also only had three "close" female acquaintances—Michele Poling, Charlene Meter, and the Norfolk go-go dancer. Charlene and the go-go dancer were serious relationships, while Michele was little more than a pen pal. Laura Hayes, a twenty-year-old who had dated Hartwig in 1988 and 1989, went unmentioned. Hayes had grown up in Cleveland and had graduated from Mount Vernon Academy. Hartwig had visited her in Washington, where she was a student when he was on the *Iowa*.

Another of Hartwig's girlfriends, Karen Doney, was also missing from the FBI list of female acquaintances. Doney told ABC News producer Mark Brender, "He [Clayton] was a very sensitive and caring guy, and if he had any negative feelings, it was just as human and just as common as anyone else would have. He was too old-fashioned to even consider leading a life as a homosexual."

According to the FBI profile, five of six individuals (three men and two women) whom Hartwig admired had "rejected" him, and the sixth (Charlene Meter) "was applying pressure on him for an intimate relationship that he was not capable of." Bryan Hoover and Daniel McElyea said they had never "rejected" Hartwig, and Kendall Truitt said that he and Hartwig had quarreled in the past but had amicably resolved their differences and were friends on April 19. Charlene Meter denied applying any pressure on Clayton to have a love affair, and his last letter to her, written the day he died, indicated that he looked forward to seeing her when the ship returned. Michele Poling and the go-go dancer didn't tell NIS they "rejected" Hartwig.

The death analysis took Hartwig to task for reading *Soldier of Fortune* magazine, legally owning two handguns, accumulating a large collection of books dealing with military subjects, playing with firecrackers and cherry bombs when he was a youth, and wearing combat fatigues when he was stationed in Cuba. The report implied that because Hartwig only had $34 in the bank, owed money on his car, and had his telephone calling card revoked, he was despondent and prone to suicide. Charlene Meter told NIS that Clayton wasn't at all concerned about his car, because he was going to London and wouldn't need it.

"Disposable Heroes" became the centerpiece to show that Hartwig was emotionally unstable. The two agents also thought it notable that Hartwig had read a book about the destruction of the Japanese battleship *Yamato*. A 72,000-ton monster, the *Yamato* was sent by the Japanese Imperial Navy to disrupt the U.S. Navy's invasion of Okinawa in April 1945. The vessel was supposed to beach herself in the midst of the U.S. landing force and blast away with her nine 18.1-inch guns (the biggest in the world) until she ran out of ammunition. At that time, she would self-destruct. But she never got a chance to do that.

U.S. submarines spotted the *Yamato* sneaking out of Japan's Inland Sea, and she and her nine escort vessels came under concerted attack by 300 U.S. carrier-based aircraft. The superbattleship was struck by five bombs and eleven torpedoes during a fierce, two-hour engagement. The *Yamato* finally lost power, rolled over, and sank, taking to the bottom most of her 2,500-member crew. The sinking of the *Yamato* was not remotely analogous to the explosion aboard the *Iowa*.

Ault and Hazelwood concluded their equivocal death analysis by terming Clayton Hartwig "a troubled young man who had low self-esteem." Hartwig could not verbally express his anger and was facing "a multitude of stressors had he returned from the cruise." He committed suicide "in a place and manner designed to obtain the respect and recognition that he felt had been denied him."

NIS PSYCHOLOGIST Tom Mountz had not waited for the FBI to complete its analysis before drafting his own. Mountz's report, finished on June 14, was a third the size of the FBI's. He described Hartwig as a reserved individual and all but declared that Hartwig was a homosexual. He used the phrase *special relations* to characterize all of Hartwig's dealings with men. Mountz also stated that there was no proof that Hartwig had ever genuinely dated a woman, disregarding Charlene Meter, Karen Doney, the Norfolk go-go dancer, and Laura Hayes.

Mountz wrote that "many suspected more than just a friendly relationship" existed between Hartwig and Truitt. He claimed that during the last days of Hartwig's life, the sailor "was reported to be reclusive, reluctant to talk or be with anyone," even though Dan Meyer, Chief Hickman, and John Mullahy all told Admiral Milligan's panel they had lengthy conversations with Hartwig the night before the explosion. These men said Hartwig appeared to be in good spirits and did not act like he was suicidal.

David Smith's testimony was cited in Mountz's report without ever disclosing that Smith had retracted a great deal of it. Mountz also made use of "Disposable Heroes." Admitting that the writer of the poem was unknown, he said, "However, the contents allude to worthlessness, hopelessness, and the aggrandizement of death and patriotism." He was saying in effect that even if Hartwig had nothing to do with the poem, its words matched the stereotype of the dead sailor that Mountz had formulated. The poem was too good not to use. The NIS psychologist ended his report by stating that Hartwig had committed suicide and took pains to make his death seem like an accident.

BRIAN MCKEE, the civilian director of NIS, was attending a luncheon at the White House on June 16 when he learned that the FBI's Behavioral Science Unit had concluded that Clayton Hartwig had caused the explosion aboard the *Iowa*. McKee received the news from William S. Sessions, director of the FBI. Sessions, McKee, and the heads of the other federal law-enforcement agencies were having their quarterly meeting with President George Bush. At the Norfolk memorial service in April, the President had promised the relatives of the dead *Iowa* sailors that the federal government would get to the bottom of the tragedy. After learning about the FBI's findings, McKee told President Bush that NIS was a lot closer to solving the case, thanks to the FBI.

DETAILS OF the FBI's equivocal death analysis began leaking immediately after the document was handed over to NIS. As the particulars surfaced, harsh criticism was leveled at the Navy, the NIS, and the FBI for relying on such an ambiguous tool to ruin a dead man's reputation. Brian McKee and several other NIS officials would later protest that they had been "sandbagged, set up by the FBI psychological profilers." "We never made our case against Hartwig, we relied too heavily on the FBI psychological profile," McKee said.

But that was not the song McKee sang during the early summer of 1989, according to the NIS commander during the initial stage of the *Iowa* investigation. "Brian was positively purring that this was the strongest, the best case, with the most solid evidence he had ever seen," Rear Admiral Gordon said. " 'We've got this guy cold,' Brian told me."

NOT LONG after the Hartwig family was devastated by Fred Francis on NBC, they began receiving more evenhanded coverage on ABC News, largely due to producer Mark Brender and Robert Zelnick, who had been the network's bureau chief in Moscow and in Tel Aviv. Brender had grown up in a Navy family and had spent three years on a frigate as a navigator. He became a public-affairs officer in 1975. After serving in the Pentagon on the staff of the Assistant Secretary of Defense for Public Affairs, Brender had been hired by ABC News in 1982 and had covered the military beat with Zelnick for three years. "I was in the Navy, and I knew about cover-ups. I knew all about institutional bias," he said.

Just as soon as NIS entered the *Iowa* case, Brender was tipped off. He learned about Fred Francis's May 24 report the morning before it aired. He watched the report and thought, "Francis blew it." He went to Zelnick, told him what he knew and what he suspected, and said that he wanted to go to Cleveland to interview the Hartwigs and talk to anyone else who knew Clayton. A former Washington bureau chief for National Public Radio and an attorney, Zelnick arranged with George Watson, the ABC News Washington bureau chief, for Brender to follow the story wherever it took him.

Before flying to Cleveland, Brender called Commander Gene Kocmich in Norfolk. Kocmich, the *Iowa*'s former weapons officer, was familiar with the Milligan and NIS investigations and said that if Hartwig had made Truitt the beneficiary of his life-insurance policy before the ship sailed to the Persian Gulf in 1987, "It would not have been that unusual." He called Hartwig and Truitt "solid citizens, close friends, but not homosexuals." Brender also reached Truitt's father, Walter Truitt, in Marion, Illinois. The senior Truitt denounced allegations that his son was gay as "pure garbage" and said the insurance-policy arrangement between Clayton and Kendall was not that novel for close friends in the military.

Brender's first stop in Cleveland was Kathy Kubicina's home. He asked her how she would react if the Navy knocked on her front door and informed her that her brother had committed suicide and was a mass murderer. "I would have to tell them they better go away, because there is no way that Clayton did it," she said. "I have portrayed my brother as a quiet, shy guy that liked to stay alone and somehow this got misinterpreted into something really vile, and they [NIS] read things into it that weren't really even there."

Kathy drove Brender to her parents' home and took him up to Clayton's attic room. The former naval officer sat on the dead sailor's bed and observed all the nautical memorabilia around him. "I thought about Clayton Hartwig having a sailing ship tattooed on his arm with USS *Iowa*, and I knew for sure then that he didn't blow up that turret," Brender said.

The ABC producer sat with Earl and Evelyn Hartwig on the couch in their living room. "Clay had three friends in that turret, and I'm sure he's not going to take three friends with him," Evelyn said. "If he was going to commit suicide, he would have jumped off the deck, or if he had a gun, he would have shot himself."

The Hartwigs provided Brender with the names and phone numbers of some of Clayton's friends. The producer talked to Harvey Allison, who had been Clayton's supervisor when he worked as a night watchman at Mount Vernon Academy. Allison, the school's maintenance director, said he had never seen Clayton depressed and that letters he had received from Clayton in the months prior to the explosion were upbeat. Allison said Clayton wrote that he was excited about being assigned to London.

Brender got in touch with Michele Poling. She said Clayton had kept to himself, was thoughtful, and never discussed suicide. She had been interviewed twice by NIS. She had only been teasing Clayton about hiding in the Navy and described her relationship with him as similar to being his "sister." Brender also interviewed Sherylin Jackson of Columbus, Ohio, who had graduated from Mount Vernon Academy a year ahead of Hartwig. She was distressed over the portrait of him that had been painted by NBC News. Jackson described Clayton as articulate, serious, and mature. "The thought of suicide is ludicrous. He was gentle, sweet, and soft spoken. He'd never hurt anyone. He never came across as gay and had plenty of girlfriends," she said.

Dan Fife, who had known Clayton since they were two years old, told Brender that NIS had been "terrorizing" Clayton's friends to keep them from coming forward and saying good things about him. "They're digging up dirt in our pasts, which had nothing to do with the case, and basically scaring us so that we won't talk and help Clayton out," Fife said. He said the agents had threatened to subpoena him if he refused to cooperate with them.

When he returned to Washington, Brender continued to track down Hartwig's relatives and friends by phone. Brender had an extended interview with Clayton's other sister, Cynthia Jane "Cindy" Werthmuller, thirty-one, who lived on a 220-acre farm near Clarksville, Iowa, just south of the Minnesota border. Seven years older than Clayton, she had talked to her brother about two weeks before his death. He told her the same thing he had told everyone else—that he was excited about going to London. Cindy was certain that her brother was not gay. "I feel like I have been robbed of my brother and am angry at the Navy for trying to pin the explosion on him," she said.

Brender also reached Daniel McElyea, Clayton's roommate in Guantanamo Bay. McElyea was living in Indianapolis and upset that Clayton's name had been "dragged in the mud." He said his former roommate had not been gay, suicidal, or depressed. During the eighteen months they roomed together, Hartwig fished a lot, read stacks of military-history books, and talked extensively about girls. "He also loved guns, but it was not an obsession," McElyea said. Gunner's Mate First Class Ron Helmer, who had bunked across the hall from Hartwig in the barracks in Cuba, told Brender that there had never been any rumors in Guantanamo Bay about Hartwig's being gay. He said Hartwig had once flipped over a Navy truck after swerving to avoid hitting a deer in the road. Hartwig had to appear at mast before his commanding officer, but all charges were dismissed. Helmer said he was at a loss to understand how a man who would risk a court-martial and wreck a government vehicle to avoid killing a deer would be capable of blowing up a gun turret and killing forty-six of his shipmates.

ZELNICK AND Brender's first story on ABC concerned the *Iowa*'s 1988 powder-storage problems and the repeated failure of Turret One's left gun to fire. Zelnick mentioned Hartwig's life-insurance policy and the breakup of the Hartwig/Truitt friendship, but he quoted Navy sources as saying, "The case against either man is weak and circumstantial." In his on-camera close, Zelnick said, "Some see the Navy compounding the disaster with unsubstantiated talk of murder or suicide. 'We were careless in storing our gunpowder,' complains one officer. 'Now it looks like we're trying to hang the tragedy on two heroes, including a corpse.' "

After the piece ended, Zelnick received a number of congratulatory calls from active-duty and retired flag officers and current and former high-ranking civilian officials. One of his callers was former Navy Secretary John Lehman, who recounted the serious powder problem on the *New Jersey* while it was bombarding Lebanon in 1983 and 1984. Lehman said the Navy had located some older but better preserved powder that was repackaged and fired aboard the *Iowa* on the Vieques gunnery range. Both the ship and the propellant had performed well, and Lehman believed at the time that the powder difficulties had been resolved. But obviously they had not. "It's a powder problem," he said, referring to the *Iowa* explosion.

Lehman claimed to Zelnick that the cover-up of the powder problems on the *Iowa* was being masterminded by Admiral Carl Trost, whom he had tried to block from becoming Chief of Naval Operations in 1986. Lehman had supported the candidacy of Admiral Frank Kelso, who was the commander of all U.S. forces in the Atlantic. "Frank Kelso has been troubled from the very beginning about the handling of this case," Lehman said. "I've seen it again and again, the whole system using the NIS to get people, to scapegoat them." Lehman encouraged Zelnick to do more hard-hitting reports on the *Iowa*, and as the months wore on, Zelnick, backed up by Mark Brender, made frequent appearances on ABC's *World News Tonight* with *Iowa* stories that never disappointed John Lehman.

DURING THE time of Mark Brender's odyssey around the country, Kendall Truitt walked off the *Iowa*'s aft gangplank with his seabag over his shoulder for the final time before driving south to Mayport, Florida, northeast of Jacksonville, for a new assignment. Truitt had not been allowed to speak with any other sailors on the *Iowa* when he went aboard to retrieve his belongings from his locker. He was escorted by a master-at-arms wherever he went and was treated with a mixture of suspicion and contempt by men who had known him for years. Ironically, despite the heinous nature of the crime Admiral Edney suspected him of committing, Truitt's job in Florida was keeping track of all manner of explosives, from grenades to torpedoes and missiles. But things worsened for him in Mayport. A gunner's mate, who had a buddy on the *Iowa*, jumped Truitt in a base parking lot and beat him up. "My husband was going to be the most hated man in the country, more than even Charles Manson and Ted Bundy. I felt very helpless," Carole Truitt said. At the suggestion of Carole's father, she and Kendall called and made an appointment to see Ellis Rubin, a Miami attorney who knew how to drum up favorable publicity for his clients.

Rubin had handled celebrity lawsuits involving Merv Griffin, actress Hedy Lamarr, and a huge, blue-eyed black man known as Yahweh Ben Yahweh, who claimed to be the son of God. Mass murderer Ted Bundy had asked Rubin to handle his death-row appeal, but the attorney turned him down. A frequent guest on the national television talk shows, Rubin said, "If the prosecutor is going to try and charge and condemn your clients on the six o'clock news, you'd better get them an appeal on the eleven o'clock news, because everything the media writes and shows makes an impression."

Rubin had been a naval officer at the end of World War II before attending the University of Miami Law School. After graduating, he set up practice in South Florida. Carole and Kendall Truitt met Rubin at the renovated Victorian mansion he used as his office near downtown Miami. Rubin said he had a personal interest in the case. He had remained in the U.S. Naval Reserves, retiring as a commander. He'd once served on a destroyer as officer-in-charge of a five-inch turret. The twin mount was much smaller and less powerful than a sixteen-inch turret, but it still gave Rubin an appreciation of what Truitt had experienced aboard the *Iowa*.

Rubin wasted no time in counterpunching the Navy and the NIS, as well as some segments of the news media, including NBC News, the *Washington Post*, and *Newsday*. He called a press conference in Miami and threatened to take legal action against anyone who attempted to connect Truitt to a murder/suicide conspiracy or to damage his reputation in any manner. He also promised to file a lawsuit against anyone who claimed that Truitt was gay. At one point, Rubin asked twenty-year-old Carole Truitt, who was chastely holding hands with her husband, if Kendall were a homosexual. "No, he is not," Carole replied. "Has he shown any tendencies?" Rubin asked shamelessly. "No, none at all," she said. The white-haired, white-bearded attorney couldn't resist the next question: "Well, was he a good lover?" Carole bobbed her head affirmatively and gushed, "Oh, yes!" Rubin announced that he was going to fly to Norfolk, where he would visit the *Iowa* and go through the interior of Turret Two with a fine-tooth comb.

After the press conference, NBC News anchor Tom Brokaw interviewed Truitt by satellite for the *Nightly News.* Brokaw asked Truitt if Hartwig had discussed the possibility of suicide or was depressed in the days preceding his death. "No. He was actually, he was very excited about his new orders coming out. He was to be transferred to London," Truitt replied. Brokaw asked the gunner's mate if he had been asked to take a polygraph. Truitt said that he had not.

Two days later, Rubin and the Truitts flew north to Norfolk, where they held two more press conferences—one at Norfolk International Airport and the other in front of the main gate of the Norfolk Naval Base. According to Rubin, the explosion had been caused by a combination of untrained sailors, unstable powder, and the powder being rammed into the chamber too fast and too far. He announced that one of Truitt's home-state congressmen, Representative Glenn Poshard, a Democrat from Illinois, had asked the House Armed Services Committee to conduct an investigation to determine who had leaked the NIS files.

The Navy refused to allow Rubin aboard the *Iowa*, but it did let him visit her sistership, the *Wisconsin*, which was also moored in Norfolk. The attorney pulled coveralls over his expensive suit and climbed up through the tail hatch of Turret Two on the *Wisconsin.* Emerging an hour later, grease-smudged, he told a group of waiting reporters that the space in the center gun room was so restricted that it would have been physically impossible for anyone to have inserted a detonator into the breech without at least three other men in the room knowing about it.

Rubin and the Truitts then flew to Washington for another press conference and an interview by the *New York Times.* Rubin intensified his public-relations campaign by appearing with the Truitts on ABC's *Good Morning America* and CNN's *Larry King Live.* Kathy Kubicina joined them via satellite. In addition to condemning the Navy and sensation-seeking journalists, Rubin also criticized Kathy for initiating the NIS investigation by writing the letters about Clayton's insurance policy. Kathy silently fumed. Rubin further insulted her by claiming that she had made a "veiled threat" by writing Truitt and asking him to turn over her brother's insurance-policy proceeds to Earl and Evelyn Hartwig. Kathy's face was flushed, but she tactfully said, "I wish there was some way I can put an end to this."

While they were in Washington, Rubin and his two clients also were guests on ABC's *Nightline*, with Ted Koppel. Kathy again participated by satellite. Both CBS and NBC had run stories the evening of the Koppel show claiming that the Navy had determined that Clayton Hartwig was suicidal and had bought a Radio Shack timer. These details had been leaked from the statement that David Smith recanted. Koppel asked Kathy if her brother had been depressed. She denied that he was. "When the Navy leaks information to the effect that a $25 timing device caused an explosion on a superbattleship, the USS *Iowa*, killing forty-seven men, that is so ridiculous that it defies description," Rubin said. Koppel complimented Rubin for getting the Truitts out of trouble so swiftly with his aggressive tactics. The anchorman asked Rubin if there were any advice that he could share with Kathy. "Yes, she should get herself an attorney who can deal with the media," he said.

At 8:15 A.M. on Sunday, two days after *Nightline*, the telephone in the Kubicina home rang. It was Ellis Rubin calling to see if Kathy could fly to Miami that day and talk about his representing her. He would pay the plane fare. Rubin said he had considerable experience dealing with the Navy and was prepared to take the case all the way to the Supreme Court. He apologized for offending her on television and predicted that the Navy and their media allies would ratchet up the pressure on her family. "They will manufacture things if they have to," he said. Kathy thanked him, saying she was sticking with Kreig Brusnahan, the Cleveland attorney retained by her parents.

Ellis Rubin's media blitzkrieg had been so effective that Brian McKee had to inform Admiral Edney that for all practical purposes, Kendall Truitt was outside the Navy's reach. McKee told the admiral that if the Navy didn't tread lightly, Rubin would file a lawsuit.

Overtly, NIS behaved, but it wasn't through with Truitt. The agency subpoenaed his telephone records, as well as those of his mother, Charlotte Truitt, and the residential and business telephone records of his father-in-law, Raymond C. Smith. Some individuals whose names and telephone numbers appeared in those records were contacted by NIS agents. Charlotte Truitt claimed that her Florida home was placed under NIS surveillance for several weeks by two agents in an unmarked car. NIS also pursued every rumor, no matter how wild, about Kendall Truitt's being gay. That went on long after Truitt was discharged from the Navy.

While the NIS continued looking for dirt on Truitt, Robert Zelnick aired another piece on ABC, saying that NIS had concluded that Truitt was innocent of murder. Zelnick said one *Iowa* crewman had told investigators that Hartwig had once discussed suicide, but that "investigators have lost confidence in that testimony, saying that it doesn't add up." Zelnick was referring to David Smith.

Ellis Rubin asked the Navy formally to clear Truitt's name. "We demand somebody in a uniform get on television or radio and with the print media and explain to the country that this was an unfortunate accusation that leaked out, and that the Navy is apologizing and is also clearing the record of this hero," Rubin said. That never happened.

The Navy had become ultrasensitive about the leaks. Vice Admiral Mike Boorda, the Chief of Naval Personnel, sent a memorandum to the families of all forty-seven men who had been killed on the *Iowa*, terming the press reports about the murder/suicide scenario "speculative." "We wish to assure these families that the Navy remains committed to a thorough and complete investigation, and it hopes the responsible public understands the need for discretion until all factors can be amassed and evaluated," Boorda wrote. But the leaks continued. In fact, they got worse, and most of them centered on Clayton Hartwig. "Now they're blaming this, or they're attempting to blame this explosion on a poor dead sailor who can't respond. That's terrible," Ellis Rubin said.

17

☆

"A Good Way to Set the Record Straight"

On May 30, 1989, a week before the *Iowa* sailed for Northern Europe and the Mediterranean, she shifted from the Norfolk Naval Base piers to "Whiskey Anchorage," the Atlantic Fleet's primary ammunition-storage facility. The ship's crew unloaded 1,800 powder bags from the magazines that had been stored on the barges on the York River. Once the tainted powder was removed, the sailors brought aboard hefty canisters filled with polyurethane-foam-covered replacement charges. Then the *Iowa* built up steam in her boilers and sailed out of the Chesapeake Bay on June 7, starting an eleven-day cruise to Kiel, Germany.

Morale was low among the 1,550 officers and sailors on the *Iowa*. Turret Two had been sealed shut like a tomb. Its guns had been forced back to the centerline and were pointing toward the bow, but they were as worthless as wooden telephone poles. Nobody was allowed inside the turret's ghostly confines. None of the gunner's and boatswain's mates, firemen, and Marines who had hauled the corpses and swabbed the gore from Turret Two had received adequate psychological counseling for the trauma they had suffered, and many were experiencing cold sweats, nightmares, and bouts of shaking. Turrets One and Three were functional and had a plentiful supply of powder and shells, but the gunner's mates could not fire their weapons without the permission of the Chief of Naval Operations.

As the *Iowa* made her way toward Europe, the sailors became more agitated than they had been after the bow had nearly been blown off during the "John Wayne Shoot." They lost confidence in their senior officers. Captain Fred Moosally was the most distrusted. Few men referred to him as the "Old Man" any more. He had lost the godlike aura attributed to every commanding officer when he takes command of a ship. Moosally was a Jonah now. Men had died serving under him. When the *Iowa* plowed up the mud banks at Thimble Shoals and almost collided with four other naval vessels, only the men on bridge watch, some of the engineers below, and the boatswain's mates on the main deck had learned that Moosally was an atrocious ship handler. Following the April 19 explosion, criticism of his ineptitude on the bridge had become widespread.

The former Annapolis lineman had attempted to deflect all blame for the fatal accident from himself. For several months after the *Iowa* sailed from Norfolk, the *Iowa*'s officers and men would not learn about Moosally's calumnies about them before Admiral Milligan's panel. When they heard, the captain became the most hated man aboard the ship.

His brazen defense had partially swayed Admiral Milligan, but Moosally knew that his career was still at risk. The Navy had a harsh tradition that said if a ship were grounded, involved in a serious collision at sea, or had more than a few of her crew members killed in an accident, the captain was culpable and could expect to be relieved of his command. In the not-too-distant past, this tradition was enforced regardless of mitigating circumstances. Once he was stripped of his command, the ex-captain could expect orders to an obscure shore posting, where his career would wither and die.

Fred Moosally desperately wanted to keep command of the *Iowa*. If he managed to complete his tour on the battleship without another accident, his sponsors told him, he still had a fairly good chance of becoming a rear admiral. He needed something noteworthy to happen on this cruise to boost his career. Perhaps some crisis would erupt in the Middle East that required the *Iowa*'s guns and missiles.

LIEUTENANT DAN Meyer was still in charge of Turret One. He had been scheduled to turn the turret over to Ensign Ephraim Garrett and take over one of the four deck divisions, but the day after the explosion, the weapons officer told Meyer to remain where he was. Commander Kissinger said things were just too sensitive to make any changes. Meyer's gunner's mates, especially Cletus Guffin, Mark Harden, and Shane Cline, were angered over news accounts blaming Clayton Hartwig for the explosion. They knew that Hartwig's body had been found in the pit below Turret Two's center gun room and that Hartwig hadn't been in a position to deposit a detonator in the powder chamber. Milling around behind Turret One with Meyer and Dale Mortensen, they said that some way had to be found to get the truth out about where Hartwig's body was actually found. They suggested going to either the news media or NIS.

Meyer pointed out that there was no way to talk to the press in the middle of the Atlantic Ocean; in fact, he speculated that the Navy had expedited the battleship's departure to keep the sailors from talking to the media. Based on their own experiences with NIS, Meyer and Mortensen said they didn't believe that agency would be interested in where Hartwig's body was actually found. Meyer said it would be wise to wait and see what Admiral Milligan's report said before talking to the press.

Meyer's men were not willing to fire the sixteen-inch guns again, especially with Chief Skelley still lurking about. Even though the top admirals had announced that there would be no more experiments aboard the *Iowa*, the men didn't believe them. They knew Skelley had defied authority in the past and gotten away with it. Hearing that the gunner's mates were jittery, Captain Moosally dropped in on Turret One and promised that he would be inside the turret with them the very next time they shot. There would be no experiments, he vowed. The men didn't believe him, either, and the captain's talk didn't lessen their reservations about the guns, the ammunition, or the competency of the ship's senior officers. Like almost all the other sailors on the battleship, Turret One's men desperately wanted off the *Iowa*. She was jinxed. When the ship arrived in Kiel, the men calmed down somewhat. The crew savored shore leave in Germany as well as in Portsmouth, England; Rota, Spain; Casablanca, Morocco; and Gibraltar. After a pleasant interlude, they would face another real crisis.

KENDALL TRUITT (who had been transferred to Florida), John Mullahy, and David Smith were not on the *Iowa* when she sailed to Germany. Just before the ship swapped her powder, Mullahy and Smith were told to pack their seabags and leave the *Iowa* without fanfare by way of the after gangplank. Smith was temporarily assigned as a driver for the commander of the Norfolk Naval Base, and he was also required to pick up trash around the facility. The Navy wanted to keep this unreliable witness incommunicado. Mullahy was informed that he was going to be thrown out of the service in a dispute over $3,000 the Navy said he owed as a result of his 1988 court-martial, even though the eighteen-year veteran had played a crucial role in keeping the *Iowa*'s powder magazines from blowing up, and he had led eleven men to safety from the base of the burning turret.

Several Norfolk-area newspapers and another one in Baltimore took up Mullahy's cause, writing that he should be awarded a medal for heroism and have his 1988 fraud conviction overturned. The newspapers stated that an officer had retaliated against Mullahy for his refusal to obey an illegal order. Doug Stuck of the *Baltimore Sun* looked into Mullahy's court-martial and reported that Lieutenant Commander Patricia Rios, who was in charge of a munitions dump at Cartagena, Spain, had ordered Mullahy to paint over the warning signs on 9,000 pounds of explosives and transport them in his own vehicle without a military escort. That was a violation of U.S. military and Spanish regulations, and Mullahy refused to comply.

Lieutenant Commander Rios then had inspected Mullahy's personnel records and determined that he had continued to draw a housing allowance after his first wife had walked out on him. Rios had him court-martialed for defrauding the government. Mullahy had claimed that divorce papers had never been served on him, and that he had repeatedly asked the disbursement office to stop the housing allowance. His defense fell on deaf ears; he was ordered to serve five months in the Philadelphia Naval Brig and was reduced two grades in rank.

Mullahy's savior turned out to be Lieutenant Commander Deborah Burnette, the Navy public-affairs officer stationed in Norfolk who was handling the *Iowa* story there. She first became acquainted with Mullahy when he was chosen to be the enlisted spokesman for the *Iowa* at the Norfolk press conference in April—only to be replaced by Kendall Truitt after the *Iowa*'s public-affairs officer learned that Mullahy had spent time behind bars. Burnette later reviewed the *Iowa*'s after-action reports and was impressed by numerous accounts of Mullahy's courage and coolness in life-threatening situations.

Burnette personally investigated Mullahy's claims that he had been persecuted in Spain and came to the conclusion that he was telling the truth. She discussed his case with Admirals Powell Carter and Frank Kelso and was instrumental in getting the Atlantic Fleet's Inspector General to reopen Mullahy's case. Largely due to Burnette's persistence, Mullahy was allowed to remain on active duty, received the Navy and Marine Corps Medal (the highest award given for heroism in a noncombat situation), regained the two grades in rank he lost after his court-martial, and was not required to repay the disputed funds. The Inspector General concluded that Lieutenant Commander Patricia Rios "made deliberate efforts to ruin" Mullahy's career and attempted to drive him out of the Navy. Shortly afterward, Rios was promoted to full commander.

THE DAY after the *Iowa* left for Germany, John Mullahy called Kathy Kubicina in Cleveland. She was so elated by his call that she drew twelve stars in her notebook above his name. This was the first time since NIS entered the case that anyone in the Hartwig family had a conversation with a sailor who had been on the *Iowa* on the day of the explosion. Mullahy told Kathy that he had talked with her brother for forty minutes the night before the explosion and told him to take plenty of pots and pans and electrical-outlet adapters when he went to London on security duty. Mullahy assured Kathy that her brother wasn't gay and that he had at least one steady girlfriend in Norfolk. She asked for and received the names of the other eleven survivors in Turret Two. Mullahy said a good person for her to talk with was Michael Drowns, but that Drowns was on the *Iowa* on his way to Germany.

"There was no way in hell that Clay could have had anything to do with causing that explosion," Mullahy said, adding that every enlisted man on the battleship held this same view. He said that Clayton was not "depressed or despondent and was excited as hell about going to London." Kathy's brother had not even been listed on the duty roster to participate in the April 19 gun shoot, Mullahy said.

Kathy asked Mullahy for his opinion of Dan Meyer and Dale Mortensen, whom she had met in the punch-and-cookie line at the reception after the memorial service. Mullahy said they were both "good guys" who had played key roles in keeping the ship from sinking and identifying and retrieving the bodies from the turret. They probably knew more about the explosion and the aftermath than anybody on the ship, and Kathy should talk with them when the *Iowa* returned. Mullahy apologized for taking so long to get in touch with her. His wife, Geli, a nurse, had prodded him to make this call for more than a month.

Following her conversation with Mullahy, Kathy drove to her parents' home to tell them that one of Turret Two's survivors was willing to help them. Later that evening, she called Mullahy from her mother's kitchen to ask more questions. Charles Bogino, a reporter for the *Daily Press/Times-Herald* in Hampton, was in Mullahy's apartment. Mullahy vouched for Bogino and put him on the phone with Kathy. Bogino told her that her nemesis Fred Francis of NBC News had recently been in Norfolk poking around and talking to NIS. She told Bogino and Mullahy that she was going to make Francis "pay for what he's done to my brother's reputation." She had written NBC News president Michael Gartner a letter complaining that Francis had attributed quotes to her that she had never made. She also claimed that Francis had "misrepresented himself" and had broken his word about keeping their conversation "off the record." Gartner wrote back, noting that "NBC and Fred Francis aggressively pursued that news so we could inform our viewers." He failed to address her complaints about Francis's fabricating quotes or his failure to honor his word to a source, ending his curt reply by saying, "So I write to tell you I understand your grief but also to try to explain why we do what we do. I hope that you understand our role."

AS THE *Iowa* neared Germany, several hundred NIS agents back in Virginia fanned out in a 200-mile semicircle around Norfolk checking Radio Shack stores to see if they could find a sales receipt proving that Clayton Hartwig had purchased an electronic timer. The fact that David Smith had recanted his statement that he had seen a Radio Shack timer in Hartwig's locker did not dampen NIS's zeal for the search. In fact, it gained added impetus after both Fred Francis on NBC and David Martin, the CBS Pentagon correspondent, broadcast stories the same night quoting an unidentified source (David Smith) as saying that Hartwig had shown him a $15 Radio Shack timer attached to a battery capable of detonating the five bags of powder in the gun barrel. Martin correctly stated that the source refused to take a polygraph test.

The *Daily Press/Times-Herald* newspaper in Hampton went so far as to publish photographs of six different models of Radio Shack timers, ranging in price from $3.99 to $19.95. But the NIS, Fred Francis, David Martin, and the Hampton newspaper never produced any evidence that Clayton Hartwig purchased a Radio Shack timer—even after Radio Shack searched its records with main-frame computers at its corporate headquarters in Texas. Nothing was found connecting Hartwig to an electronic timer. David Smith's imaginary timer nonetheless dominated the Navy's technical investigation for three months.

CAPTAIN JOSEPH Miceli had ensconced his technical support team in a small borrowed building on the Norfolk Naval Base. In addition to Navy technicians, Miceli had talked the U.S. Army into furnishing him six experts from Aberdeen Proving Ground in Maryland and Picatinny Arsenal in Pennsylvania. The Army ordnance and ballistic experts regularly associated with Miceli's team attended the Navy's daily 8 o'clock briefing; their salaries and expenses were paid by the U.S. Navy. Even with all of this cross-pollination, Miceli would later claim that the Army had conducted a totally independent investigation.

While NIS was canvassing Radio Shacks, Commander Ron Swanson, Admiral Milligan's legal counsel, told Captain Miceli to cooperate even more closely with the criminal agents. Shortly thereafter, Robert Nigro, head of the NIS *Iowa* inquiry, and agent Tom Goodman arrived at Miceli's headquarters and briefed him on the largely circumstantial case they had assembled on Hartwig. Miceli said the agents gave him a copy of a ninety-two-page statement by David Smith, but not Smith's retractions. "They [the agents] indicated that they had information that the explosion in the center gun probably was an intentional act," Miceli said, adding that Nigro and Goodman stated that Clayton Hartwig was guilty of blowing up Turret Two. He later claimed that NIS didn't inform him that David Smith had recanted his story about seeing an electronic timer until early November 1989, seven months after the explosion. "I expressed some disappointment in not hearing about it earlier. Testing is based on facts, and if those facts changed, then they should have gotten back to me," Miceli said. He said he had limited funds and would not have conducted the expensive tests at Dahlgren had he known that David Smith was a self-confessed liar.

During their initial meeting with Miceli, Nigro and Goodman urged that the testing be started at Dahlgren without delay to determine if a Radio Shack electronic timer, a nine-volt battery, and a Mark 15 primer (.30-caliber cartridge) could set off an explosion like the one in Turret Two. Miceli said he could begin within several days, and then he informed the agents that he had already pretty much eliminated one type of detonator. He had asked Captain Joseph Kennedy, head of the Navy's explosive ordnance disposal facility at Indian Head, Maryland, to see if a "compression device" was workable. When jostled by a rammer or powder bags, a chemical compression device could start a chain reaction that ended in a burst of flames. The explosives experts conducted thirteen tests and concluded that chemical devices were too volatile. "Just as soon as they entered the breech of the gun, they struck something and went off," Miceli said.

Miceli spent between $50,000 and $100,000 on each of twenty-seven tests he carried out at Dahlgren. Called "open breech burns," they were conducted in a large field with two sixteen-inch gun barrels attached to concrete platforms. The breechblocks of the weapons were left open when the powder charges were ignited, as had been the case in the *Iowa* disaster. One of the objectives of these tests was to duplicate the forty-four-inch movement of the center gun's projectile. Twenty of the test firings took place in a barrel that was virtually slick, having 93 percent of its rifling worn away. The shell movements ranged from zero to 250.875 inches, but none of them were anywhere close to the *Iowa*'s. The Navy has no idea what the barrel erosion was in three test shots. The shell failed to move at all in two of them, and it only moved 4.375 inches in the third instance. Miceli used a barrel that was 21 percent worn, comparable to the erosion in the center gun, for four test shots. The shell movements were zero, 17.25, 31.125, and 85.750 inches, respectively. Miceli came up with some strange arithmetic. He simply eliminated the shell that did not budge; then he added the movements of the remaining three shells. He divided that figure by three and calculated that the average shell movement for all twenty-seven test shots was 44.708 inches, or approximately the same as the *Iowa*'s.

Although Miceli was supposed to be testing the feasibility of igniting five powder bags with an electrical timer, he also utilized "squibs" (miniature electrically fired explosives), soldering irons, and primers to activate the blasts. All twenty-seven firings were remotely activated. Cables snaked from the open breech to a blockhouse, where electrical charges were transmitted back to an igniter in the gun barrel, making the powder bags explode. This was not realistic testing, because there was no way of knowing whether the igniters would have worked without receiving a jolt of electricity.

Miceli took videotape shots of all twenty-seven tests. He also taped shells and powder bags being loaded into sixteen-inch guns on the battleship *Wisconsin*. Navy public-relations specialists would later edit these tapes into a deceptive package to convince the families of the forty-seven dead sailors, Congress, the news media, and the American public that Clayton Hartwig had sabotaged Turret Two's center gun.

DURING THE time Miceli was conducting the "open breech burn" tests, retired Rear Admiral Ed Snyder drove down to Dahlgren from Washington to see what he could learn. At Dahlgren, he ran into a Marine gunnery sergeant who remembered Snyder from the late 1960s, when he was getting the *New Jersey* ready for Vietnam. The sergeant introduced him to some technicians who had witnessed Miceli's tests. They told him that the entire operation was a waste of time. "There's no way you can duplicate the conditions inside the gun room of a battleship with a rusted-out sewer pipe sitting in a cow pasture," one man said.

CAPTAIN MICELI worried that if an electronic timer were eliminated as an ignition device, he would have no fallback. So even though he had been satisfied in mid-May that a chemical compression device was impractical, he went back to Captain Joe Kennedy at Indian Head, Maryland, and asked him to take another crack at devising a chemical device that would not burst into flames as soon as it was inserted into the breech. Kennedy's explosives experts tried again, building chemical initiators from such exotic components as hair pomade, steel wool, swimming-pool chlorine, and brake fluid.

Caught on videotape, their efforts are instructive and often absurd. One petty officer displayed a floppy steel-wool device that looked like a large bird's nest. Addressing two colleagues, he cracked, "Can you imagine a guy carrying a piece of shit like this across the forecastle and heading toward the turret to blow it up?" All three laughed heartily. In other taped scenes, the ordnance experts tried to devise ways to prevent chemicals from prematurely intermingling and producing a "cook off." They tinkered with thin glass vials and plastic kitchen bags used to seal leftovers. And when they did succeed in setting off these improvised devices, they obtained decidedly mixed results. Sometimes, a chemical igniter would spark, blossoming into flames as soon as it was being placed in a simulated gun barrel. On other occasions, it required minutes for the chemicals to sputter and then flare. And sometimes nothing happened. The experts thought the chemical igniters were unreliable and too large to conceal. The only two chemical devices that Miceli tested at Dahlgren drove the projectiles about 250 inches up the barrel, roughly six times the shell movement in the *Iowa*'s gun.

ACCORDING TO Captain Miceli, the idea of sending the *Iowa*'s copper-nickel-alloy rotating band to the Norfolk Naval Shipyard's metallurgical laboratory for spectrographic analysis originated with Vice Admiral Joseph Donnell, the officer who had appointed Admiral Milligan to head the *Iowa* investigation. Donnell had extensive duty as an engineering officer at sea, and Miceli was happy to have his input. The rotating band, a malleable fin near the base of the projectile, folds over during firing, forming a gas-tight seal. It was peeled off the shell when it was extracted from the gun five weeks after the explosion. Admiral Donnell surmised that if an electronic timer had been in the powder chamber, microscopic particles of it might have clung to the soft alloy before the fin bent over. That assumed that both the barrel and the shell were in pristine condition before the explosion and that no contamination had been introduced into the barrel since the explosion. Such was not the case. First, cleaning fluid and metal fibers already present in the gun barrel also could have been trapped under the rotating band. Second, the projectile had been tainted as a result of the firefighting efforts and the laborious extraction of the shell after thousands of gallons of seawater, foam, lubricant, and cleaning solution were dumped down the bore.

When the rotating band—fifty inches in circumference—was removed from the *Iowa* projectile, it was cut in half. One half was used by the Norfolk Naval Shipyard for spectrographic analysis. The other half was stored for a time in a locker not designed to store evidence safely. The shipyard used up a quarter of the rotating band, carving off small sections for testing. Employing electron microscopy and X-rays, technicians claimed they detected the same chemical elements (barium, silicon, aluminum, and calcium) under some rotating bands on shells fired at Dahlgren as they had on the *Iowa* band. They were positive that an electronic timer attached to a nine-volt battery and a .30-caliber rifle cartridge primer caused the *Iowa* explosion.

NIS urged Miceli to have a non-military forensic laboratory conduct parallel tests. He agreed, and the FBI Crime Laboratory in Washington consented to help. The FBI lab received a sixteen-inch-long section of the *Iowa*'s rotating band. It also received sections of a band fired at Dahlgren with no timing device, as well as two bands that had been ignited with electronic timers. Kenneth Nimmich, chief of scientific analysis at the FBI lab, said that even before the testing began, he was concerned that the *Iowa* band had been contaminated. When the FBI technicians spread open a five-inch-wide section of the band, they realized that it was saturated and "wet" with Break-Free, a cleaning solution. Some lubricating oil was also present.

The FBI learned from *Iowa* personnel that it was routine practice to pour five gallons of Break-Free down each gun barrel after the weapon was through firing for the day. The presence of Break-Free under the rotating band was confirmation to the FBI that contamination had seeped in under the seal. The lab stated that since barium chloride is prevalent in Break-Free, "The significance of finding barium in the *Iowa* band becomes questionable." Break-Free also contains calcium sulfonate, so the FBI erased calcium from the Navy's list of "foreign elements." Nimmich said the lab identified the same "foreign elements" on rotating bands that had been fired without timers as bands that had timers. The FBI concluded that there was no scientific evidence to indicate that an electronic timing device had been present in the center gun.

The FBI lab told Miceli that he should conduct a "controlled" firing, inserting "a rare element," such as gallium or mercury, to see whether the element would be snared on the rotating band. This process would prove whether or not Miceli's testing procedures were valid. The FBI also advised the Navy technicians not to refer to silicon traces on the *Iowa* rotating band as "integrated circuit components" or "glass." Silicon was a common contaminant. The FBI found silicon particles "in significant numbers" on all the bands that the Navy had submitted, including the ones fired without a timer.

In addition to recommending the "rare-element test," the FBI encouraged Miceli to take the silicon specimens to a laboratory that specialized in microchips and see if the Norfolk Naval Shipyard scientists knew what they were talking about. Miceli rejected every one of the FBI's suggestions. Kenneth Nimmich said Miceli told the FBI to stop testing and return the unused portions of the rotating band. Nimmich told Miceli he was making a grave error. "We felt we could add significantly to the investigation, but we were not requested to do so," he said. Miceli later disputed Nimmich, saying, "One day the FBI called up and announced that they were off the case. They offered no explanation. I begged them to stay."

Apparently feeling that he had been burned by the FBI, Miceli sacked up the few remaining pieces of the *Iowa*'s rotating band and flew north to the Naval Weapons Support Center laboratory in Crane, Indiana, where he had been commanding officer from 1982 to 1985. A number of workers still remembered him "yelling at the top of his voice making people shiver in their boots," personally poking through dumpsters to see what employees were tossing out, and chasing poachers "like a mad man with a loaded gun in his car." But he still had a coterie of loyal devotees there, some of whom worked in the laboratory that would be involved in the *Iowa* testing. The laboratory was well equipped to handle such tasks as electron spectroscopy and gas chromatography.

WHILE THE *Iowa* was on her cruise and Miceli was testing at Dahlgren, Robert Zelnick and Mark Brender of ABC News decided that they had to devote more energy to reporting the Navy's mistreatment of Clayton Hartwig and his family. In a sixteen-page memorandum, written on June 27 and entitled, "Smear: The Navy and Clayton Hartwig," the two newsmen spelled out to their bosses why more airtime should be allocated to telling the Hartwig story. They took the Navy to task for refusing to correct the lies that had been liberally strewn about concerning Kendall Truitt and Clayton Hartwig. Instead of apologizing, the Navy had privately sought to convince members of Congress and some acquiescent reporters that "suicide/murder is the most likely theory of the case." Zelnick and Brender reviewed the improper storage of the *Iowa*'s gunpowder in 1988 and stated that the night before the explosion, the cooling system in the battleship's magazines had been turned off to make the powder more potent. All the sailors they interviewed told them that they couldn't imagine being in a turret filled with gunpowder with a mad man trying to blow it up, and somebody saying casually on the sound-powered phones, "We have a problem in here. We're not ready yet." The other men in the turret would have been yelling their heads off.

The Zelnick/Brender memo did a fine job of encapsulating Clayton Hartwig's boyhood, his family and neighborhood, his home, the key role his Seventh-Day Adventist religion played in his daily life, his military career, and his friends. The writers found "no evidence whatsoever of homosexuality in Hartwig's background," or anything connecting him to inserting a timer into the gun. They knew about David Smith's statement to NIS about seeing a timer, as well as Smith's refusal to take a polygraph and his retractions. They wrote that John Mullahy fully supported the Hartwig family's claim that Clayton had been screened by the Navy for a security job in London.

The two newsmen reviewed seventeen of Hartwig's letters written over a two-year period. These letters led them to an entirely different conclusion about Hartwig than that held by the FBI's Behavioral Science Unit and NIS psychologist Thomas Mountz. By sifting through Hartwig's letters with "malignant selectivity," they said, it was possible to paint a dark picture of him as a despondent, self-pitying, and perhaps suicidal individual. But a more comprehensive view of his writings "than the squalid NIS characterizations" revealed a young man of moral probity and personal integrity, decent and sensitive, "easily hurt yet easily healed."

Zelnick and Brender believed that one of Hartwig's letters, written in late March 1989, proved that Hartwig and Truitt had patched up their differences several months prior to the explosion. That was consistent with Carole Truitt's statement that the night before the *Iowa* sailed for the Caribbean, she had laundered Hartwig's dress whites. Zelnick and Brender ended their memo on this note: "Hartwig was a loving and devoted son and brother, a faithful and caring friend, a reliable correspondent. Most of all, he was a sailor. He loved the sea. He loved his ship. He loved his comrades. And he loved the United States Navy. Were he able to see the dirt the Navy has heaped upon his fresh grave, he would have good reason to be pissed off. 'Don't you think I deserve better, huh?' he might have written."

Two days after the memo was distributed to ABC's executives and anchors, Zelnick aired another piece for *World News Tonight,* saying that NIS was responsible for leaking material that fingered Kendall Truitt as a possible murderer and Clayton Hartwig as a likely suicide. Zelnick said two NIS agents had met with Truitt's attorney, Ellis Rubin, saying they were sorry about the leaks and they no longer believed that Truitt played any role in the explosion. NIS also acknowledged that Hartwig and Truitt never had a homosexual relationship. The agents told Rubin that news reports about a Radio Shack timer being found in Hartwig's personal possessions were fraudulent. Zelnick exhibited a copy of a January 18, 1989, Navy message to the *Iowa* nominating Hartwig for overseas security duty. Navy public-relations officers were still stubbornly insisting that Hartwig had fantasized the overseas posting.

AFTER THREE months of dogged reporting, Zelnick wanted to see some of the material that he and Mark Brender had assembled appear in print, either in a magazine or a Sunday newspaper. He called Kevin Klose, an editor of the *Washington Post*'s "Outlook" section, and asked him if he would be interested in an article about the Navy's besmirching of Clayton Hartwig. Klose, who had been a correspondent with Zelnick in Moscow and thought highly of his reporting, was definitely interested. The "Outlook" section included the Sunday editorial page and about ten pages of commentary and opinion pieces normally written by nonstaffers. Klose went to his boss, Jodie Allen, editor of "Outlook," and told her about Zelnick's proposal. Allen said she was excited about getting her newspaper "finally on the right side of this issue."

It didn't take Molly Moore and George Wilson long to hear that Zelnick was invading their territory with the Hartwig piece. According to Allen, Moore went to national editor Robert Kaiser and asked him to have the piece killed, claiming that she and Wilson wanted to "keep inaccuracies" out of the newspaper. She dropped by the Chief of Naval Information's office on Friday morning, June 30, and told Rear Admiral Jimmy Finkelstein that Zelnick's "Outlook" piece had definitely been spiked. But late Friday evening, Leonard Downie Jr., executive editor of the *Washington Post*, reviewed the article written by Zelnick and Brender and told Jodie Allen and other editors, "This belongs in the paper." One reporter said, "Len Downie realized that we had been dead wrong about Hartwig with our reporting, and this was a good way to set the record straight." The headline above the Sunday, July 2, piece read, "The Navy vs. Hartwig, Did Leaks from the USS *Iowa* Probe Smear a Sailor?" The article closely followed the approach in the memo that Zelnick and Brender had circulated inside ABC.

ALTHOUGH THE Zelnick/Brender article that appeared in the *Washington Post* was well received by most Pentagon correspondents, it didn't seem to make much of an impression on NBC's Fred Francis. On July 18, Francis ran another piece on the *NBC Nightly News* that was again based almost exclusively on documents leaked by an NIS agent. Francis said that the FBI Behavioral Science Unit's equivocal death analysis of Clayton Hartwig had satisfied Navy investigators "that Hartwig was a troubled homosexual who took his own life." According to Francis, Admiral Milligan's team had collected 228 exhibits of various types, one of which was a three-hour taped statement from David Smith. Francis had a transcript of Smith's statement from which he quoted liberally. Although Smith had repudiated that prior to broadcast, for some reason that repudiation was not included in the broadcast report.

Francis included verbatim passages from the FBI equivocal death analysis in his script. He said the FBI profilers considered Hartwig to be a very disturbed young man who could not vent his anger and who was under a great deal of stress, "virtually insuring some type of reaction. In this instance suicide." Even though NIS had informed attorney Ellis Rubin that they did not believe Kendall Truitt was gay or had anything to do with the *Iowa* explosion, Francis implied that a homosexual relationship existed between Truitt and Hartwig. He said investigators told him that Hartwig had made homosexual advances to David Smith the night before the explosion.

Francis ended his piece by saying, "Because the evidence against Hartwig is only circumstantial, the Navy's complete findings, due out in a few weeks, will stop short of a definitive conclusion of suicide. But one naval officer said today, 'No reasonable person can conclude otherwise.' "

18

☆

"The Men Didn't Want to Shoot Again."

THE DAY AFTER the broadcast of Fred Francis's piece containing the misleading information about David Smith, Bob Zelnick wrote another internal memo castigating Francis. "All three networks became aware of and reported on the content of his testimony back in May at which time both the Navy and the Pentagon were describing him as a witness who lacked credibility and had flunked or otherwise refused to continue with his lie detector test," Zelnick said. Despite spending $7 million on the investigation and questioning four to five hundred witnesses, he wrote, the Navy still had no hard evidence that a crime had been committed by anybody. There was no proof that Hartwig had ever engaged in homosexual activity with anybody, or that he had ever attempted suicide either in high school or aboard the *Iowa*. Zelnick and Mark Brender had obtained the *Iowa*'s "watch bill" (duty roster) for the Caribbean cruise, and Hartwig's name did not appear on it, signifying that Hartwig was near the end of his tour on the battleship and that he had been assigned to the turret by Chief Ziegler shortly before the fatal gun shoot began.

Zelnick asked two prominent Washington psychiatrists to analyze fifteen of Hartwig's letters. These psychiatrists concluded that Hartwig lacked the traits associated with suicide: helplessness, hopelessness, a feeling of victimization, trouble concentrating, uncontrollable crying, fantasies, and feelings of resentment. In anticipation of the release of Admiral Milligan's report, Zelnick recommended to Paul Friedman, executive producer of *World News Tonight,* that he and Brender interview some psychiatrists on videotape, revisit Hartwig's family and friends, and discuss the case with one or more prominent former prosecutors or Justice Department officials to obtain answers to these questions: Has the Navy established that a crime was committed? Has the Navy established probable cause to believe that Hartwig committed the crime? Could the case presented by the Navy pass muster with a grand jury? Was the Navy's evidence compelling enough so that if Hartwig were still alive, a jury would convict him of being a mass murderer?

Zelnick and Brender traveled to Norfolk and had some further discussions with John Mullahy. Mullahy confirmed that there had been multiple misfires in Turret One. He was willing to go on camera and say that. Mullahy said he did not believe that Hartwig had propositioned Smith the night before the explosion, and he considered Smith to be "a flake." The ABC newsmen also wanted to tape an interview with retired Master Chief Chuck Hill. The former gunner's mate was willing to talk with the reporters, but he didn't want to appear on camera or have his name used. He feared that the Navy might retaliate against him by cutting off his pension or recalling him to active duty. Hill told Zelnick and Brender that he didn't believe that Hartwig had anything to do with the explosion. He believed that the powder that had been improperly stored on river barges during the summer of 1988 was unsafe, and he voiced a long string of profanities at Chief Skelley for conducting illegal powder experiments the day of the explosion. Hill was unyielding in his conviction that Hartwig and Truitt had not been involved in homosexual behavior when they were wrestling on the main deck in 1987. The two sailors were goofing off on duty. That was serious, he said, but they were not sodomites. The interviews and information Zelnick and Brender obtained were incorporated into a piece that aired later in the summer.

AS REAR Admiral Richard Milligan neared the end of his investigation in early July, a senior captain who recently had been assigned to the Navy's surface warfare branch in the Pentagon was designated by Admiral Edney, Vice Chief of Naval Operations, to look over Milligan's shoulder and second-guess him if necessary. That officer was Captain Douglas Katz, a 1965 U.S. Naval Academy graduate who had recently been chosen to become a rear admiral. The primary reason that Admiral Edney used Katz to buttress Milligan was that he thought Katz knew more about sixteen-inch gunnery than Milligan did, despite the fact that both Katz and Milligan had commanded the *New Jersey* at different times.

Katz had served as commanding officer of the battleship *New Jersey* before coming to the Pentagon. His ship had been lying off the San Clemente, California, gunnery range on April 19, unlimbering her nine sixteen-inch guns, when word was flashed by the commander of the Surface Warfare Group in Long Beach, California, that the *Iowa* had experienced a major gunnery disaster in the Caribbean and that no sixteen-inch guns on any battleship could be fired until the cause of the accident could be determined. Katz turned to his weapons officer, standing beside him on the bridge, and told him to have the gun crews swivel their turrets to the centerline and then secure from battle stations.

Douglas Katz had played halfback on the Annapolis varsity football squad with Fred Moosally. Years later, he still held "the Moose" in awe, describing him as "one hell of a football player and one hell of a guy." Before Admiral Milligan's *Iowa* report was scheduled for release to the public, Katz was told by Admiral Edney and Vice Admiral Mike Boorda, Chief of Naval Personnel, that he would fly to the Mediterranean and brief Fred Moosally on its contents. Katz was also slated to go to Cleveland the day the report was released and tell the Hartwig family that the Navy considered Clayton to be a mass murderer.

AS THE *Iowa* cruised about the North Atlantic, Baltic Sea, and Mediterranean, news about the Navy's investigation continued to dribble out, sometimes generating real animosity on the battleship. On July 3, Kendall Truitt, his wife Carole, his mother, his in-laws, and his attorney, Ellis Rubin, held a press conference in Jacksonville, Florida, in which Truitt faulted the Navy for having "a motive of the week" in its explanations of how Turret Two blew up. Truitt also claimed that there had been widespread drug use on the battleship, which may have contributed to the accident. "On the *Iowa*, a lot of the guys with us had serious drug problems. It's pretty bad when your guys are dealing with gunpowder and half of the individuals are doing drugs," Truitt said. The Chief of Naval Information gave Truitt's allegations credibility by refusing to confirm or deny them.

Fred Moosally learned about Truitt's inflammatory statements when he received a cable from the same Navy press officer who had refused to comment on them. Moosally threw a tantrum, grabbing a microphone and shouting into the public-address system, "Our buddy Truitt is out there telling everybody that the *Iowa* is full of drug addicts, dopers, and we all know that's not true!" Nearly every man onboard the battleship cursed Truitt; some banged on steel bulkheads with wrenches and vowed to split Truitt's head if they ever laid eyes upon him again.

The ship carried some reminders of the ongoing investigation. Two NIS agents were aboard her for the entire voyage. They didn't interrogate anybody and kept to themselves. But even though they were stealthy, their presence was known and cast a pall over the ship. Radio messages were transmitted frequently to the captain from the Vice Chief of Naval Operations or the Chief of Naval Information. The messages were classified, but the radio operators chattered about their contents to their sidekicks, who in turn told everyone else. These messages, which I later obtained after filing a Freedom of Information Act lawsuit against the Navy, were designed to buoy Moosally's spirits and reassure him that he was still a member of the Navy's inner circle.

The battleship entered the French port city of Marseilles on July 24 for two weeks of shipyard work. Shortly after the ship docked, Fred Moosally strode off the forward gangplank for a leave in Paris, some 500 miles away, with his wife, Joan, who had flown over from Washington to meet him. Before his departure, he turned over the operation of the ship to the executive officer, Commander Morse.

A week into the repairs, Shiite Muslim kidnappers released a videotape of the gagged and bound body of Marine Corps Lieutenant Colonel William Higgins swinging from a makeshift gallows. When he was abducted in February 1988, Higgins had been the commander of a United Nations peacekeeping force in southern Lebanon. Terrorists who released the grisly tape announced that the forty-four-year-old Higgins had been executed in retaliation for Israel's kidnaping of Sheik Abdul Karim Obeid, a Muslim cleric. They also threatened to execute another hostage. A task force was being assembled off the coast of Lebanon, and the *Iowa* was ordered to join it as soon as possible. The ship might be called upon to use her two remaining sixteen-inch turrets and her Tomahawk missiles.

During the twenty-four hours it took the battleship to exit the shipyard, Commander Morse frantically tried to locate the captain. Moosally was not at the hotel where he said he would be staying, so the *Iowa* sailed from the French port on the overcast afternoon of August 2 with the executive officer in command. Getting underway was not smooth. Yard workers' tools littered the passageways and the main deck, and some equipment that might be needed in Lebanon was inoperable. Jokes flew around the bridge about the captain "missing movement." Most of the hilarity at Moosally's expense was inspired by Commander Morse, who was exuberant about being in command of the *Iowa* at sea, heading toward a possible war zone.

"Missing movement" means that when your ship sails, you aren't aboard. It's a serious offense, and sailors can be sentenced to the brig for it. Since the captain had been on authorized leave and didn't know that the ship was sailing, technically he wasn't guilty of "missing movement." But he hadn't shown sound judgment by not being registered at the hotel where he said he would be, and by failing to stay in frequent touch with the ship in case an emergency arose.

Once the *Iowa* left French waters, the U.S. State Department helped the Navy locate its missing captain. A flurry of messages ensued. Some of the traffic crossed the desk of Alvin Adams, a senior State Department officer in Washington who had just been nominated to become U.S. ambassador to Haiti. He was also the adoptive father of Tung Thanh Adams, who had been killed in the *Iowa* explosion. When Adams informed his wife that Moosally had missed the *Iowa*'s sailing, her eyes lit up. Having been married to a diplomat for twenty years, she knew from experience that bureaucracies like the Navy rarely punished one of their high-ranking officers, no matter how outrageous the offense. She found it inconceivable that even after the explosion had imperiled his career, Moosally could do something so stupid as to miss the sailing of his ship.

A DAY'S sailing from Marseilles, as the battleship prepared to enter the narrow, twenty-four-mile-long Strait of Messina separating Sicily from Italy, a Navy helicopter bearing Fred Moosally overtook the *Iowa* and landed near her fantail. Commander Morse hustled back to the flight deck to tell the captain how much he had been missed. Moosally's arrival was none too soon. Vice Admiral James Williams, commander of the U.S. Sixth Fleet, had approved the test firing of the *Iowa*'s guns after conferring with the Pentagon. Once the battleship successfully fired several missions into the sea, she could join a task force.

The *Iowa* was scheduled to test-fire her remaining six big guns the day after the captain arrived. Naval Sea Systems Command had rushed a technician, Bruce Wetzel, out to the battleship to observe her gunfire. Wetzel was a bad omen to the gunner's mates. In the past, he had shown up like clockwork just before Chief Skelley conducted one of his experiments. "The men associated Wetzel with Skelley. They still had the shakes from the explosion. The men didn't want to shoot again, and then Wetzel shows up. The gunner's mates went around moaning, 'Oh, God, not more experiments!' " Dan Meyer said.

Wetzel promised that no experiments were in the offing, but he wanted to install pressure gauges in six gun barrels. Meyer demanded that Wetzel fork over the kind of written authorization from Sea Systems Command that was required before an alteration could be made to a gun barrel. "I don't have any authorization, Mr. Meyer," Wetzel conceded. "I can't tell you who's behind this. Don't push me. You'll lose big-time." Meyer shrugged and told Wetzel that he could install the instruments.

Meyer said some of his toughest, most experienced sailors were trembling when they entered Turret One as the *Iowa* prepared to fire her first mission since Turret Two blew up. Several of the younger men wept, but nobody refused to go to his battle station. Turret One fired nine 2,700-pound, blue-painted practice projectiles in single salvos. Turret Three shot six of these shells the same way. All fifteen lacked an explosive charge. Both turrets fired on a ninety-degree angle from the bow at a make-believe target, a spot in the ocean picked by radar operators in the combat information center. This "hole in the ocean" was 16,000 yards from the ship. Only one shell from Turret One "splashed" (hit) the target. The rest of the shells missed the target by about a hundred yards. It was not spectacular shooting, but at least there were no misfired weapons or explosions.

Captain Moosally kept his word and went to Turret One and stood next to Dan Meyer and Dale Mortensen while their gun crews fired the first three shells. He then made his way back to Turret Three and observed the gunfire there, before returning to Turret One for its final three salvos.

As soon as main battery plot ordered the turrets to cease fire, the executive officer, the weapons officer, and about twenty-five chiefs and petty officers hurried to Turret One to congratulate the captain. The ship's photographer was summoned to capture this triumph on film. The picture, later printed in the ship's "cruise book," shows the captain sitting in a chair in the turret officer's booth with a blue *Iowa* baseball cap perched on his head, beaming as if his team had just scored the winning touchdown in the Super Bowl. He was surrounded by a crowd of officers and enlisted men. The gunner's mates, who wore hoods with eye slits, looked like Klansmen. These hoods and padded gauntlets were added to the gun crew's battle dress after the explosion. The garb was hot, impeded the men's movements, and probably wouldn't have provided any protection to the forty-seven men who died in Turret Two.

The *Iowa* fired her sixteen-inch guns again the next day. Seventeen practice shells (2,700-pound concrete-and-iron slugs containing no explosive charges) were fired at a rubber raft tethered to a balloon outfitted with radar reflectors some 15,000 yards away. The ship launched her remotely piloted vehicle (RPV), and the drone's television camera showed one shell raise a waterspout near the target. On August 9, the battleship fired eighteen more practice shells at a target Chief Skelley called a "killer tomato." It was a bright red inflatable target bobbing on the surface and attached to a balloon covered with radar reflectors. The "killer tomato" was located 17,500 yards from the ship. One shell punctured and sank it. The next day, the *Iowa* fired her guns for the final time before the Sixth Fleet commander came aboard to use her as his flagship. Nine shells plunged into the ocean 16,000 yards from the ship. The gun crews weren't shooting at any target, not even a "hole in the ocean." Dan Meyer said the fact that Chief Skelley was running these practice sessions rather than the senior officers further alarmed the gunner's mates. "The men felt that sooner or later something really awful was going to happen again," Meyer said.

ON AUGUST 15, Vice Admiral Williams and his Sixth Fleet staff helicoptered out to the *Iowa*, near Gibraltar, from the guided-missile cruiser USS *Belknap*. In his dress whites and with his brush-cut, steel-colored hair, Williams resembled the quintessential naval flag officer from the 1920s. He looked as though he had been born to command a fleet from the flag bridge of a battleship. Fred Moosally, wasting no time trying to ingratiate himself with the admiral, had scheduled a firepower demonstration to coincide with the admiral's first few hours aboard the *Iowa*. Turrets One and Three each fired nine 2,700-pound practice shells at a "killer tomato" drifting 15,000 yards from the ship. None of the rounds even grazed the target, but Chief Skelley contended that the ship had scored three direct hits and one near-miss, explaining that if the shells contained explosive charges, they would have "swamped" the "killer tomato."

AFTER FRED Moosally's demonstration of his ship's skill with her sixteen-inch guns, Admiral Williams ordered the captain to head her toward

Lebanon to link up with the aging carrier *Coral Sea* and the remainder of the U.S. task force. Williams hoped that this seaborne show-of-force would persuade the terrorists not to execute Joseph Cicippio, fifty-eight, an administrator at the American University of Beirut, and seven other U.S. hostages still held in Lebanon. And he had another thorny situation with which to contend. The U.S. Embassy in Beirut was surrounded by about a thousand Maronite Christian demonstrators loyal to General Michel Aoun, head of Lebanon's military government. Aoun had demanded that U.S. Ambassador John McCarthy present his diplomatic credentials to him and recognize Aoun's Christian cabinet as "the legitimate Lebanese government."

Located near the Mediterranean in Aoukar, a Christian suburb in East Beirut, the bunkerlike U.S. Embassy was ringed with concertina wire and sandbags. The United States had shut down its embassy in the Muslim sector of West Beirut and moved into a Christian enclave after pro-Iranian militants had blown it up in 1983. Patrick Tyler, then a correspondent for the *Washington Post*, was outside the embassy in August 1989, covering the demonstrations, which he termed "nonviolent." Despite Tyler's characterization of the protesters, the U.S. State Department and Admiral Williams chose to view them otherwise. Williams made plans to employ the *Iowa*'s sixteen-inch guns to deal with General Aoun's supporters.

DAN MEYER was in Turret One when the operations officer, Commander Bob Finney, entered the turret officer's booth and said he had some ballistics questions to ask Meyer. Finney said Admiral Williams wanted to drop "a ring of steel" around the embassy. The admiral wanted to "surgically rain down" sixteen-inch shells three hundred yards from the embassy. Captain Moosally had been pressing Williams to let him prove that the *Iowa* could perform such a feat. Chief Skelley had also attested to the guns' incredible accuracy. Commander Finney wanted to know how far the initial round would fall from the target. "It should miss in range by plus or minus 150 yards. It should be off in deflection by fifty yards to the left or right. Its killing radius is approximately seventy yards, depending on whether you're firing a 2,700-pound armor-piercing shell or a 1,900-pound high-explosive shell and what kind of fuse you're using. So, the first round we fire has a reasonably good chance of wiping out the embassy, Commander," Meyer said.

Meyer explained that during World War II, the guns had been set up to fire an elliptical pattern devised for fighting enemy ships. This firing pattern had never been modified, meaning that if the *Iowa* fired a three-gun salvo, the shells would be scattered in range and deflection. The turrets were not aligned, so the dispersal of the shells would worsen if Turrets One and Three fired at the same target at the same time. "And even if we don't level the embassy, we'll butcher hundreds of innocent civilians," Meyer said.

The slender operations officer took a deep breath as Meyer rattled off data. "That's terrible," Finney finally said, "but I can't tell that to the admiral. He'll have a fit. You do it, Meyer." "Me? I'm only a lieutenant," Meyer responded. "Well, somebody's got to do it, and you're designated," Finney said, as he descended the tail hatch. Meyer screwed up his courage and went to flag plot, located amidships on the port side below the Tomahawk and Harpoon missile box launchers. The compartment was filled with lieutenants and lieutenant commanders. Meyer examined their left breast pockets and felt more confident. Many of them were wearing gold Surface Warfare badges. Admiral Williams might be a nuclear submariner, but he had men around him who were bona fide ship drivers.

Meyer thought the surface officers might comprehend the principles of gunnery. He sought out the senior watch officer and gave him the same information that he had provided Commander Finney. The watch officer had Meyer repeat this to Admiral Williams's chief of staff, who told Meyer that he would personally inform the admiral of the limitations of the *Iowa*'s guns. The "ring of steel" plan was canceled. But after it was discarded, an even riskier one took its place.

DAN MEYER and Dale Mortensen learned the details of the revised plan from a handwritten memo and noted that it contained a number of Skelley's trademarks—the use of unconventional shells, illogical fire-control techniques, a failure to understand the limitations of the sixteen-inch gun system, and a near-total disregard for the safety of the ship's crew. Admiral Williams approved the new battle plan. Captain Moosally, who told the officers on the bridge that he had relatives living in Beirut, nevertheless was eager to fire the *Iowa*'s guns at General Aoun's Maronite Christian forces. Moosally wanted to prove to Admiral Williams and the Navy that his ship could handle a difficult assignment. Williams had voiced support for the *Iowa*'s captain a number of times since he had come aboard the battleship, saying that Moosally had been unfairly criticized in the press after the explosion. The admiral was willing to give Moosally a chance to bombard General Aoun's troops and thereby redeem his reputation and career.

Williams knew that Aoun had plenty of armor and could disrupt an evacuation of the U.S. Embassy. For the previous six months, Aoun's 20,000-man army had been attempting to drive 40,000 Syrian troops out of Lebanon. Aoun was losing, and he was distressed that the United States had failed to come to his aid. To prevent the Americans from abandoning the embassy, Aoun was prepared to surround it with tanks. But to do that, he had to send the tanks through a tunnel beneath a river. The Sixth Fleet staff decided that if the *Iowa*'s sixteen-inch guns could punch a hole in the tunnel or seal it shut at either end, Aoun's tanks and fighting vehicles would be neutralized.

The plan called for the *Iowa* to steam along the Lebanese coast at twenty knots. Turret One would open fire with a three-gun salvo, using Chief Skelley's experimental antisubmarine shells. The projectiles were supposed to plummet into the river flowing above the tunnel. When they detonated beneath the surface, a pressure wave would breach the concrete and reinforced-steel tunnel walls. If that didn't work, Turret One would have just thirty seconds to reload and fire another three-gun salvo of 2,700-pound armor-piercing shells at an outcrop near the tunnel's exit. These heavier shells were meant to start a landslide to block the outlet. If Aoun deployed infantry and attacked the embassy, then Turret One had to reload in thirty seconds once more and fire a three-gun salvo of antipersonnel projectiles. These shells, which were packed with bomblets, would almost certainly damage the embassy and kill a large number of Lebanese civilians surrounding the compound.

While the vessel was maneuvering parallel to the coast, she would be within the range of an eight-inch artillery piece, sited on a hill, which could rain 250-pound shells on her at will. The shells might not have enough punch to penetrate the *Iowa*'s thick flanks or her turrets, but they could make a shambles of her superstructure, kill the men on her bridge, and devastate the box launchers housing her missiles, each of which contained hundreds of pounds of high explosives. To silence the eight-inch gun, Turret Three was supposed to fire volleys of 1,900-pound high-explosive shells.

After carefully studying the Sixth Fleet battle plan, Meyer and Mortensen stared at each other in disbelief. "It won't work," Meyer said. Mortensen nodded in agreement. Meyer decided to speak with the Sixth Fleet planners to see if this scheme could be aborted, or at the very least drastically modified, before the *Iowa*, her crew, U.S. diplomats, and many, many Lebanese civilians got hurt. When Meyer arrived in flag plot, Chief Skelley was bragging about the ingenious ordnance he had designed and his impressive fire-control abilities. Meyer hushed Skelley and then explained to the staff officers that their battle plan was unrealistic. Every time you changed a shell type, from antisubmarine to armor-piercing to antipersonnel, you added an extra minute to the process of loading the guns. That ensured that Turret One could never comply with the firing timetable.

Meyer said he doubted that Skelley's antisubmarine rounds would be effective. Nor did he believe that the armor-piercing shells had much chance of hitting the stone outcrop. But if, by some miracle, they did hit the right place, it was unlikely that the three shells would cause a landslide and seal the tunnel. If the antipersonnel shells were used, hundreds of civilians would die. Meyer added that Turret Three wasn't capable of trading shots with an eight-inch artillery piece. The turret's equipment hardly ever worked, and its gunners were seldom able to get a shell to hit one of Skelley's illusionary "holes in the ocean." If the rear turret failed to deliver accurate and timely counter-battery fire and defend the ship, the *Iowa* would be subjected to appalling casualties. After Meyer completed his glum assessment, the Sixth Fleet officers informed him that they had no intention of canceling or even modifying the plan.

But the plan was never put into effect. On September 6, three helicopters swooped down on the U.S. embassy in the early morning hours and evacuated a dozen American diplomats still occupying the facility. The embassy would reopen two months later, after the situation with General Aoun's Maronite Christian forces cooled a bit. The *Iowa* departed for Gaeta, Italy, near Naples, for two weeks of rest and relaxation. For the remainder of the cruise, the ship would not be called upon to take part in another crisis.

ON JULY 15, two weeks before the *Iowa* sailed to Lebanon, Admiral Milligan signed his report and sent it up the chain of command. The report had been hastily composed by Commander Swanson, Milligan's counsel, and two other Navy attorneys in late May and had been scarcely modified since then. Swanson, who admitted that he was anxious to move on to his new job as legal counsel to the Vice Chief of Naval Operations, allowed a monumental error to occur. The order appointing Milligan to head the *Iowa* investigation specifically forbade him to blame the explosion on the "misconduct" of any "deceased members" of Turret Two. Nevertheless, Swanson allowed Milligan to submit his report charging Clayton Hartwig with mass murder, something the admiral legally could not do.

And something else was amiss with Milligan's report. At the time he signed the sixty-six-page document, the admiral did not have a scintilla of scientific proof that any kind of detonator had been present in the gun barrel. Captain Miceli was still conducting tests, but so far he had produced nothing. Miceli's tests could not be completed until the middle of October, well after the Navy had released Milligan's report to the public on September 7.

Before Milligan's report could be publicly released, the following protocol had to be followed: (1) Vice Admiral Joseph Donnell, the "convening authority," or the senior officer who put Milligan in charge of the investigation, had to review the report and agree or disagree with it; (2) Donnell's immediate superior, Admiral Powell Carter, the Atlantic Fleet commander, had to approve or reject Milligan's findings and Donnell's input; (3), Admiral Carlisle Trost, Chief of Naval Operations, had to weigh everything forwarded to him from Milligan, Donnell, and Carter and decide whether it would be released, required additional investigation, or was so flawed that it should be scrapped. This process, with attorneys supposedly reviewing every step of the way, was designed to safeguard the rights of those accused of wrongdoing and also to guarantee that valid conclusions were put forward.

Before flying from Norfolk to join his battle group at sea in Mid-July, Milligan delivered a stack of copies of his report and other documents to Admiral Donnell. On July 28, just two weeks after receiving the material from Milligan, Donnell endorsed his subordinate's report, saying that the determination that Clayton Hartwig had sabotaged the gun "leaves the reader incredulous, yet the opinion is supported by facts and analysis from which it flows logically and inevitably."

AFTER ENDORSING Milligan's report, Donnell had it delivered down the street to Admiral Powell Carter. Carter was a member of "Rickover's Navy," a carefully screened, highly disciplined, technically oriented cadre of nuclear-submarine officers who had received their training under the late Admiral Hyman G. Rickover, the "father" of the Navy's nuclear-propulsion program. As such, Carter viewed the *Iowa* and her three sisterships as hopelessly obsolete. But even though he was predisposed against battleships, Carter personally examined every scrap of paper relating to the explosion on the *Iowa.* The admiral devoted two weeks to this undertaking, to the exclusion of almost all of his other duties, before signing a five-page letter of endorsement on August 11. However, for all his attention to detail, Carter fell into the same trap that Admirals Milligan and Donnell had. He was well aware that technical tests were still ongoing, yet he didn't halt the review process, as he had a legal right to do. When he later learned that some of the test results were at variance with the conclusions he had endorsed, he did nothing about issuing a correction.

HOWEVER, ADMIRAL Carter's endorsement pointed out that there were "substantial and serious failures" by Captain Fred Moosally and his senior officers that merited disciplinary action. Carter found unconvincing Moosally's alibi that he was unaware of serious deficiencies with all three sixteen-inch turrets. In the fleet commander's opinion, the battleship's executive officer, Commander Morse, was equally blameworthy. Carter faulted the Yorktown Naval Weapons Station for improperly storing the *Iowa*'s powder in 1988, and he recommended that those responsible should be punished.

Carter wrote that the very idea that Clayton Hartwig had committed suicide and killed forty-six men he knew was "repugnant almost to the point of disbelief." However, he believed that the evidence gathered by Admiral Milligan was sufficient to overcome his doubts. He mentioned the FBI's equivocal death analysis as something that satisfied him that Hartwig was a killer. After signing his endorsement, Carter had the report hand-carried to the Pentagon to Admiral Carl Trost, so the Chief of Naval Operations could make a final decision on how to handle the painful document.

ADMIRAL TROST was another Rickover disciple. Although Rickover's officers were widely regarded as prodigies when they were recruited (normally from the ranks of the U.S. Naval Academy), their course of instruction, outlook, and management style were rigidly circumscribed by the aged admiral. Some senior officers had voiced the opinion that the domination of the service by these secretive technocrats was causing the Navy to lose its "sea dogs" (innovative surface-warfare skippers). These senior officers grumbled that Carl Trost had served so little time aboard a surface combatant that he had no concept of how a warship like the *Iowa* performed.

The task of evaluating the legal soundness of Admiral Milligan's report for Admiral Trost was handled primarily by none other than Commander Ron Swanson, who was by then Admiral Edney's counsel. According to Rear Admiral Ted Gordon, Swanson's new post meant an objective legal review of the *Iowa* investigation by Admiral Trost was impossible. "Any time there was a question raised, the report was reviewed by the man who wrote it and who gathered the material, namely Ron Swanson," Gordon said. Swanson later denied that he had reviewed the Milligan report for Admirals Trost and Edney. But Edney testified later in a civil lawsuit that Swanson had done so. Gordon said that Edney was telling the truth. The *Iowa* report remained in the CNO's offices for twenty days before Trost signed a six-page letter of endorsement on August 31.

The CNO stated that NIS had conducted "an exhaustive investigation into the backgrounds and recent behavior of not only center gun room personnel but of all relevant USS *Iowa* crew members," when the only people NIS had backgrounded had been Clayton Hartwig, Kendall Truitt, John Mullahy, and David Smith. Trost misconstrued the FBI Crime Laboratory's findings, failing to disclose that the FBI had determined that the "foreign elements" found under the rotating band came from a cleaning solution commonly used in the barrels. Like Admirals Milligan, Donnell, and Carter before him, Trost was convinced that Clayton Hartwig had blown up the center gun, concluding that Hartwig was "the individual who had motive, knowledge, and physical position [access] within the turret gun room to place a device in the powder train."

ON AUGUST 28, three days before the CNO signed the final endorsement, Captain Joseph Miceli received startling news from the Naval Weapons Support Center in Crane, Indiana. According to Crane, the FBI Crime Laboratory was correct, and the Norfolk Naval Shipyard was dead wrong. Additional testing revealed that an electronic timer, batteries, and a primer were not involved in the deadly explosion. The Norfolk Naval Shipyard's technical analyses, upon which the admirals based their judgments, were irrelevant. Captain Miceli had to throw out the results of twenty-five of the twenty-seven Dahlgren test firings, because they involved electronic timers. All that remained were two chemical firings. And those weren't germane either, because they had not replicated the shell movement that occurred in the center gun. The Crane report totally undermined Milligan's case against Clayton Hartwig.

19

☆

"You'll Never Convince Me My Son Did That!"

IN A FOUR-PAGE memo to Admiral Milligan, with copies to Admiral Edney and Vice Admiral Peter Hekman, head of Sea Systems Command, Captain Joseph Miceli broke the news that there was no chance that an electronic timer had anything to do with the *Iowa* explosion. Miceli admitted that his August 11 summary of his technical investigation was no longer valid. The technicians at Crane were now pulling out the stops to see if a chemical igniter might have been involved in the disaster. This was highly unlikely, given the fact that the ordnance experts at Indian Head had already determined that this type of igniter was impractical. "I do not expect my final report will be able to identify a specific device as the initiating mechanism," Miceli wrote.

At that point, alarm bells should have been ringing all through the Navy. The *Iowa* report and its two endorsements should have been returned to Admirals Milligan, Donnell, and Carter for another look. Admiral Trost's letter of endorsement, still not completed, should have indicated that the Dahlgren tests were no longer valid. None of this was done. Instead, the Navy went forward with its defective report, determined to unveil it at a press conference the week after Labor Day.

But before that happened, Admiral Edney sent Captain Douglas Katz to the Mediterranean to give Fred Moosally a preview of its contents and to reassure the captain that his career was not in jeopardy. Katz later said that Moosally wasn't in a bad frame of mind when he arrived on the ship. "I tried to put myself in the same position," said Katz. He told Moosally that Admiral Milligan had recommended that Moosally be relieved of command. Not to worry, Katz said, Admiral Donnell had overruled Milligan. Donnell wrote that Moosally's "poor adherence to explosive safety regulations and ordnance safety" and "his failure of leadership" were a "marked departure from an otherwise outstanding performance" and concluded that captain's relief was "unwarranted." Donnell also found that disciplinary action that Milligan proposed against Moosally's executive officer, Commander Morse, was not warranted. Admiral Carter concurred with Donnell's findings, as did Admiral Trost.

Moosally would receive a letter of admonition and perhaps a paltry fine at an admiral's mast to be conducted on the *Iowa* by Admiral Donnell after the report was released. Moosally was off the hook. He still had a chance at promotion. Katz said harsher punishments would be meted out to Commander Kissinger, the weapons officer; Commander Finney, the operations officer; and Chief Skelley. Milligan had wanted to relieve Lieutenant Commander Costigan, the gunnery officer, but since Costigan had been transferred to shore duty shortly after the explosion, this was no longer an issue. Milligan also recommended that disciplinary action be taken against Lieutenant Dan Meyer, Turret One's officer, and Lieutenant Kevin Hunt, Turret Three's officer.

THREE DAYS before the *Iowa* report was released, ABC News producers Mark Brender and Stephanie Zaharoudis and correspondent Robert Zelnick were able to track down and convince Seaman David Smith to tell them how he had concocted most of the testimony he had given to NIS. Brender left a message for Smith at his mother's home in suburban Maryland, outside Washington. Smith phoned Brender at ABC's office in the Pentagon, but he became frightened and refused to answer any questions. Zelnick and producer Zaharoudis staked out Smith's mother's home for several days. They also obtained a photograph of Smith from his high-school yearbook. Smith's mother finally came out and told Zelnick and Zaharoudis that her son would talk with them. They had hoped that the seaman would do an on-camera interview, but he refused, agreeing instead to a telephone conference call with Zaharoudis in the ABC bureau in downtown Washington and Brender and Zelnick in the Pentagon. Smith told the ABC News team that NIS agents had ground him down in sessions lasting up to seven hours and threatened to charge him with forty-seven counts of murder and accessory to murder if he did not cooperate. He said the agents put words into his mouth and distorted his testimony.

The Smith interview was a major coup for ABC News. A number of reporters, including Zelnick, had been quoting unnamed sources for three months, saying that Smith had recanted his testimony, but this was the first time that Smith had personally confirmed that fact. Once the ABC piece quoting David Smith was broadcast, Zelnick, also an attorney, strode purposefully into the office of Rear Admiral Jimmy Finkelstein, who was preparing to retire as Chief of Naval Information. Zelnick told Finkelstein, "I made a promise to myself even before I became a journalist, while I was studying law, that in my life if the opportunity ever presented itself to confront evil, I would do it. I regard the Navy's handling of the case against Clayton Hartwig as evil. You are proceeding with a case that is extremely flimsy against an individual who is not in a position to defend himself. You are marshaling a public relations effort that we can document as false . . . in every particular."

Zelnick, who had recruited a number of noted mental-health professionals to scrutinize the FBI's equivocal death analysis of Hartwig, was highly agitated by Admiral Trost's handling of the Milligan report. "By the time Trost signed off on the report, he knew that Miceli's original conclusions about an electronic timer had been proven false by the FBI and by the Navy's own laboratory in Crane, Indiana," Zelnick said. The ABC correspondent said the CNO also was aware that at the time of his death, Hartwig was being screened for a physical security position in London, and that there was no evidence that Hartwig had been assigned as Turret Two's center gun captain on the day of the explosion. But what really riled Zelnick the most was Trost's handling of David Smith's testimony. Trost knew that Smith had recanted, Zelnick said, but that didn't stop Trost from using hunks from Smith's false testimony to prop up the Navy's weak case against Hartwig. If Zelnick were correct, the CNO had either overlooked or not read crucial exculpatory evidence about Hartwig.

IN ADDITION to planning and rehearsing the Pentagon press conference where Admiral Milligan's report would be made public, the Navy had a logistical nightmare to handle. Not only did it have to sell the press and the public on the idea that Clayton Hartwig was guilty, it had a much tougher audience to convince—the wives, mothers, fathers, brothers and sisters of the other forty-six men who had died on the *Iowa* on April 19. The Navy planned to send hand-picked teams of officers, carrying copies of the Milligan report, to meet with those relatives several hours before the report was released in Washington. That was no simple task, since the *Iowa* relatives were spread all over the country. Some parents were divorced, with the mother residing in one state and the father in another. Some of the deceased men had been married, requiring the Navy to contact both the spouse and the parents, in many instances in different locations. Several of the family situations were complicated. One sailor's wife lived in Florida. His divorced mother was in Pennsylvania. His father was in prison in one state and his brother was in prison somewhere else. When all these variables were factored in, the Navy estimated that it would require sixty-seven teams to do the job.

The effort to distribute the reports to the *Iowa* families was directed by forty-nine-year-old Vice Admiral Mike Boorda, Chief of Naval Personnel. Given his background, it was amazing that Boorda had risen to vice admiral. He didn't have a Naval Academy ring and he was a "mustang," a former enlisted man. But the Navy was changing, and as Chief of Naval Personnel,

Boorda often dealt with cutting-edge issues, such as assigning women to sea duty and overhauling the Navy's draconian methods of dealing with homosexuals. Gossip in the Navy corridors of the Pentagon hinted that Boorda was a dark-horse candidate in the not-too-distant future to become CNO.

Captain Stephan Loeffler, who worked for Admiral Boorda and helped organize the distribution of the Milligan report to the *Iowa* families, said a group of officers began assembling at the Navy Annex near the Pentagon two weeks before September 7, the date selected for the release of the report. Boorda told the officers that they were not allowed to read the report. Loeffer said Boorda told them, "You are representatives of the Navy. You are not to be partisans or advocates, nor are you supposed to convince anybody of anything. If the families have any questions, you are not to answer them. Write down the questions and tell the families you will get the answers for them in Washington." Officers who worked with Boorda said he told them that strict neutrality was the only sensible course.

Neutrality wasn't going to be all that easy, because in addition to delivering the reports, Admiral Edney wanted Boorda's teams to show a propagandistic videotape to the relatives of the dead men. The tape had been spliced together by the Chief of Naval Information's office from scenes shot at Dahlgren and aboard the battleship *Wisconsin*. It also contained snippets of the amateur video taken by a Second Fleet staff officer on April 19. The tape contained "staged" scenes intended to lead viewers to believe that a simulated event was in fact a real event. The tape inaccurately stated that the Dahlgren testers had been able to duplicate the actual event in the center gun. The footage of the *Wisconsin* gun room was taken while the ship was moored in Norfolk. The powder charges seen on the tape were dummies. One sequence was particularly glaring. A *Wisconsin* gun captain is shown inserting a lead foil between two powder bags, and viewers were led to believe that this was the method Clayton Hartwig used to slip a detonator into the powder chamber. The FBI and Crane laboratories had already debunked this theory.

Not many of the officers who worked for Boorda were excited about showing the tape. Captain Loeffler said that Admiral Boorda gave the officers permission to view it. He didn't want them to be caught unaware, sitting on a sofa in a grieving parent's den, watching the tape for the first time and having their mouths fall open in shock. All of the relatives had to be contacted to see whether they owned a television set and whether their videotape player was VHS or Beta format. Some people didn't have a television set or a VCR, and Boorda's teams had to carry that equipment with them. The day before Boorda's representatives left Washington to deliver the reports and tapes, the admiral addressed them, emphasizing that timing was crucial. He wanted the families to obtain their information from the Navy first, not the news media. Boorda knew that Admiral Edney was sending Captain Douglas Katz to Cleveland to handle the Hartwig family.

Unlike the other emissaries, Katz was not supposed to be neutral. His assignment was to persuade Earl and Evelyn Hartwig that their son was a mass murderer.

REAR ADMIRAL Ted Gordon, who had headed the Naval Investigative Service when the *Iowa* inquiry first began, was aware that the Milligan report was legally defective. Therefore, Gordon was startled to learn on September 6 that the Navy had scheduled a press conference for the next day to release the report. Then functioning as acting Judge Advocate General, he decided he should try to get the event canceled. He had previously warned the Navy's top leadership that Milligan had conducted an "illegal" investigation. Milligan had not informed witnesses of their rights, had failed to keep accurate transcripts, and had not provided legal counsel to witnesses. The Navy's legal Bible, the Judge Advocate General's manual, mandated that a criminal investigation, such as this one, had to fully protect the civil rights of all witnesses and potential defendants.

All of Gordon's attempts to have the press conference canceled ended in failure. He first went to the office of the Vice Chief of Naval Operations. When he walked into the outer reception area, he ran into Admiral Edney's executive assistant, Captain Harold Gehman. Gordon told Gehman that although he was familiar with the legal framework of Milligan's report, he hadn't been given an opportunity to read and comment on the entire document. "This is crazy! Three people, myself as acting Judge Advocate General, Bud Flanagan, who is in charge of the Office of Legislative Affairs, and Brent Baker, who is Chief of Naval Information, have got to defend this thing after it is released," Gordon said. "And none of us even knows what is in the goddamned report!" Gehman simply said, "We'll see what we can do."

Gordon was bothered by his encounter with Captain Gehman, so he called the CNO's office and talked with one of Admiral Trost's assistants. Gordon didn't expect to get any help from the CNO, but he felt he had to try. "Carl Trost was an absentee landlord with very little interest in the day-to-day management of the U.S. Navy," he said. Gordon repeated the same "song and dance" that he had given Gehman. The CNO's staffer listened and said he would see what he could do. Several minutes later, Admiral Milligan phoned Gordon and said, "I've been told to call you. I don't know why."

"Milligan wanted to brief me on the phone. It was insane. I said, 'To hell with it!'" Gordon recalled. He told Milligan he was going to boycott the press conference. "There was an empty chair at their press conference. It said 'Admiral Gordon' on the back of it, but I wasn't there. Brent Baker was there, but he had no choice in the matter since it was a press conference," Gordon said. "I sure wasn't going to stick my neck out for something I hadn't even read. And sure enough, just as soon as that press conference ended all hell broke loose. The media and Congress went right after the Navy's ass, as they should."

LATE ON Wednesday afternoon before the Thursday press conference, Rear Admiral Brent Baker, along with Admirals Edney and Milligan and Pete Williams, the public-relations assistant for Secretary of Defense Dick Cheney, drove to an audiovisual production facility the Navy operated in a seedy Washington neighborhood. They planned to conduct a "murder board." Before the Navy exposed its senior officers to a press conference, it prepared them for it at a "murder board." Junior officers, posing as journalists, shouted rude, obnoxious questions at the admirals. The idea was to "murder" the flag officers, forcing them to make mistakes that could be critiqued and corrected before the actual event. Williams's role at the "murder board" and the press conference would be to introduce the admirals and provide a brief background statement. Nobody attending the "murder board" was particularly surprised to hear that Admiral Trost would not attend. Admirals Edney and Milligan, armed with elaborate charts and graphs and the propaganda tape, would attempt to convince the Pentagon press corps that the Navy had conducted a comprehensive, unbiased investigation.

After observing the "murder board," it was obvious to Baker that Edney knew nothing about gunnery, and Milligan was still obviously not comfortable in his role as a spokesperson. But at least there was one thing for which to be grateful. Captain Joseph Miceli wouldn't participate in the press conference. The ordnance officer had asked Baker to sit up front with the admirals in case there were any technical questions that Edney and Milligan couldn't handle, but Baker nixed that idea in a flash. Baker said he considered Miceli to be "like a loose cannon on the gun deck, rolling around, smashing things to bits."

After the "murder board" ended and the participants were leaving the production facility, Pete Williams said to Baker, "Are you sure you want to go through with this thing?" Baker asked Williams what he meant. "Well, you're going to have a lot of people who are not going to believe you. A lot of people will be shouting at you. You have nothing firm here, nothing conclusive," Williams said. The decision to hold the press conference was not his, Baker said.

THE NEXT morning, a nondescript government car pulled up at 9:30 in front of the white frame home of Earl and Evelyn Hartwig in Cleveland. A drawn-faced Captain Douglas Katz—wearing a short-sleeved, open-collared white uniform with six rows of ribbons and a gold Surface Warfare badge above his left breast—got out of the vehicle and dashed through an unruly throng of video cameramen and still photographers. Two Navy officers, also wearing white uniforms, struggled to keep up with the quick-stepping Katz, who carried a portmanteau containing a copy of Admiral Milligan's report, a stack of heavily excised NIS documents, and the videotape. One of the officers was Renee Lewis, a lieutenant who, back in April, had officially notified the Hartwigs that their son was dead. She was stationed in Cleveland, and the family had developed a close rapport with her. They valued her opinion and thought that she was honest, even when it hurt her career. She would later resign from the Navy, in part because of the Navy's treatment of the Hartwigs. The other officer was Commander Sam Falcona, a public-relations specialist from Washington.

Earl and Evelyn Hartwig greeted the officers at the front door and then took them through the kitchen to the living room, where Katz and Falcona were introduced to Kathy Kubicina and their attorney, Kreig Brusnahan. Lieutenant Lewis was already well acquainted with the family members and was on speaking terms with Brusnahan. Space was at a premium in the living room. Earl, Evelyn, and Brusnahan sat on a couch. Katz and Falcona were directed to rocking chairs, and Renee Lewis sat on a stool. Kathy Kubicina settled on the floor near Katz's feet. An audiotape recorder with a microphone on a plastic stand was conspicuously positioned on a coffee table between the Hartwigs and the Navy officers. Brusnahan asked Katz if it would be all right to record their conversation, and Katz consented. Brusnahan walked over to the recorder, pushed down the red "record" button, and returned to the couch.

Katz launched into a hard sales pitch to convince the Hartwigs that Clayton was a murderer. He said that the *Iowa* projectile had been driven thirty-six inches into the rifling, then he changed that to thirty-nine inches. Finally, he confessed, "I don't know exactly—about 36, 39, I've forgotten, but, you know, it was just over 36, whatever it was." Earl, Kathy, and their attorney knew that the correct distance was forty-four inches. Katz said that the ship's gunpowder had been improperly stored on barges the summer before the explosion, but he contended that it was still stable. If that were so, Evelyn Hartwig asked, then why had all of the powder been removed from the ship after the explosion? Katz claimed that even if the powder were "160 percent safe," the Navy "would still throw it overboard, because that's the safest way." Evelyn wanted to know why the Navy hadn't tested the powder that Turret Two was supposed to fire on April 19 before it blew everybody to bits. Katz danced around that question for several minutes before admitting that the Navy wasn't aware there was a problem with the powder until the accident occurred.

Of the forty-seven *Iowa* families, only the Hartwigs received copies of NIS interviews that had the names deleted and whole pages blacked out by NIS censors. Katz pulled several handfuls of this material from his bag and laid the documents on the floor within Kathy's reach. She surreptitiously scooped up some of these records and began reading them, so that she could prepare some tough questions for Katz. While Kathy was doing her research on the floor, Evelyn continued to grill Katz. Could a single lot of powder be bad? That was impossible, Katz said. However, Evelyn and Kathy had learned from talking to several naval ordnance experts that it was possible. Katz wasn't sure what kind of powder Turret Two had been using the day of the explosion. But he thought he remembered that Turret One was using "842." If he had referred to page 23 of the Milligan report, which he had in his lap, he would have known that Turret One was firing D-845 reduced charges, and Turret Two was firing D-846 full charges. Kathy knew it from talking to John Mullahy and other gunner's mates who had been on the *Iowa* on April 19. "I am not positive because I can't—I forgot what the firing plans said," Katz faltered. Katz should have known that the *Iowa* had no firing plan showing what types of powder and shells were being used on the day of the explosion. He glanced down and saw Kathy immersed in the NIS documents. His face clouded, and he raised his right foot and stomped it down hard on the mound of papers Kathy was studying. She glared at him. "I was mad as hell at the arrogant bastard, but I had the good sense not to say anything," she said later.

Evelyn asked Katz about the multiple misfires experienced by Turret One's left gun crew. Katz said that a misfire "doesn't play one way or the other." He failed to tell Evelyn that peacetime safety regulations require a captain to clear a fouled bore in one turret before commencing fire in another turret. Kreig Brusnahan asked Katz how the Navy knew that Clayton Hartwig had been standing in the gun captain's position when the blast struck him. The videotape would make that crystal clear, Katz vowed.

Without mentioning David Smith's name, Katz said NIS obtained testimony in late May establishing that Hartwig had an electronic timer in his locker on the battleship. Katz never mentioned that Smith had recanted this testimony or that he told ABC News that NIS agents had pressured him into making false statements. Katz attempted to qualify his upcoming remarks by saying, "I am no psychologist." But then he proceeded to diagnose Clayton as "a loner" and "somewhat introverted," with only three friends in the world. He said that Clayton had written many letters but hadn't been able to demonstrate his anger verbally. He kept it in, had low self-esteem, lacked aggression, and had "professional illusions." Katz referred to the picture of Clayton dressed "in a commander's uniform" to illustrate his point.

As further evidence of Clayton's delusions of grandeur, Katz said that he had made up going to London on a Navy security assignment. This statement would become very significant before the day was over. Katz claimed that Clayton had made "suicide gestures" in the past, and that the FBI's equivocal death analysis had concluded that he killed himself. Evelyn asked for a complete copy of her son's FBI profile, but Katz refused, saying that the Navy would only give her its barebones conclusions. She could ask the FBI for the report, but he was not optimistic.

Despite all the information to the contrary, Katz still maintained that the Navy had proof that a detonator had caused the blast on the *Iowa*. However, he conceded that the Navy might never know what kind of detonator was used. "We have determined it was an intentional act which was probably caused by your son," he said.

Evelyn Hartwig was on the verge of collapsing. Still, she defiantly thrust out her chin, stared Katz down, and said, "You'll never convince me my son did that! Why would he kill 47 sailors? Never! Well, does the Navy ever make mistakes or have accidents?" "Surely," Katz replied. "What about all those other accidents that have happened to battleships?" she inquired, referring to the 1924 and 1943 explosions aboard the battleship USS *Mississippi*. "None of those other accidents—we've never had an accident like this ever. Not anywhere near the same," Katz said. He was only partially accurate. None of the factors responsible for the numerous big-gun disasters that had afflicted the major navies of the world for a century were ever exactly the same, even aboard the *Mississippi*, where the same turret blew up twice. Evelyn Hartwig didn't back down. "Well, he didn't do it, and you'll never convince me he did. I am sorry," she wailed.

Katz said he also had a son in the Navy and told Evelyn that he knew what she was going through. Unable to keep her emotions in control any longer, she began weeping. "He [Clayton] loved the Navy. He was so proud of that ship. Why would he want to blow it up?" she cried. Katz asked if it would be all right to show the videotape. Brusnahan told him to go ahead, so Katz got up, slid the cassette into the VHS machine, and punched the "play" button. Earl was spellbound by the images on the television screen. And from time to time he yelled, "That's not right! . . . They made that up! . . . That's pure, unadulterated bullshit!"

When the tape ended, Kathy dragged her mother up off the couch and guided her to the kitchen, out of Katz's earshot. Evelyn's face was puffy; her hands were tightly folded to reduce the shaking; and her breathing was labored. Kathy feared that her mother might suffer a stroke or a heart attack. Nearly blinded by tears, she moaned, "Kathy, maybe he did do this? Maybe they're right?" "Don't you ever say that again! Don't you ever think that again! You might be my mother, but if you ever do, I'll slap you silly, so help me God!" Kathy hissed. "We both know what kind of boy Clay was, and he couldn't do such a thing! The Navy is just trying to frame him to cover up their own mistakes! Get yourself under control, and let's go back in there!" Evelyn straightened her back, wiped her eyes, and determinedly followed her daughter back to the living room to spar some more with Captain Katz.

WHEN EVELYN and Kathy reentered the living room, Katz was telling Earl and Brusnahan about his recent trip to the Mediterranean to talk to Fred Moosally about the Milligan report. "He [Moosally] is a superb man.

A superb man," Katz said. Even so, he continued, Moosally was answerable for the conditions on the ship that led up to the explosion. There would be an admiral's mast to discipline the captain, his senior officers, and Chief Skelley. Evelyn didn't think Moosally was "a superb man," and she didn't want to talk about him. She had more she wanted to say about her dead son. "Well, he [Clayton] led us to believe that he was proud of that ship," she said. Katz told the Hartwigs that coming to Cleveland to give them this terrible news was "probably the toughest thing I've ever had to do in my life."

Katz said that the family would be receiving a letter from the Chief of Naval Operations. When Admiral Trost's one-page letter arrived several days later, it spent an inordinate amount of space denying that the leadership of the Navy had anything to do with leaking derogatory information about Clayton. "I regret that some individuals did provide unauthorized and anonymous information prematurely to the press, but in our era of investigative journalism, I have no way to preclude that," Trost said.

As Katz concluded his presentation, Brusnahan asked him whom the Hartwigs should contact if they had any questions about the report, the videotape, or anything else connected with the investigation. Katz was taken aback for a minute, then stammered, "I think probably—I think—I think probably. Well, what I don't have for you is the exact point of contact for those kinds of things." Then he walked over to Evelyn, hugged her, kissed her on the cheek, and headed through the kitchen and out of the house with Lieutenant Lewis and Commander Falcona. Outside, he snaked his way through the obstacle course thrown up by the journalists in the front yard and was able to reach his car without uttering a word.

After the three naval officers sped away, Kathy, Earl, and Brusnahan emerged from the house and held a press conference. "We believe that when the truth comes out, it will be told that he did not do it," Earl said. "But for right now, the damage has been done. So we just have to live with that." Kathy said her family was especially galled by the Navy's assertion that her brother was despondent, emotionally unstable, and predisposed to suicide. "We talked to him seven days before he was killed. He was fine, absolutely not depressed," she said. Brusnahan said the family would seek a congressional inquiry into the Navy's leaking of false and unsubstantiated information, including the allegation that Clayton Hartwig and Kendall Truitt had a homosexual affair. Brusnahan said they would probably sue the Navy for the "intentional and negligent infliction of emotional distress" under the Federal Tort Claims Act.

The suit would be filed in 1991, on the second anniversary of the *Iowa* explosion, and as it wound its way tediously through the federal court system, it would subject the Navy to the kind of scrutiny that the service had evaded in every other venue, including Congress.

WITH FEW exceptions, the Navy's messengers were met by stunned disbelief or outright hostility when they delivered the Milligan report and showed the videotape to the families of the forty-six other men killed in Turret Two. Bob Gedeon of Cleveland subjected a Navy commander to four hours of exhaustive cross-examination, but he received no worthwhile information. "An officer came from Washington with a video that looked like a seventh-grade science film and a letter from Milligan about 'most probable cause.' I said right away that Hartwig didn't do it—the investigation was done wrong from the beginning," said Gedeon, whose son, Seaman Robert Gedeon III, died in the left gun room. "There is nothing in this report that shows me how Hartwig did it. I think he's a scapegoat," Gedeon told the commander.

Another Cleveland father, Reginald Johnson, who had retired from the Air Force in 1987, was just as put off by the report as Bob Gedeon. His son, Reginald Lee Johnson Jr., had been the primerman on the center gun and had never before participated in a firing exercise. "I just lost a lot of respect for my government," Johnson said. "The Navy men kept talking about Hartwig. They could very well be talking about my son. . . . The whole thing was tainted. How can you say somebody did something without proof? My heart goes out to the Hartwigs. I don't know how they found the fortitude to stand up to the Navy," he said. "If you understand the military and how it does things, you knew it was a cover-up."

In Akron, about forty miles south of Cleveland Susan Backherms, widow of Gunner's Mate Third Class Robert Backherms, was suspicious of the Milligan report even before she read it. When a naval officer called to say he would be coming to her home bringing the Milligan report and a videotape, Mrs. Backherms told him to leave the tape in Washington. She had no desire to see it. But the commander claimed that watching the tape would help her. After the officer arrived and had played the tape, she exclaimed, "I don't believe a word of it. I think you're just showing me what you wanted me to see!" She said the tape was a way for the Navy "to split and divide the families," and she vowed, "I'm not going to rest until I find out what really happened."

Down south, in the gently rolling foothills of eastern Tennessee in Greeneville, the parents and widow of Gunner's Mate Third Class Jack Thompson also found the Navy's explanation of the accident unacceptable. When the videotape ended, Jack's widow, Leasa, screamed, "This is bullshit! I don't believe any of this!" She got up from her seat and stormed out of her in-laws' home slamming the front door.

Sharon Ziegler, widow of Chief Reggie Ziegler, was sitting in her wheelchair in Rushville, New York, near Syracuse, when a white-clad officer arrived bearing the Milligan report and the videotape. Paralyzed from the waist down and wheelchair-bound for five years, she was withering away with cancer. Sharon had made a number of attempts to get Chief Skelley, who had been her husband's best friend on the *Iowa*, to tell her what happened, but he wouldn't respond. "Skelley knows more than he's telling," she told other *Iowa* families.

As the video ended, Sharon looked directly at the officer and said, "That tape was a joke! My father was in the Army. I know all about gunpowder being old. That's what happened, not some sad, confused boy blowing up his friends." She said the officer refused to talk substance with her. "He was very evasive and had been programmed on what to say to me," she said. When he left for Washington, Sharon phoned Kathy Kubicina and offered to help her.

When Sharon later requested a copy of Reggie's service record, the Bureau of Naval Personnel provided it on microfiche, which she could not read without special equipment. She wrote the Navy to ask for help, and they told her that for $2.50 they would send her a handheld microfiche reader. Such a cold-hearted response prompted her to say, "Reggie was definitely government property. I can't believe that a wife is so insignificant. I'm nothing in their eyes."

Out west in La Mesa, New Mexico, ten miles from the Mexican border, Emily Buch-Hague, the mother of Lieutenant Philip Buch, who was Turret Two's officer, totally supported the Milligan report. "It's worse knowing your child was killed by someone who deliberately caused this instead of it being an accident. It's very upsetting," said Mrs. Buch-Hague, a junior high school science teacher.

At Lake Wales, Florida, near Tampa, retired Chief Boatswain's Mate Robert L. Morrison was furious at the Navy he had so faithfully served for twenty years. He felt that his son, Legalman First Class Robert Kenneth Morrison, had no business being inside Turret Two on April 19. He was untrained in sixteen-inch gunnery procedures and damage control and had been shanghaied into the turret, ostensibly to reduce the manpower shortage there. He died in the rear of the right gun room, standing with nothing to do. The bald, leathery-faced Morrison watched the tape with a staff officer from Washington and then roared, "That was all pure bullshit!"

In Munnsville, New York, near Sharon Ziegler's home, Louis Fisk, who taught vocational education to emotionally disturbed children, shared Chief Morrison's view about the Navy losing its moral compass. Fisk's son, Boatswain's Mate Second Class Gary Fisk, had died while attempting to operate the faulty powder hoist in the center gun room. Louis Fisk and his wife, Barbara, who was Gary's stepmother, watched the videotape with a lieutenant commander. After it ended, Louis sprang from his seat, reacting exactly as Earl Hartwig, Chief Morrison, and Leasa Thompson had. "This is absolute bullshit!" he growled. "How did you get this job?" "I had hours and hours of indoctrination and training," the rattled officer replied. "That could have been my son you're blaming! The Navy just wants a scapegoat!" Louis fumed.

Even though they were gracious and never raised their voices, the couple that caused the Navy almost as much agony as the Hartwigs was Ambassador Alvin and Mai-Anh Adams, the adoptive parents of Fire Controlman Third Class Tung Thanh Adams. Captain Steve Loeffler, one of Admiral Boorda's chief deputies, was chosen to brief the Adamses. Loeffler was instructed by Boorda to use kid gloves in his dealings with this high-ranking official and his spouse. When Loeffler arrived at the Adamses' home in Alexandria, Virginia, outside Washington, he found the house overflowing with relatives.

Loeffler said the family asked "very, very specific questions" and wanted to know why their twenty-five-year-old son had been in the turret. Only one fire controlman was needed to fire guns, yet both Tung and Fire Controlman Richard Lewis had been in the turret at the time of the explosion. Loeffler had no explanation. He promised to get one, but he never did. Both Adamses were distressed by the tape and had to leave the room several times. "I could have torn the report to shreds if it made any difference, but they had closed minds," Ambassador Adams later said. Captain Loeffler returned to the Pentagon and informed Admirals Boorda and Edney that the Navy had a real problem with the Adams family. He was told to placate them. A series of seven or eight phone calls ensued between Loeffler and the family. Alvin and Mai-Anh remained unsatisfied with the answers they received. Finally, Loeffler arranged for the Adamses to meet with Rear Admiral Richard Milligan and Captain Douglas Katz.

The Adamses had first met Katz six years earlier, when he had commanded the destroyer USS *Deyo* and made a port call in Djibouti, where Adams was ambassador to the East African country. Katz and Adams had participated in a memorial service for fifty-six French paratroopers and the 241 U.S. Marines and sailors killed in terrorist bombings in Beirut, Lebanon, in the fall of 1983. But their prior experience with Katz didn't count for a thing when it came to obtaining additional information about the *Iowa* explosion. Even though Milligan had been in charge of the investigation, Katz did most of the talking, reassuring the family that the investigation had been "the most thorough" the Navy had ever done. If Hartwig had been so crazy, why didn't somebody notice and take some action? the ambassador asked. Neither Milligan nor Katz had a logical explanation for that. Why was Fred Moosally getting off so lightly? Mai-Anh inquired. Katz said that Moosally would be disciplined by Vice Admiral Donnell, but he didn't inform her that the captain's punishment would amount to little more than a slap on the wrist. Neither Alvin nor Mai-Anh thought the session was productive. They were discouraged, but they were nowhere near quitting.

20

"Hall Has Just Ripped the Navy a New Asshole!"

ADMIRAL BUD EDNEY and Rear Admiral Richard Milligan's press conference in a Pentagon briefing room was in many ways a replay of Captain Douglas Katz's performance in Earl and Evelyn Hartwig's living room, except that some of the most aggressive reporters assigned to the military beat were in the audience. Robert Zelnick and Mark Brender of ABC News, Jack Dorsey of the *Virginian-Pilot* and *Ledger-Star* in Norfolk, and John Hall, the gruff bureau chief of Media General News Service, intended to grill the two admirals clad in white "ice cream man suits." Pete Williams, the Pentagon's public-affairs director, announced that Admiral Edney would go first. Williams said that copies of the Milligan report and some censored NIS documents would be available after the briefing, as well as copies of a videotape that would be part of the presentation. He also introduced Rear Admiral William Schachte, who had succeeded Ted Gordon as NIS commander, and Rear Admiral Robert Ailes, the top deputy at Sea Systems Command.

There were stage props strewn around the area where Milligan and Edney would be speaking, including mock powder bags, ornate poster boards, an easel holding photographs of Turret Two's center gun room, television sets, and a videotape player. Commander Ron Swanson, now Edney's legal counsel, moved the props around, changed the posters on the easels, and operated the videotape machine. The press conference was broadcast live throughout the Pentagon on closed-circuit television. Edney insisted that the Navy had remained mute about the details of the investigation and hadn't leaked anything for the previous five months. Some reporters sniggered. Others cackled. Many stared at Fred Francis.

Milligan followed Edney, declaring that even though the center gun crew was "administratively" untrained, it was still "a capable gun crew." Such doublespeak was generously strewn through Milligan's discourse. He began his assault on Clayton Hartwig's character by hoisting the joke book, *Getting Even: The Complete Book of Dirty Tricks*, into the air. He brandished the book like a fundamentalist preacher seeking to banish Satan with the Bible. He claimed the book provided "explicit" instructions on how to construct detonators and bombs. Photographs and videotape of Milligan clutching the joke book would appear on the front pages of newspapers and on television broadcasts all over the country.

He then discussed the psychological profiles of Hartwig prepared by the FBI's Behavioral Science Unit and Lieutenant Commander Mountz, an NIS psychologist, diagnosing Hartwig as an introverted loner and loser who had no normal friendships. He said that according to the FBI's equivocal death analysis, Hartwig had killed himself in such a way as to make it appear an accident.

Milligan pointed to some of the pictures on easels and said the Navy's technical case against Hartwig rested on test firings at Dahlgren and analyses of those firings conducted at the Norfolk Naval Shipyard. One of the poster boards showed cutaways of several rotating bands. He said that "foreign material" found under the Dahlgren test bands corresponded with chemical elements on the *Iowa* band. Milligan implied that an electronic timer had caused the blast, even though he had been told otherwise. He claimed that Clayton Hartwig "was the most likely person" to have placed the detonating device in the powder chamber. At that point, Milligan turned the lectern over to Edney.

According to Edney, the Navy would have been much happier if Milligan had determined that the tragedy had been caused by a technical malfunction or an unintentional personnel error. He claimed the Navy's "exhaustive" investigation proved that the nearly half-century-old *Iowa*-class battleships were safe to operate and that the powder, much of which was older than the battleships, "is stable and ready to use." Following that fulsome endorsement of battleships, the questioning began in earnest. Milligan was asked if Clayton Hartwig had been emotionally unstable. He was stable, Milligan said, or he couldn't have performed his job as Turret Two's center gun captain. Was Hartwig gay? There was no proof of that. If Hartwig were stable, the reporter persisted, how could he have committed such a heinous crime? Milligan meandered for an extended period of time without dealing with the question. But the reporter was tenacious. Didn't the FBI's equivocal death analysis say that Hartwig was unstable? Milligan sidestepped some more before acknowledging that perhaps such terminology was in the FBI analysis. He couldn't remember all the details. "There's just reams of data," he groused.

Admiral Edney said that spotting anything awry with Hartwig would have been virtually impossible, because, "He was a clean-cut sailor. He was a bright sailor. He didn't smoke, he didn't drink, and he didn't carouse on liberty. He did his job."

Another reporter attempted to pin down Milligan on exactly what kind of detonator Hartwig had used. Had it been an electronic timer or was it pressure-activated? Milligan engaged in semantics, but the reporter persisted, asking, "Was it a timer or a pressure device?" "I can't—we have not been able to determine what it was," Milligan responded. "The issue is that there was something in that propellant charge foreign to the normal charge." Was there anything in Hartwig's locker on the *Iowa* that indicated he had the materials to construct a detonator? Milligan knew from NIS that nothing of this sort had been found, but he replied, "Well, there are a number of possible devices. I mean you are talking about thousands of different hardwares." Perceiving that Milligan was on the razor's edge of a lie, Edney stepped forward and said, "The answer to your question is no. There was nothing found."

An astute reporter asked Milligan if it weren't Navy policy to remove the lead foil from the bag before inserting it into the breech. Milligan admitted that this was so. Removal of the lead from the bag happened long before the gun shoot, outside the confines of the turret. Given those facts, the reporter observed, there was no way Hartwig could have secreted either an electronic timer or a pressure-activated device in a foil bag. Milligan looked as if he had been hit squarely between the eyes by a two-by-four. Did Milligan's choice of the phrase *principal friend* to characterize Clayton Hartwig and Kendall Truitt's relationship indicate that he thought the two sailors were homosexuals? "We have no hard evidence of homosexuality in this case," Milligan replied.

Edney stepped forward. He had been warned by his attorneys that Truitt would have a winnable libel case against the Navy if the service made any homosexual allegations against him. "There has never been any evidence of that [homosexuality]," Edney said. "I know it's been played in the press, but I would hope everybody in this audience recognizes, male or female, you can have close personal relationships with the same sex without coming to any definition on it."

Edney was asked how much pressure would have been required to detonate a device in the center gun. He wouldn't even hazard a guess. Why couldn't the Navy determine what kind of device had been used? Edney couldn't answer that, either. He mentioned that the Navy had asked the FBI Crime Laboratory for assistance, but he misrepresented what the FBI told the Navy. Did either admiral know why Hartwig had committed suicide? Neither ventured an opinion. Did Truitt have anything to do with the destruction of the turret? Edney said that Hartwig's $50,000 double-indemnity life-insurance policy, which had first drawn the attention of NIS to Truitt and Hartwig, was a red herring, having absolutely nothing to do with the explosion. Moreover, Truitt was in the magazines at the time of the explosion and could not have put a detonator or anything in the center gun.

Edney then contradicted an explanation Milligan had given earlier in the press conference for how Hartwig had initiated the blast. Edney was asked where Hartwig acquired the components for a detonator. He said the Navy bought a bunch of Radio Shack electronic timers, tested them, and determined that they were not involved in the sabotage of the gun. Edney's response demonstrated that he had read and understood Captain Joseph Miceli's Crane report. It also rocked many reporters. "What do you mean by that?" clamored one newsman. Milligan then stepped forward and said there were many different kinds of Radio Shack electronic timers, and quite possibly the Navy had tested the wrong kind. Milligan's answer meant that either he had not read the Crane report or he had read it and was being evasive.

Another reporter asked if the "foreign elements" found under the *Iowa*'s rotating band had resulted from efforts to extinguish the fire and the onerous task of removing the shell from the barrel. Milligan said the rotating band had not been contaminated, indicating that he either didn't read or didn't comprehend the FBI Crime Laboratory's report.

Was Hartwig being considered by the Bureau of Naval Personnel for an overseas security billet at the time of the explosion? Milligan said there was "every indication" that Hartwig was going to be "cleared" for such duty. That was an extraordinary admission. The Navy's public-relations officers had previously insisted that Hartwig was not being sent to London. He had "fantasized" those orders. Some reporters might not be able to understand the significance of glycols being present under the rotating band, but they had no difficulty figuring out that a twenty-four-year-old sailor receiving choice duty in London was not a likely candidate for depression.

Pete Williams tried to end the press conference, which was getting out of hand, but one reporter wasn't through yet. "What is the standard of proof to which your conclusions, judgments are addressed? Is it 'beyond a reasonable doubt' or 'preponderance of evidence'?" the reporter asked Edney. The admiral cautiously framed his response, saying that the Navy had conducted an "administrative" inquiry in which only the "preponderance of proof" was required. In effect, Edney stated that the Navy had accused Clayton Hartwig of mass murder with nothing more substantial than hearsay and scientifically suspect evidence.

SHORTLY AFTER the admirals' press conference ended, Kendall Truitt's attorney, Ellis Rubin, conducted another one in Miami. The colorful trial lawyer labeled the Navy's version of the explosion "nothing more than speculation." "Our information was that it was the Navy's negligence, untrained and unqualified crew members, and fifty-year-old technology, dangerous from day one," he said. Rubin again demanded that the Navy insert a formal letter of exoneration in Truitt's personnel records.

ONE OF the reporters put off by the admirals' tendency to distort the truth at the press conference was John Hall. Hall had been a newspaper and wire-service reporter for thirty years, twenty-seven of them in Washington, and he thought the conference was one of the most nefarious events he had ever covered. An old-fashioned, shoe-leather journalist, Hall later said that as Milligan and Edney made their pitch, he kept feeling compassion for "that poor dead sailor that they're frying up for this event without anything approaching a standard of proof, except for method of elimination." Hall said the Navy charged Hartwig with everything "except bed wetting." His coworker, Steve Goldberg, with whom he would share a number of bylines on the Navy's mishandling of the *Iowa* investigation, said he was disturbed by the admirals' use of "pop psychology" to condemn a dead man. Both reporters said that the Navy's "leakers" had been so effective that many reporters were absolutely convinced that Clayton Hartwig and Kendall Truitt were guilty of sodomy and mass murder before Milligan and Edney ever said anything.

Hall knew a lot about battleships. He had covered the congressional hearings in the early 1980s concerning the recommissioning of the four *Iowa*-class ships and had toured the *Iowa* in the Philadelphia Naval Shipyard before she was towed to Pascagoula, Mississippi, to be overhauled. He recalled thinking about how antiquated the *Iowa*'s fire-control computers were, as well as the powder and projectiles she would have to fire. He knew about the *New Jersey*'s gunnery problems in Lebanon in 1983 and 1984. He thought the controversy over whether Hartwig and Truitt were homosexual lovers benefited the Navy, because it deflected attention from the *Iowa*'s glaring safety infractions. Hall left the press conference and walked to Room 2C-332 in the Pentagon, where Pete Williams promised that copies of Milligan's report and censored NIS interviews would be available for twenty-four hours. He heaped documents into a cardboard box and estimated that it would take two more such loads for him to have everything.

Since he was riding the Metro subway's Blue Line back to his office in the National Press Building, there was no way he could manage three hefty boxes at one time. He would have to come back for the remainder the following day. As Hall was leaving the room carrying his box, he bumped into George Wilson, the *Washington Post*'s Pentagon correspondent. "Where's the gold, John?" Wilson asked, peering into Hall's carton. "It's in here someplace, if you care to read through it," Hall said. "I don't have time to read all that. Call me if you find the gold," Wilson quipped. Hall stalked off toward the Metro.

Back in the office, Hall made a decision not to write anything for a week. He wanted to get his hands on all 7,000 pages the Navy was making available, digest this material, and then write a long, analytical series. He called his editors in Richmond, informed them of his plan, and obtained their blessing. Hall's first story, published in the *Richmond Times-Dispatch* on

Sunday, September 17, and circulated throughout the country by the Associated Press, disclosed for the first time that the *Iowa* was conducting illegal powder experiments when the center gun blew up. Hall called the ill-fated battleship "a floating laboratory for high explosive experiments" and accused Sea Systems Command of having a conflict of interest for being involved in the illegal experiments and then managing the technical investigation. He discussed how Chief Skelley had drastically altered some sixteen-inch projectiles so that they would explode underwater, in the hope of sinking a submarine. Hall also disclosed that Skelley had violated safety regulations by using potent D-846 powder with 2,700-pound projectiles. "The combination of a zest for experimentation on the *Iowa*, and high turnover, inexperience, and poor management onboard, had initially attracted the attention of investigators seeking the cause of the explosion," Hall wrote. But then the homosexual issue shoved the ship's many shortcomings to the back burner.

The day after his first piece ran, John Hall overheard Gene Marlow, the deputy bureau chief, tell Steve Goldberg, "Hall has just ripped the Navy a new asshole!" Shortly after that, Hall's phone rang. It was George Wilson calling, not to congratulate Hall but to ask, "Who are your sources?" Hall thought Wilson was kidding, but he wasn't. Wilson said he really needed Hall's sources and his help. Three days after the admirals' press conference, Wilson had written a piece for the *Washington Post* headlined, "The Different Faces of Clayton Hartwig" and larded it with psychological jargon. He had quoted unnamed NIS sources who described Hartwig "as weird, a man confused about his sexual identity and about his future." Although the Navy had officially abandoned the gay issue, Wilson quoted an anonymous sailor who claimed that Hartwig was a homosexual. Wilson only identified one individual in his story, Gunner's Mate Second Class Michael Carr, who said that Hartwig was a dedicated individual, very professional, very competent. John Hall's initial piece, on the other hand, contained names, times, dates, and specific anecdotes. Wilson's editors urged him to come up with something comparable. As Wilson made his pleas, Hall said he seriously thought about slamming down the phone on his competitor, but instead he told Wilson to be sure to read his next installment. He might learn something.

Hall's second story ran on Thursday, September 28, and reported that the *Iowa*'s crewmen had been terrified when they learned that a Tomahawk cruise missile would be fired at their vessel by the cruiser *San Jacinto* as part of an experiment. Hall also wrote that the *Iowa*'s crewmen were so poorly trained that they were unable to keep many of the 14,000 valves and 250 miles of cable on the vessel functioning.

Hall's article also included congressional reaction. He said that Democratic Senator Sam Nunn of Georgia, chairman of the Senate Armed Services Committee, had decided to hold hearings about the manner in which the Navy had conducted its investigation. Democratic Senator John Glenn of Ohio had asked the General Accounting Office, Congress's technical and fiscal watchdog, to examine the unauthorized gunpowder experiments and other unconventional practices that took place on the *Iowa*. Defense Secretary Dick Cheney told Hall that he was convinced that it was safe to operate the four *Iowa*-class battleships, but he did not subscribe to the Navy's judgment about Hartwig, terming it only "a guesstimate."

Hall's third installment, which ran the next day, took a look at why U.S. battleships continued to steam around the globe two generations after every other major naval power had relegated them to the boneyard. He quoted an unnamed Navy official as saying, "A lot of us around here knew this [the *Iowa* explosion] was going to happen. We argued against the battleships and lost, and now we're stuck with them. I don't know what caused that accident. All I know is that you can't fight wars with dangerous antiques, which is what these things are." Hall cited the testimony that Captain Fred Moosally and Master Chief James Hickman had given to Admiral Milligan, saying they didn't have enough qualified sailors to operate the ship's three sixteen-inch turrets.

Hall's final piece appeared on Saturday, September 30, and painted a fuller, better-balanced portrait of Clayton Hartwig, sometimes relying on excerpts from letters he had written to his parents, his buddies, and his girlfriends. "I'm planning to stay on here to watch the ship pull out on 7 June for their six-month cruise to the Mediterranean," Hartwig wrote on April 3. "I'll probably never see these guys or the ship again so I want to wave goodbye." Hall didn't believe that letter, written sixteen days before Hartwig's death, came from someone who hated his ship or his turret mates. Kreig Brusnahan, the Hartwigs' attorney, told Hall that the Navy's case against Clayton amounted to "a collection of innuendo." Hall called the FBI and asked someone to explain exactly what the phrase *equivocal death analysis* really meant. FBI spokesman Milton Ahlerich said, "It is strictly an opinion. It is not evidence."

JOHN HALL wasn't the only journalist to doubt the Navy's objectivity and fairness, nor was he the only reporter to dig deeper or to write stories attacking the service for distorting the truth or withholding exculpatory evidence about Clayton Hartwig. In Hampton, Virginia, reporters Robert Becker and A.J. Plunkett of the *Daily Press/Times-Herald* put together a lengthy story that systematically debunked the Milligan report. They wrote: Navy records disclosed that friction had ignited powder bags aboard other battleships; poor safety practices and an incompetent gunnery training program existed on the *Iowa* long before the accident; there was evidence that the Milligan team already had reached its conclusion about Hartwig before NIS agents interviewed the Cleveland sailor's friends and family; serious doubts existed about where Hartwig's body had actually been found in the turret.

Military writer Jack Dorsey of the *Virginian-Pilot/Ledger-Star* in Norfolk took a hard look at the lack of training and the safety deficiencies aboard the *Iowa* and declared her to be "a lax ship." Dorsey disclosed that there were prohibited "spark-producing items" (six cigarette lighters, key chains, and other metal objects) found on the bodies of the men in Turret Two. He also wrote about the last minute-substitution of untrained personnel in the turret, the absence of accurate training records, and the outlawed but routine practice of opening flameproof doors inside the turrets after powder bags had been removed from the magazines.

THE DAY that Admirals Edney and Milligan held their press conference, the *Iowa* was anchored in the harbor of the picturesque little resort town of Gaeta, Italy. About a third of the crewmen were off the ship on liberty when a team of officers from the Bureau of Naval Personnel arrived to buck up Captain Fred Moosally's spirits. These Washington-based officers were also in Gaeta to ensure that the captain didn't stray from the official line in case he was approached by a reporter. Once the Pentagon press conference ended, Moosally got on the ship's public-address system and provided the men still aboard a condensed version of what had been said in Washington. Most sailors dismissed Moosally's briefing as more disinformation.

Passivity turned to anger several days later, when the men began receiving newspaper clippings from their wives, girlfriends, and parents concerning the Pentagon press conference and questions that had been raised about the impartiality of the Navy's investigation. Gunner's Mate Third Class Cletus Guffin bristled over Milligan's assault on Clayton Hartwig. "Nobody believed it," he said.

Dale Mortensen wasn't surprised that Milligan had adopted the suicide theory. The admiral had received his technical data from Captain Joseph Miceli, and Mortensen thought that Miceli's "biggest thing was to prove that the gun and ammunition were not at fault." The men in Turret One were in a defiant mood. "My men were saying, 'We know it wasn't Clayton Hartwig. His body was in the wrong place,'" Meyer said. "Nobody bought the theory of a bomb-throwing fag. The idea of malicious conduct was not believed, not accepted." Meyer asked the men to "hang tough" a little longer and see if the system righted itself. Very few sailors were happy about that.

Brian Scanio, the first man to enter Turret Two while the fires still raged, chafed at the fact that Edney and Milligan had blamed Hartwig. "Bull! It's not true!" he raged. He had seen Hartwig's body in the pit below the center gun and pledged to raise as much hell as it took to get somebody in authority who was unbiased to hear him out. His division officer, Lieutenant George Anderson, had a number of other men who had also fought fires inside the turret and felt exactly the same.

ONE OF the most provocative news accounts received by some of the *Iowa* officers and sailors was written by Robert Zelnick. An article by the ABC News reporter appeared on Monday, September 11, on the op-ed page of the *New York Times*. Headlined, "The Navy Scapegoats a Dead Seaman," the article stated that accused rapists, killers, and drug dealers enjoy the presumption of innocence until proven guilty, but that Clayton Hartwig had been branded a mass murderer with meager evidence. Zelnick wrote that Hartwig had been subjected to a "process of guilt by fiat." He claimed that the evidence against the sailor was so weak that it would never have sustained a grand jury indictment, much less a criminal conviction.

That was pretty strong stuff, and it caught the practiced eye of Mike Wallace, the star correspondent of CBS News's highly successful newsmagazine, *60 Minutes*. Wallace had been drawn to the *Iowa* story for months. A naval officer in the South Pacific during World War II, Mike had visited the *Iowa* in Norfolk in 1986 when Captain Larry Seaquist had commanded her. What really hooked Mike on this story was the fact that it was about little people getting the stuffing pounded out of them by a huge bully.

Like Mike, I had once been a naval officer. Trained as a gunnery and fire-control officer, I served two tours of duty in Vietnam, one of them as a naval gunfire spotter, artillery observer, and forward air controller in the First Air Naval Gunfire Liaison Company (ANGLICO). ANGLICO was an elite outfit that provided the U.S. Army and the Korean and Vietnamese military with the same kind of gunfire and naval air support that U.S. Marines received.

After I was discharged, I kept up my interest in the military. When the *Iowa* explosion occurred, I had been covering this subject on an almost full-time basis for a decade. My Navy background, continued interest in gunnery, and the fact that I produced numerous television news stories about the military were the reasons I received that phone call from the Turret One gunner's mate a week after the explosion. He said that he had asked an officer he knew in Norfolk if there was anybody in the news media who was familiar with naval gunnery. The officer had met me and gave the sailor my name and home phone number.

The day Zelnick's piece ran in the *New York Times*, I was sitting in an office down the hall from Mike Wallace on West 57th Street in New York. I was writing a script about a defense contractor who sold a small, defective part to the U.S. Air Force, thus transforming a high-tech missile designed to lock on and destroy enemy radars into an expensive, useless piece of junk. Mike bounded into the office where I sat and tossed a ragged-edged newspaper article in my direction. I snatched it as it fluttered down, glancing at it and realizing that it was the Zelnick *Iowa* piece I had read earlier that morning. "You've been dying to do this story for months," Mike said. "Let's see if your friend Zelnick is right. We'll do the story."

I had stayed fairly current with the *Iowa* story, but I had some catching-up to do. I hadn't attended the admirals' press conference, but I did have a transcript and a tape of it. I read the transcript and then watched the tape. Questions about the Navy's testing procedures and what kind of detonator (if any) had been used leapt out at me. I thought that if I were going to do this story justice, I had better get some first-class people to help me. My initial call was to Paul Hoven. Paul had flown helicopters in Vietnam, where he had completed 1,400 combat missions, earning the Distinguished Flying Cross and thirty-two Air Medals. He had worked as an analyst for two Washington think tanks and had been a military consultant for two television networks, ABC and CBS.

Paul, a firearms expert, was a voracious reader of military history. He had a well-developed sense of irony, and zero tolerance for anyone with inflated self-esteem. Paul informed me several years earlier that he had very little use for naval officers. "They're all effete snobs or assholes," he said. However, he said he was willing to make an exception for me, because I had provided gunfire and close air support to "grunts" in Vietnam. I told Paul that I was going to ask retired Rear Admiral Ed Snyder, who had commanded the *New Jersey* in Vietnam, to help us. If the admiral agreed, would Paul give him "a pass" too? He wouldn't make any promises. He told me he'd start by calling Tony Battista and Chuck Bernard, who had worked with Captain Joseph Miceli at Dahlgren.

My next call was to a researcher in the *60 Minutes* Washington office, twenty-five-year-old Ariadne "Ari" Allan. Ari quickly pointed out that she knew very little about the Navy and next to nothing about battleships. That could be an advantage, I said, because Paul and I might take too much for granted, while someone with no preconceptions could listen to us and say, "I don't understand a word of what you're saying. Put it in plain English." She said she would call the Chief of Naval Information's office and go to the Pentagon to obtain the 7,000 documents the Navy said were available. She coaxed a young naval lieutenant in the document room into filling three boxes with records and then carting them out and loading them into the trunk of a waiting cab.

My final call was to Ed Snyder. I had first met him in 1975 when he was the Navy's oceanographer, and I had followed his campaign, occasionally as the Navy's official spokesman, for recommissioning the *Iowa*-class battleships in the early 1980s. I hadn't seen his name mentioned in the press concerning the *Iowa* investigation—which was puzzling, given the fact that he was the preeminent expert on sixteen-inch gunnery.

But before we got very deep into the subject of the *Iowa* explosion, he laid down some ground rules. Admiral Snyder would not appear on-camera, because he didn't want to disparage the Navy in public, no matter how much he was at odds with its handling of this case. He didn't want to be paid anything. He said he would pull out of the project if he sensed that we were putting together an exploitative piece. I assured him that wasn't going to happen, but if it did, I'd be out the door before he was.

ARI ALLAN, Admiral Ed Snyder, Paul Hoven, and I met at the *60 Minutes* office in northwest Washington. Paul and the admiral drifted back to an empty office and talked for about fifteen minutes. When they emerged, they were smiling and swapping war stories. The four of us began work by separately examining the files that Ari had obtained at the Pentagon. We reassembled every couple of hours to compare notes. Admiral Snyder had the transcript of Fred Moosally's interviews with Milligan's team. Paul had Chief Skelley's interviews, and Ari and I split the NIS records.

The first time we got back together, the admiral was fuming about Moosally. "He's the worst sort of naval officer, the kind of captain who blamed everything that goes wrong on his ship on his crew!" "How many commands did Moosally have before he got the *Iowa*?" he inquired. "Just one, a destroyer," I said. "Then how in the hell did he get a major command like the *Iowa*?" he exclaimed. Before I could answer, he lowered his voice and said, "You don't have to answer that. It's obvious he got that ship through political wheeling and dealing."

"He's a nutty little squirrel," Paul said, belatedly explaining that he was referring to Chief Skelley. Paul said Skelley ducked every question put to him by Admiral Milligan and his team about who had given him permission to ignore safety regulations. Skelley's and Moosally's testimony confirmed Admiral Snyder's hypothesis that conditions had been "terribly wrong" aboard the *Iowa* long before the accident.

Ari said the records she and I went through led to the inescapable conclusion that the paramount goal of NIS had been to establish that Clayton Hartwig was a homosexual. No matter whom the NIS agents interviewed, even Clayton Hartwig's mother, the issue of homosexuality invariably was raised. Some witnesses apparently had been informed that they might be charged with sodomy if they didn't testify that Clayton Hartwig and Kendall Truitt were gay. David Smith's marathon interrogations reminded us of the confessions extracted from prisoners of war by brutal interrogators in Pyongyang, North Korea, during the early 1950s and in Hanoi, North Vietnam, in the 1960s. The fact that the NIS agents hadn't informed the FBI's psychological profilers about Smith's recantation of his derogatory testimony against Hartwig was unethical at best and criminal at worst.

PAUL SAID that Tony Battista and Chuck Bernard told him that because Joseph Miceli had been such a controversial, contentious character when they worked with him at Dahlgren, they had kept close track of his naval career since then. After Miceli had been promoted to captain, he had been given command of the Naval Weapons Support Center at Crane, where he supervised the commingling and rebagging of the gunpowder for the recommissioned battleships. That powder was later blamed for the *New Jersey*'s grossly inaccurate gunfire in Lebanon. Miceli was then ordered to find some reliable powder and rebag it for the sixteen-inch guns. He managed to do this, but this was the same powder that was being used on the *Iowa* when the center gun in Turret Two exploded. Ari, Admiral Snyder, and I were goggle-eyed at this information. We were now fully aware that Miceli had a major stake in having the powder vindicated. He should have had nothing to do with the technical investigation. If Paul was able to unearth these facts, why wasn't the Navy aware of them?

AS WE walked back to the office after lunch, I asked Admiral Snyder to read the Milligan report. It was not very thick. After that, would he review the transcript of Edney and Milligan's press conference and watch the videotape? I'd already done this, but I wanted a professional opinion. He said that he'd do it. Paul offered to read the newspaper stories and television scripts, and Ari said she would study Clayton Hartwig's letters. I would evaluate the Milligan panel's interviews of Dan Meyer, Dale Mortensen, Kendall Truitt, John Mullahy, Lieutenant Commander Costigan (the gunnery officer), and Commander Kissinger (the weapons officer). After two hours of poring over this material, we got together again.

Admiral Snyder said that it was evident that the Navy had no idea what kind of a detonator had been employed, or even if one had been used. He expressed disbelief at Milligan's claim that the five bags of powder in the center gun had been rammed at a normal speed of 1.5 feet per second rather than at the fast speed of 14 feet per second used to ram projectiles. "There is no way Milligan could know how fast the powder was rammed. Even if the control handle was found in the slow speed position after the explosion, that doesn't prove anything. The rammerman could have realized that he had made a mistake by ramming too fast and yanked the handle back to the slow speed position just before he died," the admiral said.

The former *New Jersey* skipper couldn't understand why the turret's sprinkler system did not work, why almost none of the men in the three turrets had gas masks, or why powder that had been corrupted by being improperly stored in 1988 had been allowed back aboard the *Iowa*. As a consummate professional, he was outraged by the lack of crew training. And as a scientist, he was vexed by some of Captain Miceli's tests, considering them to be balderdash. Paul was stewing over the Navy's campaign of leaks and character assassination directed against Clayton Hartwig. He was also offended by the Navy's making such a big issue about Clayton Hartwig's being "a loner." "He was a member of the Seventh-Day Adventist Church, for Christ's sake! He joined when he was three years old. When other kids were playing on Saturdays, he was in church with his mother and father," Paul said. "I know a lot of people who are Seventh-Day Adventists, and they are all quality folks." Wagging an accusatory finger at Admiral Snyder and me, he said, "I hate to tell you guys, but the Navy's full of bigots!"

Ari changed the subject, stating that the Navy had misused Clayton Hartwig's letters. The FBI profilers had cited his Sunday, April 16, 1989, letter to Charlene Meter, the last letter he ever wrote to anybody, as evidence that he lived in a fantasy world. Clayton provided Charlene with specific details about his upcoming foreign assignment, even informing her that he had to attend a five-week "physical security school" in San Antonio, Texas. Admiral Milligan announced at the Navy press conference that Hartwig really was supposed to get that overseas assignment. Even so, the FBI's equivocal death analysis, with its garbled conclusions about that letter, continued to be circulated by the Navy to the media and Congress as "proof" that Hartwig was cuckoo. The four of us were amazed that, after devoting so much time and manpower to trying to prove that Hartwig and Truitt had been homosexual lovers, Admirals Milligan and Edney would then insist that homosexuality had never been an issue.

I told the other three that the *Iowa*'s weapons officer, Commander Kissinger, had not seemed to be embarrassed about admitting to the Milligan panel that he knew next to nothing about sixteen-inch gunnery. The testimony of Lieutenant Dan Meyer and Gunner's Mate First Class Dale Mortensen convinced me that they were two people who did seem to know what they were doing. Meyer, Turret One's officer, had spoken candidly to Milligan's panel about Chief Skelley's "kitchen-sink" experiments and other safety problems that seemed routinely to plague the *Iowa*. Meyer's testimony also provided a sense of how horrifying it must have been when he entered the powder flats and saw the clusters of dead bodies and powder bags glowing like charcoal. Reading Mortensen's transcript, I reflected that if he hadn't been on the battleship that fateful day, Turret One might have caught fire and Turret Two would have suffered even more damage.

On page 33 of Mortensen's transcript, he discussed something that gripped me. He said the gas ejection air did not work in Turret Two's center gun. He said that somebody climbed down into the pit to inspect the valve that regulated the compressed air. While that person was below fiddling with the valve, the explosion ripped through the turret. Who was that person? Mortensen didn't say, but he made it very clear that he was describing a real person and a real event. Admiral Milligan tried to convince Mortensen that nothing of the sort had happened, but the gunner's mate refused to retreat. The Navy hadn't said anything about a body being found near the compressed-air valve in the pit below the center gun. Was Mortensen talking about Clayton Hartwig? It was imperative for us to talk with Meyer and Mortensen, but it would take more than two years for that to happen.

Before we called it quits that day, we all looked at the Navy tape that had been shown to the *Iowa* families. At first glance, we couldn't pick up the trick edits. We played it several times, froze it on some suspicious frames, and spotted several sleights of hand. Even so, after more than twenty years in network television, I knew that unless you have outtakes (material that was shot but not aired) or are aided by the person who put the tape together, it's almost impossible to detect the deception. But there is another way—obtain the documents describing what really happened and compare those with the narration in the tape. It took some time, but we were able to obtain the records to prove that Navy videotape was dishonest.

21

☆

"The Navy Is Still in the Fag-Bashing Business."

A NUMBER OF powerful legislators on both sides of Capitol Hill prepared to hold the Navy accountable for botching the *Iowa* investigation. Two of the senators who pushed hardest for hearings were Howard Metzenbaum and John Glenn, both Democrats from Ohio. Metzenbaum, a silver-haired former business executive from Cleveland, and Glenn, a retired Marine colonel, World War II and Korea fighter pilot, and the first American to orbit the earth, were incensed by what Admirals Edney and Milligan said at their press conference. Clayton Hartwig was one of their constituents. Neither of the Ohio lawmakers nor any of their colleagues with whom they discussed the case thought the Navy had the kind of concrete evidence that was required to accuse an individual of mass murder. "It was so preposterous that it drove Senator Metzenbaum wild. And then the Navy's case started unraveling," said Richard Woodruff, Metzenbaum's deputy. "It was beyond the pale. It was not plausible, and the Navy knew it."

Woodruff had been a Senate employee for ten years. Metzenbaum told Woodruff that the Navy's overt homophobia disgusted him. Metzenbaum wanted to have the Senate Judiciary Committee, of which he chaired a subcommittee, conduct the *Iowa* hearings, but Woodruff told him that the hearings would have more impact if they were held by the Senate Armed Services Committee, which controlled the Navy's budget. That meant that Metzenbaum had to call Senator Sam Nunn, chairman of the Armed Services Committee, and ask him to intervene.

"You've got to look into this!" Metzenbaum told Nunn. "This is absurd! There is no way this could have happened!" Metzenbaum said the Navy's technical investigation was so bogus that another sixteen-inch gun might blow up on another battleship, killing more men. That did it. Nunn agreed to hold oversight hearings, but his counsel, Richard DeBobes, was initially displeased with that decision. DeBobes had spent almost all of his adult life in the Navy, retiring as a captain, and he hated to see anything done that might discredit the service.

The first meeting between the Senate staffers and Navy representatives took place in the Russell Senate Office Building in mid-September. Three officers showed up—Rear Admiral Milligan, Captain Roger Pitkin of the Navy's Office of Legislative Affairs (known as the "Navy's mouthpiece on the Hill"), and Rear Admiral William Schachte, who commanded NIS. "Pitkin kept away from us as much as possible. He was not a schmoozer. He was tough, reluctant to turn anything over to us," Woodruff said. "When you work on the Hill for a while you grow to despise these legislative affairs guys. I expected Pitkin to be just as he was, not very cooperative, a real tight ass."

Schachte kept his mouth shut. Milligan did almost all of the talking during the meeting, while Pitkin took copious notes. Milligan hauled out the joke book that he'd held up at his press conference and waved it around again. The congressional aides had previously scrutinized the book and were aware that the author's formula for making a "dog doo-doo bomb" was the most harmful thing it contained. Milligan next repulsed the staffers by "stating flat out" that Clayton Hartwig and Kendall Truitt were "faggots." "Everybody winced," Woodruff said. The admiral proclaimed that there was "evidence" to prove that an electronic timer had been planted in the barrel by Hartwig. Woodruff and the other staffers recoiled, realizing that Milligan had restated something that had been rejected by Admiral Edney at the press conference. "Everybody was dumbstruck by his presentation. We were open-mouthed that this was what the Navy was trying to pull over everybody," Woodruff said.

RICHARD DEBOBES set up a number of meetings between Captain Joseph Miceli and the twenty congressional staffers assigned to the case. Captain Pitkin tried to prevent Miceli and other naval personnel from being interrogated by the Armed Services Committee, and he also dug in his heels about turning over documents. After being threatened with subpoenas and told he personally would be cited for contempt of Congress, Pitkin became more compliant. During a rancorous series of meetings with Captain Miceli, Pitkin took notes while Miceli bickered, sidestepped, and puffed up like a toad whenever his word was disputed. "Joe [Miceli] took this very personally," DeBobes said. For several months, DeBobes said, Miceli called him with "his theory of the day." "He [Miceli] was 150 percent sure of one thing one day, and the next day he was 150 percent sure of something else," the committee counsel said. DeBobes eventually wearied of Miceli's kooky theories and decided that he "had outlived his usefulness." DeBobes told Pitkin to get somebody who wasn't considered a scoundrel to represent the

Navy on technical issues or suffer the consequences in diminished credibility with Senator Nunn. DeBobes's advice went unheeded.

THE CONGRESSIONAL staffers cackled after reading Chief Skelley's statements to Admiral Milligan and learning just how slender his credentials were. "We were laughing at Skelley. People had referred to him as 'the genius of gunnery,' and the guy sold pots and pans," Woodruff said. NIS administrators and the agents who handled the *Iowa* case were called back often and grilled by the staffers. "We didn't find NIS's theory plausible. It was incredible. The perception of NIS up here [in Congress] is terrible, as it perhaps is in the rest of the country," DeBobes said.

NIS agents Tom Goodman and Ed Goodwin, as well as Robert Powers, who headed the NIS criminal investigations division, were several times put through the wringer by the congressional staffers. "We beat the hell out of those two guys [Goodman and Goodwin]. We got them to admit that they only wrote down summaries of what witnesses told them. They had no verbatim transcripts," Woodruff said. A number of witnesses who had been interviewed by NIS told reporters and Armed Services Committee staffers that the agents had falsified large portions of their statements, showing them agreeing to details on paper that they had emphatically denied in person. Goodman and Goodwin stuck by their reports. NIS acknowledged that it had provided the FBI psychological profilers with selected material concerning Hartwig, deleting exculpatory evidence, such as the fact that David Smith had retracted the derogatory things he'd said about Hartwig. The agency refused to budge on its "gay theory" that Hartwig had sabotaged the gun after his alleged love affair with Truitt soured.

WHILE THE Senate Armed Services Committee staffers were turning the tables on the NIS agents, their counterparts from the House Armed Services Committee were preparing to do the same. The stimulus for the House investigation had come from Mary Rose Oakar—the Democratic congresswoman from Cleveland who had convinced Kathy Kubicina to talk with Molly Moore of the *Washington Post* back in May in the hope that the unsubstantiated rumors might be spiked, or at least to try to contain the family's side of the story. Oakar had suffered through a four-hour discourse by Admiral Milligan in her office several days after his press conference. She was unimpressed, saying, "I have not seen one iota of circumstantial or any form of evidence that would indicate that Clayton Hartwig committed that crime. . . . How they can conclude, based on the information that they have supplied, the so-called psychological profile, a couple of magazines, that this individual committed a deliberate crime, not only killing himself, but forty-six other individuals, is beyond my comprehension!"

Oakar was so irritated by Milligan's refusal to consider any cause for the explosion other than as an intentional act by Clayton Hartwig that she contacted Representative Nicholas Mavroules, a Massachusetts Democrat who was chairman of the Investigations Subcommittee of the House Armed Services Committee. Mavroules told Oakar that his investigators had done some preliminary work and were convinced that the Navy had trampled on the constitutional rights of the Hartwig family and Kendall Truitt. He said he would instruct his staffers to "aggressively pursue" the case.

MARY ROSE Oakar received a promising lead when a letter from Mrs. Mary Wahler of Oxon Hill, Maryland, a Washington suburb, arrived in her office in the Rayburn Building during the second week of September. Mrs. Wahler was the aunt of Gunner's Mate Third Class Jack Thompson Jr. of Greeneville, Tennessee. She said that while Jack was home on Easter leave he had talked to one of his uncles about a sequence of near-disasters that had occurred on the *Iowa*. According to Mrs. Wahler's letter, Jack said, "They have modified it [the gun turret] into a death trap."

Oakar said that Admiral Milligan was going to be on Capitol Hill in the next few days, and that she intended to question him about the Jack Thompson situation. When Oakar met with Milligan, she handed him a copy of Mary Wahler's letter. As Oakar described it later, "He pooh-poohed the whole notion that this young man was afraid and that he had witnessed various unsafe, hazardous occasions while on board that battleship."

VICE ADMIRAL Joseph Donnell flew to the Mediterranean to admonish Captain Fred Moosally; Commander Kissinger, the weapons officer; Commander Finney, the operations officer; and Chief Skelley for their roles in the events leading up to the April disaster. The Navy had no interest in seeing Donnell's trip publicized. Normally, when a three-star admiral comes aboard a capital ship, gongs and whistles go off. But many officers and enlisted men who were on the *Iowa* on October 3, as she prepared to enter the harbor at Istanbul, Turkey, said they were unaware that Donnell ever was on the ship. Others say that he arrived in mufti. The Atlantic Fleet's surface forces commander handed Captain Moosally a nonpunitive "letter of admonition" that wouldn't even be entered into his personnel file. Commander Finney received a similar letter. Moosally had dodged the bullet.

Admiral Donnell tendered Commander Kissinger and Chief Skelley slightly harsher punitive "letters of admonition" for dereliction of duty. Kissinger was also fined $2,000, and Skelley $1,000, but Donnell suspended both fines. As word filtered out to the fleet about Donnell's indulgent treatment of the *Iowa*'s commanding officer, most officers were astounded that Moosally received more lenient punishment than his subordinates. The Navy tried to defend this by releasing a statement claiming that Moosally had been judged on his "overall command policies," while his underlings had been judged on how they performed their duties. When that failed to offset criticism that Moosally's "slap on the wrist" was yet another example of the Navy's whitewashing the tragedy, the service issued another statement claiming that the numerous safety violations aboard the battleship, and the meager training of the sailors, were totally unrelated to the tragedy.

The *Iowa*'s crew was not that affected by the news that the captain had received almost painless punishment. The men's morale was already low and did not drop any farther. But that all changed after a story was published in the October 8 issue of *Navy Times*. Although *Navy Times* is an independently owned weekly publication, the newspaper is viewed in the fleet as a semiofficial organ. Promotion lists were printed in it before they appear anywhere else. Bits and pieces of Moosally's testimony to Admiral Milligan's panel had already appeared in other publications, but the captain's most spiteful remarks about his ship, his officers, his crew, and his predecessor had received no coverage. The *Navy Times* article, which included those remarks, landed on the battleship like a nine-gun broadside from an enemy dreadnought.

"I heard the men mutter, 'That two-faced bastard,' over and over whenever Moosally's name came up," Dan Meyer said. "The captain really shot himself in the foot by trashing the crew. Any thoughts to save the ship's honor were now over." Some remarks about the captain were homicidal. A number of officers and sailors later said that Moosally was smart to keep a Marine orderly, with a holstered and chambered .45-caliber semiautomatic pistol, at his side whenever he left the sanctuary of his sea cabin or the bridge.

The story of Moosally's backstabbing of his crew was picked up from *Navy Times* and republished by a number of major newspapers around the country. Admiral Edney fired off a barbed letter to Tom Philpott, editor of *Navy Times*. Edney complained about the headline, "*Iowa* CO Rips Quality of Officers, Crew." That's what Moosally had done, but Edney protested that writing about it amounted to "sensationalism." He accused the newspaper of selectively editing Moosally's transcript. Why didn't reporter William Matthews extol the crew's gallant firefighting efforts on April 19 instead of focusing on Moosally's malicious remarks? Edney praised Moosally, referring to him as "a man who loves his ship and crew." He ended his tirade by saying that Moosally and the *Iowa* had performed "in a superior manner" during the recent deployment to the Mediterranean.

SHORTLY AFTER Fred Moosally became a pariah on his own ship, he again summoned Dan Meyer to his sea cabin and informed him that he was "disloyal" and would pay the consequences for his treachery. First of all, Meyer wouldn't receive the gold Surface Warfare device; second, Meyer and Dale Mortensen would not get the Navy and Marine Corps Medal for their heroism on April 19; third, the executive officer, Commander Morse, would hand Meyer a "nonpunitive letter of caution" for being on bridge watch on the day of the explosion rather than inside Turret One. Meyer had been assigned to the bridge by Commander Finney, the operations officer, and had obtained permission from his superior, Commander Kissinger, the weapons officer, to be outside his turret during the gun shoot. These extenuating circumstances made no difference to "the Moose," who sat behind his desk, partially concealed by a stack of transcripts. In that stack were Meyer's and Mortensen's statements to Admiral Milligan's panel and six statements from sailors who were assigned to Turret One.

Moosally said he couldn't understand why Meyer had not followed the guidelines given by the ship's legal officer about what he could say and what he should avoid saying to Admiral Milligan's panel. Meyer had shot his mouth off. Mortensen and the gunner's mates had done the same thing. Moosally and Meyer had already gone over this same ground months earlier. Meyer reminded the captain again that he had not attended the legal officer's tutorials. He had been busy identifying bodies in Turret Two. That explanation made no difference to the captain. Moosally was furious that Meyer, Mortensen, and their petty officers talked to Admiral Milligan about finding a body (Clayton Hartwig's) in the pit below the center gun. "Don't tell anyone that the body was in the bottom of the pit in the turret!" Moosally shouted. As Meyer departed Moosally's cabin, the captain hollered, "You're not helping me Meyer!" Meyer was stunned. He was supposed to be helping find out why the explosion occurred, not helping the captain save his career.

Moreover, Moosally had just ordered Meyer not to furnish evidence in a murder case. A gunner's mate had been accused of mass murder, primarily because he was in the right place at the right time. And the captain knew that there were witnesses who would swear that the body of the accused person (Hartwig) was found in a location where it would have been impossible for him to have committed the murders.

NAVY TIMES articles about the Milligan report inspired one of the ship's former officers to write an impassioned letter to Senator John Glenn in mid-September, saying that Admiral Milligan's report reads "like a cheap tabloid and is *wrong*!" The letter came from Lieutenant Commander James Danner, who had been the Catholic chaplain on the *Iowa* from July 1987 through July 1989. Danner had volunteered for a gruesome job following the explosion. He attempted to identify and tag the bodies once they were removed from the turret. On that terrible day, young sailors came up to the priest with severed hands in clear plastic bags, gory jawbones, and other severed parts, asking him, "Father, what do I do with this?"

Danner had been "Iron Mike" Fahey's frequent drinking companion. Some of the Catholic relatives of the dead sailors thought that Danner had gone way beyond the call of duty in comforting them in their time of grief. Gene and Mary Lou Blakey, the parents of Gunner's Mate Third Class Scot Blakey, were among this group. The Blakeys had received a letter from Danner shortly after the Milligan report was released, saying, "I don't believe it. I know for a fact that he [Hartwig] didn't do it."

Danner wrote Senator Glenn from the island of Okinawa, where he was a regimental chaplain assigned to the Third Marine Division. Declaring that even though he was bound by the confidentiality of the confessional, he knew from nonconfidential sources that "Clayton Hartwig and Captain Fred Moosally are convenient scapegoats for the U.S. Navy. Shipmates don't kill shipmates." Danner wrote another letter to Earl and Evelyn Hartwig in which he said, "I do not, nor will I ever believe that your son Clayton had anything to do with causing the explosion! There are some things in life that are unexplainable and known only to God, but the Navy refuses to accept that possibility." He told the Hartwigs that Kathy Kubicina's letters about her brother's life insurance policy "put the spotlight on Clayton, and therefore the Navy made the facts fit the letter."

Danner's letters to Senator Glenn, the Hartwigs, and the Blakeys cheered the *Iowa* relatives who were dejected about the Milligan report. But the chaplain frittered away the goodwill he had engendered by sending another letter to Earl and Evelyn Hartwig, saying that their daughter's primary motivation in writing the letters about her brother's insurance policy was not justice, "but rather greed." He claimed that once Kathy knew that she had lost the battle for the $100,000 insurance money, she lashed out at the Navy. Evelyn responded to Danner, denying that her daughter was greedy and saying that Kathy "has our full approval on all she is doing to clear her brother's name."

Mary Welden, a Catholic, who was the mother of Gunner's Mate Second Class Stephen Welden, wrote Danner that her son had been assigned to Turret Two only six weeks before the explosion and announced shortly after arriving there, "I'm going to die in that hole!" "You were on the ship at the time and you were good friends with many of the men who died," Welden said. "What did you do to help them? You were in a position of authority, knowing about the misfire [in Turret One] and knowing about the men's fears, what did you do?"

Nancy Jo Lewis, whose son, Fire Controlman Richard Lewis, died in the turret officer's booth, wrote Danner, "I have spoken with four [*Iowa*] families today that do not believe that you wrote this [last] letter. They think the Navy composed it for you." Danner, who was later promoted to full commander, never answered Welden's or Lewis's letters. Vice Admiral Boorda, the Chief of Naval Personnel, sent a letter to all of the *Iowa* families, reproaching Danner for his lack of discretion and for making unfounded accusations against Kathy Kubicina. "The chaplain was out of line in my opinion, and he certainly does not speak for the Navy or on behalf of anyone but himself," Boorda wrote.

WHILE THE controversy over Chaplain Danner's letters swirled around the Navy and the *Iowa* families, Admiral Snyder and I closely inspected Captain Joseph Miceli's technical documents, comparing them with the

Milligan report and the statements made by Admirals Milligan and Edney at their press conference. We discovered so many discrepancies that we decided to submit a lengthy series of technical questions, much like legal interrogatories, to the Navy and see if they would respond.

One of the things we were most anxious to obtain from the Navy was a summary table of the twenty-seven Dahlgren test shots that included: (1) How far the shell moved; (2) the point of ignition; (3) the ignition source; (4) whether a lead-foil packet that could have conceivably concealed a detonaten was inserted each time; (5) the extent of barrel erosion. We never thought that the Navy would be foolish enough to provide this information, but when it arrived over our fax machine, we were ecstatic. This document proved that Captain Miceli had never come close to replicating the *Iowa* explosion. From a number of sources, including Admiral Edney's remarks at the press conference, we knew that the Navy had abandoned the idea that an electronic timer was involved in the blast. We now had evidence that Miceli had squandered twenty-five of his twenty-seven Dahlgren shots involving electronic timers, leaving only two tests involving chemical igniters.

Armed with this summary table, we took another look at the Navy's videotape. We were able to identify which test shots the Navy editors had dubbed into their finished product. We compared the relevant data (shell movement, source of ignition, barrel erosion, etc.) of these test shots with the actual event. While he viewed the tape, something else dawned on us. When the center gun blew up in Turret Two, the rammer chain parted. The disconnected links flew back like grapeshot, destroying the rammer motor and assembly housing. But that hadn't happened in any of the twenty-seven Dahlgren test shots. That meant that the technicians didn't use a real rammer. We also noticed something else peculiar. The powder bags in every Dahlgren shot were roped together before they were thrust into the powder chamber. Nothing like that had ever happened on any *Iowa*-class battleship that Admiral Snyder knew about.

Admiral Snyder applied his scientific skills to determine whether the "foreign materials" the Navy claimed were found under the *Iowa*'s rotating band could have come from sources that were normally present in a gun room. The Navy listed glycol as "significant foreign material" that might have been associated with a chemical igniter. The admiral disagreed. Glycol is a component of Break-Free, the solution used to swab out gun barrels. The Navy also made much about finding calcium. From his time as skipper of the *New Jersey*, Snyder knew that calcium was consistent with routine cleaning operations inside a turret. He also thought the Navy was mistaken in listing copper, aluminum, and lead as "foreign materials." Traces of these metals normally were present after a gun fired.

Admiral Snyder couldn't understand why so many men had died in Turret Two. The admiral could understand the deaths of the men in the center gun room, and perhaps even those in the turret officer's booth, but not what happened in the other gun rooms and all the way down to the powder flats. To find out why the casualties were so high, we sought from the Navy the autopsy reports of all forty-seven men, without success. However, we did obtain Clayton Hartwig's autopsy report from his family and later received autopsy reports from a number of other families.

Studying Hartwig's autopsy report, we were shocked to learn that his body contained five times the lethal dosage of cyanide. In addition to Hartwig's autopsy, we had another clue as to why mortality rate was so high. It was Exhibit #2019 of the Milligan report, an eleven-page synopsis prepared by Dr. Richard Froede, the Armed Forces Medical Examiner. It listed the causes of death for all forty-seven men and what chemicals were in their bodies. The cyanide levels of twenty-nine of the other men were elevated. Dr. Froede wrote that he couldn't account for the source of the cyanide, but he assumed that it came from burning paint.

We needed some help from a medical examiner, so I called Dr. John Feegel in Tampa, Florida, a forensic pathologist and an attorney who had been a medical examiner in Denver, Tampa, and Atlanta. I told John why I was calling. "The Navy is still in the fag-bashing business," John said, with obvious distaste. He told me to fax Hartwig's autopsy and Dr. Froede's report, and he would take a look.

John called back several hours later. "So, the Navy is saying that this kid popped a handful of cyanide pills and then tossed a detonator into the barrel just for good measure?" John chuckled. "Seriously, since many of those dead men in that turret had a lot of cyanide in their bodies, you need to look for the source. Was there by any chance any polyurethane foam in that turret?" "Yes, the powder bags were covered with polyurethane foam," I said. "The breech was open, and the burning fumes probably spread throughout the turret. There were also some powder bags at the bottom of the turret that caught fire." "Get in touch with Underwriters Laboratories," John suggested. "You'll find out that in many hotel and office building fires, a large number of people die due to burning upholstered furniture stuffed with polyurethane foam." While I had John on the phone, I asked him if it were possible to rely on the information contained in Hartwig's autopsy report and place his body in an exact position within the turret. "That's nonsense," he said. "I'd like to see the autopsy photos, but the damage to the torso, as it's described in the protocol, doesn't seem extensive enough to put him directly in the path of the blast." "The Armed Forces Institute of Pathology says he was peering into the breech when the blast occurred," I said. "Rubbish," he replied.

We discovered that Sea Systems Command had failed to issue warnings to the four battleships that polyurethane foam jackets could be lethal if they ignited outside an airtight chamber—even after we informed them of this potential hazard. Captain Miceli had begun the use of the "wear-reducing" foam jackets when he had been the commanding officer of the Naval Weapons Support Center in Crane. This was yet another conflict of interest for Miceli. "If the magazines on the *Iowa* had caught fire, even though they did not explode, the whole crew could have perished anyway from cyanide," Admiral Snyder said. "The captains of those four battleships had a right to know about this potential hazard, so they could properly direct their damage-control efforts in the event of a fire."

WHILE WE were swamping the Navy with technical questions, other news organizations kept Lieutenant Commander Deborah Burnette busy with requests for interviews and information. Burnette, the deputy public-affairs officer in Norfolk, went to her boss, Captain Paul Hanley, and to Captain Ed Ellis, the Atlantic Fleet's top legal officer, and told them she wanted to look at all of the material the Milligan panel used in deciding Clayton Hartwig's guilt. She said that without doing this, she could no longer in good conscience answer the news media's questions. Admiral Milligan's documents were still being stored in a small courtroom on the Norfolk Naval Base, and both men told her to feel free to rummage through the boxes. Burnette began with Hartwig's letters and quickly decided that sections of them had been shamelessly taken out of context by the Milligan panel. She thumbed through the copy of *Getting Even: The Complete Book of Dirty Tricks,* which she termed a "stupid practical-joke book." She decided that it didn't contain enough information "to tell me how to blow up my neighbor's house, much less devastate the inside of a sixteen-inch gun turret."

She looked at the photograph of Hartwig as a teenager dressed up for a costume party as the captain of *The Love Boat.* It was clear to her that Hartwig had been much too young to have been in the Navy when the picture was taken. Yet Admiral Milligan and the psychological profilers had announced to the world that this innocent snapshot showed that Hartwig had been impersonating an officer and had delusions of grandeur.

Something else bothered Burnette. One of Captain Miceli's men, who had labored for five weeks to free the 2,700-pound projectile from Turret Two's center gun, wrote an article for a technical publication about that task. Burnette had been asked by Captain Hanley to review the article for accuracy before it could be published. The article recounted how tremendous quantities of Break-Free and seawater had been poured down the barrel of the center gun, and a sledge and huge drill had pummeled the projectile and bored out its base. Burnette asked the author of the article how tons of fluids, metal scraps, shavings, steel wool, and other extraneous material had been isolated, so that the rotating band wasn't contaminated. The man didn't know, so she looked at the technical team's notes and found nothing relating to that subject. "The evidence under the rotating band had to be tainted! This was terrible, monstrous!" Burnette told Hanley.

Because she was also unable to find backup data for some metallurgical tests that had been conducted on the rotating band, Burnette asked Hanley's permission to call another member of Miceli's team. This man was unable to shed any light on the subject, except to say that he doubted that backup data had ever existed.

IN LATE September, Sea Systems Command and Captain Joseph Miceli became supersensitive as the congressional investigators and the news media poked large holes in the Navy's technical case. One senior officer decided that something needed to be done to restore confidence in the command. The officer was Captain Al Becker, the chief of public affairs at Sea Systems Command. As a lieutenant, Becker's mentor had been Captain Vince Thomas, who had been one of the Navy's smoothest press operatives in the late 1960s and early 1970s. Although retired to South Florida, he often traveled to Washington to visit friends at the Pentagon and have a drink with some prominent journalists.

During one of Thomas's trips north, he met with Becker, who told him that Captain Miceli had been griping that some of George Wilson's articles about the *Iowa* investigation were "factually incorrect," and that Miceli wanted "to straighten this reporter out."

Putting George Wilson in touch with Captain Miceli might serve two purposes, Becker said. Miceli could settle his disagreements with Wilson, and Sea Systems Command (through Miceli) could promote its current theory that a chemical igniter, not an electronic timer, caused the *Iowa* explosion. Becker asked Thomas to call Wilson and see if the reporter would attend a Saturday brunch and "a deep backgrounder" with Miceli at Becker's Arlington, Virginia, home. A deep backgrounder meant Wilson was free to report what Miceli told him, but he couldn't tell his readers his source's identity or indicate that he might have an ax to grind. Miceli later disputed Becker's definition of "a deep backgrounder," claiming that Wilson wasn't even allowed to use the information.

Becker went to Vice Admiral Peter Hekman, head of Sea Systems Command, and informed him that "a deep backgrounder" between Miceli and Wilson had been arranged. Hekman asked Becker if the briefing had been approved by Rear Admiral Brent Baker, the Chief of Naval Information. Becker told him that it had been, and Hekman gave his permission to proceed. Becker later admitted that he lied to Hekman. Brent Baker knew nothing about the session with Wilson. If he had known, he never would have allowed Miceli to attend, because he considered Miceli to be "an unguided missile."

George Wilson, Vince Thomas, and Joseph Miceli arrived at Al Becker's home at approximately 10 A.M. on Saturday, October 7. They remained there four hours. Miceli brought videotapes, pictures, and pieces of the *Iowa*'s rotating band to show Wilson. He told Wilson how a chemical compression detonator worked. He also showed the reporter a draft copy of his final technical report, which hadn't been released. Becker later said he was suffused in a warm, fuzzy glow, believing that the brunch had been an even bigger success than he expected. If Wilson's article turned out as he hoped, he might have a chance to escape Sea Systems Command and become chief of public affairs for the Pacific Fleet in Hawaii.

FIVE DAYS later, Captain Miceli was seated in an office in the Russell Senate Office Building, providing the identical information to Dick Woodruff and other Senate staffers that he had already leaked to George Wilson. Miceli mentioned that he needed to conduct some additional tests using chemical igniters. These devices could be constructed from materials that were easily obtained aboard ship, such as four tablespoons of a commercial cleaning compound containing chlorine, steel wool, and two ounces of glycol. "Where in the world would a sailor would find two ounces of glycol on the battleship?" one staffer asked. "It's in Brylcreem," Miceli replied. This once-popular male hair ointment contains propylene glycol. Millions of tubes of the gooey white pomade had been sold in large measure due to its snappy advertising jingle: "A little dab will do ya." Woodruff ridiculed Miceli: "Captain, are you telling us that Hartwig tossed a chemical device into the breech, and then yelled, 'A little dab will do ya.'?"

Shortly after Miceli left Capitol Hill, Dick Woodruff called to tell me about the "Brylcreem bomb." Mike Wallace was sitting in my office when I took the call. He had come down from New York to meet Admiral Snyder, obtain a progress report, and agree on some interview dates and locations. Mike asked us if it would be all right for him to run some of our material by a high-ranking naval officer whom he'd met through Admiral William J. Crowe Jr., the former chairman of the Joint Chiefs of Staff. None of us objected. I only knew this officer by reputation, which was exemplary. Mike reached him and told him what we were finding. The officer told Mike that he knew about these horror stories, which were all true. Then, according to Mike, the officer said, "I'm ashamed to say this, but the Navy is conducting a cover-up at the very highest levels. I hope you're not planning on abandoning your story, because if that happened, you'd be doing both your viewers and the United States Navy a tremendous disservice."

The same day that Miceli was on Capitol Hill trying to peddle his "Brylcreem bomb" theory, Dick Woodruff received a call from George Wilson, who said he'd heard that the Senate Armed Services Committee was investigating whether a "chemical bomb" was responsible for the destruction aboard the *Iowa*. Woodruff was evasive, so Wilson told him that he knew Captain Miceli had been up on Capitol Hill and talked to Woodruff and other staffers. Wilson asked if any other news organizations were looking into this angle, and Woodruff said they were. Wilson thanked him and hung up. He had begun encountering resistance from his editors over his stories about the *Iowa*. He had recently submitted another story, "The Mind of a

Navy Investigator," which purported to explain how a technical investigator (Captain Joseph Miceli) solved the *Iowa* explosion. Editors on his newspaper's national desk had rejected Wilson's proposal out of hand. Wilson was not worried that his "chemical bomb" story would stir up a controversy. He had a scoop from an official source and a semiconfirmation from another source, and other news organizations were sniffing about.

During the second week in October, the day before George Wilson's article on a "chemical bomb" ran in the *Washington Post*, Al Becker called Joseph Miceli and cried, "I've lost control of George Wilson!" Becker had spoken with Wilson and learned that his article was written in such a way that even though Miceli's name was not mentioned, it would be obvious to the Navy, to competing news organizations, and to the investigators from the House and Senate Armed Services Committees that Miceli was the source of the leak. The Navy was paranoid about leaks. For one thing, Senator Nunn had threatened to figuratively hang the top admirals from a yardarm if there were any more major unauthorized disclosures. The Georgia Democrat was not one with whom to trifle. He and his committee had the power to punish the Navy financially for its transgressions. Becker said he pleaded with Wilson to delete any mention of the fact that anybody in the Navy had supplied him any information. But Wilson stubbornly refused. Miceli accused Becker of ambushing him. "I felt betrayed by Captain Becker," Miceli said later.

Miceli wasn't the only one who felt double-crossed by Becker. The day George Wilson's article ran, Rear Admiral Brent Baker summoned Becker to his Pentagon office and chewed him out. "What the hell did you do and what were you thinking? Why didn't you tell us?" Baker shouted. Becker was whipped. "I never had any intention of having Miceli identified as the source," he said in a hushed voice. "I suffer from hubris."

The day after Becker's meeting with Brent Baker, Miceli, Becker, and Admiral Hekman were notified by Admiral Edney's flag lieutenant to report as soon as possible to Edney's Pentagon office. As the trio entered the sanctum of the Vice Chief of Naval Operations, they saw Brent Baker and Captain Harold Gehman, Edney's executive assistant. Gehman had a legal pad and was preparing to take notes. Edney was rabid over the publication of the "chemical bomb" story—not only because of the leak but also because Miceli could not prove that any kind of detonator was involved. "What the hell is going on?" Edney thundered. Everyone began trying to pin the blame on someone else.

Edney gruffly told Miceli that if he had any more brilliant ideas, he had better run them by Admiral Hekman before leaking them to George Wilson or any other reporter. Baker, Miceli, Becker, and Hekman left Edney's office with the distinct understanding that their careers were in limbo. During the short drive back to Crystal City in his government limousine, Hekman seethed. It was obvious that the admiral wasn't through with Becker. The next day, Becker was ordered to report to the office of Rear Admiral Malcolm MacKinnon, Admiral Hekman's chief deputy. Admiral MacKinnon informed Becker that he had been working too hard lately and was noticeably under strain. He told Becker to accompany the flag secretary downstairs. When Becker arrived on the ground floor, he was hustled from the lobby into a waiting staff car. Several sources said that a Marine sentry wearing a holstered .45-caliber pistol got into the back seat next to Becker, and that the driver, a lieutenant commander, sped away toward Bethesda Naval Hospital in Maryland. At Bethesda, Becker was ushered into a locked psychiatric ward, where he remained for three months.

Becker had not seen a psychiatrist or clinical psychologist prior to going to the hospital. No one from the Navy had consulted with his wife about the plan to commit him. Becker had no lengthy absences from work, or any unexplained long lunches. He had exhibited no irrational behavior and apparently only suffered from sleeplessness. Following his hospitalization, he was fired from his job at Sea Systems Command and later was medically discharged from the service. He was then hired by the Pentagon as a civilian public-affairs specialist.

22

☆

"I Wouldn't Classify It as Pooh-Poohing."

MIKE WALLACE HAD once done a story involving the Naval Investigative Service. While far from being laudatory, it was fair and balanced and was appreciated as such by Brian McKee, the civilian head of the agency. Mike called McKee and arranged for me to meet the men who ran NIS that afternoon at the Washington Navy Yard.

Seated around a rectangular table were Brian McKee; Robert Powers, the agency's chief of criminal investigations; Gary Cumberford, the public-affairs director; and Rear Admiral William Schachte, the NIS commanding officer. Admiral Schachte did most of the talking during the hour-long session, and it was apparent that he wasn't up to speed on the evidence. McKee and Powers frowned knowingly at each other whenever Schachte was off-target.

Schachte said the mere fact that Clayton Hartwig had drawn up a will was "strange." This statement was strange in itself, since the Navy encouraged everyone aboard a ship to have an up-to-date will before embarking upon a cruise. Schachte also found it peculiar that Hartwig would make Kendall Truitt the beneficiary of his life-insurance policy. I asked him how many other sailors on the *Iowa* had named friends as their beneficiaries. He said he had no idea, because NIS had only checked Hartwig's records. Hartwig was not a homosexual, nor was Kendall Truitt, he said, because an exhaustive investigation had cleared them.

Schachte said Hartwig's autopsy report confirmed that he was the gun captain and had been "peering into the breech" at the time of the explosion. He then bounced off the Richter scale of falsehood, stating, "They only recovered forty pounds of mush [Hartwig's body] and the rest of the casket was filled with about 180 pounds of sand." He claimed that his agents were distressed over the leaks, which had been "counterproductive." NIS had absolutely nothing to do with the leaks, he said, adding that the guilty party should be prosecuted.

MIKE WALLACE and I started our videotaped interviews in Norfolk with John Mullahy. The thirty-five-year-old gunner's mate described Clayton Hartwig as a rational, lucid, functional character. He recounted his fifty-minute conversation with Hartwig the night before the explosion in which Hartwig asked Mullahy for advice on what he should take to London when he went there on security duty. Mullahy said that when he joined the *Iowa*'s crew, he had heard rumors that Hartwig and Truitt were both gay, but that he later got to meet several of Hartwig's girlfriends. Telling about overhearing Errick Lawrence's last words from the center gun room on the sound-powered phones, he said that Lawrence didn't seem terrorized. "No panic in that turret. You heard no panic in that turret prior to the explosion?" Mike asked. "Not prior to the explosion. None," Mullahy replied. He told us about the "John Wayne Shoot" when Turret Two fired over Turret One, frightening everyone when the fireballs enveloped the forward turret.

Later, Mullahy discussed how defenseless he'd felt being six decks below the explosion. He told about rescuing three sailors trapped in a smoke-filled compartment and peeking inside the blazing powder flats to see if anyone in there were still alive. The men in there were all dead—either roasted alive or poisoned, or both. There was nothing that Mullahy could do, so he banged shut the armored hatch and fled. He talked about flooding the magazines to keep them from exploding, about administering first aid, about carrying to safety the damage-control officer who had been overcome by smoke, and about combing through the wreckage in the turret trying to recover the mangled bodies of his comrades.

Our next interviews took place in Miami with Kendall and Carole Truitt and their attorney, Ellis Rubin. As good an interview subject as John Mullahy had been, Kendall Truitt was better. He was more articulate. He had nothing but good to say about Clayton Hartwig. "He was a good guy. He didn't drink. I mean, we would go out and maybe have a daiquiri once in a while, but I mean, we wouldn't come back trashed like everybody else," Truitt said.

Truitt said that Chief Skelley's illegal experimentation with the D-846 powder and 2,700-pound projectiles was fraught with danger, because the fast-burning powder could build up too much pressure behind the shell and shatter the barrel. He took issue with Milligan's statement that Hartwig had been leaning over, staring into the breech at the time of the explosion. "Actually, when you ram powder, you don't have to bend over. You can stand there and you can look at it. You can see from every position in there. The rammerman can see how far it goes. The gun captain can see just by standing there."

Truitt said that the center gun's rammer had not functioned properly in almost a year and would often "take off" on its own at a high speed. He had seen that happen once when a projectile was unintentionally rammed. If powder had been present, an explosion would have resulted. Truitt said that he had told Admiral Milligan about the defective rammer.

After Mike finished interviewing Kendall and Carole Truitt, the crews turned the two cameras around, relit the room, and prepared to interview attorney Ellis Rubin. Rubin claimed the Navy had singled out Clayton Hartwig and Kendall Truitt because it needed scapegoats. The admirals didn't want to admit that the fifty-year-old battleship technology was obsolete and couldn't be safely modernized, or that Fred Moosally hadn't made sure that his crew was properly trained. The defense attorney flatly rejected the Navy's claims that it had discovered trace elements of a detonator under the rotating band. He said that since Captain Joseph Miceli's team hadn't maintained a proper chain of custody of the band, the trace elements could have been added later. Mike told Rubin that he was going to interview Admiral Schachte, commander of NIS, the next day. Was there anything Rubin wanted him to ask Schachte? Ask the admiral why NIS continued to make false statements to the media, said Rubin.

I TOLD Mike that we might have some difficulty getting Admiral Schachte to talk about leaks. The Inspector General of the Defense Department, June Gibbs Brown, had reported that it was possible that the leaks had come from NIS. However, she theorized that the leaks had originated from uniformed Navy sources who had been provided investigative material by NIS. "The leaks stopped when NIS stopped briefing Navy management and started again after dissemination of investigative reports," Brown wrote. I was sure that Schachte would hide behind the Brown report.

We arrived at NIS headquarters on a bright, warm Sunday afternoon in mid-October and were conducted to the same conference room on the second floor of the "Gun Factory" where I'd met with Admiral Schachte and his staff. The same cast of characters was present. During the half hour that it took the camera crews to set up their equipment and light the room, the atmosphere was strained. Later, I obtained a copy of the script that Schachte attempted to follow during the interview. Rear Admiral Brent Baker and his staff had drafted it. Baker later told me that Schachte had to memorize the script and undergo a "murder board" before he was allowed to go on-camera with Mike.

The admiral answered Mike's first few questions with scripted bromides. However, it didn't take long for Mike's go-for-the-jugular style of cross-examination to render Schachte's script worthless. Mike asked Schachte what Hartwig's motive was for blowing up the gun. "Mike, we don't know the answer to that," Schachte responded. "But if you don't know the answer, then how can you finger a man? You can't put a man in jail for life for murder unless you have a motive. And unless it's been proved in a court of law," Mike persisted. "Mike, we have got plenty, believe me, of evidence. Call it circumstantial evidence, but evidence as to what happened on that awful day," the NIS commander replied.

And then Mike caused Schachte to stumble. He had Schachte agree with Admiral Milligan's statements that by May 9, all natural causes for the explosion had been eliminated. Once Schachte agreed to that, Mike produced a copy of Captain Joseph Miceli's May 25 technical report, stating that friction was considered to be the most likely cause of the explosion. Schachte said that he was ignorant about the technical aspects of the investigation. Mike then reminded Schachte that as late as June 28, Miceli was still running tests to see if natural causes, such as friction and electronic emissions, had caused the blast. If every natural cause had really been eliminated by May 9, why was Miceli continuing to test more of them six weeks later? Schachte looked as if he had been bushwhacked, but he had no answer.

Mike changed the direction of his questioning. What was it in Hartwig's background that led NIS to conclude that he was a mass murderer? There was nothing particular that you could point to, Schachte said, adding that as a youth Hartwig had blown up stumps in his backyard with cherry bombs. Mike noted that it was "a long haul from blowing up stumps in your backyard to murdering forty-six friends."

Was Hartwig a homosexual? Schachte said NIS had no evidence that he was. Then why was it leaked that Hartwig was a homosexual? "Mike, the leaks were unfortunate," Schachte said haltingly. Where did the leaks come from? Schachte said he didn't know. How important was the FBI's equivocal death analysis? "It wasn't something that tipped the scale," the admiral replied. Would this case hold up in a court of law? Since he was an attorney, Schachte was cautious, saying that the Navy was not in a court of law. Mike asked again why the Navy was so convinced that Hartwig was guilty. "You have to look at the entire investigation, Mike," Schachte said. "I have! I have! And I'm still at a loss," Mike countered.

Was Schachte saying that Hartwig was suicidal? Yes, there was some evidence from witnesses about that. "But why?" Mike asked. He had spent time the night before the explosion chatting with John Mullahy about going to London. Schachte said Hartwig hadn't received those transfer orders yet. Mike said that Admiral Milligan had announced at his press conference that Hartwig was getting those orders to London. Was Schachte accusing Milligan of making a mistake? No, Schachte said, he was simply confused.

Mike asked the admiral if his agents had leaked information about Hartwig's and Truitt's alleged homosexuality to NBC correspondent Fred Francis. Schachte emphatically denied it, and then launched into an involved monologue about how well educated, how well trained, and how scrupulous his agents were. When Schachte finished, Mike shrugged and said we had interviewed a source who said that "active-duty NIS agents" had provided confidential material to NBC and other organizations. This source described some of the NIS agents as "homophobic paranoids," who went so far as to describe to our source the exact model of the electronic timer that NIS claimed Hartwig used to blow up the turret. Was this person lying to us? Schachte told Mike to give him the name of our source and NIS would check him out. Mike snorted and said we had no intention of turning over any of our sources to NIS.

Our cameraman, Bob Peterson, displayed the picture of Clayton Hartwig dressed as the captain of *The Love Boat* on a monitor we had brought especially for this purpose. Mike said this picture had been taken when Hartwig was sixteen. Had Schachte ever dressed up and gone to a costume party like these three young men had? Schachte said that he had. Then why was NIS using this old picture as evidence that Hartwig was a homosexual mass murderer? The picture was just one of many things that NIS had collected, Schachte responded.

Had NIS agents ever engaged in so-called pressure tactics? Never, Schachte asserted. Well, how did he account for David Smith's recanting his testimony, claiming that he had been coerced by NIS agents into giving it in the first place? Schachte denied that any pressure had ever been put on Smith. Did Schachte consider Smith to be a credible witness? He wasn't sure. Mike returned to the subject of leaks. How could Fred Francis imply in his news reports that Hartwig and Truitt were homosexuals if he hadn't been leaked NIS documents on a silver platter? Schachte dodged behind the Pentagon Inspector General's report, saying he was pleased that NIS had been given "such a clean bill of health on this thing [leaks]."

Schachte told Mike there was "no substance" to claims by Jack Thompson's family in Tennessee that Turret Two was a "death trap." Mike said we had talked to members of the Thompson family, who said that NIS agents had visited them twice, employing "strong-arm tactics," harassing them, and warning them not to talk about Jack's statements that the *Iowa* was an unsafe ship. According to the Thompsons, NIS seemed "more interested in hushing up the information about the accident than in investigating." Schachte said that wasn't true.

Mike said we had submitted Clayton Hartwig's autopsy report to two independent forensic pathologists, who ridiculed the Navy's opinion that Hartwig was peering into the breech at the time of his death. Schachte said he remained satisfied with the findings of the Armed Forces Institute of Pathology. Why had so many sailors died of cyanide poisoning? Schachte was caught unaware. He knew nothing about cyanide. Mike asked Schachte if the Navy was claiming that Clayton Hartwig had been insane. The Navy would never know the answer to that question, Schachte said. If you don't have a motive, how could the Chief of Naval Operations send such a heartbreaking letter to Earl and Evelyn Hartwig, telling them that their only son had killed himself and murdered forty-six colleagues? "Mike, we know an awful lot. We know an awful lot," Schachte replied. "Well, then tell us about it," Mike demanded. "I can assure you, we had no ax to grind! We had no motivation other than—any of us—other than finding out what happened!" Schachte said, his voice cracking.

"I've talked with a high-ranking Pentagon official, who told me that he believes that this was a conspiracy and a cover-up at the highest levels of the Navy. He said it involved collusion among NIS, the Navy, the Chief of Naval Information, and many high-ranking naval officials," Mike said. "Now these are hard charges, especially coming from an individual with considerable naval background." "I totally disagree! I couldn't disagree more with anything I've ever heard in my life!" retorted Schachte. Was there anything else the admiral wanted to say before we turned off the lights and cameras? No, he said. Mike asked the other NIS representatives in the room if they'd like to sit down and say something on-camera. There were no takers.

WHILE WE were working on our story, Robert Zelnick and Mark Brender of ABC News continued trying to prove that the Navy's case against Clayton Hartwig was irreparably flawed. Zelnick devoted a great deal of time to trying to discredit the FBI's equivocal death analysis and the NIS psychological autopsy. He and Brender were aided by Dr. Douglas Jacobs, professor of psychiatry at Harvard Medical School and director of the Suicide Education Institute of Boston. In Jacobs's opinion, for the federal investigators to conclude that Hartwig had intentionally caused the explosion, they had to demonstrate not only that he was suicidal but also that he was homicidal. After examining the case files, Jacobs concluded that there was no evidence to support either conclusion. He faulted the FBI and NIS profilers for not conducting their own interviews and for relying exclusively upon secondhand data.

Jacobs said the FBI and NIS had been wrong in saying that Hartwig had low self-esteem. He described the twenty-four-year-old sailor as a romantic and said Hartwig's letters in the last month of his life didn't reveal any of the following symptoms associated with a suicidal person: turmoil, hopelessness, helplessness, anger, frustration, depression, psychosis, or confusion. According to Jacobs, Hartwig's letters were the best available evidence of his mental stability. The Harvard psychiatrist scolded the profilers for utilization of the observations of Hartwig's mental state by nonprofessionals as conclusions; an overemphasis on the subject of homosexuality; the inability to find a clear motivation for suicide; the lack of evidence of psychotic behavior in which murder/suicide can occur. Jacobs stated, "Finally, there is an implication that Clayton Hartwig killed himself and others to achieve the power and recognition that he felt he lacked. Clayton Hartwig's ego-ideal was connected with the Navy. Unless there is unequivocal evidence that Clayton

Hartwig felt betrayed by the Navy, the hypothesis of the NIS report is invalid." He said the FBI should have assigned a clinically trained "suicidologist" to the case.

Zelnick also contacted Dr. David Trachtenberg, a prominent psychiatrist practicing in Montgomery County, Maryland, outside of Washington. In Dr. Trachtenberg's opinion, Clayton Hartwig was "a slightly immature young man," but there was nothing in the Navy documents to suggest any existing or developing mental disorder or derangement. "I found no evidence of preexisting or developing depression, mania, paranoia, or schizophrenia," he said. Hartwig's correspondence indicated "a young man of general good spirits, proud of his ship, proud of the Navy."

Trachtenberg methodically dismantled the NIS psychological autopsy and the FBI's equivocal death analysis of Hartwig. He thought it was perfectly normal for a gunner's mate on a battleship to be interested in firearms, explosives, and naval warfare. As for Hartwig's affinity for *Soldier of Fortune* magazine, Dr. Trachtenberg said that many normal young men read that publication. NIS thought it bizarre that Hartwig aspired to become a police officer or FBI agent. "I know a lot of nice people who want to be in the FBI or even a police officer," the psychiatrist said. He spurned the notion that Hartwig's collections of model ships, guns, and military books and videotapes meant "that he had a fantasy life that went far beyond the realities of his true life." He said this was characteristic behavior for young men in Hartwig's age-group who were members of the armed forces. "There is no evidence that Hartwig suffered from anything even close to the degree of disease, disorder, or derangement that would precipitate so extreme an act of violence, not only against himself, but against his own shipmates and against the Navy of which he seemed so proud," Trachtenberg concluded.

Zelnick furnished a summary of the Jacobs and Trachtenberg analyses to staff investigators Warren Nelson and Bill Fleshman of the House Armed Services Committee, suggesting that the two psychiatrists might make compelling witnesses at future *Iowa* hearings. Nelson and Fleshman accepted Zelnick's invitation and did him one better. In addition to using Doctors Jacobs and Trachtenberg, they contacted the American Psychological Association and asked that a panel of nationally recognized mental-health experts be assembled to evaluate the government's psychological profiles of Clayton Hartwig. Fourteen professionals in the fields of forensic psychology, suicidology, and neuropsychology soon set about determining how fair, accurate, and scientifically valid the NIS and FBI profiles had been. Although four of the professionals believed the murder/suicide theory was plausible, ten of fourteen professional psychologists contradicted the equivocal death analysis, and all fourteen criticized the technique as being "too speculative."

Zelnick and his producer, Mark Brender, were also working for my competition, the ABC newsmagazine *20/20*, and I had distinctly mixed feelings about that. I left CBS News in 1978 to help found that show, and I had remained there almost eleven years. I had been back at CBS less than a year. I called Mike Wallace and told him about *20/20*. He didn't seem very concerned, telling me to put together the best piece I could. The two broad casts would probably complement each other and have more impact, he predicted.

JOHN HALL continued to pursue the *Iowa* story after he had finished writing his four-part series on illegal experiments, broken equipment, untrained crewmen, unstable powder, and a cockeyed investigation. Hall wrote a column bearing the headline, "Navy Could Have Admiral Kafka." "The government has trapped a dead sailor in an intricate web of shifting facts, inspired leaks, and guesswork," Hall wrote. "This case would inspire another chapter of *The Trial* on the absurdity of individual powerlessness against the apparatus of authority."

Hall scolded the Navy for leaking the "chemical bomb" theory to George Wilson. "No matter what evidence is brought to the Navy, its answer is the same. The ship was being used for unauthorized and dangerous high explosive tests. The ship was undermanned. Its crew was poorly trained. Its officers were negligent. Its equipment was nearly a half-century old and some of it in poor repair." The Navy didn't deny these charges, he wrote, but rather it claimed that none of these abnormalities caused the explosion. The Navy was so out of control that the Inspector General's report on leaks was leaked so that NIS could put out its own spin on the report. "Kafka couldn't have conjured up such a nightmare for a dead man in a land of inalienable rights."

Through persistence, Hall's partner, Steve Goldberg, got the FBI's top administrators to turn on the Navy and reveal that its laboratory had failed to find any evidence that an electronic device was involved in the *Iowa* explosion. That was a major breakthrough, because until then, the Navy had staunchly insisted that the FBI's tests were merely "inconclusive."

Goldberg teamed up with John Hall to write a nationally syndicated story that caused an uproar on Capitol Hill with the House and Senate committees investigating the *Iowa*, with other journalists, and with every one of the families of the forty-seven men who died in Turret Two—because it caught the Navy in a blatant lie.

BY SIMPLY reporting the facts, Hall and Goldberg and dozens of other journalists turned editorial opinion against the Navy for botching the *Iowa* case. The *Plain Dealer* in Cleveland ran a cartoon of an admiral staring at a piece of paper stamped, "USS *Iowa* Investigation." Behind him was a picture of the Navy's official mascot, "the Scapegoat." Spread around the admiral were such farcical causes for the explosion as: "The Japanese did it in a sneak attack that went unnoticed"; "The cleaning woman did it"; "The son of Captain Queeg did it"; "It was done by the crew to prevent Bob Hope from entertaining them"; "Whoever it was will be on the *Oprah Winfrey Show*." Another cartoon, which appeared in the *Baltimore Sun*, showed a seedy mob of print and television reporters attempting to interview a tombstone engraved HARTWIG. One newsman holding a microphone demanded, "Seaman Hartwig, how do you respond to charges that you blew up a gun turret on the USS *Iowa*, killing forty-six sailors in order to kill yourself?"

AS THE heat increased on the Navy in editorial pages around the country, and on Capitol Hill, where the House and Senate Armed Services Committees were nearly ready for their *Iowa* hearings, I kept expecting my phone to ring and to have Admiral Brent Baker inform me that Mike Wallace's interview with Admiral Milligan had been canceled. But that call never came.

It was essential during the interview to have Admiral Milligan compare his investigation with a legal proceeding. Once he did that, Mike could ask Milligan if he thought his evidence could survive the challenges it would undoubtedly be subjected to in either a military or a civilian court of law. Was Milligan's evidence convincing enough to secure a first-degree murder indictment?

Milligan wasn't an attorney, and he had a reputation for arrogance. He might just take the bait. Brent Baker and his deputy, Captain Gordon Peterson, greeted us as we entered the Pentagon. They took us to the room where the interview would take place. Admiral Milligan was there, as well as Admiral Edney. The Vice Chief of Naval Operations announced that before the interview could proceed, he, Milligan, and Baker had to talk to Mike in private. Producers and researchers were excluded.

Baker later said that Edney was well aware that television newsmagazine producers did most of the research and writing, and the correspondent depended on them for the details of the story. Separate Mike Wallace from his support staff, and Edney thought he might be able to fluster Mike and peddle the Navy's version of the tragedy. After about twenty minutes, Mike, the three admirals, and their aides emerged.

"You'll find that he's [Hartwig] a very troubled individual, very much a loner, a man who had few principal friendships throughout his life, very limited numbers at one time, and was very depressed on the loss of those friendships," Milligan said. "He was a man who was not financially well off at all. He's a man who talked of suicide to four individual witnesses." "When? Where?" Mike asked. Milligan said that Hartwig had made a suicide "gesture" in high school. Where did he obtain that information? Milligan said it came from some witnesses "back in the Cleveland area."

Did the admiral know what kind of device had been used to ignite the powder bags in Turret Two? Milligan said he had no idea. Was he aware that Captain Joseph Miceli, his technical-investigation director, had told Senate investigators that a "Brylcreem bomb" was the most likely detonator? That was Miceli's personal opinion, Milligan said. Was he aware that Miceli had also bragged that the Navy's lab in Crane, Indiana, would soon be able to tell precisely which manufacturing lot the Brylcreem came from? Milligan seemed offended and repeated what he had said earlier—that it was Miceli's personal opinion.

Did he have any idea when Hartwig found out he was going to be gun captain? Milligan said nobody knew for sure, because all the witnesses died in the explosion. Mike next sprang the legal trap, asking, "Do you think that the case the Navy makes against Hartwig would be sufficient to obtain a criminal indictment against Clayton Hartwig?" "Personally, yes," he replied. Brent Baker grimaced, squirming in his chair. The Navy's public-affairs chief knew that Milligan had leapt into the lion's den. "You do?" Mike asked. "Yes, I think the case that we have in this investigation is very solid. I think the evidence is there. The findings and facts and opinions support the conclusion," Milligan stated.

"At best, this is a circumstantial case that you're talking about, and yet you say that you believe that you could get a criminal indictment against him. It is circumstantial. You have no witnesses," Mike said. Milligan agreed with Mike, but he claimed that Hartwig had "the opportunity to commit the crime."

Why had Milligan made such an issue out of the practical-joke book at his press conference? Because there was one dirty trick in the book involving fireworks and electrical light bulbs. Mike handed him the joke book and asked the admiral to locate the offensive prank. Milligan flipped to pages 86 and 87. Headlined, "Explosives," the pages apprised the potential prankster to first "gently" break the glass on a large-watt light bulb. Mike took the book back from Milligan and read, "Do not disturb the filament. Even more gently attached to the filament is the fuse of the M-80 [a large firecracker]. Screw the bulb carefully back into a ceiling socket. Finally, move a bag of feces up and around the light fixture. Be certain the fuse and the filament do not touch the feces." All of us, even Brent Baker and the other naval officers present in the room, struggled not to laugh. Milligan didn't crack a smile. Didn't the admiral think that equating a "doo-doo bomb" to the sabotage of a gun turret was a bit farfetched? Mike inquired. That irony went right over Milligan's head. He stiffly replied that since the joke book was "irrelevant to his [Hartwig's] job as a gunner's mate," he had no business keeping it in his locker on the battleship.

Mike said the Navy leaks had emotionally crippled the Hartwig family and traumatized Kendall Truitt and his wife, Carole. "When I tell people I'm doing a story about the *Iowa*, they say, 'You mean about the homosexual?' " Milligan pointed out that his official report made no mention of homosexuality. Mike said we had interviewed a source who told us that the rumor about Hartwig and Truitt being gay had been leaked to him by NIS agents. "I cannot confirm that. I have no idea," Milligan said. "I wish I did know where it came from." Mike said Representative Mary Rose Oakar claimed that Milligan had "pooh-poohed" the account by Jack Thompson's family that Turret Two had been "modified into a death trap." "I wouldn't classify it as pooh-poohing," Milligan replied.

Mike asked about Captain Fred Moosally's testimony that the *Iowa* was filled with dopers, marginal performers, and men who constantly took unauthorized absences? Milligan took issue with the *Iowa* captain, saying that the battleship was manned with a "very positive crew." Percentage-wise, the vessel didn't have any more drug addicts than any other ship in the Navy. He said that there had not been an accident aboard the *Iowa* in February, overlooking the "John Wayne Shoot." Why did Milligan think there was such skepticism of his investigation by the press and in the Congress? It was due to his taking an unpopular position. The easy solution would have been to say, "We don't know what happened." His conscience, however, wouldn't let him do that. But Milligan had no fingerprints, nothing tangible, no scientific evidence to support his murder accusations against Hartwig, Mike said. Milligan ended the interview by saying, "Mike, there is no other cause of this accident. We have looked at everything. We've ruled out everything. We conducted a thorough investigation, and it all comes together to the only conclusion that I could and I did make, and that's the one that you're well aware of. This was a deliberate act, most likely done by Petty Officer Hartwig."

DAVID SMITH had recently been discharged from the Navy and was working as a security guard for IBM in Maryland. He agreed to come to our office after work and be interviewed by Mike. Smith told Mike about eating breakfast with Hartwig the morning of the explosion and being edgy about participating in his first gun shoot. He was also apprehensive that the Tomahawk experiment would take place and the *Iowa* would be clobbered by a missile. Hartwig told Smith that the turret's thick armor would protect him. Smith said he knew nothing about how the explosion occurred. Even so, two NIS agents accused him of withholding information and told him that if he didn't swear that Hartwig had constructed a detonator, he would be charged with forty-seven counts of accessory to murder, as well as perjury and obstruction of justice.

Smith denied that he'd ever seen a Radio Shack electronic timer in Hartwig's locker, and he also said that Hartwig had never made homosexual advances toward him. He admitted that he had provided false testimony against Hartwig, only because he was bullied by the NIS agents and had been deprived of sleep for several days. He also told Mike that after the *Iowa* returned to Norfolk, he had been assigned to help extract the shell stuck in Turret Two's center gun. Several gunner's mates poked wire brushes into the barrel and scoured out the rifling. "There was all kinds of dirt. There was all kinds of debris in there. I don't honestly think any foreign material would have come from a detonating device," Smith said. Mike asked whether Clayton Hartwig had ever told him that he was going to blow up the turret. Certainly not, Smith replied.

The only person that we still wanted to interview before completing our piece was Clayton's father, Earl Hartwig. Earl and Mike, who got along well when they met, had several things in common. They were reasonably close in age and both had served in the Navy during World War II. Mike asked Earl to describe Clayton. Earl said that Clayton was a normal boy who had been educated in Seventh-Day Adventist schools, enjoyed camping, and had many school friends, He added, "And his biggest thing in life was enlisting in the Navy."

Earl denied that his son was a "loner" but said that Clayton would "sooner read a book or listen to music" than play with the neighborhood kids. Mike asked about Clayton's low self-esteem, often mentioned by Admiral Milligan. Earl said that was drivel, because Clayton knew what he wanted and went out and got it. Was Clayton depressed? "I've never seen the boy depressed," Earl said. From his own days aboard a warship, Earl said he knew that if his son had been psychotic, somebody would have noticed and reported it.

Did Clayton ever discuss committing suicide with Earl? "As his father for twenty-four years, I've never heard the boy say anything about suicide or do anything that would look like he's attempting to end his life or anything," Earl said. Why did Earl think the Navy seemed so determined to blame his dead son? "Four battleships that are on the line would be the main reason, because if they found them defective, I don't think the government would support an antiquated piece of equipment that may kill hundreds of other people down the line," he said. "They had to have a scapegoat, and that was the bottom line."

What was Clayton's opinion about the *Iowa*? "He loved the *Iowa*. And he was proud of her," Earl said. Clayton had taken him on several tours of Turret Two, showing him the center gun room, the mechanical and electrical decks, the projectile decks, and the powder flats. Did Earl find it strange that Clayton had made Kendall Truitt the beneficiary of his life-insurance policy? No, he said, it was a fairly common practice during World War II. Buddies would sign their policies over to each other, because they didn't believe they were going to die.

Earl said that Kathy's letters about the insurance policy had focused the investigation on Clayton. Once Kathy's letters were turned over to Admiral

Milligan, he sent NIS agents all over the country, "checking about the insurance policy and the gay part of it." Earl said NIS had done much worse things than spreading false rumors about his son's sex life. Agents had also gone to the Norfolk Police Department and other Virginia law-enforcement agencies seeking unsolved bombings and murders they could tie to Clayton and Kendall. They were unsuccessful, but they stirred up more malicious gossip.

23

"It's Bad. It's Worse Than I Thought."

THE VOICE ON the other end of the telephone was agitated. The caller gave his name as "Navy Captain Pete Frank." Somewhat melodramatically, he said, "The *Iowa* whitewash continues." According to "Captain Frank," a selection board composed of thirteen flag officers had just met and unanimously voted that the *Iowa*'s skipper, Captain Fred Moosally, was "superbly fit" to receive another major command, such as a squadron of destroyers. Although Moosally's selection didn't mean that he would automatically become an admiral, he couldn't be considered for that rank without the blessing of this board.

His selection occurred just two weeks after Vice Admiral Joseph Donnell, commander of Surface Forces Atlantic, had flown out to the Mediterranean and handed Moosally a "letter of admonition" for dereliction of duty, because he had failed to train his crew or to ensure that they obeyed safety regulations. If what "Captain Frank" told me was true, then Moosally's selection was certainly irregular, but the caller claimed that something even more inappropriate had occurred. One of the thirteen senior officers who had voted for Moosally was none other than Rear Admiral Richard Milligan. In his final *Iowa* report, Milligan had recommended that Vice Admiral Donnell or Admiral Powell Carter, commander of the Atlantic Fleet, relieve Moosally as the *Iowa*'s commanding officer. That recommendation had been vetoed by Donnell.

Because what "Captain Frank" said was so alien to everything I had learned in the Navy about the accountability of captains of naval vessels, I was cautious and asked him how I could confirm the selection-board results. He gave me the name and telephone number of a personnel captain who was responsible for assigning surface officers to billets. After that, he hung up.

I made several calls to the Pentagon to see if there really was a "Captain Pete Frank" and was able to determine that there was no officer with that rank and name in the Navy. Then I called the Chief of Naval Information. Brent Baker wanted to know if I planned to include the selection board's handling of Moosally in our story. We hadn't decided, I said, emphasizing that the information I was seeking was "time-sensitive." I expected either a confirmation or a denial from him within two hours. I next called Vice Admiral Boorda, the Chief of Naval Personnel. Boorda wasn't available, but his public-affairs officer listened to what I had to say and promised a speedy reply. The personnel captain whose name I had been given by "Captain Frank" refused to talk with me. An hour after I'd talked to Baker, he called back, confirming everything. "It happened. It was an error. Moosally's name has been withdrawn," Baker said, adding that Milligan had voted for Moosally. Shortly after that, Boorda's assistant called, confirming Baker's account.

THAT SAME evening, ABC's *20/20* opened its broadcast with correspondent Tom Jarriel and producer Martin Clancy's *Iowa* piece, entitled, "Convicted in the Grave." Correspondent Jarriel asked Milligan if the Navy had any investigation underway to determine "who was leaking this slander on this man [Hartwig]." "None that I'm aware of," Milligan replied. Jarriel assailed the admiral for relying on the FBI's equivocal death analysis, saying, "Equivocal, as I understand it, means two or more possible interpretations." Milligan didn't put up an argument. "So it's not worth much?" Jarriel asked. "The fact that it was an equivocal analysis was considered," Milligan said. "In the Navy, would a Navy officer ever fire at an equivocal target?" Jarriel baited. "I'm not sure I understand the question," Milligan replied. Jarriel said the equivocal death analysis seemed to be important in this case, because the Navy had essentially staked its reputation on the controversial procedure. It had destroyed the reputation of a dead sailor, using "an equivocal report backed up by circumstantial evidence." "Backed up by the evidence of the entire investigation," Milligan responded. Jarriel ended the piece by saying that Pentagon sources had informed ABC News that the Navy had an institutional stake in seeing an individual blamed rather than faulting the weapon or the gunpowder.

TWO NIGHTS later, our *60 Minutes* piece aired. The report was constructed around the following exchange between Mike Wallace and Admiral Milligan: "Do you think that the case that the Navy makes against Hartwig would be sufficient to obtain a criminal indictment against Clayton Hartwig?" "Personally, yes." "You do?" "Yes, I think the case that we have in this investigation is very solid." If Admiral Milligan really had enough hard evidence to obtain a criminal indictment, Mike pointed out, he should have reasonable answers to four questions. What was Hartwig's motive? Did he have the opportunity to blow up the gun? What method did he employ? And finally, was the explosion a criminal act at all, or was it an accident? Mike stated that the Navy did not know Hartwig's motive; his opportunity to sabotage the gun was debatable; the Navy could not explain the method he used; and there was abundant evidence that the explosion was an accident. "If you have the most flimsy, circumstantial, so-called evidence pinpointing this young man as having done this ill deed, and he's not here to defend himself, it's the family against the United States Navy," Representative Mary Rose Oakar said.

The day after our piece ran, Brent Baker expedited copies of it and the *20/20* piece to Captain Fred Moosally on the *Iowa*. Baker also sent Moosally a three-page message, saying that neither broadcast had any real impact. He offered to send public-relations specialists out to the battleship to brief her crew on what to expect from the news media when they returned to Norfolk at the end of the six-month deployment. Although he appreciated Baker's offer, Moosally felt public-relations training was a luxury he couldn't afford at the time. He had a much more pressing matter with which to deal. A team from the General Accounting Office (GAO) was on its way to the *Iowa* to observe her firing her sixteen-inch guns. If this gun shoot didn't go smoothly, the *Iowa* and her three sister battleships could be headed back to the boneyards from which they emerged in the early 1980s.

In late November, the two GAO investigators, Tim Stone and Jerry Hurley, arrived on the *Iowa* with Captain Joseph Miceli to spend several days aboard the battleship and watch her fire twelve rounds into the ocean. Stone, a former Army artilleryman, and Hurley, a former naval gunnery officer, were well informed about the Navy's continuing troubles with its sixteen-inch gunpowder.

Chief Skelley explained to the GAO representatives that the ship would fire two rounds from each gun in Turrets One and Three. The 1,900-pound high-explosive shells would be propelled by six powder bags. No experimentation was allowed. Everything had to be by-the-book. Skelley would be aiming at a patch of ocean 20,000 yards away from the ship. He would use radar to tell him where the shells splashed, and he would score as a hit any shell that impacted within sixty-five yards of the "target." Dan Meyer and Dale Mortensen's forward turret would fire first. Stone and Hurley hurried up to the bridge to observe the firing of the first six shells. Turret One was told to load three rounds, but there was an extended delay. Captain Moosally became petulant. Some of the sailors who had been on the bridge on the day of the explosion were overwhelmed by a sickening feeling of déjà vu. Finally, one of the men wearing sound-powered phones informed the captain that the forward turret was experiencing mechanical difficulties.

Without speaking to anyone, Captain Joseph Miceli left the bridge. He emerged on the starboard side of the main deck, walking past Turret Two. He crouched under the rear of Turret One and rapped loudly on the sealed tail hatch, seeking entry. A gunner's mate lowered the hatch, and Miceli climbed into the turret officer's booth. The turret was darkened except for pools of light supplied by battery-powered "battle lanterns."

Miceli asked Meyer and Mortensen what the problem was, and they told him that the master circuit board on the electrical deck had shorted out. They said this happened periodically. The circuit board, which had been installed during World War II, was too brittle to withstand the crushing pressure created by the booming sixteen-inch guns. Back in the early 1940s, this flaw had been understood, and the Navy had intended to replace the circuit boards in all three turrets just as soon as wartime shortages eased, but somewhere along the line, that plan had been shelved. Without the master circuit board, the turret had no power to train or elevate the guns, lift the shells and powder up to the gun rooms, or operate the sprinklers and firefighting hoses.

Miceli was aghast. He couldn't tell Stone and Hurley or Fred Moosally that Turret One was out of action. "We have to impress our visitors. We can't have them thinking there are any problems with the guns," Miceli said. Meyer said he had seen a circuit board jump started in Turret Three. He reached for the phone to the bridge to talk to the weapons officer. Miceli stopped him. He ordered Mortensen to jump start the circuit board, even though this order violated safety regulations. Mortensen slipped on a pair of rubber gloves, picked up some alligator clips, and headed down to the electrical deck. He could have used a helper, but he didn't want any of his sailors to see him violating safety regulations. Or, in the event he electrocuted himself, he didn't want any witnesses. Mortensen knew that the concussion of the guns might cause the alligator clips to become unfastened and the circuit board to short out again. If that happened, the following were distinct possibilities: (1) A shell in the hoist or bags of powder could free fall and detonate; (2) the turret could rotate to the right, fire, and tear up the superstructure; (3) the turret could swing to the left and shear off the bow; (4) a fire could start inside the turret, and the crew would be powerless to extinguish it.

Once Mortensen had finished jury-rigging the circuit board, Miceli had Dan Meyer inform the bridge that Turret One was ready to load. Only one of Turret One's six shells actually struck the "target." Two more dropped within sixty yards, making them "hits" in Chief Skelley's book. Five of Turret Three's shells went far afield, but one plunged forty yards from the "target." Stone and Hurley entered Turret One during a break to observe the crewmen loading and firing the last three rounds. Once the exercise was completed and Miceli returned to the bridge, Mortensen told the two GAO representatives that Miceli had ordered him illegally to jury-rig the circuit board so the gun shoot could proceed. Stone and Hurley were impressed with Mortensen's integrity and technical skills, and they asked the Navy to assign him to their team. The Navy agreed. "Nobody ever questioned Mortensen's abilities. He was a very good source to us," Hurley said. Stone and Hurley subsequently told the Senate Armed Services Committee staffers that Miceli was untrustworthy and had shown reckless disregard for the safety of Turret One's gun crews.

As THE House and Senate Armed Services Committee hearings on the *Iowa* drew near, Rowan Scarborough of the *Washington Times* made life disagreeable for the Navy's public-relations staff. Scarborough had been talking with Kathy Kubicina on a regular basis since early September. He also chatted with John Mullahy. Kathy and the former *Iowa* sailor told Scarborough about the looting that had occurred in Turret Two's berthing compartment while the fires raged and before the bodies had been removed from the devastated turret. Kathy also gave Scarborough a copy of a letter sent to her by Ensign Ephraim Garrett, who had been in Turret One when the explosion rocked the battleship. Garrett had written, "You are correct that there was looting while the damage control efforts were ongoing on 19 April." He also said that those who had been caught looting had either been disciplined by Captain Moosally at mast or had received special court-martials.

Scarborough located other references to the looting in the NIS reports. One sailor was quoted as saying the masters-at-arms (ship's police) had arrested an individual for breaking into the lockers of the deceased men. Two parents of dead sailors, Robert Gedeon and Nancy Jo Lewis, told Scarborough that they had been informed by men still on the *Iowa* that the looting had definitely occurred. Before writing his story, Scarborough asked the Navy for a comment. "It is absolutely false," said Lieutenant Commander Craig Quigley, who worked for Rear Admiral Brent Baker. "There was nobody caught. There was no break-in. There was no evidence of looting."

Because plundering a dead shipmate's personal property was so inimical to the Navy's public image, Scarborough's story caused an uproar in the Chief of Naval Information's office. Admiral Baker's deputies wasted no time attacking the story and challenging Scarborough's veracity. "There is no record whatsoever of any tampering with crew lockers. There was no one seen in the berthing area. There was nothing strewn around the crew quarters," Lieutenant Commander Quigley said. He went so far as to deny that the NIS interviews of *Iowa* personnel confirming the looting were accurate. During the same time that Brent Baker's staff was bad-mouthing Scarborough, Baker sent a message to Fred Moosally inquiring about the looting. Baker said his staff had labeled Scarborough's story as being totally false, based on information provided by Admirals Donnell and Milligan. "I am now told that a flat denial might not be correct," Baker added. Moosally agreed with Baker.

A MONTH after our *60 Minutes* piece ran, a large volume of mail—the majority of it from Navy veterans—continued to pour into our New York office, protesting the Navy's treatment of Clayton Hartwig. I called Admiral Snyder and read him some of the letters. He said he had obtained some archival material for me and would give it to me the next morning when he gave me a ride to the office. As I got in the front seat of Admiral Snyder's diesel-powered Volkswagen, he dropped a thick, crumbling legal folder on my lap. "What's that?" I asked. He said it contained the transcripts of the courts of inquiry into the 1924 and 1943 explosions in Turret Two aboard the battleship USS *Mississippi*. Admiral Milligan and some of the Navy's public-relations officers had been insisting that the two *Mississippi* disasters were totally different from the *Iowa* blast. Admiral Snyder located the *Mississippi* files so we could see for ourselves.

In the admiral's opinion, the most significant piece of paper in the folder was the final endorsement signed by the Chief of the Bureau of Ordnance General regarding the 1943 accident in the Pacific. The chief had written that the explosion in the fourteen-inch gun that killed forty-three men and injured twenty others probably resulted from friction generated by the rammer shoving bags of powder over loose grains of propellant. In late May 1989, Captain Joseph Miceli's technical team had reached virtually the same conclusion about the *Iowa*, concluding that friction was the most likely cause. However, there was one crucial difference between the 1943 and 1989 incidents. The *Mississippi*'s center gun in Turret Two had been "hot"—meaning that twelve rounds had already been fired from the weapon, and the crew was in the process of loading round number thirteen when a fireball spewed from the breech. The *Iowa*'s center gun in Turret Two, on the other hand, had been "cold"—meaning that it had not been fired. Hot gases and burning debris in the *Mississippi*'s gun barrel may have been contributory factors, while that was not so in the *Iowa* mishap.

When asked about the relevance of the *Mississippi* disasters, one of the Navy's public-relations officers said he wasn't sure whether the Navy had even looked at the *Mississippi* court of inquiry records while contemplating the cause of the *Iowa* explosion. But in his opinion, the *Mississippi* inquiry, completed in 1944, was not applicable. "I think our investigative techniques, our investigative equipment have far advanced since 1944. We looked at the friction aspect, and it was ruled out. The techniques and the equipment used have advanced immensely since 1944," he said. But in response to a follow-up question, the officer expostulated, "How do you get friction? You rub things together."

DURING THE late fall of 1989 and early winter of 1990, a hard-nosed Navy flag officer painstakingly reviewed certain aspects of the *Iowa* disaster. Rear Admiral Ming Chang, the Navy's Inspector General, had been ordered by the Chief of Naval Operations to look into the unauthorized gunnery experiments that had taken place aboard the *Iowa*. Like many other detectives, Admiral Chang became intrigued by details outside his mandate and began looking into areas already explored by Admiral Milligan. Chang questioned the competence of most of the Navy's laboratories and test facilities to produce the kind of precise data that Milligan required to arrive at his verdict. Early in his inquiry, Chang curtly told Milligan and Captain Miceli, "I can't believe the Chief of Naval Operations signed off on this garbage [their *Iowa* report]."

The highest-ranking Asian-American in the Navy, Chang had known both Milligan and Miceli for two decades. He had been the commander of Cruiser/Destroyer Group Two, which was patrolling off the Lebanese coast when Milligan arrived in the fall of 1983 aboard the battleship *New Jersey*. Chang was aware of the *New Jersey*'s ineffectual gunnery in Lebanon. For that reason alone, he felt that Milligan should never have been assigned to head an investigation in which faulty gunpowder was an issue.

And the Inspector General thought Miceli was a poor choice to be technical director. Before becoming Inspector General, Chang had been in charge of development and procurement of the Navy's weapons at Sea Systems Command, and as such, he had been Miceli's superior. He thought that Miceli had botched the bagging of the sixteen-inch gunpowder when the four *Iowa*-class battleships were recommissioned in the early 1980s, when Miceli had commanded the Naval Weapons Support Center in Crane. The Inspector General asked Miceli to conduct more tests to see if friction had ignited the *Iowa*'s powder, and Miceli flatly refused.

Chang and his staff, consisting of one captain and four commanders, flew to the Mediterranean to take sworn testimony from Chief Skelley and the *Iowa*'s senior officers. Chang's reputation preceded him, and officers in the battleship's wardroom talked in cowed terms about the arrival of "Ming the Merciless." Once aboard the *Iowa*, Chang's staff started with Skelley. The master chief fire controlman provided the names of four civilians who worked at naval weapons facilities and assisted him with his unauthorized experiments. Skelley said that similar experiments had taken place on the ship in November 1987, when Captain Larry Seaquist was commanding officer. Captain Fred Moosally swore that he was unaware that Skelley and the ship's former gunnery officer, Lieutenant Commander Costigan, planned to conduct illegal experiments on the day of the explosion. Commander Kissinger, the ship's weapons officer, testified that he knew about the powder experiments but had failed to inform the captain.

When Chang and his staff returned to Norfolk, they questioned Lieutenant Commander Costigan, the *Iowa*'s former gunnery officer. Costigan said the experiments were designed to gather "range data" for the technicians at Dahlgren; the information was of "no use" to the crew of the *Iowa*. Costigan confirmed that he didn't obtain permission from Captain Moosally before scheduling the experiments.

Chang interviewed a number of civilian technicians who helped facilitate Skelley's unauthorized projects. John McEachren, the ordnance specialist with Sea Systems Command, said the experiments had been discussed at the Battleship Gunnery Improvement Conferences in 1988 and 1989 in Crystal City, Virginia. However, he said the officers and enlisted men at those conferences had been informed that firing less than six-bag loads had not been approved by the Chief of Naval Operations.

Chief Skelley had justified his violations of safety regulations by claiming that some battleships had fired "partial loads" during World War II and that Captain Larry Seaquist had permitted him to conduct similar experiments in 1987. Admiral Chang thought it was time to call Seaquist into his headquarters at the Washington Navy Shipyard and see what the former *Iowa* skipper had to say for himself. Seaquist called the Judge Advocate General and obtained permission to have Lieutenant Commander Steve Stallings, who had been his legal officer on the *Iowa*, attend the interview with him.

Chang said he wanted Seaquist's candid opinion of Chief Skelley. He was also interested in finding out whether Seaquist had sought permission from anyone in higher authority before allowing Skelley to conduct the experiments aboard the *Iowa* in 1987. Seaquist said Skelley was a walking encyclopedia of battleship trivia, but he had no "street smarts." He said that while the ship was sailing from Trondheim, Norway, to Rota, Spain, Skelley wanted to fire six 1,900-pound projectiles with five-bag loads of D-846 powder and twelve 2,700-pound projectiles with five-bag loads of either D-846 or D-839 powder. Commander Gene Kocmich, the ship's weapons officer, was away on leave, and Master Chief Chuck Hill, Skelley's immediate superior, was adamantly opposed to Skelley's scheme, saying that it was contrary to the safety manual for sixteen-inch guns.

Seaquist went to Rear Admiral Richard Milligan, who had been aboard the ship for several days, serving as the battle group commander, and told him about the experiment. Seaquist informed Milligan that he was not about to do anything contrary to regulations without the admiral's knowing and approving it. He and Milligan talked about the experiments for two days before Milligan assented. The experiments were spelled out in the firing plan, which was submitted to Milligan. Seaquist said he was "absolutely certain" that when Milligan had condoned the experiments, he was fully aware that they entailed violating safety regulations.

Near the end of the interview, Chang informed Seaquist that he could be considered a "target" of the investigation, because he had failed to stop the illegal experiments. Driving back to the Pentagon, Seaquist told Steve Stallings, "I might be the only officer in this whole affair to face the prospect of a general court martial, which is an irony, because I wasn't even on the ship at the time of the explosion."

Chang called in Seaquist again. The Inspector General pointed a forefinger at Seaquist and shouted, "Where's the piece of paper authorizing you to conduct such experiments?" Seaquist had no such piece of paper with him and was rightfully frightened. Chang dismissed Seaquist and summoned Admiral Milligan to explain his role in the unauthorized 1987 experiments when he was aboard the *Iowa*. Chang didn't treat Milligan with any more deference than he had shown Seaquist. Milligan said he could recall being aboard the battleship from October 20 to November 10, 1987, but that was about it. Chang later said, "I decided that Rich Milligan was lying. I told him, 'I can't believe you didn't know.' I went over it with him four or five times." Chang said he thought it incredible that Milligan had included details about the 1987 experiments in his report but didn't mention that he had been on the *Iowa* when they took place.

WHILE ADMIRAL Chang continued his investigation, the Senate Armed Services Committee held a one-day hearing on November 16. Admiral Carl Trost, the Chief of Naval Operations, devoted most of his testimony to defend what he called the Navy's admirable "overall" safety record. He ticked off a list of ships that hadn't been involved in an accident, as if to say that would offset the list of ships that had been in collisions, groundings, and other types of mishaps. Senator John Warner, a Republican from Virginia who had been Secretary of the Navy, told the CNO, "I want you to know that America has the utmost confidence in you as the senior sailor." Warner tossed a puffball question to the CNO about whether or not the *Iowa* investigation had been a cover-up. Trost glowered, assuring Warner that he wouldn't countenance such monkey business.

Senator John Glenn said he held Trost accountable for the lack of training on the *Iowa*, calling it "an appalling, appalling situation aboard a capital ship of the U.S. Navy." Trost did not respond. Once Trost left the witness table, and Admiral Milligan, Captain Miceli, and Robert Powers of NIS took his place, they came under fire from Senator Alan Dixon, an Illinois Democrat. Dixon said their *Iowa* report was "based on supposition and guesswork, rather than fact and physical evidence." He accused NIS of allowing "a series of leaks that reflects poorly on the professionalism" of the agency.

Senator John McCain, an Arizona Republican and former naval aviator who had been a prisoner of war in North Vietnam for six years, read the following headline, "The FBI Fails to Find Cause of Explosion Aboard USS *Iowa*." An Annapolis graduate whose father and grandfather had been admirals, McCain said such negative coverage ought to prod the Navy into asking the FBI Crime Lab to conduct further tests. Admiral Milligan said he had no problem with the FBI's looking at what the Navy was doing. However, he never did anything to implement that.

Senator James Exon, a Nebraska Democrat and an implacable foe of the battleship reactivation program since its inception, asked about the age and stability of the gunpowder. Milligan said the propellant was World War II vintage and that it had been rebagged in the early 1980s. He pointedly failed to mention that it had been improperly stored during the summer of 1988 or that it had been destroyed as a safety precaution following the *Iowa* explosion. Senator Dixon noted that one hundred NIS agents had interviewed three hundred witnesses worldwide and had not come up with a shred of credible evidence that Kendall Truitt and Clayton Hartwig were homosexuals. "I did not classify or even suggest either one of these gentlemen were homosexuals," Milligan replied.

Senator Glenn asked Milligan if the ignorance of Captain Fred Moosally and the senior officers about the illegal experiments, and the lack of training of the *Iowa*'s crewmen, meant that the "whole fleet" was in similarly bad shape. Milligan assured the senator that the other ships were combat-ready.

Senator Dixon said some sailors on the *Iowa* claimed that the center gun's rammer had a lengthy history of unpredictable behavior. It sometimes darted forward at a high rate of speed and other times refused to budge. Milligan said his technical team combed through Turret Two's maintenance records and found no reference to any rammer malfunctions. Dixon asked Milligan if "some other independent, separate agency" ought to be in charge of the investigation. "I do not know who could be more interested in finding the actual cause of this accident than the Navy itself. It is our problem," Milligan responded.

THE *Iowa* arrived back in Norfolk at 1 P.M. on Pearl Harbor Day, December 7, from her six-month deployment to the North Atlantic and Mediterranean. A Navy public-relations release boasted that the ship had transited twelve seas, five gulfs, eleven bays, seven straits, and eight channels. She had sailed 35,661 miles and consumed 195,000 gallons of fuel.

Once the ship was tied up, Captain Fred Moosally held a brief press conference. He maintained that critical comments he made about his officers and crewmen in his testimony to Admiral Milligan had been taken out of context by the news media. "Absolutely, some mistakes were made on the ship. I am not perfect. My crew is not perfect. We make mistakes. But the mistakes are not commensurate with the label we got," he said. The captain discussed his forthcoming testimony before the Senate Armed Services Committee by saying, "My objective at that hearing is to convince the Congress, the American people and most importantly the families of our deceased and fallen shipmates that the *Iowa* described in the press never existed."

After his press conference, Moosally left the ship to visit the Naval Legal Services Office on the base, to review the documents collected by Admiral Milligan. He also went to the Norfolk Naval Shipyard to look at the test data. It was nearly midnight when he slowly ascended the forward brow. The boatswain's mate of the watch saluted the captain when he stepped on the teak-covered main deck. Suddenly, the captain told the petty officer that he had gone through the evidence related to the explosion. "It's bad. It's worse than I thought," he said in a choked voice. The sailor was startled. Captains don't ordinarily discuss such sensitive matters with boatswain's mates.

The next morning, the captain's chief yeoman found Lieutenant Dan Meyer in the wardroom and said that Moosally wanted Meyer to help him prepare his testimony for the Senate Armed Services Committee. Meyer had no choice but to agree. After Meyer finished writing a two-page summary of the points he thought the captain should deal with, he met with Moosally and Commander Kissinger, the weapons officer, in Moosally's cabin. Meyer and Kissinger differed over how much the captain should reveal to Congress about what had occurred on the ship prior to the explosion. "It amounts to how far you want to separate yourself from the official Navy position, Captain," Meyer said. Moosally remained poker-faced, giving no clue about what he intended to do.

Following his talk with Kissinger and Meyer, Moosally drove north in his red Mazda to his home outside Washington. Captain Joseph Miceli was aboard the ship, sitting in a comfortable corner of the *Iowa*'s wardroom, holding court. He loudly proclaimed several times, "The Navy sinks or swims on the murder/suicide theory." Miceli's refusal to consider any cause for the explosion other than sabotage dismayed Meyer and several other junior officers, although Miceli's unwavering support of the theory that Hartwig did it was readily accepted by some officers and sailors, most notably Chief Skelley. Skelley worried that congressional hearings on Admiral Milligan's findings, coupled with Admiral Chang's inquiry into illegal powder experiments, might cause the cancellation of the battleship program. He held one person directly responsible—Kathy Kubicina. She was continually appearing on network television and in the newspapers, heaping abuse on the Navy and the battleships. Skelley told anybody on the ship who would listen that Kubicina wasn't so much interested in clearing her brother's name as she was in extorting money from the Navy. He even had bumper stickers printed up reading, "Save the *Iowa*, Sink Kathy Kubicina." Since he didn't own a car, he plastered one of the stickers on a bulkhead in his office. He offered others to crewmen, but there were few takers.

FRED MOOSALLY'S two-story brick home in Oakton, Virginia, became a well-trafficked spot during the weekend that the *Iowa* captain prepared his congressional testimony. Flag officers regularly came and went. Rumors spread through the upper ranks of the Navy that "the Moose" was fighting mad, convinced that he had been abandoned by the top admirals, and was contemplating a counterattack on the Navy on Capitol Hill. He had some formidable allies in the House of Representatives, including chairmen of subcommittees essential to the Navy's interests. Admiral Edney told a number of flag officers to visit Moosally and make sure he didn't jump ship.

One of Moosally's visitors was Rear Admiral Ted Gordon. "I went over to Moosally's home the night before his testimony to tell him to cool it, to watch it," Gordon said. "What he was talking about doing was not good for the Navy, not good for his own career. I told him I thought he would still make admiral, no matter what had happened to the *Iowa*." Another one of Moosally's callers was Rear Admiral William "Bud" Flanagan, the Chief of Legislative Affairs. Moosally had served as executive officer of the frigate USS *Bronstein* under Flanagan. The two men were close. Flanagan assured Moosally that he was still in favor with the admirals who counted. He also talked to Moosally's wife, Joan, asking her to use her influence to keep her husband from doing anything indiscreet.

Moosally and Flanagan, both attired in dress-blue uniforms with rows of multicolored ribbons and golden Surface Warfare badges pinned on their left breasts, appeared at 9 A.M. on Monday, December 11, in the Hart Senate Office Building. In addition to swarms of print and television reporters, congressional aides, and other spectators, there were several people seated in the audience who had a special interest in the proceedings. Earl and Evelyn Hartwig and Frank and Kathy Kubicina were there, hoping to confront Fred Moosally once he finished his testimony. Before Moosally was called, Senator Sam Nunn announced that Sandia National Laboratories in Albuquerque, New Mexico, had agreed to test the *Iowa*'s rotating band to see if there might be a natural explanation, such as friction, for the explosion. This was a significant development, because Sandia had impeccable scientific credentials and, unlike the Navy, had no stake in the outcome. Senator John Warner then trumpeted the fact that he had talked with Admiral Carl Trost earlier that very morning, and the CNO said he "welcomed" Captain Moosally's testimony and stood "foursquare" behind what Admiral Milligan had already disclosed.

Moosally was allowed to enter into the record a self-serving and at times misleading statement. He claimed that his crew had been well trained, but that the ship's recordkeeping was in such sorry shape that training was hardly ever written down. He prevaricated when he said that the *Iowa* had never conducted gunpowder experiments while he was commanding officer.

Moosally attempted to renege on some of the testimony he had given to Admiral Milligan about the quality of his crew. He insisted that his statement had been misunderstood. He had been describing the conditions of the ship as they existed when he assumed command in 1988. Senator Nunn called his hand for failing to mention that he had kicked hundreds of men off the ship in his first ten months as commanding officer. Moosally admitted that he had "cleaned those people out," but he claimed that "those conditions do not exist today."

Senator Nunn asked Moosally if he agreed with the Navy's oft-stated conclusion that Clayton Hartwig "most probably" blew up the gun. Moosally's answer made headlines the next morning. "I would not come out and say that," he said. "I would not make an unqualified statement that Petty Officer Hartwig is the guy who committed the wrongful act. I do not think I can do that." "You, yourself, cannot do that?" Nunn asked. "No, Sir," Moosally replied. The committee chairman asked Moosally if he believed Admiral Milligan was in a position to conclude that Hartwig was guilty. "I cannot answer that question, Mr. Chairman," Moosally said. "You are saying you, yourself, cannot judge that?" Nunn inquired. "I am saying myself, I cannot," Moosally responded. Kathy Kubicina was so elated by this exchange that she almost jabbed her mother in the ribs.

Senator Warner sought to get Moosally to back the Navy's line, but he only succeeded in getting the captain to say that he believed the blast "was the direct result of a deliberate act." But try as he might, Warner could not convince Moosally to say that a specific sailor, Clayton Hartwig, was responsible. Moosally said that he lacked the scientific and technical expertise to arrive at such a conclusion. Warner noted that Moosally had twenty-three years on active duty and had commanded another ship. "How is it that you lack the expertise to either agree or disagree with that conclusion?" he demanded petulantly. Moosally answered that he wasn't a munitions expert and didn't have the time to evaluate all of the laboratory and forensic results. Well, was Admiral Milligan a munitions expert? Warner inquired. No, Milligan wasn't. Warner asked if Moosally had some other explanation for the tragedy that he was withholding from the committee. Moosally said he had no such information.

Senator William Cohen, a Republican from Maine who would go on to become Secretary of Defense in 1997, asked Moosally if he were given six months with nothing else to do but analyze the test results, would he be able to "affirm the results or the conclusions reached by the Navy"? He said he didn't have the qualifications to do it.

Senator Alan Dixon, a former trial lawyer, reminded Moosally that Chief Skelley had no formal training in gunnery or ballistics and "for a living he sold pots and pans" when he was not on active duty. Moosally, who had told Admiral Milligan that Chief Skelley drove him "nuts," weakly defended Skelley by saying, "He is pretty much an expert." Then, Senator Nunn asked Moosally whether he was satisfied that the explosion had been an intentional act. He agreed it was. Asked whether he had formed a conclusion about who might be the guilty party, Moosally said he had not.

Fred Moosally had just terminated his career. Shortly thereafter, Rear Admiral Flanagan called Admiral Edney and told him that Moosally had repeatedly refused to support the Navy's position. His retirement papers would be processed within days.

While Moosally was standing near the witness table following the hearing, surrounded by still and video cameramen, Kathy Kubicina and her mother crept up and got between the *Iowa* captain and the newspeople. Evelyn Hartwig looked Moosally straight in the eyes and, in a quivering voice, said, "My son loved the Navy and that ship as much as you do." "I know. I know he did, Mrs. Hartwig," Moosally replied. "Well, how could you say that he killed his forty-six shipmates?" she said, her voice rising. "I didn't," he softly protested. Moosally reached over and grasped Evelyn around the shoulder, drawing her to him. He gave her a bear hug and said, "God bless you!" And then he kissed her on the cheek. She wept, and the former Annapolis football star fought back his own tears.

24

☆

"I Depart in Rage, in Anger, and in Frustration."

RICHARD AULT AND Roy Hazelwood, the FBI psychological profilers who put together Clayton Hartwig's equivocal death analysis, had a rough time when they appeared before the Senate Armed Services Committee. The agents read statements claiming that they had the "depth" to make psychological determinations about criminal suspects that "the academic community does not have." Ault admitted to Senator Alan Dixon that the Navy had only provided him with fragments of the evidence assembled against Hartwig. Ault was asked whether the poem "Disposable Heroes" was in Hartwig's handwriting. He didn't know. Was he aware that other gunner's mates had told Admiral Milligan that another sailor, Jay White, had written the poem? Roy Hazelwood answered that whether or not Hartwig had written the poem was "immaterial," because Hartwig "had the potential of seeing it."

Dixon asked both agents if they were aware that David Smith had recanted the testimony they used in Hartwig's equivocal death analysis. They said they were aware of that but were unsure exactly what Smith had retracted. Had they personally interviewed any witnesses? No, they had relied solely upon the Naval Investigative Service for their information. Dixon asked if Ault had "any hard evidence, any evidence that would support the idea that Hartwig actually carried out this act." "No, Sir," Ault responded. "This opinion that we submitted is based on a half scientific, half art form."

Senator William Cohen asked the FBI agents if the NIS team had a "predisposition" to believe that Hartwig was guilty when Ault and Hazelwood first met with them in early May. "Yes. Yes, in fact they did," Ault said, adding, "The evidence that we accepted from the Navy that there was no accident was also the same kind of evidence on which they stated that the only guy in a position to do any damage was Clayton Hartwig. That is why we only looked at Hartwig."

The newspaper reaction to Ault's and Hazelwood's statements was ferocious. Lars-Erik Nelson began a column in the *New York Daily News* this way: "Deep within the FBI there exists a unit of people who—without ever talking to you or anyone who knows you—are prepared to go into court and testify that you are a homicidal maniac."

An editorial in the *Washington Post* said, "Long distance personality analysis by experts who have never met the subject are almost always ludicrous. But when the subject is dead, cannot defend himself and is found to be guilty of a horrendous crime, opinions like this are deserving of contempt."

THE HOUSE Armed Services Committee was even tougher on the Navy and the FBI Behavioral Science Unit witnesses than the Senate had been. Admiral Milligan stated once again that the explosion was an intentional act, "most probably done by Petty Officer Hartwig." "Most probably?" Congressman Nicholas Mavroules (D—Massachusetts) asked sarcastically. "But you cannot say without any doubt whatsoever that it was Mr. Hartwig?"

Representative Joseph Brennan (D—Maine) brought up Captain Fred Moosally's recent testimony in the Senate. Why had Moosally stubbornly refused to agree that Hartwig was responsible for the explosion? According to Milligan, Moosally hadn't had the time to review all of the investigative documents. Brennan asked Milligan if he had ever directed any other investigation involving a large loss of life. The admiral said that when he was a junior officer, he had participated in a minor inquiry involving no casualties. "But essentially you do not have a lot of experience in investigations?" Brennan asked. Milligan insisted that his captaincy of the *New Jersey* qualified him to investigate the *Iowa* disaster.

DR. RICHARD Froede, the Armed Forces Medical Examiner, provided some testimony that proved later to be extremely valuable. Yet at the time, only one man, Captain Joseph Miceli, grasped the significance of Froede's words. Congressman Nicholas Mavroules asked Froede if, shortly after the disaster, he had listed the cause of death as accidental for all forty-seven men killed in Turret Two. Froede agreed he had. Why hadn't he changed the causes on the death certificates to murder and suicide once the Navy announced that Clayton Hartwig intentionally caused the explosion? Froede said that nobody had offered him any convincing evidence to make him change his earlier findings.

Mavroules stated that the pressure wave generated inside the turret by the explosion had been an astonishing 4,000 pounds per square inch and that the temperature had soared to 3,000°F. Given that force and heat, how confident was Froede about where the sailors were prior to the blast? Froede attempted to explain how he arrived at his determinations by comparing the conditions of two bodies, Clayton Hartwig and Reginald Johnson. Johnson, who was the primerman, stood on a platform below the gun and inserted a .30-caliber cartridge into the breechblock. Froede said that unburned powder was embedded in both Hartwig's and Johnson's bodies. He called this a "stipple effect," saying that if you took a pistol and fired it near a person, some of the powder would stick to that person's body. "But as you move the gun farther from the target, then you won't see that powder deposit that comes out of the muzzle." Froede said that since the bodies of both Hartwig and Johnson had similar "stippling," they must have been standing closest to the breech.

There had never been any doubt about where Johnson had been prior to the explosion. Dan Meyer and Dale Mortensen and several others who entered the turret after the explosion discovered Johnson's body on the primerman's platform below the gun.

Congressman Larry Hopkins (R—Kentucky) said that some official Navy accounts had Hartwig looking into the open breech with his arms extended when the fireball caught him, while other accounts had him standing to the side of the weapon. Which one was true? Dr. Froede said he didn't know. That answer contradicted a May 26 memo from Froede to Captain Miceli, which stated, "Clayton M. Hartwig's injuries are consistent with those of an individual standing on the gun captain's platform, bending over and looking into the open breech of the gun at the time of the explosion."

After the hearings, Captain Miceli wrote Dr. Froede a "Dear Dick" letter, enclosing copies of his testimony and Froede's May 26 memo. Miceli wrote that there were some "slight inconsistencies" in Froede's testimony that he might like to change "when you mark up your statement." Froede said he never made those changes. Admiral Edney later testified that Miceli had far exceeded the scope of his authority by asking Froede to revise his testimony.

ON DECEMBER 21, the third and final day of the hearings held in the Rayburn House Office Building, FBI psychological profiler Richard Ault was asked by Representative Mavroules if he had discussed the case with Dr. Froede. Ault said he had not. Had he even examined the autopsy reports? He hadn't done that, either. Mavroules told Ault that the medical examiner had ruled that all forty-seven deaths were accidental. "That is his opinion, and we have our opinion," Ault said, somewhat churlishly. Mavroules asked Hazelwood if he were sure that the material NIS had provided him was factual. "No, Sir," Hazelwood replied, adding that it wasn't his job to corroborate information.

Representative Norman Sisisky (D—Virginia) asked Hazelwood if he had drawn up psychological profiles on anyone else in Turret Two. Hazelwood said he hadn't. The FBI agents stated that Hartwig exaggerated a lot. Sisisky ridiculed the notion that there was anything abnormal about a young, healthy sailor like Hartwig exaggerating his experience or even the type of ship on which he served. It happened all the time in the Navy. Sisisky said that he learned that firsthand when he had been a Navy seaman in boot camp at Bainbridge, Maryland, at the end of World War II. Sisisky said Ault and Hazelwood had described Hartwig "as not sufficiently aggressive to be a good leader, immature and lacking in other leadership skills." Hartwig was a second class petty officer and a gun captain, the congressman noted. If Hartwig had no leadership abilities, how did he get promoted? "Beats me," Ault said. "I don't know how the Navy works."

AS THE year ended, Rear Admiral Ming Chang, the Navy's Inspector General, put the final touches on his report about unauthorized powder experimentation aboard the *Iowa*. Chang informed Admiral Edney that his report would reveal that Rear Admiral Richard Milligan had personally approved illegal gunnery experiments while he was aboard the *Iowa* serving as battle group commander in 1987. Edney was outraged. If Milligan's indiscretion appeared in Chang's report, Milligan's credibility would be greatly impaired. According to regulations, however, even though Edney outranked Chang, he was not allowed to meddle in the affairs of the Inspector General's office. Chang was supposed to submit them directly to the Secretary of the Navy. This system had been set up to insulate the Inspector General from pressure by high-ranking officers, such as the Vice Chief of Naval Operations, who might want to dilute or even suppress an embarrassing or politically sensitive report.

As Chang prepared to submit his report to Secretary of the Navy Lawrence Garrett, he learned from the unofficial "flag-officer grapevine" that Secretary Garrett had no stomach for it. Chang was instructed by Garrett's aides to give it to Edney. Edney ordered Chang to overhaul his report and make it "a one-officer informal investigation." This same arrangement had been used by Milligan, and it permitted Edney to keep Chang's report under wraps indefinitely. "The bottom line is that he [Edney] buried my goddamned report!" Chang railed. "I expected a firestorm, but the press missed it."

The only newspaper to report anything about the report was a small daily, the *Free Lance-Star*, in Fredericksburg, Virginia. Reporter Laura Moyer filed a Freedom of Information Act request and received five hundred pages of Chang's report. Even though most of the pages were heavily censored, there was still enough information for Moyer to piece together several highly readable articles. Moyer related how several officials at Sea Systems Command and at Dahlgren had intentionally concealed the facts of unauthorized powder tests on the *Iowa* so that their superiors wouldn't abort the experiments. She quoted Chang as saying, "Disregard of standard Navy gunnery safety and test procedures . . . could conceivably have placed the safety of the crew of the USS *Iowa* in jeopardy." She revealed that Admiral Milligan had been aboard the *Iowa* in November 1987 when the unauthorized experiments began. Moyer asked the Navy if she could speak to Milligan, but she was turned down.

Admiral Edney had a memo released, claiming that Chang determined that the "test firings [unauthorized experiments] on USS *Iowa* were safe and presented no undue risk to the crew." But apparently no reporters from any major newspapers or television networks read Moyer's articles, so Edney was never called upon to explain the inconsistencies between his memo and Chang's report.

DURING THE winter and early spring of 1990, Captain Joseph Miceli began meeting regularly with a group of about forty scientists from Sandia National Laboratories, the institution retained by the Senate Armed Services Committee to take a second look at the Navy's technical investigation of the *Iowa* explosion. The scientists were led by Dr. Richard Schwoebel, who had been at Sandia nearly three decades. Schwoebel sent Miceli a four-page, single-spaced list, seeking twenty-seven items, including specimens of chlorinated cleaning powder used on the *Iowa* at the time of the explosion, thirty Mark 15 primers, an inventory of all electrical malfunctions that had ever occurred in Turret Two, copies of the Navy's sixteen-inch gunnery manuals, and samples of Break-Free cleaning solution taken from the *Iowa*'s storerooms.

Schwoebel and his colleagues had familiarized themselves with the operation of the three sixteen-inch gun turrets on the *Iowa*, where they had been helped by Dan Meyer and Dale Mortensen. They had also collected wipings from Turrets One and Three on the *Iowa* and from the turrets of her sisterships, the *Wisconsin* and the *New Jersey*. They asked Captain Miceli to take a look at the projectiles that had been stuck in the right and left guns of Turret Two on the *Iowa* on April 19. They were informed by Miceli that both 2,700-pound shells inexplicably had disappeared.

Sandia's chemical-analysis group, headed by Dr. James Borders, looked into any evidence that could prove or disprove the Navy's prevailing theory that a chemical igniter had caused the explosion. The Navy said it had located three types of "foreign elements" under the *Iowa*'s rotating band: minute steel-wool fibers encrusted with calcium and chlorine; a fragment of polyethylene terephthalate (PET), commonly used in plastic bags; and three different glycols—chemicals found in brake fluid, antifreeze, and Brylcreem. Borders's group detected identical metal fibers in another *Iowa* turret, as well as in turrets aboard the *New Jersey* and the *Wisconsin*. They informed the Navy that seawater is a plentiful source of both calcium and chlorine. Calcium is also present in Break-Free cleaning and lubricating solution, which had been poured down the gun barrel during the five weeks that the projectile was being freed. Borders visited the Navy laboratory in Crane, Indiana, and asked to examine a scorched iron fiber coated with high concentrations of calcium and chlorine, which had been discovered under the *Iowa*'s rotating band. The fiber was minuscule, just a few thousandths of an inch in diameter and a few hundredths of an inch long. It was the only physical evidence the Navy had to support its claim that a chemical device had initiated the *Iowa* blast. A Crane technician brought out an envelope, opened it, and shook it. Nothing emerged. The Navy was never able to locate the fiber or to explain how it vanished.

Sandia technicians examined portions of the *Iowa*'s rotating band with electron microscopes and were unable to find any traces of the plastic "Seal-a-Meal" bag the Navy claimed had contained the chemical detonator. However, they did locate traces of foreign elements the Navy claimed were part of an ignition device in wipings taken elsewhere in Turret Two, as well as from samples in the *New Jersey*'s and *Wisconsin*'s turrets. Sandia determined that these traces came from ballpoint pens, eyeglass frames, buttons, ID badges, and other plastic items routinely carried into the turrets by crewmen. Borders eliminated one of the glycols, deciding that it was a component of Break-Free. Another glycol had been misidentified by the Navy. It was actually a phenol, also a component of Break-Free. Although Borders couldn't say with absolute certainty that no chemical device had been in the powder chamber, he cast grave doubts on the Navy's theory.

In February, Dr. Karl Schuler, a member of the Sandia team, went aboard the *Iowa* and entered Turret Two. In addition to having his doctorate in mechanics from the Illinois Institute of Technology, Schuler had worked at the Brooklyn Naval Shipyard as an engineer for five years. Schuler took some exacting measurements and determined that the Navy had miscalculated when it said that the five powder bags had been rammed into the barrel twenty-one inches farther than they should have been. The distance of the overram was significant, because if the Navy's figure was correct, the bags could not have been crushed against the base of the projectile. Schuler was able to prove that the bags had actually been rammed twenty-four inches into the barrel. After spending fifty hours on a Cray supercomputer at Sandia, Schuler's team was convinced that the twenty-four-inch overram, combined with 2,800 pounds of pressure produced by the rammer, had compressed the powder bags to the point that they had ignited.

Schuler also picked up on something abnormal that had happened in the center gun room the morning of the disaster. The powder hoist, which carried the powder bags from the powder flats to the gun room, hadn't been lowered after being unloaded, as it should have been. Robert Backherms, the rammerman, had to use one hand to operate a lever that shut the hoist door and lowered the "powder car," while using his other hand to control the variable-speed rammer. During the loading process, Backherms had to shove the rammer lever all the way down to push the projectile firmly into the bore at about fourteen feet per second. After withdrawing the rammer, and with the powder bags in place on the tray, Backherms would have to gently—very gently—ease the lever slightly forward and nudge the bags forward at no more than two feet per second. If Backherms became disoriented, he could have rammed the powder too far and too fast.

ANOTHER GROUP of Sandia investigators, Paul Cooper and his explosives team, received a dozen bags of D-846 powder from the same lot that was involved in the accident on the *Iowa*. Each bag contained about 1,800 thumb-size pellets stacked in eight layers of 225 pellets. When the sixteen-inch battleship propellant had been rebagged in the mid-1980s, a trim or "tare" layer had been added. The "tare" layer, which was supposed to contain from fifteen to sixty-five grains reclining on their sides, was added to ensure that every bag weighed the same. The *Iowa*'s gunners mates were told nothing about the "tare" layer. Cooper was distrustful of this layer, because it was on the top of each bag and could scrape against a red silk pouch filled with black powder on the end of the next bag. Cooper first began with small-scale drop tests with nitrocellulose pellets to measure their stability.

With help from Karl Schuler, Cooper conducted 450 drop tests, often working from sunup to sundown and on weekends. A pattern began to emerge. "We predicted that if you had something like five or ten or fifteen pellets on that ["tare"] layer, between the first and second bag, and if the gun were overrammed, and overrammed at high speed, then there was a very high probability of getting ignition," Cooper said. The fewer pellets there were in the "tare" layer, the more freedom they had to slip about, become fractured, and generate sparks. Schuler and Cooper briefed Captain Miceli about their test results. Miceli wasn't impressed, because they had been using models that were much smaller than an actual powder charge. Miceli said that their research wasn't relevant to the *Iowa* situation, but still he agreed to schedule drop tests at Dahlgren, using five actual bags of powder compressed into a steel cylinder the same diameter as a sixteen-inch gun.

THE HOUSE Armed Services Committee released its report, "USS *Iowa* Tragedy: An Investigative Failure," in early March 1990. The report laid into the Navy for failing to test and eliminate every possible natural cause before leaping to the conclusion that the explosion had been an intentional act. The Navy was criticized for allowing the turret and the projectile to become contaminated, for permitting evidence to be thrown overboard, and for failing honestly to disclose the nature of its disagreement with the FBI Crime Laboratory over substances found on the rotating band. The FBI's equivocal death analysis was labeled the "single major fault in this investigation."

In the committee's opinion, the Navy didn't have enough credible evidence to accuse Clayton Hartwig of "being a suicidal mass-murderer." If the Navy followed accepted judicial standards, Hartwig would never be convicted of any crime. NIS's participation in the case was termed "flawed." NIS devoted almost all of its manpower and resources to Hartwig, trying to prove that he was a homosexual mass murderer, "without adequately investigating other crew members or persuasively detailing why other suspects were not credible." The NIS agents assigned to the case were criticized for their shoddy interviewing techniques. The Navy and NIS were censured for the wholesale leaking of sensitive documents and inaccurate information. The committee accused Admiral Milligan of being unfit to oversee a major criminal investigation. Milligan's repeated failures to preserve evidence and to maintain an accurate chain of custody of the evidence were among the reasons given for this stern assessment.

SHORTLY AFTER the House Armed Services Committee report was released, Lieutenant Dan Meyer was arrested when one of his former gun captains turned over some evidence to a scientist working for Sandia National Laboratories. William Chambers, a member of Jim Borders's team, was aboard the *Iowa* looking around Turret Two. As Chambers was preparing to leave the ship on a sunny Friday afternoon, he asked a group of officers and enlisted men on the main deck if they still had any of the powder grains from the day of the explosion. It was important to find these grains, because Dr. Richard Schwoebel, head of the Sandia team, strongly suspected that Captain Joseph Miceli was providing propellant from lots that were not involved in the *Iowa* explosion. That would compromise Sandia's findings.

Several sailors said they had discovered some unburned pellets under the deck plates in the center gun room after Turret Two had been washed out and painted. One of the men, Gunner's Mate Second Class John Keerl, rushed below to his berthing space and got some of these pellets out of his locker. Keerl put them in a "peanut-butter glass jar" and carried them up to the quarterdeck.

As Keerl handed Chambers the jar, the officer of the deck, Lieutenant Kevin Hunt, tried to snatch it back, screaming that it was evidence. Chambers ignored Hunt and walked off the forward gangplank, clutching the jar. Hunt sought out the gunnery officer, Lieutenant Commander Larry Dodson, and complained that Meyer had put Keerl up to giving Chambers the powder. Meyer and Hunt, who shared a stateroom, had been bickering with each other for months about gunnery practices on the battleship. Dodson, who became gunnery officer six months after the explosion, knew that Meyer had been in his office, nowhere near the main deck, when Keerl gave the jar to Chambers. There were no grounds that Dodson could see for him to take any disciplinary action against Meyer, so he allowed the lieutenant to leave the ship at 4:30 P.M. to spend the weekend at his parents' home in Virginia Beach.

By the time Meyer arrived back on the ship about 6:30 A.M. on Monday, the situation had worsened. Captain Moosally was aboard and had received a telex from Captain Joseph Miceli, complaining that the ship had provided evidence to Sandia without first clearing it with him. Moosally said that heads would roll. Meyer was in his office about 8:30 A.M., sorting mail with Gunner's Mate Third Class Warren Mayberry, who acted as Meyer's clerk, when the phone rang. It was a clerk in the legal office, calling to tip off Mayberry that the ship's top cop, Senior Master-at-Arms Chief Robert Porter, and two of his deputies toting handcuffs were on their way to arrest Meyer. Porter arrived several minutes later and informed Meyer that he was escorting the lieutenant to the captain's cabin. Meyer looked at the handcuffs. "Senior Chief, are those handcuffs absolutely necessary?" Porter instructed his men not to shackle Meyer's wrists.

Meyer knew he was in deep trouble when he entered the captain's cabin and saw the angry expression on Moosally's face. Lieutenant Commander Dodson and Commander Kissinger, the weapons officer, also were there. "Did you give some evidence to Sandia on Friday?" Moosally shouted. Meyer said that he had not. He admitted taking Chambers on a tour of Turret Two, but he said that once he left the turret, he had turned the Sandia scientist over to other officers and had gone to his office. He had later heard that Keerl had given Chambers some propellant, but he denied having had anything to do with that. "Bullshit! You're under arrest!" the captain bellowed. Moosally told Chief Porter to lock up Meyer.

In the passageway outside the captain's cabin, Meyer asked the master-at-arms, "Senior Chief, are you going to lock me up in the brig?" "No, Mr. Meyer, I'm going to put you in my personal office," Porter replied. When they reached Porter's small office, the chief read Meyer his rights. He also said that a team of NIS agents was on its way to charge Meyer with some unspecified crime and to interrogate him. Meyer asked if Porter really had to lock the door, and the chief said he was sorry, but he had to follow the captain's orders. After the chief and his men left, Meyer went over to Porter's desk and picked up the telephone. It worked. Incredibly, it was one of only four outside lines on the entire ship. The first call he made was to Warren Mayberry. He told the clerk to make sure the men assigned to Turret One knew that even though he had been arrested, he was in good shape and there was nothing to worry about. Then he dialed his father and said in a quavering voice, "Dad, I'm under arrest pending court-martial. I really need your advice. I don't want to go to Leavenworth [military prison]. I want to go to law school once I get out of the Navy."

Retired Captain Donald Meyer told his son that he wasn't quite sure what he was going to do, but he would definitely do something. Donald Meyer thought about getting in touch with his Annapolis classmate and good friend, Admiral Carl Trost, the Chief of Naval Operations. The CNO had sent a personal note to his old classmate, informing him that he had read Dan's testimony to Admiral Milligan and thought that Dan had handled himself commendably.

About noon, Dan Meyer called Lieutenant Commander Dodson, saying he was hungry and asking Dodson to please send a sandwich and a glass of milk up to Chief Porter's office. Dodson said Meyer could eat in the wardroom as long as he was accompanied by armed guards. Following lunch, Meyer was escorted back to the master-of-arms's office. Mayberry slipped some magazines under the locked door. Meyer read them for a time. A week before, Meyer called the Bureau of Naval Personnel in Washington to see what jobs were available once he left the *Iowa*. He had no doubt that Captain Moosally would get rid of him. The personnel officer with whom he talked said that a communications billet would soon be open aboard the USS *La Salle*, a command-and-control ship based in Bahrain. Nicknamed "The Great White Ghost of the Arabian Coast," she served as the flagship of the commander of the U.S. Middle East Force. Meyer was told that if he took that job, he had to complete a two-month communications course in Newport, Rhode Island.

The afternoon wore on, and no NIS agents showed up. Lieutenant Commander Dodson entered the office about 5 P.M. and told Meyer that he was free to leave. No charges would be filed. He would not be court-martialed. When Meyer opened the front door to his parents' home, his mother rushed to him, hugging him tightly. She told him how frantic she had been when she heard about his incarceration. "I don't want to see you get hurt over this," she said.

WHEN MEYER reported aboard the ship the next morning, he was told by the officer of the deck that transfer orders were awaiting him in the ship's administrative office. He opened the orders and saw that he was being sent to the *Tarawa*, a helicopter assault ship, as an engineering officer. He called the personnel officer with whom he had spoken the previous day and told him about the order. "Somebody really wants you off that ship in the worst sort of way," the officer remarked. The personnel officer arranged to have Meyer's orders changed to the *La Salle*.

During Meyer's remaining forty-eight hours on the *Iowa*, almost all of the officers shunned him. It was nothing personal. The policy was mandated from above. Meyer would have been forced to eat in isolation, except that Lieutenant Mike Weaver, an electronics warfare officer from Texas, decided that this was uncouth behavior, so he made a point of sitting next to Meyer in the wardroom for all his meals. Before Meyer left the ship for the final time, he was handed an unfavorable fitness report signed by Fred Moosally. As Meyer trudged down Pier 7 carrying his gear, a sizable number of officers, chiefs, and sailors standing near the forecastle yelled, "Keep up the good work, Dan!" "Way to go, Dan!" "We're gonna miss you, Man!"

ALMOST AS soon as Meyer started communications school in preparation for his assignment on the *La Salle*, he submitted a letter of resignation to the Bureau of Naval Personnel. He owed the Navy one more tour of duty in return for his ROTC scholarship at Cornell, but once he completed that, he wanted out. Meyer's letter would cause a sensation. He wrote that the sixteen-inch guns were still unsafe in August 1989, when the Navy lifted the ban on firing them. "The primary concern was not the safety of my men nor the defense of the American Embassy in Beirut, but of the survival of the budgets assigned to the battleship program." Meyer declared that the forty-seven men in Turret Two "died not for nation, family, or creed, but in defense of institutionalized interests." He defined those "interests" as the shore installations that advocated and funded Chief Skelley's illegal gunpowder experimentation. "I depart in rage, in anger, and in frustration," he wrote. "The professional ethic is corrupt and irreconcilable with my personal beliefs. As such, the only responsible action is to resign."

The very day Meyer's letter of resignation arrived at the Bureau of Naval Personnel, it was handed to Vice Admiral Mike Boorda. Boorda picked up the phone and called Donald Meyer in Virginia Beach to ask where Dan was. Boorda savored the kind of salty language commonly used on the mess decks and berthing spaces aboard a warship. He liberally spiced his everyday speech with such profanity. Donald Meyer, a straight-laced fellow, grimaced each time Boorda uttered another expletive. Finally, he told Boorda that he didn't appreciate his gutter mouth and also found it disconcerting that a three-star admiral, the man in charge of all the Navy's personnel, had to call a retired captain to locate one of his own officers. After that, Meyer gave Boorda his son's phone number in Newport.

Dan Meyer was attending a communications class when he was told that Vice Admiral Boorda's personal assistant was on the line, waiting to talk to him. "Lieutenant Meyer, the admiral would like to speak with you. Please hold on a minute," the assistant said. "Hey, Asshole," Boorda irreverently began the conversation. Meyer couldn't believe what he was hearing. He had met Boorda once when the admiral had commanded the battle group to which the *Iowa* belonged. He didn't think that admirals talked that way to junior officers they barely knew. "I've got your letter in front of me," Boorda continued. "We've got to talk. You're going to be here in my office tomorrow for lunch. There are tickets reserved in your name at the airport. Don't be late."

The next day, Meyer flew to Washington and met with Boorda. The short admiral hopped up from his chair when Meyer entered his office and walked around his desk to pump the former turret officer's hand. Meyer was a captive audience for Boorda for the next three hours. The first hour was devoted to Boorda's biography, which he had transformed into a Horatio Alger–style tale on how to succeed in the Navy. Following this inspirational warm-up, Boorda got down to serious business, asking Meyer if he could "absolutely" prove that the Navy shore installations were in any way responsible for the *Iowa* explosion. Meyer told Boorda there were extensive communications between Chief Skelley and Sea Systems Command personnel before each illegal experiment. Boorda tried to convince Meyer that his accusations were without merit. "Let me spell it out to you," Boorda said. "You go out to the *La Salle* and do great. Clean up your record. I'm going to sit on this hotheaded letter, and then in six or eight months, you can join my staff, wherever I may be." "Sir, there are rumors that you might become Chief of Naval Operations. Is this offer still good if you're CNO?" Meyer asked. "We don't talk about those kinds of rumors around here," Boorda replied, grinning. "Sir, if I did what you're asking, I'd have to be very quiet for the next eighteen months," Meyer said. "You'd have to behave like a naval officer," Boorda curtly responded. "Sir, this all sounds like a quid pro quo to me," Meyer said. "It's nothing of the sort! Just think about what I've offered you!" Boorda barked, hastily dismissing Meyer.

Flying back to Rhode Island, Meyer knew there was no way he could accept Boorda's deal. He wasn't about to stop campaigning against the Navy's *Iowa* conclusions. Before leaving for the Middle East, Meyer provided the Senate Armed Services Committee with details about how Captain Joseph Miceli had biased the technical investigation. He also began furnishing bits and pieces of information to some of the relatives of the men who were killed on the *Iowa*. Meyer never expected that Boorda would monkey with his letter of resignation. But as he discovered when he received his discharge papers in 1991, that's what had happened. The references to the misconduct of the three naval shore installations had been deleted. His statement that the professional ethic of the Navy "is corrupt and irreconcilable with my personal beliefs" had also disappeared.

25

☆

"This Is Shit, Really Shit, Really Lousy Science!"

THE NAVY TRIED to downplay the first anniversary of the *Iowa* disaster. The relatives of the forty-seven men who perished in the turret explosion had to pay their own travel expenses to Norfolk to attend a simple memorial service aboard the battleship. But at least they were given discounted rates at the Navy Lodge, a rundown motel located on the Norfolk Naval Base. Captain Fred Moosally, scheduled to retire from the Navy within several weeks, thanked the families for making regular calls and sending letters to the ship, telling them, "You have helped the memory of your sons, husbands, and fathers live in us." Sailors stood in respectful silence atop the three sixteen-inch gun turrets and along the port and starboard sides of the gray vessel. Vice Admiral Jerome Johnson, the Second Fleet commander who had been on the bridge when the accident occurred, said, "I have been a witness to this tragedy since that first terrible moment one year ago. I have seen the differing, often conflicting emotions everyone has felt, strength and sorrow, dedication and despair, comfort and confusion." After a plaque inscribed with the names of the deceased men was attached to Turret Two, some of the family members made their way into the turret.

FOUR DAYS after the first anniversary of the *Iowa* explosion, *U.S. News & World Report* devoted its cover and ten full pages inside the magazine to an exhaustive inquiry of the accident. The article was written by Peter Cary, a former Navy officer who had completed the service's rugged explosive ordnance disposal (EOD) schools in Key West, Florida, and Indian Head, Maryland. For at least six months after the explosion aboard the *Iowa*, Cary thought the Navy had done a competent investigation. But after looking into Admiral Milligan's investigation, he changed his mind. He decided to do a story, bringing to the assignment an expertise that no other reporter had. He knew how to build a detonator.

Cary asked scientific experts such as Lee Grodzins, a physics professor at the Massachusetts Institute of Technology, to evaluate the Navy's work. Grodzins told Cary, "This is shit, really shit, really lousy science!" The professor said the Navy failed to prove scientifically the existence of brake fluid (a component of the alleged chemical device). "You couldn't present this thing in court. You'd be thrown out," Grodzins said.

Cary decided to assemble chemical detonators similar to the one the Navy suggested Hartwig had used. His first models were constructed in the laboratory of Professor Walter Rowe, who taught forensic sciences at George Washington University. Two failed to ignite, another began sputtering after two and a half minutes, and the most successful flared in ninety seconds. Then Cary decided to try some tests outside the laboratory. He drove out to a shopping center in suburban Virginia and purchased steel wool at a grocery store, brake fluid at an auto-supply firm, and chlorinated bleach at a swimming-pool company. He parked near a dumpster and constructed his detonator behind the shopping center. He triggered it and waited several agonizing minutes before there was a "poof," followed by flames and a cloud of white smoke. "I thought, 'Holy shit! What am I doing? If the cops come by and see me with this stuff, they're going to haul me off to jail as a terrorist,'" Cary said. "These chemical devices didn't work well or reliably," he said. "They weren't all that small, and I didn't see how Hartwig could have sneaked one of them into the gun room without everybody in there knowing what he was doing."

Cary attended both the Senate and the House hearings on the *Iowa* and concluded, "The Navy's technical investigation was warped." He wanted to learn more about Clayton Hartwig's personality, so he flew to Cleveland, interviewed Earl and Evelyn Hartwig, and examined Clayton's attic room. "I looked around, and I was stunned. Clearly the FBI and NIS portrayals of Clayton Hartwig were distorted. It was eminently clear to me that this was a real travesty," Cary said.

STANDING UNDER dark clouds on the main deck of the vessel he had commanded for two tumultuous years, Captain Fred Moosally condemned the Navy for mismanaging the investigation of the gunnery explosion aboard the *Iowa*. Moosally's Friday, May 4, 1990, change-of-command ceremony was periodically interrupted by cloudbursts. "After the investigation report was released, it is too bad that the ball was handed off to people most concerned about an image and therefore unable to bring themselves to admit that the investigation report is irreconcilable with the results of every inspection held on [the] *Iowa* before and after April 19th [1989]." Moosally went on: "How could this have happened in our Navy? The explosion in Turret Two was a dual tragedy—forty-seven men died and the 1,500 survivors were made victims when they should have been heroes."

Rear Admiral George Gee, the *Iowa*'s battle group commander, pinned the Navy's Legion of Merit on Moosally's uniform blouse, which was sodden from the rain, praising his accomplishments in the year following the explosion. Commander John Morse, the battleship's executive officer, was made commanding officer for the remaining months that it would take to get the *Iowa* ready to return to mothballs. After a reception, Moosally was piped off the ship with full honors. Then he drove north with his family to his home outside Washington. Shortly after that, he went to work for a major defense contractor.

MANY OF the relatives of the men killed in Turret Two didn't know what to make of Fred Moosally's sudden about-face. Nancy Jo Lewis, mother of Fire Controlman Richard Lewis, said his remarks were "not what I expected him to say. I would just say that he has joined the ranks of many of the rest of us on how the [Milligan] report was handled. I'm glad to see he said it." Kathy Kubicina was overly optimistic, saying, "We've got Captain Fred on our side now. This is it. By the end of the year, there isn't going to be anybody that believes that stupid story." Kreig Brusnahan, the Hartwigs' attorney, said that Moosally hadn't told the whole truth when he testified at the Senate Armed Services Committee hearing in December. "He was still in the Navy and he had to toe the line. Now that he's retired, he's making his true feelings heard," Brusnahan said.

FRED MOOSALLY'S farewell speech motivated Lieutenant Dan Meyer in Rhode Island to call the Senate Armed Services Committee. Identifying himself as the Turret One officer on the *Iowa* on the day of the explosion, Meyer asked to speak to the staffer who was in charge of the inquiry. He was told that person was Richard DeBobes, the committee's counsel, but DeBobes wouldn't be able to speak with him for an hour. Could Meyer please call back? He could and did. When Meyer spoke with DeBobes, he was unaware that the counsel was a retired Navy captain and legal officer who had worked for Admiral William Crowe when Crowe had been chairman of the Joint Chiefs of Staff. Meyer told DeBobes that Captain Joseph Miceli first arrived at a conclusion and then altered evidence to make it fit. "If there is a stink in the investigation, Miceli is the guy who knows all about the stink," Meyer said.

Meyer wasn't the only person who contacted DeBobes out of the blue. Brian Scanio, who had been the first person to enter Turret Two when it was still ablaze, paid a visit to DeBobes's office in the Russell Senate Office Building. Scanio had witnessed grisly scenes that no one else on the ship had. He had provided graphic testimony to Admiral Milligan, but he believed that Milligan had largely ignored what he had to say. He decided to travel to Washington and talk to somebody who worked for the Senate Armed Services Committee.

Denied leave, Scanio left the ship without permission and contacted ABC News producer Mark Brender when he arrived in Washington. Brender took Scanio up to Capitol Hill to talk to DeBobes, who wasn't pleased that Scanio had taken an unauthorized absence (UA) from the *Iowa*. The former Navy captain was more interested in getting Scanio back to the battleship than in listening to the sailor's story. DeBobes called the *Iowa* and said he was making sure that Scanio returned to Norfolk. He learned that Scanio was broke, so he bought him a meal and lent him enough money to buy a bus ticket.

When Scanio reported aboard the *Iowa* after twelve days of UA, he was told by a sailor standing at the after brow, "You're in a lot of trouble!" Rather than being locked up in the brig and facing a court-martial, Scanio was hustled off the ship and taken to the Portsmouth, Virginia, Naval Hospital, where he was placed in a psychiatric ward and diagnosed as having post-traumatic stress disorder (PTSD, sometimes referred as "shell shock"). He told an evaluation panel of three Navy psychiatrists that he was "haunted by the sight of dead comrades, some of them close friends, as well as by his own danger from the fire, explosion, and live electrical equipment." He also complained that his testimony had been ignored by the "official investigation."

The doctors wrote that Scanio had a "neatly groomed appearance," that "his speech was spontaneous and of a normal rate and rhythm," and that his thought processes "were logical and goal directed." He wasn't experiencing hallucinations or delusions, and his memory and cognitive skills weren't impaired. They were awed by the heroism that Scanio had displayed in the turret. They recommended that he be placed on six months of limited duty and estimated he should be fit for duty at the end of that time.

ON THURSDAY, May 24, three weeks after Captain Fred Moosally had retired from the Navy and one day prior to the scheduled testimony of Dr. Richard Schwoebel of Sandia National Laboratories before the Senate Armed Services Committee, the Navy was conducting the last of its drop tests at the Surface Warfare Center at Dahlgren, Virginia, using five D-846 propellant bags. Miceli had conducted sixteen tests, all of which were a bust. Karl Schuler and Paul Cooper of Sandia drove down to Dahlgren from Washington to attend the final day of testing. Five powder bags were stacked vertically under an 860-pound weight and dropped three feet onto a steel plate to simulate a high-speed overram in a sixteen-inch gun barrel.

Viewing the seventeenth test from inside a concrete bunker, Schuler and Cooper were discouraged when the bags crashed into the steel plate and nothing happened. Schuler asked Miceli if he and Cooper could go out and check the bags and rearrange some of the "tare layers" before the eighteenth test. "Go ahead, be my guest!" Miceli replied, confident that nothing would have any effect on the bags. Dahlgren workers unfastened the five bags, each of which had the pellets bunched near the center of the "tare layer." Schuler noticed that all five pellets in the "tare layer" in one bag had been crushed. "One of the pellets actually looked like it had shot out some hot little particles," Schuler said. He thought the pellets were too near each other to ignite. So he spread them out. The bags were resealed and restacked. Schuler and Cooper returned to the bunker and told Miceli to drop the weight and the bags.

Smiling faintly, Miceli started the countdown: "Four . . . three . . . two . . . one . . . fire . . . ." The weight and propellant dropped on the steel plate. A ball of yellow flame enveloped the bags, accompanied by a huge "kaboom." The metal structure that had supported the weight and bags was blown apart. The entire event was captured on videotape, which revealed that the ignition had occurred between powder bags two and three. Schuler said for nearly thirty seconds, everyone in the bunker remained silent, and then Paul Cooper exclaimed, "Oh, shit!" Some of the technicians snickered. Captain Miceli charged out of the blockhouse, nervously pacing round and round the structure for about ten minutes. Finally, he came back inside and called Vice Admiral Peter Hekman, head of Sea Systems Command, informing the admiral about the detonation. Miceli and Hekman agreed that an order had to be issued immediately, halting the firing of all sixteen-inch guns. They also surmised correctly that the Navy would be forced to reopen the *Iowa* investigation.

Dr. Schwoebel was excited when Schuler and Cooper phoned him and told him what had happened. When Schuler and Cooper arrived in Washington, they called Richard DeBobes to make sure that Senator Sam Nunn, the Armed Services Committee chairman, knew about the events at Dahlgren. Admiral Edney had claimed "that Sandia's work was all horseshit," DeBobes said.

THE SENATE hearing began at 9 A.M. on Friday, May 25, in Room 216 of the Hart Senate Office Building. In his opening remarks, Senator Nunn got straight to the point, saying, "The testimony today will essentially eviscerate the Navy's conclusion that the explosion on the USS *Iowa* was the result of a wrongful intentional act." He said "grave doubts" would be cast on the Navy's findings concerning the presence of "foreign material" on the *Iowa*'s rotating band. It would also be shown that very serious deficiencies existed in the Navy's training of its sixteen-inch gun crews.

Senator John Warner contended that it was much too early to rush to judgment, to use the phrase *cover-up*, or to consider apologizing to Clayton Hartwig's family. He praised the Navy for halting the firing of battleship guns and for agreeing to reopen the investigation. Senator William Cohen said the only rush to judgment had been made by the Navy when it blamed Clayton Hartwig. "I think that the Navy will have to do a great deal to rehabilitate itself in terms of its investigative activities," Cohen added. The committee's eldest member, Senator Strom Thurmond, the eighty-seven-year-old Republican from South Carolina, inserted a tough statement into the record. Thurmond called the detonation at Dahlgren "a first step in clearing the name of the sailor so maligned by the Navy's findings."

Richard Schwoebel, Karl Schuler, Paul Cooper, and Jim Borders came next. Schwoebel said the Navy hadn't produced credible evidence to prove that a chemical detonator had caused the blast. According to the Sandia Laboratory, the explosion had been either an accident due to human error or an equipment failure. Senator Nunn asked Schwoebel what he thought of Admiral Milligan's statement that, "No plausible accidental cause of ignition could be found." "We think that there is a plausible other way in which the explosion could be initiated," Schwoebel responded.

Senator John Glenn said he was distressed about the way the Navy had come to choose Clayton Hartwig as the culprit. "There was a willingness, because of lack of information, to go ahead and blame this basically on a personality profile, and to assign blame and say it could not have been anything else," Glenn said. In his closing remarks, Nunn rejected Admiral Milligan's conclusion that the explosion had occurred because of a wrongful, intentional act. This was not supported "by reliable, probative, and substantial evidence," Nunn said.

CAUTIOUS AND conservative, Sam Nunn was regarded with near-awe by his colleagues in Congress and the Bush administration. Nunn was desirous of a swift, equitable resolution to this case, including an apology to the Hartwig family. Richard DeBobes visited the Navy's Office of Legislative Affairs and advised the officers there to make sure that anyone who had been associated with the first investigation didn't participate in the second. One of the officers he specifically mentioned was Admiral Milligan. Flag officers, such as Milligan, could not be promoted without being confirmed by the Senate, and Senator Howard Metzenbaum had asked his fellow lawmakers to put a "permanent hold" on Milligan, "in the event that his name comes up for promotion."

DeBobes also informed the Navy that Captain Joseph Miceli had overstayed his welcome, spending most of his time defending his own conclusions. Milligan had nothing to do with the reinvestigation, but Miceli did. Astonishingly, he was put in total charge of the reinvestigation, although he was supposed to confer with Vice Admiral Hekman and a flag board composed of three of Hekman's subordinates and a retired admiral. The flag board proved to be a toothless tiger. It rarely met, didn't get involved in Miceli's day-to-day operations, and never insisted that Miceli speed up his work. About all the board did was provide the Navy with a smokescreen, allowing it to claim that Miceli wasn't a one-man band. But that's what he was. Every time Sandia announced that it had another breakthrough, Miceli stalled and stalled until he could find something with which to discredit his opposition. He even scoffed at the qualifications of Sandia's experts, claiming that its laboratories and personnel had no experience in crime-solving. The Navy announced that the new investigation would be completed in six weeks. But that didn't happen. It would drag on for seventeen months.

THE EXPLOSION at Dahlgren and Senator Nunn's hearing received front-page treatment in many of the country's major newspapers and led the network news broadcasts. They were also given prominent play by the overseas news media. Mike Wallace was in Paris during this time, and he read about the developments in the *International Herald-Tribune* and saw replays of the blast on CNN. As he was getting ready to leave his hotel, Mike ran into Navy Secretary Lawrence Garrett and tried to pin down Garrett about whether the Navy was going to apologize to Clayton Hartwig's family. Garrett refused to tell Wallace anything and briskly walked away from the correspondent. Following that encounter, Mike called me in Washington and told me to go to New York to update the *Iowa* piece we had aired in November. He would head back and join me, and we would rerun the piece on Sunday night.

ONCE ADMIRAL Frank Kelso relieved Admiral Trost as Chief of Naval Operations and Admiral Jerome Johnson replaced Admiral Bud Edney as Vice Chief of Naval Operations on June 30, 1990, the Navy's unwavering position about the cause of the *Iowa* disaster began to change. Admiral Kelso, from the very beginning, had not liked the Navy's decision that Clayton Hartwig had blown up the center gun. According to an assistant, Kelso said, "This is one of a number of possible conclusions. It's not right for the Navy to lay this at the feet of a petty officer." Admiral Johnson, who had been on the bridge with Fred Moosally at the time of the explosion, also had been firmly against the decision to accuse Hartwig. Johnson said, "I told Frank Kelso that I had investigated a number of catastrophic airplane explosions, and it was my experience that you sometimes can't reconstruct the cause." Johnson felt that the *Iowa* explosion could never be reconstructed, and he said that one of his priorities as the number-two man in the Navy would be to overturn the verdict against Hartwig and to try to make amends to his family.

Shortly after Frank Kelso became CNO, Richard DeBobes visited him in the Pentagon and said the Navy was making "a major mistake" in allowing Captain Miceli to remain in charge of the *Iowa* reinvestigation. "The Navy got rid of Milligan. You need to get rid of anybody who is tainted like Miceli," said DeBobes. Kelso listened but allowed Miceli to remain in control.

AS IT turned out, Miceli wasn't the only major player in the first *Iowa* investigation who managed to wangle his way into the second. Commander Ronald Swanson, who had been Admiral Milligan's counsel, and as such had drafted most of the *Iowa* report, remained counsel to Admiral Johnson. In the summer of 1990, when Rear Admiral Gordon, the Navy's Judge Advocate General, heard that Swanson was working on the reinvestigation, he went to Admiral Kelso and said that Swanson had a blatant conflict of interest and should be removed promptly. The CNO agreed and had Swanson transferred.

BY AUGUST of 1990, Kathy Kubicina had tired of relying on reporters, congressional investigators, and NIS agents as her principal sources of information. She decided that before the *Iowa* went back into mothballs and her crew was dispersed, she should drive to Norfolk and do some gumshoeing on her own. Didi Price, whose brother, Matt Price, had died in the explosion, told Kubicina that her boyfriend, Gunner's Mate Third Class Cletus Guffin, a former Turret One gun captain, was "positive" that Clayton Hartwig's body was not found where the Navy claimed it was. Guffin also said that Turret One's former officer, Lieutenant Dan Meyer, knew where the body was actually found, but he had instructed the men assigned to his turret to keep their mouths shut. Guffin shared an apartment away from the ship with Gunner's Mate Second Class John Keerl, who had provided unburned gunpowder grains from Turret Two's center gun to a Sandia scientist, thereby prompting the arrest of Lieutenant Meyer. Didi suggested that it would be a good idea for Kathy to visit Guffin and Keerl and hear what they had to say.

Kathy wanted somebody to accompany her, somebody who knew the case well and could be a reliable witness as to what was said. Kathy got Nancy Jo Lewis, a Northville, Michigan, accountant, to go. Lewis's twenty-four-year-old son, Richard Lewis, a fire controlman, had been killed after being aboard the *Iowa* a mere two weeks. Lewis had begun a newsletter for the relatives of the other men who had perished in the turret, and she had interviewed gunpowder experts, computer specialists, and radar technicians. She became familiar with the initial muzzle velocities of shells, understood how an analog fire-control computer worked, knew how far the Navy's OP-3565 manual required an AN/WSC-3 antenna to be from a gun turret, and could rattle off the cyanide and carbon monoxide levels found in the bodies of the forty-seven crewmen.

When Kathy and Nancy visited John Keerl at his apartment, they found him to be supportive but uptight. The criminal charges of obstruction of justice, relating to his giving powder grains to a Sandia scientist, had just been dropped, and he had been cautioned by several officers to avoid any future involvement in the *Iowa* investigation. Even so, Keerl told the two women that not a single gunner's mate on the ship believed that Clayton Hartwig was guilty. He stated that the explosion resulted from a high-speed overram. Shortly before the disaster, Keerl said, he and Dale Mortensen had coffee with Ernie Hanyecz, Turret Two's leading petty officer. On their way to their respective turrets, Hanyecz stated that if there were going to be any problems during the gun shoot, they would involve Turret Two's center gun, because Errick Lawrence was assigned as gun captain there. Keerl then produced a letter he had recently received from Dan Meyer, who was serving aboard the USS *La Salle* in Bahrain, along with a copy of Meyer's letter of resignation, which Vice Admiral Boorda had advised Meyer to rescind. Meyer had asked Keerl to make sure that the gunner's mates in Turret One read the letter. "For the gunnermates of Turret Two, I deeply regret that they died not for nation, family, or creed but in defense of the institutionalized interests at Crane, Indiana, Dahlgren, Virginia, and Louisville, Kentucky."

Kathy pulled her brother's autopsy photo from a folder and handed it to Keerl. He took it reluctantly, staring at it for several minutes without saying anything. "Is that the body you saw in the pit below the gun?" Kathy asked. The clean-cut second-class gunner's mate remained speechless. "Well, is it?" she demanded. He beat around the bush. "It could be. I'm just not sure." Cletus Guffin, Keerl's roommate, who had been listening quietly to the exchange, screamed at Keerl, "Just tell them what you told me last week about being sure that Hartwig's body was down in the pit below the gun! What are you afraid of?" Keerl still refused to speak up.

ON FRIDAY, October 26, 1990, the *Iowa* was decommissioned for the third time. The morning before the midday ceremony, the skies over the Norfolk Naval Air Station were clear, the waters of the Chesapeake Bay were calm, and the weather was temperate. Sailors lined up row after row of brown metal folding chairs on the teak-covered main deck to accommodate the thousand or so former crewmen, some from World War II and Korea, and family members who were expected to attend the formalities. As the guests clambered up the forward and aft gangplanks, a northeaster blew in with gale-force winds, knocking hundreds of chairs over the side, into the water and onto Pier 12. The temperature dropped abruptly and torrential rains soaked the ship, her crewmen, and visitors. High wind gusts made it essential to get everyone off the main deck and inside the ship. Admiral Johnson, the Vice Chief of Naval Operations, climbed to the bridge and delivered the farewell address on the ship's public-address system. Former crewmen and visitors collected under loudspeakers inside the ship and listened to the admiral's address.

"You here today and your fallen shipmates have taught us that sacrifice, heroism, and courage live," Johnson said. "Decommissioning of a Navy ship is always a bittersweet occasion," he said. "Most of all, there's the sense of pride of having been a member of a small group of people that have served in a ship that helped write the history of the United States." Commander John Morse, the ship's commanding officer, said, "We shall not forget this is our ship. The queen of the fleet. She will always be a symbol of peace, hope, and fear," he said. "A fast ship, and ready still to go in harm's way. Fear God and Dreadnought!"

AT A morning hearing conducted by Representative Mary Rose Oakar on November 8, 1990, Vice Admiral Peter Hekman, head of Sea Systems Command, vowed that the reinvestigation of the *Iowa* explosion would be completed in several months. Hekman said a battleship "was not what we would call a high-tech ship." About 70 percent of its crewmen held low rank, as compared to a guided-missile cruiser, where fewer than fifty out of five hundred men held inferior ranks. "These ships were designed in the 1930s for an average education level in the Navy at that time of fifth grade. They are designed to withstand an eighteen-inch shell. They are tough and reliable, but simple systems," Hekman said. Audible gasps emanated from the place in the audience where the family members of the dead *Iowa* sailors were clustered. Some of these family members later said they took Hekman's words to mean that a man would really have to be a moron to serve aboard a battleship. "We don't have a class system in the Navy, do we?" Oakar scornfully asked. "It is not a class system," Hekman replied, swiftly backpedaling. The congresswoman reminded the admiral that three of her constituents had died aboard the *Iowa*, and all had been reasonably well educated. Was he implying that young men such as these hadn't been as valuable to the Navy as the sailors serving aboard high-tech guided-missile cruisers? Not at all. He certainly hadn't meant to classify the *Iowa*'s crewmen as "untrainable." Oakar asked if these men had been trained to operate their battleship within the Navy's safety standards. Hekman was unable to answer that question.

Oakar asked if the Secretary of the Navy and the Chief of Naval Operations intended to apologize, "or is the Navy too arrogant to indicate that it may have made a mistake in the handling of this?" "It is not too arrogant. If they feel a mistake has been made, I feel rather confident that they would apologize," Hekman said.

REAR ADMIRAL Douglas Katz called Kathy Kubicina soon after the Navy announced that it was lifting the firing restrictions on the *Wisconsin* and the *Missouri*, so those two remaining battleships could participate in the Gulf War with Iraq. Katz said that this wasn't being done without a lot of thought. She asked him if defective powder would ever cause another battleship disaster. "Absolutely never," he said. "Never, never, never." When would the *Iowa* reinvestigation be concluded? Katz said there was no firm timetable. Kathy told him about the interviews that she and Nancy Lewis had conducted in Norfolk, and the fact that she had obtained Clayton's autopsy photo in order to compare it with those of other men who had been killed in the turret. "His body, although it is in bad condition, is not in as bad a condition as the rest of the bodies are," she said. Katz urged her to do nothing with this material until the technical inquiry was finally over. Katz said that he was getting ready to leave the Pentagon and probably wouldn't be talking to Kathy again. He went to the Middle East, where he would command a carrier battle group during the war with Iraq. But he was wrong about not talking to Kathy again. He would be ordered to return to Cleveland to deliver a very different message to the Hartwig family than the one he had imparted in 1989.

PAUL COOPER, Sandia's explosives expert, had never ceased searching for the projectiles that were lodged in Turret Two's left and right guns when the center gun blew up. It had required a tremendous effort to remove these shells from the barrels and then hoist them from the turret. Captain Joseph Miceli claimed that the two gargantuan shells had simply vanished. One day in early December 1990, as Cooper was wandering through a warehouse at Dahlgren, he asked a technician about the missing projectiles. The man led Cooper to a storage area where Cooper spied two 2,700-pound projectiles standing upright. They were painted light blue, just like the center projectile, and were battered and scarred. Cooper examined them closely and discovered that they were covered with the same minute metal fibers that the Navy claimed had been part of the detonator used in the center gun.

Cooper informed the other members of the Sandia team about his find, and tests were scheduled. The fibers on all three shells were the same. Grease and debris removed from under the rotating bands of the right and left projectiles had calcium and chlorine levels identical to those in the center shell. Glycol levels were similar on all three projectiles. "It should have ended the Navy's case against Hartwig right then and there," Dr. Schwoebel said.

BY EARLY December 1990, after serving for six months aboard the USS *La Salle*, Dan Meyer decided that he had found a home. She had been the flagship for the commander of the Navy's Middle East Force for two decades. Her skipper was Captain John Nathman, destined to become an admiral. The day that Meyer arrived to become radio signals officer, he provided Captain Nathman and the executive officer with a synopsis of the *Iowa* disaster, the Navy's and Sandia's investigations, and his roles in them. He told his superiors about his arrest and his meeting with the Chief of Naval Personnel, Vice Admiral Boorda. Meyer correctly assumed that if the captain and executive officer were aware of his past, they wouldn't overreact if NIS agents, Senate investigators, or somebody from Sandia unexpectedly appeared on the quarterdeck and asked to speak with him.

Meyer prospered on the *La Salle*. He had been promoted and was now wearing the twin silver bars, or "tracks," of a full lieutenant on the collars of his khaki work shirt. Since communications was one of the *La Salle*'s most important functions, the radio signals officer had one of the busiest jobs on the ship. Meyer enjoyed it, even though there were times when he missed the pumping adrenaline that preceded the ear-splitting booms of the sixteen-inch guns.

On December 5, while Meyer was assigning priorities and security classifications to stacks of outgoing messages in radio central, he was called by Lieutenant Matt Anderson, the *La Salle*'s legal officer. "Dude, you've got a problem. NIS is on the ship, and I've just talked with them," Anderson said. "They asked for 'Ensign Meyer,' and I said, 'You mean Lieutenant Meyer.' And they said, 'Maybe he's a lieutenant for now, but not for long.'" Anderson told Meyer that he didn't have to leave the ship with the agents unless he agreed to do so. Meyer had just received a letter from Kathy Kubicina, informing him that NIS was going to interview Cletus Guffin and Nancy Lewis about where Clayton Hartwig's body was actually found, so he was pretty sure he knew why the agents were here. For the previous five months, he had been corresponding regularly with Kathy, Nancy Lewis, Peggy Price, and some of the other families of the *Iowa* victims.

Lieutenant Anderson escorted NIS Special Agents Mark Prugh and Robert Grosson, from the NIS Bahrain office into the locked and air-conditioned confines of the radio compartment. The NIS men insisted that Meyer leave the ship and accompany them to their office. Meyer put on his blue-and-gold-lettered *La Salle* baseball cap and followed them off the ship without protest. Once they arrived at NIS headquarters, the agents asked Meyer if he had publicly stated that only three bodies had been found in Turret Two's center gun room instead of four, as Admiral Milligan had claimed in his report. Meyer said that was true. Did he tell his men not to discuss where Clayton Hartwig's body had been found? Meyer said he informed his men that if they didn't agree with any aspect of the Navy's investigation, including the location of Hartwig's body, that they should tell him, and he would make sure that a federal investigative agency with no stake in the outcome, such as Congress or the General Accounting Office or Sandia, received the information. Any gag orders, he said, would have come from Captain Fred Moosally. That ended the interview. The agents drove Meyer back to the *La Salle*, where they faced several indignant senior officers who demanded to know why they had "kidnapped" one of their subordinates. Meyer continued to receive the letters from Kathy Kubicina and the other relatives for the next six months, but he wouldn't hear from NIS again until he had been discharged from the Navy and was in law school.

26

☆

"We Made a Bad Mistake, and We're Sorry."

IN EARLY SEPTEMBER of 1991, Dan Meyer was unpacking his belongings in his apartment in Bloomington, Indiana, where he was preparing to attend Indiana University School of Law, when I called and asked if I could go there and talk to him. Meyer said that even though he was a civilian, he wanted to check with the Chief of Naval Information before giving me an answer. Meyer had little difficulty getting Rear Admiral Brent Baker on the phone. He told Baker about my interview request and asked if he could cooperate with me. Baker said he had no objections. Meyer called me back, and we arranged to meet that weekend. The day before I arrived in Bloomington, Meyer received a call from Captain Joseph Miceli, who said he had heard from "someone in Brent Baker's office" that Meyer planned to talk with me. That was bad, very bad, Miceli said. Meyer should have nothing to do with me. Meyer told Miceli that he was a civilian, and he could talk with anyone he pleased.

After I arrived on campus, Meyer walked me through what he had seen and heard the day of the explosion. He described his trips into the lower part of the turret and discussed the conditions of the bodies he found in Turret Two. The body of Lieutenant Philip Buch, the turret officer, was in three parts. Chief Ziegler had been beheaded. There were definitely only three bodies—not four, as the Navy claimed—in the center gun room. They were barely recognizable, especially the rammerman's. "Hartwig was down in the pit," he said. He talked with Dale Mortensen and John Keerl, who had closely examined the body there. They said Hartwig had been down there turning on the gas ejection air. I pulled out Clayton Hartwig's autopsy photographs and handed them to Meyer. He looked at them for a long time and then said they looked like the body he had seen at the bottom of the pit.

"The body in these pictures is certainly in much better shape than the other three bodies I found in the center gun room," he added. Before I left Bloomington, Meyer also agreed to do a television interview with Mike Wallace.

IT WAS now time to do another *Iowa* piece on *60 Minutes*. I planned to call Brent Baker to see if I could arrange an interview with Admiral Kelso. But before I did that, Baker called me. We met and spent most of the time talking about Captain Joseph Miceli, whom Baker referred to as "an out-of-control zealot" and "a real loose cannon on the gun deck." He quoted Miceli as saying, "I know Hartwig did it [blew up the gun]. He was running an experiment with Chief Skelley. He put a detonator in the gun for Skelley to check out how much stress the barrel could take." Baker said that Miceli wanted NIS to arrest Skelley. Baker said he was appalled by this preposterous idea, and when he told Admiral Kelso about it, the CNO blanched. According to Baker, Kelso said, "If we've been basing our investigation on this kind of crap, then it's time for us to apologize."

I asked Baker if he would have lunch with Mike Wallace. He was willing, so the three of us met at the Palm Restaurant in Washington. Looking dapper in his white uniform with gold shoulder boards, Baker told Mike everything that he had told me earlier about Miceli's bizarre behavior. Baker said that he would schedule a lunch with us and Admiral Kelso at the Pentagon, where we could discuss the proposed apology to the Hartwig family and ascertain whether the CNO would agree to sit down with Mike on-camera after he delivered the apology.

THE WEEKEND before our luncheon with Admiral Kelso, the Navy became enmeshed in a seamy scandal that became known as "Tailhook." (Tailhook was named after the hook at the rear of an aircraft that snags a wire when the plane lands on an aircraft carrier and keeps it from hurtling down the flight deck.) Some 5,000 active duty, reserve, and retired Navy and Marine Corps aviators, defense contractors, and groupies attended the 1991 Tailhook conference at the Las Vegas, Nevada, Hilton. Washington dignitaries and flag officers, including Navy Secretary Lawrence Garrett and Admiral Frank Kelso, were also on hand. Previous Tailhook conventions had been described as "grossly appalling" by flag officers who attended them. But this one was far worse than the others. The fallout from the drunken orgy lasted three years, turned the Navy upside down, cost Secretary Garrett and a number of flag officers their jobs, and almost caused the Naval Investigative Service to be abolished. Admiral Kelso would have his reputation besmirched and be forced to resign before the end of his second tour as CNO.

Most of the misbehavior took place in twenty-two hospitality suites on the third floor of the hotel. All of them furnished unlimited quantities of free booze, twenty-four hours a day. For the young male officers, the convention's main highlight was something called "the gauntlet." Hundreds of drunken males, shouting obscenities, lined both sides of a curving hallway on the third floor and groped, fondled, and pinched women on their breasts, buttocks, and crotch areas. Some of the women had their clothes ripped off in the gauntlet. Others were physically picked up and passed along over the heads of the howling mob. Some of the men exposed themselves. The Defense Department's Inspector General later estimated that there were fifty-three aggravated assaults during the gauntlet, nine more in hotel suites, and six on the pool patio. Several participants later testified that a number of flag officers were aware of the sexual assaults but did nothing to halt them.

MIKE AND I sat down to lunch with Admiral Kelso on Monday, September 9, just two days after "the gauntlet" took place in Las Vegas. We were in the admiral's private dining room in the Pentagon to discuss an apology in the *Iowa* case and had no idea about Tailhook. Both of us were familiar with Kelso's service record and respected him.

A country boy with a "common touch," Kelso was also regarded as an intellectual by his peers. Kelso's aides had repeatedly told us that he didn't concur with Admiral Milligan's conclusions about the *Iowa* disaster, and that he was committed to reversing those conclusions.

Admiral Kelso never promised that he would extend a candid apology to the Hartwigs, but he led us to believe that he might. He was also noncommittal about whether he would sit down and do an interview with us after the apology. However, he did say, "We made a bad mistake, and we're sorry."

Admiral Brent Baker drafted a letter for Admiral Kelso to be sent to the Hartwigs. For a time, Kelso thought it was fine, because he initialed it. The letter said, "It is my conclusion, as Chief of Naval Operations, that there is no credible Navy technical evidence to point to your son, Petty Officer Clayton M. Hartwig, or any of his shipmates, as having caused this explosion. We will never know with absolute certainty exactly what happened in Turret Two. I wish to apologize to you and your family for any emotional distress the Navy has caused you. Your son died while serving his country."

REAR ADMIRAL Douglas Katz arrived at Earl and Evelyn Hartwig's Cleveland home at 9:30 A.M. on October 17, 1991, bearing the Navy's apology. Katz strode briskly through a shouting swarm of reporters and camera crews on the Hartwigs' front lawn. He was trailed by Commander Sam Falcona, the same public-relations officer who had accompanied Katz here in 1989, and Lieutenant Karen Ford, who had taken over for Lieutenant Renee Lewis as the Hartwigs' casualty assistance officer. Kathy Kubicina, Earl and Evelyn Hartwig, and their attorney, Kreig Brusnahan, greeted the three naval officers at the front door. Katz hugged and kissed Evelyn, telling her that he was bringing better news than the last time. Brusnahan had a cassette tape recorder sitting prominently on a coffee table to make sure that there would be no disagreements later about what was said. Before reading Admiral Kelso's apology, Katz distributed copies of the final reports from Sandia National Laboratories and Sea Systems Command.

Admiral Kelso's letter differed significantly from the draft prepared by Admiral Baker. It said the Navy had been unable to prove or disprove Sandia's theory that the explosion had been initiated by ramming the five bags of gunpowder too fast and too far. The Navy had also been unable to prove or disprove its original conclusion that Clayton Hartwig had blown up the gun. "Without this clear and convincing proof, the opinion that your son may have intentionally caused his own death and the deaths of his shipmates is not appropriate," the letter stated. Kelso said the Navy's final position was "that the exact cause [of the explosion] cannot be determined." The initial investigation contained "a qualified opinion that implicated" Petty Officer Hartwig, the letter continued, and that opinion had been interpreted by many as being "conclusive." "For this, on behalf of the United States Navy, I ask you to accept my sincere regrets."

Kathy and her parents had mixed feelings as they listened to Katz read the letter. They realized that this wasn't "a real apology," but they also knew that the public and press would consider it to be one. Kreig Brusnahan, who had lodged a $40 million damage complaint against the Navy for its treatment of the Hartwigs, told Katz that he had a message he wanted delivered to the CNO. The Navy hadn't responded to Brusnahan's complaint for the "intentional and negligent infliction of emotional distress," and the statutory deadline for doing so was about to run out. Unless there was some movement on the Navy's part to settle the complaint, Brusnahan would have to file a lawsuit in U.S. District Court in Cleveland.

"I don't want this going through the courts for the next five or ten or fifteen years. It's not going to do anybody any good," Brusnahan said. Katz said he would inform Admiral Kelso that Brusnahan preferred to negotiate the claim with the Navy rather than litigate it. As Katz prepared to depart, he said, "Well, I would love to see you all again, but I'd just as soon it not be here." "We hope we never have to see you again," Evelyn shot back. Just as soon as the three naval officers left the house, they were surrounded by reporters and photographers. Smiling, Katz told the reporters: "We sincerely regretted implicating their son; we apologize. We apologize for the burden of this whole thing. It was hard on them and hard on us."

ADMIRAL FRANK Kelso's apology and press conference took place minutes after Admiral Katz left the Hartwigs' home in Cleveland. Kelso stated that despite spending $25 million and more than two years of testing, the Navy had uncovered no evidence to suggest that the gun had been operated improperly, nor had it established a plausible accidental cause for the explosion. But he also emphasized that there was no evidence that anybody had blown up the gun. He announced that he was changing the rules for investigating major accidents involving fatalities. The Navy would never again use an informal board composed of a single officer, as it had done in this case. The hope was that this would ensure that no officer or sailor in the future would be accused of wrongdoing without overwhelming evidence.

Admiral Kelso walked directly from the press conference to another room in the Pentagon, where Mike Wallace, Ari Allan, I, and our two camera crews were waiting to interview him. Mike shook Kelso's hand when he entered the room. Bob Peterson, our chief photographer, turned on the lights and made sure that two cameras were synchronized. One was trained on Mike and the other on Kelso. Once the interview began, Mike made it clear that he was interested in where Clayton Hartwig's body had actually been found. He said that in order for Hartwig to have inserted a detonator into the breech, he had to have been standing in the gun captain's position. Kelso concurred, but he pointed out that he wasn't accusing Hartwig of doing anything wrong. "No, but you're saying that you still are not sure. You've apologized to the Hartwig family, but you've not said, 'He couldn't have been there, he couldn't have done it, because he wasn't in a position to do it,'" Mike said. "What I'm saying is that I do not know exactly what happened," Kelso countered.

"But what if Hartwig wasn't at that position at the time the accident took place, and what if the Navy knew it?" Mike asked. Kelso said he had seen no evidence to suggest that the Navy knew that Hartwig had been anywhere but in the gun captain's position. Mike asked one of our technicians to play excerpts from Brian Scanio's and Dan Meyer's interviews. We had interviewed Scanio in front of Turret Two aboard the *Iowa,* moored in the Philadelphia Navy Shipyard, and Meyer on a destroyer in New York Harbor. Scanio appeared on the monitor, saying that Hartwig's body was found in the pit below the gun, not in the gun captain's position. Meyer appeared next. He was seen examining Hartwig's autopsy photos and then declaring that this was the same corpse he'd seen in the pit. He also stated that it was common knowledge among the *Iowa*'s sailors that Hartwig's body was found in the pit.

Admiral Kelso called Scanio "a very heroic young man" who had been decorated, but he said there were opinions differing from his about the location of Hartwig's body. Kelso said he had personally talked to a doctor at the Armed Forces Institute of Pathology about the matter. "Which one, the first or the second?" Mike asked. Kelso said he didn't know, he couldn't remember the man's name.

Kelso said that once he learned that we had interviewed Brian Scanio in Philadelphia about the *Iowa,* he read the transcript of Scanio's testimony before Admiral Milligan's panel. Scanio hadn't been able to identify the body in the pit, Kelso declared. If Kelso had really studied the transcript of Scanio's testimony, he would have discovered that the former *Iowa* sailor had told Milligan's legal officer, Commander Ronald Swanson, that he had seen two bodies in the pit.

Mike interrogated Kelso about the leaks of derogatory information about Clayton Hartwig and Kendall Truitt. "Who leaked what to whom and what was the reason for the leaks?" Mike demanded. Kelso said he "abhorred leaks" and had no idea who was responsible for them. Mike pounced, referring to Captain Joseph Miceli's dealings with Captain Al Becker and George Wilson of the *Washington Post* at Becker's Virginia home in the fall of 1989. Miceli allegedly had told Wilson, "The Navy has the goods on Hartwig." Kelso reluctantly admitted that he knew about the incident. "You would have no objection, then, if Captain Joe Miceli talked to us?" Mike asked. "We will consider it," Kelso said.

Pointing at Brent Baker, Mike told Kelso that his public-affairs chief had described Miceli to us as "a zealot, and a loose cannon completely out of control." Kelso made a faint attempt at defending Miceli. Mike asked Baker if he'd like to expand on his comments. The camera that had been trained on Kelso slewed around and focused on Baker. One of our audio technicians pointed a "shotgun" microphone on a metal pole in Baker's direction. Kelso sat dumbstruck while Mike toyed with Baker. "I don't believe I told you he was 'out of control' or a 'zealot,' did I?" Baker said faintly. "In my presence, and in the presence of my colleague Charlie Thompson. I was there. I heard you say it," Mike shouted. "I told you he [Miceli] was . . . that he had very determined opinions on this issue. He is an expert on guns," Baker sidestepped.

We had also brought along a videotape of the May 24, 1989, NBC News Fred Francis piece, which relied upon leaked NIS documents. If Kelso had seemed uncomfortable before, he was positively squirming in his seat as he listened to the NBC correspondent discuss the "special relationship" between Hartwig and Truitt and say, "Navy sources tell NBC News that some disturbing facts have been uncovered about Truitt." After the tape ended, Mike asked who had leaked the material to Fred Francis. Kelso said he had no idea. But why hadn't the Navy come forward after this piece and said, "This is baloney. Nobody from the Navy says this. It is absolutely untrue"? Why had the Navy remained silent and let the public believe that this kind of stuff was true? Kelso said he didn't know.

Mike pursued Baker again. "Admiral Baker, did you leak anything to NBC about Clayton Hartwig?" "Absolutely not," Baker said. Mike then told Admiral Kelso that the Navy would have saved a great deal of time and money if it had ever made an honest attempt to determine where Hartwig's body was actually found. Kelso repeated that the forensic pathologist, whose name he still couldn't remember, had been able to verify the location of Hartwig's body. "Was Clayton Hartwig the gun captain that day?" Mike inquired. "I . . . I . . . the . . . ," Kelso reeled. "We're told he wasn't, by people aboard the ship," Mike said. Kelso acknowledged that several people who had been on the ship had testified that Hartwig was not the gun captain. "That's part of the things that I can't explain with conclusive proof," he said. Mike asked Kelso if he had discussed the apology with his predecessor, Admiral Carl Trost. Kelso said he had not. "You're in the unenviable position of cleaning up after your predecessor," Mike observed. "No, I would not say that. I knew when I came to this job that I was going to have to face the *Iowa* investigation some day. That's part of the job. I'm doing what I think is right," Kelso said.

ON JUNE 30, 1992, attorney Kreig Brusnahan filed a lawsuit in U.S. District Court in Cleveland against the Navy for intentionally inflicting emotional distress on the Hartwigs. His filing came two months after the Navy sent a letter to Clayton Hartwig's parents' home in Cleveland, inviting the dead sailor to join the Naval Reserve. The Navy promised the following benefits for enlisting: extra income every month; travel; leadership and advancement opportunities; subsidized education; retirement; and "life insurance (optional)." "Needless to say, my parents were traumatized," Kathy Kubicina said of the Navy solicitation. "My father at first thought it was a joke. My mother, of course, has been heartbroken." Admiral Frank Kelso dashed off another letter of apology to the Hartwigs after reporters asked Brent Baker about this latest screw-up.

BRUSNAHAN SCALED back the amount of money he sought from the Navy from $40 million to $12 million. He asked for $3 million each for Earl and Evelyn Hartwig and $3 million each for Kathy Kubicina and her sister, Cindy Werthmuller. By claiming that the Navy had deliberately injured the four family members rather than Clayton, Brusnahan avoided a legal obstacle known as the "Feres Doctrine." A 1950 U.S. Supreme Court decision, the Feres Doctrine states that members of the military who are injured on active duty do not have the same rights as other citizens do to sue the government. Thirty-eight of the *Iowa* families had also filed a lawsuit against the Navy in U.S. District Court in Alexandria, Virginia, seeking $2.35 billion in damages. But their attorneys made a calculated decision to mount a frontal assault on the Feres Doctrine. U.S. District Judge Claude M. Hilton summarily dismissed their suit. The Hartwigs' suit remained virtually dormant for a year. During that time, the U.S. Justice Department, which represented the Navy, attempted to have the suit dismissed on the grounds of "sovereign immunity," alleging that no citizen could sue the government without the government's permission. In May 1993, U.S. District Judge Paul R. Matia ruled in Cleveland that the Justice Department was wrong, and he allowed the Hartwigs' suit to proceed.

The Hartwigs also sued NBC News for $10 million. They claimed that reports by Fred Francis, NBC's Pentagon correspondent, had falsely portrayed Clayton Hartwig as a suicidal mass murderer, and that his broadcasts had inflicted emotional distress on the family. NBC defended itself by claiming that Francis couldn't be held liable, because he had based his reports on leaked official government records. The network argued that even if the bootlegged NIS files that Francis used contained defamatory information, he wasn't responsible for disseminating those misrepresentations. The federal judge finally dismissed the Hartwigs' NBC suit before either side had taken any testimony.

BY THE summer of 1993, it had become clear that despite his hard work and loyalty, Kreig Brusnahan needed some help with the Hartwigs' lawsuit against the Navy. "I simply didn't have the resources to fight the entire United States Navy," Brusnahan said. I asked Kathy Kubicina if she would like me to talk to Cleveland attorney Terence Clark, a longtime friend, to see if he'd consider representing her family. After meeting with Clark, the Hartwigs chose his firm, Squire, Sanders & Dempsey, to represent them.

When Terence Clark entered the case, he brought with him two top-flight attorneys. The first was Richard Gurbst, a Squire, Sanders & Dempsey partner who had worked for the Legal Aid Society of Cleveland for eleven years, where he handled criminal, juvenile, and civil matters for clients who couldn't afford a private attorney. The third member of the legal team was Paula Christ, who had clerked for the chief federal judge in Cleveland before joining the law firm. The Navy's case was handled by Marie Louise Hagen and Steven Snyder, attorneys who worked for the Justice Department's Civil Division in Washington.

JUST BEFORE Thanksgiving in 1993, Marie Hagen began playing hardball. She brought back NIS agent Tom Goodman from his duty station in Europe to assist her with the lawsuit as an investigator. Goodman called Carole Truitt, now Kendall Truitt's ex-wife, in Florida and attempted to get her to say that Kendall and Clayton Hartwig had been homosexual lovers while they served aboard the *Iowa*. He told her that he was working for the Justice Department, which was defending the Navy in the Hartwig lawsuit. "You're divorced now. Is there anything you might remember in the four and half years since the explosion?" Carole quoted Goodman as saying. She told Goodman she didn't want to have anything more to do with him and warned him never to call her again. When she hung up, she phoned Evelyn Hartwig in Cleveland.

"They're back at it again! They're going around trying to get people to say that Ken and Clay were gay, only they've got the Justice Department helping them this time!" Carole cried, excitedly. She told Evelyn that she would do anything she could to help, including testifying in court. "They're terrible people! Somebody's got to stop them!" she exclaimed.

SHORTLY AFTER agent Tom Goodman returned to his home base at La Maddalena on the Italian island of Sardinia, after doing detective work for

Marie Hagen, he made arrangements to visit John Mullahy. Mullahy had moved to Cartagena, Spain, when he retired from the Navy in 1991. After leaving the *Iowa*, Mullahy had served with distinction aboard two carriers and had been promoted to chief petty officer. He had selected Cartagena so that his wife, Geli, could be near her family. He was employed by a Spanish contractor making ship repairs for the U.S. Navy.

Mullahy was instantly on guard when Goodman called to say he was coming to Cartagena to treat him to lunch. Goodman wasted no time honing in on the homosexuality issue. Had Clayton Hartwig and Kendall Truitt been homosexual lovers on the battleship? It had been more than four years since the explosion. Maybe Mullahy had felt sorry for Hartwig and covered for him when he talked with Admiral Milligan and testified before Congress? Mullahy was out of the Navy, Goodman said, and nobody would charge him with anything if he changed his story. Mullahy exploded and began swearing. He told Goodman that he wasn't changing anything, because he had told the truth.

But Goodman wouldn't stop there. He asked more questions about the sexual orientation of Hartwig and Truitt, and Mullahy cursed more. Goodman wanted to know if Mullahy knew where Truitt was. Mullahy said he hadn't talked with Truitt in years and didn't know where he was. As they left the restaurant, Goodman handed him a card and asked if Mullahy planned to testify for the Hartwigs. Mullahy said he didn't know, but there was no way he would ever testify for the Navy. He said the Navy had killed forty-seven men, falsely accused one of the dead men of being a mass murderer, and then attempted to cover up everything.

THE TWO Justice Department attorneys did everything they could to halt the flow of subpoenaed documents. Lawyers hate to start deposing witnesses until they have custody of every relevant document. Thus, Hagen and Snyder had effectively shut down the case. The two federal attorneys had no incentive to speed things up. In fact, it was contrary to their interests. By stalling, they could win this case without ever having to try it in court. After putting up with Hagen and Snyder's dilatory tactics for more than a year, Terence Clark and his colleagues asked Magistrate Judge David Perelman for relief. Perelman was in charge of overseeing "discovery" (the exchange of documents by both sides and the taking of testimony prior to trial) for Chief U.S. Judge George W. White.

Magistrate Perelman's ruling was a humiliating defeat for Hagen and Snyder. The judge was disdainful of their refusal to release a category of documents called "lessons learned." "Were the 'lessons learned' by the Navy from the *Iowa* tragedy and its aftermath the positive ones to be more vigilant and precise, in general or in specific regards, as to modes of operation aboard war vessels?" he wrote. "Or were they perhaps less laudable ones, such as not to engage in a cover-up after a screw-up; to be more circumspect in choosing a scapegoat when attempting a whitewash; to more carefully rehearse those dealing with the media to avoid a bad case of foot-in-mouth; or that it is not quite as easy to mislead the public as might be assumed?"

During the summer of 1995, Terence Clark took a deposition from a Naval Criminal Investigative Service (NCIS) agent named James Whitener. The Naval Investigative Service (NIS), badly disgraced during the Tailhook scandal, had slightly altered its name. In addition to switching its name, the agency would now be headed by a civilian instead of an admiral. Members of other federal law-enforcement agencies quickly pointed out that these cosmetic changes weren't likely to remedy the organization's ingrained habits. "Same ole, same ole," said one federal agent who had worked with the Navy sleuths in the past.

Terence Clark was deposing Whitener because Navy sources suspected him of providing computer diskettes containing *Iowa* investigative files to Len Tepper and Fred Francis of NBC News. These same sources said that Whitener had come under scrutiny for leaking sensitive files to these newsmen in another case.

Wearing a plum-colored shirt, flower-print tie, and greenish brown suit, Whitener made it known when he entered the room that he wasn't happy about being deposed. His state of mind was important, since he had a 9-mm semiautomatic pistol strapped to his belt in a holster on his right side. Several times, when he was annoyed by a question, Whitener stood up, brushed back his coat like an old-fashioned gunslinger, and displayed the weapon for everyone in the room to see. Clark repeatedly told Whitener to take off the firearm. The NCIS agent, who was represented by Steven Snyder of the Justice Department, treated the matter as a joke. But the court reporter didn't. She later told me that she had taken scores of depositions of federal agents and had never seen one behave like this with a gun. "I was really frightened," she said.

A computer buff, Whitener testified that he'd been stationed in Norfolk in 1989 and had volunteered to work on the *Iowa* investigation. Computer literacy had been practically nonexistent among his fellow agents back then, so Whitener took charge of transferring all the field reports and interviews to diskettes. He was probably the only agent in the Norfolk office who had the capability to retrieve and duplicate the computerized *Iowa* data.

When NBC News and *Newsday* broadcast and published verbatim portions of the *Iowa* files, Whitener had come under suspicion. Sharply questioned by his superiors about the leaks, he had denied any wrongdoing, but he claimed that Robert Powers, who was in charge of all NIS criminal investigations, would probably hold him responsible anyway, because there was bad blood between them.

As the deposition ended, Clark informed Whitener that he planned to call him back as a witness at a later date. Whitener hopped to his feet, again brushing back his coat to reveal his holstered pistol. Whitener's right hand snaked toward the weapon but stopped just short of grabbing the butt. He shouted that if he had to come back, Clark would have to track him down and serve him with a subpoena. "Where do I serve you then?" Clark asked. "That's your problem." "Well, I'll catch you at home then." "Feel free. Oh, by the way, no one in my family is empowered to accept . . . ." Then, glancing in the direction of the court reporter typing away on her laptop computer, he said, "I thought we were off the record." "I want to hear your nasty comments on the record," Clark said. "No one in my family is empowered to accept service, nor is anyone in my agency or my office empowered. If you want to serve, you serve," Whitener blustered. "Check your gun the next time you get up here. I don't want you coming in this office anymore with a gun," Clark said. Whitener's face reddened. He began cursing. Then he did something strange. He seized the court reporter's exhibits, piled on a table in front of her, and dashed from the room, clutching the exhibits. Loudly swearing, he made his way toward a bank of elevators, with Snyder trying to keep pace. Attorneys, paralegals, and secretaries rubbernecked in the sedate Washington office of Squire, Sanders & Dempsey. Clark later furnished the court reporter a duplicate set of exhibits. Whitener never returned the originals.

Admiral Mike Boorda inserted himself back into the *Iowa* saga on September 6, 1995. The former Chief of Naval Personnel, Boorda had taken over from Admiral Frank Kelso as Chief of Naval Operations in the spring of 1994. Boorda appeared on a nationally syndicated radio talk show hosted by Diane Rehm and discussed the case. A caller from San Antonio told the CNO that every time he heard the word *Navy*, the first thing he thought about was the *Iowa* disaster. Boorda said that handling high explosives and ordnance was a risky business. "That round going off inside the turret of the *Iowa*, which so tragically killed so many sailors, also obliterated an awful lot of the evidence, and it was a big explosion inside an enclosed space that was meant to stay enclosed," he said. The cause of the explosion would probably never be known. "We ought not speculate about it," he added.

"But there was an awful lot of speculation at the time including the labeling of one of those sailors as perhaps having been a homosexual," Diane Rehm said. "The families were terribly disturbed. It appeared as though the Navy was trying to cover its own tracks." Boorda blamed investigators who stumbled over each other and reporters who got their facts wrong because of deadline pressures and cutthroat competition. "I think finally when the Navy came out and said, 'We really don't know,' that was the most honest answer we could have come up with, and we truly, really don't know," he said.

WHEN VICE Admiral Douglas Katz arrived at a Norfolk law office in December 1995 to have his deposition taken, he was not his normal good-humored self. In the six years since he had first visited the Hartwig family in Cleveland, Katz's naval career had prospered. He had risen from captain to vice admiral. He had commanded a carrier battle group during the Gulf War with Iraq and was currently in charge of all the Navy's surface forces in the Atlantic. He could reasonably expect to attain four-star rank. However, the *Iowa* case had become a tar baby, sticking to him no matter where he went or how high he ascended. In addition to the Justice Department lawyers who represented him, his superiors had dispatched an attorney, a Navy captain, to take notes and report back on Katz's performance. One slip of the tongue here, and his career plans could be dashed.

During the deposition, Katz several times informed Richard Gurbst, one of the Hartwigs' attorneys, that he was not familiar with various aspects of sixteen-inch gunnery. Gurbst was incredulous, since Katz had commanded the battleship *New Jersey*. Katz could not explain the projectile and powder ramming process and wasn't sure whether four, five, or six bags constituted the standard load for firing a gun.

When he extended the Navy's apology to the Hartwigs in 1991, Katz had given the family the distinct impression that he believed Clayton was innocent. "We might make a few mistakes along the way, but we always generally try to come back and correct them; better that than the alternative," Katz had told the family then. However, in the course of his deposition, Katz repeatedly said he still personally believed that Clayton Hartwig sabotaged the center gun. Upon what standard of proof did he base his belief? Nothing. It was just a feeling.

RETIRED ADMIRAL Edney, the former Vice Chief of Naval Operations, was deposed for two days during September 1996. Terry Clark asked the sixty-one-year-old admiral if he believed the *Iowa* explosion had been an accident. There was no possibility of that, he responded. Edney admitted that he once had become furious at Captain Joseph Miceli, who had headed the *Iowa* technical investigation, for leaking classified information to George Wilson of the *Washington Post*. "I was extremely unhappy and reacted to it . . . and I was unhappy. When I'm unhappy, there's no doubt in anybody's mind," he said. Had Edney ordered the Naval Investigative Service to go back and try harder to make a criminal case against Kendall Truitt, even though top NIS officials advised him that there was no credible evidence to connect Truitt with the explosion? At first, Edney said that he couldn't recall, but then he added, "But I would not be surprised at that [happening]."

Captain Joseph Miceli was deposed by Paula Christ over a four-day period in December 1996. Now retired, the sixty-three-year-old Miceli claimed that shortly after being appointed technical director of the investigation, he phoned a captain in Norfolk working for the Atlantic Fleet's surface forces commander, Vice Admiral Joseph Donnell, and told that officer to make sure that the remains of the forty-seven dead sailors weren't removed from the turret. He also told the captain "to take a zillion pictures." "Pictures of what?" Christ asked. "Equipment, people, where the people were before they were touched. The remains," he replied. "Why were the locations of the remains important to you?" "In the analysis of the event, people are one of the most important factors that you have to consider to analyze with regards to probable cause," Miceli said. What else did he hope to learn from these photographs? "Well, the first thing I want to know is where everybody was. After the explosion. You don't know where they were before the explosion, but I want to know where everybody was after the explosion, because it avoids any arguments later on who was where," he answered. He said no one heeded his advice. The bodies were moved and no pictures were taken.

Miceli testified that thorough testing had established several months prior to the Navy's September 7, 1989, press conference that a chemical compression detonator wasn't a realistic way to set off a blast. He had given this information to Admiral Milligan, but during Milligan's press conference, the admiral still insinuated that a chemical device was a distinct possibility. Miceli also said the Naval Weapons Support Center in Crane, Indiana, concurred with the FBI Crime Laboratory's assessment that an electronic device was not involved in the explosion. Miceli said he had personally given a written report to this effect to Admiral Milligan well before the press conference.

DURING LATE 1996 and early 1997, Marie Hagen and Steven Snyder, the Justice Department attorneys who were defending the Navy, adopted the NIS line in attempting to prove during the depositions of Earl and Evelyn Hartwig and Kathy Kubicina that their son and brother had been a homosexual. The government attorneys also sought to show that the family had suffered no emotional trauma as a result of the murder accusations the Navy had first leveled and then retracted against Clayton. The lawyers didn't deny that it had been improper to leak the raw NIS files, but they took the position that since the identity of the leaker couldn't be positively established by the government, the Navy bore no responsibility for the damages.

One of the first questions Snyder asked Earl Hartwig was, "Mr. Hartwig, do you know for sure if your son was a homosexual?" "I know for sure he wasn't," Earl replied. During a punishing, six-day deposition, Kathy Kubicina was asked again and again by Marie Hagen if her brother had been gay. "You believe it smeared your brother's name that he was labeled a homosexual?" Marie Hagen asked. "Only because he wasn't. If he would have been, it would have been fine," Kathy countered. Hagen later read excerpts from an NIS interview of a sailor who claimed that Clayton was gay. "They shouldn't have been so selective in their interviews. They should have interviewed more of his friends instead of one or two people that said he was a homosexual. That's what they should have done," Kathy said. Hagen then produced an anonymous letter stating that Clayton had been "a practicing homosexual." Kathy called it rubbish.

Hagen then asked Kathy how having an undertrained crew and tainted gunpowder aboard the *Iowa* had damaged the Hartwig family. Kathy stared at Hagen incredulously, as though she had just arrived in a flying saucer from Mars. A bulb seemed to go on in Hagen's head, and she quickly added, "Okay. So this goes to your theory that a lot of little things contributed to setting the stage for the accident?" "Exactly," Kathy snapped. Hagen next asked, "Let's assume the Navy had made all the same mistakes they made, conflicts of interest, didn't talk to all the witnesses, Miceli manipulated evidence, all the things we've talked about, and came to the conclusion that we just don't know, we can't tell, would that have caused you the same distress?" "As opposed to them blaming my brother? I would have to say, no, I probably wouldn't have suffered this much," Kathy said. "I wouldn't have dealt with what I've had to deal with. I wouldn't have gone through what I've gone through. Things would have been so much different if they would have come back and said it was an accident that they couldn't explain." She closed the deposition by saying, "And I know I can speak for my parents, because I know this is how they feel. We accepted his [Clayton's] death as an accident. What we can't accept is the way the investigation was handled."

Marie Hagen and Steven Snyder subjected sixty-six-year-old Evelyn Hartwig to a lengthy cross-examination. "Did you ever suspect your son was a homosexual?" Snyder asked. Evelyn began to crumble. "No," she said, her voice quivering. "Never in your life?" "No," she said, tears streaming down her face. "Would it hurt you if he was a homosexual?" "No. Why would it?" she replied, her hands trembling. "You seem very angry." "I don't know why this homosexual thing is—the Navy must have a vendetta about these poor—problems—these kids have with their sexuality," Evelyn sniffled. Then she put her head on the table and sobbed. After she had regained a measure of control, Snyder barraged her for another ten minutes with a spate of questions about her son's alleged homosexuality.

Then he asked her what she knew about the condition of her son's body following the explosion. "I had the impression there was nothing left of my son. He was blown to bits. So I tried to adjust to that," she said. She later learned that Clayton hadn't been in the center gun room. He had been in the pit below the gun, turning on the gas ejection air. Kathy had obtained Clayton's autopsy report and photographs. However, Evelyn said she couldn't bring herself to look at the pictures. "I was strong enough to listen to what happened to his face, his beautiful arms, his legs, but he wasn't burned," she said. "And he had his tattoo they identified. I didn't want him to get it. He wanted to get a tattoo to be a sailor like his dad, USS *Iowa's* name [was] on his body. So why would he blow up the USS *Iowa*? That's the name of the ship."

Evelyn came unglued again. Snyder pointedly ignored her fragile emotional state, but Marie Hagen had a horrified expression. "I sent him in there whole and they give him back to me in pieces!" Evelyn screamed. "I'm not sure if I got all his pieces! I don't trust the Navy and my government so much on account of this! I don't even know if I got my son's body! I wish I could go there myself and dig it up by hand and look at it!"

Marie Hagen began sobbing, and she, Kathy Kubicina, Paula Christ, and Terry Clark encircled Evelyn and consoled her. Snyder did not budge from his chair.

EPILOGUE

☆

"For One Thing, It Broke My Heart."

THE EXPLOSION ABOARD the USS *Iowa* ended the lives of forty-seven men. It ruined the careers of a number of officers or put them under a cloud. It also psychologically scarred many of the crewmen who extinguished the fires and removed the bodies from Turret Two, and it deeply affected the families of the deceased sailors. Here's what has happened to some of the characters mentioned in this book.

ADMIRAL FRANK KELSO. During the fall of 1993 and winter of 1994, the "Tailhook" scandal erupted again during a legal proceeding, scorching Admiral Frank Kelso so badly that he was forced to resign. William T. Vest Jr., the Navy judge, claimed that Kelso had a "personal interest" in the way Tailhook had been prosecuted and should have removed himself from the case. He took Kelso to task for shielding his own and other high-ranking officers' misconduct and using "unlawful command influence" to steer the investigation to his personal advantage. Kelso was mortified when he learned of the judge's decision. For a week, he fought hard to save his job, then capitulated. He announced at a Pentagon press conference that he would retire at the end of April 1994, two months ahead of schedule.

When retired Admiral Frank Kelso limped into the room in downtown Washington to be deposed in the Hartwigs' lawsuit, he looked like a wounded eagle. It had been two and a half years since he had resigned as Chief of Naval Operations. He partially supported himself with an aluminum crutch, which was attached to his right arm by a semicircular cuff. Not long after he retired from the Navy, he had been stricken by a degenerative muscular disease that had kept him confined to a wheelchair for months. His pale blue eyes still gleamed, but his old self-assurance was missing. He was as courtly as always, introducing himself to everyone in the room as "Frank Kelso." It would never occur to him to say, "Admiral Frank Kelso."

Once the deposition began, Terence Clark, the Hartwigs' attorney, asked the admiral if he had any idea how much pain Earl and Evelyn Hartwig and their two daughters had endured since the Navy claimed their son was a mass murderer. "I'm sure this family experienced a lot of pain. There's no question in my mind that they did," he said. "But I want to make it very clear to you that my judgment was that there was not clear and convincing evidence that any human caused this accident. And therefore, I was telling them [in 1991] that I regretted they have gone through this period of time till we came to this conclusion."

The former CNO became uncomfortable whenever Clark brought up the widespread leaks that had so characterized the *Iowa* investigation. "I've tried a—a lot of people have tried to stop leaks, and they don't stop for some reason, because there is a whole cottage industry in this town [Washington] to create leaks," he said. The Navy had determined that Clayton Hartwig wasn't a homosexual, Kelso said. He had rejected the FBI's "equivocal death analysis," as well as Admiral Milligan's report claiming that Clayton Hartwig had placed a detonator in the gun. Sabotage had been a theory, not a proven fact.

Admiral Jeremy "Mike" Boorda. The Pentagon announced that Admiral Kelso would be succeeded by Admiral Mike Boorda, who headed the North Atlantic Treaty Organization's military operations in and around Bosnia. During his two tumultuous years as CNO, Boorda proved time and again that although he was a politician, he managed to offend almost every constituency in the Navy, with the exception of the enlisted personnel, with whom he had an affinity, having served six years in the ranks. He often tried personally to solve sailors' problems.

Early in Admiral Boorda's second year as CNO, while I was checking the background of a flag officer involved in the *Iowa* investigation, I stumbled across one of Boorda's most sensitive secrets. A friend, who was a former naval officer and an authority on military decorations, told me that Admiral Boorda was wearing unauthorized combat "V" devices on two of his ribbons. The Navy had known about it since 1987 and had told Boorda to get rid of the devices, but he had failed to comply. One of the unauthorized "Vs" was on the Navy Achievement Medal, which Boorda had earned as weapons officer aboard the destroyer USS *John R. Craig* in 1965 off the coast of South Vietnam. The second "V" was pinned to the Navy Commendation Medal, which Boorda received as executive officer of the frigate USS *Brooke* from 1971 to 1973. The vessel briefly had been in the South China Sea off the coast of Vietnam during those years. The citations accompanying the two medals didn't authorize Boorda to wear the bronze devices, which would have indicated that he had earned them while under enemy fire.

I often shared information with Roger Charles, a retired Marine lieutenant colonel and Annapolis graduate and Vietnam veteran, and I told him about Boorda's unapproved "V" devices. Roger was working on a story about Boorda and asked if it would be all right for him to file a Freedom of Information Act request for the records of all Boorda's decorations. I told him to go ahead.

Once Roger Charles received the records of Boorda's decorations, he obtained a recent color photograph of the admiral wearing the two challenged "Vs." He visited the archives and studied every regulation governing awards from 1963 to 1996, and he perused the deck logs and official histories of the two vessels to which Boorda had been assigned when he obtained the medals. Once Roger satisfied himself that there was no possible justification for Boorda to wear the two devices, he called David Hackworth to tell him what he had found. A retired Army colonel who had been awarded more than a hundred medals—two-thirds of them related to combat—Hackworth was a best-selling author and *Newsweek* columnist who often skewered military brass in print for abusing their troops and soaking the taxpayers to subsidize regal lifestyles.

Hackworth called a well-placed Navy source, who said he was on the right track. He also discussed the case with a retired Marine general, who said he had only encountered one similar situation during his thirty-five-year career—and that officer had been summarily drummed out of the Marine Corps. An interview was set up between Hackworth and Admiral Boorda at 1 P.M. on Thursday, May 16, 1996, in the CNO's office. However, Hackworth was experiencing the after-effects of oral surgery, so Evan Thomas, *Newsweek*'s Washington bureau chief, and John Barry, a veteran national-security correspondent for *Newsweek*, agreed to do the interview. Rear Admiral Kendall Pease, the Chief of Naval Information, called Hackworth at his Montana home and said that since the former colonel was not going to participate in the interview, Boorda wanted to postpone it. Evan Thomas called Pease shortly after that and said the interview was too important to delay. Pease asked why, and Thomas told him the interview concerned Boorda's "V" devices.

About 12:15 P.M. on May 16, Pease entered the CNO's office and informed him that the *Newsweek* correspondents would ask him about the "Vs." Boorda knew about Roger Charles's FOIA request and had been told by the Navy's lawyers that he wasn't entitled to wear the tiny devices. He had already removed them from his ribbons. Pease said the meeting with the two correspondents had been slipped to 2:30 P.M. At about 12:30 P.M., Boorda announced that he was going to his official residence, Tingey House, on the grounds of the Washington Navy Yard, about fifteen minutes away. He said he would be back at 2:15 P.M., in time for the interview. He arrived at Tingey House at 1:05 P.M. and wrote two letters on his computer—one of love and regret to his wife, Bettie, and another addressed, "To my sailors." In the second note, Boorda confessed that he had no right to wear the "Vs." He also said how much he loved the Navy and how proud he was of its enlisted personnel. Then he picked up a five-shot .38-caliber Smith & Wesson revolver and walked outside into a garden. Dressed in a white uniform, he placed the gun barrel on his chest over his heart and pulled the trigger. He was taken to D.C. General Hospital, where he was declared dead at 2:30 P.M.

In June 1998, Navy Secretary John Dalton put a letter in Admiral Boorda's personnel file from retired Admiral Elmo Zumwalt, the Chief of Naval Operations during the end of the Vietnam War, saying it was "appropriate, justified and proper" for Admiral Boorda to attach the "Vs" to the ribbons on his uniform. However, the Navy said that this did not constitute a formal ruling by the service on whether Admiral Boorda was entitled to the decorations. Such a determination, a Navy spokesman said, could come only from the Board of Correction of Naval Records, which had not been petitioned to review the case.

ADMIRAL LEON "BUD" EDNEY. In some ways, Edney acquired more influence in the Navy after his retirement than when he had been a four-star admiral. He was the éminence grise, a senior fellow at both the Center of Naval Analysis and the National Defense University, and a consultant to a firm called the Defense Group, which worked on policies affecting the armed forces in the next century. He had been commandant of midshipmen at Annapolis during the early 1980s, and he remained involved in the affairs of the academy, serving on a board of inquiry that investigated wholesale cheating at Annapolis.

Some Annapolis alumni were dismayed that Admiral Charles R. Larson, the superintendent of the Naval Academy, had selected Edney in April 1997 to fill the newly created post of Distinguished Professor of Leadership. A press release said that Edney would "teach core leadership and ethics courses and promote moral development and leadership education." Part of Edney's job would be to inspire midshipmen and mentor faculty members. When Kathy Kubicina heard about Edney's appointment, she said, "I am appalled that the Naval Academy would take the man who ensured that my brother was falsely accused of mass murder and put him in charge of teaching ethics and leadership to thousands of future officers. But it doesn't surprise me, given what I have witnessed about the Navy's sense of values during all these years."

On December 1, 1998, Edney appeared as an expert witness on the subject of ethics before the House Judiciary Committee, then debating whether President Clinton should be impeached for allegedly committing perjury and obstructing justice. The retired admiral vowed that cover-ups and lying would never be tolerated in the Navy, which he said had a higher standard of ethics and morality than did society as a whole. Shortly after that, Edney was named chairman of the board of the Retired Officers' Association. Edney promised to promote diversity in the 400,000-member organization.

Captain Fred Moosally. After retiring from the Navy in 1990, Moosally went to work for a major defense contractor and has since been hired by another. He is still a popular figure on Capitol Hill, especially on the House side. He lives in Oakton, Virginia. When he attended the Norfolk, Virginia, dedication of a plaque to the dead *Iowa* sailors in 1994, marking the fifth anniversary of the explosion, he was shunned by most of the former crewmen, who were still incensed over what he had told Admiral Milligan about them.

Captain Larry Seaquist. Seaquist retired from the Navy in 1994 and runs an international consulting firm in Washington. On May 22, 1995, he submitted a seventy-page memorandum to Steven S. Honigman, General Counsel of the Navy, urging that the *Iowa* case by reopened. It was Honigman who requested the memo. Rear Admiral R.E. Grant, the Navy's Judge Advocate General, assigned an experienced military attorney to assist Seaquist and to protect his rights. Grant promised that copies of the document would not be provided to high-ranking naval officers or civilian officials whom Seaquist named either as botching the previous investigations or as being involved in cover-ups. Grant also assured Seaquist that no retaliation would be taken against him, and that the Navy would treat his memo seriously.

Seaquist divided his memo into five sections: (1) Major gaps in the original investigation, such as the failure to mention equipment failures and previous near-disasters in Turret Two; (2) Official misconduct by such figures as former Secretary of the Navy Lawrence Garrett, Admiral Carl Trost, Admiral Frank Kelso, Admiral Bud Edney, Admiral Mike Boorda, Admiral Powell Carter, Vice Admiral Joseph Donnell, Vice Admiral Douglas Katz, Rear Admiral Richard Milligan, Captain Joseph Miceli, Captain Fred Moosally, Captain Michael Fahey, Captain Ron Swanson, Rear Admiral William Schachte, and several other former Naval Investigative Service administrators and agents; (3) Unexplained and unnecessary deaths, such as cyanide poisoning, inoperative firefighting equipment, and the chronic lack of emergency breathing devices; (4) Official misrepresentations to the families, such as the fact that the Navy wasn't positive about the identification of the bodies when they were sent home for burial, and false notifications of the causes of death; (5) Other information, such as Captain Mike Fahey's verbally and physically assaulting members of the *Iowa*'s crew when he was executive officer of the battleship.

Each of Seaquist's subsections contained numerous sources whom the Navy could contact to confirm his data. The former *Iowa* commanding officer sent copies of his report to a group of active-duty and retired admirals and recommended that the Navy appoint a "Blue Ribbon Panel" of admirals to look into his charges. "The single most important implication of the *Iowa* case to date is that the Navy has yet to stand up to its own professional ethics and its moral obligations," Seaquist wrote. If the Navy opted to do nothing, he said, "This information is so extensive and so persuasive that it will inevitably find a public hearing." Honigman wrote Seaquist on June 30, 1995, saying that he was reviewing Seaquist's memo. He vowed to "advise you of the results of the review as soon as possible." Even though Seaquist repeatedly called Honigman's office, he never was able to talk with him—nor did he ever hear back from him. Honigman, a Yale Law School classmate of President and Mrs. Clinton, moved to the White House in 1998 to be in charge of "encryption policy" concerning computers.

Captain Mike Fahey. After commanding a destroyer squadron in Norfolk, Fahey became commanding officer of the Naval ROTC detachment at the University of South Carolina in Columbia. He retired in 1998.

Rear Admiral Richard Milligan. Senator Howard Metzenbaum's "hold" on Milligan's promotion to vice admiral stuck, and he retired in 1992. He taught economics at the Naval Postgraduate School in Monterey, California, then moved back to Washington to become vice president of a national insurance company. He now lives in Pawleys Island, South Carolina.

Rear Admiral William Schachte. In 1992, Schachte became the acting Judge Advocate General and almost got the job, but he attempted to minimize his involvement in the *Iowa* affair. After committee staffers produced NIS records and transcripts of interviews Schachte gave in 1989 concerning the investigation of Clayton Hartwig, he was forced to withdraw his candidacy. He retired in 1993 and practices law in his hometown of Charleston, South Carolina.

Rear Admiral Ming Chang. Disgusted that Admiral Edney had buried his *Iowa* investigation, Chang retired in 1990. He is the vice president and principal sales representative in Asia for a major defense contractor based in Lexington, Massachusetts.

Rear Admiral John E. "Ted" Gordon. After retiring in 1992, Gordon took a job with a major defense contractor in Arlington, Virginia, and is in charge of legislative affairs. He lives in Vienna, Virginia.

Rear Admiral Brent Baker. Baker became head of the Communications Department at Boston University when he retired in 1992. He lives in Natick, Massachusetts.

Admiral Jerome Johnson. After completing his tour as Vice Chief of Naval Operations, Johnson was named president of the Navy-Marine

Corps Relief Society, based in Arlington, Virginia. He lives in Fairfax, Virginia.

Other Navy Flag Officers. All of them are retired. Admiral Carl Trost lives in Potomac, Maryland; Admiral Powell Carter in Harpers Ferry, West Virginia; Vice Admiral Joseph Donnell in Virginia Beach, Virginia; Vice Admiral Douglas Katz in Annapolis, Maryland; and Vice Admiral Peter Hekman in Alexandria, Virginia.

Commander Ronald Swanson. After Swanson was removed from the *Iowa* reinvestigation due to the appearance of a conflict of interest, he was promoted to captain and put in charge of the Navy Legal Services Office in Pensacola, Florida. He retired in 1995 and is an assistant prosecutor in Escambia County, Florida.

Commander Deborah Burnette. Soon after Frank Kelso resigned as CNO, Burnette was promoted to captain and became the commanding officer of the Naval Media Center in Washington. Burnette then became commanding officer of the Navy's regional public-affairs center in Atlanta. She retired in 1997 and is living in Atlanta, where she is raising three young children she has adopted. She also does freelance public relations.

Captain Joseph Miceli. After spending three years investigating the *Iowa* explosion, Miceli retired in 1992.

NIS Officials and Agents. Brian McKee retired in 1990 and operates a motel in Malone, New York. Robert Powers retired in 1993 and lives in Alexandria, Virginia. Both McKee and Powers occasionally do security consulting work. Robert Nigro is a supervisory special agent in the Washington office. Mike Dorsey is assigned to the counterintelligence branch in Washington. Tom Goodman is assigned to Cecil Field in Jacksonville, Florida. Both Ed Goodwin and James Whitener are stationed in the Norfolk area.

The FBI Psychological Profilers. Richard Ault and Roy Hazelwood retired in 1994. They are both vice presidents of the Academy Group, an association of former members of the Behavioral Science Unit. They frequently provide expert testimony and advice in civil cases where violence has occurred in apartment complexes or shopping malls.

Lieutenant Dan Meyer. After graduating from Indiana University School of Law in Bloomington, Meyer took up the practice of law in Washington, D.C. He lives near South Mountain in Maryland's Catoctin Valley.

Gunner's Mate First Class Dale Mortensen. After the *Iowa* was decommissioned, Mortensen was transferred to Newport, Rhode Island, and joined the master-at-arms force. His primary duty was collecting urine samples to see if sailors were using drugs. "I went from being one of the best sixteen-inch turret captains in the Navy to collecting bottles of piss," he said bitterly in 1992. He left Newport and served his last three years of active duty at the Vieques gunnery range. When he retired in 1995, he moved back to his hometown of Pontiac, Michigan, and now works in a factory.

Master Chief Stephen Skelley. Skelley was transferred to the battleship USS *Wisconsin* shortly before the onset of the Gulf War with Iraq. He helped direct the firing of fifty 1,900-pound shells on February 7, 1991, blowing up a pier and heavily damaging sixteen boats at a marina in Kuwait. After the *Wisconsin* was decommissioned, he received orders to Dahlgren, where he did what he described in 1993 as "make work." He was then assigned to the aircraft carrier USS *Theodore Roosevelt*.

Gunner's Mate Third Class Kendall Truitt. Truitt attended deep-sea diving school in Houston and was a diver for a brief period of time, before deciding that diving was almost as dangerous as being inside Turret Two on the *Iowa*. He is in the landscaping business in Apex, North Carolina, near Raleigh. He says he has long since spent all of Clayton Hartwig's insurance money, with a big chunk of it having gone to Miami attorney Ellis Rubin for Truitt's legal defense.

Fireman Brian Scanio. Scanio joined the Peace Corps and was stationed in the Philippines. After contracting appendicitis and a tropical disease, he was evacuated back to the United States. He works as an insurance salesman in Pittsburgh, Pennsylvania, and still suffers traumatic bouts of shaking and cold sweats due to the time he spent fighting fires amid the carnage in Turret Two.

Seaman David Smith. Smith enlisted in the U.S. Army in 1990, was stationed in Schofield Barracks in Honolulu, Hawaii, and was promoted to sergeant. Discharged in 1995, he moved back to his hometown of Rockville, Maryland, and then to Morehead City, North Carolina. He has said many times that he wants to call Earl and Evelyn Hartwig and tell them how sorry he is for lying about their son to NIS, but he never has.

Other *Iowa* Officers. All of them have either retired or resigned from the service. Commander John Morse was promoted to captain after the *Iowa* was mothballed. He was stationed in the Middle East and now lives in Fairfax Station, Virginia. Commander Jerry Ware lives in Manlius, New York, near Syracuse, and is a senior engineer for a major defense contractor.

Commander Gene Kocmich is a defense consultant, living in Hampton, Virginia. Lieutenant Commander Dana Griffin, promoted to commander after leaving the *Iowa*, now works for an international aerospace company. He lives in Silver Spring, Maryland. Commander Robert Kissinger is employed by a subcontractor servicing the Navy's Tomahawk missile. He lives in Virginia Beach. Lieutenant Commander Kenneth Costigan is in the insurance business and also lives in Virginia Beach. Lieutenant Terry McGinn, a contracting officer for the U.S. Marine Corps, lives in Fredericksburg, Virginia.

OTHER *IOWA* CREWMEN. All of them have either retired or resigned from the service. Master Chief Chuck Hill splits his time between his farm outside Chesapeake, Virginia, and Key West, Florida. Master Chief James Hickman is a deputy sheriff and jail guard in Norfolk. Gunner's Mate Third Class John Mullahy, who was promoted to chief before his retirement in 1991, lives in Cartagena, Spain. Gunner's Mate Third Class Cletus Guffin moved back home to South Dakota.

MEMBERS OF CONGRESS, STAFFERS, AND INVESTIGATORS. Senator Howard Metzenbaum retired from the Senate in 1994 and is chairman of the board of the Consumer Federation of America. Senator Sam Nunn retired in 1996 and is a senior partner in the Atlanta law firm of King & Spaulding. He is also a member of many corporate boards. Richard DeBobes still is employed by the Senate Armed Services Committee. Richard Woodruff is head of legislative affairs for the National Endowment for the Arts. Congresswoman Mary Rose Oakar was defeated for reelection in 1992 and runs a political consulting firm in Cleveland and Washington. Warren Nelson is a consultant for the Pentagon. Bill Fleshman is a businessman in Roanoke, Virginia. Tim Stone and Jerry Hurley still work for the General Accounting Office. All the members of the Sandia team—Dr. Richard Schwoebel, Dr. James Borders, Paul Cooper, and Dr. Karl Schuler—are retired. The first three live in Albuquerque, New Mexico; Schuler resides in Texas.

THE MEDIA. Fred Francis is still a correspondent for NBC News. Len Tepper now works for the ABC News investigative unit. Molly Moore is a correspondent for the *Washington Post*, based in Mexico. George Wilson left the *Washington Post* and is a columnist for Army Times Publishing Company. Jack Dorsey, Tony Germanotta, and Dave Addis are still with the *Virginian-Pilot/Ledger-Star*. Germanotta and Addis are editors, and Dorsey continues to give rides to hitchhiking sailors, thereby obtaining information for his column. Robert Kessler still covers Brooklyn-based federal law-enforcement agencies for *Newsday*. John Hall remains the Washington bureau chief of Media General News Service, and Steve Goldberg is associate editor of *Kiplinger's Personal Finance Magazine*. Robert Zelnick left

ABC News in 1998, and now teaches journalism at Boston University. Mark Brender left ABC shortly after Zelnick and is now the Washington head of a major satellite imaging firm. Peter Cary is assistant managing editor of *U.S. News & World Report*, in charge of investigations. Jack Davis was promoted to publisher of the *Daily Press* in Hampton, Virginia. A.J. Plunkett is the night metro editor of the *Richmond Times-Dispatch*. Charles Bogino attended Catholic University Law School in Washington and is an attorney. At eighty, Mike Wallace is still going strong at *60 Minutes*. Paul Hoven is a military consultant and Ari Allan is a documentary producer. Both of them live in the Washington area. Admiral Ed Snyder and I make a point of eating lunch together once a week at a fast-food restaurant and talking about the *Iowa* explosion.

THE *IOWA* FAMILIES. Ambassador Alvin Adams, the adoptive father of Fire Controlman Third Class Thanh Adams, was named U.S. ambassador to Peru after completing his tour in Haiti. Adams was president of the United Nations Association of the United States, a UN lobbying group and then retired in 1995. He and his wife, Mai-Anh, live in New York. Sharon Ziegler, widow of Senior Chief Reggie Ziegler, Jack Thompson Sr., father of Gunner's Mate Third Class Jack Thompson Jr., and retired Chief Boatswain's Mate Robert Morrison, father of Legalman First Class Robert K. Morrison, all have died. Gene and Mary Lou Blakey, the parents of Gunner's Mate Third Class Scot Blakey, moved from Eaton Rapids, Michigan, to Virginia Beach to be near three of their four surviving children. Gene Blakey had spearheaded the lawsuit that was joined by the majority of the *Iowa* families. The suit was dismissed due to the Feres Doctrine, and Blakey wrote to President Bill Clinton in 1994, " Just think, the Navy admitted they were wrong and was still able to get away with all this injustice by hiding behind the Feres Doctrine. This is very scary, because it isn't the first or the last time this doctrine has been (or will be) a convenient carpet to sweep all wrongdoings under, to hide and forget about." Blakey never received a response from Clinton. Peggy Price, the mother of Gunner's Mate Third Class Matt Price, wrote Clinton in 1993, "I will get justice if I have to pursue this till my dying day." She also received no response. She had Crohn's disease, a thickening of the intestinal wall and a hardening and narrowing of the passageway, and had to have radical surgery to relieve her condition. Her doctors said this was caused by the stress of Matt's death and her distress over how the Navy handled the investigation. She told her husband, Butch, and four other children, "I will never give up on trying to get the Navy to do the right thing, and after my passing, if there are still no results, you are to carry on."

CLAYTON HARTWIG'S CLOSE FRIENDS. Bryan Hoover lives in Springfield, Ohio, with his wife, Monique, and their three children. He is a respiratory therapist and she is a nurse. Charlene Meter, a massage therapist, is attending Cleveland State University. She shares a house with Kathy Kubicina's oldest daughter, Jami.

The Hartwig Family. Cindy Werthmuller, Clayton's other sister, lives on a farm in Clarksville, Iowa, with her husband, John, and works as a home-health-care technician. Kathy Kubicina lives in a Cleveland suburb with her husband, Frank, and two younger children. She wrote Defense Secretary William Cohen—who criticized the Navy's handling of the *Iowa* investigation during Senate Armed Services Committee hearings in 1989 and 1990—asking him to read Larry Seaquist's report. She also wrote Attorney General Janet Reno, asking her to do the same thing. Neither replied. Earl Hartwig now suffers from Parkinson's disease, and Evelyn Hartwig has Bell's palsy, which temporarily paralyzes her face when she is under stress. When she was asked by Justice Department attorneys how the Navy injured her, Evelyn replied, "For one thing, it broke my heart."

Afer sitting for two years on a motion by the Justice Department to dismiss the Hartwig family's lawsuit against the Navy, U.S. Magistrate David S. Perelman ruled on January 26, 1999, that the Navy had immunity and did not have to pay damages. Perelman recommended that U.S. District Judge George W. White toss out the family's $12 million suit for intentional infliction of emotional distress, stating that the Federal Torts Claims Acts shielded the Navy from claims that it leaked confidential information about Clayton Hartwig, conducted a sham investigation of the explosion aboard the *Iowa*, carried out an illegal search and seizure at the Hartwig home, suppressed evidence that made Clayton Hartwig look good, and falsified evidence that made him appear guilty. Judge White, who was retiring from the bench, asked the court clerk to reassign the case to another jurist. The Hartwigs' attorney, Terence Clark, appealed the ruling and informed his clients that, due to the clogged docket, it might take two years or more before a new judge could hear their appeal. Kathy Kubicina was nonplussed by the delay . "I've got ten years invested in this. Another ten is no problem," she said. "I truly believe that we'll win this case, if we don't give up hope. If you make the Navy pay for what it did, it's not likely to commit another atrocity like this."

Sources

I RELIED ON more than 25,000 documents, including the material generated by Rear Admiral Richard Milligan; Captain Joseph Miceli's technical inquiry; the U.S. Army's input; the Naval Investigative Service's reports, interviews and handwritten notes; tests and analyses done by Sandia National Laboratories; Rear Admiral Ming Chang's investigation, interviews, and supporting documentation; reports from the FBI Crime Laboratory, the FBI Behavioral Science Unit, and the FBI Disaster Squad; autopsy reports and toxicological studies from the Armed Forces Institute of Pathology for all forty-seven men killed in the explosion; the General Accounting Office conclusions; the investigation of the USS *New Jersey*'s gunnery problems in Lebanon in 1983–84, caused by defective powder; the courts of inquiry into the 1924 and 1943 explosions aboard the USS *Mississippi*; the Navy's investigation of every large-caliber gunnery disaster in this century; and reports of the 1950 grounding of the USS *Missouri* on Thimble Shoals. In addition, I obtained the deck logs and message traffic to and from the *Iowa*, or any other vessels or commands (such as the Second Fleet) that were involved in events described in this book; the journals, diaries, and letters of Dan Meyer, Reggie Ziegler, Kathy Kubicina, Philip Buch, Clayton Hartwig, Jack Thompson, Matt Price, Errick Lawrence, and Terry McGinn; the records and notes of Mary Rose Oakar, Larry Seaquist, Ed Snyder, Dick Woodruff, Robert Zelnick, Mark Brender, Charles Bogino, A.J. Plunkett, Peter Cary, Roger Charles, Don Price, John Hall, Steve Goldberg, Jack Dorsey, Tony Germanotta, Warren Nelson, and Bill Fleshman. I also made use of Master Chief Stephen Skelley's diagrams and handwritten notes describing his gunpowder experimentation and the reconfigured shells he had conceived; Skelley's records of every sixteen-inch shell fired aboard the *Iowa* while she was in commission from 1984 to 1990; the *Iowa*'s training schedules for 1988 and 1989; her manning levels in the three sixteen-inch turrets for the same time period; and memos proving that the *Iowa* had functioned as a "test platform" in 1988. None of this material was examined by Admiral Milligan. The *Iowa*'s newspaper, her "plan-of-the-day," and "cruise books" were very useful.

Much of my best information came from people, either in interviews I conducted personally or from official statements they provided to the Navy, when they testified to Congress, or during the lawsuit filed by the Hartwig family. I've listed this in two categories: interviews and statements and/or testimony. Many people fell into both categories.

Interviews	***Statements and/or Testimony***
Dale Mortensen	Dale Mortensen
Jerome Johnson	Dan Meyer
Dan Meyer	Gene Kocmich
Gene Kocmich	Fred Moosally
David Smith	David Smith
Scott Ragan	Toby Larkin
Stephen Skelley	Stephen Skelley
Larry Seaquist	Larry Seaquist
Joseph Metcalf	Emmett C. Dunn Jr.
John Lehman	J.C. Miller
G.E. Gneckow	Kevin Hunt
Chuck Hill	Charles Fulcher
Dana Griffin	Bob Finney
Jerry Ware	Robert Kissinger
Dennis Brooks	Kenneth Costigan
Tom Carey	Leo Walsh
Terry McGinn	Dale Miller
Bob Sumrall	John McEachren
Carla Seaquist	Shane Cline
Sharon Ziegler	Mark Harden
Emily Buch-Hague	John Morse
James Hickman	James Hickman
Leslie Ware	John Mullahy
John Mullahy	Kendall Truitt
Kendall Truitt	Ron Griffith
Donald Meyer	Robert Reimann
Susan Backherms	Donald Schultz
Carole Truitt	Robert Enochs
Mildred Thompson	Ephraim Spencer Garrett
Leasa Thompson	Vergil Marshall
Jack Thompson Sr.	Carlos Washington
Dick Lawrence	John Brush
Paula Lawrence	Cletus Guffin
Mary Lou Blakey	Murray Cunningham
Gene Blakey	Benjamin Droweinga

Interviews

Didi Price
Butch Price
Peggy Price
Reginald Johnson Sr.
Louis Fisk
Barbara Fisk
Ernest Hanyecz Sr.
Shelly White
Robert Morrison
Cletus Guffin
Thomas Kilcline Jr.
Michael Estes
John Keerl
Wilfred Patnaude
George Anderson
Brian Scanio
Paul Bopp
Alvin Adams
Mai-Anh Adams
Nancy Lewis
Darleen Schelin
Dale Schelin
Richard Bagley
Richard Milligan
Ted Gordon
Bill Fogarty
Tim McNulty
Don Price
Ed Snyder
Ronald Swanson
Ed Ellis
Warren Nelson
Dorothy Williams
Linda Williams
Lucille Young
Mary Coleman Chambers
Mary Ogden
Jimmy Pappas
Paul Hanley
Steve Burnett
Jimmy Finkelstein
Joseph Miceli
Chuck Bernard
Tony Battista

Statements and/or Testimony

John Keerl
Robert Burch
Cecil Croft
Patrick Shedd
Michael Estes
Ricky Frambo
Verlin Allen
Kenneth MacArthur
Oliver Demery
Jeffrey Bolander
Bruce Richardson
Timothy Blackie
William Barbra
Brian Scanio
Thad Harms
Noah Melendez
James Drake
Eugene Smallwood Jr.
Carl Trost
Joseph Donnell
Richard Milligan
Bud Edney
Ronald Swanson
Donovan Housley
Harry Freeman
Frank Gerstenslager
Ronald Robb
Joseph Miceli
Earl Hartwig
Evelyn Hartwig
Kathy Kubicina
Michael Carr
Tom Goodman
Ed Goodwin
Charlene Meter
Stephen Stallings
Bryan Hoover
Michael Mielens
Michele Lee Poling
Deborah Burnette
Thomas Mountz
Richard Ault
Roy Hazelwood
Dan McElyea

Interviews

Ming Chang
Deborah Burnette
Earl Hartwig
Evelyn Hartwig
Kathy Kubicina
Frank Kubicina
Howard Metzenbaum
Mary Welden
Dick Woodruff
Karen Fetterman
Mary Rose Oakar
Charles Macloskie
Ronald Kessler
Brian McKee
Charlene Meter
Stephen Stallings
Bryan Hoover
Jack Dorsey
Tony Germanotta
David Addis
Molly Moore
A.J. Plunkett
Charles Bogino
Jack Davis
Mark Brender
Robert Zelnick
Bob Gedeon
Linda Gedeon
Patsy McMullen
John Greenya
Kreig Brusnahan
Cynthia Werthmuller
Frank Kelso
Ellis Rubin
Jodie Allen
William Arkin
Peter Cary
Douglas Katz
Dr. Richard Froede
Nicholas Mavroules
Dr. Richard Schwoebel
Richard DeBobes
Dr. James Borders
Dr. Karl Schuler

Statements and/or Testimony

Frank Kelso
Kenneth Nimmich
Douglas Katz
Bruce Wetzel
Al Becker
Robert Powers
James Whitener

Interviews

Dr. John Feegel
Paul Cooper
John Hall
Steve Goldberg
Stephanie Zaharoudis
Patrick Tyler
Steve Loeffler
William Schachte
William Fleshman
Al Becker
Vince Thomas
Robert Powers
Martin Clancy
Tom Jarriel
Tim Stone
Jerry Hurley
Rowan Scarborough
Stan Sirmans
Jeff Styron
Pat Brogan

☆

Bibliography

Baer, George W. *The US Navy, 1890-1990, One Hundred Years of Sea Power.* Stanford, California: Stanford University Press, 1994.

Barnett, Correlli. *Engage the Enemy More Closely: The Royal Navy in the Second World War.* New York: W.W. Norton & Company, 1991.

Beach, Edward L. *The United States Navy: 200 Years.* New York: Henry Holt, 1986.

Bearden, Bill, and Bill Wedetz. *The Bluejackets' Manual.* Annapolis, Maryland: Naval Institute Press, 1978.

Breuer, William B. *Sea Wolf: A Biography of John D. Bulkeley, USN.* Novato, California: Presidio Press, 1989.

Butler, John A. *Strike Able-Peter: The Stranding and Salvage of the USS Missouri.* Annapolis, Maryland: Naval Institute Press, 1995.

Crenshaw, R.S., Jr. *Naval Shiphandling.* Annapolis, Maryland: Naval Institute Press, 1975.

Crowe, William, J., Jr. *The Line of Fire.* New York: Simon & Schuster, 1993.

Cutler, Thomas J. *The Battle of Leyte Gulf: 23-26 October 1944.* New York: HarperCollins, 1994.

Evans Robley D. A *Sailor's Log.* New York: D. Appleton and Company, 1901.

Friedman, Norman. *U.S. Battleships.* Annapolis, Maryland: Naval Institute Press, 1985.

Garzke, William H., Jr., and Robert O. Dulin, Jr. *Battleships.* 3 vols. Annapolis, Maryland: Naval Institute Press, 1990-95.

Gray, Colin, S. *The Leverage of Sea Power*. New York: The Free Press, 1992.

Hagan, Kenneth J. *This People's Navy: The Making of American Sea Power*. New York: The Free Press, 1991.

Hayduke, George. *Getting Even: The Complete Book of Dirty Tricks*. Secaucus, New Jersey: Lyle Stuart, 1980.

Howarth, Stephen. *To Shining Sea: A History of the Untied States Navy 1775-1991*. New York: Random House, 1991.

Hughes, Wayne P., Jr. *Fleet Tactics: Theory and Practice*. Annapolis, Maryland: Naval Institute Press, 1986.

Isenberg, Michael T. *Shield of the Republic*. New York: St. Martin's Press, 1993.

Kessler, Ronald. *Moscow Station*. New York: Pocket Books, 1990.

———. *The FBI*. New York: Pocket Books, 1993.

Knox, Dudley W. *The History of the United States Navy*. New York: G.P. Putnam's Sons, 1936.

Lehman, John F., Jr. *Making War*. New York: Charles Scribner's Sons, 1992.

———. *Command of the Seas*. New York: Charles Scribner's Sons, 1988.

Mack, William P., with Thomas D. Paulsen. *The Naval Officer's Guide*. Annapolis, Maryland: Naval Institute Press, 1991.

———, and Albert H. Konetzni, Jr. *Command at Sea*. Annapolis, Maryland: Naval Institute Press, 1982.

Massie, Robert K. *Dreadnought*. New York: Random House, 1991.

Moore, Molly. *A Woman at War: Storming Kuwait with the U.S. Marines*. New York: Charles Scribner's Sons, 1993.

Morison, Samuel Eliot. *The Two-Ocean War*. Boston: Little, Brown & Company, 1963.

Muir, Malcolm. *The Iowa Class Battleships*. New York: Sterling Publishing Company, 1987.

Musicant, Ivan. *Battleship at War: The Epic Story of the USS Washington*. New York: Harcourt Brace Jovanovich Publishers, 1986.

Noel, John V., Jr. and Edward L. Beach. *Naval Terms Dictionary*. Annapolis, Maryland: Naval Institute Press, 1988.

———, and James Stavridis. *Division Officer's Guide*. Annapolis, Maryland: Naval Institute Press, 1989.

O'Connell, Robert L. *Sacred Vessels: The Cult of the Battleship and the Rise of the U.S. Navy*. Boulder, Colorado: Westview Press, 1991.

Polmar, Norman, and Thomas B. Allen. *Rickover*. New York: Simon & Schuster, 1982.

Reckner, James R. *Teddy Roosevelt's Great White Fleet*. Annapolis, Maryland: Naval Institute Press, 1988.

Reilly, John, C., Jr. *Operational Experience of Fast Battleships: World War II, Korea, Vietnam*. Washington, DC: Naval Historical Center, 1989.

Rubin, Ellis, and Dary Matera. *"Get Me Ellis Rubin!"* New York: St. Martin's Press, 1989.

Shilts, Randy. *Conduct Unbecoming: Gays and Lesbians in the U.S. Military*. New York: St. Martin's Press, 1993.

Stavridis, James. *Watch Officer's Guide: A Handbook for All Deck Watch Officers*. Annapolis, Maryland: Naval Institute Press, 1992.

Stillwell, Paul. *Battleship Missouri*. Annapolis, Maryland: Naval Institute Press, 1996.

———. *Battleship New Jersey*. Annapolis, Maryland: Naval Institute Press, 1986.

Sumrall, Robert F. *Iowa Class Battleships: Their Design, Weapons, and Equipment*. Annapolis, Maryland: Naval Institute Press, 1988.

Vistica, Gregory L. *Fall From Glory: The Men Who Sank the U.S. Navy*. New York: Simon & Schuster, 1995.

Wallace, Mike, and Gary Paul Gates. *Close Encounters: Mike Wallace's Own Story*. New York: William Morrow and Company, 1984.

Wilson, George C. *Super Carrier*. New York: Macmillan Publishing Company, 1986.

Wouk, Herman. *The Caine Mutiny*. Garden City, New York: Doubleday & Company, 1951.

Zumwalt, Elmo R., Jr. *On Watch*. New York: Quadrangle, 1976.

Index